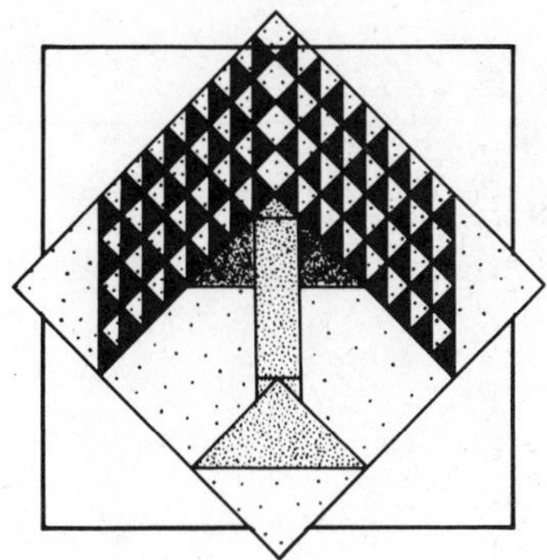

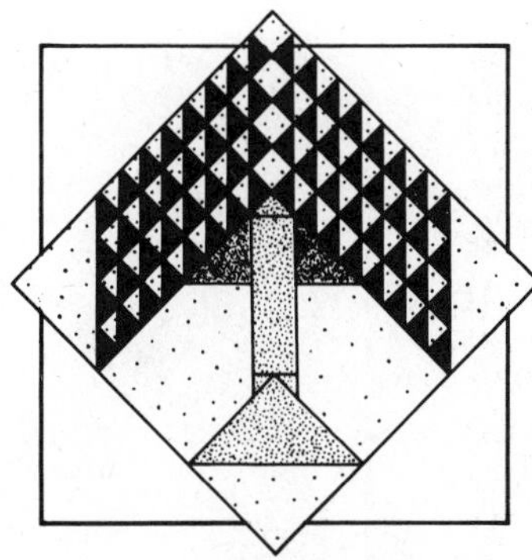

# FAMILY RELATIONS

## *A Reader*

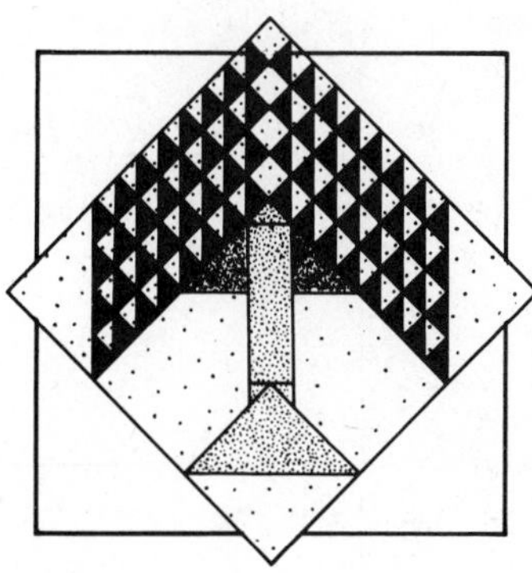

**Consulting Editor**

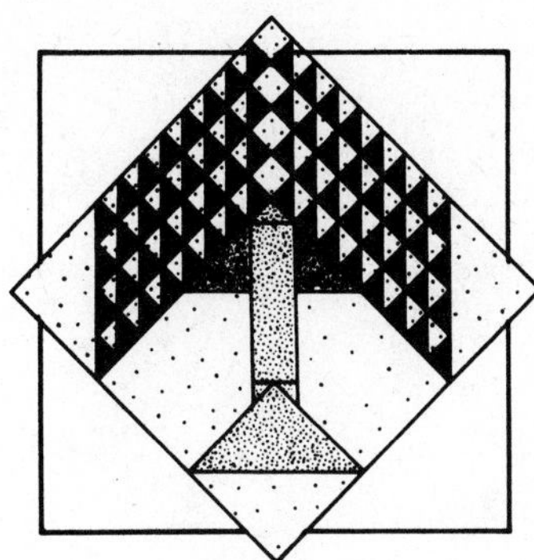

*Norval D. Glenn*
*Marion Tolbert Coleman*
*Both of the University of Texas at Austin*

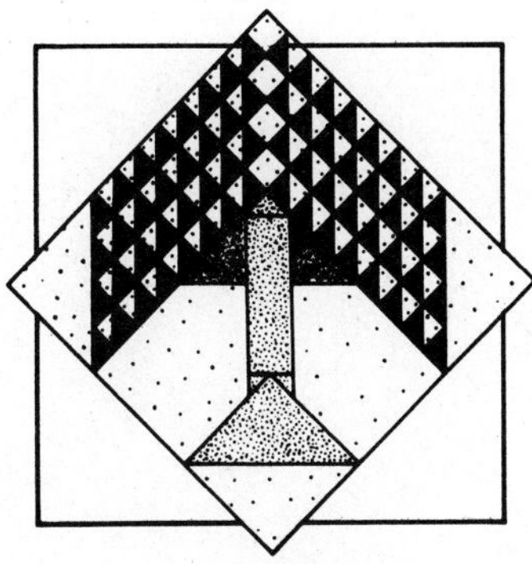

# FAMILY RELATIONS

## *A Reader*

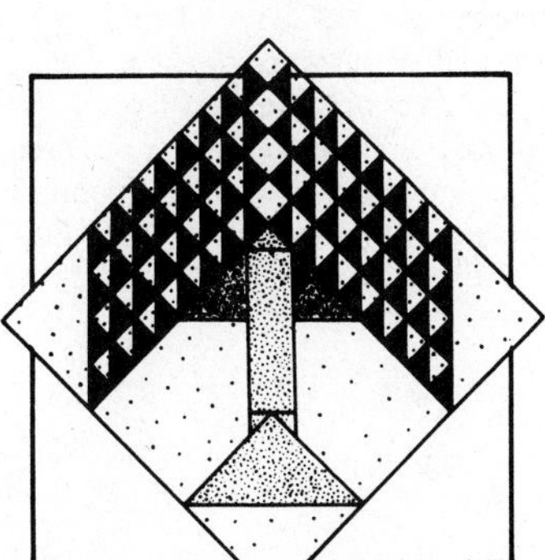

Wadsworth Publishing Company
Belmont, California
A Division of Wadsworth, Inc.

Acquisitions editor: Paul O'Connell
Project editor: Waivah Clement
Production manager: Charles J. Hess
Designer: Keith J. McPherson
Artist: Alice B. Thiede
Compositor: The Saybrook Press
Typeface: 10/12 Garamond Light
Printer: Malloy Lithographing, Inc.

ISBN 0-534-10545-9 (previously ISBN 0-256-05649-8)

Library of Congress Catalog Card No. 87–71670

*Printed in the United States of America*

3 4 5 6 7 8 9 0 ML 5 4 3 2 1 0 9

The cover design was inspired by an Ohio Amish quilt pattern entitled "Tree of Life." The tree represented on the cover is the pine. The pine had special importance to early settlers and their families. To them it was the essential of life, for pine trees became their homes and furniture and were used as a symbol of their coins, flags, and documents. It also represented loyalty and steadfastness. The basic form of the design is the same in all areas of the country and generally appears in only two colors—red, blue or green on white field. "The Pine Tree" pattern is also known as "Temperance Tree," "Tree of Paradise," and "Tall Pine Tree."

# Preface

This book grew out of our experience in teaching the general undergraduate course in the sociology of the family. In these classes we have found that a reader, used in combination with a textbook, can enormously enhance a course by enlarging upon the survey information offered in the textbook and by broadening the kinds of sociological material to which students are exposed beyond that dictated by the textbook format. We have drawn upon our prior, positive experiences with readers in compiling this one. Its design reflects our own teaching needs and preferences, which we believe are similar to those of many other instructors in the family course. We hope instructors will find our organization to be flexible, the subjects compatible with those they feel to be important, and the readings of high scholarly content and value. At the same time, we believe that the readings will be of interest to students and will provide them with insights into both the family as a social institution and their personal family experiences.

The selections are grouped into several parts or sections. With three exceptions (Sections One, Two, and Eight), the organization reflects a life cycle approach to family, an approach compatible with most family texts. The first two sections on historical and comparative family systems are important because these tend to be areas that family texts deal with only in generalities, if at all. We believe that we can understand the contemporary family in the North American culture only when we understand the historical and comparative contexts.

The final section (Eight) is an eclectic group of recent writings that are particularly intriguing because of their controversial viewpoints. We believe that students should be exposed to differing views on major issues, so these and many of the other selections throughout the book present views with which not all family social scientists agree. It is also important that students in the family course be exposed to materials written from a variety of theoretical and ideological perspectives, and the selections have been chosen accordingly. They are not consistently "functionalist," or consistently "feminist," or consistently anything else. However, we have tried to identify controversial views for what they are rather than to present them as "truth." Our goal is not to propagandize for particular points of view, but rather to encourage students to think for themselves.

In our main departure from existing readers, we have given each selection its own introduction rather than writing one overarching introduction for each section or part. This arrangement allows instructors to assign the readings in any sequence, since each selection and its introduction can stand alone. The introductions attempt to set the stage for the piece rather than to summarize its content. For instance, students are advised when the argument presented in a selection is highly controversial. The addition of these introductions should greatly enhance students' understanding of and appreciation for the readings.

Finally, our objective has been to include materials that conform to high scholarly and intellectual standards while remaining understandable to students who lack strong backgrounds in sociology and statistics. Therefore, selections that are either journalistic and simplistic or filled with jargon and arcane statistics have been avoided. We have tried to include interesting selections, but only those that will stimulate students to think about family issues in a sophisticated manner.

We find the study of the American family to be fascinating, and if this book helps to engender a similar fascination on the part of students, we will consider our efforts in producing it to have been successful.

*Norval D. Glenn*
*Marion Tolbert Coleman*

# Acknowledgments

The work on this volume was a challenging and enriching experience due to the involvement and support of a number of individuals. We would like to thank Chuck Bonjean, Sociology Editor for Dorsey Press and our colleague, for asking us to take on this project. His enthusiasm and guidance from the earliest conversations about the book kept our energy levels high. Paul O'Connell, Senior Editor at Dorsey Press, was both persistent and patient with us. The reader was greatly improved by the suggestions of our critical readers, Mary Ann Lamanna, The University of Nebraska at Omaha; Patrick McHenry, The Ohio State University; Steven L. Nock, The University of Virginia; and Jill Sobel Quadagno, Florida State University. Finally, we thank Annamaria Sergi for her diligent clerical assistance. Her careful attention to the myriad details involved in compiling this text saved us many hours and much sanity.

*N.D.G.*
*M.T.C.*

# Contents

*Section One*

# A Historical Perspective

# 1

STUART A. QUEEN, ROBERT W. HABENSTEIN, AND JILL S. QUADAGNO

# The Family of the Ancient Romans

*The family of the ancient Romans, and the changes that occurred in that family as the Republic gave way to the Empire and Roman civilization reached its zenith, inspire special interest because many observers have noted similarities between the changes in the Roman family and changes in the family systems of modern Western civilization in the past century. In both cases, authority weakened within the family, movement toward equality of men and women took place, the enforcement of restrictive sex norms broke down, and a historically rare condition emerged whereby either husband or wife could divorce the other at will.*

*Some cyclical change theorists believe that civilizations evolve through predictable stages of development and decline analogous to those of a biological organism. Some of these theorists, in turn, consider the changes that occurred in both the Roman and Western civilizations to characterize a rather late stage of the life cycle of civilizations and thus to indicate the incipient decline and impending death of a civilization. However, not all of these changes have occurred in other great civilizations—or at least the changes have not been well-documented. One important divergence between the seemingly parallel changes in the family structure in the Roman and modern Western civilizations is that they occurred only in the patrician (upper) class in Rome but have occurred at all social levels in the modern West.*

*Studying parallel changes in the Roman and Western families may or may not provide insight into the rise and fall of civilizations, but it does suggest that affluence and attendant liberation from a struggle for subsistence tend to engender a hedonism—a pleasure orientation—that permeates family relations, as well as other aspects of life.*



---

The Roman family in early times was like that of the ancient Hebrews in being primarily a household or a kinship group dominated by a male head, yet the two peoples differed sharply in that the early Romans were strictly monogamous, never approving polygyny or concubinage. In both cultures, important changes occurred. Among the Jews, these were associated with the destruction of their nation, among the Romans, with successful wars of conquest, called the Punic Wars, and accumulated wealth.

Of course, there was no sudden change in customs, traditions, and mores in either Judah or Rome, but there are many reasons for considering the Punic Wars as a turning point in the history of the Roman family. Long absences of men serving in the army, growth of the capital city, rise of a leisure class, importation of slaves, and other changes in the structure of Roman society inevitably led to changes in family life. Many of the innovations were regarded as vicious and degenerate, both by Roman satirists and later by Christian apostles. Hence it may be held that early Christian standards of family life drew heavily on the patriarchal tradition represented by the Jews and the Romans, but they also constituted a reaction against the innovations and the disorganization evident especially in the upper classes of imperial Rome.

## THE ROMAN FAMILY BEFORE THE PUNIC WARS

### Family Structure

Before the Punic Wars, which were fought in the third and second centuries B.C., the Roman family was patrilineal, patrilocal, and patriarchal. Dominance of the *paterfamilia* (father of a family) was not identical with that of the head of a Hebrew family, but it was no less complete.

The Roman *familia*, or household, included all those persons who were subject to the authority of the paterfamilias. These might be wife; unmarried daughters; sons and adopted sons (whether married or not) and their wives, sons, and unmarried daughters; and even remoter descendants, but always counted in the male line. In later centuries, *familia* included slaves and clients. Such a household usually broke up only on the death of its head. When this occurred, there might be as many new *familiae* as there were males directly subject to the *patria potestas*, a term meaning that the paterfamilias had absolute power over the members of the family. Individuals could become detached from the household by marriage, adoption, or emancipation without destroying the group as a whole.

The Roman *gens*, which we have called "clan" in the description of other cultures, was a group of households tracing their descent through males from a common ancestor. Membership in the Roman gens was indicated by the *nomen*, usually the second of three names that a citizen commonly possessed. Certain gentes were supposed to be descended from *patres* who in the days of the kings constituted the senate. Others had a later origin. The gens seems to have been much more than a listing of kinsmen, as frequently is the case in our culture. It was a group that provided guardians for minor children, the insane, and spendthrifts; it took over property left by members who died without any heirs; it conducted certain religious services and sometimes had a common burial plot; it even passed resolutions that were binding on its members.

As in ancient Judah, there was no place in early Roman society for detached persons. Everyone was supposed to belong to a household and to be under the control of its paterfamilias. When the paterfamilias died, each of the adult males under his direct control might become the head of a new household, inheriting a share of the estate. Estates sometimes were kept intact instead of being divided. This was managed by agreement of the heirs or, in later years, by provisions in the father's will. Minor children who were left orphans or half-orphans and unmarried grown daughters were commony placed under a guardian (*tutor*) selected by their gens. In later times, when daughters sometimes inherited property, they were not permitted to marry without consent of the gens, nor could their share of the family lands be alienated from the gens. If there were no immediate heirs, property was supposed to be divided among the nearest *agnati* (relatives descended from a common ancestor through the male line).

In all this, we see again that early Roman society was organized in kinship groups—household and gens—that apparently were stable and not often broken up. However, individuals could be detached from these groups. When a girl married, she usually became a member of her husband's *familia* and gens. A boy or man might be emancipated or adopted.

### Family Cycle

**Mate selection.** In general, mate selection in Rome was arranged by the fathers of the young couple. As among the Greeks, Hebrews, and other ancient peoples, romance had little to do with the approach to marriage. Roman fathers chose wives for their sons and husbands for their daughters without necessary consideration of their children's wishes. If the young people knew and were fond of each other, certainly that was no obstacle, but neither was it essential. When the Roman law spoke on consensus (consent of both parties), it meant agreement of the fathers, not of the bride and bridegroom. However, the *patres* were not entirely free. Law and the mores required that both parties to a marriage be physically mature, unmarried, and not too closely related.

Formal betrothal, although not required by law, was considered good form. In the *sponsalia* (betrothal), the girl was promised by her paterfamilias or *tutor* to the paterfamilias of her husband-to-be. Only if either party to the engagement was an independent person (*sui juris*) was the pledge made by or to him or her. There was sometimes a ceremony in the atrium of the girl's home: certain formulas were repeated; gifts were exchanged; perhaps the man gave the girl a ring to wear on the third finger of her left hand; and finally came congratulations, refreshments, and a "social hour." If there was later dissatisfaction with the engagement, it was most likely to be canceled by the girl's paterfamilias. If the boy's family wanted to break the engagement, they could not recover any of the presents. How regularly betrothal was followed by a wedding and how often engagements were broken we do not know, but we may suppose that in this early period such agreements were usually kept. We may also suppose that the formalities mentioned were observed in patrician rather than in plebeian homes.

Marriages were of two general kinds. If bride and bridegroom were both Roman citizens, their marriage was called *justae nuptiae* or *matrimonium justum* (regular marriage). The children would be citizens and possess all civil rights. If one of the mates was a Roman citizen and the other belonged to a group with *jus conubii* (privilege of marrying Romans) but without citizenship, the marriage was still called *matrimonium justum*, but the children acquired the civil status of the father. Marriage contracted between a man and a woman of different rank—for example, a patrician and a plebeian—was legal and the children were legitimate, but they took the civil status of the parent of lower degree. This second form of marriage was called *injustae nuptiae* or *matrimonium injustum*. The *jus conubii* was gradually extended, first to plebeians in 442 B.C., then to inhabitants of various Italian cities, and long after the Punic Wars to former slaves, or freedmen.

For the solemnization of a marriage, no legal forms were necessary in the sense of a license to be procured from a magistrate or ceremonies to be performed by persons authorized by the state. The only real essential was consensus—that is, agreement of both parties if they were *sui juris*, but usually of their patresfamilias. The acts considered most important in a wedding ceremony were the joining of hands in the presence of witnesses, the escorting of the bride to her husband's house, and, in later times, the signing of a marriage contract. Great pains were taken to select a lucky day. Auspices were taken and the results reported before the rest of the ceremonies proceeded. On the eve of her wedding day, the bride dedicated to the *lares*, or family gods of her father's house, her girlhood garments and ornaments. The next morning, she was dressed for the wedding by her mother. She wore a long, one-piece tunic fastened around the waist with a woolen band tied in the "knot of Hercules," which only the husband was privileged to untie. Over the tunic, she wore a brightly colored veil. Finally, there was a special coiffure and a wreath of flowers.

The ceremony associated with *matrimonium justim* could take one of several forms. The one most commonly used by patricians in early times was called *confarreatio*. In the girl's home, the bride and bridegroom were brought together by a once-married matron living with her husband in undisturbed wedlock. They joined hands in the presence of 10 witnesses, after which the bride repeated the words *Quando tu Gaius, ego Gaia* ("Wherever you are Gaius, I am Gaia"). Then the bride and groom sat side by side on stools covered with the skin of a sacrificed sheep. An offering was made to Jupiter of a cake of spelt (*far*), from which the ceremony got its name. Then the cake was eaten by the bride and groom, and a prayer was offered to Juno and some other deities. The couple then was congratulated, and the main ceremony was over.

Another type of ceremony was called *coemptio*. This was a fictitious sale of the girl made in the presence of five witnesses. A coin was laid on some scales that had to be held ceremoniously. Then followed the joining of hands and word of consent, as in the *confarreatio*. A prayer was recited, perhaps a sacrifice was offered, and then came congratulations.

The third form of ceremony was called *usus*. We have very little information about its details, although it appears that hands were clasped, words of consent spoken, and congratulations offered. If the wife then remained in her husband's house, not absenting herself for as many as three nights in succession for a year, she came under his authority. *Usus* appears to have been the ceremony most frequently employed by plebeians, although they also used *coemptio*. Marriage through any of these forms was defined as marriage with *manus*, meaning that a husband had power over his wife and rights to her property. *Manus* was akin to *patria potestas*.

After the principal ceremony, the bridegroom, with a show of force, tore the bride from her mother's arms and set forth in a public procession to his own house. Accompanied by torchbearers and flute players, the couple passed through the streets amid singing and feasting. On the way, the bride offered one coin to the gods of the crossroads and gave two coins to the bridegroom—one as a symbol of her dowry, the other as a gift to his household gods. The groom scattered nuts through the crowd. When the procession reached the groom's house, the bride wound bands of wool about the doorposts, after which she was carefully lifted over the threshold. Only invited guests accompanied the couple into the house, the rest of the crowd dispersing. In the atrium, the husband offered his wife fire and water. With a torch, she lighted a fire on the hearth and then recited a prayer. Finally, she was placed by the attending matrons on the marriage bed, which stood in the atrium.

It seems to have been a matter of some importance for the Roman bride to bring her husband a dowry (*dos*). The dowry usually was provided by her paterfamilias and became the property of her husband or of his paterfamilias.

The customs involved in mate selection and marriage were not similar in all times or for all social levels. Among people of modest means, the betrothal and wedding ceremonies must have been much simpler than those described. Among slaves, there was probably little or no formality.

**Child rearing.** As among the ancient Hebrews, children were desired, especially boys, in order to continue the family line, religious ritual, and property. The first important event in the life of a patrician child was its acceptance as a member of the family. It was customary to lay the newborn baby at the father's feet. If he took it in his arms, he thereby acknowledged it as his own and admitted it to the rights and privileges of membership in the family. If he refused to accept the newborn, the child became an outcast and probably would be exposed by the roadside. It might perish, or it might be taken away and reared by someone who wanted a foster child or a slave. It appears that such exposure was less frequent in Rome than it was in Greece and that the sale of children, which was permitted by law, rarely occurred in fact.

On the ninth day after birth, called *Dies Lustricus*, the child was given its individual name (*praenomen*), and various domestic rituals were performed. This was a festive occasion, with congratulations and gifts from friends and relatives. A string of beads was placed around the baby's neck, partly as a magical protection and partly as a means of identification. Often a locket, which was worn until the end of childhood, was also hung around the child's neck.

In earliest times, single names were apparently the rule, but double names were also used. Somewhat later, although still long before the Punic Wars, freemen often had three names. First came the *praenomen*, which, like our first name, indicated the individual. Next was the *nomen*, which indicated the gens, and third was the *cognomen*, which indicated the *familia*. This order was not always followed, and occasionally additional names were given. There were never more than 30 praenomena in use, hence they appeared over and over again. Fathers of patrician families were at some pains to avoid praenomena used by members of their gens whose social standing was low. Some of the plebeian branches of large families used no cognomen. Women less frequently had three names. Instead of having a praenomen, a woman was called *maxima* or *minor*, *secunda* or *tertia*. It should be noted that this is the first culture we have described in which family names appear somewhat in the manner that is familiar to contemporary Americans.

In those early centuries, Roman babies were usually nursed by their mothers. However, the care of the child was often shared by slaves who washed and dressed it, told it stories, sang to it, and rocked it in a cradle. Roman children played with dolls, blocks, carts, hoops, stilts, and other toys that would be familiar to many an American child. They had pets, too—dogs and birds, especially. They played games of many kinds.

Training of the children was conducted by both parents. Special stress was placed on moral development, reverence for the gods, respect for law, obedience to authority, and self-reliance. Most of this education was informal and came from steady association with the parents. In early days, children not only sat at the table with their elders, but also helped to serve the meals. For the more formal part of their education, Roman boys and girls apparently were taught the elements of reading, writing, and arithmetic by their mothers. Girls received almost all their education from the mother, while boys at the age of seven became their fathers' companions. If the father was a farmer, his son helped in the fields. If he was a man of affairs living in the capital city, his son joined him in receiving guests and visiting the forum and otherwise acquainted himself with business and government. If a father was too busy to give his son much attention, he might turn him over to a slave, who not infrequently was a more competent teacher than the father. Sometimes a number of other men would send their sons to be taught by the same slave. But in general, the training of Roman children was the responsibility of their parents.

No special ceremony marked the passing of the girls into womanhood, but an important celebration marked that of boys into manhood. Usually on the March 17 nearest his seventeenth birthday, the boy formally laid aside his boyhood toga and put on the garb of a man. A sacrifice was offered, and there was a procession to the forum. Every effort was expended to make this an impressive occasion. If it was on the feast day called *Liberalia*, the forum was sure to be crowded, an offering was made in the temple of Liber, and the day ended with a feast at the father's house.

Again, the records and narratives that have come down to us appear to describe the growing up and the ceremonies experienced by the sons of patricians. We can only surmise how differently things went for the children of plebeians, and slaves. In any case, growing up in early Roman society seems to have been fairly serious business, relieved, however, by affectionate ties within the family and a considerable degree of security.

**Breaking family ties.** Family ties sometimes were broken deliberately. As we have seen when a girl married, she usually joined her husband's *familia*. Even a boy might leave his parental home and parents' control through emancipation or adoption. *Emancipation* involved a ceremony of fictitious sale whereby a son was set free from the *patria potestas* and detached completely from his family. *Adoption* involved the formal transfer of a person from one household to another. The Romans adopted not only small boys, but even grown men; the adopting group hoped to ensure itself a successor to a previously heirless head, and the adopted person, to gain security and status.

Like the household and gens in which it was embedded, the conjugal family, or marriage group, seems to have been very stable before the Punic Wars. The first Roman divorce of which we have definite information occurred about 300 B.C.,[1] but there seems to have been earlier provision in the law.

As among the early Hebrews, only men could take the initiative to terminate an unsatisfactory marriage. In contrast to a Hebrew husband, however, a Roman was restricted in a number of ways. If the marriage had been celebrated with the formal ceremony called *confarreatio*, it could be dissolved only with considerable difficulty and a corresponding ceremony called *difarreatio*. If a man was contemplating the dismissal of his wife, he was required by law to assemble a council of his and her male relatives, unless he had caught her in adultery, in which case his hands were free and he might punish her even with death. The grounds for divorce were, in addition to adultery, making poison, drinking wine, and possibly counterfeiting house keys. Toward

[1]James Donaldson, *Woman: Her Position and Influence in Ancient Greece and Rome, and among the Early Christians* (London and New York: Longmans, Green, 1907), pp. 116–17.

the end of this period, less serious grounds were used as a basis for divorce. One man dismissed his wife with the charge that she had appeared in the streets without a veil, and another complained that his wife had gone to the public games without informing him. Divorce was essentially a private matter, and the right to it was a privilege of the husband or his father; nevertheless, if he got rid of his wife on other than recognized grounds, he might be severely reproved by the censor as well as by his kinsmen and the general public. The power of the paterfamilias was so great that he not only could divorce his own wife, but also could arrange the divorce of his son with or without the son's consent.

**Family Controls**

Theoretically, the Roman father had absolute power over his children and his sons' children: he decided whether the newborn child was to be accepted into the family; he punished misconduct by often severe penalties; he alone could acquire and exchange property; he could claim the earnings of his offspring; and he alone could proceed against anyone who injured or abducted his children. In a sense, the members of the family were his chattels. However, this theoretically absolute power was restricted in practice, at first by custom and later by law. Very early, the right to expose or kill a child was limited, although the father continued to decide whether a child should be admitted to his household. Custom also put a check on arbitrary and cruel punishments. It obliged the paterfamilias to call a council of relatives whenever he contemplated inflicting severe penalties on a child, and public sentiment probably forced him to accept the council's verdict. In regard to the ownership of property, the father was not so much an individual titleholder as a trustee for the family as a whole. Finally, he was a kind of priest responsible for sacrifices to the gods, offerings to the spirits of dead ancestors, and family worship in general. His power (*patria potestas*) might be extinguished in several ways—obviously by death, but also by loss of citizenship. The marriage of his daughter usually removed her from the family and transferred her to the authority of her husband. The emancipation or adoption of a child freed it from the father's power.

We have observed that within the family, the paterfamilias had authority to arrange marriages and divorces, but always subject to certain mores and laws. Thus he was required to see that bride and groom were physically mature, unmarried, and not too close of kin. He was restricted in the matter of divorce by the necessity of calling a council of his and his wife's relatives if his marriage had been celebrated by the ceremony called *confarreatio*.

The sexual mores of the early Romans constituted a stern code that seems to have been rather generally followed. If a wife was caught in adultery, she might be killed at once, and an unchaste betrothed girl might be punished in the same way. Concubinage was disapproved. By the third century B.C., the Romans seem to have had a double standard, for Cato is quoted as having said, "If you were to catch your wife in adultery, you would kill her with impunity without trial; but if she were to catch you, she would not dare to lay a finger upon you."[2]

Before the Punic Wars, family controls were chiefly internal, although not entirely so. Moreover, they seem to have been quite effective throughout most of this period. A sense of unity comparable with that of the early Hebrew family accompanied the controls. It bound together not only husband and wife, parents and children, but very often a three-generation household under *patria potestas*. As among the Hebrews, a wife was legally subject to her husband's rule, but she was in fact his companion and partner, and respected and loved as a person.

## THE ROMAN FAMILY AFTER THE PUNIC WARS

In the third and second centuries B.C., there were three long wars with Carthage that took Roman men away from home for years at a time. During those years of war, women inevitably assumed many responsibilities and found some freedom from the usual control of their husbands and fathers. Responsibility and freedom probably were the opening wedges for the "emancipation" of women and the establishment of a more egalitarian pattern of family life. The wartime experiences of men in the army and of women left behind contributed also to the breakdown of the old code of sexual mores. The family system was inevitably affected by the changing economic situation in Rome. Wealth poured in from tribute levied on conquered peoples. There was an increase of idle rich at one end of the scale and of slaves and landless freemen at the other. When the republic finally gave way to the empire, extravagance, conspicuous consumption, and domestic intrigue had become notorious—at least among the upper classes.

During the Punic Wars, the sex ratio appears to have changed from one of male to one of female predominance. Whether this new ratio continued and whether it contributed significantly to the rising number of unmarried adults we do not know, but by the beginning of the Christian era, there was a considerable number of bachelors and of unmarried women. With increasing frequency, women who did marry remained legally members of their fathers' families. Thus the power of the husbands was greatly reduced, while wives became more independent. Although we have no statistics on the subject, there is no doubt that divorce became more frequent. In general, marriage and the family became less important and less stable. Even the atrium reflected the declining significance of the family, for family gods often were tucked away, the hearth sometimes was removed, and meals were eaten in various parts of the house.

### Growing Instability of the Family Structure

Enough has already been presented to demonstrate that there were significant changes in attitudes and practices affecting marriage and the family.

---

[2]Quoted in Willystine Goodsell, *A History of Marriage and the Family* (New York: Macmillan, 1934), p. 126.

Change does not necessarily signify deterioration, of course, but during the Punic Wars, there *was* an increase in family disorganization and instability.

To begin with, some marriages were contracted without the expectation of an enduring union. Although our information on this point is very limited, it is alleged by some historians that upper-class Romans occasionally entered into what might be called *companionate marriages*—that is, husband and wife agreed openly or tacitly to continue their marriage only as long as it suited them.

It is also true that after the Punic Wars divorce became easier to obtain and more frequent than it had been in earlier times. Some prominent Romans divorced their wives on the grounds of mere suspicion or were really motivated by desires to marry younger or wealthier women or to secure political advantages. Women now found it possible to secure divorces. We do not know how widespread divorce really became. It is likely that the numbers have been much exaggerated. In any case, much publicity has been given to the divorces of socially prominent persons, as is the case in contemporary America. It appears that Ovid and the younger Pliny each married three times; Cleopatra and Antony, four times; Sulla and Pompeii, five time. Juvenal tells about a woman who had 8 husbands in 5 years, and Martial tells of another who had 10 husbands. However, there is no good reason to suppose that frequent divorce and remarriage was representative of the common people.

**Economic changes.** The custom of a dowry (*dos*) provided by the wife's family continued from early times. However, instead of being the unquestioned property of the husband or his paterfamilias, it was the husband's to use only while the marriage lasted. If the marriage was broken by death or divorce, the dowry usually reverted to the wife, her father, or her heirs, depending on a number of circumstances. If, however, a divorce was caused by some fault of the wife, her husband could retain part of the *dos*. In the later imperial period there developed another sort of matrimonial property—"gift for the sake of marriage" (*donatio propter nuptias*). It was presented by the husband, but it remained his property both during and after the marriage unless there was a divorce in which he was held to be at fault. In that case, all or part of the *donatio propter nuptias* could be claimed by the injured wife. Both the *dos* and the *donatio* appear to have contributed to the financial stability of the family, but the arrangements just mentioned indicate that enough marriages were expected to end in divorce to necessitate some definite provision for disposing of this property.

There were other departures from past customs and laws that concerned the title to property and its inheritance, especially by women. As we noted in our review of the earlier period, property was commonly thought of as belonging to the family as a whole, but it was usually administered by the paterfamilias. In the later period, there was an increasing emphasis on individual ownership and disposition of property.

Fathers who had means frequently left large sums in trust for their daughters. Husbands sometimes willed property to their widows. Thus arose a class of wealthy women. This seemed such an anomaly to some Romans that they tried to check it. A law of 169 B.C. forbade a citizen who owned property worth more than 100,000 asses to make a woman his heir. Under other laws, the woman who remained a member of her father's family, instead of being transferred to her husband's, had only a limited right of inheritance from her husband if he died intestate. In this case, she received no consideration until her husband's relatives as remote as second cousins had received a share of his property.

**Changing status of women.** The changes in customary practices and the attempts at legal control imply radical changes in the status and roles of the sexes. Women were described as following "male pursuits," including such activities as attending military maneuvers, playing politics, studying philosophy, and joining new religious movements.

With the gradual disappearance of marriage with *manus*, the accumulation of independent wealth in the hands of women, and the participation of women in many activities outside the home, the relative status of the sexes changed from one of complete masculine dominance to one of near egalitarianism. This change was greatly resented by some conservative Roman men, who gave vent to their feelings in statements both picturesque and exaggerated. Thus the elder Cato is quoted as having said, "All men rule over women, we Romans rule over all men, and our wives rule over us."[3]

**Changing sexual mores.** Changes in sexual mores also occurred. Many lurid details have been reported about the corruption of morals in imperial Rome. According to some tales, concubinage and prostitution grew, abortion and infanticide became common, and adultery was all but universal. Upper-class women attended the theater and the circus and witnessed licentious dances. At banquets, women as well as men reclined while they sometimes ate and drank to excess or were entertained with ribald songs and plays. A Roman lady occasionally ran away with a gladiator. Upper-class women often displayed themselves in the streets and wore clothing that attracted attention to their physical charms. Clearly, there was enough of this sort of behavior to stir some moralists to express themselves vigorously. Thus Juvenal in his sixth satire was presumably urging a certain man to refrain from marriage on the grounds of women's faithlessness, intrigues, orgies, and extravagances when he wrote, "Chastity has long since left the earth. . . . No woman is content with a single lover nowadays." Nevertheless, the penalties for adultery continued to be severe, although they may not have been regularly imposed. Not only an adulterous wife, but also her husband, was deemed guilty of the crime. If 60 days after her offense had become known neither her husband nor her father had started legal action, any interested citizen might prosecute. If she was found guilty, she

[3]Quoted in ibid., p. 135.

was supposed to lose one-half of her dowry and one-third of her other property and to suffer banishment to a desert island. In certain cases, the father of a woman could kill both her and her lover. The husband had similar privileges, but he could instead claim compensation from the offending man and hold him until he paid. If a man was found guilty of adultery, he could be condemned to lose one-half of his property, to restore all of his wife's dowry, and to suffer banishment.

**Family Cycle**

Fathers continued to arrange the marriages of their children, but with the growth of the metropolis, there was an increasing tendency to resort to professional matchmakers. A betrothal arranged by a matchmaker was a contract, but not a personal relationship. Seneca is quoted as having said, "Any animal or slave, or every article of clothes or dish is tested before purchase, but never the bride by her groom. Any vices she may have of passion, stupidity, misshapedness, or evil breath one learnt only after marriage."[4] Although a betrothal was a contract, it apparently created no legal right like those on which breach-of-promise suits are based in our culture. If the contract specified that a finaicial penalty might be imposed in case of breach, such a provision was considered disgraceful. If anyone entered into an engagement while betrothed to another, however, he or she was deemed infamous. Moreover, if the engagement was broken, either party might reclaim whatever presents he or she had given the other. It is difficult to determine what inferences should be drawn from these data, but it is probably safe to say that a good many betrothals were broken and that young men and women enjoyed more freedom of choice than they had in earlier times.

Marriage without *manus* gradually became customary, and the three formal ceremonies that had accompanied *matrimonium justum* disappeared. The contracting of marriage continued to be a private affair, for it did not require the participation of any civil officer or religious functionary. The old-fashioned family council often was convened in order to obtain its consent, but emphasis was increasingly placed on the consent of the bride and groom. This did not eliminate bargaining, nor did it always make for a stable marriage; instead of considering such basic matters as affection, health, personal habits, and continuance of the family line, the young couple was often concerned with political and economic advantages of a temporary nature. When the particular purpose of the marriage had been achieved, either or both partners might secure a divorce and seek new marital ventures.

Many people ceased to regard marriage as a sacred obligation to family and state. Not only did they contract and dissolve marriages more lightly than in the past, but increasing numbers did not marry at all. The early Romans, like the Hebrews and most nonliterate peoples, had had practically no place for

[4]Quoted in Ludwig Friedlander, *Roman Life and Manners under the Early Empire* (New York: Dutton, 1908–13), vol. 1, p. 234.

unmarried adults. However, the growth of Rome into a great city, the accumulation of wealth—at least in the hands of certain classes—and the consequent possibility of maintaining oneself comfortably and respectably outside of marriage changed matters. Undoubtedly, some men and some women, too, sought freedom from family cares. It has been alleged that Roman men abstained from marriage because of resentment against the growing independence of ambitious women. This sounds, however, very much like rationalization. Even if the actual number of celibates was not very great, their existence stirred the government into imposing various penalties on unmarried adults.

It is evident that the authority of a paterfamilias over his children and grandchildren gradually diminished. He was still entitled to their earnings or other acquisitions, but his authority to punish was limited to "moderate chastisement." A son who committed a serious offense was turned over to the civil courts instead of to a family council. Quite apart from legal changes restricting paternal control, there appears to have been a shifting away from stern discipline toward moderation and even indulgence. Thus we read of children being spoiled and growing up to be "idlers and wastrels." No doubt this occurred, but again we lack specific accounts.

Many upper-class mothers turned over the care of their small children to nursemaids and slaves who fed them, supervised their play, told them fairy tales, and taught them. Girls learned to spin, weave, make clothes, and perform various household tasks. Some of them were also taught music and dancing and how to develop good posture. Their brothers were either tutored at home or sent to school, where they studied grammar, rhetoric, literature, and sports of various kinds. There is, however, good reason to believe that the majority of Roman children were still educated informally through observing and helping their elders. At least, there must have been a wide discrepancy in the lives of children on different socioeconomic levels. Unfortunately, our information is very sketchy. Most of what has come down to us pertains to those in the higher strata. These accounts primarily discuss the general conditions of children's upbringing rather than the children themselves. Ancient Rome had no nursery schools, child-guidance clinics, or juvenile courts to record the actual behavior of youngsters of any social class.

**Family Controls**

From the foregoing, it is evident that the old controls over family life not only were slipping from the paterfamilias, but also were not being effectively transferred to religious or civil authorities. Some of the efforts to replace "internal" family controls with "external" social controls have been noted. A few others will be mentioned here.

As early as 131 B.C., one of the censors recommended the adoption of a law compelling everybody to marry, observing that "if it were possible to have no wives at all, everybody would gladly escape that annoyance, but since nature had so ordained that it was not possible to live agreeably with them, nor to live at all without them, regard must be had rather to permanent welfare than to transitory pleasure."[5] Actual legislation came later, extending privileges to men and women in accordance with the number of their children and imposing penalties on bachelors. The *lex julia et papia pappaea* of A.D. 9 made unmarried women between the ages of 20 and 50 and unmarried men between 25 and 60 ineligible to receive estates or legacies, except from near relatives, unless they married within a short time. We do not know whether such laws had any important effects, but they provide indirect evidence of a decline in the importance that earlier had been attached to marriage and family life.

In the attempt to reduce the number of divorces, Augustus required "the active party" to execute a written document (*repudium*) in the presence of seven witnesses, all full Roman citizens. This apparently remained the law for some 500 years, although its effectiveness has not been determined.

**Family Functions**

Until the Punic Wars, the functions of the Roman *familia*—household, often of three generations, controlled by the paterfamilias—were quite inclusive. The household was at once a religious, an educational, an economic, and a legal institution. Each family had a system of worship of its own. Family gods and spirits of deceased ancestors required attention. The head of a Roman family was bound to offer food and drink to the departed for as long as he lived and to provide for the continuation of these acts of affection and piety after his death by perpetuating his family line. It was, therefore, a solemn religious duty to marry and have children; the religious and the procreational functions of the family were entwined. As we have noted, the greater part of a boy's education took place in the home, and practically all of the girl's training was given by her mother. Early households were largely self-sufficient. Hard work was a virtue engaged in by all. The property, while held by the paterfamilias, was regarded as belonging to the family as a whole. Finally, the paterfamilias exercised judicial functions. Alone or in consultation with his kinsmen, he judged the guilt of members of the family, and in accordance with his decision imposed punishment. The Roman family, therefore, was in many respects the most important institution in that culture during its early history.

After the Punic Wars, the Roman *familia* lost some of its importance, at least among the upper classes. Internal family controls were replaced by external laws made by religious and civil authorities, and the family lost ground as an agency of social control. It was less often the center of religious ceremonies and training, and sometimes ceased to be an economic unit. Fewer people married, and it became easier to dissolve an existing marriage. The authority of the father over his children and grandchildren diminished. Education of the young was more often carried on by tutors, some of whom were slaves, and some upper-class children were sent to school. It appears that the family underwent less change among common people, who continued to regard it as

---

[5]Quoted in James Bryce, *Studies in History and Jurisprudence* (Oxford: Oxford University Press [Clarendon Press], 1901), vol. 2, p. 801.

the arena for a rather inclusive array of activities and services—procreation, child rearing, economic support, religious observance, and social control.

## REFERENCES


Bryce, James. *Studies in History and Jurisprudence*. Oxford: Oxford University Press (Clarendon Press), 1901. See especially volume 2, chapter 16.

Carcopino, Jerome. *Daily Life in Ancient Rome*. New Haven, Conn.: Yale University Press, 1940. See especially chapter 4.

Donaldson, James. *Woman: Her Position and Influence in Ancient Greece and Rome, and among the Early Christians*. London and New York: Longmans, Green, 1907. See especially book 2.

Friedlander, Ludwig. *Roman Life and Manners under the Early Empire*. New York: Dutton, 1908–13. See espcially volume 1, chapter 5.

Goodsell, Willystine. *A History of Marriage and the Family*. New York: Macmillan, 1934. See especially chapter 4.

Johnston, Harold W. *The Private Life of the Romans*. (Revised edition by Mary Johnston.) Chicago: Scott, Foresman, 1903 and 1932.

Juvenal. *Satires*. See any convenient translation, especially of satires 2, 6, and 14.

Leffingwell, Georgia W. *Social and Private Life at Rome in the Time of Plautus and Terrance*. New York: Columbia University Press, 1918.

McDaniel, Walton B. *Roman Private Life and its Survivals*. Boston: Marshall Jones, 1924.

Ovid. *The Art of Love*. See any convenient translation.

Pliny, the Younger. *Letters*. See any convenient translation, especially of book 1, letter 14; book 2, letters 4 and 20; book 3, letter 16; book 4, letters 2, 10, and 19; book 5, letter 16; book 6, letter 4; and book 7, letter 5.

Roby, Henry J. *Roman Private Law in the Times of Cicero and of the Antonines*. Cambridge: Cambridge University Press, 1902.

Rogers, H. L., and Harley, T. R. *Roman Home Life and Religion*. Oxford: Oxford University Press (Clarendon Press), 1923.

# 2

WILLIAM M. KEPHART

# The Oneida Community

*Of the four theoretically possible forms of marriage, only three are known ever to have been institutionalized in human societies. In all known societies, a majority of the marriages have been monogamous, that is, one man has been married to one woman. In many societies, only monogamy has been allowed. However, a majority of known societies have allowed polygyny, the marriage of one man simultaneously to two or more women, and a very few societies have featured polyandry, the marriage of one woman simultaneously to two or more men. The remaining theoretically possible form is group marriage, the marriage of two or more men simultaneously to two or more women. Despite considerable experimentation with group mating, no clearcut evidence suggests that group marriage has ever been successfully established (institutionalized) in any society.*

*The usual explanation for the apparent absence of group marriage in past societies, and for an extraordinary degree of instability in experimental group matings in modern societies, is that sexual competition in a group mating tends to prevent the cooperation necessary for the group to function as a cohesive unit. However, evidence that some form of marriage other than monogamy, polygyny, or polyandry might be workable under certain special conditions comes from the Oneida Community. This was a group of about 300 adults who practiced both economic and sexual communism from 1849 until 1881 in upstate New York under the leadership of John Humphrey Noyes, a theologian who believed that humankind could be without sin. Whether the "complex marriage" of the Oneida Community was really a group marriage or simply an arrangement to provide socially approved sexual relations without marriage is debatable. Still, its existence for more than thirty years suggests that social order and cohesion do not necessarily require one of the three historical forms of marriage. In Oneida, the purpose of the sexual communism was to promote social cohesion by keeping loyalties focused on the group rather than on specific other persons, and it seems to have served that purpose well for several years.*

*However, the "complex marriage" was not successfully institutionalized in the sense of being transmitted to the next generation, and Oneida was not a total society, but rather was a small community surrounded by a society that allowed only monogamous marriage. The latter condition may have helped to preserve the sexual communism for a few years, since dissatisfied members of the comunity could leave at will, but hostility from the larger society contributed eventually to the abandonment of the unusual sexual practices.*



---

The world remembers the followers of John Humphrey Noyes not for their social or economic system, but for their practice of complex marriage. Rightly or wrongly, just as the term Mormon brings to mind polygamy, so the term Oneida conjures up thoughts of the "advanced" sex practices of the Community. It was Noyes himself who coined the phrase "free love," although because of adverse implications the phraseology was discarded in favor of complex marriage.

According to Noyes, it was natural for all men to love all women, and for all women to love all men. He felt that any social institution which flouted this truism was harmful to the human spirit. Romantic love—or "special love," as the Oneidans called it—was harmful because it was a selfish act. Monogamous marriage was harmful because it excluded others from sharing in connubial affection. The answer, obviously, was group marriage, and throughout the whole of their existence, this was what the Oneidans practiced.

Noyes's views on matrimony were also based on biblical interpretation. In the *Bible Argument*, published by the Oneida Community, the following statement appears:

> In the kingdom of heaven, the institution of marriage—which assigns the exclusive possession of one woman to one man—does not exist (Matt. 22:23-30).
>
> In the kingdom of heaven, the intimate union, which in the world is limited to pairs, extends through the whole body of believers (John 17:21). The new commandment is that we love one another, not by pairs, as in the World, but en masse.[1]

Over and over again, on both secular and religious grounds, John Humphrey Noyes criticized monogamy and extolled the virtues of group marriage.

---

[1]From Constance Noyes Robertson, ed. *Oneida Community: An Autobiography, 1851–1876* (Syracuse, N.Y.: Syracuse University Press, 1970), p. 267.

> The human heart is capable of loving any number of times and any number of persons. This is the law of nature. There is no occasion to find fault with it. Variety is in the nature of things, as beautiful and as useful in love as in eating and drinking. . . . We need love as much as we need food and clothing, and God knows it; and if we trust Him for those things, why not for love?[2]

Although he did not say it in so many words, Noyes hoped that the sharing of partners would serve as yet another element in the establishment of group solidarity. That he was able to succeed in this realm—despite the fact that the bulk of his followers had Puritan backgrounds—attests to his leadership capacity.

The system of complex marriage was relatively uncomplicated. Sexual relations were easy to arrange inasmuch as all the men and women lived in the Mansion House. If a man desired sexual intercourse with a particular woman, he simply asked her. If she consented, he would go to her room at bedtime and stay overnight. Once in a while, because of a shortage of single rooms, the above arrangements were not practicable, in which case the couple could use one of the "social" rooms set aside for that purpose.

**Sexual regulations.** Sex is never a simple matter (among humans, at least), and from the very beginning, complex marriage was ringed with prohibitions and restrictions. Other modifications arose over the years. By the early 1860s a fairly elaborate set of regulations was in force, so that throughout most of the Community's existence, sexual relations were not nearly so "free" and all-encompassing as outsiders believed.

Noyes taught that sex was not to be considered a "wifely duty," that is, something accepted by the female to satisfy the male. The notion was stated in positive terms in the *Handbook* [the book of rules and principles Noyes wrote for his followers]:

> The liberty of monogamous marriage, as commonly understood, is the liberty of a man to sleep habitually with a woman, liberty to please himself alone in his dealings with her, liberty to expose her to child-bearing without care or consultation.
>
> The term Free Love, as understood by the Oneida Community, does not mean any such freedom of sexual proceedings. The theory of sexual interchange which governs all the general measures of the Community is that which in ordinary society governs the proceedings in courtship.
>
> It is the theory that love after marriage should be what it is *before* marriage—a glowing attraction on both sides, and not the odious obligation of one party, and the sensual recklessness of the other. (p. 42)

Noyes went to great pains in his discourses to separate the "amative" from the "propagative" functions of sex. It was only when the two were separated, he said, that the true goals of Perfectionism could be attained. In practice, this meant that males could have sexual intercourse up to, but not including, ejaculation. (Females, of course, could achieve sexual climax at any time.)

---

[2]From Robert Parker, *A Yankee Saint* (New York: Putnam, 1935), pp. 182–183.

There were two exceptions to the nonejaculatory rule: (a) when the male was having intercourse with a female who was past menopause, and (b) when a child was desired. Authorization for childbearing involved a special procedure. However, by permitting males to achieve ejaculation only with postmenopausal females, the Perfectionists not only were employing a novel method of birth control—effective, as it turned out—but were using an ingenious method of providing the older, less attractive women with sex partners.

The *Handbook* also points up the desirability of courtship, and there is no doubt that in the Oneida Community sustained courtship was the order of the day. Men were eager to win the ladies' favor, so they acted accordingly. And the ladies evidently found it refreshing to be wooed by the men. Pierrepont Noyes [a son of John Humphrey Noyes] catches the full flavor of the relationship in the following passage:

> There has survived in my memory an impression, a dim recognition, that the relation between our grown folks had a quality intimate and personal, a quality that made life romantic. Unquestionably, the sexual relations of the members under the Community system inspired a lively interest in each other, but I believe that the opportunity for romantic friendships also played a part in rendering life more colorful than elsewhere.
>
> Even elderly people, whose physical passions had burned low, preserved the fine essence of earlier associations; child as I was, I sensed a spirit of high romance surrounding them, a vivid, youthful interest in life that looked from their eyes and spoke in their voices and manners.[3]

As in society at large, the men were apparently more enthusiastic than the women, at least in a strictly sexual connotation. The practice of having the man ask the woman for sex relations, therefore, was soon replaced by a new system.

**Use of a go-between.** Under the new system, the man would make his request known to a central member—usually an older woman—who in turn would pass on the request. In practice, the use of a go-between served a number of purposes. It spared the women—it was they who suggested the system—the embarrassment of having to voice a direct refusal or conjure up an excuse. As one of the interviewees told me: "Sex relations in the community were always voluntary. There was never any hint at coercion. But after they started using a go-between, it made things easier for everybody."

Employment of a go-between also gave the Community a measure of control over the sexual system. For example, the Perfectionists were ever on guard against two of their members falling in love—special love, as they called it. So if a particular couple were having too-frequent relations, the go-between would simply disallow further meetings between them. In the matter of procreation, too, it was important that the Community be able to establish pater-

[3]Pierrepont Noyes, *My Father's House: An Oneida Boyhood* (Gloucester, Mass.: Peter Smith, 1966), p. 131.

nity. And while this was not always possible, the go-between greatly facilitated the identification process.

It should be mentioned that the Oneidans considered sex to be a private matter. Aside from the particular go-between involved, "who was having relations with whom" never became common knowledge. Indeed, the subject itself was taboo. Public displays of affection, vulgarity of any kind, sexual discussions or innuendoes, immodest behavior—all were forbidden. During the many decades of their existence, the Perfectionists had but one unpleasant experience along these lines.

William Mills was accepted into the Community during the early 1860s. A rather vulgar person, it soon became obvious that he was a misfit. The women would have nothing to do with him. As a consequence, he started to cultivate the friendship of teenage girls. Breaking the Perfectionist taboo, Mills would discuss sexual matters openly with them, asking them about their amours and boasting of his own. The situation soon became intolerable, and he was asked to leave. He refused. The central members were in a quandary: from time to time others had been requested to leave, but none had ever refused. After several discussions, it was decided—in an almost literal sense—to take the bull by the horns. According to Robert Parker:

> Mills found himself, one winter night, suddenly, unceremoniously, and horizontally propelled through an open window, and shot—harmlessly but ignominiously—into the depths of a snowdrift. It was the first and only forcible expulsion in the history of the community.[4]

Taken collectively, the regulations concerning sex were designed to permit maximum freedom for the individual without jeopardizing the harmony of the group as a whole. This involved a delicate balance of rights and responsibilities, and Noyes was well aware of this fact. He strove mightily to keep sex "within bounds," and whenever there were excesses he moved to correct them.

To take one example, the original procedure had been for the man to go to the woman's room and remain all night. Some of the women evidently complained that the practice was too "tiring," and Noyes saw to it that a change was made. Henceforth, the man would stay for an hour or so and then return to his own room. This was the procedure followed throughout most of the Community's existence.

Along these same lines, the Perfectionist leader constantly inveighed against the so-called fatiguing aspects of sexual intercourse. Instead of advocating *coitus reservatus*, for instance, he could have endorsed *coitus interruptus*—both being equally effective as birth-control techniques. But Noyes was convinced that ejaculation had a debilitating effect on the male, hence he preached against its danger.

He was also against *coitus interruptus* on theological grounds, since the practice is condemned in the Bible. That is, when Onan had intercourse with

---

[4]Parker, *A Yankee Saint*, p. 223.

his deceased brother's wife, he refused to ejaculate in natural fashion. Instead, he "spilled it on the ground, lest that he should give seed to his brother. And the thing which he did displeased the Lord." (Gen. 38:9-10)

Additionally, Noyes totally rejected all forms of contraception. For reasons best known to himself, he looked upon them as "machinations of the French" and refused even to consider them. To be acceptable, birth control had to include a strong element of (male) self-control.

Interestingly enough—and in spite of some rather questionable logic—John Humphrey Noyes' ideas about sex and birth control proved workable. His goal was to provide complex marriage with a spiritual base, and he apparently succeeded. Throughout the whole of the Community's existence, there were no elopements, no orgies, no exhibitionism. Nor was there any instance of incest, sadism, masochism, or any other sexual activity that would have been considered reprehensible by the standards then current.

**Ascending fellowship.** Complex marriage did pose one problem that Noyes went to great pains to solve: how to keep the older, less attractive members of the community from being by-passed in favor of the younger members. True, it was only with postmenopausal women that men were allowed to achieve ejaculation, but this restriction provided an inadequate answer to the problem. The real answer was to be found in the principle of ascending fellowship.

According to this principle, members were ranked from least to most perfect. Any follower who wished to improve himself, therefore, was advised to associate with someone higher on the spiritual scale. (Noyes taught that a high-ranking person would not in any way be downgraded by associating with a person of lower rank.) Since it took time and experience to achieve high spiritual rank, those at the upper end of the scale were nearly always the older, more mature members. It was these older Perfectionists rather than the younger members who were thus regarded as the desirable partners.

The Oneida *Handbook* contains the following explanation:

> According to the Principle of Ascending Fellowship, it is regarded as better—in the early stages of passional experience—for the young of both sexes to associate in love with persons older than themselves, and if possible with those who are spiritual and have been some time in the school of self-control—and who are thus able to make love safe and edifying.
>
> This is only another form of the popular principle of contrasts. It is well understood by physiologists that it is undesirable for persons of similar character and temperament to mate together. Communists have discovered that it is undesirable for two inexperienced and unspiritual persons to rush into fellowship with each other; that it is better for both to associate with persons of mature character and sound sense. (p. 39)

There is no doubt that age was shown great respect in the Community. This is the way Noyes wanted it, and this is the way it was. In addition, the fact that younger men were encouraged to have sexual relations with older women served to strengthen the birth-control measures that were used.

## UNANSWERED QUESTIONS ABOUT COMPLEX MARRIAGE

The foregoing pages give the broad outlines of the sexual system employed by the Oneidans. But many questions remain unanswered. To what extent did the women refuse sexual requests? Was a go-between really used, or was this a formality which was easily by-passed? Did women as well as men initiate sexual requests? Was not the factor of male jealousy a problem? Did the Community women have difficulty adjusting sexually to a large number of different partners? I have attempted to find answers to these questions, but with limited success. One of those interviewed made the following points:

> I grant the questions are of sociological interest, but look at it from our view. If somebody came to you and asked questions concerning the sex life of your parents and grandparents, you'd have a tough time answering. The same with us. When the old Community broke up, there was a natural reluctance to discuss sex. Former members didn't discuss their own sex lives, and naturally their children and grandchildren didn't pry.
>
> I often wish the old people had had a regular system of marriage. Then we wouldn't have had such bad publicity—most of it incorrect or misleading. If it weren't for the sex part, the Oneida Community might have been forgotten long ago.

One of the officers of Oneida Ltd. [the company formed when the Oneida Community disbanded] supplied some interesting information. During the decades of the Community's existence, many of the Oneidans were in the habit of keeping diaries. (Diary keeping was evidently much more common in the nineteenth century than it is today.) Some of the Perfectionists also accumulated bundles of personal letters. After the Community broke up, and as the members died over the years, the question arose as to what to do with all these documents. Since so much of the material was of a personal and sexual nature, since names were named, and inasmuch as the people's children and grandchildren were still living, it was decided to store all the old diaries, letters, and other personal documents in the vaults of Oneida Ltd. Several years ago, this officer received permission to examine the material in order to see what should be done with it.

> I went through some of the stuff—old diaries and things— and a lot of it was awfully personal. Names and specific happenings were mentioned—that kind of thing. Anyway, I reported these facts to the company, and it was decided that in view of the nature of the material, it should all be destroyed.
>
> So, one morning we got a truck—and believe me, there was so much stuff we needed a truck—loaded all the material on, and took it out to the dump and burned it. We felt that divulging the contents wouldn't have done ourselves or anybody else any good.

While there is no doubt that the burned material would have shed much light on the sexual behavior of the Perfectionists, the action taken by the company is understandable. Oneida Ltd. is not in business to further the cause of sociological research, and regardless of how much the material might have benefited social scientists, there was always the possibility that the contents would have proved embarrassing to the company or to some of the direct descendants.

The diary-burning episode has been mentioned in some detail in order to show how difficult it is to answer sexual questions of the kind posed above. The interview information presented here should be thought of as a series of clues rather than as a set of definitive answers.

To what extend did the Oneida women refuse sexual requests? The company official who had examined some of the material to be burned reported that there was nothing therein to suggest a high refusal rate. Another male respondent stated that he had been informed by an old Community member that the man "had never been refused." One female interviewee felt that refusal was a problem "in some instances." Most of those interviewed, however, had no specific information to offer. My impression is that female refusal was not a major problem, although the issue probably arose from time to time.

Was a go-between really used, or was this a formality which was easily bypassed? None of those interviewed had any direct evidence to offer. All that can be said is that there were no *reported* instances where the rule was broken. Since the matter was never raised by the Oneidans themselves, it is doubtful whether a real issue was involved. Given the religious orientation and esprit de corps of the members, there is every reason to suppose that the stipulated procedure was followed.

Did the Oneida women, as well as the men, initiate sexual requests? This question drew a generally negative answer from all the respondents. Several said they knew of some coquetry on the part of certain women, but they had never heard of anything more direct. Two of the older female respondents stated that there was one known case where a woman went to a man and asked to have a child by him. In this instance, however, the implication is not clear, since the Perfectionists differentiated sharply between amative and procreative aspects of sex. All reports considered, it appears that the Oneida females were no more disposed to assume the role of active partner than were females in society at large.

Was male jealously a problem? Apparently not; at least, none of the interviewees knew of any major flareups. One respondent put it as follows:

> I don't think it was much of a problem. Certainly the old folks, when they talked about the Community, never made any issue of it. Their religious teachings emphasized spiritual equality, and their whole way of life was aimed at stamping out feelings of jealously.
>
> Also, with so many women to choose from, why would a man experience feelings of jealousy? Once in a while a man and woman would be suspected of falling in love—"special love" they called it—but it happend infrequently. When it did, the couple were separated. One would be sent to Wallingford, Connecticut—we had a small branch there....

Noyes himself constantly preached against the dangers of male jealousy. On one occasion he remarked, "No matter what his other qualifications may be, if a man cannot love a woman and be happy seeing her loved by others, he is a selfish man, and his place is with the potsherds of the earth.[5] On another occasion—referring to a man who was becoming romantically involved with a particular woman—he said, "You do not love her, you love happiness."[6]

It is likely that male jealousy was at most a minor problem, though it did receive a certain amount of attention. Female jealousy was evidently no problem at all. It was not mentioned by any of those interviewed, nor, so far as I could ascertain, was the matter ever raised during the Community's existence.

Did the women of the Community have difficulty in adjusting sexually to a large number of different partners? Respondents had little or nothing to report on this matter—which is unfortunate, since the question is an intriguing one. The Oneida women were encouraged to have sex with a variety of men but were not supposed to become emotionally involved with any of them.

The average American woman tends to emotionalize and romanticize her sexual experience, and the Perfectionist system—in which monogamous love played no part in the sex act—might well seem incongruous to her. In the case of the Oneida women, one can but conjecture. If they were indeed gratified by sexual variety, all human experience would be in for a contradiction. And yet, given the prevailing system—and their willingness to follow Noyes' teachings—who is to say what feminine feelings really were?

In the absence of the diary material, it is tempting to conclude that answers to such questions as these will never be found. Nevertheless, interest in present-day communes is great, and it is likely that investigation of historical groups like the Oneidans will continue.

---

[5]W. T. Hedden, "Communism in New York, 1848–1879," *The American Scholar,* 14 (Summer 1945), p. 287.

[6]From Raymond L. Muncy, *Sex and Marriage in Utopian Communities* (Bloomington: Indiana University Press, 1973), p. 176.

3

EDMUND S. MORGAN

# The Puritans and Sex

*Some people believe that the movement toward permissive premarital sex standards in the United States in the past two or three decades continues a long-term trend, that it is the latest phase of "progress" or "enlightenment." In fact, sex standards in Western societies have not always trended in one direction, and in the United States, as well as in several other societies, periods of relative permissiveness have alternated with periods of relative restrictiveness. The early colonial period in Puritan New England was a time of relative restrictiveness, but according to the selection that follows, the Puritans were not as sexually restrictive or as prudish as we tend to believe they were. One meaning of the term* puritanical *is prudish, the definition given by* Webster's New Collegiate Dictionary *being, "of, relating to, or characterized by a rigid morality." However, Morgan presents evidence that at least regarding sexual matters, the Puritans were not especially puritanical. This is but one of many instances in which careful historical research has revealed inaccuracies in popular views of family and sexual relations at various times in the past.*

Source: Reprinted from "The Puritans and Sex" by Edmund S. Morgan in *The New England Quarterly* 15, no. 4, (December 1942), pp. 591–607. 

Henry Adams once observed that Americans have "ostentatiously ignored" sex. He could think of only two American writers who touched upon the subject with any degree of boldness—Walt Whitman and Bret Harte. Since the time when Adams made this penetrating observation, American writers have been making up for lost time in a way that would make Bret Harte, if not Whitman, blush. And yet there is still more truth than falsehood in Adam's statement. Americans, by comparison with Europeans or Asiatics, are squeamish when confronted with the facts of life. My purpose is not to account for this squeamishness, but simply to point out that the Puritans, those bogeymen of the modern intellectual, are not responsible for it.

At the outset, consider the Puritans' attitude toward marriage and the role of sex in marriage. The popular assumption might be that the Puritans frowned on marriage and tried to hush up the physical aspect of it as much as possible, but listen to what they themselves had to say. Samuel Willard, minister of the Old South Church in the latter part of the seventeenth century and author of the most complete textbook of Puritan divinity, more than once expressed his horror at "that Popish conceit of the Excellency of Virginity."[1] Another minister, John Cotton, wrote that

> Women are Creatures without which there is no comfortable Living for man: it is true of them what is wont to be said of Governments, *That bad ones are better than none*: They are a sort of Blasphemers then who dispise and decry them, and call them *a necessary Evil*, for they are *a necessary Good*.[2]

These sentiments did not arise from an interpretation of marriage as a spiritual partnership, in which sexual intercourse was a minor or incidental matter. Cotton gave his opinion of "Platonic love" when he recalled the case of

> One who immediately upon marriage, without ever approaching the *Nuptial Bed*, indented with the *Bride*, that by mutual consent they might both live such a life, and according did sequestring themselves according to the custom of those times, from the rest of mankind, and afterwards from one another too, in their retired Cells, giving themselves up to a Contemplative life; and this is recorded as an instance of no little or ordinary Vertue; but I must be pardoned in it, if I can account it no other than an effort of blind zeal, for they are the dictates of a blind mind they follow therein, and not of that Holy Spirit, which saith *It is not good that man should be alone*.[3]

Here is as healthy an attitude as one could hope to find anywhere. Cotton certainly cannot be accused of ignoring human nature. Nor was he an isolated example among the Puritans. Another minister stated plainly that "the Use of the Marriage Bed" is "founded in mans Nature," and that consequently any withdrawal from sexual intercourse upon the part of husband or wife "Denies all reliefe in Wedlock vnto Human necessity: and sends it for supply vnto Beas-

---

[1]Samuel Willard, *A Compleat Body of Divinity* (Boston, 1726), 125 and 608–613.
[2]John Cotton, *A Meet Help* (Boston, 1699), 14–15.
[3]*A Meet Help*, 16.

tiality when God gives not the gift of Continency."[4] In other words, sexual intercourse was a human necessity and marriage the only proper supply for it. These were the views of the New England clergy, the acknowledged leaders of the community, the most Puritanical of the Puritans. As proof that their congregations concurred with them, one may cite the case in which the members of the First Church of Boston expelled James Mattock because, among other offenses, "he denyed Coniugall fellowship vnto his wife for the space of 2 years together vpon pretense of taking Revenge upon himself for his abusing of her before marryage."[5] So strongly did the Puritans insist upon the sexual character of marriage that one New Englander considered himself slandered when it was reported "that he Brock his deceased wife's hart with Greife, that he wold be absent from her 3 weeks together when he was at home, and wold never come nere her, and such Like."[6]

There was just one limitation which the Puritans placed upon sexual relations in marriage: sex must not interfere with religion. Man's chief end was to glorify God, and all earthly delights must promote that end, not hinder it. Love for a wife was carried too far when it led a man to neglect his God:

> . . . sometimes a man hath a good affection to Religion, but the love of his wife carries him away, a man may bee so transported to his wife, that hee dare not bee forward in Religion, lest hee displease his wife, and so the wife, lest shee displease her husband, and this is an inordinate love, when it exceeds measure.[7]

Sexual pleasures, in this respect, were treated like other kinds of pleasure. On a day of fast, when all comforts were supposed to be foregone in behalf of religious contemplation, not only were tasty food and drink to be abandoned but sexual intercourse, too. On other occasions, when food, drink and recreation were allowable, sexual intercourse was allowable too, though of course only between persons who were married to each other. The Puritans were not ascetics; they never wished to prevent the enjoyment of earthly delights. They merely demanded that the pleasures of the flesh be subordinated to the greater glory of God: husband and wife must not become "so transported with affection, that they look at no higher end than marriage it self." "Let such as have wives," said the ministers, "look at them not for their own ends, but to be fitted for Gods service, and bring them nearer to God."[8]

Toward sexual intercourse outside marriage the Puritans were as frankly hostile as they were favorable to it in marriage. They passed laws to punish adultery with death, and fornication with whipping. Yet they had no miscon-

---

[4]Edward Taylor, Commonplace Book (manuscript in the library of the Massachusetts Historical Society).

[5]Records of the First Church in Boston (manuscript copy in the library of the Massachusetts Historical Society), 12.

[6]Middlesex County Court Files, folder 42.

[7]John Cotton, *A Practical Commentary . . . upon the First Epistle Generall of John* (London, 1656), 126.

[8]*A Practical Commentary*, 126.

ceptions as to the capacity of human beings to obey such laws. Although the laws were commands of God, it was only natural—since the fall of Adam—for human beings to break them. Breaches must be punished lest the community suffer the wrath of God, but no offense, sexual or otherwise, could be occasion for surprise or for hushed tones of voice. How calmly the inhabitants of seventeenth-century New England could contemplate rape or attempted rape is evident in the following testimony offered before the Middlesex County Court of Massachusetts:

> The examination of Edward Wire taken the 7th of october and alsoe Zachery Johnson, who sayeth that Edward Wires mayd being sent into the towne about busenes meeting with a man that dogd hir from about Joseph Kettles house to goody marches. She came into William Johnsones and desired Zachery Johnson to goe home with her for that the man dogd hir. accordingly he went with her and being then as far as Samuell Phips his house the man over tooke them. which man caled himselfe by the name of peter grant would have led the mayd but she oposed itt three times: and coming to Edward Wires house the said grant would have kist hir but she refused itt: wire being at prayer grant dragd the mayd between the said wiers and Nathanill frothinghams house. hee then flung the mayd downe in the streete and got atop hir; Johnson seeing it hee caled vppon the fellow to be sivill and not abuse the mayd then Edward wire came forth and ran to the said grant and took hold of him asking him what he did to his mayd, the said grant asked whether she was his wife for he did nothing to his wife: the said grant swearing he would be the death of the said wire. when he came of the mayd; he swore he would bring ten men to pul down his house and soe ran away and they followed him as far as good[y] phipses house where they mett with John Terry and George Chin with clubs in there hands and soe they went away together. Zachy Johnson going to Constable Heamans, and wire going home. there came John Terry to his house to ask for beer and grant was in the streete but afterward departed into the towne, both Johnson and Wire both aferme that when grant was vppon the mayd she cryed out severall times.
>
> Deborah hadlocke being examined sayth that she mett with the man that cals himselfe peeter grant about good prichards that he dogd hir and followed hir to hir masters and there threw hir downe and lay vppon hir but had not the use of hir body but swore several othes that he would ly with hir and gett hir with child before she got home.
>
> Grant being present denys all saying he was drunk and did not know what he did.[9]

The Puritans became inured to sexual offenses, because there were so many. The impression which one gets from reading the records of seventeenth-century New England courts is that illicit sexual intercourse was fairly common. The testimony given in cases of fornication and adultery—by far the most numerous class of criminal cases in the records—suggests that many of the early New Englanders possessed a high degree of virility and very few inhibitions. Besides the case of Peter Grant, take the testimony of Elizabeth Knight about the manner of Richard Nevars's advances toward her:

---

[9]Middlesex Files, folder 48.

> The last publique day of Thanksgiving (in the year 1674) in the evening as I was milking Richard Nevars came to me, and offered me abuse in putting his hand, under my coates, but I turning aside with much adoe, saved my self, and when I was settled to milking he agen took me by the shoulder and pulled me backward almost, but I clapped one hand on the Ground and held fast the Cows teatt with the other hand, and cryed out, and then came to mee Jonathan Abbot one of my Masters Servants, whome the said Never asked wherefore he came, the said Abbot said to look after you, what you doe unto the Maid, but the said Never bid Abbot goe about his businesse but I bade the lad to stay.[10]

One reason for the abundance of sexual offenses was the number of men in the colonies who were unable to gratify their sexual desires in marriage.[11] Many of the first settlers had wives in England. They had come to the new world to make a fortune, expecting either to bring their families after them or to return to England with some of the riches of America. Although these men left their wives behind, they brought their sexual appetites with them; and in spite of laws which required them to return to their families, they continued to stay, and more continued to arrive, as indictments against them throughout the seventeenth century clearly indicate.

Servants formed another group of men, and women too, who could not ordinarily find supply for human necessity within the bounds of marriage. Most servants lived in the homes of their masters and could not marry without their consent, a consent which was not likely to be given unless the prospective husband or wife also belonged to the master's household. This situation will be better understood if it is recalled that most servants at this time were engaged by contract for a stated period. They were, in the language of the time, "covenant servants," who had agreed to stay with their masters for a number of years in return for a specified recompense, such as transportation to New England or education in some trade (the latter, of course, were known more specifically as apprentices). Even hired servants who worked for wages were usually single, for as soon as a man had enough money to buy or build a house of his own and to get married, he would set up in farming or trade for himself. It must be emphasized, however, that anyone who was not in business for himself was necessarily a servant. The economic organization of seventeenth-century New England had no place for the independent proletarian workman with a family of his own. All production was carried on in the household by the master of the family and his servants, so that most men were either servants or masters of servants; and the former, of course, were more numerous than the latter. Probably most of the inhabitants of Puritan New England could remember a time when they had been servants.

Theoretically no servant had a right to a private life. His time, day or night, belonged to his master, and both religion and law required that he obey his

---

[10]Middlesex Files, folder 71.

[11]Another reason was suggested by Charles Francis Adams in his scholarly article, "Some Phases of Sexual Morality and Church Discipline in Colonial New England," *Proceedings* of the Massachusetts Historical Society, xxvi, 477–516.

master scrupulously.[12] But neither religion nor law could restrain the sexual impulses of youth, and if those impulses could not be expressed in marriage, they had to be given vent outside marriage. Servants had little difficulty in finding the occasions. Though they might be kept at work all day, it was easy enough to slip away at night. Once out of the house, there were several ways of meeting with a maid. The simplest way was to go to her bedchamber, if she was so fortunate as to have a private one of her own. Thus Jock, Mr. Solomon Phipps's Negro man, confessed in court

> that on the sixteenth day of May, 1682, in the morning, betweene 12 and one of the clock, he did force open the back doores of the House of Laurence Hammond in Charlestowne, and came in to the House, and went up into the garret to Marie the Negro.
>
> He doth likewise acknowledge that one night the last week he forced into the House the same way, and went up to the Negro Woman Marie and that the like he hath done at severall other times before.[13]

Joshua Fletcher took a more romantic way of visiting his lady:

> Joshua Fletcher . . . doth confesse and acknowledge that three severall nights, after bedtime, he went into Mr. Fiskes Dwelling house at Chelmsford, at an open window by a ladder that he brought with him. the said windo opening into a chamber, whose was the lodging place of Gresill Juell servant to mr. Fiske. and there he kept company with the said mayd. she sometimes having her cloathes on, and one time he found her in her bed.[14]

Sometimes a maidservant might entertain callers in the parlor while the family were sleeping upstairs. John Knight described what was perhaps a common experience for masters. The crying of his child awakened him in the middle of the night, and he called to his maid, one Sarah Crouch, who was supposed to be sleeping with the child. Receiving no answer, he arose and

> went downe the stayres, and at the stair foot, the latch of doore was pulled in. I called severall times and at the last said if shee would not open the dore, I would breake it open, and when she opened the doore shee was all undressed and Sarah Largin with her undressed, also the said Sarah went out of doores and Dropped some of her clothes as shee went out. I enquired of Sarah Crouch what men they were, which was with them. Shee made mee no answer for some space of time, but at last shee told me Peeter Brigs was with them, I asked her whether Thomas Jones was not there, but shee would give mee no answer.[15]

In the temperate climate of New England it was not always necessary to seek out a maid at her home. Rachel Smith was seduced in an open field "about

---

[12]On the position of servants in early New England see *More Books*, XVII (September, 1942), 311–328.

[13]Middlesex Files, folder 99.

[14]Middlesex Files, folder 47.

[15]Middlesex Files, folder 52.

nine of the clock at night, being darke, neither moone nor starrs shineing." She was walking through the field when she met a man who

> asked her where shee lived, and what her name was and shee told him. and then shee asked his name, and he told her Saijing that was old Good-man Shepards man. Also shee saith he gave her strong liquors, and told her that it was not the first time he had been with maydes after his master was in bed.[16]

Sometimes, of course, it was not necessary for a servant to go outside his master's house in order to satisfy his sexual urges. Many cases of fornication are on record between servants living in the same house. Even where servants had no private bedroom, even where the whole family slept in a single room, it was not impossible to make love. In fact many love affairs must have had their consummation upon a bed in which other people were sleeping. Take for example the case of Sarah Lepingwell. When Sarah was brought into court for having an illegitimate child, she related that one night when her master's brother, Thomas Hawes, was visiting the family, she went to bed early. Later, after Hawes had gone to bed, he called to her to get him a pipe of tobacco. After refusing for some time,

> at the last I arose and did lite his pipe and cam and lay doune one my one bead and smoaked about half the pip and siting vp in my bead to giue him his pip my bead being a trundell bead at the sid of his bead he reached beyond the pip and Cauth me by the wrist and pulled me on the side of his bead but I biding him let me goe he bid me hold my peas folks wold here me and if it be replyed come why did you not call out I Ansar I was posesed with fear of my mastar least my master shold think I did it only to bring a scandall on his brothar and thinking thay wold all beare witnes agaynst me but the thing is true that he did then begete me with child at that tim and the Child is Thomas Hauses and noe mans but his.

In his defense Hawes offered the testimony of another man who was sleeping "on the same side of the bed," but the jury nevertheless accepted Sarah's story.[17]

The fact that Sarah was intimidated by her master's brother suggests that maidservants may have been subject to sexual abuse by their masters. The records show that sometimes masters did take advantage of their position to force unwanted attentions upon their female servants. The case of Elizabeth Dickerman is a good example. She complained to the Middlesex County Court,

> against her master John Harris senior for profiring abus to her by way of forsing her to be naught with him: . . . he has tould her that if she tould her dame: what cariag he did show to her shee had as good be hanged and shee replyed then shee would run away and he sayd run the way is befor you: . . . she says if she should liwe ther shee shall be in fear of her lif.[18]

---

[16]Middlesex Files, folder 44.

[17]Middlesex Files, folder 47.

[18]Middlesex Files, folder 94.

The court accepted Elizabeth's complaint and ordered her master to be whipped twenty stripes.

So numerous did cases of fornication and adultery become in seventeenth-century New England that the problem of caring for the children of extra-marital unions was a serious one. The Puritans solved it, but in such a way as to increase rather than decrease the temptation to sin. In 1668 the General Court of Massachusetts ordered:

> that where any man is legally convicted to be the Father of a Bastard childe, he shall be at the care and charge to maintain and bring up the same, by such assistance of the Mother as nature requireth, and as the Court from time to time (according to circumstances) shall see meet to Order: and in case the Father of a Bastard, by confession or other manifest proof, upon trial of the case, do not appear to the Courts satisfaction, then the Man charged by the Woman to be the Father, shee holding constant in it, (especially being put upon the real discovery of the truth of it in the time of her Travail) shall be the reputed Father, and accordingly be liable to the charge of maintenance as aforesaid (though not to other punishment) notwithstanding his denial, unless the circumstances of the case and pleas be such, on the behalf of the man charged, as that the Court that have the cognizance thereon shall see reason to acquit him, and otherwise dispose of the Childe and education thereof.[19]

As a result of this law a girl could give way to temptation without the fear of having to care for an illegitimate child by herself. Furthermore, she could, by a little simple lying, spare her lover the expense of supporting the child. When Elizabeth Wells bore a child, less than a year after this statute was passed, she laid it to James Tufts, her master's son. Goodman Tufts affirmed that Andrew Robinson, servant to Goodman Dexter, was the real father, and he brought the following testimony as evidence:

> Wee Elizabeth Jefts aged 15 ears and Mary tufts aged 14 ears doe testyfie that their being one at our hous sumtime the last winter who sayed that thear was a new law made concerning bastards that If aney man wear aqused with a bastard and the woman which had aqused him did stand vnto it in her labor that he should bee the reputed father of it and should mayntaine it Elizabeth Wells hearing of the sayd law she sayed vnto vs that If shee should bee with Child shee would bee sure to lay it vn to won who was rich enugh abell to mayntayne it wheather it wear his or no and shee farder sayed Elizabeth Jefts would not you doe so likewise If it weare your case and I sayed no by no means for right must tacke place: and the sayd Elizabeth wells sayed If it wear my Caus I think I should doe so.[20]

A tragic unsigned letter that somehow found its way into the files of the Middlesex County Court gives more direct evidence of the practice which Elizabeth Wells professed:

---

[19]William H. Whitmore, editor, *The Colonial Laws of Massachusetts. Reprinted from the Edition of 1660* (Boston, 1889), 257.

[20]Middlesex Files, folder 52.

> der loue i remember my loue to you hoping your welfar and i hop to imbras the but now i rit to you to let you nowe that i am a child by you and i wil ether kil it or lay it to an other and you shal have no blame at al for I haue had many children and none have none of them. . . . [*i.e.*, none of their fathers is supporting any of them.][21]

In face of the wholesale violation of the sexual codes to which all these cases give testimony, the Puritans could not maintain the severe penalties which their laws provided. Although cases of adultery occurred every year, the death penalty is not known to have been applied more than three times. The usual punishment was a whipping or a fine, or both, and perhaps a branding, combined with a symbolical execution in the form of standing on the gallows for an hour with a rope about the neck. Fornication met with a lighter whipping or a lighter fine, while rape was treated in the same way as adultery. Though the Puritans established a code of laws which demanded perfection—which demanded, in other words, strict obedience to the will of God, they nevertheless knew that frail human beings could never live up to the code. When fornication, adultery, rape, or even buggery and sodomy appeared, they were not surprised, nor were they so severe with the offenders as their codes of law would lead one to believe. Sodomy, to be sure, they usually punished with death; but rape, adultery, and fornication they regarded as pardonable human weaknesses, all the more likely to appear in a religious community, where the normal course of sin was stopped by wholesome laws. Governor Bradford, in recounting the details of an epidemic of sexual misdemeanors in Plymouth, wrote resignedly:

> it may be in this case as it is with waters when their streames are stopped or damned up, when they gett passage they flow with more violence, and make more noys and disturbance, then when they are suffered to rune quietly in their owne chanels. So wickednes being here more stopped by strict laws, and the same more nerly looked unto, so as it cannot rune in a comòne road of liberty as it would, and is inclined, it searches every wher, and at last breaks out wher it getts vente.[22]

The estimate of human capacities here expressed led the Puritans not only to deal leniently with sexual offenses but also to take every precaution to prevent such offenses, rather than wait for the necessity of punishment. One precaution was to see that children got married as soon as possible. The wrong way to promote virtue, the Puritans thought, was to "ensnare" children in vows of virginity, as the Catholics did. As a result of such vows, children, "not being able to contain," would be guilty of "unnatural pollutions, and other filthy practices in secret: and too oft of horrid Murthers of the fruit of their bodies," said Thomas Cobbett.[23] The way to avoid fornication and perversion was for parents to provide suitable husbands and wives for their children:

---

[21]Middlesex Files, folder 30.

[22]William Bradford, *History of Plymouth Plantation* (Boston, 1912), II, 309.

[23]Thomas Cobbett, *A Fruitfull and Usefull Discourse touching the Honour due from Children to Parents and the Duty of Parents towards their Children* (London, 1656), 174.

> Lot was to blame that looked not out seasonably for some fit matches for his two daughters, which had formerly minded marriage (witness the contract between them and two men in *Sodom*, called therfore for his Sons in Law, which had married his daughters, Gen. 19.14.) for they seeing no man like to come into them in a conjugall way . . . then they plotted that incestuous course, whereby their Father was so highly dishonoured. . . .[24]

As marriage was the way to prevent fornication, successful marriage was the way to prevent adultery. The Puritans did not wait for adultery to appear; instead, they took every means possible to make husbands and wives live together and respect each other. If a husband deserted his wife and remained within the jurisdiction of a Puritan government, he was promptly sent back to her. Where the wife had been left in England, the offense did not always come to light until the wayward husband had committed fornication or bigamy, and of course there must have been many offenses which never came to light. But where both husband and wife lived in New England, neither had much chance of leaving the other without being returned by order of the county court at its next sitting. When John Smith of Medfield left his wife and went to live with Patience Rawlins, he was sent home poorer by ten pounds and richer by thirty stripes. Similarly Mary Drury, who deserted her husband on the pretense that he was impotent, failed to convince the court that he actually was so, and had to return to him as well as to pay a fine of five pounds. The wife of Phillip Pointing received lighter treatment: when the court thought that she had overstayed her leave in Boston, they simply ordered her "to depart the Towne and goe to Tanton to her husband." The courts, moreover, were not satisfied with mere cohabitation; they insisted that it be peaceful cohabitation. Husbands and wives were forbidden by law to strike one another, and the law was enforced on numerous occasions. But the courts did not stop there. Henry Flood was required to give bond for good behavior because he had abused his wife simply by "ill words calling her whore and cursing of her." The wife of Christopher Collins was presented for railing at her husband and calling him "Gurley gutted divill." Apparently in this case the court thought that Mistress Collins was right, for although the fact was proved by two witnesses, she was discharged. On another occasion the court favored the husband: Jacob Pudeator, fined for striking and kicking his wife, had the sentence moderated when the court was informed that she was a woman "of great provocation."[25]

Wherever there was strong suspicion that an illicit relation might arise between two persons, the authorities removed the temptation by forbidding the two to come together. As early as November 1630, the Court of Assistants of Massachusetts prohibited a Mr. Clark from "cohabitacion and frequent keeping company with Mrs. Freeman, vnder paine of such punishment as the Court shall thinke meete to inflict." Mr. Clark and Mrs. Freeman were both bound "in

---

[24]Cobbett, 177.

[25]Samuel E. Morison and Zechariah Chafee, editors. *Records of the Suffolk County Court, 1671–1680. Publications* of the Colonial Society of Massachusetts. XXIX and XXX. 121, 410, 524, 837–841, and 1158: George F. Dow, editor, *Records and Files of the Quarterly Courts of Essex County, Massachusetts* (Salem, 1911–1921), I, 274; and V. 377.

XX £ apeece that Mr. Clearke shall make his personall appearance att the nexte Court to be holden in March nexte, and in the meane tyme to carry himselfe in good behavior towards all people and espetially towards Mrs. Freeman, concerneing whome there is stronge suspicion of incontinency." Forty-five years later the Suffolk County Court took the same kind of measure to protect the husbands of Dorchester from the temptations offered by the daughter of Robert Spurr. Spurr was presented by the grand jury

> for entertaining persons at his house at unseasonable times both by day and night to the greife of theire wives and Relations &c The Court having heard what was alleaged and testified against him do Sentence him to bee admonish't and to pay Fees of Court and charge him upon his perill not to entertain any married men to keepe company with his daughter especially James Minott and Joseph Belcher.

In like manner Walter Hickson was forbidden to keep company with Mary Bedwell, "And if at any time hereafter hee bee taken in company of the saide Mary Bedwell without other company to bee forthwith apprehended by the Constable and to be whip't with ten stripes." Elizabeth Wheeler and Joanna Peirce were admonished "for theire disorderly carriage in the house of Thomas Watts being married women and founde sitting in other mens Laps with theire Armes about theire Necks." How little confidence the Puritans had in human nature is even more clearly displayed by another case, in which Edmond Maddock and his wife were brought in court "to answere to all such matters as shalbe objected against them concerning Haarkwoody and Ezekiell Eurells being at their house at unseasonable tyme of the night and her being up with them after her husband was gone to bed." Haarkwoody and Everell had been found "by the Constable Henry Bridghame about tenn of the Clock at night sitting by the fyre at the house of Edmond Maddocks with his wyfe a suspicious weoman her husband being on sleepe [*sic*] on the bedd." A similar distrust of human ability to resist temptation is evident in the following order of the Connecticut Particular Court:

> James Hallett is to returne from the Correction house to his master Barclyt, who is to keepe him to hard labor, and course dyet during the pleasure of the Court provided that Barclet is first to remove his daughter from his family, before the sayd James enter therein.

These precautions, as we have already seen, did not eliminate fornication, adultery, or other sexual offenses, but they doubtless reduced the number from what it would otherwise have been.[26]

In sum, the Puritan attitude toward sex, though directed by a belief in absolute, God-given moral values, never neglected human nature. The rules of conduct which the Puritans regarded as divinely ordained had been formulated for men, not for angels and not for beasts. God had created mankind in two sexes; He had ordained marriage as desirable for all, and sexual intercourse as essen-

---

[26]*Records of the Suffolk County Court,* 442–443 and 676; John Noble, editor, *Records of the Court of Assistants of the Colony of Massachusetts Bay* (Boston, 1901–1928), II, 8; *Records of the Particular Court of Connecticut, Collections* of the Connecticut Historical Society, XXII, 20; and a photostat in the Library of the Massachusetts Historical Society, dated March 29, 1653.

tial to marriage. On the other hand, He had forbidden sexual intercourse outside of marriage. These were the moral principles which the Puritans sought to enforce in New England. But in their enforcement they took cognizance of human nature. They knew well enough that human beings since the fall of Adam were incapable of obeying perfectly the laws of God. Consequently, in the endeavor to enforce those laws they treated offenders with patience and understanding, and concentrated their efforts on prevention more than on punishment. The result was not a society in which most of us would care to live, for the methods of prevention often caused serious interference with personal liberty. It must nevertheless be admitted that in matters of sex the Puritans showed none of the blind zeal of narrow-minded bigotry which is too often supposed to have been characteristic of them. The more one learns about these people, the less do they appear to have resembled the sad and sour portraits which their modern critics have drawn of them.

4

CARL N. DEGLER

# The Emergence of the Modern American Family

*Carl Degler begins his preface to* At Odds *with the comment that the book is "an exercise in foolhardiness." His first reason for suggesting this label is that the work is an attempt to deal with two different historical subjects, the history of the family and the history of women, neither of which he feels has had sufficient development in either the formulation of theories or the collection of data. If this were not enough, Degler adds what he considers a more serious reason for his feelings, namely that the goal of the book is to integrate the two areas over a long period of time. This is difficult, because study of the two areas has been almost completely separated, in spite of clear overlaps between the two subjects.*

*Regardless of his feelings, Degler does bring together these two bodies of literature and the result is a book that not only intertwines the two subjects but "show(s) as concretely and analytically as possible how the interaction has shaped the family and the life of women down to the present."[1] His basic argument is that women's struggle for equality and their placement in the home sphere are inherently "at odds."*

*Degler argues that the modern American family as we define it today emerged in the years between the American Revolution and about 1830. This new family form had at least four general characteristics that clearly distinguished it from earlier families. In these new families:*

*1. Marriage was based on affection and mutual respect between partners.*

[1]Degler, At Odds, p. vi.

*Moreover, wives had increasing influence and autonomy within the family.*

2. *The wife's primary role was childcare and household maintenance. In such a role she was viewed as being morally superior to her husband while he in turn was seen as her legal and social superior. This division of labor and control were justified through the ideology that men and women maintain separate spheres of influence.*
3. *Childhood became sharply distinguished from adulthood, and both parents carried a major responsibility for rearing their children.*
4. *Average family size decreased significantly compared to previous centuries.*

*Using both statistical data and personal documents, Degler traces the development of these four features of the modern American family. The selection that follows is the portion of the book that examines the emergence of affection and mutual respect in the mating process.*



---

Let us begin to look at the emergence of the modern American family in the order in which the family itself began—with the decision to marry. How was the choice of marital partner made and what was the significance of the basis of the choice? In the half-century after the Revolution the bases of marriage began to change in a decidedly modern direction. Increasingly, free choice by the partners became the basis of family formation. Today it is axiomatic that personal happiness and the affection of the two partners for each other are the only proper foundation for a marriage and the family that follows. Such a conception of marriage has not always been the way in which families were established. Affection was most unlikely to be a basis of marriage if the families of origin of the young people held large amounts of property. For to permit a marriage to take place on the basis of personal or individual preference or whim, rather than by reference to family needs and prospects, threatened a family's holdings and perhaps its long-term future. That was why European crowned heads and noble families insisted that the marriage choices of children be in the hands of parents. Lesser men and women also insisted upon it. In 16th-century Protestant Geneva, for instance, a man could not marry under the age of twenty without his father's consent, or, in case the father was dead, that of his mother or relative. In Catholic France, royal edicts stipulated that parental consent to marry was necessary for a woman until twenty-five and for a man until thirty. As late as 1639 even a son who was over age in France could be disinherited if he married for the first time against his parents' wishes. Historian Lawrence Stone tells of one Michael Wentworth, who, in 1558, stipulated in his will that if any of his daughters did not accept the choice of marital partner named by his executors "but of their own fantastical brain bestow themselves upon a light person" their estate would be reduced from 100 to 66 pounds. Stone called this "powerful posthumous economic blackmail," a practice that American fathers of the 17th century were not hesitant to follow.[1] In Andover, Massachusetts, for instance, fathers who owned land used their control over it to influence, if not to shape, their sons' decisions about marriage. By delaying the turning over of their land to their sons, fathers could determine when and perhaps whom sons would marry.

By the 18th century, however, parental control over the marital choices of their children weakened. Philip Greven, who studied colonial Andover, found that by the mid-18th century fathers were not using their land so frequently to influence their sons' marital decisions. A clearer measure of the decline in parental control over grown children and the corresponding improvement in the children's freedom of choice in marriage is provided by Daniel Scott Smith's study of another colonial town, Hingham, Massachusetts. Smith found that in marriages contracted before 1780 the age of the bridegroom, on the average, was almost two years higher if the father died after age 60 than it was with men whose fathers died before 60. That is, if the father lived beyond the median age of fathers at the marriage of the oldest son (60 years), then the sons' time of marriage was delayed, presumably because the fathers would not let them marry or would not give them the land necessary for the support of a wife and family. In the marriages formed between 1781 and 1840, however, the average difference in the ages of marriage of the two sets of sons was negligible—only three months. This suggests that by the last two decades of the 18th and the opening of the 19th century, a father's influence over a son's choice of decision was much less than it had been before the American Revolution. A study of Concord, Massachusetts, has come up with the same results, though using 1760 as the dividing date. After that date the difference in age of marriage was less than ten months, but before 1760 the difference was 1.5 to 2 years. Moreover, the Concord study found that prior to 1770 the eldest son was twice as likely to succeed to his father's occupation as would be expected by chance. After 1770, the other brothers were more likely to do so than the eldest son, suggesting that the father no longer was able to consider only his own preferences.[2]

In an as yet unpublished investigation of some 100 upper-class families in North Carolina between 1830 and 1860, Jane Turner Censer found that by that period almost no fathers used their power to withhold inheritance from their sons. She reported that even sons who disobeyed their fathers, usually by wasting resources, were not disinherited. Almost half of the fathers actually passed on substantial amounts of property, usually in the form of land, to their sons long before their own deaths, thus facilitating a son's wish to marry without parental influence. Finally, of the 92 wills Censer examined, only two specified a particular occupation that a son ought to follow, but even in these two cases the father added provisions to the will which permitted the son to escape having to follow his father's expectations! In short, even among very wealthy planter families in the South, who certainly had property to conserve, parental power over a son's decisions was not exercised.

Parental control over daughters similarly declined from the 18th to the 19th century. Smith, in his study of Hingham, was able to demonstrate the shift by an examination of the order in which daughters married. He began with the assumption that a father preferred to have his daughters marry in the order of birth; otherwise a propective suitor might well think something was wrong with an unmarried older daughter. When Smith divided the marriages of daughters according to periods, he discovered that between 1650 and 1750 less than 11 percent of daughters married out of birth order. But after 1741 over 18 percent did so, suggesting a substantial increase in the freedom of choice of daughters. Censer in her study of some 100 upper-class families in North Carolina found a similar degree of freedom of choice for daughters. Of 85 women marrying between 1795 and 1865 in 25 families, 30 percent of them married out of birth order; yet these were families in which the conservation of and control over their substantial wealth certainly gave the father reasons for seeking to control marital choices as well as providing the wherewithal by which to exercise such power.

Finally, Smith advanced a third measure of the shift in parental control from between the 18th to the 19th century. He showed that in Hingham, in the early years of the 19th century, daughters of wealthy parents were actually marrying at a later age than those of poorer parents, though, a hundred years before, the pattern had been just the opposite. Smith's explanation was that in the early colonial period parents with money could marry off their daughters earlier than less wealthy parents simply because the rich had dowries to offer. But by the end of the 18th and opening of the 19th century, young women were making their own decision, and were not permitting their parents to rush them into matrimony any faster than daughters of less well-to-do parents.

By the early years of the 19th century, parental control over the choice of marriage partners of their children was no more than a veto, as it is essentially today in the 20th century. Parents obviously had influence, as in the case of Catharine Beecher, who broke off an engagement with a young man, even though her father, Lyman Beecher, clearly approved of the match. Her father ws able to prevail upon her to reopen the relation, and in due course she made a commitment to marry the young man, but the young man's death in an accident intervened. It is nevertheless significant that Catharine never married. Even in the more traditional South, apparently, parental control was weak. Juliet Janin, writing in later life about her own betrothal in 1832 in New Orleans, explained that her suitor, because he was a foreigner, asked her father for her hand before he asked her. "In those days in N.O.," she wrote, "a girl brought up in a measure according to french usages though not coerced was apt to be influenced by . . . the wishes and advice" of her parents or guardian. This, too, was a wealthy family, but clearly considerations of family fortune were not expected to take precedence over the preferences of the young.[3]

If a parent strongly disapproved of his daughter's choice, his principal recourse was either to send her away from home or move the whole family. The second option was apparently being followed by one father in 1857, as recounted by a diarist. The diary-keeper met the daughter on a river boat, where she showed the diarist "the pictures of her lover, from whom she had been ruthlessly torn. Her family actually came West to get her away from him," the diarist wrote indignantly. The limited role of parents and kin in marriage choices is evident, too, in Mary Robart's explanation to cousin Mary Jones of Georgia in 1855, as to why Robart's sister Louisa did not consult the Joneses when she decided to marry a widower with eight children. "Having gained Mother's consent and mine," Robart wrote, Louisa "asked no one else, as she felt she was the best judge of what would promote her own happiness."[4]

Earlier in the century, Elizabeth Southgate, vacationing at a spa far from her parents, met a young man she fell in love with, and though she did not think she could agree to marry him until he had consulted her parents, she knew that her feelings were decisive with her parents. After assuring her mother of her love for the young man, she submitted "herself wholly to the wishes of my Father and you, convinced that my happiness is your warmest wish . . . ." They checked out the young man's reputation and prospects and quickly agreed to the marriage. Even more reflective of the daughter's freedom of choice was the reaction of Mary Peirce's father to the request of Henry Poor for his daughter's hand. Poor had already obtained Mary's consent, he assured the father. Since the Peirces had complete confidence in her judgment, Peirce wrote back, "we submit the subject suggested in your communication entirely to her decision. . . ."[5]

The references to personal happiness in both Mary Robart's and Elizabeth Southgate's letters are significant, for they reveal the goal behind a couple's freedom of choice. Southgate put the matter quite baldly, she thought her suitor "better calculated to promote my happiness than any person I have yet seen." This expression of individualism, as against the collective interest of the family, was made in 1802, and with her parents' tacit acknowledgment of its rightness. The journal of Sarah Ripley of Massachusetts between 1810 and 1812, in which she recorded her movement toward matrimony, also noted that happiness was the expected objective of marriage. Although at one point her meetings with her male friend were less promising than she would have liked, she believed that "hope still soothes my heart and whispers happiness to come." Significant, too, was the fact that throughout the long courtship—five years—her father seemed to play no role at all, except to provide the job that made the marriage possible. Clearly, parents as well as children considered personal, individual happiness the goal of marriage. "There is nothing on his earth that interests me so much as that he may in all respects be worthy of her," wrote a North Carolina planter in 1838 to his son about the suitor of his daughter, "and calculated in mind and morals to make her happy. This is my greatest solicitude."[6]

The role parents played by the latter half of the 19th century was well summed up in a letter in 1871 from Hyland Rice, a young physician, to Robert W. Waterman. In formal, even stilted language, Rice asked Waterman's permission to marry his daughter. "She and I have discovered our mutual affection and have concluded, with the permission of her mother and yourself, to run the two courses of our lives into one." Rice asked permission even though he acknowledged, as he put it in the letter, that Waterman did not think he was "the man suitable above all other men to make her life happier." Nevertheless, Rice promised to do his best to ensure her happiness and to mend his ways in order to achieve that goal. Once again it is clear that happiness was the purpose of marriage and that mutual affection was its justification. Whatever Waterman's earlier objections to Rice may have been, he did not withhold his consent, and apparently Rice had not expected him to once Mary's agreement had been gained. (Something of the weight accorded the personal choice of a son or daughter is measured in the remark of a North Carolina woman on an impending marriage between the daughter of a wealthy planter and a Roman Catholic suitor: "the family (one and all) dislike the match exceedingly," but it went forward nonetheless.)[7]

When people in the 19th century spoke of the purposes of marriage, they were most likely to refer to "love" or affection as the basis of the attraction between marital partners and the beginnings of family formation. Love as the basis for marrying was the purest form of individualism; it subordinated all familial, social, or group considerations to personal preference. The idea of love, to be sure, was not new in the 19th century. The Middle Ages had certainly known of it, and the troubadours had sung of courtly love. But significantly enough, not as a basis for marriage. For as Andreas Capellanus, the 12th-century writer, put the matter in his *Art of Courtly Love*, "Everybody knows that love can have no place between husband and wife." Or as he phrased it a little later in the same work: "We declare and hold as firmly established that love cannot exert its powers between two people who are married to each other."[8] In short, love was extra-marital. The idea that love should be the cement of marriages does not figure prominently in Western marriage customs until at least the 17th century. Historian Lawrence Stone tells us that King Charles I and Queen Henrietta Maria were the first English royal couple to be celebrated as a domestic pair rather than as the result of dynastic considerations. Others would follow in subsequent centuries until the high point of royal conjugal love would be reached with Victoria and Albert in the 19th century.

More important as a sign of a new emphasis upon affection within marriage in the 17th century was the stress Puritans placed upon it in their sermons and writings. The Puritan conception was not so much that love ought to be the foundation or origin of marriage as that the couple could expect that time would bring love into their relationship. The Puritan divines asserted the importance of affection, intimacy, and loyalty within marriage, elements that would, of course, become central to the ideal of marriage in America in the 19th century. Margaret Winthrop expressed the idea in quite Puritanical terms when she told her husband, John, the 17th-century governor of the Massachusetts Bay Colony, that the two chief reasons she loved him were "first because thou lovest God; and, secondly, because that thou lovest me. If these two were wanting, all the rest would be eclipsed. But I must leave this discourse," she quickly interjected, "and go about my household affairs. I am a bad housewife to be so long from them; but I must needs borrow a little time to talk with thee, my sweet heart." John's affection for Margaret was no less. In an extant fragment of a letter to her he made clear that she came first in his life. "The largeness and truth of my love to thee makes me always mindful of thy welfare," he began, "and sets me on work to begin to write before I hear from thee. The very thought of thee affords me many a kind refreshment: What will then be the enjoying of thy sweet society, which I prize above all wordly comforts?" The two most popular handbooks on domestic duties in 17th-century England, Lawrence Stone reports, asserted that the purpose of marriage was spiritual intimacy and the avoidance of adultery and fornication outside it. Protestantism, by abandoning the Catholic ideal of celibacy, gave a new emphasis in Christianity to sexual expression, which it then tied to the family.[9]

One consequence of emphasizing affection and loyalty between spouses was an improvement in the position of a woman in marriage. Even in male-dominated Calvinistic Geneva, for example, women were encouraged to sing hymns in church and the old masculine custom of wife-beating was frowned upon. Puritans in Old and New England alike gave recognition to the individual interests of women by making marriage itself a contract, which implied equality. As a contract, rather than a sacrament, marriage could now be dissolved; thus divorce became a matter of public policy, not of religious doctrine. Even so, as John Milton found out, divorce was not easy to obtain, even for a man. But the first step in making marriage responsive to the needs and desires of individuals had been made by Protestantism. Nowhere in the Western world was a divorce easier to obtain than in 17th-century New England.

It is all too easy, of course, to exaggerate the ways in which the Puritans' stress upon personal affection in marriage improved the position of women. To put the proposition into perspective it is only necessary to recollect the explusion of Anne Hutchinson from the Massachusetts Bay Colony in 1638 for presuming to preach. Yet it is worth remembering that it was the Puritans' encouragement for women's participation in church affairs that made it possible for Hutchinson to begin her teaching at all. Protestantism's part in improving the place of women inside and outside the family is best observed in the Quakers, who were, after all, a kind of latter-day Puritans. In them the implications of Puritanism reached their fullest expression. Among the Quakers, women were the religious peers of men. In fact, some of the earliest Quaker missionaries to Puritan Boston were women.

Protestantism's and Puritanism's emphases upon affection in marriage and upon a degree of autonomy for women within the family may have been strong and important, but it would be erroneous to think that the typical American marriage or family even in the 18th century exemplified these ideals. Yet changes were surely in process. In the years after the American Revolution there were more and more signs that affection between spouses and greater freedom for women within marriage were a growing part of family life. Lawrence Stone in his recent history of the family in Britain describes the emergence by the end of the 18th century of what might be called a marriage of companions. And though England is not America, the two countries certainly influenced one another, if only through their common language and common reading. Stone points out that by the end of the 18th century, sons of peers were much less likely to marry wealthy women than in earlier times, a sign of the rise of what he terms "affective individualism." The increase in the expectation of affection in marriage, Stone argues, was also measured in the upsurge in the number of romantic novels published toward the end of the 18th century. Between 1760 and 1779 fewer than twenty such novels were published each year. In the years 1780–89, however, the annual rate was up to almost fifty; by the last decade of the century the figure reached eighty per year. Significantly, many of the novels were written by women—as they would be in the United States in the early 19th century. "Romantic love and the romantic novel grew together after 1780," Stone concluded, "and the problem of cause and effect is one that is impossible to resolve. All that can be said is that for the first time in history, romantic love became a respectable motive for marriage among the propertied classes."[10]

The romantic novel does not become common in America until the 19th century, but in the late 18th century examples of marriages based upon affection and future companionship are not difficult to find. John Dickinson of Pennsylvania wrote his wife of fifteen years in 1784 that she was the "best of women, best of wives, and best of friends."[11] John and Abigail Adams in their correspondence often addressed each other as "friend." The rise in individual affection as a basis for marriage is also measured in a study of some 220 petitions for divorce in 18th-century Massachusetts. As the century advanced, the study makes clear, the number of petitions increased, even though the law, or the grounds for divorce remained substantially unchanged. More important, the grounds advanced by the petitioners shift as the century moves on. Before 1765 not a single one of the petitioners, male or female, mentioned loss of conjugal affection as a reason for divorce, though they did make other personal accusations, such as that the other party wasted goods or neglected the family. Between 1776 and 1786, however, fully 10 percent of the 121 suits in that period referred to loss of affection as a justification for divorce. "Ceased to cherish her," said one; another alleged that his wife "almost broke his heart."

Apparently this increased emphasis upon affection in marriage had an effect upon the courts and therefore upon society, much to the benefit of women. Before 1773 not a single petition for divorce by a woman in Massachusetts on the grounds of adultery by a husband was accepted by the courts, though many had been from husbands alleging such behavior on the part of their wives. In 1773, however, two women won full divorces, not merely separations, on the specific ground of adultery by their husbands. Thereafter, other women began to petition, as they had not done before, on the sole ground of adultery, and many now won their cause. In fact, the women's rate of success in divorce petitions in general went from 49 percent for the years before 1774 to 70 percent for the years thereafter. During that same period the men's rate of success advanced only from 66 percent to 73 percent. In sum, by the end of the 18th century, women's rate of success was almost equal to that of men, pointing to one area in which women's position in marriage, at least in Massachusetts, had come abreast of men's.[12]

Moreover, the increased use by women of the grounds of a husband's adultery clearly reflected a growing emphasis upon personal love and respect as the basis of a marriage. It was putting into practice what the Puritan writers of the 17th century had advocated when they opposed the double standard and defined marriage as a relationship of mutual respect, affection, and companionship. By the last quarter of the 18th century, funeral sermons, too, testified to the ideal of the complementarity of the marital relation and the emotional bonds between marital partners. No longer were women the Eve-temptresses against whom many divines had warned men in earlier times.[13]

Popular writings also reflected this rising emphasis upon love in marriage. A survey of some fifteen magazines published in New England during the last fifty years of the 18th century disclosed that romantic love was widely believed by the writers to be the heart of an ideal marriage. Indeed, the concept was so broadly apparent in the popular literature of the time that it surprised the modern sociologists who were conducting the content analysis of the magazines. They had associated the idea of romantic love with the needs and functioning of an industrial society—that is, a society in which wealth was sufficiently available to permit personal feelings to be the basis of choice of marital partners.[14]

The growing acceptance of affection as the primary ground for family formation was an important stage in the evolution of women's place within the family and in our understanding of how the family has altered over time. It is quite true, as modern observers have pointed out, that most relationships between people involve the exercise of power, and certainly the relationship of marriage is no exception. Yet once affection is a basis of marriage, the marital relation becomes significantly different from other relationships between superiors and inferiors. To begin with, unlike any other subordinate, such as a slave or an employee, a young woman comtemplating marriage did have some choice as to who her new master would be. Clearly unsatisfactory possibilities could be ruled out completely, and, from acquaintance at courtship, she had an opportunity to learn who were the undesirable partners. After the marriage, the woman also had an advantage that few slaves or employees enjoyed in dealing with their masters or employers. She was able to appeal to her husband's affection for her, and she, in turn, could use that affection in extracting concessions that a slave or an employee could not. In short, by the very nature of the relation, a woman in the family of affection had more power or influence than any other subordinate one can think of . This is but another way of saying that, simply because women are a sex, the analysis of the history of the family and of women must differ significantly from the ways in which we analyze the behavior of other social groups. Certainly there are valuable analogies to be drawn between the subordination of women and the subordination of other groups, as has often been pointed out. Yet it is essential that the unique elements in the relation between men and women not be forgotten or minimized. By the same token, this caveat should not be read as an invitation to sentimentalize the relations between the sexes; that would only be retrogressive in the study of women or the family.

This modern emphasis upon love in marriage, which by the early 19th century increasingly characterized marriages, was neatly enunciated in 1802 by a young Massachusetts matron of twenty-six when she said that marriage could be a "galling chain. Souls must be kindred to make the bond silken. All others I call unions of *hands*, not *hearts*. I rejoice," she continued, "that the knot which binds me was not tied with any mercenary feelings, and that my *heart* is under the same subjection as my *hand*."[15]

Marriage for love only was the ideal, and one that many young women tried to put into practice. Mollie Dorsey, in her diary written during the 1850s, epitomized the conflict between love and money as a basis for marriage when the family of origin was not wealthy and, at the same time, the way in which that conflict was probably resolved in most cases. "Aunt Eliza wonders why I don't try to captivate Mr. Rucker, as he is rich," Mollie wrote in her journal. Aunt Eliza had admitted that he was not as "nice-looking" as Mollie's lover Byron, "but then, he *owns a farm*, and bless my old darling, he don't own much of anything except those lots and—myself." An indication of how marriages were actually completed comes in her next observation. "My Aunt likes money, but *she* married for love," for her husband had been an impoverished itinerent minister when he asked her to marry him. Aunt Eliza's experience was recapitulated in the marriage of Mollie's sister Dora. Three weeks after Mollie was married, Dora, who was only seventeen, married a man she met for the first time at Mollie's wedding. Her mother was not "reconciled to the suddenness of the affair," Mollie admitted, but her father quietly gathered together a trousseau for Dora, and the wedding went off as and when Dora wished.

Although there is more than a suggestion in Mollie's description that Dora's decision to marry was more emotional than thoughtful, Mollie's own path to matrimony made evident that young women in the middle of the 19th century not only had a choice but also usually exercised it thoughtfully and with realistic expectations. There is no doubt that affection was central to Mollie's decision to marry Byron Sanford. He "loves me tenderly, truly, and . . . I know now that I can place my hand in his and go with him thro life, be path smooth or stormy," she wrote in her diary the night he proposed to her. She fully recognized that their relationship had not been like those depicted in the sentimental novels of the time. "We did not fall madly in love as I had always expected to, but have gradually 'grown into love,'" as the preceding entries in her diary certainly make evident.[16]

Simply because affection was a chief basis for marital choices, courtship in the 19th century was an important stage in family formation. At perhaps no other point in the course of a marriage was a woman's autonomy greater or more individualistically exercised. A brief examination of actual courtships provides some insight into not only how marriages were arranged but what marriage meant for women in the 19th century.

Contrary to what is sometimes thought about the Victorian years, courtship did not have to be formal, excessively restricted, or even chaperoned. Not until late in the 19th century and then only among the urban upper classes was the European practice of chaperoning at all well known. It is true that premarital sexual relations, today so commonplace in America, were rare among all classes of Americans. Even in the 18th century, when premarital pregnancies reached a high not equaled until the late 20th century, no more than 10 per cent of women conceived children that were born less than nine months after the marriage ceremony. And according to the few historical studies on the subject, the proportion of bridal pregnancies in the 19th century was even smaller. Only among black families were premarital pregnancies proportionately high at the end of the 19th century. But even then, the great majority of black couples waited until marriage before conceiving children.[17] Illegitimate births were also low for all groups of society, though of course they occurred.

Means of contraception were rather well known in the 19th century, but they were not sufficiently reliable to protect women from the social stigma which fell like a hammer on those whose sexual relations outside marriage were revealed by illegitimate births. Finally, it should be remembered that premarital sexual relations have not been typical of American courtships for most of the 20th century, either.

If we leave aside premarital sexual experience as a measure of the freedom of courtship, then the Victorian courtship is far from staid. Indeed, as Alexis de Tocqueville and other foreign travelers in America in the 1830s and 1840s pointed out, unmarried women were much freer in public than their married sisters. Middle- and lower-class women moved about not only without chaperones, but also with a certain amount of abandon. Mollie Dorsey, while traveling with her family on a river boat in the late 1850s, reported that she and a newly found female friend "have splendid times—flirt all day." It was not unusual for a young woman to accompany a young man on fishing trips, with no one else along, or to accept invitations for walks together, discussing personal matters. "I am sorry to tell you," one young woman wrote a female friend in 1822, "that I feel remarkably dull this evening having just returned from a long walk of three miles out of town . . . for I was with a gentleman who I am somewhat afraid of, as he is most appallingly sensible and intellectual, and I have been exerting every facility to say something smart." Mollie Dorsey also took a long walk; she stayed out so late with her lover that her father came looking for her. She felt "sheepish to be patrolled home," and her father's reproof "rather spoiled the romance of the thing," she complained. A young man's diary of 1861 similarly revealed young women who were hardly bashful. He told of going to a "Sewing Circle of the North Baptist Church," where he "went over the river with Miss Hutchins. 3 couples of us remained there until 1½ in the morning. Came up with Lizzie Green. I don't know how many kisses I had that evening, was almost smothered with sweet things." Two days later he spent an evening with a Miss Albert, who gave "me a sweet kiss before I was aware of the fact; went home with my lady. She too gave me a farewell salute." A dozen years later Anna Haskell in California told in her journal of the several boys who rather regularly came to her room at college at night, even though the practice was quite against the rules. Sometimes Anna would go off alone with one for a walk and talk. Nor was it always necessary for couples to sneak off in order to obtain privacy. When callers came to Mollie Dorsey's house, all her relatives and family quickly left the room so that the couple could be alone.[18]

Late night courting was not limited to the new country or to forward young men. Indeed, as Lester Frank Ward's diary written during the same years in rural eastern Pennsylvania shows, courting in Victorian America could be freer than many have supposed. Again and again Ward reported that he and "his girl," as he referred to the young woman who later became his wife, kissed and caressed each other until the early morning hours. On a Monday night in 1860, when he was nineteen, he left her only "at half past three . . . amid thousands of kisses." Then on the following Wednesday he escorted her home, not leaving again until 3:00 a.m. During that stay, he reported they spent "an hour embracing, caressing, hugging, and kissing. O bliss! O love! O passion, pure, sweet and profound! What more do I want than you?"

Nor was all the initiative his. On a subsequent visit, after an absence of several days, he found her most captivated by him. "She looked at me so gently and spoke so tenderly. 'I love you,' she said, kissing me on the mouth. 'I love this mouth, I love those dear eyes, I love this head,' and a thousand other little caressing pet-names." At around 3:00 A.M., when they became sleepy, they arranged the chairs in such a way that they could lie lengthwise facing each other and he opened his shirt, placing her hand on his bare chest. She said she thought she might be doing something wrong, but, significantly, she did not stop. "As we lay in this position," he noted, "the cocks crowed." Quickly he slipped off to work, where he caught up on his lost sleep. After another equally loving visit, at 4:30 in the morning they heard her father jumping out of bed. Hurriedly they kissed and he ran home.

By early 1861 their physical attraction to one another had become so strong that it began to worry them. "I had a very affectionate time with the girl, kissing her almost all over and loving her very deeply and she *does* me." Two weeks later Ward referred to a "very secret time" with her. "I kissed her on her soft breasts, and took too many liberties with her sweet person, and we are going to stop. It is a very fascinating practice and fills us with very sweet, tender and familiar sentiments, and consequently makes us happy." They talked about their fear that "we might become so addicted in that direction that we might go too deep and possibly confound ourselves by the standards of virtue." Even when he was not with her, he dreamed about her and during the day fantasized about "kissing her sweet breasts and sleeping in her arms." A week later he characteristically, if enigmatically wrote, "I slept in her arms; yes, I lay with her, but did nothing wrong."

Yet, despite the intimacy, the relationship between them was not yet settled, for she was still seeing other young men, a practice that inevitably aroused Ward's jealousy and temporarily reduced her ardor. Gradually, after a long talk, they recognized their mutual attraction and dependence; weeping and kissing, they re-established their old, close relation. Ward was thrown into despair some nights later when he called on her only to find that her brother was home, preventing their usual love-making. Ward managed to get a note to her asking if he could return later. To his delight she wrote back that she wanted to kiss him. When he did return, "closely held in loving arms we lay, embraced, and kissed all night (not going to bed until five in the morning). We have never acted in such a way before. All that we did I shall not tell here, but it was all very sweet and loving and nothing infamous," he assured himself. By the end of that year of rather steady courtship little restraint was left on their emotions. "When I arrived at the house of sweetness, she received me in her loving arms and pressed me to her honey-form, and our lips touched and we entered Paradise together . . . . That evening and night we tasted the joys of love and happiness which only belong to a married life." Early the next year, in 1862, they were married.[19]

Ward's diary is unusually explicit about the physical side of a mid-19th-century courtship; yet even it, by late 20th-century standards, is noticeably circumspect, suggesting the difficulty 19th-century people had in discussing such matters, even privately. It is worth noting, too, that the diary was originally written by Ward in French, a fact that probably accounts for his uncommon explicitness of language. But there is no reason to believe that the behavior he described was rare or exceptional.

The courtship of an older couple, even at the end of the century, could be quite different, though revealing of what marriage meant to certain women. Jerome Hart in 1896 was forty-two years old, but he had never married. Only five years before he had become editor of the *Argonaut*, an important weekly in San Francisco, and a measure of his success as a journalist. In the last month of 1895 he met Ann Clark, a graduate of the University of California Law School and a legal adviser in an insurance and real estate agency in San José, some 45 miles south of San Francisco. Their correspondence over the course of the four years it took them to move from first acquaintance to husband and wife documents the formality that could occur even between lovers, especially when one was a career woman. For the first three months of their correspondence he addressed her only as "my dear Miss Clark." Probably because of her own career, Ann Clark was slow to accept Hart's proposal of marriage. Certainly she gave testimony to the conflict that could arise with the conventional view of marriage when a woman pursued a career. At one point Hart complained that at their last meeting she had seemed cold toward him. She explained herself by writing that "At the last moment how I yearned to say 'Stay' yet you think I do not care for you. You can never realize the terrible temptation I was under to let myself glide into those strong arms of yours and to take all the love and protection you offer me." She then referred to the burdens borne by a single woman in an age when marriage for women was the expected role. "No more would I have to meet perplexities and stumble along in the dark alone."[20]

The courtship of Charlotte Perkins Stetson, the feminist writer, and Houghton Gilman, which took place at about the same time on the opposite side of the continent, was at once different from and similar to that of Hart and Ann

Clark. It was different in that in the Stetson-Gilman case the woman was the older of the two by seven years; in 1900, at the time of her second marriage, Charlotte Stetson was forty. It is different, too, in that Stetson was a mother by a previous marriage, and divorced. Like Ann Hart, Charlotte was a career woman who spent much time traveling and lecturing on behalf of women's causes. Houghton was a lawyer and Charlotte's first cousin.

Like Ann Hart, Charlotte Stetson was not prepared to fall in love, though it is also clear that she wanted that love desperately. "O sweetheart—is it true? Aren't you sorry yet? Surely you could have done better. I ought not to have let you throw yourself away so. You could have had so much happier a life with a *whole* woman who would have been all yours." The last is a reference to her commitment, which Houghton accepted, to her work as feminist and lecturer. but she promised anew that, if she could not be like other wives, "that piece of me from time to time—even most of the time—will make you as happy as all of some one else would. I shall tenderly and remorsefully try to make the piece large and sweet-full of raisins!" At the same time she found it difficult that she was, because of her commitment to Houghton, no longer a complete entity, but now "greatly lacking my other half. It seems vague and funny. I wonder if it will go away. If we have been playing—dreaming—and it will all pass!"

The conflict between the memories of her first marriage, the commitment to her career, and her deep desire to marry Houghton gave a poignancy to this courtship that was probably not usual, but nonetheless illustrative of the ambiguity that many, though certainly not most women of the late 19th century felt about marriage. Charlotte herself had decided that the marriage would not take place for two years, when she had paid off all her accumulated debts. It is also evident that her work came first. "Dear, if I had to choose today between you and my work—two hearts might break, and I might die of the breaking, but I could not choose other than the one way. If I can harmonize love and home with this great calling I shall be happy beyond my wildest hopes." There were also conflicts still in her mind about a wife's proper role, for, as she said in that same letter, she felt "so remorseful and ashamed to think that you, my dear, dear love, are not my first and only. All the piled up ancestral womanheartedness—cries out Treason! I feel I am not truly loving you." In a subsequent letter, when she learned that Houghton's regiment would not be sent to Cuba to fight, she exulted in the sense of security the news brought her. "Guess I'm a woman all right—just like the rest of 'em. 'Tisn't any fun, either," she concluded ruefully. But always there was the commitment to her work, even when it created tension. "If I should lose you, the wound would go deeper than any other of the many I have had. But under and over and around all that poor little woman's heart of mine is this great strong boundless thing that loves and works for all the world. I can't help it—that's me."[21]

Courtship is only one way of gaining an insight into the nature and bases of marriage in 19th-century America. After all, it is only the beginning of a marriage, and, in some ways, the ideal as opposed to the real expression of what marriage meant.

## NOTES

1. Natalie Zemon Davis, "Ghosts, Kin, and Progeny: Some Features of Family Life in Early Modern France," *Daedalus 106* (Spring 1977), 107; Lawrence Stone, "The Rise of the Nuclear Family in Early Modern England," in Charles E. Rosenberg (ed.), *The Family in History* (Philadelphia, 1975), pp. 45, 48–49.

2. Philip J. Greven, Jr., *Four Generations, Population, Land, and Family in Colonial Andover, Massachusetts* (Ithaca, 1970), pp. 222–23; Daniel Scott Smith, "Parental Control and Marriage Patterns: An Analysis of Historical Trends in Hingham, Massachusetts," *Journal of Marriage and the Family 35* (August 1973), pp. 423–24; Robert A. Gross, *The Minutemen and Their World* (New York, 1976), pp. 211n, 235n.

3. Kathryn Kish Sklar, *Catharine Beecher: A Study in American Domesticity* (New Haven, 1973), p. 36; Ms. biography of Louis Alexander Janin, Box 20, Folder 22, Janin Family Collection, Huntington Library, San Marino, Ca.

4. Donald F. Danker (ed.), *Mollie: The Journal of Mollie Dorsey Sanford in Nebraska and Colorado Territories, 1857–1866* (Lincoln, 1959), p. 7; Robert Manson Myers (ed.), *The Children of Pride: A True Story of Georgia and the Civil War* (New Haven, 1972), p. 118.

5. Clarence Cook (ed.), *A Girl's Life Eighty Years Ago: Selections from the Letters of Eliza Southgate Bowne* (New York, 1887), p. 140; see also Janet Wilson James, "Changing Ideas about Women in the United States, 1776–1825," unpublished dissertation, Harvard University, 1954, p. 141; James R. McGovern, *Yankee Family* (New Orleans, 1975), p. 59.

6. Journal of Sarah Ripley Stearns, February 2, 17, May 26, October 24, 1810, February 1, November 10, 1812, Stearns Papers, Schlesinger Library, Radcliffe College; North Carolina planter's remark quoted in unpublished paper of Jane Turner Censer presented at meetings of Southern Historical Association, November 1977. I am indebted to Ms. Censer for permitting me to use the results of her research.

7. Hyland Rice to R. W. Waterman, September 25, 1871, Robert Waterman Papers, Bancroft Library, University of California, Berkeley; Censer's unpublished paper, Southern Historical Association, 1977.

8. Quoted in E. William Monter, "The Pedestal and the Stake: Courtly Love and Witchcraft," in Renate Bridenthal and Claudia Koonz (eds.), *Becoming Visible: Women in European History* (Boston, 1977), p. 123.

9. Robert C. Winthrop (ed.), *Life and Letters of John Winthrop* (2 vols., Boston, 1864), I, 247, 292; Stone, "Rise of the Nuclear Family," pp. 26–28, 30–31.

10. Lawrence Stone, *The Family, Sex, and Marriage in England, 1500–1800* (New York, 1977), pp. 318, 284.

11. *Ibid.*, p. 372.

12. Nancy F. Cott, "Eighteenth Century Family and Social Life Revealed in Massachusetts Divorce Records," *Journal of Social History 10* (Fall 1976), p. 32; Nancy F. Cott, "Divorce and the Changing Status of Women in Eighteenth Century Massachusetts," *William and Mary Quarterly*, 3rd Series, *33* (October 1976), pp. 586–614.

13. *Ibid.*, pp. 599–600, 613.

14. Herman R. Lantz *et al.*, "Pre-industrial Patterns in the Colonial Family in America: A Content Analysis of Colonial Magazines," *American Sociological Review 33* (June 1968), pp. 413–26.

15. Quoted in Nancy F. Cott, *Bonds of Womanhood: "Women's Sphere" in New England, 1780–1835* (New Haven, 1977), p. 18. See also Michael Gordon and M. Charles Bernstein, "Mate Choice and Domestic Life in the Nineteenth Century Marriage Manual," *Journal of Marriage and the Family 32* (1970), pp. 668–69.

16. Danker (ed.), *Mollie*, pp. 103, 113, 65.

17. Daniel Scott Smith and Michael S. Hindus, "Premarital Pregnancy in America, 1640–1971; An Overview and Interpretation," *Journal of Interdisciplinary History 4* (Spring 1975), pp. 537–70;

Herbert G. Gutman, *The Black Family in Slavery and Freedom*, 1750–1925 (New York, 1976), pp. 64–65, 504, Table A–30.

18. Danker (ed.), *Mollie*, pp. 7, 20, 36, 47; Mary Cogswell to Weltha Brown, April 2, 1822, Brown Correspondence, Hooker Collection, Schlesinger Library, Radcliffe College; quotations from young man's diary in Ernest Earnest, *The American Eve in Fact and Fiction, 1775–1914* (Urbana, 1974); Diaries of Anna Haskell, March 15, 1876, Haskell Family Collection, Bancroft Library, University of California, Berkeley.

19. Bernhard J. Stern (ed.), *Young Ward's Diary* (New York, 1935), pp. 10, 14–15, 18–19, 33, 35–37, 44, 80.

20. Hart-Clark Correspondence, especially Jerome Hart to Ann Clark, May 22, July 23, 1896, May 19, 1897, Ann Clark to Jerome Hart, May 22, 1896, April 1, 13, 1897, Bancroft Library, University of California, Berkeley.

21. Charlotte Perkins Stetson to Houghton Gilman, May 5, 3, 9, 13, 1898, Charlotte Perkins Gilman Papers, Schlesinger Library, Radcliffe College.

## 5

ROBERT L. GRISWOLD

# Sexual Cruelty and the Case for Divorce in Victorian America

*In 1978, John Rideout made national headlines as the first man charged by his wife with raping her while they still lived together. He was subsequently acquitted by an Oregon Circuit Court. Greta Rideout's accusation and the court's decision began a debate that still continues. By the end of 1986, twenty-four states had altered their rape laws to permit prosecution of men for raping their wives. The exact form of the abolishment of this exemption, however, shows some variation. For instance, several states now prohibit marital rape only in the form of first-degree forcible rape, while others permit prosecution only if the spouses are separated. In any case, in the few years since the Rideout decision, marital rape has become a legal reality.*

*Historian Robert Griswold, whose work parallels that of Carl Degler (see the introduction to Reading 4), has devoted much study to the history of sexual and mental cruelty in divorce proceedings. He suggests that the major changes in the nature of modern marriages, and specifically the emergence of romantic marriages, were accompanied by womens' increasing intolerance of their husbands' insensitive or abusive behaviors. Griswold's research shows that by the latter half of the nineteenth century, judges "grew more sensitive to the issue of sexual cruelty and more willing to break a marriage when either spouse, but especially husbands, offended the sexual sensibilities of their mates."*[1] *Divorce rates during this time increased dramatically, and cruelty*

---

[1]From Robert L. Griswold, "Law, Sex, Cruelty, and Divorce in Victorian America, 1840–1900," *American Quarterly* 35, no. 5 (Winter 1986), pp. 721–745.

*was second only to nonsupport in increase as the legal grounds for divorce.*

*Thus, while women could not press the charge of marital rape, they could file for divorce on the basis of cruelty. Judges, however, ruled inconsistently on cruelty cases, a situation that Griswold suggests reflects confusion and ambiguity about the nature of marriages. Thus, the recent changes incorporating marital rape into the laws of many states closes a gap that has existed for over a hundred years.*

*The following selection describes a case that Griswold found in his research on sexual cruelty. It fascinated him because it was an exception to the general pattern of rulings at the time. However, it illustrates both the ambiguity of such complaints and the growing commitment to the new ideals about family life.*

Source: Robert L. Griswold, "Sexual Cruelty and the Case for Divorce in Victorian America" (*Signs: Journal of Women in Culture and Society* 1986, vol. 11, no. 3)

---

In February 1876, Abigail English filed for a legal separation from her husband John on the ground of extreme cruelty. Specifically, the New Jersey resident described the physical suffering she incurred because of her husband's excessive sexual demands: oblivious to her pleas for restraint, insensitive to her uterine disease, which made intercourse painful, unmindful of a physician's recommendation of sexual abstinence, he relentlessly insisted on sexual intercourse. When she resisted, he used brute strength to force her to submit to his lust. Despite the judge's hope that the recovery of her health might someday permit a reconciliation, the New Jersey Court of Chancery decided that his behavior constituted extreme cruelty under the statute and granted Abigail a divorce *mensa et thoro*.[1]

The decision seemed eminently reasonable under the circumstances and dovetailed with late nineteenth-century assumptions about male lust and the need to promote male continence within and outside marriage. After all, here was a brutish husband so heedless of his wife's well-being as to threaten her already delicate health in order to satisfy his base desires. While no court explicitly recognized marital rape as a ground for separation or divorce, an increasing number of late nineteenth-century jurisdictions recognized sexual incontinence as sufficient to prove cruelty if such behavior harmed the health of the wife. This recognition of the damage caused by sexual excesses was part of a more general expansion in the legal definition of marital cruelty that began in the middle decades of the nineteenth century. Prior to about 1840, the law defined cruelty as either violence or threats of violence, a narrow concep-

---

[1]English v. English, 27 *New Jersey Equity Reports* 71–75 (1876). A divorce *a mensa et thoro* is a divorce from bed and board or, in other words, a legal separation without the right of remarriage.

tion that gave way under the impact of changing conceptions of gender roles, family life, social class, and mental health. Thereafter, an increasing number of states recognized the sufficiency of petitions based not on violence but on a much wider range of behavior, including verbal epithets, that undermined the health of the wife. By the last two decades of the century, a few jurisdictions even recognized that cruelty sufficient for a divorce might consist solely of mental torment.[2] The favorable hearing given to Abigail English's complaint in Chancery Court reflected these changes and represented a victory for women wedded to tyrannical men.

The February 1876 decision was not the end of the story, however. Four months later the case appeared on appeal, and this time the New Jersey Court of Errors and Appeals overturned the Chancery Court's decision, in the process noting that most women experienced pain during intercourse, that John English generally treated his wife with kindness and affection, and most important, that he felt genuine remorse for his conduct and fervently desired to reunite his family. His expressions of love, his promises of reform, his repentance for wrongdoing, his behavior since she separated from him, all convinced the court that he posed no further threat to his wife's health; consequently, a divided court reversed the earlier decision and dismissed her suit.[3]

Her successful complaint followed by his successful appeal and reversal offer more than access to the personal misery of one New Jersey couple. When Abigail walked into court armed with her divorce complaint, the judge of her suit immediately became an arbiter of Victorian culture. To him fell the responsibility of deciding whether John English's behavior corresponded to acceptable standards of marital behavior or whether his behavior warranted the legal separation of a husband and wife. The judge and, later, the justices of the appellate court made their decisions in light of legal precedent but also against the backdrop of larger cultural issues involving the regulation of sexuality in nineteenth-century America, the definition of Victorian manhood and womanhood, and the relationship between relatively new family values and older commitments to family stability.

Certainly John English's behavior confirmed the emerging belief that cruelty

---

[2]On the history of the legal definition of matrimonial cruelty, see Robert L. Griswold, "The Evolution of the Doctrine of Mental Cruelty in Victorian American Divorce, 1790–1900," *Journal of Social History* (Fall 1986), pp. 127–48.

[3]English v. English, 580–86. The historical literature on violence against women and on marital cruelty is rather slim. Several essays, however, have recently appeared on the problem, including three by Elizabeth Pleck: "Wife-Beating in Nineteenth-Century America," *Victimology* 4 (Fall 1979): 62–74, "Feminist Responses to 'Crimes against Women,' 1868–1896," *Signs: Journal of Women in Culture and Society* 8, no. 3 (Spring 1983): 451–70, and "The Whipping Post for Wife Beaters, 1876–1906," in *Essays on the Family and Historical Change*, ed. Leslie P. Moch and Gary D. Stark (College Station: Texas A&M University Press, 1983), 127–49. Two books on divorce in late nineteenth-, early twentieth-century California discuss changing perceptions of unacceptable marital behavior: Elaine T. May, *Great Expectations: Marriage and Divorce in Post-Victorian America* (Chicago: University of Chicago Press, 1980), 75–91; and Robert L. Griswold, *Family and Divorce in California, 1850–1890: Victorian Illusions and Everyday Realities* (Albany: State University of New York Press, 1982), chap. 6. On English legal attitudes about marital cruelty, see John M. Biggs, *The Concept of Matrimonial Cruelty* (London: Athlone Press, 1962).

sufficient for divorce could take an almost endless variety of forms. By mid-century an increasingly complex understanding of matrimonial cruelty was taking shape. Many jurists began arguing that misery, whatever its source, that was detrimental to the health of a spouse justified a divorce, and thus the pain experienced by Abigail English during sexual intercourse—pain traceable to problems caused by a long, difficult, forceps-aided delivery—carried legal weight not present just a half-century earlier. She had tried to avoid his advances and had begged him to desist, but her remonstrances had had no effect, and he had continued to insist on frequent intercourse. In so doing, English not only caused his wife real physical suffering but confirmed Victorian suspicions about the dangers of unregulated sexuality: physicians, feminists, religious thinkers, moral conservatives, and utopians all voiced concern about unbridled male sexuality and proffered ideas on how often and by whose initiative sexual intercourse should take place, its impact upon body and mind, and whether and how such energy might be turned to more constructive pursuits. Although disagreements punctuated this debate—for some, sexual intercourse symbolized the triumph of the carnal over the spiritual; for others, sexual relations expressed the most profound spiritual union possible between a husband and wife—after mid-century a more repressive ideology (though not necessarily more repressive behavior) began to take shape. Led by physicians such as William Acton, moral advisers emphasized women's disinterest in sex and feared the danger indulgence posed to both male and female vitality.

As a corollary to the growing emphasis on female passionlessness, a variety of reformers emphasized the importance of male sexual control. Feminists of various persuasions found themselves allied on this point not only with those favorably disposed to femaly sexuality but also with prudish purity crusaders intent on establishing a repressive sexual ideology for men and women. In feminist pamphlets, Women's Christian Temperance Union "white life" campaigns, and anti-prostitution crusades led by moral conservatives, the call went out to alter male sexual behavior by harnessing and rechanneling destructive sexual energy to more ennobling pursuits.[4]

Thus, John English's behavior ran badly afoul of the emerging ideology. To the lower court, his actions likely symbolized the rampant egotistic individualism and male deviancy so troubling to nineteenth century reformers: drunken,

---

[4]The growing literature on nineteenth-century sexuality is reviewed by Estelle B. Freedman in "Sexuality in Nineteenth-Century America: Behavior, Ideology, and Politics," in *The Promise of American History: Progress and Prospects*, ed. Stanley Katz and Stanley Kutler (Baltimore: Johns Hopkins University Press, 1982), 196–215. The emphasis on male continence is discussed by many authors: see, e.g., Carl Degler, *At Odds: Women and the Family in America from the Revolution to the Present* (London and New York: Oxford University Press, 1980), 279–97; David Pivar, *Purity Crusade: Sexual Morality and Social Control, 1868–1900* (Westport, Conn.: Greenwood Press, 1973), passim; Carroll Smith-Rosenberg, "Beauty, the Beast, and the Militant Woman," *American Quarterly* 23 (October 1971): 562–84; Barbara Berg, *The Remembered Gate: Origins of American Feminism: The Woman and the City, 1800–1860* (London and New York: Oxford University Press, 1978), 182–85, 190, 210–12; William Leach, *True Love and Perfect Union: The Feminist Reform of Sex and Society* (New York: Basic Books, 1980), 81–98; Mary Ryan, *Cradle of the Middle Class: The Family in Oneida County, New York, 1790–1865* (Cambridge: Cambridge University Press, 1981), 116–27.

gambling, irreligious, and sexually incontinent men were all far out of step with a nascent middle-class ethic that emphasized self-control and self-restraint.[5] But English failed in other ways as well. The campaigns against intemperate, impious, and incontinent males represented the more public, more organized effort to redefine the nature of manhood. Within the private world of sentiment, another revolution, fueled by domestic ideology, was under way that hoped to "feminize" male attitudes about personal relations.

Understandably, historians have focused on the impact of domestic ideology upon women, but what most have largely ignored is the ideology's message to men. Several scholars, however, have found that domestic moralists also sought to redefine manhood and, to this end, portrayed the ideal mid-nineteenth-century husbands as affectionate, considerate, loving, and sensitive: his psychological commitment to his wife and children complemented his wife's even greater devotion to her husband and offspring. In essence, the ideology of domesticity tried to alter conceptions of manhood in directions that would minimize the psychological distance between husbands and wives. It was no accident, as Mary Kelley pointed out in her analysis of nineteenth-century domestic fiction, that ideal men in these popular stories were feminized men, for such a vision helped bridge the gap between the public world of man the provider and the private world of woman the domestic. From this perspective, John English violated all that men were to be: his brutal insensitivity represented both an assault upon the sensibilities of his wife and an affront to new standards of manhood taking shape at mid-century.[6]

Yet, the denouement to this case was more complicated than the neat correlation between new standards of manhood and deviant male behavior leading to the award of a legal separation. The high court, by a vote of nine to five, reversed the lower court's decision and refused to award a legal separation. Why? Certainly the answer does not lie in the court's condonation of his behavior, a point made by the justices at the end of their opinion. Given legal precedents, the general direction of American divorce law, and basic conceptions of equity, the justices had good reason to grant Abigail English relief: the husband clearly posed a threat to the health of his wife, and thus her case met well-

---

[5]Ryan, chap. 4; Daniel T. Rodgers, "Socializing Middle-Class Children: Institutions, Fables, and Work Values in Nineteenth-Century America," *Journal of Social History* 13 (Spring 1980): 354–67; Ronald P. Byars, "The Making of the Self-made Man: The Development of Masculine Roles and Images in Ante-Bellum America" (Ph.D. diss., Michigan State University, 1979), 64–65, 70–94, 104–15.

[6]Several scholars have begun analysing the redefinition of manhood in Victorian America: Mary Kelley, "The Sentimentalists: Promise and Betrayal in the Home," *Signs* 4 (1979): 434–46; Degler, 26–51; Griswold, *Family and Divorce*, chaps. 5, 6; Leach, 9–10, 32–34, 65, 89–90, 99–101, 134 ff., 143–47, 158 ff.; Blanche Hersh, *The Slavery of Sex: Female Abolitionists in America* (Champaign: University of Illinois Press, 1978), 200–209; Anthony Rotundo, "Body and Soul: Changing Ideals of American Middle-Class Manhood, 1770–1920," *Journal of Social History* 16 (Summer 1983): 23–38; Karen Halttunen, *Confidence Men and Painted Women: A Study of Middle Class Culture in America, 1830–1870* (New Haven, Conn.: Yale University Press, 1982), 1–32.

established criteria for granting a divorce or separation on the ground of cruelty.[7]

The justices, however, chose not to do so. In part, their decision reflected the well-established precedent that marriages should be ended only for "grave and weighty" reasons that posed a threat to the future safety or health of the wronged spouse: otherwise, husbands and wives might divorce simply out of mere unhappiness, misery, or want of romance, a situation that ultimately invited social disaster. Such assumptions were especially strong in New Jersey, among the most conservative of the states in terms of divorce law, one of only six states that did not allow an absolute divorce on the ground of cruelty, and home to key supporters of the late nineteenth-century effort to establish uniform divorce laws in order to limit the accessibility of divorce.[8] New Jersey's unwillingness to include cruelty as a ground for absolute divorce suggests that the state's lawmakers placed a higher premium on social order than on personal happiness, a point made most forcefully in this case when the appellate judges even denied Abigail a separation. Although the court implied that she might indeed "live more comfortably at her father's house, with a liberal allowance for alimony," the real question, said the court, was whether her husband's behavior released her from her "duty as a wife."

As an answer, the court decided that duty came before happiness; moreover, the court defended this position by arguing that John English, despite his cruel and despicable past behavior, posed no further threat to his wife. What had Abigail's husband done to gain such confidence? Apparently, since his wife had left him, he had shown to the high court's satisfaction proper adherence to the new standards of manhood and family life that he had so brazenly ignored only months before. The Court of Errors and Appeals took pains to trace the Englishes' history, noting that they had overcome class, educational, and religious differences and even parental opposition to establish a marriage characterized by affection and "fond endearments." Moreover, since the separation, he had been miserable and had begged forgiveness: his tender letters, requests for ministerial intervention, expressions of love and affection, and promises of reform—coupled with a sanguine prognosis for his wife's physical recovery—convinced the court that Abigail faced little danger of future injury. In short, the hope of male reform outweighed the fear of female vulnerability

The documents that follow, albeit intrinsically more interesting than most, are just two of literally hundreds of divorce cases available in state appellate reports. Like so many others, the case of Abigail versus John English offers

---

[7]In 1845, the Connecticut Supreme Court refused a wife's divorce complaint because of her husband's sexual excesses on the ground that he supposedly did not know his behavior threatened his wife's health: Shaw v. Shaw, 17 *Connecticut Reports* 196 (1845). Yet most courts found sexual excesses to be cruelty warranting a divorce: see Melvin v. Melvin, 58 *New Hampshire Reports* 571 (1879); Walsh v. Walsh, 61 *Michigan Reports* 557 (1886); Mayhew v. Mayhew, 61 *Connecticut Reports* 235 (1891); Grant v. Grant, 53 *Minnesota Reports* 181–82 (1893).

[8]May, 4–5; Lynn Halem, *Divorce Reform: Changing Legal and Social Perspectives* (New York: Free Press, 1980), 34–39; and Carroll D. Wright, *A Report on Marriage and Divorce in the United States, 1867–1886* (Washington, D.C.: Government Printing Office, 1889), 114.

access to the private lives of common Americans and to the thinking of Victorian judges as they tried, within the context of changing definitions of gender, to balance the claims of family stability against those of individual autonomy and happiness. Although this decision came down on the side of family stability, it did so only because John English convinced the court that he sincerely regretted his past behavior, truly loved his family, and posed no further threat to the well-being of his wife. Thus, although at first look the appellate decision appears to subordinate personal happiness to family duty, the story is not quite so straightforward: in defending their rejection of a separation, the justices placed less emphasis on family stability—though that theme is present—and more on the husband's allegiance to new ideals about manhood and family life. The appellate case, for all of its apparent conservatism, thus contained within it many assumptions held by defenders of more expansive divorce laws. These two cases, then, not only show the complicated tensions between the need for family stability and desires for personal happiness but also suggest the complexity of the relationship among family, gender, and law in Victorian America.

*English* v. *English*
Cases in Chancery
27 New Jersey Equity Reports 71–75
February Term, 1876

The Chancellor:

The bill is filed for a divorce *a mensa et thoro*, on the ground of extreme cruelty. The main charge is gross abuse of marital rights.... The case is of such a nature, and the relations with which it deals are of so delicate a character, that the court would gladly have been spared the necessity of judging between the parties. The complainant, however, has invoked its aid and protection, and the defendant denies her right to it; it therefore becomes the duty of the court, however unpleasant the task, to dispose of the questions presented for determination. The parties were married in 1867. The complainant is, and since June, 1873, the date of the birth of her third child, has been, afflicted with a uterine disease of such a character as to make connubial intercourse very distressing to her. She speaks of it as "agonizing," and as causing her intense suffering, indescribable pain. Notwithstanding her condition, and in spite of her remonstrances and entreaties, the defendant has, ever since that time, insisted on having intercourse with her, frequently even using force to accomplish his purpose. To her entreaties and expressions of apprehension that the intercourse would be fatal to her, he would reply, "No fear of its killing you; you will not die until your time comes; you know how I am—I cannot control myself;" or, "You have stood it before and will stand it again; you know I cannot help it;" or, "It is the same old story; I am sick of hearing it." She swears, that from June, 1873, to November, 1875, (on the 6th of which last-mentioned month she left his house and went to her father's,) with the exception of two weeks after the birth of her child in the first-mentioned month, and the two weeks after her miscarriage in 1874, he had intercourse with her every night when her catamenia [menses] were not upon her, (and it appears that he did not spare her even then,) and frequently twice and sometimes three times in a night; and she says she had been kept awake "many and many a night" by the pain she has suffered during and after intercourse.

This treatment continued up to the night of the 2d of November, 1875, when, after he had had intercourse with her against her remonstrance, which she urged on account of the pain which the act would cause her, he sought it twice again, once at about midnight, and the last time at about three o'clock in the morning, when he strove to accomplish his purpose by force, and only desisted at the crying of her and the children. She swears, that he then struck her in the back with his fist, and that, subsequently, when they had both got out of bed, he, violently striking his fist on the mantle piece, said to her, "I'll fix you, you can make up your mind to that," and this, she says, he repeated several times. She testifies, that when he commenced that night, she told him she could not stand it, that she felt unusually ill, and he replied, "You will have to stand it." She says she told him she felt so sick and weak that she was afraid she would not live long if he persisted as he had done lately; to which he answered, "That there was no fear of her; that she would not die till her time came," and she says he then held her down to the bed and accomplished his design. She adds, that she suffered the most excruciating pain, and that she cried and told him of her sufferings; she says also, that in holding her down he bruised her limbs so that they were lame and sore for more than two weeks afterwards. The character of his conduct on that occasion, is shown by the fact that from that time until the 6th of November, when she left the house, and went to her father's with her two children, he was morose and sullen, and did not notice her or the children. He admits that this was caused by her refusal to submit herself to him on the night of the 2d. Such gross and reprehensible abuse of marital rights as that of which he has been guilty, is just ground for a divorce from bed and board. *Moores* v. *Moores, 1 C.E. Green 275; Shaw* v. *Shaw, 17 Conn. 189; 1 Bishop on Marr. and Div., 760.*

But it is insisted by the defendant's counsel, that if the divorce prayed for be granted, it will be in contravention of the settled rule of the court, that a divorce will not be granted on the testimony of the complainant alone.

The testimony of the complainant does not stand alone, however. Strong corroboration of it is found in that of both of the physicians as to her physical condition, and also in the defendant's own testimony. He says that eight or nine months prior to July 1st, 1875, she assigned her delicate health and weakness as a cause of her unwillingness to submit herself to him; that she assigned her feebleness as an objection; that she was in delicate health between July and November, 1875; that she told him that her physician said she should have rest, that she should abstain from intercourse with him; that on the night of the 2d of November, 1875, she told him she was not very strong, that she felt delicate, and that she did not want him to have intercourse with her; that he struggled with her in bed, that night, in his endeavor to effect his purpose; that she cried when she jumped out of the bed, and that she cried because she did not want him to have connection with her. He further admits that she often tried, by physical means, to protect herself against him, and that she complained that his intercourse with her injured her, that it made her weak.

There can be no doubt that she was so diseased that connubial intercourse inflicted great and distressing pain upon her; nor can there be any doubt that her condition was known to him. According to his own testimony, he insisted on having connection with her against her will, and her remonstrance and entreaties, urged on the ground of her delicate and diseased condition; and he even, by his own admission, struggled with her to effect his purpose. The rule which he invokes in his aid, cannot avail him. In the light of all the testimony, her statements are entitled to credit, and if so, she is entitled to the relief which she seeks. He has been guilty of extreme cruelty towards her, so as to render it unsafe for her, under existing circumstances, to cohabit with him or to be under his dominion or control.

A divorce from bed and board forever, will be decreed. The complainant's health, however, may hereafter be restored, and it may become desirable that they should again live together. In order that the decree now pronounced may not be an insuperable obstacle to such a re-union, leave will be given to the parties to apply, by mutual, free, and voluntary consent, to be discharged from this decree.

*English* v. *English*
Court of Errors and Appeals
27 New Jersey Equity Reports 580–86
June Term, 1876

The opinion of the court was delivered by
SCUDDER, J.

Upon a bill filed by Abby L. English for divorce *a mensa et thoro*, on the ground of the extreme cruelty of her husband, John English, a decree has been made that they be separated from bed and board forever; provided, however, that the parties may, at any time thereafter, by their joint and mutually free and voluntary act, apply to the Court of Chancery for leave to be discharged from the decretal order. The custody of infant son and daughter of the parties was given to the complainant; and it was further adjudged and decreed that the defendant pay to the complainant $25, in weekly payments, for the support of herself and their children. From this decree an appeal has been taken to this court.

Our statute (Rev., 1874, 5, p. 255), enacts that for extreme cruelty in either of the parties, the Court of Chancery may decree a divorce from bed and board forever thereafter, or for a limited time, as shall seem just and reasonable.

In *Moores v. Moores, 1 C.E. Green 279*, it is stated that a gross abuse of marital rights, resulting in injury or suffering to the wife, may constitute "cruelty" in the eye of the law, and justify the wife in separating herself from her husband. The law, at the time of this opinion, did not differ from the present statute, and the learned Chancellor meant that such conduct would constitute "extreme cruelty" within the terms of the statute.

This is the charge made in the complainant's bill, which as been proven in the judgment of the Court of Chancery; and upon the authority of the above-cited case, this decree of perpetual separation has been made, unless the parties shall voluntarily apply for a discharge. So far as the action of the court is concerned, it is a separation of this husband and wife forever.

The act of separation is so important in its consequences to the parties and to their children; it is so contrary to the policy of the law, which rather seeks to "set the solitary families," and keep them thus united for their own good and for the welfare of society, that it is important in every case to examine carefully whether those cogent reasons are to be found which constrain the court to allow and order such separation.

We shall adopt the specific definition of extreme cruelty which has been approved in this case, and inquire whether there has been a gross abuse of marital rights. Such abuse must be attended with suffering, injury to the health, and be against the will of the wife.

The case shows that from the time of the marriage, on August 21st, 1867, to June, 1873, there is no complaint that she was abused in this respect. But from that date up to the 6th day of November, 1875, when she left her husband's house, taking with her their two little children, she says that he has thus injured her. On June 3d, 1873, the third child was born, and in the long and difficult delivery, which was effected with instruments, she sustained such hurt that she was a sufferer until after she left her home, and may be so still. She so testifies, and although her husband denies all knowledge of any disorder, she is corroborated by two physicians, who have examined her since the separation, and describe her condition. Since June 3d, 1873, the husband had access to her frequently, when he must have known that she suffered, and was weakened by his acts. It is not requisite to give the particulars. Much of the case on this point depends, necessarily, upon her own evidence, which is sustained by the family physician to the extent that she needed rest for her recovery from the delivery, the disorder that followed it, and a subsequent miscarriage in November, 1874. The wife made no complaint to any one excepting her husband, and continued to occupy the bed with him until within three days of her leaving. The evidence of Theodore G. Thomas, a physician who has made women's diseases a specialty, is that while in the situation in which he found her, soon after the separation, moderate indulgence would not damage her, yet that excessive indulgence would. He further says, although there would be pain, that a large proportion of married women assent under exactly those circumstances.

It is obvious that there should be an affectionate forebearance on the part of the husband when the wife is thus affected, and a selfish, lustful persistence, without regard to consequences, is unkind, even where no decided objection is made. But, in this case, it is charged that objections have been made, and considerable rudeness, if not force, used at times, to effect the purpose. This is the wife's statement; but it is denied by the husband, who says that the complaints were that she did not wish to have more children. She is a woman of a nervous and rather delicate constitution, and while her account may be exaggerated, we are satisfied that it is substantially correct. This evidence does not stand upon the wife's testimony alone: it is corroborated by other facts in the case, founded mainly on the defendant's own qualifications and denials of her statements.

On the night of November 3d, 1875, she complains that he was persistent and violent in his efforts, and as she arose from the bed, after his failure to succeed, he struck her in the back with his fist. She says that her cries awoke the children, and were heard by the servant. The children are too young to be examined as witnesses, and the servant, although in the employment of the complainant, is not produced. The brother of the complainant, however, testifies that the defendant told him, soon after the separation, that on that night she cried out, and left the bed. The wife remained home on Wednesday, Thursday, and Friday following this November 2d, during which time they were separated at night, and spoke to each other but little through the day. On Saturday, November 6th, she left, taking with her the two little children, and went to her father's house, where she has since remained. These facts are a general statement of the complainant's case.

It is important to consider the relations of the parties during their marriage, and some facts since their separation, to arrive at a just conclusion in this peculiarly delicate and painful case.

It appears that the parents of the wife objected to the marriage because of the difference of their religion. He is a Catholic, and she is a Protestant. But this difference did not, apparently, cause any trouble after their marriage, for she went to church with him, or elsewhere, as she pleased. The parents also objected to some inequality in their station in life, but this was based mainly on the fact that she had received a better education, while he, working at his trade of tinsmith, was comparatively unlearned, but, by prudent management, had accumulated a moderate fortune.

After the marriage, he was always kind and affectionate, with the exception of the matters of this complaint. He provided a good home for her, and gave her every reasonable indulgence and allowance, excepting in two or three unimportant particulars, about which there is conflicting testimony. The relatives, friends and servants who have been called as witnesses, all testify that they were fond in their endearments, even in the presence of others, and that they were remarkably affectionate. The wife says that she loved him until the day after November 2d, when he was morose and sullen in his conduct. His affection for her appears to have been always strong, and continues, so that he describes himself as miserable in his separation from his wife and children, and he says he is willing to make any reasonable concessions if she will return. That he is sincere, appears from the fact that after his wife left on Saturday afternoon while he was at his work, on Sunday morning he went to see her at her father's house, asked her forgiveness and begged her to return home with the children. He continued to call afterwards, repeatedly, with the same requests. November 10th, he sent her a letter, asking her to return, describing his pain at her leaving him, avowing his love for her, his only happiness to be with her and the children, and promising that every trouble, so far as it depended on him, should be removed; that he was willing to leave the only complaint she had ever made against him to their doctor. He is not a scholar, but this letter is a most tender appeal to a wife, under any circumstances. In the same month of November, he requested Spencer M. Rice, a Protestant Episcopal clergyman, whose church his wife had sometimes attended, to see her, and endeavor to get her to come back to her home. Mr. Rice went and had a long conversation with the wife and her mother. He says the wife gave no decided answer, but her mother told him to say that the result of the interview was unsatisfactory.

On November 10, 1875, Mrs. English was examined by the family physician, Dr. Latkins, at her father's house. The bill of complaint for the divorce was sworn to by her and filed the same day. This action was promptly begun while the husband was attempting to arrange for a settlement of the family troubles. He has used no threats, nor has he been offensive in his efforts to secure the return of his family; on the contrary, he has used entreaties for forgiveness, and promises of self-denial and forbearance. After this suit was commenced, on the day before Christmas, he sent the usual presents to his wife and children, with a most pathetic letter, in which he says that no Christmas present would be so good to him as to see them all back in their home again. This letter would, ordinarily, have little or no effect in a cause that had been already commenced, but in determining the character of the man, in connection with all the facts of the case, it has significance, and if it be a true expression of his feeling, will go far to satisfy a court that the wife will not be unsafe if within the power of such a husband.

The point for determination is not whether the husband, in his rudeness, has injured his wife without sufficient thought or care of her physical health, while doing an act which, in ordinary cases, is not unlawful, infurious or dangerous, for it must be conceded under the facts of this case, that he has thus abused his marital rights; but the true inquiry is whether the conduct of the husband has been such as to raise a reasonably apprehension that further acts of the same abuse will be committed if the wife should return to him. The court must be satisfied that the wife is in danger of bodily harm if she go back to him, or, to use the language in *Close* v. *Close, 10 C.E. Green 529*, that he has done and will continue to do such acts as will endanger her health, or render her life one of such extreme discomfort and wretchedness as to incapacitate her to discharge the duties of a wife. It is not the question whether she will live more comfortably at her father's house, with a liberal allowance for alimony, but whether she is released from her duty as a wife by the extreme cruelty of her husband, and the reasonable apprehension that it will continue. The principle which must decide this case does not affect these parties alone: it is of the utmost importance to all, that these bonds should not be lightly severed.

A separation from bed and board is not decreed only as a punishment for past misconduct, but mainly as a protection against future probable acts of cruelty; this probability being based upon the former conduct, and the character and disposition of the parties. *Bishop's Mar. and Div., 719, &c.*

*In Shaw* v. *Shaw, 17 Conn. 189*, it was stated by the court that the wife had just reason to fear that her husband would compel her to occupy the same bed with him, regardless of the consequences to her health, and yet the divorce was refused. It is not necessary, if we were disposed, to go so far in this case, for we see no reasonable ground to apprehend that this defendant, whose disposition appears to be affectionate towards his family, and who has been already subjected to distress, exposure and expense, as the consequences of his misconduct, will again transgress, with the certainty that he will, with such aggravation, be perpetually separated from his wife.

The health of the wife has also been considered. By the testimony of both physicians who have been examined, the ailment from which she has suffered is curable with proper medical treatment, and she may be in her usual good health at this time. But if it were otherwise, it is not believed that, with the knowledge he now has of her condition, he would attempt to treat her cruelly.

In conclusion, it must be clearly stated that the action of the court is not based upon any approval of the acts of this husband, of which his wife complains, nor upon his requests for her return, nor upon any formal security that he can offer for his future good behavior. Our action is founded on the history of the married life of these parties, the affection this husband has always manifested for his wife, and his repentance for his misconduct; so far as we can judge of human conduct, he is sincere, and looking at the entire case, with its own peculiar circumstances, we are of the opinion that this divorce should now be refused.

The decree is reversed, and the bill will be dismissed without prejudice, so that the facts urged in this complaint may be used if the case should again be brought before the court.

For reversal—DALRIMPLE, DEPUE, DIXON, LATHROP, LILLY, SCUDDER, VAN SYCKEL, WALES, WOODHULL. 9.

For affirmance—BEASLEY, C. J. CLEMENT, DODD, KNAPP, REED. 5.

*Section Two*

# A Comparative Perspective

6

WESLEY A. FISHER

# Courtship in Russia and the USSR

*Although Karl Marx paid little attention in his theoretical writings to the family system as it existed under capitalism and as it might exist under communism, his colleague Frederick Engels did consider the questions of family formation and maintenance. His writings, including especially* The Origin of the Family, Private Property, and the State, *and* The Condition of the Working Class in England in 1844, *give clear statements of the Marxist perception of the family and its relation to the overarching economic system. To these writings the Soviet government has, through the years, turned as it has enacted various family policies, hoping to empower the kind of ideal family system that Engels envisioned under communism.*

*Marx envisioned capitalist society as comprised primarily of two classes, the Bourgeoisie, who own capital, and the Proletariat, who own only their own labor. Regarding families specifically, Engels believed that neither bourgeois nor proletarian families could be truly happy under capitalism. Because the bourgeois family is based on property, and marriage arrangements are guided solely by the desire for accumulation of more property, he held that love between husband and wife is impossible. Furthermore, relations between parents and children are also tarnished by the question of inheritance of property. Engels stated that the bourgeois family is characterized by greed, oppression, and exploitation, and he suggested that the class structure of capitalist society is reflected within the microcosm of the bourgeois family, with the wives, unable to own or inherit property, being a proletariat under their husbands' bourgeois power.*

*Engels painted an equally dismal portrait of the proletarian family under the capitalist system. In spite of the potential for love among husband, wife, and children that the absence of property makes possible, the meager circumstances of the family's day-to-day existence coupled with the dehumanizing capitalist industrial system leave the family helpless and demoralized. Thus, even though the proletariat do not own property, the system of private ownership nevertheless ultimately destroys all chance for happiness among these families, as well.*

*With Engels targeting private property as the evil that destroys both bourgeois and proletarian families, his prediction is not surprising that, under communism, the family would grow strong and true love could emerge. With class lines removed and property in the hands of the state, men and women could join in marital unions based solely on love.*

*The Soviet government has from its beginning passed laws designed to mold the family into the ideal love match Engels foresaw. One might expect that these laws, viewed over the course of the twentieth century, would reveal continuous change in one direction with each successive law refining or updating previous ones. However, this has not been the case. Reversals in family policy have meant, for instance, that for one generation of Soviets, abortion was legal, while for another it was outlawed, and for still another, procreation was rewarded. At one time, free love was espoused, adultery condoned, and divorce discouraged. Later, those who strayed from the monogamous bed suffered punishment and divorces were readily granted to the betrayed spouses.*

*On one aspect of marital policy, mate selection, Marxist thought has not wavered. Reviewing Engels' position on the family under capitalism, it is not surprising that the Western "marriage market" view of the mate-selection process is abhorrent to Marxists. Rather, the official position holds that marriage choice is based solely on love and that entrance into marriage is spontaneous and based on emotion.*

*In* The Soviet Marriage Market, *Wesley Fisher overviews contemporary attitudes on and behaviors in mate-selection in the USSR. In the chapter excerpted here, he looks closely at the many aspects of courtship and addresses the question of whether or not Soviet young people strictly adhere to the love-based marriage ideal.*



---

This paper examines the extent to which the various peoples of the USSR have adopted the ideological stance of the Soviet regime regarding mate-selection and criteria of mate-selection. Romantic conceptions of love and belief in love are widespread throughout Soviet society. The majority of the Soviet population has by now accepted the ideological principle that marriage should be contracted only out of love; but as with other areas of the ideology, this idea is accepted more in the abstract than in concrete reference to one's own fate.

Not only do most people in the USSR agree that love in a general sense exists, but they tend to believe in the possibility of a "grand" love, a "great" love. The responses of some 15,000 persons surveyed in various areas of central Russia and the Tatar ASSR in 1968–71 concerning beliefs in love reveal that the overwhelming majority of respondents were ready to say that real "great" love exists or to admit that they earlier believed in its existence but are now disillusioned. Evidently belief in romantic love at least at some point in the life cycle is extremely widespread in a society that only a century ago Sir Donald Mackenzie Wallace characterized as evidencing little romance or sentimentality regarding family relations among the peasant majority (Wallace 1912: 91).

The young and those currently in occupations that involve more contact with the ideology are a little more likely to believe that "great" love exists. Students in higher education and secondary-school teachers are somewhat more likely to be romantic than manual workers or engineering personnel. Seventy-five to 85 percent of all groups, however, believe at some time in their lives in "great" love, which implies that indoctrination with romantic conceptions is highly successful at young ages, followed by some rejection of romantic ideas in later life. Such belief in an aspect of the ideology in early years followed by disillusionment is similar to the situation regarding the career aspirations and expectations of Soviet youth (Yanowitch and Dodge 1968). The importance of exposure to the ideology is perhaps also shown by the fact that of the manual workers surveyed, those in the Moscow area were more likely to value love than were workers elsewhere (Fainburg 1972 :6).

When asked whether in principle marriage should be based on love, a very substantial proportion of the population parrots back the official ideology. Thus when asked "Do you believe in principle that marriage should only be concluded on the basis of love?," 94 percent of a sample of 271 workers, engineers, doctors, and librarians in Minsk in the late 1960s answered affirmatively (Iurkevich 1970a: 95, and 1970b: 101). Similar belief in love as the basis of marriage as an ideal matter was shown in Anatolii Kharchev's study of 500 couples in the Leningrad Palace of Weddings in 1962. In answer to the question "What is in your opinion the main condition for a stable and happy marriage?," 76.2 percent claimed love or love and common views, trust, sincerity, friendship, and the like; 13.2 percent claimed equal rights and mutual respect; 4 percent love and housing conditions; 1.6 percent love and material goods; 0.6 percent presence of children; 0.2 percent "realistic views of life;" and 4.2 percent gave no answer (Kharchev 1964: 179). When asked to rank in order of importance the reasons for establishing a family, eighth-graders and graduating secondary-school students in the Estonian SSR in the late 1960s generally ranked "being together with a person one loves" highest.

Belief in love as the basis of marriage is connected to other value orientations. The choice is not simply love versus material calculations as constantly juxtaposed in Soviet ideology, but rather a notion that if one marries not for love that other psychological motives should nonetheless be most important. Thus when a Minsk sample of workers, engineers, doctors, and librarians (N = 221) was asked "If for some reason there was no basis to hope rationally to marry for love, which of the motives listed below would be sufficient in your opinion?," 86 percent answered congeniality, friendship, or respect (Iurkevich 1970a: 95). There is some evidence that belief in love tends to be accompanied by other approved Soviet values. Those in a 1966–67 study in Perm who claimed to have married for love were more likely to value such things as a clear conscience and satisfaction with work, while those who claimed that they had entered marriage as a matter of calculation were more likely to be oriented to promotion in their careers, "getting ahead," and material security (Fainburg 1970: 73–75).

Moving from commitment to abstract ideal values to the motives that Soviet citizens claim as the reasons they entered their own marriages, it seems likely that at the time of their weddings the vast majority of couples believe that they are marrying for love. In surveys of newlyweds in Palaces of Weddings and registration bureaus, virtually all couples claim they are marrying for love (see, for example, Kharchev and Emel'ianova 1970: 63). Among couples already married much depends on the wording of the question. Asked whether they had entered marriage because of love, because everyone does so, or because of some sort of calculation, some 70 to 80 percent of married respondents in Fainburg's sample of 15,000 in central Russia and the Tatar ASSR claimed that they had entered marriage because of love. Students in higher education were particularly likely to claim love as the reason they had married (see Fainburg 1970). This study has been interpreted to mean that about one-fourth of Soviet couples marry for reasons other than love (Riurikov 1974). What it does show is that when confronted with a choice of responses directly ideological in nature, very few people in the Soviet Union are willing to say that they entered into their marriage through some sort of calculation. A somewhat larger percentage are willing to say that they married "because everyone does so."

Open-ended questions concerning the marriage motives of those already married for some time tend to elicit love as an answer in fewer cases than do closed-ended questions, although the majority of men and women still claim that they married for psychological rather than material or other reasons. The results of studies of marriage motives in various regions of the USSR among manual workers in Minsk, young couples in Leningrad, families with children in Moscow, and in a sample of married Kirgiz men and women show that, as already stated, a majority of couples believe that they married because of love or other psychological reasons. This conclusion also holds true for a survey of collective farmers in Byelorussia (Kolokol'nikov 1976: 80). It is particularly interesting to note that the sample of Kirgiz men and women does not differ substantially in this respect from the samples in the Slavic areas of the country—evidently the ideology of love as the basis for marriage has penetrated even the Moslem Central Asian areas of the country. Studies of newlyweds in the Buryat ASSR and Dagestan ASSR also confirm the acceptance of the ideology by the nonSlavic population. (See Khitynov 1974: 15; Agaev 1972: 8.)

Judging by these various surveys, women tend to be more romantic than men and to claim love as the reason for having married more than their husbands do. This is in accordance with the findings by sex regarding Estonian students' views of the reasons for establishing a family. Men are more likely to feel that they entered a shotgun marriage, that they had to marry because they had fathered an illegitimate child.

There is evidence that those with higher education and more exposure to the ideology are more likely to claim that they married for love in answer to open-ended as well as closed-ended questions. The pilot study for the Minsk survey consisted primarily of respondents who were white-collar employees with some amount of higher education. Seventy percent of them (N = 253) claimed that they had married for love as opposed to only 47.9 percent and 57.4 percent of men and women respectively among manual workers in factories in the eventual study itself (Iurkevich 1970a: 96).

It is important to distinguish ideals regarding family patterns from actual behavior. Much of the Soviet population's adoption of the ideal of love as a basis for marriage is adoption only in terms of voiced attitudes. As will be seen, many other factors come into play in mate-selection in the USSR than love and romantic attachment alone. At least one Soviet article has recognized that the responses favoring love in such surveys as those reviewed above are ideological in nature rather than a statement of personal conviction ("60,000,000 semei" 1970), and there is evidence of a certain cynicism on the part of the Soviet population toward the value of love as a basis for relations between men and women. In a recent Soviet joke, for example, a prostitute is asked whether she gave her services for love or money. "For love, of course," she answers. "How can you call $3.00 money?" (Many prostitutes work for foreign currency.)

It would be a mistake, however, to dismiss the verbal acceptance by the Soviet population of a romantic basis for marriage, as is implicitly done in arguments that the emergence in the USSR of romantic criteria of mate-selection is unlikely since the society is still not free from material want (see Hollander 1973: 257). The fact that the Soviet population says it believes in romantic love to the extent that it does, even if such statements are only superficial voicing of what is ideologically and politically acceptable, arguably serves to reduce the number of marriages made for economic and other reasons unconnected to love.

Soviet ideology also has had a clear effect on the criteria that people use in selecting a mate. Surveys that have asked what people are looking for in a future spouse uniformly have found characteristics such as "loving" or psychological traits to be chosen first among traits desirable in a spouse. Choices further down the list tend to vary depending on the sex of the respondent, but it is striking how low nationality, occupation, and financial status tend to be among attributes considered salient.

For two different groups of Estonian students for both sexes, the relations between the respondent and future spouse are the most important consideration; that is to say, whether the future spouse loves the respondent and whether the respondent loves the future spouse are considered to be the most important criteria in mate-selection. Very important also is the character or personality of the future spouse. Beyond mutual love and the character of the ideal mate, however, there is a split to some extent in the criteria used by men and women. In what looks very much like a typical Western market exchange, the Estonian men tend to give more importance to appearance as a criterion in choosing a future wife, whereas women are somewhat more likely to place importance on the education of a future husband. There is thus an asymmetry in the criteria used by men and women, with men tending to favor "typically feminine" traits as elsewhere in the world, and women tending to place somewhat more emphasis on the education—and perhaps therefore future occupation—of their desired mates. It is remarkable, however, that the occupation as such, financial status, and nationality of the future spouse are considered to be highly unimportant by both men and women. It thus would seem that the ideology has had quite an effect on attitudes in underplaying these characteristics.

Elsewhere in the Baltics, a poll of women students in Vilnius State University in the fall of 1973 found the trait considered to be most important in a future husband to be intelligentnost', or essentially "being cultured." The second most important trait was that a future husband treat a woman as a friend equal in all ways to him, and the third was that a future husband have a caring attitude toward his family and children. Other traits mentioned were belief in self, love of work, sobriety, sense of humor, and a striving for all-around perfection. These Lithuanian female students thought the ability to understand a husband was the most important attribute of a wife. The emphasis on psychological characteristics and on relationships was considered by the researcher to be evidence of change in the concept of manly strength from physical or economic prowess to essentially intellectual strength (Solov'ev 1973: 13).

Studies elsewhere in the USSR show generally similar results. A thousand students in the second year of higher education and in specialized academic institutions in Simferopol in 1975 were asked to name the three main traits that attract them in a future spouse. Men named love for husband and children first, then fidelity, then ability to run a household and create a comfortable home. Women named "loving" and "a good family man" as the most desirable attributes in a husband, then named a series of character traits. As in the case of the Estonian students, women were somewhat more likely to desire education in a future husband than men were to desire education in a future wife, and also as in the Estonian case, men tended to place more importance on appearance than did women (Ermishin 1976). Women workers in a textile factory in Minsk chose devotion and industriousness as the qualities most desirable in a husband and also thought that the same qualities were most desirable in a wife (N = 500. Bangerskaia 1975). In like manner, 50 women who had been married for some time who were interviewed in Leningrad in the late 1960s claimed to have valued primarily intelligence and "seriousness" in their husbands prior to entrance into marriage (Kharchev and Emel'ianova 1970: 63).

On the other hand, while in those areas of the USSR traditionally lacking in development of a love complex, voiced criteria of mate-selection now are less concentrated on economic matters, less stress is placed on the psychological characteristics of the spouse. Thus in a survey of rural Kirgizia in the early 1970s only 9.7 percent of the respondents thought the material well-being of the family of bride or groom to be most important, but only somewhat over a quarter of the sample emphasized the character of the future spouse while fully 56 percent thought the spouse's appearance was most important. (N = 430. Achylova 1972: 10.)

At least in voiced attitudes most of the Soviet population agrees with the official ideology and believes that the most important criteria in mate-selection are the psychological characteristics of the future spouse. The acceptance of the ideology is clearest regarding those traits most desired and those most disregarded. Thus most important among the criteria of mate-selection are love and the psychological characteristics of the future spouse, while at the other end of the scale, the financial status of the spouse is most underplayed. In between, the effect of the ideology is not quite so clear. Beauty and personal appearance, for example, are disliked as criteria of prestige and of mate-selection by the official moralists of Soviet society, and for many years the evil heroines of socialist realism were presented as very attractive while the good women were portrayed as plain and unconcerned with their looks (Hollander 1973: 240–41). Notwithstanding this official line, however, Soviet men still place importance on the appearance of their future wives.

Similarly, the importance given to education among attributes of an ideal mate cannot be explained simply by the contribution of education to psychological and personal characteristics as has been argued by Soviet writers (Kuznetsova 1973: 13), but is connected to the role of education in advancement in social status in a bureaucratic society such as the USSR. From time to time there is recognition in the Soviet press of the extent to which the use of education as a criterion in mate-selection represents a desire to advance in social status rather than a concern for the personal characteristics of the spouse. In a letter to the editors of *Sovetskaia kul'tura*, a young male metalworker in love with a student complained:

> When she and I were among her comrades she would tell them that I was also a student at another institute. I found it unpleasant that she seemed to be ashamed of me, even though, frankly speaking, I did not feel any sense of inferiority when I was among students. Their conversations and interests were not alien to me. In Tonia's opinion, however, my lack of a student's identification card practically compromised her. She said, "It doesn't matter which one, but you should graduate from an institute."
>
> In conclusion, despite my regrets, I had to break with the girl I loved. My entry into a higher school kept being delayed, and her demand became a burden.
>
> I am now 26 years old; I am a student in a correspondence course, married and raising one son. It would seem that it is long past time to forget the sad story, but I am continually reminded of it by the conversations of my fellow workers

> and fellow students. Many of them do not hide the fact that they entered higher school not out of any sense of vocation, but rather for calculating reasons. They do care what sort of specialists they become; they are concerned with their "future position in society." They are not attracted to people in workers' occupations. If one of them marries, the first thing he or she reports is not what sort of person his or her spouse is, but rather who he or she is. If he is an engineer, that means the marriage is a successful one. If not, the person has made a stupid mistake. ("Not Simply Love" 1976)

Although no surveys have asked questions regarding attitudes toward the class origins of a potential spouse, it is clear that the class background of a future wife or husband is often taken into account even when the couple themselves are essentially similar in their own education and general socioeconomic status. Two recent popular Soviet plays have revolved around the question of parental opposition to marriages between couples of varying social origins, even though in both instances the would-be bride and groom are essentially similar in all other characteristics, in particular in education. In Vladimir Konstantinov's and Boris Ratser's play *Unequal Marriage*, the son of a well-known philologist falls in love with the daughter of a house painter, and the parents of both conspire to separate the couple. "We are not the right color," the house painter says (see the description of this play in Saikowski 1970). Similarly, in Mikhail Roshchin's play *Valentin and Valentina*, the daughter of an aristocratic family falls in love with the son of a female railroad attendant who warns her son, "She is not a proper match for you." (Roshchin 1971. See also Kaiser 1976: 38–40.) As is to be expected given the constrictions of socilist realism, the two plays end happily for the couples involved, but the point is that class origin is still maintained as a criterion in mate-selection, at least where parents are concerned.

There is little attention paid in Soviet writings to the extent to which men take the occupation of their future mates into account in choosing a wife. Although it is clear that women's occupations are important in actual behavior of mate-selection, there is almost no discussion of the matter except perhaps for claims that "the girl with the job has not lost her appeal" (*Soviet Life* 1973). From indications in the surveys discussed above and other evidence available, it is clear that a man's occupation is a considerably more important criterion in mate-selection than a woman's occupation, notwithstanding the great participation of women in the Soviet labor force. A content analysis of descriptions of marriage and love in two popular youth magazines, *Iunost'* and *Sel'skaia molodezh'*, found that in only 8.6 percent of the stories did the authors give no information concerning the professions of the male characters, whereas in the case of women the percentage was fully 48.2 percent. In other words, in Soviet discussions of marriage and love it is impossible to imagine a man without an occupation, but it is possible to imagine a woman without one (Semenov 1973: 170). In like manner it is claimed that a woman still "wants to see in a man a being of a somewhat higher order in level of knowledge, professional and career achievement than she herself" (Kuznetsova 1973).

Of interest is the veritable absence today of open discussion of political criteria in mate-selection. While in earlier more turbulent times the suitability of a mate was seen as in part resulting from proper political views—heroes of the socialist-realist novels of the Stalin era, such as Korchagin in Nikolai Ostrovskii's novel, *How the Steel Was Tempered* (Ostrovskii 1936), would throw over potential mates for their lack of true communist views—politics no longer seems to be a major consideration when courtship is discussed. This is not to say that political attitudes do not play a role in mate-selection or a role in people's decisions to marry, but in terms of their predominance among criteria of mate-selection and in public discussion of mate-selection they seem to have fallen by the wayside. Certainly no published mention is made of the idea that a future husband or wife should be a member of the Komsomol or Communist Party. To some extent this may be because such criteria as education may be assumed to include such political matters.

The gist of the above discussion is that on the level of voiced attitudes the Soviet population has to a very great extent accepted official Marxist-Leninist ideology concerning motives for mate-selection and criteria of mate-selection. As will be seen, a marriage market exists in the Soviet Union in many ways similar to marriage markets elsewhere, but the point here is that Soviets do not consciously feel themselves to be driving a bargain: although bargains are struck, people do not think of themselves as bargaining. Although such a split between consciousness and behavior is typical of other courtship systems as well (Goode 1964: 32), it is arguable that in the Soviet case the greater elaboration and rigidity of ideology has meant that those entering marriage are even less aware of a market structure to courtship than persons in other countries with institutionalized romantic love complexes. Additional evidence that this is so may be found in Soviet practices of almost casual entrance into marriage and the decline of such institutions as engagements.

The counterargument is that in a system where ideology concerning mate-selection is so rigid and codified and comparisons are constantly made between the hideous bourgeois past, when "marriages of calculation" were supposedly rampant, and the good socialist present when love prevails, the population is repeatedly reminded that calculation in mate-selection is in fact possible. The constant assertions that marriages in the Soviet Union are not based on considerations other than love bring to mind the idea that perhaps it would indeed be possible to marry for reasons other than love.

That this is so in a sizable minority of cases can be seen from the prevalence of so-called fictitious marriages: marriages that have been legally contracted but are not consummated or at least where the parties have no intention of establishing a family. The distinction between fictitious marriages and marriages of calculation often is not very sharp. Under Soviet law fictitious marriages may be recognized as invalid (Kodeks o brake i sem'e RSFSR, 1975: article 43). Under article 20 of the RSFSR Criminal Code it is possible to punish the parties to such marriages with up to a year of corrective labor at their place of work for violating the rules for registering acts of civil status, and further criminal punishment for such persons has been urged (Feofanov 1971). Thus often it is not enough simply to register a marriage to gain the desired calculated end, but a pretense at conjugal relations must be made or actual marital relations established to fool the neighbors and the authorities. Examination of different sorts of fictitious marriages serves as a way of understanding the various self-interested motivations Soviet couples may have in entering marriage.

Fictitious marriages are nothing new in Russia: they have their origins in the practices of the revolutionaries of the 1860s and 1870s who would marry so that the women involved could obtain separate passports to go abroad (Elnett 1926: 83; see also Stites 1978: 91, 132). A number of regulations in contemporary Soviet life have spawned several sorts of fictitious marriages. The most frequent types are marriages contracted to gain living space and/or obtain residence permits to live in the larger cities. It is not permitted to bring a member of the opposite sex into your room or apartment to live with you if you are not registered as married, nor is it possible to live with someone in one of the larger cities if that person does not have the appropriate residence permit. While such restrictions can be breached where separate apartments or private houses are concerned, the shortage of housing means that neighbors in already overcrowded communal apartments take a definite interest in the matter. Thus from the standpoint of obtaining housing and living in the major cities, there is a definite incentive to register marriages.

Many such marriages are, of course, not strictly speaking fictitious marriages: given the difficulties of finding places for sexual contact outside of marriage, many young people marry for lack of privacy in the overcrowded apartments they share with parents and others ("The Young Marrieds" 1964). In studies of marriage motives in Perm, the percentage of those claiming to have entered their marriages "by calculation" was twice as high among those who at the time of the survey were living in their own house as among those who were living in communal apartments (Fainburg 1970: 71).

From time to time the Soviet press reports trials of those who have entered into fictitious marriages to obtain housing or residence permits. Usually such matters find their way into the courts because of the interest of some third party in having the marriage declared fictitious. Thus *Pravda* has reported the case of a Kiev woman doctor who in order to remain in Kiev and obtain housing arranged to marry one of her patients fictitiously, but made the mistake of using a man who already had a wife (Shatunovskii 1969). At times the relationships can become quite complicated. *Izvestiia* reported a case involving a man who after hatching several fictitious marriages for himself, proceeded to run a kind of marriage bureau for such marriages:

> Everything began back in 1962 when Baku resident Leonid Kazakevich decided to move to Moscow. He could not live at the Kursk Railroad Station or Vnukovo Airport, nor could he obtain a residence permit. At this point Leonid Kazakevich hatched the idea of a phony marriage. He registered his marriage with one Marina and was subsequently assigned living quarters, even though he and his fake wife had blithely separated. True, he had provided the woman with a Volga automobile as her part of the deal.
>
> Leonid decided to recover his expenses, using the same methods on the seas of matrimony. He proceeded to enter into fictitious wedlock with women named

> Liuba, Natasha and Margarita. In return for permits to take up residence at his address, Kazakevich received up to 1,000 rubles from his brides. He even wanted to legitimately marry Margarita, "for she's a very nice person, and my wife and I no longer see eye to eye." Financial plans vanquished tender affection, however.

In addition to his own numerous fictitious marriages, Kazakevich became responsible for uniting ten couples in return for some 7,300 rubles and was eventually sentenced for dishonest matchmaking (Feofanov 1971).

Many fictitious marriages for residence permits or housing are simply indispensable for persons who have been transferred to major cities for jobs but are unable to obtain housing for one reason or another (Beliavskii and Finn 1973: 77–83). They also are common among students who are trying to escape government reassignment to the provinces upon graduation and wish to stay in the larger cities (Feofanov 1971; Smith 1976: 9). The prices paid for the privilege of entering into such marriages vary, but the general black market price seems to range from about 1,000 to 2,000 rubles, or in other words, it costs about a year's average salary to enter into such marriages.

About the same amount of money purchases a fictitious marriage to Jews, through whom it is possible to leave the country. Presumably at least some marriages to foreigners also are fictitious and are contracted solely to leave the country. Another type of fictitious marriage involving travel abroad is that between persons who have the opportunity to travel for one reason or another and find that because they are unmarried the state is unwilling to let them go. It is rare that both husband and wife are allowed abroad together, presumably so as to ensure that the spouse will behave abroad and return to the USSR.

Another type of fictitious marriage occurs in order to save one's reputation in the eyes of relatives and close friends because of pregnancy. Such marriages were especially frequent during the period from 1944 to 1968, when a factual state of discrimination against illegitimate children existed as a result of then prevailing Soviet law. Thus in 1955 a woman's letter introduced into a divorce case in Minsk read:

> I need a father for my daughter, be it only in documents I am agreeable to the conclusion of a marriage with anyone regardless of age, position, or appearance. To the person with whom I conclude a marriage and who will adopt my daughter, I can provide a large reward and promise full peace and quiet. That is, depending on his desire, I will immediately hide myself so that it will *never* be remembered that I exist. (Iurkevich 1970a: 100)

In view of the continuing problems of illegitimate children even since legal changes in 1968 (Madison 1977), it is likely that fictitious marriages to avoid discrimination against out-of-wedlock children still exist. There is evidence that a certain proportion of Soviet marriages are considered by those in them to be shotgun marriages.

As in other societies, of course, marriages or promises of marriage are sometimes used to entice persons into things they would not otherwise do. Thus a 1968 *Izvestiia* article recounted how an athletic coach enticed women champion rowers from Saratov to join his team in Kiev by promising to marry them (Proletkin 1968).

Many of the above fictitious marriages are just one end of a spectrum that includes marriages for love that also may include some of these calculating motives. By making various social benefits dependent on the marital status of the parties involved, the Soviet regime sponsors the abuse of possibilities for marrying. While such abuses exist in other countries—such as fictitious marriages to immigrate into the United States, to dodge taxes, and the like—the plethora of such regulations in a bureaucratic, rule-ridden society makes the likelihood of such marriages perhaps greater than in the West. Over time as housing becomes more available, conditions improve, standards of living in various parts of the country become more equal, and foreign travel becomes freer for couples, it can be expected that the number of such marriages will decrease. Up to now, however, these types of arrangements are indicative of ways in which the Soviet Union has sponsored marriages of calculation rather than sought structurally to destroy the possibility for them, even if unintentionally.

## CONTROL OF TRANSACTIONS IN MATE-SELECTION

Parental control over mate-selection historically was extensive throughout all the various geographic regions that now comprise the USSR. Among the Russian peasantry until the end of the nineteenth century, marriages were concluded primarily according to parental choice and economic considerations played the major role. The main goal was to find a bride who would be a good worker, and the feelings of young people usually were not taken into consideration to any great extent. As a result there was a frequent practice of elopement or what was alternatively known as samokhodka, ubeg, or samokrutka, a pattern according to which the couple would be married in secret and then after some time would return to the parents to ask for their blessing and forgiveness (Aleksandrov et al. 1964: 469).

Marriages were arranged through the use of matchmakers or svaty, usually elder relatives of the groom who would visit the bride's family at night so as not to be seen, and the marriage arrangements had very definite elements of purchase and sale. Grooms throughout Russia generally paid a kladka or contribution to the expenses of the wedding and the bride's clothes (this has been claimed to be a survival of a bride-price, see Aleksandrov et al. 1964: 470), and in return the size of the bride's dowry was determined. Typically there also was inspection of the groom's house.

In addition to the actual economic contract between the parties, many customs in the traditional Russian peasant wedding ritual were of a somewhat mercenary nature. Thus when the groom's party would set out for the wedding, the bride's relatives would set up various obstacles that the best man then had to buy off with gifts of wine and sweets. Also, the place next to the bride was sold to the best man by the bride's younger brother. In some areas of Russia the bride was ritually purchased from the bridesmaids (Aleksandrov et al. 1964: 469–72; Dunn and Dunn 1967: 96–99).

By the end of the ninteenth century and beginning of the twentieth, matches began to be made more often with the consent of the parties involved. Although parental consent and matchmaking continued, they tended to take on somewhat more of a ritualistic aspect, and the traditional ways in which young people might meet each other increased in importance. Young people would meet in winter at so-called posidelki or sit-downs, spinning-bees. The girls of a village would gather, after which the boys of the village, sometimes within specific age-groups, would arrive to sing and dance with them. To some extent there were aspects of village endogamy, since only those who were residents of the village had the right to sit-down, even though those from other villages attended. In summertime the posidelka was replaced by the gulianie or walk, stroll. These often took the form of a kind of mass outing at which prospective brides and grooms and their parents could have a look at one another (Dunn and Dunn 1967: 23–24).

Although courtship in the towns also included parental consent and matchmaking, there existed something more of a love pattern. Young workers or members of the merchant class would meet at evening parties, at gulianiia, or, very frequently, in church. Indeed, by the turn of the century priests were complaining that the churches were being turned into meetinghouses for young people (Zhirnova 1975). Although selection might be made by the couple themselves, an official agreement or ritual matchmaking persisted even where the matchmaker had not actually done anything. In the towns relatives were sometimes replaced by fellow workers or professional women matchmakers (svakhi) in the bargaining process. As in the countryside a dowry generally was provided by the bride's side, and the groom had to pay everything necessary for the brides' wedding dress. Urban wedding ceremonies also contained the same elements of purchase of the bride as among the peasantry (Aleksandrov et al. 1964: 476).

In general, the same patterns characterized the Ukrainian and Byelorussian areas of the country, but it would seem that something more of a love pattern was institutionalized in the rural regions of those areas than was the case in central Russia. Although the consent of those entering marriage was not necessary to conclude a marriage among either the Ukrainians or Byelorussians, as a factual matter it generally was taken into account. The consent of parents was, however, necessary. As among the Russians the groom would send emissaries to conclude an agreement with the parents of the bride, and as among the Russians a dowry generally was provided, though the latter was of less importance in urban areas (Aleksandrov et al. 1964: 688, 692, 867, 870).

In the Baltic areas of the country youth historically had more of a say in the selection process. This was particularly the case in the Protestant regions. Thus following confirmation Estonian youth would become acquainted at work and in leisure activities. In contrast, the role of parents, particularly the father, in Latvia and Lithuania seems to have been somewhat greater in concluding marriages. While in Estonia the ability of a wife to be a good worker was important, economic considerations seem to have been somewhat more of a concern in Latvia and Lithuania. Throughout the Baltics the tradition of having a matchmaker sent by the groom to conclude all agreements existed, as well as wedding customs similar to those in Slavic areas in which the bride was "bought."

As in much of Western Europe the bride had the right of control over the dowry she brought to her marriage (Belitser et al. 1964: 73–76, 173–75, 280–82).

In the Caucasus and Central Asia the role of parents in mate-selection was considerably greater historically than in the Slavic and Baltic areas, particularly among Moslem peoples. Daughters often were given into marriage while still children, and rarely were the wishes of the future partners taken into account. Thus even at the beginning of the 20th century Armenians

> did not pay any attention whatsoever to the mutual consent of those entering into marriage and even thought that it was ill-mannered for young people to be interested in this question or to express their desire. The choice was made by their parents—when choosing a girl they looked at her mother, when choosing a boy at his father. (Lalaian 1906, cited in Ter-Sarkisiants 1972: 126)

In Central Asia a girl's father decided whom and when she would marry, and in many respects the marriage of a Central Asian girl was a forced marriage (Massell 1974: 111). Primarily an economic transaction between two families negotiated by the fathers, courtship in many parts of these areas involved open haggling over the bride-price or kalym. Exorbitant kalym often led to marriage by abduction (Luzbetak 1951: 76–99; Massell 1974: 112–14). In some areas of the Caucasus by the beginning of the 20th century, purchase of brides had fallen by the wayside, but haggling for dowries remained (Ter-Sarkisiants 1972: 137–38).

Soviet laws and changes in the socioeconomic structure of the USSR have brought about a situation whereby the majority of brides and grooms now enter into marriage by mutual consent. Although it seems clear that most couples do now enter into marriage of their own free will—to compel persons to marry against their will is a crime in Soviet law—parents and kin still play a large role in the decision to marry. Such authority of parents in mate-selection varies by geographic region along the lines historically existing before the Revolution: although it has been reduced throughout the entire USSR, kin control of mate-selection remains greater in the Caucasus and Central Asia.

The continuing participation of parents in the marital choices of their children in the Slavic areas is connected to a large extent to the problems of the housing shortage and the fact that most newlyweds anticipate living with one or the other set of parents after marriage. Of the 500 couples interviewed in 1962 at the Leningrad Palace of Weddings, 79.6 percent asked the consent of their parents to their marriage, while some 38 percent of all couples expected to live with their parents immediately after marriage (Kharchev 1964: 180). Among women interviewed in the same location in the late 1960s, over three-fourths had introduced their future spouses to their parents, while over 50 percent of them were helped financially by their parents and lived with their parents immediately after marriage (Kharchev and Emel'ianova 1970: 62). Ninety-three percent of the parents of a sample of rural Byelorussian couples surveyed in the early 1970s knew of the young people's decision, and 79.6 percent approved of it (Kolokol'nikov 1976: 81). While these have been the only surveys that have asked a question concerning parental consent directly, it is clear that the same relationship with parents must be true for other areas of the country. Thus over half the newlyweds in Kiev in 1970 intended to live with one or the other set of parents after marrying, and over two-thirds of the brides and over half the grooms were receiving material help from their parents as of the time of entrance into marriage (Chuiko 1975: 89–90). It is hard to see how under such circumstances newlyweds could avoid taking into account the opinions of their parents or of others with whom they plan to live.

Since parents are less likely than those actually entering into marriage to stress the psychological characteristics of a potential spouse among criteria of mate-selection, the fact that so many newlyweds live with their parents decreases the chances that couples will enter into marriage as a result of love. Couples interviewed in Perm in 1966–67 were less likely to say that they had married for love if they were living with their parents (Fainburg 1970: 71).

It is interesting to note that where Soviet parents have disapproved of their children's marital choices, it has been overwhelmingly the groom's parents who have been dissatisfied. Among Kharchev's 1962 sample of Leningrad couples, the parents who objected to their children's marriage were all parents of the groom (Kharchev 1964: 186), and in the study of women in Leningrad as of the late 1960s, 12 percent of the bride's parents objected to her marriage, whereas 28 percent of the groom's parents objected to his (Kharchev and Emel'ianova 1970: 62). From time to time the Soviet press prints articles attacking parents for interfering in their children's choice of a spouse, and in almost all cases these are instances of parents of the groom objecting to their son's marriage. Very rarely does an article appear concerning objections by the parents of the bride. Such articles concern, for example, a father's maneuvers in trying to get a ZAGS registration worker fired for registering the marriage of his son (Kotelevskaia 1968), or a young student's refusal to stand up to the objections of his father to his marriage where the father had been newly chosen first secretary of the Party Raikom and felt snobbish toward his daughter-in-law (Chachin 1971). In general discussions of parental opposition to the choice of a spouse, the examples used are almost exclusively that of opposition by the grooms' parents (see Ovchinnikova 1970).

The explanation as to why the concern of grooms' parents would be greater than the concern of brides' is to be found in the far greater value of men than of women in the Soviet marriage market. The great shortage of men in the postwar era has meant that it has been much harder for women to find husbands than for men to find wives, and presumably the parents of brides have been more ready to settle for anyone their daughter could get. A common attitude in Soviet society is that if a woman is single she is to be pitied, and it is usually thought that a single woman is unable to find a mate while a bachelor is thought to be single by choice (Svetlanova 1969). Comparison of the two Leningrad surveys gives some reason to suppose that the objections of grooms' parents have become more vociferous over the years: that is to say, there is some evidence that as the sex ratio has normalized and the value of men on the Soviet marriage market has fallen, parents used to the idea that a man can acquire pretty much anyone he wants have more and more objected to their sons' choices of brides.

While parental consent still is frequently sought in the USSR, mates are now generally found outside the home. In the European areas of the country very few now meet through parents and other relatives: only 3.3 percent of the Leningrad couples interviewed in 1962 and only 2 percent of the women interviewed in Leningrad in the late 1960s had met through relatives (Kharchev 1964: 197; Kharchev and Emel'ianova 1970: 62). Kin are more likely to have introduced newlyweds to each other in the areas in which parental control over mate-selection was traditionally very strong, such as the Caucasus and Central Asia. It would seem, however, that as of the present time only a minority of couples even in these areas now meet through parents and other relatives. Thus in a survey done of couples in rural Kirgizia in the early 1970s, only 23.2 percent had met through parents and relatives, and only 15.8 percent of those working in urban industry had so met (Achylova 1972: 8–9).

In urban areas throughout the country something close to 40 percent of couples now meet through school or work. In studies in Leningrad, Kiev, and Frunze, 17.5 percent, 15.7 percent, and 18.4 percent respectively of couples met in school; 21 percent, 22.1 percent, and 22 percent respectively met at work. A growing number meet at places of leisure, such as the cinema, clubs, and the like; such places accounted for 27.2 percent of Leningrad couples in 1962, 21.6 percent of newlyweds in Kiev in 1970, and even 20.1 percent of couples in rural Kirgizia in the early 1970s. A small but growing proportion meet by accident on the street or in other locations (Kharchev 1964: 197; Chuiko 1975: 98; Achylova 1972: 8–9).

Those with incomplete higher or higher education are more likely to have met in school than those with only secondary or incomplete secondary education, while the latter are more likely to have met at work. It is primarily those with secondary education who meet in places of leisure. The proportion of those meeting on the street decreases with more education. These relationships provide some support for the idea that those higher up in the society are more concerned with their choice of spouse and are less likely to meet randomly.

Although self-selection has become the norm throughout the USSR even in those areas that traditionally had strong kin control over marriage and/or formal matchmaking, it is interesting to note that matchmaking still persists in certain groups and is widely practiced as a ritual matter in weddings. While any matchmaking that does not take into account to consent of the parties is strongly condemned and punished by political authorities, matchmaking with the consent of the parties still exists in several settings where partners have been unable to find mates with specific desirable characteristics, although it is subject to government harassment. Attempts sometimes are made to put matchmakers on trial, but matchmaking as such is not a crime under Soviet law as long as there is mutual consent of the parties. (For a description of such a case see Beliavskii and Finn 1973: 42–48.) Campaigns have been held against the practice of matchmaking in Jewish synagogues (Shabad 1962). Matchmaking has remained a part of rural wedding ceremonies in most areas of the USSR, but now has a humorous character and generally is limited to the details of the wedding arrangements (Aleksandrov et al. 1964: 491; Pushkareva and Shmeleva 1959; Ter-Sarkisiants 1972: 128; and others).

Of interest is the fact that although matchmaking and arranged marriages have declined, popular demand has increased for such things as marriage bureaus, compatibility services, and computer matchmaking. The poor sex ratios after the war and the fact that women often tend to be concentrated in industries such as textiles where they have little chance of meeting men, while "bachelor cities" with disproportionate numbers of men abound in the far north and at construction sites (Perevedentsev 1977), has meant that many people, particularly those in the older ages, have found themselves lonely and unable to find a mate in a society where close personal relations play a great role in people's lives. In the period immediately following the war, the flight of young women from the countryside to the cities in search of husbands was a common occurrence. With normalization of the sex ratio, such mobility in search of a mate ceased to be so prevalent. As of 1959 Khrushchev announced that it had more or less ended ("Farms Cultivate Love, Khrushchev Declares" 1959), but the problem still continues to some extent. Thus complaints are raised from time to time in the press regarding labor turnover among women workers in textile towns ("The Young Women Are Leaving Krasavino" 1975). There also has been a high labor turnover among rural women schoolteachers (Perevedentsev 1971a).

In like manner there are a limited number of places where young people can spend their free time and meet each other. The number of ways to spend leisure time is not well developed in the Soviet Union and a source of complaint in the Soviet press. Clubs, films, and concerts are claimed by young people to be too structured and uninteresting to provide a place to meet, while bars, cafes, and the like are insufficient in number and provide little opportunity for private conversation (Fisher 1974). As a result, dance halls and something akin to the old narodnoe gulianie prevail in many towns. A few years ago a 100-meter strip on Kirov Street in Astrakhan became the object of much discussion since crowds of young people were gathering to meet there, and a by-product of this custom was drunkenness, fistfights, and the like (Vyzhutovich 1975). Such difficulties also are noted at dance halls. In keeping with the general concept of order in Soviet life, along with recognition of the need for such meeting places, suggestions are made regarding the ways in which they should be organized. Thus in spite of young people's desire to meet in unstructured places, suggestions are made that "the dancers themselves could be made responsible for keeping order at the dances: the dance hall could become a dance club with its own rules and *aktiv* . . . " (Briman 1975).

As of the late 1960s public demand for marriage bureaus and electronic matchmaking began to grow quite strong in the USSR. From 1969 to 1971 a debate raged on the pages of *Literaturnaia gazeta* concerning the advisability of such services. One of the first of the articles to appear bemoaned the plight of single women in the USSR and advocated the use of computers for finding single women husbands:

> . . . and so a husband must be found for Galochka. Traditional matchmaking techniques are brought into play with the approval of public opinion. Valya and Vanya meet at the home of someone who invited them for that purpose. But mention computers as a possible aid to finding a marriage partner—God forbid! Public opinion doesn't approve. Computers cannot make decisions, but they can take account of a person's requirements and help two compatible people to meet. The conservatism of public opinion must be overcome. Who knows, computers may help lower the divorce rate. (Svetlanova 1969)

Five articles and a vast number of letters to the editor followed. Academician A. Berg, chairman of the Scientific Council on Cybernetics of the USSR Academy of Sciences, endorsed the use of computers for matchmaking in an article entitled "Concerning Love Machines and Oracles," claiming that the only thing a computer would do would be to reduce the unlikeliness of a man living in Moscow becoming acquainted with a possible wife living somewhere in Vladivostok (Berg 1970). In the scholarly press as well, marriage bureaus and even newspapers in which persons could advertise for desired partners were advocated (Kharchev and Emel'ianova 1970: 62).

The final article in the debate in *Literaturnaia gazeta* was entitled "Acquaintanceships and Weddings," and was written by sociologist Vladimir Shliapentokh. Shliapentokh noted that over 75 percent of those who had written letters to *Literaturnaia gazeta* were in favor of marriage bureaus and almost half of them voiced a personal interest in using such marriage bureaus. Women aged 30 to 50 were most in favor while young students did not think that they personally needed such services. Only the elderly, those over 60 years of age, were highly opposed to such matchmaking. Educated urban dwellers were more agreeable to the idea of matchmaking by computer than those with less education and those from rural areas. Those writing letters expressed the view that matchmaking by computer would be a tremendous help to women living in predominantly female textile towns and to men living in predominantly male mining towns in Siberia, and stressed the difficulty of meeting people in contemporary urban settings (Shliapentokh 1971).

Six days after Shliapentokh's article appeared, *Pravda* published an article that ended all discussion of computer dating. *Pravda*'s main point of contention with Shliapentokh's article was that there was no mention of love:

> What did this "analysis" offer those who are burdened with loneliness and dream of finding happiness in marriage? Nothing less than an omnipotent, super-efficient, "electronic matchmaker"—a "marriage bureau" employing the latest equipment . . . . Could this learned sociologist, and with him the editors of the newspaper, really believe that the public activeness of Soviet people can find worthy application in fussing over the arrangement of a marriage bureau with an electronic matchmaker ejecting a mechanical list of the virtues of an optimal partner?
>
> Incredible!
>
> *Literaturnaia gazeta*'s discussion, useful in intent, about marriage and the family can hardly be said to have culminated in the best way. *Literaturnaia* should have hardly used its columns to propagate an idea alien to our Soviet

> moral outlook, the idea of arranging a marriage and family by calculation even if electronic calculation. ("Marriages Arranged by Electronic Matchmaker" 1971)

It seems clear that what was objectionable in the proposal of marriage bureaus to Soviet officialdom was not so much the use of new techniques for letting people become acquainted but rather the fact that any questionnaire designed for purposes of establishing some compatibility of partners would have to take into account characteristics and traits that are alien to the conception of romantic love and lack of calculation in marriage. A number of the articles published by *Literaturnaia gazeta* had dealt with the question of what should be contained in such a questionnaire. In describing the beginnings of a family service in Tartu, Estonia, one author had indeed gone so far as to argue that the more questions placed into a questionnaire for such computer matchmaking the better, including such things as living conditions and property status—things clearly not supposed to be taken into account when marrying in the USSR (Voina 1970).

For several years after the *Pravda* article there was little open discussion of such compatibility services. At the same time a certain amount of premarital counseling became available in Leningrad and in some cities of the Baltic republics, but was not officially sponsored nor part of the economic plan (see Danilov 1972; Verb 1975). In the summer of 1974, however, *Literaturnaia gazeta* again picked up the topic with an article by Iurii Riurikov that advocated a kind of compatibility service that would be both a consultation service for married couples and also a bureau through which it would be possible to meet persons of the opposite sex (Riurikov 1974). Debates similar to that in *Literaturnaia gazeta* began to appear on the pages of *Moskovskii komsomolets* and *Nedelia* with the participation of such scholars as S. I. Golod and I. S. Kon. Perhaps as a result of the *Pravda* response to the older *Literatrunaia gazeta* debate, the accent in the discussion began to be less on the prognosis of compatibility and love than simply on the use of computers and "get-acquainted services" for introducing people to each other (see, for example, Kon 1976).

In November 1976, *Literaturnaia gazeta* decided to run as an experiment two marriage notices in response to pressure by readers for some service of this sort. The notices, which evidently were fictitious, read as follows:

> Single man, age 48, height 166 cm., education in the humanities, homebody, would like to meet blonde woman under 35 who loves the theater and symphonic music. Moscow, No.1.
>
> Divorced woman, age 32, height 162 cm., has 6-year-old child, construction technician, wants to meet man who loves sports, is cheerful and doesn't drink. Voronezh, No. 2. ("Let's Get Acquainted" 1976).

The response to the notices, so out of the ordinary in Soviet life, was tremendous. The newspaper received some 10,000 letters, over 99 percent of which were in favor of establishing get-acquainted services, more than in the 1969–70 debate. Shliapentokh was asked to analyze the letters and carry out a survey of 1,600 subscribers to *Literaturnaia gazeta*. He found that only 20 percent of the letters were from men, an indication of the advantageous position of Soviet men in finding marriage partners, and that respondents to the survey would have preferred the notices to contain more information on personal character traits. Preference was expressed for get-acquainted clubs over such notices or computer matchmaking or, in other words, for services that would involve face-to-face contact (Shilapentokh 1977).

One of the main reactions to the publication of the notices, however, was fatigue with the whole debate. As one woman put it, the discussion "began when my daughter was only 24. Now she is 32, and I don't know if I'll live to see the end of the debate or until my nice, well-educated daughter meets a proper man" ("Get Acquainted!" 1976). Clubs for those over 30 years of age and so-called friendship clubs have been formed in the last few years in Leningrad, Kiev, Taganrog, Rostov-on-Don, Tashkent, Ust Ilim, Lipetsk, Tomsk, Barnaul, Krasnodar, Minsk, Poltava, Novosibirsk, and other cities. Most importantly, the Bureau of the Moscow City Party Committee and the Moscow City Soviet Executive Committee adopted a resolution at the very end of 1977 to stimulate population growth in Moscow that included the organization of a get-acquainted service (Malinovskii 1976; Radzinskii 1977; "First Steps toward Family Service" 1977; " 'He,' 'She' and 'They' " 1978; Fedoseeva 1978; Mushkina 1978). While such services are still considered to be troublesome from aesthetic and moral points of view, they seem to have been accepted now as necessary (Radzinskii 1977; Rubinov 1978). Indeed, there now is some discussion of organizing singles vacation hotels, tour groups, and parties ("The Family and Its Members" 1978).

Public demand for new forms of courtship has been sufficiently great as to change official attitudes. It seems likely, however, that development of such services will be slow, and it remains to be seen to what extent the Soviet population actually will use them.

Reduction in the authority of parents and control of kin over the mate choices of their children generally is associated with a reduction in the importance of dowry and bride-price systems, since such investments cannot be protected (Goode 1963: 34). While the practice of paying dowries and bride-prices has been greatly reduced and indeed eliminated in many areas of the USSR—payment of a bride-price is a criminal act under article 232 of the RSFSR Criminal Code—such customs are still common in the Soviet Union, particularly in Central Asia. This continued existence of dowries and bride-prices is perhaps not surprising in view of the continued importance of parental approval of marriages, if not full control over mate-selection as discussed above.

A Turkmen poetess, Esenova, recently complained that convictions in the Turkmen SSR for payment of kalym total only three or four per year, "when we all know that many more instances of bride purchase occur." Evidently there is a great deal of concealment before the authorities and participation in, or at least overlooking of, the practice by many party and government officials. The size of kalym varies greatly: recent reported cases range from 250 rubles plus seven suits of clothes and 16 pieces of fabric, to a full 16,000 rubles plus 100 oriental gowns and some poultry. The size of kalym depends on the status and value both of the bride and her family, with an uneducated girl reportedly valued more highly than an educated one since girls with university education are considered to know too much and would not submit to their husbands as obedient servants. Families with many sons claim to spend their lives in poverty trying to save money for kalym. It is unclear just how widespread the practice of kalym is, but it seems to be generally approved in Central Asia on the ground that the custom gives newlyweds a start in life since in-laws repay them part of the kalym in necessary household furnishings (Esenova 1974; Esenov 1977; Murtazakulov 1975).

The amounts of money involved in kalym have been increasing over the years. In the mid-1960s they began to soar. Thus a hospital attendant near Dushanbe who paid some 50 rubles for his bride in 1966 complained, "They used to be cheaper. My brother Safar a few years ago paid only 250. Now for some reason or other they would not take less than 500 rubles" (quoted in Lorince, 1966: 869; see also Urusova 1973). It seems likely that this raise in bride-prices is partly due to greater affluence and partly due to changes in the sex ratio. As the sex ratio has normalized in the Moslem areas of Central Asia and the Caucasus, the supply of brides relative to grooms has become less plentiful, and the price for brides therefore has increased.

The effect of changing sex ratios also is visible as regards the size of dowries. Just as the closing of nunneries in the sixteenth and seventeenth centuries in England increased the number of women available for marriage among the English nobility, thereby increasing the size of dowries (Stone 1961), so too there is evidence that dowries in postwar Armenia increased in comparison with their prewar levels (Ter-Sarkisiants 1972: 137–38). Ethnographic reports of rural Latvia and central Russia in the 1950s and early 1960s reported the custom of giving a dowry as still very much in effect (Belitser et al. 1964: 177; Kushner 1958: 277), as might be expected given the great shortage of eligible men in those areas.

In spite of general ideological agreement that self-selection should be the basis of marriage, considerable parental and kin participation in the decision to marry has remained in postwar Soviet Union, particularly in those rural areas where parental control of mate-selection historically was very strong. Continuing parental influence in mate selection is not the result of tradition alone, however. Poor housing conditions that have meant that newlyweds generally have had to live with their parents, the poor sex ratios following the war and the consequent difficulties in finding a partner, and the economic utility in the countryside of adding a new member to the family all have helped to maintain some parental authority in courtship.

## REFERENCES


Achylova, R. "Izmenenie polozheniia zhenshchin pri sotsialisme kak faktor formirovaniia novykh vzaimootnoshenii mezhdu suprugami v kirgizskikh sem'iakh." In Sovetskaia Sotsiologicheskaia Assotsiatsiia et al., *Dinamika izmeneniia polozheniia zhenshchiny i sem'ia*. Moscow: 1972.

Agaev, M-B. Kh. "Razvitie brachno-semeinykh otnoshenii v usloviiakh stroitel'stva kommunizma (na materialakh Dagestanskoi ASSR)." Candidate of Philosophical Sciences dissertation abstract, Makhachkala, 1972.

Aleksandrov, V. A., et al., eds. *Narody evropeiskoi chasti SSSR*. I. Moscow: Nauka, 1964.

Bangerskaia, T., "Who Is Head of the House?" *Soviet Life* 12 (December 1975): 49–50.

Beliavskii, Al'bert V., and Finn, Emil' A. *Liubov'i kodeks*. Moscow: Sovetskaia Rossiia, 1973.

Belitser, V. N., et al., eds. *Narody evropeiskoi chasti SSSR*.II. Moscow: Nauka, 1964.

Berg, A. "O liubvi, mashinakh i orakulakh." *Literaturnaia gazeta*, March 18, 1970: 12–13.

Briman, M. "The Dance Hall: Light and Shadows." *Sovetskaia kul'tura* May 30, 1975: 5. Translated in *CDSP* 27: 7.

Chachin, V. "Myl'nyi puzyr'." *Pravda*, December 6, 1971: 6.

Chuiko, Liubov' V. *Braki i razvody*. Moscow: Statistika, 1975.

Danilov, A. "Do You Want to Be Happy?" *Komosomolskaia pravda*, November 29, 1972: 2. Translated in *CDSP* 25, 8: 18.

Dunn, Stephen P., and Dunn, Ethel. *The Peasants of Great Russia*. New York: Holt, Rinehart and Winston, 1967.

Elnett, Elaine. *Historic Origin and Social Development of Family Life in Russia*. New York: Columbia University Press, 1926.

Ermishin, P. "Ideal'nyi muzh ili razborchivaia nevesta?" *Literaturnaia gazeta*, June 16, 1976: 12.

Esenov, R. "After Paying the Bride-Price." *Pravda*, February 7, 1977: 4. Translated in *CDSP* 29, 6: 23.

Esenova, T. "Nenavistyi kalym." *Literaturnaia gazeta*, May 22, 1974.

Fainburg, Z. I. "K voprosu ob eticheskoi motivatsii braka." In G. V. Osipov et al., eds., *Problemy braka, semi'i i demografii. Sotsial'nye issledovaniia, vypusk 4*, Moscow: Nauka, 1970.

———. "Vliianie emotsional'nykh otnoshenii v sem'e na ee stabilizatsiiu." Paper read at the XII International Seminar on Family Research, Moscow, 1972.

"The Family and its Members." *Literaturnaia gazeta*, May 1, 1975: 12. Translated in *CDSP* 30, 18: 18.

"Farms Cultivate Love, Khrushchev Declares." *New York Times*, October 18, 1959: 22.

Fedoseeva, E. "SM–120 Would Like to Make a Date with SZh–40." *Literaturnaia gazeta*, October 25, 1978: 13. Translated in *CDSP* 30, 44: 6, 20.

Feofanov, Iu. "Suprug dlia zhilploshchadi." *Izvestiia*, December 20, 1971: 6. Translated in *CDSP* 22, 51: 30.

"First Steps toward Family Service." *Nedelia* 52 (1977): 7. Translated in *CDSP* 30, 1: 13.

Fisher, Wesley A. *The Moscow Gourmet*. Ann Arbor, Mich.: Ardis, 1974.

"Get Acquainted!" *Literaturnaia gazeta*, December 22, 1976: 13. Translated in *CDSP* 28, 52: 12–13.

Goode, William J. *World Revolution and Family Patterns*. New York: Free Press, 1963.

———. *The Family*. Englewood Cliffs, N.J.: Prentice-Hall, 1964.

" 'He,' 'She' and 'They'." *Literaturnaia gazeta*, January 18, 1978: 12. Translated in *CDSP* 30, 5: 17.

Hollander, Paul. *Soviet and American Society: A Comparison*. New York: Oxford University Press, 1973.

Iurkevich, Nikolai G. *Sovetskaia sem'ia*. Minsk: Izdatel'stvo BGU im. V. I. Lenina, 1970a.

———. "Motivy zakliucheniia i stabil'nost' braka." In N. Solov'ev et al., eds., *Problemy byta, braka i sem'i*. Vilnius: Mintis, 1970b.

Kaiser, Robert G. *Russia: The People and the Power*. New York: Atheneum, 1976.

Kharchev, Anatolii G. *Brak i sem'ia v SSSR: opyt sotsiologicheckogo issledovaniia.* Moscow: Mysl', 1964. Also 2d ed., 1979.

———, and Emel'ianova, K. L. "Brak: ideal i deistvitel'nost'." In *Problemy braka, sem'i i demografii. Sotsial'nye issledovaniia, vypusk 4.* Moscow: Nauka, 1970.

Khitynov, Maksim B. "Osobennosti formirovaniia i razvitiia sotsialisticheskoi sem'i u ranee otstalykh narodov (po materialam Buriatskoi ASSR)." Candidate of Philosophical Sciences dissertation abstract, Alma-Ata, 1974.

*Kodeks o brake i sem'e RSFSR.* Moscow: Iuridicheskaia literatura, 1975.

Kolokol'nikov, V. T. "Brachno-semeinye otnosheniia v srede kolkhoznogo krest'ianstva." *Sotsiologiche skie issledovaniia* 3 (1976): 78–87.

Kon, I. S. "Sputnik zhizni." *Nedelia* 5 (1976): 16.

Kotelevskaia, L. "Ne tol'ko bestaktnost'." *Izvestiia*, February 13, 1968: 3.

Kushner, P. I., ed. *Selo Viriatino v proshlom i nastoiashchem: Opyt etnograficheskogo izucheniia russkoi kolkhoznoi derevni.* Moscow: 1958.

Kuznetsova, L. "Kogo my liubim." *Literaturnaia gazeta*, September 5, 1973: 13.

Lalaian, E. "Vaoits-dzor." *Azgagrakan handes* 13 (1906): 143.

"Let's Get Acquainted." *Literaturnaia gazeta*, November 17, 1976: 13. Translated in *CDSP* 28, 47: 7.

Lorince, G. "Brides for Sale." *New Statesman*, June 17, 1966: 169–70.

Luzbetak, Louis J. *Marriage and the Family in Caucasia.* Vienna-Modling: St. Gabriel's Mission Press, 1951.

Madison, B. "Social Services to Women and Children: Problems and Priorities." In Dorothy Atkinson, et al., eds., *Women in Russia.* Stanford: Stanford University Press, 1977.

Malinovskii, L. "'Friendship' Correspondence Club." *Literaturnaia gazeta*, December 22, 1976: 13. Translated in *CDSP* 28, 52: 13.

"Marriages Arranged by Electronic Matchmaker." *Pravda*, June 15, 1971: 3. Translated in *CDSP* 23, 24: 10.

Massell, Gregory J. *The Surrogate Proletariat: Moslem Women and Revolutionary Strategies in Soviet Central Asia: 1919–1929.* Princeton, N.J.: Princeton University Press, 1974.

Murtazakulov, I. "Make Atheistic Work Highly Militant." *Turkmenskaia iskra*, April 16, 1975: 2. Translated in *CDSP* 27, 38: 18.

Mushkina, E. "Great Expectations." *Zhurnalist* 12 (1978): 49–51. Translated in *CDSP* 31, 8: 12–130.

"Not Simply Love." *Sovetskaia kul'tura*, April 27, 1976: 6. Translated in *CDSP* 28, 18: 11.

Ostrovskii, Nikolai A. *Kak zakalialas' stal'.* Moscow: Molodaia gvardiia, 1936.

Ovchinnikova, I. "Potomu chto schastliv." *Izvestiia*, April 12, 1970: 4.

Perevedentsev, V. I. "Budet li svad'ba?" *Literaturnia gazeta*, February 24, 1971a: 13.

———. "Bachelor Cities." *Literaturnaia gazeta*, February 16, 1977: 13. Translated in *CDSP* 29, 7: 16.

Proletkin, V. "Kradenye nevesty." *Izvestiia*, March 16, 1968: 3.

Pushkareva, L. A., and Shmeleva, M. N. "Sovremennaia russkaia krestianskaia svad'ba." *Sovetskaia etnografiia* 3 (1959): 47–56.

Radzinskii, E. "Differing Faces of Loneliness." *Literaturnaia gazeta*, January 12, 1977: 13. Translated in *CDSP* 23, 3: 16.

Riurikov, Iu. "Tol'ko li liubov'?" *Literaturnaia gazeta*, July 17, 1974: 13.

Roshchin, Mikhail. "Valentin i Valentina." *Teatr* (1971): 157–86.

Rubinov, A. "Happiness Is So Possible." *Literaturnaia gazeta*, March 8, 1978: 12. Translated in *CDSP* 30, 10: 14–15.

Saikowski, C. "Boy Meets Girl as Moscow Laughs." *Christian Science Monitor*, December 12, 1970.

Semenov, V. E. "Obrazy braka i liubvi v molodezhnykh zhurnalakh (Opyt kontentanaliza)." In *Molodezh': Obrazovanie, vospitanie, professional'naia deiatel'-nost'.* Leningrad: Nauka, 1973.

Shabad, T. "Moscow Rabbi Says Visitors Abet Black Market." *New York Times*, October 5, 1962: 4.

Shatunovskii, I. "Kak ishchut prostakov." *Pravda*, August 17, 1969: 6.

Shliapentokh, Vladimir E. "Zankomstva i svad'by." *Literaturnaia gazeta*, June 9, 1971: 12.

———. "Their Own Problems and Others'." *Literaturnaia gazeta*, November 30, 1977: 12. Translated in *CDSP* 29, 48: 15–16.

"60,000,000 semei." *Literaturnaia gazeta*, July 1, 1970: 11.

Smith, Hedrick. *The Russians*. New York: Quadrangle, 1976.

Solov'ev, Nikolai la. "Kto nravitsia devushkam . . . " *Literaturnaia gazeta*, December 19, 1973: 13.

*Soviet Life*, March 1973: 20.

Stites, Richard. *The Women's Liberation Movement in Russia: Feminism, Nihilism, and Bolshevism 1860–1930*. Princeton, N.J.: Princeton University Press, 1978.

Stone, L. "Marriage among the English Nobility in the 16th and 17th Centuries." *Comparative Studies in Society and History* 3 (1961): 182–206.

Svetlanova, E. "Muzh dlia Galochki." *Literaturnaia gazeta*, January 8, 1969: 12. Translated in CDSP 1, 9: 13–14.

Ter-Sarkisiants, Alla E. *Sovremennaia sem'ia u armian*. Moscow: Nauka, 1972.

Urusova, A. "Traditsii nastoiashchie i mnimye." *Izvestiia*, October 20, 1973: 5.

Verb, Lidiia Ia. "Kul'tura vzaimotnoshenii muzhchiny i zhenshchiny." In *Sovetskii etiket*. Leningrad: Znanie, 1971.

Voina, V. "Razvodov ne budet." *Literaturnaia gazeta*, June 3, 1970: 13.

Vyzhutovich, V. "The Hundred-Meter Strip." *Komsomolskaia pravda*, July 13, 1975: 2–3. Translated in *CDSP* 27, 33: 6.

Wallace, Sir Donald Mackenzie. *Russia*. London: 1912.

Yanowitch, M., and Dodge, N. "Social Class and Education: Soviet Findings and Reactions." *Comparative Education Review* (October 1968): 248–67.

"The Young Marrieds." *New Statesman*, September 4, 1964: 304.

"The Young Women Are Leaving Krasavino." *Pravda*, March 26, 1975: 2. Translated in *CDSP* 27, 12: 22.

Zhirnova, G. V. "Traditsionnye mesta vstrech molodezhi v gorode: seredina XIX—nachalo XX v." In *Polevye issledovaniia Instituta Etnografii 1974*. Moscow: Nauka, 1975.

7

DAVID POPENOE

# What Is Happening to the Family in Sweden?

*Until recently, nonmarital cohabitation was rare in the United States, but its acceptance and prevalence have grown rapidly since around 1970. Recent data from marriage records in one county in Oregon suggest that the percentage of marrying couples who had cohabited rose from 13 in 1970 to 53 in 1980,[1] and of course many couples who cohabit never marry one another.*

*Although it is still too soon to know how this new living arrangement will affect family formation and dissolution, there is some suggestive evidence. For instance, the U.S. marriage rate has dropped steadily in recent years, and most of the change apparently reflects a later average age at marriage. For one reason, couples may be postponing marriage because they are already living together.*

*The probable eventual impact of cohabitation in this country is suggested by conditions in Sweden, where cohabitation has been common for a long time. That country specially interests sociologists and demographers because of its excellent government records and the trends those records reveal. Nonmarital cohabitation is only one of several aspects of family life and intimate relations that Popenoe discusses in the following selection, but that aspect is of special interest.*

This article is an abridged and modified version of "Beyond the Nuclear Family: A Statistical Portrait of the Changing Family in Sweden" in *Journal of Marriage and the Family* 49 (February 1987): 173–183, Copyrighted (1987) by the National Council on Family Relations, 1910 West County Road B, Suite 147, St. Paul, Minnesota 55113. Reprinted by permission.

[1]Patricia A. Gwartney-Gibbs, "The Institutionalization of Premarital Cohabitation: Estimates from Marriage License Applications, 1970 and 1980," *Journal of Marriage and the Family* 48 (May 1986), p. 423.

In recent political and cultural debate in Sweden the "condition" of the Swedish family has been given increasing attention. Surprisingly, however, only the material or economic condition has been the focus of concern. What is also of interest, at least to the outside world, is the non-material or social condition of the Swedish family. About this dimension of the family Swedes, at least in public, have been virtually silent.

Concerning the Swedish family's social condition a crossnational examination of recent demographic and social data reveals some significant developments. The Swedish marriage rate is now the lowest in the industrial world, and the non-marital cohabitation rate is the highest in the industrial world. These facts will come as no surprise to most Swedes. More surprising, however, is that the rate of family dissolution in Sweden may also have become the highest in the industrial world. These three rates and the social reality they measure, which are discussed in this article, signify important, continuing changes in the Swedish family that go well beyond its economic condition.

## MARRIAGE

Until recent decades the history of nuptuality in Sweden had not shown any remarkable differences from comparable European nations, except for somewhat lower rates of marriage during some time periods. Swedish marriage records go back to 1749 and it is possible to compute the crude marriage rate for every year since then. The proportion of married women in the age group 20–44 years, for example, was 59.4 in 1750 and then dropped (although with many ups and downs) to 52.1 in 1900, which was a low point. During this century the marriage rate rose rapidly, however, passing its earlier high and reaching a peak in the mid-1960s. The percentage of married women in the 20–44 age group in 1970 was 70.4. Prior to 1900 more men than women married, but in this century the pattern reversed itself with the number of married women outdistancing married men (in 1970 only 61.5 percent of Swedish men in the age group 20–49 years were married). But the important point is that marriage was never so popular with either sex as it was in the 1950s and early 1960s, and this was as true of Sweden as it was of other countries.

Beginning in the mid-1960s, however, the picture changed with startling rapidity. While the marriage rate in most other advanced nations leveled off or in some cases continued to increase, Sweden's began to drop sharply. During a seven- or eight-year period following 1966, according to calculations made by Swedish family sociologist Jan Trost, the marriage rate decreased by about 40 percent, a decrease which he believes has not occurred "anywhere else or at any other time." The drop was even greater for the younger age groups. For women aged 20–24, the marriage rate per thousand women dropped from 194 in 1966 to 91 in 1973, and for women aged 25–29 the comparable drop was from 175 to 96. By 1980 these rates had dropped much further still, to 53 for the 20–24 age group and 78 for the 25–29 age group. An international comparison with Sweden's 1980 marriage rate of 78 for persons in the 25–29 age group shows Denmark, 99; Japan, 109; France, 117; the U.S., 127; and England and Wales, 168. The 1980 Swedish rate was also considerably below the other countries in the 20–24 and 30–34 age groups. The declining marriage rates in Sweden (as elsewhere) reflect a rising average age of marriage. But in addition, a growing number of Swedes are not marrying at all.

Today, Sweden has the lowest marriage rate in the industrial world and at the same time one of the highest mean ages of first marriage—30 for men and 27 for women (1983), compared to 25.5 for men and 23.3 for women in the U.S. (1985). The marriage rate in Sweden increased slightly in the mid-1970s and since then has continued to drop, although in the total number of marriages per year has followed a slightly different trend, with some increase in the early 1980s.

## NONMARITAL COHABITATION

One must not assume, however, that since marriage is going out of fashion in Sweden, people there no longer are "coupling." What has happened is that marriage is gradually being replaced by nonmarital cohabitation, also called "consensual unions" or "living together in an unmarried state." Although precise data on the amount of nonmarital cohabitation in Sweden today are not available, few Swedish experts would contest the proposition that the rate is the highest in the industrial world.

Due to the lack of legal registry and a fixed date of inception, data on nonmarital cohabitation are much more difficult to assemble than marriage data, and making comparisons among nations is also fraught with difficulty. Many careful estimates of the amount of nonmarital cohabitation in Sweden have been made, however. Unmarried couples as a percent of all couples in Sweden were estimated at 1 percent in 1960, 7 percent in 1970, 13 percent in 1975, and 21 percent in 1983. Projecting these data, an educated guess about the situation today is close to 25 percent. Comparable estimates for other European nations are 7 percent in the late-1970s for the Netherlands, 2.5 percent for Britain, and 13 percent for France. (In this and many other aspects of family life, Denmark is only a few steps behind Sweden.) For the United States, unmarried couples as a percentage of all couples in 1981 were estimated at 4 percent and today the figure is probably about 5 percent. Interestingly, the U.S. percentage apparently did not increase between 1984 and 1985, whereas in Sweden there is no statistical indication of any diminution of this trend.

The data given above for Sweden refer to couples of all ages. If one looks at the younger age groupings the picture changes considerably. In 1980, the percent of unmarried women ages 20–24 living with someone else was 68 percent (79 percent for men) and in the 25–29 age bracket, the percent was 35 percent (49 percent for men). Moreover, virtually all Swedes now cohabit before marriage (only an estimated 2 percent of marriages today were not preceded by nonmarital cohabitation, compared to nearly 50 percent among women born in the 1930s).

Living together before marriage is an old custom in Sweden; Swedes have long been permissive in matters of premarital sex in terms of allowing "engaged" couples not to have to wait until the actual marriage takes place, and marriages commonly occurred around the time the couples' first children were coming due. By one estimate a third of all marriages in 1963 involved a pregnant bride. But it is only in this sense that nonmarital cohabitation has been a widespread Swedish tradition, and the situation today has changed considerably. Nonmarital cohabitation is now regarded legally and culturally as an accepted alternative rather than a prelude to marriage. This is reflected in the fact that the average length of time couples remain unmarried lengthens each year, with a growing number, as noted above, never marrying at all. According to one recent study only 20 percent of young, childless women born in the 1950s married their cohabiting partner within eight years, compared to 80 percent of those born at the end of the 1930s.

One of the most striking changes in the cohabitation scene today is that children no longer are much of a reason to get married; in other words, the expectation or birth of a child affects only marginally the chances that a couple will marry, and this applies to both first and second children. The rapidly declining influence of childbirth on marriage is brought into relief by the data on the percentage of children born out of wedlock. Officially, the concept of children born out of wedlock was dropped from all Swedish legislation in the early 1970s (the term illegitimate was dropped in 1917), and children of such unions have exactly the same rights as children of married unions. From Swedish population registration records, however, one can calculate the percentage of all children born in a given year to unmarried mothers. This figure has climbed sharply in recent years, from 10 percent in 1956, 22 percent in 1971, and 32 percent in 1975. In 1984 the percentage stood at 45 percent, giving foreign journalists the occasion to state that nearly half of all births in Sweden today are to unmarried parents. The comparable figure for the United States (1983) is 20 percent. (It should be emphasized that in Sweden, due to the high rate of nonmarital cohabitation, the concept "born to an unmarried parent" usually does not mean "born to a single parent.")

What, in general, is the social significance of the decline in marriage and the rise of nonmarital cohabitation? Many Swedes (especially younger Swedes) see little if any significance. And it has been government policy since the change in divorce laws of the early 1970s, according to the interpretation of some Swedish experts, to be officially "neutral" between the two forms of living together. Some observers maintain that nonmarital cohabitation has become an institution almost equivalent to that of marriage; the two social institutions do not compete with each other, but they exist along side each other. This near equivalence was reflected in recent changes in Swedish family law. A great many different reasons are invoked by Swedish nonmarital cohabitors to account for their not getting married: freedom from oppressive tradition, freedom from state control, and more commonly, "what difference does it make; it is our love that counts." A typical response to the question, "Why not marry?" is "Why marry?"

Yet because it is such a radical departure from cultural practice throughout world history, this Swedish deinstitutionalization of marriage surely deserves more analysis and public discussion, in terms of possible long-run social implications, than it has received. In all of human history, after all, marriage has been the basis of the family as a social institution. Virtually all societies heretofore have made the marriage ceremony one of the most significant ceremonies in their members' lives. It has been a ceremony in which family, religion, and society express their approval of and hopes for, as well as setting down the moral and legal rights and duties of, a union between two people who are expected to contribute to the continuance of the society through legitimized procreation.

In Sweden such a social expression is disappearing; it is reasonable to say that most Swedish young people today are merely drifting away from their families of orientation, usually in stages, and eventually settling with someone else, all seemingly without any form of public or social recognition. Gone for the most part are engagement parties, weddings, and even an appropriate time at which one can say "congratulations." Indeed, the life course of marriage-like relationships in Sweden is not easy to bring into focus. This is pointed up by a "marital history" that one Swedish couple gave to me: They met in 1967, moved in together in 1969, exchanged rings in 1973 (this was around the time their first child was born and was for the purpose of showing others that they were attached), and married in 1977. When asked what anniversary they celebrated, they responded, "the day we met."

The most important social consequence of nonmarital cohabitation may be a behavioral one. As noted by Swedish demographers Jan Hoem and Bo Rennermalm, "the distinction between nonmarital cohabitation and marriage is still important for individual conduct in Sweden. . . . the universal acceptance of previously unconventional living arrangements has not erased differentials in behavior." They are referring particularly to the high rate of family dissolution among unmarried couples as compared to married couples.

## FAMILY DISSOLUTION

Under this heading first consideration is typically given to the dissolution of marriage as reflected in official divorce statistics. The divorce rate has never been a very adequate indicator of family dissolution in a society (to say nothing of the level of marital happiness) but its adequacy has improved in recent decades as the legal bases for divorce in advanced societies have liberalized. Divorce rates have shown a long-term increase in most western nations since around the turn of the 20th century; they reached a high point in many countries right after the World War II, then declined through the 'fifties only to begin rising again during the 'sixties to their current high level, probably the highest in the modern history of these nations. The Swedish divorce rate was one of the highest in Europe following World War II and since then, beginning in 1963, it has climbed faster than in most other countries and is still climbing. Sweden's rate of divorced persons per 100 married persons in recent years (9.69) falls just behind that of the western world's acknowledged divorce leader, the United States (11.28).

Of the many different rates of divorce that can be calculated, one of the most useful is the proportion of marriages expected to end in divorce over the life course of a given cohort (rather than ending in the death of one of the partners). For the cohort of people born in the United States in 1945 the proportion of marriages (for males) ending in divorce is expected to be 42 percent, while in Sweden the figure is 36 percent. For other countries examined the rates are: England and Wales, 27 percent; Switzerland, 14 percent; and Belgium, 12 percent.

The high Swedish divorce rate is surprising because so many of the factors traditionally associated with divorce in the United States are mitigated in Sweden, including such factors as poverty, teen pregnancies, early marriage, interethnic and interfaith unions, and high residential mobility. But perhaps the most surprising thing about the high Swedish divorce rate concerns the amount of nonmarital cohabitation. One could think of many such nonmarital unions as "trial marriages" in which the step of formal marriage is taken only after the union has matured and the couple desires to signify a certain permanence to the relationship. As the thesis was put by one scholar some years ago, "the decrease in the marriage rate is the result of an increase in trial marriages, and therefore. . . . those marriages being formed will be "happier' and thus the divorce rate, ceterus paribus, will be lower." Based on information currently available this thesis is far from correct. The marriage rate continues to drop while the divorce rate continues to climb.

Because so many Swedes no longer marry, however, the use of divorce rates to measure family dissolution in Sweden becomes rather meaningless, especially when making comparisons with nations where the amount of nonmarital cohabitation is relatively low. What is needed is the addition of some measure of the break-up rate of couples living outside of marriage in consensual unions. Yet if it is difficult to get data about the formation of such unions, it is even more difficult to get information about their break-up. There are also numerous problems in comparing the break-up rate of nonmarital cohabitors with that of married couples because, as noted above, marriages in Sweden today represent a kind of final stage of a cohabiting relationship; that is, almost all marriages are preceded by a stage of nonmarital cohabitation.

To avoid including "casual cohabitation" in the measure of family dissolution, which one expects by definition would have a much higher break-up rate than marriages, it is useful to look at the break-up rate of couples, both married and unmarried, who have had a child. This, in fact, has been done for a special sample of 4,300 Swedish women, born between 1936 and 1960, who were asked retrospective questions about their life histories. The findings showed the dissolution rate of cohabiting couples with one child to be three times the dissolution rate of comparable married couples, on the average. For cohorts coming of marriageable age today, because of recent increases in nonmarital cohabitation and its wider cultural acceptance, this difference in dissolution rates has undoubtedly diminished. Yet it is unlikely that the difference has disappeared (differences of similar magnitude have been found in a number of other, smaller scale studies) and it seems a well-based conclusion that nonmarital cohabitation, at least at the present time, simply does not have the durability of marital cohabitation.

If the nonmarital cohabitation dissolution rate is added to Sweden's already high and growing divorce rate, it is reasonable to put forth the following proposition: Sweden may have the highest rate of family break-up in the industrialized world. That a society so resolutely devoted to social welfare and the good life should have achieved such a position has received remarkably little discussion. Family dissolution is a subject Swedes do not like to talk about; unlike almost every other common "social problem," for example, it has never been the focus of a major, government sponsored investigation.

Of course the significance of such a comparatively high rate of family dissolution, in terms of its personal and social consequences, is a matter of widely conflicting opinion. On the positive side are those who maintain that adults are better off psychologically because of it, that it shows how strained many marriages actually were before the time of easy divorce, and that it represents a positive good in helping to destroy an oppressive institution. Arguments on the negative side include a loss of "family values," a weakening in the "social control" of adolescents, and especially psychological damage to the children and youths who are involved. Children under 18 are involved in about two thirds of all divorce actions in Sweden (the comparable number for nonmarital cohabitation dissolutions is not known). It is the opinion of many social scientists that, while recognizing there are numerous cases where children of dissolution are better off than in deeply troubled families, family break-up can create lasting psychological problems in children. On this most Swedes with whom I have spoken agree, and the opinion also seems widely held in other advanced countries.

Sometimes it is pointed out that the percentage of broken families today is little different from what it was at the turn of the century. This is increasingly less true, however, as the rate of family dissolution increases. More importantly, the statement is based on equating the high death rate of spouses in 1900 with the high divorce rate today, thus masking what many believe are profound psychological and social differences (especially for children) between death and divorce.

Closely related to family dissolution is another feature of contemporary Swedish life that has been widely commented on in the West: the high percentage of single-parent families. In 1980, single-parent families amounted to 18 percent of all households with children (with another 11 percent of households with children consisting of step-families). This percentage of single parent families is very high by European standards, but not quite as high as the 21.5 percent of all families with children in the United States in 1980. Sweden takes the lead, however, if one discounts the data for U.S. blacks, an ethnic group that is extremely small in Sweden. In 1980, 17 percent of American white families with children had only a single parent compared to 52 percent of black families. Both nations have seen a sharp increase in the number of single parent families in recent years, and in both nations women make up the overwhelming majority of these families' heads. (It should be noted that the economic and social situation of the single parent family in Sweden, although worse than that of complete families there, is not characterized by the high level of relative deprivation that is found in the United States.)

## CONCLUSION

What is happening to the Swedish family? The facts noted above indicate that something important is happening, and it is not just that Swedes living in families are less well-off economically compared to Swedes living outside of families. There is nothing in the data I have seen to suggest that the Swedish family is in a state of "collapse," or anywhere near such a state. But the data do suggest, in my opinion, that there should be much more research and public discussion about the possible consequences of current Swedish family trends, especially the personal and social consequences of such a high rate of family dissolution.

# 8

MARGERY WOLF

# Marriage, Family, and the State in Contemporary China

❦

*To fully appreciate the enormity of the changes the Communist Revolution brought to the family in China, one must first understand the traditional patriarchal family system that had been in place virtually unchanged for the previous 2,000 years. The family was the most important social and political unit in pre-Communist China. Families provided for virtually every aspect of their members' lives including education, medical care, and legal counsel. Taxes were paid to the family rather than the government.*

*In this extremely patriarchal culture, the most important relationship was that between father and son. Fileal piety, duty to the father, continued even after death in the form of ancestor worship. Daughters, on the other hand, were considered liabilities by parents. Enormous dowries were required of brides' families. After marriage(most likely to someone whom she had never seen until the ceremony), the main requirement of a wife was that she produce male children. A husband who found his wife to be barren or a producer only of daughters could take on a concubine or additional wives. In contrast, a woman whose husband died could not remarry, and it was acceptable for a childless widow to commit suicide since no role was left for her in society.*

*The ideals and practices of this system clearly oppose the ideals of communism. Soon after the revolution, the Marriage Law of 1950 was enacted. This law abolished the old marriage practices and established a new system based on equal rights for men and women, freedom of choice in mate selection, and monogamy. Since then, other laws have more fully developed this new model of marriage. Only in the last few years, since lines of communication have reopened between China and the West, have social scientists been able to assess the effects of communism and the new laws on the Chinese family. As Wolf notes in the following selection, Chinese citizens carefully repeat the government-sanctioned responses when questioned. However, her research suggests that old ways are hard to change and that reality does not correspond exactly with the ideal.*

Source: Adapted from "Marriage, Family, and the State in Contemporary China" by Margery Wolf in *Pacific Affairs* 57, no. 2 (Summer 1984) pp. 213–36. 

---

In most, if not all, peasant societies the development of the state as a political force has meant conflict with the family.[1] China has not been an exception. The state in traditional China strongly supported the values of the old family system, even when those values on occasion required that family needs take priority over state needs.[2] The ideology of the family system and the ideology of the state were mutually supporting, both being based on a Confucian morality that held sacred a system of generation, age, and gender hierarchies. As Maurice Freedman explained:

> From the point of view of the state, a man's obligations to it were in fact both qualified and mediated by his kinship relations. They were qualified in the sense that obligations springing from filial piety and mourning duties were held to modify duties owed to the state. An official who lost a parent was supposed to retire during his mourning. People related to one another in close bonds of kinship were so far regarded by the written law to require solidarity among them that the Code provided that certain relatives might legitimately conceal the offenses of one another (except in cases of high treason and rebellion), either escaping punishment altogether or suffering a penalty reduced in accordance with the closeness of the relationship; and that it was an offence generally for close kinsmen to lay even just accusations against one another. There was built into the system the principle that close patrilineal kinship set up special rights and duties standing apart from the rights and duties between men and the state.[3]

The imperial state came into conflict with the family system when families were joined together in lineages, and lineages were strong enough to control territory. In the years before Liberation, both anticommunist Westerners and the ruling Guomindang warned that the Chinese Communist Party was intent upon "destroying the family." In truth, the communists were bent on destroying the *ideology* of the old family system; they recognized, as did their imperial

---

[1]This paper was originally prepared for a conference, "Contemporary Marriage: Comparative Perspectives on a Changing Institution," sponsored by the Center for Advanced Study in the Behavioral Sciences and the Russell Sage Foundation. I am very grateful to the co-organizers of that conference, Amyra Grossbard-Shechtman and Kingsley Davis, for their comments. Although I must bear full responsibility for the paper's failings, its strengths come from the careful readings given it by Carol A. Smith, Emily Honig, William L. Parish, Martin King Whyte, Muriel Bell, and Arthur Wolf.

[2]By "family system," I mean the group of men who shared or assumed they shared a common ancestor, and because of this relationship were bound together by rights, duties, and ideology. In some areas of China, these groups were both large and well-organized, forming patrilineal descent groups that controlled whole villages or even groups of villages.

[3]Maurice Freedman, "The Family in China, Past and Present," in *The Study of Chinese Society: Essays by Maurice Freedman* (Stanford, California: Stanford University Press, 1979), pp. 241–42.

predecessors, that it was this ideology that led to the organization of ever larger and more powerful groups of kin—the lineages that might be a threat to the new state's political organization. The Communists had no intention of destroying the family as a domestic unit, for it was as essential to their society as to the one they displaced.

In the thirty-some years since Liberation, the new state has been in quiet contest with the old family system for the loyalty of its citizens. In the cities, the state has manipulated everything from ideology to housing in order to break the old bonds of moral debt and filial duty to patrilineal kinsmen. Its success has been impressive, perhaps because much of the urban population—in particular, that majority to whom the revolution was addressed—had already begun to question the old truths. In the countryside, those old truths were the only truths until a rival ideology was brought in by the revolution. The Chinese countryside has undergone massive social transformation, but the Communists learned early on that family reform is a touchy issue—that landlords and organized lineages might be destroyed, but the bonds of kinship are a force to be used, not attacked.

This essay will look closely at the struggle between family and state as it affects marriage formation. Again and again, the reader will find me qualifying statements by stating whether they are applicable to the city or to the countryside. The gulf that now exists between rural and urban society is a fairly new feature in China's social landscape. F.W. Mote expresses the old relations between country and city elegantly when he explains:

> The rural component of Chinese civilization was more or less uniform, and it extended everywhere that Chinese civilization penetrated. It, and not the cities, defined the Chinese way of life. It was like the net in which the cities and towns of China were suspended. The fabric of this net was the stuff of Chinese civilization, sustaining it and giving it its fundamental character. To extend this metaphor, China's cities were but knots of the same material, of one piece with the net.[4]

Unlike Europeans, Chinese did not see their cities as "beleaguered islands in a sea of barbarism" (again quoting Mote), but as part of a whole with considerable movement on the part of the intellectual and elite population between rural family homes and their urban branches. This continuity began to erode in the late nineteenth century when the break-up of the civil service drained the vitality out of the rural elite. One might have expected Mao's peasant revolution to rebuild the ties between country and city, but in his efforts to destroy the class system, Mao destroyed the rural elite; and in his need to control urban unemployment, he put an end to the migration of rural people to the cities, in effect ending meaningful social interaction between the two populations. Over the last thirty years, the rural people in China have become second-class citizens in all but the rhetoric of the state. This has had, as we shall see, considerable influence on their willingness to conform to state policy.

---

[4]F.W. Mote, "The Transformation of Nanking, 1350–1400," in G. William Skinner, ed. *The City in Late Imperial China* (Stanford, California: Stanford University Press, 1977), p. 105.

## THE MEANING OF MARRIAGE

In traditional China, marriage was but a building block in the basic institution of society, the family. One of the most sacred duties of a son was to provide descendants for his and his father's ancestors. To do so, he must marry. Wealthy families and land-owning peasants used marriages to form ties with other families that might be useful in times of trouble or advantageous in commercial or political arenas. Poor families saw the marriages of their children as a necessary step in providing for their old age. The wedding itself was a major social event in the life of a family and, even though a proper wedding might bring parents to the verge of bankruptcy, the brideprice, dowry, gifts, and feasting could not be foregone if the family wished to remain a part of the moral community. The pair who were being wed were minor actors. Ordinarily they were not consulted about whom they would marry or when, but were presented with a mate at the time deemed appropriate by the senior generations. Some parents, out of poverty or callousness, gave their daughter to whichever family offered the most for her; many others tried to avoid marriages that would cause their daughters grief. Parents of sons chose brides who would meet the needs of the family first and of their sons second. Even the young people accepted this as the parents' and their own filial duty.

Except for a highly Westernized, highly politicized urban elite, the traditional attitudes toward marriage were not seriously questioned until the Communists' victory in 1949. In the first half of this century, family reform was an issue among the articulate minority who had contact with foreigners, but it did not extend into the countryside until the revolutionaries were forced out of the cities in the late 1920s. Even then, the pressure for change was weak, circumscribed by the need for political support from a conservative male peasantry. Nonetheless, the first law the Communists promulgated after the revolution was the Marriage Law of 1950, and it was designed to intervene at a basic level in the intimate affairs of the family. The opening paragraph reads, the "supremacy of man over woman . . . is abolished"—a political commitment many women in the West have yet to win. Subsequent paragraphs ban polygyny, child betrothal, brideprices and dowries, and the coercion of either party to the union.

The immediate impact of this law has been described elsewhere.[5] Suffice it to say here that when the campaign to enforce the law was launched in 1953, it quickly became clear that the Communists would have to temper their efforts to "liberate" women and the younger generation, if they were to retain their support in the rural areas. Local cadres perceived the law as a threat to their

---

[5]See Judith Stacey, *Patriarchy and Socialist Revolution in China* (Berkeley and Los Angeles: University of California Press, 1983); Kay Ann Johnson, *Women, the Family, and Peasant Revolution in China* (Chicago: University of Chicago Press, 1983); Delia Davin, *Women-Work: Women and the Party in Revolutionary China* (Oxford: Clarendon Press, 1976); Elisabeth Croll, *Feminism and Socialism in China* (New York: Schocken Books, 1978); M.J. Meijer, *Marriage Law and Policy in the Chinese People's Republic* (Hong Kong: Hong Kong University Press, 1971).

patriarchal powers, and grew suspicious of a government that was giving with one hand and taking away with the other. The campaign was abandoned, but the law was not. In the cities, workplace study groups continued to discuss the various aspects of the law, and the state slowly began to implement them; but minimal pressure for compliance was exerted on rural people.

Mao's policy regarding the family had multiple purposes. He sought to free women from their subjugation to men and from the oppression resulting from their lowly status within the family. He also wished to release the younger generation from the tyranny of their elders. Mao spoke to this point long before Liberation in his celebrated *Report on an Investigation into the Peasant Movement in Hunan*, written in 1927:

> A man in China is usually subjected to the domination of three systems of authority: (1) the system of the state (political authority) . . . (2) the system of the clan (clan authority) . . . and (3) the system of gods and spirits (theocratic authority) . . . As to women, apart from being dominated by the three systems mentioned above, they are further dominated by men (the authority of the husband). These four kinds of authority—political authority, clan authority, theocratic authority, and the authority of the husband—represent the whole ideology and institution of feudalism and patriarchy, and are the four enormous cords that have bound the Chinese people and particularly the peasants.[6]

The rural class-structure depended on the patriarchal power of the lineage (translated "clan" in the above quotation). To destroy it and consolidate the power of the communists, Mao encouraged those most oppressed by the system to speak out and take power. He also recognized the economic potential of women, referring to it in speeches on several occasions:

> Women comprise half of the population. The economic status of working women and the fact of their being specially oppressed prove not only that women urgently need revolution but also that they are a decisive force in the success or failure of the revolution.[7]

And, less idealistically: "China's women are a vast reserve of labor power. This reserve should be tapped and used in the struggle to build a mighty socialist country."[8]

Communist policies were aimed at destroying the old family-system and the patriarchal ideology that supported it, not at destroying the family as a domestic unit. Nor were the Communists intent on degrading the domestic unit in favor of the marital bond. A handbook about marriage registration put out by the civil office of the Ministry of Interior states:

---

[6]Mao Tse-tung, *Report of an Investigation into the Peasant Movement in Hunan* (Peking: Foreign Languages Press, 1953), p. 40.

[7]Quoted by Hsu Kwang, "Women's Liberation Is a Component Part of Proletarian Revolution," *Peking Review* (March 22, 1974), p. 17.

[8]Mao Tse-tung, "China's Women Are a Vast Reserve of Labor Power," quoted in Sybilla Green Dorros, "Marriage Reform in the People's Republic of China," *Philippine Law Journal*, vol. 51 (1976), p. 351.

> Through work of marriage registration we help to build and strengthen new democratic and united families and further develop the cause of socialist construction. We all know that once a couple becomes man and wife through marriage, they will build a family. After they build a family, not only will they bear children, but they may also have to live with other relatives and take care of elderly parents and younger brothers and sisters. *This kind of family relationship is much broader and more pervasive than the relationship between husband and wife.*[9]

The family has been one of the few sources of welfare services available in a poor country determined (at least until recently) to develop itself without foreign assistance. To retain the Chinese family without the old Chinese family-system, and to maintain the ideology of mutual obligation yet shed the patriarchal ideology of the old system, required restructuring—and marriage reform was a critical first step.

In normative terms, marriages are still formed to serve the interests of a larger group. Formerly that group was the family and the lineage; now it is the collective or society. A carefully defined and controlled marriage registration system was set up to place the formation of marriages firmly under the control of the Party. The Party, not the family, has the final word on who may marry whom, when they may marry, how their union will be celebrated, etc. Those in charge of marriage registration are instructed to make sure not only that each marriage meets the requirements of the Marriage Law, but that the principals to each marriage understand the rights granted them by virtue of that law.[10] The orientation of both parties to a marriage is expected to be towards the larger group—i.e., the collective—and the content of that relationship should be one of unswerving selflessness. In a guide for young people issued in 1964, *The Correct Handling of Love, Marriage and Family Problems*, the writer cautions young people "consciously [to] put the revolutionary cause in first place."[11] Lu Yang tells them:

> Marriage problems, when compared to the revolutionary cause, are minor matters and should be put in second place; but speaking in terms of the life of an individual, love, marriage, and the organization of a new family are, after all, serious matters. Whether they are treated well or not will concern not only an individual's progress and the happiness of family life, but also all of society.[12]

In reading the various guides and handbooks relating to issues of marriage and divorce, one detects tension regarding expressions of individualism.[13]

---

[9]Civil Office of the Ministry of Interior, "How to Manage Marriage Registration Work Well," *Chinese Sociology and Anthropology*, vol. 1 (Winter 1968), p. 14 (emphasis added).

[10]Dorros, "Marriage Reform," p. 371.

[11]Lu Yang, *The Correct Handling of Love, Marriage, and Family Problems* (Chi Nan: Shantung People's Publishing House, 1964), reprinted in *Chinese Sociology and Anthropology*, vol. 1, Spring 1969, p. 8.

[12]*Ibid.*, p. 11.

[13]Two years after the essay quoted above was published, it came under Party attack for being "revisionist" and, worse yet, for suggesting that, in the matter of marriage, individual concerns might be ranked as high as society's needs.

Freed from the oppression of the "feudal" family, people are expected to transfer their loyalties from that collective to one organized by the state. Young people were to choose their own mates, and the young bride was no longer subject to her mother-in-law's rule. Therein lies a contradiction and an anxiety. If society encourages a strong relationship between husband and wife, one by its very nature likely to be emotionally charged, there is a risk of comrades in socialist nation-building turning into self-indulgent lovers. The guidebooks insist that love is shared labor, mutual support in studying, mutual criticism, and comradely solidarity—a companionate marriage without the romance.

These are the official formulations, but what in fact does marriage mean to the post-Liberation generations getting married? In 1980–81, some thirty years after the Marriage Law was promulgated, I interviewed 300 women in two cities and four rural communes about their work lives, their domestic lives, and their social lives. Because of the restraints Chinese officialdom placed on me and my informants, these were often formal and stiff interview sessions. But from them, and from informal interactions not sanctioned by my hosts, I was able to get some sense of what marriage means now in China. Women in the two cities, Beijing and Shaoxing, willingly gave me the official version of the purpose of marriage. They told me that a good marriage was one in which both parties were willing to work for the good of the country, studied hard to increase their knowledge so they could contribute more to their work units, and were not afraid of hard work. When I agreed that this was the official definition and asked for more personal opinions, many added that a spouse should "show concern" for his or her mate, be even-tempered, and get along with other people. However, before the interview drew to a close, I also asked how they had chosen their own husbands, who did various kinds of household chores, etc., and their amused answers to these questions revealed more about the content of the new marriages. Love was an ideal occasionally mentioned, but few could define it. Certainly, they had little opportunity to develop it or any other intimate feelings before marriage. Even in the cities, Chinese "courtships," i.e., the events that lead up to an engagement, are often short and embarrassing. When choosing a spouse, a woman looks to see if the man she is attracted to or has been introduced to has a good class background (i.e., no landlords or intellectuals), good family conditions (e.g., few dependents), good earning-power, and good looks. Some women told me, laughingly, that the last two factors were most important, and quoted a saying to the effect that men only care about a woman's looks and women only care about a man's earnings.

The sad thing about many of the new marriages is that the young couples often seem as mismatched as they were in the old days, when marriages were arbitrary matches arranged by the parents. The young person who is taught that his or her spouse will be a best friend and lifelong companion often finds, "after the rice is cooked," that they have very little in common. Even though marriage is delayed until both parties are in their mid or late twenties, both are usually sexually inexperienced, and, from all reports, many women wish they had stayed that way.[14] The urban housing situation is very tight, so couples must either delay their marriages until housing is available (sometimes for years) or move into the already cramped quarters of the husband's (less commonly the wife's) family. In the latter case, as one woman told me, if you want to have an argument, you either take a walk or resign yourself to involving the whole family. In a society where until recently any inessential interaction between husband and wife in front of others was considered the ultimate in poor taste, a young couple living cheek by jowl with parents and siblings has limited opportunity to form that private culture most Western couples consider intrinsic to marriage.

Young people who do manage to get a room of their own often find it less a love-nest than a staging ground for separate lives centered on their workplaces. The workplace (or unit, as the more literal translation of the Chinese reads) is one of several means by which the state achieves control over its citizenry. Until you have a unit, that is, have been assigned a job, you cannot marry because your unit, not your family, gives you permission to marry. It is also your unit that gives you permission to get on a list at the Housing Bureau for living space, that gives you the chits allowing you to buy furniture for it, and that gives you the ration cards for everything from rice to cotton cloth. It is at your unit that you participate in political-study classes, learn of changes in policy, are given your contraceptives, and are told when you are eligible to become pregnant. I do not know if there is a conscious effort by the Party to transfer the center of a person's life from her home to the unit where she works, but the end result is just that.

In short, marriage for urban women is a necessary step in the passage from one stage of life to another. The two stages are often described as "before you have children" and "after you have children," and for both economic and social reasons one must marry in order to have children. When I asked why people have children at all in view of the population problem so often invoked in China now, I was told that the state needs another generation of workers (just as the family once needed another generation of worshippers). When I pressed further, I was told, often with giggles, that everyone wants a baby to play with. As in the past, a child is the only individual toward whom one can openly display affection. I think women clearly hope (or, in the case of the women I interviewed, hoped) to find in their husbands someone with whom they can share their innermost feelings: the study-group documents, editorials, and advice manuals have told them this is the inevitable result of free-choice marriages. Most women indicated in one way or another that they had been disappointed in this hope. To my initial surprise, more of the older women—women married to men chosen by their parents—described to me relation-

---

[14]See Gail Hershatter and Emily Honig, "Chinese Women," unpublished paper delivered at the National Women's Studies Association Meetings, June 1982. See, also, the articles by Gail Hershatter and Emily Honig in *Pacific Affairs* 57, no. 2 (Summer 1984).

ships that were clearly warm and close. I suspect that, once the initial disappointments are past, many of these young marriages will also mellow into affectionate companionship. Unlike North Americans, they do not have the option of the quick divorce and new search for a more satisfactory mate that also precludes the possibility of learned happiness.

Both happily and unhappily married Chinese farm women in Taiwan in the "old days" gave the impression of being submissive to the strictures and patriarchal ideology of the traditional family system. Their behavior, nonetheless, revealed their recognition that the male social structure was not in their best interests, and that it was up to them to provide for their own future security.[15] It took me a good many years of relaxed field-work in Taiwan to reach this revisionist view of the Chinese family system, and it is highly unlikely that I shall ever have the opportunity to do that kind of field-work in China. However, it does seem to me that rural women in China take many of the Party promises less seriously than do men. Certainly they are aware that the decree that women are no longer subordinate to men is parroted and ignored like many other slogans. A woman in Shaanxi whom I asked about the 1953 Marriage Law campaign told me that she had young children in those years and was not able to go to meetings. She could not remember anything about it. At another commune, I attended the final award-giving session of a campaign to improve mother-in-law/daughter-in-law relations. There was a big turnout (a cadre told me later the women would "get in trouble" if they failed to show up), but few paid much attention to the speakers: the audience chatted among themselves, mended clothes, and attended to their children. A young woman from Beijing who was traveling with me thought they were inattentive because they were too ignorant to understand. It was painfully obvious to me that they were bored to tears, and expressing it in the direct way that rural people have.

Farm women are fun to interview. In China they were, if anything, more nervous about the Beijing cadres than the foreign interviewer. If I asked a question they were afraid to answer, they simply refused to respond, whereas the urban women tried to placate me and the cadres with any slogans they could think of that might come somewhere near the topic. When I asked rural women about marriage in new China, they were sincere in their appreciation of their new power to veto marriages suggested by their parents. Even though many of them had met their husbands only once or twice before marrying them, they insisted in their conversations with me that their marriages were quite different from the old *baoban* (arranged) marriages. Somehow their nod of agreement put them and their marriages in a category different from that of their parents. It created slightly different expectations about the relationship between husband and wife. No one could quite articulate for me what that difference was, but it seemed to follow from the fiction that they had chosen each other and hence must already have some emotional tie or commitment.

---

[15]See Margery Wolf, *Women and the Family in Rural Taiwan* (Stanford, California: Stanford University Press, 1972).

In the main, marriage in rural China is still viewed primarily as an event in the life of the family, much as it was in pre-Liberation China. The state has laid out a new set of rules to be worked around, but the needs of the family can usually be met within those regulations or by bending them to fit. If marriage in the city is the process that makes adults out of children, in the country it is still the means by which a woman is transferred from one family to another. City women, married or unmarried, are paid by the state at their place of employment; rural women earn workpoints that are entered in the accounts of their fathers before marriage or of their fathers-in-law after marriage. The majority of the guests at an urban wedding are friends and fellow workers; the "master of ceremonies" is likely to be the head of the man's unit. In a country wedding, kinsmen outnumber friends, and the important guests are representatives not of the state but of the families and their affines.

China's urban marriages have a misleading similarity in form to Western marriages. However, for women in China marriage is the necessary transitional act in achieving adulthood. It is inevitable, and it is recognized by both the participants and their parents as the end of the easy years. Choosing a husband is a serious affair and has little resemblance to the sentimental romance that Westerners associate with courtship. Rural marriages are less easily confused with the Western model. Through the Marriage Law, the state has placed more emphasis on relations between the two people who are marrying; but, by and large, rural marriage is still a matter of families, not lovers.

Since Liberation, then, marriage has taken on different meanings in rural and urban China, a state of affairs that I believe was neither conscious nor desired on the part of the present government. The state's successes have been in the cities. It is there that the new ideology about the content of a proper marriage found fertile or at least friable soil in which to take root. In the countryside, to continue the metaphor, the state's teachings fell on hard ground. In competing for their loyalties, the state has thus far not managed to provide rural people with that which they most value—security. Men and women, old and young, have found much for which they are grateful to the new government; but matters of the family have always been matters for the family. As we shall see in the pages ahead, rural people have managed at nearly every turn to modify or outwait the state's attempts at interference.

## FREE CHOICE MARRIAGE

The freedom to choose the person with whom one will live out one's adult life is the core of the Marriage Law and, for many Chinese, may be all they know about it. Many words have been devoted to the hows and whys of it, and much propaganda has been distributed to the outside world about the success of it. Not surprisingly, when I asked women in my two urban samples, Beijing and Shaoxing, who had arranged their marriages, the younger women all denied vehemently that anyone had. They had made "free-choice marriages." To say otherwise, of course, would have been to say they had broken the law. Less direct questioning indicated that in the cities, the program has been fairly effective. By and large, urban senior generations do not present their offspring with spouses, although they may arrange for someone to introduce them to a few prospective mates. A Beijing mother told me that most young people met someone on their own or through work or school, but "well-behaved" girls or "shy" boys might need their relatives' help to locate someone suitable. In Shaoxing, a city less dominated by politics, women were divided over questions designed to elicit how much influence parents should have in their daughters' marriages. Twenty-three out of forty-one women said they felt the girls should find their own mates, but eighteen said that they should have some parental help or at least parental approval before taking any final steps. Probably the mothers of many young women are very much involved in the final decision, but it is not something they are willing to discuss with a foreign interviewer in the presence of local officials.

As usual, the rural interviews were not the same. Women answered more frankly, and also very differently. The data presented in Table 1 tells the story. Just after Liberation, the number of women who said they decided for themselves who they would marry jumped to around a quarter of the women in the cohort marrying in the 1950s (now aged 40–49). There has been little change since. Only a fourth of the country women who married in the last decade claimed to have found husbands on their own. In a social setting that still suspects sexual involvement between any two people of the opposite sex seen in casual conversation or walking alone together, to meet, get to know, and decide to marry without disqualifying oneself as a decent and acceptable mate takes a lot of ingenuity.

Since who influences decisions is difficult to judge even for the people making the decisions, in three of the rural sites I also asked a simpler question, one designed to give me some sense of how much autonomy women actually exercised in selecting their mates: "When did you first meet your husband?" Of the 112 rural women who married under the protection of the Marriage Law, 38 percent (43) knew their husbands before they became engaged to them; 29 percent (32) met them only after they were engaged (an act nearly as binding as marriage); and 33 per cent (37) did not meet them until the day of their marriage.

These data serve to indicate perhaps more strongly than what has gone before how much the family still controls marriage in the rural areas. In the

**TABLE 1** ***Husband Selection: Rural***

| | *Age in 1980–81* | | | | |
|---|---|---|---|---|---|
| | *20–29* | *30–39* | *40–49* | *50–59* | *60+* |
| (n) | (60) | (48) | (29) | (20) | (21) |
| Selected by self (%) | 27 | 26 | 25 | 5 | 9 |
| Selected by parents (%) | 55 | 65 | 68 | 95 | 90 |
| Selected by both (%) | 17 | 10 | 7 | 0 | 0 |

cities, parents still serve in an advisory capacity, but the larger family—the uncles, grandfathers, and cousins who make up a local lineage—is irrelevant to marriage unless called upon by a worried parent to "introduce" someone. In the rural areas, the extended kin are important actors in what will be a major social event, and from an individual woman's perspective they are determining agents in the quality of her adult life.

## THE COST OF MARRIAGE

Foreign visitors to pre-Liberation China and Taiwan were often shocked at the enormous expense to which the Chinese went to marry their young and bury their dead. A decent wedding in Taiwan cost somewhat more than an adult farmer could expect to earn in a year. From an economic perspective, it was a horrendous waste of money, but money was not all that was involved. Marriages could be had, and were had, considerably cheaper. What was being bought was not a bride, as the Communists have insisted, but status for two families. The bigger the show, the more status for the groom's family; the bigger the dowry, the more status for the bride's family. The relatives of both shared in the reflected glory and in the good food. The entire village shared in the excitement of strangers coming and going, the worth of dowries to estimate, the number of guests and the quality of the food to be evaluated, and a helpless bride to be teased and examined. To be the center of this excitement and gain the face of having done it properly, families who could ill afford it competed with each other in almost potlatch proportions. Many a family has impoverished itself with the marriage of an eldest son.

The Communists sought to do away with this in Article Two of the Marriage Law, which prohibited "the exaction of money or gifts in connection with marriage." Their success was both brief and limited. During the Cultural Revolution, when all "feudal" practices came under the close scrutiny of the Chinese Moral Majority, the austere tea-and-speeches weddings of the cities were sometimes found in the country; but, even then, many families managed to have inconspicuous banquets, secretly exchange bride-prices, and smuggle dowries. Parish and Whyte were told that the gifts (including but not limited to money) given to the parents of the bride had increased in value since Liberation, whereas the dowry taken by the bride to her new home had decreased substantially.[16] They felt that this was a direct consequence of the new earning power of young women, which made them an asset to their own families as well as to their husbands'. The hypothesis is a good one, but my informants insist that the size and cost of the dowries expected have gone *up*, not down. When I asked country people why they thought the cost of marriages had gone up. they said it was because times were better so people could afford more. When I asked city people, they said that people in the countryside spent much more than did those in the city, and it was because this was the only time a country girl would be able to get new clothes, quilts, and a wristwatch, since

---

[16]Parish and Whyte, *Village*, pp. 180–92.

she did not have a job like city girls. The explanations for the high costs of city weddings ranged anywhere from a shortage of girls to a shortage of boys, from interference by feudal parents to greedy young women, from the taste for bourgeois luxuries learned from the Gang of Four to the natural desire of the young couple to celebrate.

My data again show differences in the rural and urban settings. The stronger influence of the family in rural China is clearly exhibited in the way marriages are currently celebrated. Times are good, comparatively, and rural families are back to demonstrating rank and status. Weddings are a traditional way of doing so. But the rules have changed. Women are no longer valued for their reproductive capacity alone, so their side has another counter in the bargaining process, thereby inflating the requirements on both sides. Moreover, young people are more likely to be aware of the degree to which they are being exploited by their fathers: the patriarchal family-system remains in place and their earnings to support it. They may with good reason see this as an opportunity to take out their share.

Urban young people are less likely than their rural counterparts to be advertising their family's rank and status with fancy wedding parties, but they are nonetheless having elaborate, expensive marriage celebrations. The foreign press in China has had great fun documenting the cynicism and malaise under which urban youths now labor. In one decade, young people have seen their life-sacrificing idealism hailed by the country's leaders and then condemned as a national disaster. The more articulate tell one another (and some foreigners) that they believe in nothing, certainly not in Party propaganda. The less articulate say little and indulge themselves when opportunities arise. Their eyes have dropped from the horizon of China's potential greatness to their personal prospects. Having worked for the glory of the Party and found that, for many, its rewards were hard labor in a distant border region, they have now turned to working for their own security in a not very secure social world. Material possessions and the enjoyment of one day at a time are becoming the Beijing style, and that style includes lavish wedding parties and as many gifts as the young couple's marketability can command. In the cities, the state has managed to invalidate the belief system behind the elaborate traditional marriage, but the frequent vacillations within the ideology that was intended to replace the old beliefs have caused many to lose faith. I do not think the return of the old marriage customs says much about old family ideology, but it does say a great deal about the current strength of the state's hold on the urban youths' imaginations.

## HOUSEHOLD COMPOSITION AFTER MARRIAGE

Ideally, in traditional China, families searched out wives for their sons and brought them home to live with them. The more married sons and the more generations under one roof, the greater the prestige of the family. Inevitably, friction developed between married brothers or married sons of brothers and the extended family divided, creating two or more smaller units. Among the

**TABLE 2** ***Percentage of Women Forming Neolocal Households at Marriage***

| | *Age in 1980–81* | | | | | *Total* | |
|---|---|---|---|---|---|---|---|
| | *20–29* | *30–39* | *40–49* | *50–59* | *60+* | *20–49* | *50+* |
| | % *(n)* | % *(n)* | % *(n)* | % *(n)* | % *(n)* | % *(n)* | % *(n)* |
| Urban | 38 (16) | 31 (26) | 57 (21) | 33 (15) | 27 (22) | 42 (63) | 30 (37) |
| Rural | 0 (40) | 11 (57) | 5 (40) | 13 (40) | 13 (38) | 5 (137) | 13 (78) |

common people, extended households rarely lasted beyond the marriage of the second son—if they formed at all. Among the poor (the great majority in traditional China), one or more brothers often had to leave the family home in search of work elsewhere, returning once a year, and sometimes returning to find that other family members had also gone their separate ways in search of a living.

Since the Chinese Communists wished to end the domination of the old family system, I would not have been unduly surprised had my informants assured me that they, like most Westerners, formed upon marriage a separate domestic unit or neolocal family. Such was not the case, as the data in Table 2 indicate. In the urban sample, a larger number of women in the cohorts marrying under the Marriage Law formed neolocal families by their marriages (42 percent) than did those who married before its protection (30 percent). It would appear from a look at the cohort-by-cohort increase that this was a gradual rather than an abrupt change. The larger number (57 percent) in the cohort marrying just after Liberation undoubtedly results from the fact that during this period large numbers of soldiers flocked to the cities in search of work and then married there. In the last decade, one of the constraints on marrying couples has been poor housing. According to the young people, even though they would prefer to live alone, if they are to marry before they are middle-aged, they must resign themselves to squeezing into an apartment with the husband's family—unless one or the other of them has influential relatives or factory housing. It seems likely that the percentage of urban couples forming new families in the cohort aged 20–29 would be considerably higher were the housing available.

The rural samples show a startling *decrease* in the number of marrying couples forming neolocal families, dropping from 13 percent of those marrying before Liberation to only 5 percent of those marrying afterward. Not one of the 40 rural women marrying in the last decade formed a separate household with her spouse. The urban officials who traveled with me to China's countryside were genuinely impressed by the luxury of space that rural living provided when compared to the cities. Teams and families were building houses in every commune I visited, and we were told that at some point in their lives every married couple, save a youngest or only son and his wife, could count on having a house of their own. (The youngest or only son is expected to live with and take care of aging parents.) It is not insufficient housing, but controlled migration and prosperity that accounts for the decrease in neolocal families. In the old days, a fair number of men found themselves bereft of family, either because of early deaths or delayed marriages or because they or the other members of their families had taken to the roads in search of work. Of necessity, when they married they formed neolocal families. With better times and the stiff regulation controlling migration, rural families have reverted to the traditional pattern of a successful family—i.e., housing its married young under the roof and authority of the patriarch.

Ironically, in not building more urban workers' housing, the state is forcing young people who would prefer to break with the old family system either to delay marriage or to live under the (reduced) authority of their parents. Yet in the country, the collectives (often a group of relatives) are helping people build new houses to shelter a modernized version of the traditional family.

## THE NEW MARRIAGE LAW OF 1980

The Third Session of the Fifth National People's Congress, which met in 1980, passed a new marriage law, raising the minimum age for marriage by two years, making family planning mandatory, and, among other things, rendering into law some of the customary family obligations of the traditional society. When I asked officials why the minimum age for marriage had not been raised to the current "appropriate" age for marriage, I was told that it was kept low out of consideration for the national minorities who have no population problem, hence need not delay marriage. I suspect it was also not raised beyond a level the state knew it could enforce. The requirement to practise family planning appears in two separate articles, one saying it will be practised and the other saying it is mandatory for both men and women. Again, the precise requirements are not spelled out, because the family-limitation program operates with different rules in different areas, with the biggest differences occurring between country and city.

Of particular interest to us in terms of the topic of this paper are the new statements of obligation among family members. In traditional China, the duties of children to parents and grandparents were heavy and binding. Lifelong support was basic, and the inculcation of filial piety—the encompassing concept—was so thorough that parents of adopted children tried to keep from them the identity of their biological parents, because it was assumed they would feel dual obligations, even if they had not seen the parents since infancy. In contemporary rural China, sons are expected to support their parents, grandparents, and younger siblings if the need exists. These obligations are not incumbent on daughters, for the woman transfers her filial duties to her husband's family at marriage. A widow who does not remarry assumes her former husband's debt to his parents. When I asked what a production team might do if a man refused to support his parents, the cadres told me that they would garnishee his workpoint account. They would not garnishee that of a married daughter, however, because she "belongs to another family." In contemporary urban China, the rules are less clear. The first response to my question was usually that the old people have pensions now (many do), but a review of the household budgets I collected shows that contributions to the support of the separate-living elderly are made by the sons, with lesser amounts contributed by a few daughters with particularly good jobs. When urban parents were living with adult children, the children were their sons, not their daughters, although I was struck by the warm relations and frequent contact between mothers and daughters, a rarity in the old society.

The new Marriage Law not only places children under the same financial obligations as in the traditional society, it also adds a generation omitted from the Marriage Law of 1950. Grandchildren "who have the capacity to bear the relevant costs have the duty to support and assist their grandparents." But it breaks with traditional customary law in that it extends this obligation of the younger generation to the maternal grandparents as well. The Marriage Law of 1950 referred only to the parents and was interpreted by everyone with whom I spoke as the obligation of sons and their wives. However, the new birth-limitation program creates serious problems for couples whose single allowed child is a girl. Unless the girl and her husband are obliged to support her parents as well as his, her parents face an uncertain old age. If daughters can (and must) fulfill the same functions as sons, the disaster of bearing a female child will be at least partially alleviated.

In sum, in the cities the new law serves to restore one aspect of the old family ideology in order to support the government's desperate attempt to control population growth. At the same time, it strikes a blow at the patrilineal orientation of the Chinese family by equating the rights of the maternal relatives with those of the paternal. In the cities it may work; I doubt that it will in the countryside. Extending the range of obligation to the generation of grandparents involves no real change in rural China, but extending the economic responsibility of a couple to the parents of the wife seems unenforceable. The women's parents live in another brigade and belong to another surname group. To obtain contributions from an unwilling couple, two power blocs must be confronted: the bureaucracy of the collective and another kin group. Those who have tried to work in any capacity in China will shudder at the prospect of having to cross from one bureaucracy to another in any kind of negotiation. When these two bureaucracies are peopled by different kinsmen—by definition in opposition—the negotiations will be long and tedious at best. When the content of the negotiation is a threat by the state to traditional family ideology, success seems a most unlikely prospect.

## CONCLUSIONS

In a 1937 essay titled "On Contradiction," Mao Tsel Tong wrote:

> When the superstructure (politics, culture, etc.) obstructs the development of the economic base,political and cultural changes become principal and decisive. Are we going against materialism when we say this? No. The reason is that while we recognize that in the general development of history the material determines the mental and social being determines social consciousness, we also—and in-

> deed must—recognize the reaction of mental on material things, of social consciousness on social being and of the superstructure on the economic base.[17]

After Liberation, while Mao was struggling to develop the economic base of a country impoverished by wars and mismanagement, he made full use of the organization and communication skills he and his army had learned in the Jiangxi soviets and in the Yanan base-camps to turn the class structure upside down. However, in the conservative northern border regions, he must have made a decision, perhaps an essential one, about priorities. One might "recognize" the salutary action of a transformed superstructure on the economic base under some circumstances, but in regard to women, the traditional Marxist approach must suffice. As Kay Ann Johnson so ably sums it up:

> The dominant Chinese view of the status of women asserts that after the political victory of the revolutionary movement, once women are brought in to renunmerative social (i.e., non-domestic) production, interrelated and liberating changes in all other areas of society and family life will naturally occur: women's traditional dependence on men will be broken, they will become both more socially valuable and valued for their economic contribution to family and society, they will wield more authority in their communities and family, and eventually the entire cultural superstructure of male superiority and female subordination will give way to new norms of equality and female worth which realistically reflect women's new relationship to production.[18]

When discontent among rural cadres over the "liberation" of their womenfolk expressed itself in ways similar to those Mao had witnessed in Yanan, the campaign of 1953 to implement the Marriage Law was allowed to die. Instead of pressing for family reform, he for once did follow the lead of the masses and allowed the "restoration" of the old family system that many an impoverished peasant had, in fact, barely experienced. As a result, changes in marriage in the rural areas have been limited, at most giving the young some say in their marriages and giving women some presence in the family decision-making processes. The patrilineal family remains strong. The state, in a sense, has been preempted by the family both in authority over individuals and even in economic organization—rural collectives often were superimposed over existing villages that were also likely to be single-surname villages.[19] Lineage structure, insofar as it was controlled by the landlord class, was destroyed; but the social and kin relationships persist to this day, retarding and sometimes deflecting ideological change. Many of the changes that have occurred in the countryside seem to have come about through coercion and fear of the consequences of

---

[17]Mao Tse-tung, "On Contradiction," a speech delivered in 1937 and published in 1952. Published in translation in *Selected Works of Mao Tse-tung* (Peking: Foreign Languages Press, 1967), p. 336.

[18]Kay Ann Johnson, "The Politics of Women's Rights and Family Reform in China," (Ph.D. diss., University of Wisconsin—Madison, 1976), p. 105. See, also, her book, *Women, the Family, and Peasant Revolution*.

[19]Norma Diamond, "Collectivization, Kinship, and the Status of Women in Rural China," *Bulletin of Concerned Asian Scholars* (January–March 1975), p. 25 ff.

noncompliance for both the collective and the individual. This is a slow way to alter the superstructure, and a good way to change vague distrust of the unknown into conscious opposition to a perceived threat.

Urban changes have been greater and less superficial. Ideological education has been more persuasive and more pervasive. Study groups in the workplace, textbooks in the schools, and editorials in the newspapers, can make whatever reform is underway uppermost (or at least unavoidable) in the minds of an urban citizenry in ways impossible in the countryside. Moreover, the young in the cities receive from the hands of the state what they used to receive (and in the country still do receive) from the family. Permission to marry comes from the work unit; the job that makes marriage and adulthood possible comes from the state, not by way of father's land or uncle's rice shop. Where the rural patriarchs have, for the time being at least, kept much of their authority over women and younger generations, among city-dwellers paternal authority has been thoroughly undermined by the state's taking to itself many of the sanctions and indulgences the patriarchy once had exclusive rights to dispense.

To be sure, such structural factors as low incomes, inadequate housing, increased educational opportunities, and a serious unemployment problem have a strong influence, as they do in other developing countries, on the various changes occurring in urban marriages I have addressed in the pages above. However, these factors are manipulated by the government just as surely as are propaganda campaigns. A conscious decision on the part of the state could provide more housing, less education, higher wages, or more jobs, although obviously other economic and social considerations must be and have been taken into consideration. The fact remains that the state's control in the urban areas over things material as well as things ideological has allowed it to prevail in its struggle with the family in a way that has not yet been possible in the countryside.

# 9

ELEANOR HOLMES NORTON

# Restoring the Traditional Black Family

*The following selection deals with one of the most important and sensitive of the current issues within American family relations. The facts Norton reports about the lower-class black family are undeniable; her interpretation of them is controversial, though less so than it would have been twenty, or even ten, years ago. Perhaps the most debatable of her claims is that the growth of female-headed black families and the increase in the proportion of black births that are out of wedlock reflects a "self-perpetuating culture of the ghetto." According to this widely held view, female-headed, single-parent families would remain prevalent even in the absence of high black male unemployment and other conditions that almost everyone agrees ultimately create such families. This view has not been tested because the situational bases of black "family pathology" have never been absent. Furthermore, Norton does not mention some possible situational determinants of lower-class black family relations, such as a low sex ratio (a large number of females relative to the number of males).*

*Although Norton's article is unusually sophisticated for a journalistic treatment of an aspect of American family relations, one of her factual statements must be corrected. She writes: "Half of all marriages in this country end in divorce. . . ." Accuracy requires that the statement be reworded such that* if *recent and current divorce and death rates continue for the next several decades, about half of all marriages entered into in recent years will eventually end in divorce. We will not know how many of these marriages end in divorce*

***until all of them have ended through either divorce or the death of a spouse, and that will be several decades from now.***

Source: Eleanor Holmes Norton, "Restoring the Traditional Black Family" *The New York Times Magizine* (June 2, 1985), pp. 43, 79, 93, and 96. 

---

What would society be like if the family found it difficult to perform its most basic functions? We are beginning to find out. Half of all marriages in this country end in divorce, and half of all children will spend a significant period with only one parent.

Starting and unsettling changes have already occurred in black family life, especially among the poor. Since the 1960s, birth rates among blacks have fallen dramatically, but two out of every three black women having a first child are single, compared to one out of every six white women. Today, well over half of black children in this country are born to single women. Why are female-headed households multiplying now, when there is less discrimination and poverty than a couple of generations ago, when black family life was stronger?

The disruption of the black family today is, in exaggerated microcosm, a reflection of what has happened to American family life in general. Public anxiety has mounted with the near-doubling of the proportion of white children living with one parent (from 9 percent to 17 percent) since 1970. Single parents of all backgrounds are feeling the pressures—the sheer economics of raising children primarily on the depressed income of the mother (a large component of the so-called "feminization of poverty"); the psychological and physical toll when one person, however advantaged, must be both mother and father, and the effects on children.

The stress on Amerian family life was recently addressed by Senator Daniel P. Moynihan, Democrat of New York, on the 20th anniversary of his controversial "Moynihan Report." The original report confined its analysis to the black family. Moynihan, who in April delivered a series of lectures at Harvard on the family said, "I want to make clear this is not a black issue." Indeed, just last month, the problem of increasing poverty among all the nation's children was underscored in a major report from two federal agencies.

Yet until recently, many blacks have had an almost visceral reaction to mention of black family problems. Wounds to the family were seen as the most painful effect of American racism. Many blacks and their supporters have regarded talk of black family weakness as tantamount to insult and smear. Some conservatives have taken signs of trouble in the black family as proof that the remaining problems of race are internal and have announced the equivalent of "Physician, heal thyself."

At the heart of the crisis lies the self-perpetuating culture of the ghetto. This destructive ethos began to surface 40 years ago with the appearance of permanent joblessness and the devaluation of working-class black men. As this nation's post-World War II economy has helped produced a black middle class, it has also, ironically, been destroying the black working class and its family structure. Today, the process has advanced so far that renewal of the black family goes beyond the indispensable economic ingredients. The family's return to its historic strength will require the over-throw of the complicated, predatory ghetto subculture, a feat demanding not only new government approaches but active black leadership and community participation and commitment.

While this crisis was building, it received almost no public attention, in part because of the notorious sensitivity of the subject. Yet 20 years ago, Martin Luther King Jr. spoke candidly about the black family, spelling out the "alarming" statistics on "the rate of illegitimacy," the increase in female-headed households and the rise in families on welfare. The black family, King asserted, had become "fragile, deprived and often psychopathic."

King relied in part on the Moynihan report, written when the Senator was an Assistant Secretary of Labor. Many were stunned by what one critic called the reports's "salacious 'discovery' "—its discussion of illegitimacy, matriachy, and welfare and its view that black family structure had become, in its own words, a "tangle of pathology" capable of perpetuating itself without assistance from the white world. As a result, the report's concern with remedies, including jobs, and its call for a national family policy were eclipsed.

The delay has been costly to blacks and to the country. When King spoke out, the statistics he characterized as alarming showed that two-and-a-half times as many black families as white ones were headed by women. Today, it is almost three-and-a-half times as many—43 percent of black families compared with 13 percent of white families. Since 1970, out-of-wedlock births have become more prevalent throughout society, almost doubling among whites to 11 percent. But among blacks, births to single women have risen from 38 percent in 1970 to 57 percent in 1982.

While families headed by women have often proved just as effective as two-parent families in raising children, the most critical danger facing female-headed households is poverty. Seventy percent of black children under the age of 18 who live in female-headed families are being brought up in poverty. In 1983, the median income for such households was $7,999, compared to almost $32,107 for two-parent families of all races, in which both spouses worked. Without the large increase in female-headed households, black family income would have increased by 11 percent in the 1970s. Instead, it fell by 5 percent.

As last month's report from the Congressional Research Service and the Congressional Budget Office pointed out, "The average black child can expect to spend more than five years of his childhood in poverty; the average white child, 10 months."

Buried beneath the statistics is a world of complexity originating in the historic atrocity of slavery and linked to modern discrimination and its continuing effects. What has obscured the problem is its delicacy and its uniqueness. The black family has been an issue in search of leadership. Discussion of problems in the black family has been qualitatively different from debates on voting rights or job discrimination. Fear of generating a new racism has foreclosed whatever opportunity there may have been to search for relief, driving the issue from the public agenda and delaying for a generation the search for workable solutions. Today, when nearly half of all black children are being raised in poverty, further delay is unthinkable.

Blacks themselves have been stunned by recent disclosures of the extent of the growth of poor, alienated female-headed households. The phenomenon is outside the personal experience of many black adults. Many have overcome deep poverty and discrimination only because of the protection and care of stable traditional and extended families. As recently as the early 1960s, 75 percent of black households were husband-and-wife families. The figure represents remarkble continuity—it is about the same as those reported in census records from the late 19th century. Indeed, the evidence suggests that most slaves grew up in two-parent families reinforced by ties to large extended families.

The sharp rise in female-headed households involves mostly those with young children and began in the mid-1960s. The phenomenon—while by no means a trend that permeates the entire black community—affects a significant portion of young people today, many of whom are separated economically, culturally, and socially from the black mainstream. They have been raised in the worst of the rapidly deteriorating ghettos of the 1960s, 1970s, and 1980s, in cities or neighborhoods that lost first the white and then the black middle and working classes. Drugs, crime, and pimps took over many of the old communities. Blacks remaining were often trapped and isolated, cut off from the values of the black working poor and middle class—where husbands often work two jobs, wives return to work almost immediately after childbirth and extended families of interdependent kin are still more prevalent than among whites.

A complete explanation of black family disruption does not emerge from a roundup of the usual suspects, including the many factors that make American family life generally less stable these days: the ease and relative acceptance of separation, divorce, and childbirth outside of marriage; the decline of religion and other traditional family-reinforcing insitutions, and welfare rules that discourage family unity and penalize economic initiative. Anecdotal explanations—the girl-mothers are said to want to love and receive affection from a baby; the boy-fathers reportedly brag about making babies—are also inadequate. Such anecdotes do not explain how the strong presumption in favor of marriage before childbearing has been overcome so often.

The emergence of single women as the primary guardians of the majority of black children is a pronounced departure that began to take shape following World War II. Ironically, the women and children—the most visible manifestations of the change—do not provide the key to the transformation. The breakdown begins with working-class black men, whose loss of function in the post–World-War II economy has led directly to their loss of function in the family.

In the booming post–World-War I economy, black men with few skills could find work. Even the white South, which denied the black man a place in its wage economy, could not deprive him of an economic role in the farm family. The poorest, most meanly treated sharecropper was at the center of the work it took to produce the annual crop.

As refugees from the South, the generation of World War I migrants differed in crucial respects from the World War II generation. The World War I arrivals were enthusiastic, voluntary migrants, poor in resources but frequently middle class in aspiration. They were at the bottom of a society that denied them the right to move up very far, but they got a foothold in a burgeoning economy.

Family stability was the rule. According to a 1925 study in New York City, five out of six children under the age of six lived with both parents. Nationally, a small middle class emerged, later augmented by the jobs generated by World War II, service in the armed forces, and the postwar prosperity that sometimes filtered down to urban blacks.

Today's inner-city blacks were not a part of these historical processes. Some are the victims of the flight of manufacturing jobs. Others were part of the last wave of Southern migrants or their offspring, arriving in the 1950s and 1960s. They often migrated not because of new opportunities but because of the evaporation of old ones. Mechanized farming made their labor superfluous in agriculture, but unlike the blacks of earlier generations and European immigrants, later black migrants were also superfluous in the postwar cities as manufacturing work for the less-skilled and poorly educated declined. Today's postindustrial society, demanding sophisticated preparation and training, has only exacerbated these problems.

This permanent, generational joblessness is at the core of the meaning of the American ghetto. The resulting, powerful aberration transforms life in poor black communities and forces everything else to adapt to it. The female-headed household is only one consequence. The underground economy, the drug culture, epidemic crime, and even a highly unusual disparity between the actual number of men and women—all owe their existence to the cumulative effect of chronic joblessness among men. Over time, deep structural changes have taken hold and created a different ethos.

An entire stratum of black men, many of them young, no longer performs its historic role in supporting a family. Many are unemployed because of the absence of jobs, or unemployable because their ghetto origins leave them unprepared for the job market. Others have adapted to the demands of the ghetto—the hustle, the crime, the drugs. But the skills necessary to survive in the streets are those least acceptable in the outside world.

The macho role cultivated in the ghetto makes it difficult for many black men, unable to earn a respectable living, to form households and assume the roles of husband and father. Generationally entrenched joblessness joined with the predatory underground economy form the bases of a marginal life style. Relationships without the commitments of husband and father result.

This qualitative change in fundamental family relationships could have occurred only under extreme and unrelentingly destructive conditions. Neither poverty nor cyclical unemployment alone could have had this impact. After all, poverty afflicts most of the world's people. If economic and social hardships could in themselves destroy family life, the family could not have survived as the basic human unit throughout the world.

The transformation in poor black communities goes beyond poverty. These deep changes are anchored in a pervasively middle-class society that associates manhood with money. Shocking figures show a long, steep, and apparently permanent decline in black men's participation in the labor force, even at peak earning ages. In 1948, before the erosion of unskilled and semiskilled city and rural jobs had become pronounced, black male participation in the labor force was 87 percent, almost a full point higher than that of white males.

In the generation since 1960, however, black men have experienced a dramatic loss of jobs—dropping from an employment rate of 74 percent to 55 percent in 1982, according to the Center for the Study of Social Policy in Washington. While white male employment slipped in that period, much of the white decline, unlike that of the blacks is attributed to early retirement. Since 1960, the black male population over the age of 18 has doubled, but the number employed has lagged badly.

These figures tell a story not only of structural unemployment, but of structural changes in low-income black families. The unemployment rates of young blacks have been the most devastating and militate against the establishment of stable marriages. This year, for instance, black teen-agers overall had an unemployment rate of 39 percent, two-and-a-half times that of white teen-agers. The loss of roles as workers has led to the acceptance of other roles for financial gain, many of them antisocial. With large numbers of young men imprisoned, disabled by drugs, or otherwise marginal and unavailable as marriage partners, there is an unusual disparity between the sheer numbers of black men and black women. Among whites, the ratio of men to women does not change significantly until age 50, when men's shorter life expectancy creates a gap. But among blacks, beginning at age 20, women outnumber men significantly enough to have a major impact upon the possibility of marriage.

Some argue persuasively that the female-headed family is an adaptation that facilitates coping with hardship and demographics. This seems undeniable as an explanation, but unsatisfactory as a response. Are we willing to accept an adaptation that leaves the majority of black children under the age of 6—the crucial foundation years of life—living in poverty? Given a real choice, poor blacks, like everybody else, would hardly choose coping mechanisms over jobs, educational opportunity, and family stability.

Yet, the remedy for ghetto conditions is not as simple as providing necessities and opportunities. The ghetto is not simply a place. It has become a way of life. Just as it took a complex of social forces to produce ghetto conditions, it will take a range of remedies to dissolve them. The primary actors unavoidably are the government and the black community itself.

The government is deeply implicated in black family problems. Its laws enforced slavery before the Civil War and afterward created and sanctioned pervasive public and private discrimination. The effects on the black family continue to this day. Given the same opportunities as others, blacks would almost certainly have sustained the powerful family traditions they brought with them from Africa, where society itself is organized around family.

Quite apart from its historical role, the government cannot avoid present responsibility. It can choose, as it now does, to ignore and delay the search for ways to break the hold of the ghetto, such as early intervention with young children and training and education for the hard-core poor. Although programs capable of penetrating ghetto conditions have proved elusive, the current government posture of disengagement is folly. With the poor growing at a faster rate than the middle class, the prospect is that succeeding generations will yield more, not fewer, disadvantaged blacks. An American version of a *lumpenproletariat* (the so-called underclass), without work and without hope, existing at the margins of society, could bring down the great cities, sap resources and strength from the entire society and, lacking the usual means to survive, prey upon those who possess them.

Perhaps the greatest gap in corrective strategies has been the failure to focus on prevention. Remedies for deep-rooted problems—from teen-age pregnancy to functional illiteracy—are bound to fail when we leave the water running while we struggle to check the overflow. A primary incubator for ghetto problems is the poor, female-headed household. Stopping its proliferation would prevent a spectrum of often-intractable social and economic problems.

Remedies often focus at opposite ends—either on the provision of income or of services. Neither seems wholly applicable to entrenched ghetto conditions. Public assistance alone, leaving people in the same defeatist environment, may reinforce the status quo. The service orientation has been criticized for using a disproportionate amount of the available resources relative to the results obtained.

More appropriate solutions may lie between income and service strategies. Programs are likely to be more successful if they provide a rigorous progression through a series of steps leading to "graduation." This process, including a period of weaning from public assistance, might prove more successful in achieving personal independence. Such programs would be far more disciplined than services to the poor generally have been. They would concentrate on changing life styles as well as imparting skills and education. The test of their effectiveness would be the recipients' progess in achieving economic self-sufficiency.

To reach boys and men, especially the hard-cord unemployed, more work needs to be done to cull the successful aspects of training and job programs. Effective training models need to be systematically replicated. It is untenable to abandon the hard-core unemployed, as the Reagan Administration has done, by moving to a jobs program that focuses on the most, rather than the least, trainable. Ghetto males will not simply go away. As we now see, they will multiply themselves.

The welfare program—a brilliant New Deal invention now stretched to respond to a range of problems never envisioned for it—often deepens dependence and lowers self-esteem. Although welfare enjoys little support anywhere along the political spectrum, it continues for lack of an alternative.

Reconceived, a public-assistance program could reach single mothers and offer them vehicles to self-sufficiency. The counterparts of young women on welfare are working downtown or attending high school or junior college on grants to low-income students. Far from foreclosing such opportunities because a woman has a child, public assistance should be converted from the present model of passive maintenance to a program built around education or work and prospective graduation.

Studies of the hard-core unemployed have shown women on welfare to be the most desirous of, open to, and successful with training and work. Some, especially with young children, will remain at home, but most want work or training because it is the only way out of the welfare life. Some promising experiments in work and welfare are underway in such cities as San Diego and Baltimore. But the old "workfare" approach, when adminstered as another form of welfare with no attempt to break the cycle of dependency, is self-defeating. Gainful employment, even if in public jobs for those unaccommodated by the private sector, would have beneficial effects beyond earning a living. Jobs and training would augment self-esteem by exposing women to the values and discipline associated with work, allowing them to pass on to their children more than their own disadvantages.

The ghetto, more than most circumscribed cultures, seeks to perpetuate itself and is ruthless in its demand for conformity. However, it contains institutions of the larger society—schools, churches, community groups. With minor additional resources, schools, for example, could imcorporate more vigorous and focused ways to prevent teen-age pregnancy. If pregnancy occurs, girls could be motivated to remain in school, even after childbirth, thus allowing an existing institution to accomplish what training programs in later life do more expensively and with greater difficulty.

Schools and other community institutions also need to become much more aggressive with boys on the true meaning and responsibilities of manhood, and the link between manhood and family. Otherwise, many boys meet little resistance to the ghetto message that associates manhood with sex but no responsibility.

Most important, nothing can substitute for or have a greater impact than the full-scale involvement of the black community. Respect for the black family tradition compels black initiative. Today, blacks are responding. Many black organizations are already involved, including the National Urban League, the Nationl Association for the Advancement of Colored People, the National Council of Negro Women and the National Urban Coalition. In 1983, the country's major black leaders endorsed a frank statement of the problems of the black family and a call for solutions. The statement, published by the Joint Center for Political Studies, a black research center in Washington, represented the first consensus view by black leadership on the problems of the black family. Significantly, it went beyond a call for government help, stressing the need for black leadership and community efforts.

With the increase in the number of black public officials, many black mayors, legislators and appointed officials control some of the resources that could help shape change. Although they cannot redesign the welfare system by themselves, for example, some are in a position to experiment with model projects that could lead to more workable programs—such as supplementing welfare with training grants or work opportunities for single mothers; promoting family responsibilty and pregnancy prevention for boys and girls through local institutions, and encouraging the completion of school for single teenaged parents.

The new black middle class, a product of the same period that saw the weakening of the black family, still has roots in the ghetto through relatives and friends. From churches, Girl Scout troops, and settlement houses to civil-rights organizations, Boy's Clubs, and athletic teams, the work of family reinforcement can be shared widely. The possibilities for creative community intervention are many—from family planning and counseling and various roles as surrogate parents and grandparents, to sex education, community day care, and simple, but crucial, consciousness-raising. Most important is passing on the enduring values that form the central content of the black American heritage: hard work, education, respect for family, and, notwithstanding the denial of personal opportunity, achieving a better life for one's children.

*Section Three*

# Premarital Relationships and Mate Selection

# 10

ELAINE HATFIELD AND SUSAN SPRECHER

# Romantic Beginnings

*Since she conducted her first study of the dynamics of interpersonal attraction in 1966, research by Elaine Hatfield and her colleagues has enormously expanded what we know about physical appearance and its influence in the formation of relationships. A large research literure builds on the findings of that now-classic study—one that Hatfield initially considered "a flop."*

*In the 1966 study, Hatfield used her assignment as "Freshman Welcome Week" coordinator at a major midwestern university to conduct research. One of the activities she planned for the week was a "computer" dance, at which students were told their dates had been scientifically selected for them. In truth, names were drawn out of a fishbowl. Hatfield hoped that through this random selection of partners she could learn more about what makes people desirable to each other.*

*She had access to the scores these freshmen had made on aptitude and personality assessment tests and to their grade-point averages—indicators of traits that previous studies suggested should make persons attractive. These were combined into a Social Desirability Score. Students were then asked how they liked their specially chosen dates. Hatfield and her colleagues expected that people who were closely matched on social desirability would find each other more attractive and get along better than those who were mismatched. At the last minute, Hatfield added one other variable. She asked the students selling tickets to note their impressions of the purchasers' physical attractiveness.*

*Hatfield then analyzed her data and, upon seeing the results, deemed the study a failure. Neither intelligence, personality, nor social skills made any difference in judgements of the desirability of the date. Matched persons were not any more likely than mismatched ones to like their partners. Only physical attractiveness was significant in whether or not the person, male or female, was liked.*

*Mirror, Mirror . . . overviews the literature that has accumulated since the 1966 study and examines such topics as what we as a society define as beautiful or ugly, how appearance affects casual dating and more serious relationships, how aging affects the body and our definition of beauty, and can attempts at improving appearance improve life? The importance of physical attractiveness is underscored in a poignant vignette Hatfield and Sprecher give near the end of the book. Eleanor Roosevelt and playwright Lillian Hellman, two of the world's most famous women, were asked if they had any regrets in life. They both gave the same answer, "Just one. I wish I had been pretty."*[1]

*The selection included here summarizes research findings on the role of beauty in the early stages of dating. One interesting aspect of the paper is its inclusion of a sociobiological explanation of gender differences. This theoretical perspective is often overlooked, and exposure to it in the context of a specific argument is important, regardless of whether or not one agrees with it.*



---

Recently, *Nutshell* magazine investigated the fantasies and realities of college romance. Following are two views—first from a man's perspective, then from a woman's:

> That's the way all of us are. Even the shy, sweet ones. Like everyone else, we college men are products of our environment. . . We're warped by the media. We're conditioned by Charlie's Angels, by *Playboy* Advisor and *Penthouse* Forum and the *Sports Illustrated* bathing suit issue, by all those impossibly smooth air-brushed centerfolds, by rock 'n' roll lyrics and TV ads. We've got all that glamour coming at us, but we've also got a completely separate thing going with the Girl Next Door, who's healthy and wholesome and fun. We batter, bash, tug, and heave, but we can't quite seem to reconcile the two.
>
> . . . Mitchell, who's a little more cynical than most, says right away that the only thing college men want is to sleep with beautiful college women. . . . That is the way it is. Everbody has his own private rating system—not just 8's and 10's, but for some guys a real obsession. That's what college teaches us: how to gather and correlate data. Dan blames his attitude on a course he took during his sophomore year, "Game-Playing and Decision-Making"; now he assigns attractive women coefficients and plots out probabilities like a technician in the Pentagon war room. . . . An accounting student I once knew used a sliding scale based on 100. "I'd be happy," he would tell me, "with an 80." Sure—who wouldn't be? (Luke Whisnant, a graduate student at Washington University, Schwartzbaum & Whisnant, 1982, 44)

---

[1]Hatfield and Sprecher, *Mirror, Mirror . . .*, p. 324.

> I thought college men would be tall and wear flannel shirts. I thought they'd play Frisbee and quote Hesse; I thought they'd be good kissers and drink wine. Some of them, I fancied, might smoke pipes. One of them, I dreamed, might win my heart.
>
> But as I searched, they seemed to grow shorter, t-shirt season ended only when the ski parkas came out. Frisbee was played with their dogs; pipes were more often of the water variety, and kissing was passe. The vogue, they would have had me believe, was to go directly from vertical activities (such as first-time introductions) to horizontal activities (such as could easily be accomplished in our co-ed dorms).
>
> . . . Why should I have thought college men would miraculously be older, cuter, and more sophisticated than the guys who had finished high school with me just two months before?
>
> Why? Because hope springs eternal. Because I was on my own, away from home for the first time, with a new Indian-print bedspread, a high school graduation gift—stereo, my own checking account, and a stack of fat college-issue fashion magazines filled with hundreds of examples of what to wear on campus to attract tall, cute, flannel-shirted, pipe-smoking, wine-drinking, sophisticated, good-kissing men (Hesse quotations optional).
>
> Getting those hopes dashed did not take long. A week of orientation, a few into-the-night blab sessions with my suitemates, a disastrous mixer or two, a few close encounters of the nerd kind, and the dazzling truth began to seep in: These guys were human. Just like us, but shorter. (Lisa Schwartzbaum, a freelance writer, in Schwartzbaum & Whisnant, 1982 p. 42)

Men want to date ravishing women. Women want their dates to be handsome as well as competent and TALL. But dreams are not the same as reality. The interplay between fantasy and reality will be the theme of this paper.

Before we discuss how physical attractiveness operates in both the fantasy and reality of the dating marketplace, let's begin at the beginning. Just how many people are out there bargaining in the marketplace, and who are they?

## THE" LONELY HEARTS" ARE NOW "SWINGING SINGLES"

Remember "Old Maid"? Whoever got stuck with the homely old crone was clearly the loser. This card game symbolizes the stigma once attached to being single, particularly if one was a woman. Single women, "old maids," or "spinsters," were assumed to have no choice in the matter—they were single because no one found them attractive enough to marry. Single men were "bachelors"; it was assumed they chose to remain single because they loved an exciting life.

Today, it is more acceptable to remain single—even for women. In fact, in 1978 about 48 million adult Americans (about one-third the adult population) were single. Here are some other facts:

- Most college students are single.
- More than one-half of Americans aged 18 to 39 are single.
- At any age, there are more single women than single men. This gap increases with age. For people in their forties, there are 233 unattached

(never married, divorced, widowed) women for every 100 men. (Blumstein and Schwartz 1983; Francaeur 1982).

Today, many people are choosing to remain single for a longer period (or all) their adulthood. There are several reasons why they are choosing not to marry. Many women find this choice gives them greater freedom to pursue a career. Other individuals have developed negative attitudes about marriage, perhaps from growing up in a broken home. Some develop such negative attitudes about attachment to one person that they choose to be "creatively single." Roger Libby (1977) defines a "creatively single" person as one who chooses not to be dependent on any one person—emotionally, financially, or sexually.

Other people, however, are reluctantly alone. Rather than choosing not to select, they are not selected. These people may have problems being selected because of unattractiveness or lack of social skills. The emptiness and despair of such singles is portrayed in the following comment by a young, single man:

> I have cried over my general inability to meet women—once even in my car in the parking lot of a disco in L.A. after having an extremely difficult time conversing with a number of girls who I was really attracted to (which is rare). I have been intrigued with the subject of suicide and realize that it is the most effective way to cure one's depression. . . . My depressions always center around my inability to meet women. Period. I really envy guys who have the "gift of gab" and who can just walk up to strange women and start a conversation. If I had that ability, it would solve all my problems, I'm convinced of it. (Hite 1981, 255–256)

Although many single people are involved in romantic relationships, many are not. There are many adults truly unattached. Although they may not always stay home on Saturday night, there really is no special person in their lives. They are the *Availables*.

## THE DATING GAME

Imagine that a friend has given you a six-month membership to a video dating service. Such services have been springing up all around the country. They go by names such as "Great Expectations," "Couple Company," and "People Resources" (Kellogg 1982). During your orientation meeting, the service asks you to submit a small snapshot and a handwritten autobiography. The second step, which may seem a little more intimidating, is to make an appointment for an interview that will be videotaped. You will sit down face-to-face with the interviewer and answer a series of questions–ranging from your views on politics to your views on relationships. Your interview then becomes part of a film library, available for viewing by other members.

Your membership also allows you to browse through the pictures, autobiographies, and videotapes of the other members. Any time you have some free time, you can drop in to the video dating center, and leaf through a large catalogue, which contains the other members' photographs and biographical material. From all those faces and stories, you pick out the very few whose videotapes you want to view. From those few videotapes, you have to decide just who you might be interested in meeting and possibly dating. Momentous decisions to be made.

As the newest member, you probably have some questions swirling through your mind:

1. How should I look for my videotaping? How should I dress—casually or in my best?
2. How should I present myself? Should I reveal my strengths *and* weaknesses? Or should I lie and make myself seem *really* desirable?
3. Who should I go out with? (All those videotapes!) What factors are important in a date or mate anyway? Should I care what my date looks like? Should I ask out the date I *want* (no harm in trying) or one I think I can *get*?

The questions spill out, one after the other. Luckily, social scientists have something to say about these issues. In this paper we will present evidence on just how important attractiveness is in the getting together stage of dating. We discuss how much difference other characteristics, such as intelligence and personality, make. We discuss both the *fantasy* of the dating marketplace, what men and women would like if a genie granted them three wishes, and the *reality* of the dating marketplace, what people are willing to settle for after they realize they can not get all they want. We will see which matches tend to be good ones, which not.

**How Important Are Looks In Romantic Beginnings?**

Looks are important in most areas of life, but at the beginning of romance there is probably nothing that counts more. The men and women who sign up for video dating services are well aware of this importance. Most attempt to look their best for the taping. Women apply their makeup more carefully than usual and wear their best clothes. Men get fresh haircuts, shave, and dress more carefully than usual.

What do really homely people do? There are always the jokes:

> "I'm planning to put a paper bag over my head and come as the mystery videodate."
>
> "I've hired Jeff to stand in for me."
>
> "Now that you mention it, I guess I'll cash my membership and invest my money in something more profitable—perhaps in a money market account."

These are wry remarks, but the concern behind them is well-placed. Beauty may be only skin deep, but in romantic beginnings apparently the surfaces are what count. There is dramatic evidence indicating how important looks are in the beginning stages of dating.

**Oh great computer in the sky, match me with someone attractive.** In the 1960s, Elaine Hatfield and colleagues (Hatfield [Walster] et al. 1966) organized a dance for freshman at the University of Minnesota. The men and women were told that computer would match them with a blind date who would be just right for them. In truth, we matched couples on a more mundane basis—we simple drew names out of a fishbowl.

In the backs of our minds, we were expecting people to like their dates best if they were matched by "social desirability." Tom Sellecks would like Bo Dereks, Plain Joes would like Plain Janes, and, if by chance a gorgeous person and a homely person were matched, both would feel uncomfortable.

When the men and women arrived to purchase their tickets for the dance, we set out to assess their general social desirability. We assumed social desirability was influenced by attributes such as physical attractiveness, intelligence, personality, and social skills. Meticulously, we measured each of these personal characteristics. Participants' attractiveness was secretly assessed by four ticket sellers. Intelligence was assessed by high school grades and by scores on the Minnesota Scholastic Aptitude Test. To measure personality, we gave men and women a battery of personality tests, including the prestigious Minnesota Multiphasic Personality Test and the California Personality Inventory. We also assessed their social skills.

At the dance a few days later, the four hundred couples who attended did what people always do at dances—they danced, talked, and got to know one another. Then, during the 10:30 p.m. intermission, we swept through the building, rounding up couples from the dance floor, lavatories, fire escapes—even adjoining buildings. We asked them to tell us frankly (and in confidence) what they thought of their dates.

What do you think we found? Perhaps you will be in a better position to answer this question if you return to the video dating scenario we set up for you. Imagine you have just viewed several videotapes. You have seen the whole range—everyone from the stunning actor (or actress), who promises cruises on his (or her) yacht, to the balding, pudgy mortician, who admits his (or her) hobby is collecting dead baby jokes. If you were guaranteed a date of your choice, who would you select—the actor (actress), the mortician, or someone in between? How attractive, personable, socially skilled, or intelligent would you want your date to be?

Here are some of the things we found:

1. If you are like the freshman who attended our dance, ideally you would prefer (in fact, insist) on going out with the most appealing dates available. Virtually everyone, including the homeliest men and women, asked to be matched with good-looking blind dates.
2. Everyone, good-looking or not, insisted their dates be exceptionally charming, bright, and socially skilled! ("To dream the impossible dream.")
3. Those whom fate matched up with a beautiful or handsome date wanted to pursue the dream. They wanted to see their computer match again. When we contacted couples six months after the dance to find out the extent to which people had, in fact, pursued their dreams, we also found that daters—good-looking or homely—had continued to pursue the best. The prettier the woman, the more she was pursued by everyone, homely or not.

4. Every effort to find anything else that mattered failed! Men and women with exceptional IQs and social skills, for example, were *not* liked any better than those less well-endowed.
5. Finally, both men and women cared equally about their dates' looks. (See also Curran and Lippold [1975].) They secured similar results.

The inordinate importance of good looks in blind date settings has been substantiated by other investigators (see Brislin and Lewis 1966; and Tesser and Brodie 1971).

Some time ago, we asked you to think about what you wanted in a video date. How did your reaction compare with the preceding results? Of course, in your case you merely said what you would *like*. How would you feel if you were really going to ask the person out and if they could turn down your invitation? Let's carry the exercise a little further.

**Possibility for turndown = Turnoff.** In the video dating scenario we presented, we guaranteed you a date with the person of your choice. In the computer dating study we actually conducted, the students were also pretty much guaranteed a date for the evening. But rarely does true life contain guarantees. The *reality* of the dating marketplace is somewhat different.

In fact, a video dating service generally operates as follows: For your membership fee you are allowed to send an invitation to only five or six members each month. If they so desire, these individuals can screen *your* videotape in return, and, *if* they are interested, a mutual selection is made and names/phone numbers are given to both parties. Obviously, invitations are not always reciprocated. Particularly desirable candidates, flooded with invitations, will not have the time to respond to all of them. Particularly unappealing candidates may issue five to six invitations, but no one may return their interest. Rejection is a possibility in all interpersonal interactions but is particulary characteristic of the getting-together stage of dating.

Would the knowledge that there has to be "mutual selection" affect your decisions about to whom you would send invitations? If you are like most people, it will. You may be tempted to aspire for the best, but rejection stings; you may settle for someone you think you can get. As we predicted several years ago, one's romantic aspirations are influenced by "the desirability of the goal and the perceived probability of attaining it" (Hatfield [Walster] et al. 1966).

Age and experience probably help people get a good sense of what is out there for them. A very experienced gay friend of Elaine Hatfield's observed that:

> Gay men who do a great deal of "cruising," can tell in the flicker of an eyelash who'd be interested in them, who'd not. In a bar or on the street, looks is all that matters; everyone has an exquisitely fine-tuned sense of who's available, who's not. There's a real pecking order.

Experiments indicate that, when there is a possibility of rejection, people become a little more realistic in their dating choices. In one study (Huston 1973), men were shown color Polaroid pictures of six women and asked to select one as a date. The women varied markedly in physical attractiveness. Men were also told either that the women had already seen a picture of them and had said they would be willing to date them *or* were given no information as to whether or not she was likely to date them. What type of woman were men most likely to select? Men were more likely to select a good-looking date when confident she would accept them rather than when they were uncertain about whether or not she would be interested.

The men in this study given no information about the women's desires were asked to estimate whether or not each woman would want to date them. The men assumed the beautiful women would be "harder to get." Furthermore, handsome men perceived their chances of acceptance by the women to be greater than did unattractive men.

Other researchers (Shanteau and Nagy 1979) have also examined whether the probability of acceptance is important in choosing a date. Women were asked to examine the photographs of several pairs of men and, in each case, to choose the one they would prefer to date. The men varied markedly in attractiveness. Below each photograph was a phrase indicating how certain (or uncertain) the man was that he wanted to date *her* —a conclusion he had supposedly reached after seeing her photograph. Both the attractiveness of the men and the probability of acceptance were found to be important. A man who was both attractive and willing to accept the date was seen as very desirable. A man who was unattractive and unlikely to accept a date was seen as particularly undesirable. (Other experiments, however, have been less conclusive in indicating the effects of the possibility of rejection. See, for example, Berscheid, Dion, Hatfield [Walster] and Walster [1971].)

This research indicates that, ideally, people would prefer to date very attractive others, but, because rejection is costly, they end up choosing someone of about their same level of attractiveness. Social psychologist Bernard Murstein (1971) describes how the risk of rejection moderates dating aspirations:

> A man who is physically unattractive (liability), for example, might desire a woman who has the asset of beauty. Assuming, however, that his nonphysical qualities are no more rewarding than hers, she gains less profit than he does from the relationship and thus his suit is likely to be rejected. Rejection is a cost to him because it may lower his self-esteem and increase his fear of failure in future encounters; hence he may decide to avoid courting women he perceives as much above him in attractiveness. (p. 113–114)

That people do seem affected by the chances of rejection was also demonstrated in a study conducted in the naturalistic setting of singles bars (Glenwick, Jason, and Elman 1978). If men in singles bars follow an "idealistic" strategy (following their dreams), attractive women should be approached more frequently than unattractive women. On the other hand, if men follow a more "realistic" strategy (and fear rejection), the attractive and unattractive women should be approached equally often. Using four single bars in Rochester, New York, the researchers observed unattached women and recorded how attractive each woman was, how many men initiated contact with her, and how long the contact lasted. The researchers found that men seemed to be choosing a strategy to minimize rejection: Attractive women were not approached more often—or for longer periods of time—than less attractive women.

**In Sum**

While the students who participated in our early computer dating study (Hatfield [Walster] et al. 1966) desired the most attractive date, they were guaranteed the date and did not have to face possible rejection. Other studies indicate that the possibility of rejection lowers men and women's aspirations somewhat. If you actually had to send a limited number of invitations to other video date members and "mutual selection" was necessary before names were exchanged, you would also probably be willing to settle for others of about your own level of attractiveness (or risk ending up with no one to call). We are all affected by the possibility of rejection. The dynamics of the marketplace operate to bring people together who are matched in physical attractiveness. Yet, there is no question most of us would prefer the most attractive partner we can possibly get.

## DO THINGS BESIDES PHYSICAL ATTRACTIVENESS MATTER?

Most video daters know how they want to look during their interview—as appealing as possible. But how do they act? What personality traits, attitudes, and interests should they display? And does it really matter how they act, given the importance of physical attractiveness? Here are the kinds of questions that perplex video daters:

> How should I present myself? Maybe I should fake it. After all, my friend invested $350 in this for me. I want to be sure *someone* asks me out. But how do I fake it? Should I demonstrate superior intelligence, or well that just scare possible dates away? (And my God, how would I even know how to act intelligently?) Should I act self-confident, or shy and modest? (Maybe I should be a natural leader, yet someone who can blend into a crowd? Brilliant, but not too "heady." Strong and vulnerable? Uhhuh.)
>
> On the other hand, maybe I don't want to try to be something I am not (even if I could figure out just what *that* was). What good does it do to fake it, to attract someone who loves what you *say* you are but can't stand *you* . To discover too late that your perfect match never even took a second look at you, because you were busy pretending to be someone you thought he/she would like better.
>
> What to do? Maybe I'll just shade the truth a little.

In this section, we will present the bits of evidence social scientists have collected on what men and women want in those they date.

## INTELLIGENCE, PERSONALITY, AND FRIENDLINESS DO SEEM TO MATTER

Many women are afraid that if they sound too bright they might scare dates off. While we would not recommend claiming degrees, honors, or IQ points one does not have, it does not hurt, and probably helps to take opportunities to demonstrate brilliance and competence. Experiments indicate people are more attracted to men and women who seem intelligent and competent (Aronson, Willerman, and Floyd 1966; Helmreich, Aronson, and LeFan 1970; Solomon and Saxe 1977).

It also seems to pay to act friendly. Dale Carnegie, who wrote *How to Win Friends and Influence People* (1936) several decades ago, gives just such advice. In his book, he offers six ways to make others like you:

Rule 1: Become genuinely interested in other people.
Rule 2: Smile.
Rule 3: Remember that a man's name is to him the sweetest and most important sound in any language.
Rule 4: Be a good listener. Encourage others to talk about themselves.
Rule 5: Talk in terms of the other man's interest.
Rule 6: Make the other person feel important—and do it sincerely.

Millions of copies of Carnegie's book have been sold. This success is probably because such advice is generally effective. Men and women like all the conventionally appealing things your parents (and Dale Carnegie) said they would. They like to be around "nice" and "friendly" people and those who have generally pleasant and agreeable characteristics (Kaplan and Anderson 1973). People also like those who like them. If Abigail learns that Benjamin likes her, probably Abigail will like Benjamin in return (Mette and Aronson 1974). (See Hatfield and Walster [1978] for a review of this literature.)

On the other hand, according to folklore, we should never "throw ourselves" at the people we find apealing. Socrates, Ovid, the *Kama Sutra*, Bertrand Russell, and "Dear Abby" all agree: Passion is stimulated by excitement and challenge. To find authors in such rare accord is refreshing. Luckily, research clearly shows that, this time, the sages are wrong. Researchers have conducted a number of experiments designed to demonstrate that men and women value hard-to-get dates more than easy-to-get ones. Inevitably, these experiments failed. They all had the same results: If anything, hard-to-get dates are liked less than easy-to-get dates. In general, then, there is no point in pretending to be what you are not. Some people prefer secure, easy-to-get dates; others like the excitement of a hard-to-get partner. It all balances out (see Hatfield [Walster] et al. 1973). (Some people like impossible-to-get partners most of all, making for a somewhat distant relationship.)

## BUT SUCH INNER QUALITIES DO NOT SEEM TO MATTER AS MUCH AS PHYSICAL ATTRACTIVENESS

In the computer dance study (Hatfield [Walster] et al. 1966), we found that everyone hoped for the best. They wanted a stunningly good-looking partner—who was also bright and sparkling, with a wonderful personality. But rarely is life so accommodating. When people have to make compromises (which is most of the time), what is really most important—"superficial" appearances or more meaningful things such as intelligence, warmth, considerateness, and personality? In romantic beginnings, seemingly superficial appearances are what matter. The discovery that someone has a "great personality" *seems* to matter very little. Let us consider the research that leads to this conclusion.

In the computer dating study we just described, for most of the young people physical attractiveness was everything; but, maybe that is not so surprising. In certain settings—noisy mixers, singles bars, loud new-wave discos, or computer dances—about all daters can perceive is what their dates look like. In the midst of the din, daters certainly do not have much chance to display their knowledge of world affairs or advanced calculus. In such settings, about all people can go on is looks.

But in other settings, people do get a chance to find out more about one another. A video dating service gives one a chance to do just that. So do church discussion groups, encounter groups, and small parties. What about these settings? What matters most in such settings—how you look or what you are like? Let's see.

### What People Say They Want

When teenagers and young adults are asked what characteristics are important in a date, they *say* there are many factors more important than looks. In one of the earliest studies conducted on dating relationships (Perrin 1921), men and women were asked to list the characteristics they cared about in a date. Men were more willing than women to admit they cared about looks, but it was not a very important item for anyone. For example, men insisted that a woman's "sincerity," "individuality," and "affectional disposition" were more important than her looks. (Similar results were secured in another early study by Hill [1945].)

Half a century has not changed these preferences to any great extent. In recent studies (conducted in 1956, 1967, and 1977), when men and women were asked to rate 18 personal characteristics they desire in a date or mate, good looks ranged from being 9th to 18th in importance (Hudson and Henze 1969; Hudson and Hoyt 1981; McGinnis 1958). Men and women said what they really valued was "dependable character" and "emotional stability." Other investigators have found similar results (Miller and Rivenbark 1970; Tesser and Brodie 1971).

People generally *say* looks are not too important to them, but their actions belie their statements.

### Actions Speak Louder than Words: What People Do Value

A variety of experiments suggest that looks are more important than people are able or willing to admit. In such studies, men and women are shown photographs of potential dates, who range from fairly homely to breathtakingly appealing. They are also given a brief personality sketch of each date. The potential date is described as having either a desirable personality trait or its opposite. Researchers conducted these experiments to see if attractiveness still has a powerful effect, even when compared to other powerful factors.

These studies suggest that looks overshadow everything else. It seems to matter very little to men (all the subjects in these studies have been male) if they are told their potential date is independent versus dependent (Meredith

1972), trustworthy versus untrustworthy (Shepard 1973), relaxed versus anxious (Mathes 1975), or boastful versus modest (Stretch and Figley 1980). Attractive dates were overwhelmingly preferred to unattractive ones, while trustworthy or honest or independent dates were preferred only slightly more (or sometimes not any more) than untrustworthy or dishonest or dependent dates.

Other evidence also confirms that good looks are more important than good character or personality in the dating marketplace. Elaine Hatfield and colleagues (Hatfield [Walster] et al. 1966) asked more than seven hundred young men and women, "How popular are you with the opposite sex?" and "How many dates have you had in the last six months?" As you might expect, attractive men and women were more popular and dated more often. In this same study, intelligence, personality, and social skills seemed to have little impact on popularity (similar results were found by Berscheid et al. 1971).

What can we conclude from all these studies? In romantic beginnings, attractiveness is exceedingly important. We are aroused by others who are physically and personally appealing. Appearance, which we tend to think of as only a superficial trait, appears to be far more critical in the dating marketplace than traits we think of as of deeper importance—such as intelligence, personality, and social skills. Why?

## WHY DO WE PREFER A "10" TO A "6"?

We have documented that men and women do prefer "10s" over "6s," but we have not addressed *why* this is so. There are at least three reasons:

**1. Aesthetic appeal.** Just as it is pleasant to live in a beautiful environment, possess appealing paintings, and collect beautiful objects, it is also pleasant to be around beautiful people. Infants as young as four months prefer good looks to ugliness. Investigators (Kagan et al. 1966) showed infants faces that were either normal or terribly distorted. The infants were content to gaze at the normal face, but they reacted with anxiety, fear, and crying when shown the distorted face. Aesthetic concerns probably increase as we become older.

**2. The glow of beauty.** Good looks radiate. Appearance influences how we think about others, nonphysical characteristics. Most people presume the Bo Dereks and Tom Sellecks of the world are perfect in every way. Attractive people are assumed to be unusually sensitive, kind, interesting, strong, poised, modest, sociable, outgoing, more exciting dates, and sexually warm and responsive (Berscheid and Hatfield [Walster] 1974). Elsewhere, we provided evidence that attractive people are perceived more positively in a wide variety of settings—in schools, on the job, by the mental health system, in the courtroom, and so on. It is not surprising, then, that attractive people are preferred as dating partners, for they are expected to have a monopoly on all the good things life has to offer.

Also, of course, the stereotypes about good-looking people just may contain a "kernel of truth." Possibly good-looking people, who are treated so graciously by others, actually become the beautiful and the best—sort of a self-fulfilling prophecy.

This explanation for why a "10" is preferred over a "6," therefore, suggests it has nothing to do with good looks, per se. The preference exists because of the inner qualities that are assumed to develop (or actually do develop) as a result of having an appealing exterior.

**3. Beauty "rubs off",.** There is also a selfish reason for wanting to associate with attractive people. Attractive men and women may be preferred because our self-esteem and prestige are bolstered when irresistable people find us irresistable. Sociologist Willard Waller (1937) spoke about this process in his discussion of the "rating and dating" complex. In describing college campuses several decades ago, he said men and women rated potential dates (1 to 10) and tried to date the best. Their success or failure at this game provided evidence to themselves and to others about just how valuable they were.

The "rating and dating" complex is not just a quaint reminder of the past. Even today, people gain by merely being seen with someone good-looking. In one study, for example, men were asked their first impression of another man. Tucked in at the man's side was a girlfriend, either ravishingly beautiful or exceedingly homely. (Sometimes the man was alone.) When a man was accompanied by a beauty, he was evaluated most favorably. Indeed, a man was better off being seen alone than when associated with a homely woman (Sigall and Landy 1973).

Do women gain just as much by being seen with a handsome man? Not necessarily. In another study (Bar-Tal and Saxe 1976a), men and women looked at a series of slides of married couples and judged the husband and wife on several dimensions. If an ugly man had an unusually beautiful wife, the judges assumed he must have *something* to offer. They assumed he must be unusually bright, rich, or professionally successful. The same assumptions were not made for the women. If an ugly woman had an unusually handsome husband, she gained nothing in how she was judged. She was evaluated strictly on her own merit.

Physical attractiveness matters, then, and we have considered some of the reasons why. But is physical attractiveness equally important to everyone? Is it equally important in all settings?

## THERE ARE SOME LIMITS TO THE PREFERENCE FOR THE MOST ATTRACTIVE

Probably everyone, then, cares about looks a little. But surely there is variation among people in just how important physical attractiveness is. The importance of physical attractiveness should also vary across situations. In this section, we will discuss how physical attractiveness may be more important: (1) to some people than to others; and (2) in certain settings. We will present what past research indicates and will also speculate a little on our own. This area is one in which much more research is clearly needed. Certainly, there are many homely men and women eager to find out the exceptions to the general preference for good looks.

**For Some People, Looks Do Not Matter Quite So Much**

Some people seem to care far more about looks than do others. We will consider four characteristics that may influence how important a good-looking dating partner is: (1) age; (2) self-esteem; (3) personality; and (4) gender.

**Youth: When Hope Springs Eternal**

Young people are often especially concerned about looks. At least, our personal experiences would suggest this is so.

> Elaine Hatfield once gave a surprise birthday party for Michelle, a 12-year old who was staying at her house. Since Michelle is an unusually adult little girl, rather than inviting Michelle's friends, we invited a collection of older people—including some well-known authors, psychologists, artists, and craftspeople. As we sat talking after dinner, Michelle was asked how she liked junior high school. She said that, at first, as a newcomer, she had been considered "A Nothing" . . . but, she said blithely, "it is just a matter of time until I'm one of the most popular girls."
>
> Intrigued by her confidence, a physicist asked, "What does it take to be a 'super-star'? Michelle answered matter-of-factly, "Girls have to have big breasts; boys have to be athletes." (She considered her own budding breasts to be big; we could barely see their lines under her dress.) The table suddenly became very quiet. The "adults" were reminded of their own painful high school experiences. "Surely," said the physicist (who was obviously not an athlete) with uneasy enthusiasm, "there are other ways for a boy to be popular. What if he has a great sense of humor?" Michelle pronounced with finality, "Well, he could be a *friend*, but no one would want him for a *boyfriend* ." The laws of the dating jungle are relentless, and there is perhaps no worse time than junior high and high school for those who don't "stack up."

Looks may be especially important to young people because of their need to conform in order to be popular (or at least to be accepted) by their peers. While it may sound bizarre today, when Elaine Hatfield was an undergraduate at the University of Michigan in the late 1950s, one of the prestigious sororities fined sisters who dared to "damage the house reputation" by dating ugly men. While sororities today probably no longer have fines for "dating down," there is still a great deal of pressure to date men from the right fraternities (that have good-looking men!). Young men have the same kinds of pressures to date beautiful women.

We suspect that by the time men and women reach middle age, they have learned that looks matter less, while wit, intelligence, personality, and character matter more. Although common sense suggests that looks matter more to younger people than to older individuals, little evidence exists to verify this notion. Unfortunately, no computer dating studies have been conducted with senior citizens. One study that did look at older people's general impressions of physically attractive versus physically unattractive people found that older people are not immune to the physical attractiveness stereotype. Age does not seem to diminish the belief that "what is beautiful is good" (Adams and Huston 1975). However, only further research will indicate whether older people are as likely as younger people to insist on the most attractive dating partner they can get.

**Self-Esteem**

Fundamental to how we feel about others is how we feel about ourselves. Just how is self-esteem related to dating choice? There really is not a simple answer. Self-esteem could have two different effects.

First, people with low self-esteem are often afraid they well be rejected. They fear stepping out of line and being different. They seek social approval. Shy teenagers, unsure of themselves, find it very difficult to date a person friends find unappealing. High self-esteem individuals, on the other hand, are not so desperate for social approval. They can afford to date someone much less attractive than they are. They have enough prestige "credits" to be unconcerned about the "rating and dating" complex we described earlier. (Gergen [1974] discusses self-esteem and interpersonal attraction.)

But there is another possibility. When people have high self-esteem, they have the confidence to approach anyone they desire. Thus, they are more likely to take a chance and approach a good-looking man or woman (who is also intelligent, charming, and considerate). In a delightful experiment, Sara Kiesler and Roberta Baral (1970) demonstrated this hypothesis—the greater a person's self-esteem, the more likely he or she is to approach striking dates. The researcher recruited college men to participate in a study on intelligence testing. After the men completed the first portion of the IQ test, they were told how they were doing. The researchers tried to raise the self-esteem of some of the men by giving them fake IQ test results indicating they had done very well. The self-esteem of the other men was temporarily lowered by telling them they had done poorly. At intermission, the experimenter suggested they take a coffee break. They walked to a nearby canteen and sat down. Once they were seated the experimenter's assistant walked over and joined them. On some days, the assistant was beautifully made up and dressed. On other days, she was made up to be downright ugly. (She wore heavy glasses and her hair was pulled back with a rubber band. Her blouse and skirt clashed and were sloppily arranged.) During the coffee break, the experimenter left, ostensibly to make a phone call. The man was left alone with the woman. The assistant carefully noted how much interest the man expressed in her. Did her offer to buy her a Coke? Did he ask for her phone number? Did he even go so far as to ask her out? When the man's self-esteem was unusually high, he was most romantic with the attractive woman. On the other hand, if his self-regard was at rock bottom, he was more comfortable approaching the homely woman.

What can we conclude about the possible effects of self-esteem on responsiveness to physical attractiveness? We would hypothesize that if individuals do not have to risk rejection (for example, women have traditionally been asked out rather than doing the asking), then a deficit of self-esteem will lead them to aspire to the most attractive partner possible. Because their esteem needs are unfulfilled, such persons are especially in need of any prestige that could "rub-off" on them. On the other hand, if people have to risk the chance of rejection (they have to do the asking and are not sure of the outcome), impoverished self-esteem might lead them to flee any chance of having their self-esteem assaulted even further.

**The Macho Personality**

Are there certain personality types especially captivated by looks? One study examined the relationship between having a "macho" personality and reacting to physically attractive versus unattractive persons of the opposite sex (Touhey 1979). Men and women were asked to complete the Macho Scale, which measures the extent to which people possess traditonal sexist stereotypes, attitudes, and behaviors. What are macho men and women? In general, these individuals agree with statements such as:

1. It's alright that most women are more interested in getting married than in making something of themselves.
2. A wife shouldn't contradict her husband in public.
3. I would not want to be part of a couple where the male was considerably shorter than the female.
4. For the most part, it is better to be a man than to be a woman.
5. "Henpecked" is a good word for describing some husbands.

(from the Macho Scale by Villemez and Touhey 1977)

The researchers showed men and women a photograph of someone of the opposite sex who was either attractive ("neatly groomed, smiling, relaxed, and approachable") or unappealing ("discheveled and squinting . . . sported a less inviting demeanor"). They were also given biographical information. Finally, they were asked how much they liked this person of the opposite sex and if they wanted to date him or her.

First, it must be pointed out that most of the men and women cared at least a little about looks. In general, an attractive model was liked more than a homely one. However, it was the highly macho men and women who cared most desperately. They were unusually eager to date good-looking partners and unusually quick to reject homely ones. They seemed less influenced by the biographical information. In fact, they had a hard time even remembering what was in it. The nonmachos were far less swayed by looks and did remember the contents of the biographical information.

Another recent study (Anderson and Bem 1981) produced similar results. Men and women who were sex-typed, adhering tightly to traditional male/female roles, (as measured by the Bem Sex-Role Inventory) were more likely than androgynous men and women to be more responsive to attractive than unattractive strangers.

**Gender: Do Men Care More than Women?**

> The ideal beauties teach women that their looks are a commodity to be bartered in exchange for a man, not only for food, clothing, and shelter, but for love. Women learn early that if you are unlovely, you are unloved. The homely girl prepares to be an old maid, because beauty is what makes a man fall in love. . . .

> A man's love is beauty deep. Beauty is man's only and sufficient reason for lusting, loving, and marrying a woman. Doesn't a man always say you're beautiful before he says I love you? Don't we all think it strange when he marries a dumb girl who isn't pretty and not at all strange when he marries a dumb beauty? Is it therefore surprising that even the great beauty fears a man's love will not survive her looks, and the average woman is convinced that no man can really love her? (Stannard 1971, 124).

According to popular belief, in the dating and mating game men care more than women about having a good-looking romantic partner. This assumption is so built into our belief systems that if the words "man" and "woman" were switched in the above paragraph, it would seem very strange indeed. Try it:

> The ideal muscle men teach men that their looks are a commodity to be bartered in exchange for a woman, not only for food, clothing, and shelter, but for love. Men learn early that if you are unlovely, you are unloved. The homely boy prepares to be a bachelor, because looks are what makes a woman fall in love. . . .

Is physical attractiveness really more important to men than to women, or is this mere belief? Theorists have assumed that men are more obsessed than women with appearance. Sociobiologists contend that men and women are *genetically* programmed to desire different things from their intimate relations (see Hagen 1979; Symons 1979; and Wilson 1975). Symons (1979) argues that gender differences are probably the most powerful determinants of how people behave sexually. Symon's sociobiological argument proceeds as follows: According to evolutionary biology, animals inherit characteristics that ensure they will transmit a maximum number of their genes to the next generation. It is to men and women's advantage to produce as many surviving children as possible. But man and women differ in one critical respect—to produce a child, men need only invest a trivial amount of energy; a single man can conceivably father an almost unlimited number of children. On the other hand, a woman can conceive only a limited number of children. It is to a woman's advantage to ensure the survival of the children she does conceive. Symons observes, "The enormous sex differences in minimum parental investment and in reproductive opportunities and constraints explain why *Homo sapiens*, a species with only moderate sex differences in structure, exhibits profound sex differences in psyche" (p. 27).

What are the gender differences Symons insists are "wired in"? According to Symons,

1. Men desire a variety of sex partners; women do not.
2. Men are inclined to be polygamous (possessing many wives). Women are more malleable in this respect; they are equally satisfied in polygamous, monogamous, or polyandrous marriages (possessing many husbands).
3. Men are sexually jealous. Women are more malleable in this respect; they are concerned with security—not fidelity.
4. Men are sexually aroused by the sight of women and women's genitals; women are not aroused by men's appearance.

5. For men, "sexual attractiveness" equals "youth." For women, "sexual attractiveness" equals "political and economic power."
6. Men have every reason to pursue women actively. They are programmed to impregnate as many women as possible. Women have every reason to be "coy." It takes time to decide if a man is a good genetic risk—is likely to be nurturant and protective.
7. Men are intensely competitive with one another. Competition over women is the most frequent cause of violence. Women are far less competitive.

Presumably, men are genetically "wired up" to care about beauty and youth in their lovers. Women, on the other hand, are attracted by political and economic power instead. (Henry Kissinger once observed that "power is the best aphrodisiac.")

The sociobiologists' arguments sound good, but there is a more compelling, albeit a more prosaic, explanation for why beauty is so important to men. Traditionally, men have had more social and economic power than have women. Thus, men can afford to select a beautiful and sexy mate without worrying too much about her other assets. Women have to be more practical. As one shrewd observer (Waller 1938, 162) noted: "There is this difference between the man and the woman in the pattern of middle-class family life: a man, when he marries, chooses a companion and perhaps a helpmate, but a woman chooses a companion and at the same time a standard of living. It is necessary for a woman to be mercenary." Feminist Arlie Hochschild (1975) agrees.

Other theorists (Bar-Tal and Saxe 1976b) have observed that, traditionally, women are expected to provide the husband with affection, to be sexually responsive, to be good housekeepers, and to take care of the children. Thus, beauty provides an important external cue as to whether or not a woman can adequately fulfill her traditional role. In contrast, women look for men who will be good providers—they search for men of good education and occupation rather than men of good looks.

Theorists believe that men *are* more concerned about beauty than women—but *are* they? They are. When men and women are asked what they want in a date, men admit they are more concerned about appearances than are women. Several years ago, one thousand college men and women were asked what qualities they desired in a dating partner (Coombs and Kenkel 1966). Men were more insistent on having a good-looking partner. In answer to the question, "To what extent is it important that your date be good looking or attractive?" 22 percent of the men, but only 7 percent of the women said it was "very important." What did women want? They were more likely than men to expect all the following qualities in a date: he should be of the same race, the same religion, a good dancer, possess high campus status, high scholastic ability, wear stylish clothes, and belong to a fraternity. A variety of other studies indicate that men are more concerned than women with appearances in a variety of settings—first encounters, work, dating, and marriage (Coombs and Kenkel 1966; Hewitt 1958; Miller and Rivenbark 1970; Stroebe, Insko, Thompson, and Layton 1971; Vail and Staudt 1950; Williamson 1966).

Men's concern with beauty is also reflected in their behavior. Two researchers (Harrison and Saeed 1977) examined over 800 lonely hearts advertisements that appeared in a national weekly tabloid. Such ads are placed in all types of newspapers and go something like the following:

> NON-GENERIC MALE, 36, wants to meet pretty, slim, working woman; 25–35 ish; must be well read, articulate, witty, with a finely tuned sense of the absurd. No Psychobabble, please. Write Chuck, Box 403 B
>
> GAY? I am dissatified with the gay bar scene; frustrated by the lack of constructive human contact. I wish to meet a like-minded gay man. If you're interested too, call Bill at 658–0965.
>
> WOMAN, tired of the obsession with superficial appearances, wants man who is concerned with deeper qualities—one who possesses spiritual concerns, a passion for life. . . . Send picture.
>
> PRETTY WOMAN, I WOULD LIKE TO MEET YOU. I know beauty is only skin deep. I did not used to care so much about beauty, but now I will not settle for less than the best. I also treasure an alert mind, w/serious interests (whether they be electrical engineering or scuba diving). Kindness and basic human decency. In the past, I wanted a woman who was an outstanding success; now I care more about personal qualities. Filing clerk, unemployed artist, fallen woman, or fast track exec.—it's the person rather than the occupation I care about. Write Oscar, Box 921.

The researchers found that men and women are well aware of men's special concern with appearances. As expected, they found that women were more likely than men to offer attractiveness, while men were more likely to seek it. As far as financial security, women were more likely to seek it, while men were more likely to offer it. Finally, another major sex difference was that women were likely to seek someone older, while men were likely to seek someone younger.

Other evidence indicates that attractiveness is more tightly linked to dating popularity for women than for men (Berscheid et al. 1971; Krebs and Adinolfi 1975; Hatfield [Walster] et al, 1966). Beautiful women have more dates than homely women, while a man's attractiveness (or lack thereof) is not as important in determining how busy his social calendar is.

This greater obsession in men with looks is not limited to our society. Interestingly, Ford and Beach (1951), who studied men and women in 190 societies, also concluded: "One interesting generalization is that in most societies, the physical beauty of the female receives more explicit consideration than does the handsomeness of the male. The attractiveness of the man usually depends predominantly upon his skills of prowess rather than upon his physical appearance" (p. 86).

One observation: Traditionally, men have cared about beauty while women were concerned with finding a good provider. These gender differences, however, may be on their way out. As women begin to have successful careers and become financially independent, they may have the luxury of insisting that their men be handsome and athletic (consider the popular song by Diana Ross, "I Want Muscles"). Many men may decide to accept the changes women are demanding. They may be willing to sacrifice having a beautiful date in order to have someone who can share the expenses. In the future, we may start to see less traditional and more individually tailored matches.

In conclusion, then, if you want to capitalize on your looks, you should spend your time with young people who have "appropriate" levels of self-esteem and who hold traditional macho values (and it helps if you are a woman). On the other hand, if you do not want your dating success to be totally determined by your looks, seek out people with the opposite characteristics.

## REFERENCES


Adams, G. R. and T. L. Huston. 1975. Social perception of middle-aged persons varying in physical attractiveness. *Developmental Psychology* 11: 657–658.

Anderson, S. M. and S. L. Bem. 1981. Sex typing and androgyny in dyadic interaction: Individual differences in responsiveness to physical attractiveness. *Journal of Personality and Social Psychology* 41:74–86.

Aronson, E., B. Willerman, and J. Floyd. 1966. The effect of a pratfall on increasing interpersonal attractiveness. Psychonomic Science 4: 157–158.

Bar-Tal, D. and L. Saxe. 1976a. Perceptions of similarly and dissimilarly attractive couples and individuals. *Journal of Personality and Social Psychology* 33: 772–781.

Bar-Tal, D. and L. Saxe. 1976b. Physical attractiveness and its relationship to sex-role stereotyping. *Sex Roles* 2: 123–133.

Berscheid, E., K. Dion, E. Hatfield (Walster), and G. W. Walster. 1971. Physical attractiveness and dating choice: A test of the matching hypothesis. *Journal of Experimental Social Psychology* 7: 173–189.

Berscheid, E. and E. Hatfield (Walster). 1974. Physical attractiveness. In *Advances in experimental social psychology* , ed. L. Berkowitz, vol. 7: 157–215, New York: Academic Press.

Blumstein, P. and P. Schwartz. 1983. *American Couples*. New York: William Morrow.

Brislin, R. W. and S. A. Lewis. 1966. Dating and physical attractiveness: A replication. *Psychological Reports* 22: 976.

Carnegie, D. 1936. *How to win friends and influence people*. New York: Simon & Schuster.

Coombs, R. H., and W. F. Kenkel. 1966. Sex differences in dating aspirations and satisfaction with computer-selected partners. *Journal of Marriage and the Family* 28: 62–66.

Curran, J. P., and S. Lippold. 1975. The effects of physical attractiveness and attitude similarity on attraction in dating dyads. *Journal of Personality* 43: 528–539.

Ford, C. S., and F. A. Beach. 1951. *Patterns of sexual behavior* . New York: Harper & Row.

Francaeur, R. T. 1982. *Becoming a sexual person*. New York: John Wiley & Sons.

Gergen, K. J. 1974. The self and interpersonal behavior. In *Social psychology for sociologists* , ed. D. Fields: 83–100. New York: John Wiley & Sons.

Glenwick, D. S., L. A. Jason and D. Elman. 1978. Physical attractiveness and social contact in the singles bar. *Journal of Social Psychology* 105: 311–312.

Hagen, R. 1979. *The bio-sexual factor*. New York: Doubleday.

Harrison, A. A., and L. Saeed. 1977. Let's make a deal: An analysis of revelations and stipulations in lonely hearts advertisements. *Journal of Personality and Social Psychology* 35: 257–264.

Hatfield (Walster), E.,V. Aronson, D. Abrahams, and L. Rottman, 1966. Importance of physical attractiveness in dating behavior. *Journal of Personality and Social Psychology* 5: 508–516.

Hatfield (Walster), E., G. W. Walster, J. Pilliavin, and L. Schmidt, 1973. Playing hard-to-get: Understanding an elusive phenomenon. *Journal of Personality and Social Psychology* 26: 113–121.

Hatfield, E., and G. W. Walster. 1978. *A new look at love*. Lantham, Mass.: University Press of America.

Helmreich, R., E. M. Aronson, and J. Lefan 1970. To err is humanizing—sometimes: Effects of self-esteem competence and pratfall on interpersonal attraction. *Journal of Personality and Social Psychology* 16: 259–264.

Hewitt, L. E., 1958. Students' perceptions of traits desired in themselves as dating and marriage partners. *Marriage and Family Living* 20: 344–349.

Hill, R. 1945. Campus values in mate selection. *Journal of Home Economics* 37, pp. 554–558.

Hite, S. 1981. *The Hite report on male sexuality* . New York: Alfred A. Knopf.

Hochchild, A. R. 1975. Attending to, codifying, and managing feelings: Sex differences in love. Paper presented at the American Sociological Association meetings, 29 August, San Francisco.

Hudson, J. W., and L. F. Henze. 1969. Campus values in mate selection: A replication. *Journal of Marriage and the Family* 31: 772–775.

Hudson, J. W., and L. L. Hoyt. 1981. Personal characeteristics in mate preference among college students. *Social Behavior and Personality* 9: 93–96.

Huston, T. L. 1973. Ambiguity of acceptance, social desirability, and dating choice. *Journal of Experimental Social Psychology* 9: 32–42.

Kagan, J., B. A. Henker, A. Hen-Tou, J. Levine, and M. Lewis. 1966. Infants' differential reactions to familiar and distorted faces. *Child Development* 37: 519–532.

Kaplan, J. F., and N. H. Anderson. 1973. Information integration theory and reinforecement theory as approaches to interpersonal attraction. *Journal of Personality and Social Psychology* 28: 301–312.

Kellogg, M. A. 1982. Could it be love at first cassette? *TV Guide*, 26 June: 33–36.

Kiesler, S. B., and R. L. Baral. 1970. The search for a romantic partner: The effects of self-esteem and physical attractiveness on romantic behavior. In *Personality and Social Behavior*, ed. K. J. Gerger and D. Marlow: 155–165. Reading, Mass.: Addison-Wesley.

Krebs, D., and A. A. Adinolfi. 1975. Physical attractiveness, social relations, and personality style. *Journal of Personality and Social Psychology* 31: 245–253.

Libby, R., 1977. Creative singlehood as a sexual lifestyle: Beyond marriage as a rite of passage. In *Marriage and attractiveness: Exploring intimate relationships*, eds. R. W. Libby and R. Whitehurst. Glenview, Ill.: Scott, Foresman.

Mathes, E. W. 1975. The effects of physical attractiveness and anxiety on heterosexual attraction over a series of five encounters. *Journal of Marriage and the Family* 37: 769–773.

McGinnis, R. 1958. Campus values in mate selection: A repeat study. *Social Forces* 36: 368–373.

Meredith, M. 1972. The influence of physical attractiveness, independence, and honesty on date selection. Dept. of Psychology. Western Illinois University. Macomb, Illinois. Photocopy.

Mettee, D. R., and E. Aronson. 1974. Affective reactions to appraisal from others. In *Foundations of interpersonal attraction* , ed. T. L. Huston: 235–283. New York: Academic Press.

Miller, H. L., and W. H. Rivenbark III. 1970. Sexual differences in physical attractiveness as a determinant of heterosexual liking. *Psychological Reports* 27: 701–702.

Murstein, B. I. 1971. Critique of models of dyadic attraction. In *Theories of attraction and love* , B. I. Murstein: 1–30. New York: Springer.

Perrin, F. A. C. 1921. Physical attractiveness and marriage adjustment in older American couples. *Journal of Psychology* 105: 247–252.

Schwarzbaum, L., and L. Whisnant (eds.). 1982. Can you find true love on campus? Nutshell: 41–46. Knoxville, Tenn.: 13-30 Corporation.

Shanteau, J., and G. F. Nagy. 1979. Probabilty of acceptance in dating choice. *Journal of Personality and Social Psychology* 37: 522-533.

Shepard, M. 1973. The effects of physical attractiveness and trustworthiness in long and short-term dating selection. Department of Psychology, Western Illinois University, Macomb, Illinois. Photocopy.

Sigall, H., and D. Landy. 1973. Radiating beauty: The effects of having a physically attractive partner on person perception. *Journal of Personality and Social Psychology* 28: 218–224.

Solomon, S., and L. Saxe. 1977. What is intelligent, as well as attractive, is good. *Personality and Social Psychology Bulletin* 3: 670–673.

Stannard, U. 1971. The mask of beauty. In *Women in sexist society: Studies in power and powerlessness*, ed. V. Gormick and B. K. Moran: 118–130. New York: Basic Books.

Stretch, R. H., and C. R. Figley. 1980. Beauty and the beast: Predictors of interpersonal attraction in a dating experiment. *Psychology, A Quarterly Journal of Human Behavior* 17: 35–43.

Stroebe, W., C. A. Insko, V. D. Thompson, and B. D. Layton. 1971. Effects of physical attractiveness, attitude similarity, and sex on various aspects of interpersonal attraction. *Journal of Personality and Social Psychology* 18: 79–91.

Symons, D. 1979. *The evolution of human sexuality* .New York: Oxford Press.

Tesser, A., and M. Brodie. 1971. A note on the evaluation of a computer date. *Psychonomic Science* 23: 300.

Touhey, J. C. 1979. Sex-role stereotyping and individual differences in liking for the physically attractive. *Social Psychology Quarterly* 42: 285–289.

Vail, J. P., and V. M. Staudt. 1950. Attitudes of college students toward marriage and related problems: I. Dating and marriage selection. *Journal of Psychology* 30: 171–182.

Villemez, W. J., and J. C. Touhey. 1977. A measure of individual differences in sex-stereotyping and sex discrimination. *Psychological Reports* 41: 411–415.

Waller, W. 1937. The rating and dating complex. *American Sociological Review* 2: 727–734.

Waller, W. 1938. *The family: A dynamic interpretation* . New York: Dryden.

Williamson, R. L. 1966. *Marriage and family relations* . New York: John Wiley & Sons.

Wilson E. O. 1975. *Sociobiology* . Cambridge, Mass: Belknap Press.

11

NAOMI B. McCORMICK AND CLINTON J. JESSER

# The Courtship Game: Power in the Sexual Encounter

*The old saying "A man chases a women until she lets him catch her" has long been a fairly accurate, although sexist, summary of American courtship. Most of us have personally experienced the emotional toll that the picking and changing of partners takes on its participants. One would expect courtship norms and behaviors to have changed dramatically in recent years, reflecting the impacts of the women's movement and the sexual revolution.*

*The following selection analyzes contemporary courting from the standpoint of equity theory and, more specifically, the variable "power." Equity theory predicts "that people prefer relationships in which each party receives equal relative gains."*[1] *Continuing or dissolving a relationship hinges largely on the participants' perceptions of fairness in what they receive from it as compared to what they must invest. Individuals strive for a balanced relationship and may become as distressed when receiving too much as when receiving too little. McCormick and Jesser suggest that, in situations where one of the parties decides the relationship has become extremely inequitable or unfair, that person may, through power ploys, attempt to better his or her position.*

*Using findings from a wide range of recent studies, McCormick and Jesser examine whether or not the relative balance of power in courtship pairs has changed in step with or in response to other liberating societal trends. Because of the breadth of these studies, the authors can trace the role of power through*

[1]McCormick and Jesser, "The Courtship Game," p. 74.

*the course of a relationship from initial flirtation through seduction or rejection.*

Source: "The Courtship Game: Power in the Sexual Encounter" by Naomi B. McCormick and Clinton J. Jesser in *Changing Boundaries: Gender Roles and sexual Behavior,* edited by Elizabeth Rice Allgeier and Naomi B. McCormick, by permission of Mayfield Publishing Company. 

---

The boundaries of heterosexual courtship—the institutional way that men and women become acquainted before marriage—have changed dramatically since a physician (Robinson, 1929, p. 262) offered the following advice:

> Fortunate are you, my young girl friend, if you come from a well-sheltered home.... But if you have lost your mother at an early age, or if your mother is not the right sort... if you have to shift for yourself, if you have to work in a shop, in an office, and particularly if you live alone and not with your parents, then temptations in the shape of men, young and old, will encounter you at every step; they will swarm about you like flies about a lump of sugar; they will stick to you like bees to a bunch of honeysuckle.

In the 1800s and the beginning of this century, courtship among middle-class North Americans was a sober process that strongly emphasized the end goal of marriage. Almost everyone, including feminists, valued sexual self-control (Hersh, 1980). Unmarried people were severely restricted as to *whom* they might court and *what* went on during courtship (Gordon, 1980). Because the respectable unmarried woman was constantly supervised by older adults, sexual experience with her courtship partner was unlikely (Kinsey et al., 1953).

Power—the ability to influence another person's attitudes or behavior—is an essential component of courtship. As societies become increasingly industrialized and urbanized, family and kin exercise less power over the young. "The world, as a whole, seems to be moving toward the idea of free choice in marriage" (Murstein, 1980, p. 778). The absence of parental power does not imply that courtship has become a free-for-all. Now, unmarried people have most of the power in determining the course of their own courtship.

To some extent, the sexual revolution is the result of this shift in power. As premarital sex has gained peer acceptance, increasing numbers of youthful North Americans, especially women, have sexual intercourse before marriage (Zelnik & Kantner, 1977, 1979, 1980). Sex and intimacy, not always leading to marriage, may be the new end goals of courtship.

In this paper, we look at the ways people use power in courtship. Given the limited research in the area, some of our discussion is more relevant to never-married, heterosexual, middle-class youth than to other groups. We examine gender differences in using and responding to power, and explore all levels of courtship, from meeting someone to having sex. In this paper, we focus predominantly on new dating relationships (such as how people flirt and ask dates out). We ask who holds most of the power in a dating relationship, the man or the woman. After this inquiry, we subject the sexual encounter itself to rigorous power analysis. We view sexual expression in political terms. And we inquire how and why people use particular strategies for having and avoiding sex and prefer some coital positions over others.

## POWER AND COURTSHIP

Power is one person's ability to impose wishes on another more than that other can impose his or her wishes (Weber, 1964, p. 152). The exercise of power is effective when one person succeeds in changing another person's thoughts, attitudes, or behavior (Raven, 1965, 1971). People acquire power and dominance in many ways. Sometimes they acquire and use power in a heavy-handed way. They use physical strength, social position in organizations and politics, and control over land and money, and often take unfair advantage of an influencee, or target (Collins & Raven, 1968; French & Raven, 1959).

Rape occurs when an influencing agent uses physical strength or the threat of violence to influence a victim (influencee) to have sex. Using superior wealth or the authority one has acquired as the boss or leader to convince a less-than-willing influencee to have sex is also heavy-handed. In the very least, such a use of power is sexual harassment. At its most extreme, it is rape.

Students sometimes balk when we suggest that nice people, not just sadists, use power during courtship. "If both the man and the woman like each other or want sex," they argue, "then power is irrelevant." According to these romantic students, lovers just happen to meet, just happen to get carried away and have sex. Characteristic of this attitude, some California college students are unable to relate to the question "Assuming you are very desirous of sexual intercourse . . . describe how you would try to influence your date to have sex" (McCormick, author's files):

- I don't think I would try to influence my date to have sex. If it's time and everything is right, sex will follow in its own pattern.
- I would not try. In time we would make it.
- It must come about naturally. No persuasion should be necessary. Otherwise, lovemaking is not a sign of affection but rather a disgusting sexual act.

Not everyone sees dating and mating in the same romantic light as these three students. Many, ourselves included, speculate that people are able to plan strategies carefully for attracting and seducing sexual partners. Power, the potential to influence another person's attitudes or behavior, may be an essential component of any romantic attraction or sexual relationship.

As we said before, there is more than one way to acquire and use power. The development of skills and knowledge, being perceived as attractive and likeable, and even acting helpless or "needy" can all be used to influence someone else (Collins & Raven, 1968; French & Raven, 1959). Often, these less obvious kinds of power are more effective because they avoid hitting the influencee over the head.

People often assume that their behavior is self-motivated when they receive relatively little feedback indicating that they are being influenced by someone else (Bem, 1972). For this reason, the effective strategies for influencing courtship tend to be subtle enough to convince a partner that he or she wanted what happened as much as the influencing agent wanted it. Flirtation in bars is an excellent example:

> We begin with a woman entering the bar. She is nicely dressed, and perhaps she expects to meet someone. As she enters, she characteristically stops, and nearly always adjusts some item of clothing, an accessory, or her hair. Then she looks around the bar, a deliberate scan, not a casual glance.... Then, she goes to the bar itself, walking directly to it and ends up standing next to some man.... If he fails to look at her, or if he turns away, the interaction is likely to cease immediately. But we assume that he moves slightly, perhaps looking at her briefly, perhaps just shifting his weight. His seeming trivial action is essential, since it has communicated to her that she has been noticed.... If things go further, he may well believe that *he* picked up *her*. [Perper & Fox, 1980a, p. 12]

## MEN AS PURSUERS, WOMEN AS PURSUED

Sex and the broader conditions of life cannot be separated. This fact is especially important today with the changing circumstances and opportunities in men's and women's lives. Because societies vary greatly, it is difficult to generalize about the relationship between sex and power.

Where or under what conditions do women have the most control over their sexual lives? Generally speaking, in five specific situations women have greater say over who they have sex with and how they have sex (see Hacker, 1975, pp. 212–214). First, women enjoy more sexual freedom where there is little or no emphasis on warfare and militarism. Second, women control their own sexuality more where men participate in child rearing or where child-care services are available. Third, women have greater power in their sexual relationships when they have political representation. Fourth, women enjoy greater sexual freedom where they have helped mold the mythology, religious beliefs, and world view of their groups. Finally, women are more sexually emancipated where they have economically productive roles such as control over tools, land, produce, and products.

In most societies, women's sexuality is more restricted than that of men (Safilios-Rothschild, 1977). A *double standard*—the expectation that premarital and extramarital sex is more permissible for men—has been employed. The cultural conditions just cited modify the extent to which the double standard is enforced. On the other hand, cultures that emphasize male dominance in society as a whole severely penalize premarital sex by women (Safilios-Rothschild, 1977). For example, in some Arab societies, women who break sexual conventions may be executed, sometimes by their brothers or fathers (Critchfield, 1980, p. 67).

Fortunately, not all societies oppress the sexual choices of women. The more power women have in society as a whole, the weaker the double standard is. The double standard is weak or absent in matrilineal societies, where descent and inheritance occur through the mother and land is owned or controlled by women (see Jesser, 1972, pp. 248–249). The double standard is also on the wane in societies that reward women for bearing children by encouraging them to be sexually permissive, as in Polynesia. Finally, the double standard dies in societies that have an overabundance of men. For example, in the Marquesa Islands, where men greatly outnumbered women at one time, men did all the work, including housework and child care. In contrast, Marquesan women spent their time attracting and pleasing sexual partners. In glaring contrast to North American culture, Marquesan men catered to women's whims, women were viewed as hypersexual, and sex started only after the woman gave the signal (Leibowitz, 1978).

Intriguing as they were, the Marquesans were unusual. Most societies are politically controlled by men. Consequently, sexual access to women is part of the property system (see Stephens, 1963, pp. 240–259). In societies in which women are regarded as property, men try to "enrich" themselves by having sex as frequently and with as many women as possible. Correspondingly, women try to keep themselves "precious" by staying beautiful or desirable while they refuse to give themselves to any but the "right" men—their present or future husbands (Safilios-Rothschild, 1977).

Male-dominated societies seem to permit men to use power to have sex with women while women are allowed to exercise power only to avoid sex with unsuitable partners. In such a society, a woman who uses power to seduce a man openly is regarded as "bad" and possibly dangerous. A man who uses power to avoid sex with a "turned-on" woman is regarded as "religious" at best, and inept, stupid, and unmanly at worst. This paper explores the extent to which this value system about power in sexual encounters survives in North American society.

## POLITICS OF COURTSHIP IN NORTH AMERICA

It would be difficult to describe adequately the conditions of North American society that have affected the status of women and, consequently, their sexual relations with men. Essentially, what happened is that the industrial system has become so successful during the last 70 years that men's and women's spheres of work have separated. Except for lower-class women and during times of war, many women were eliminated from the expanding workforce. Place of work and place of residence separated under industrialization, and for the "secure and successful" workforce, a man's paycheck became adequate for the support of the family (see Deckard, 1975, pp. 199–375). A "cult of domesticity" emerged (Degler, 1980), supposedly reigned over by women. This involved the attempt on the part of the middle class to upgrade (professionalize) full-time housework.

Such developments were not without strains, which have become especially noticeable within the last 25 years. Middle-class women became dissatisfied with the "gilded cage"—the house—in the midst of their declining and unrewarded domestic functions. More educated than ever before and trying their best to manage while the family's income was eaten away by inflation, housewives did not find their lot easy. As a more companionate marriage of equality became the ideal, middle-class homemakers became even more sharply aware of their unhappiness.

Divorce, when it did break the trap, sometimes resulted in more difficulties than it solved. Outside employment or going back to college also posed dilemmas for women. Domestic duties could be reduced but not completely eliminated (Davidson & Kramer-Gordon, 1979); instead of having one job, working and student mothers now had two. Eager to pacify insecure husbands, employed women retained major responsibility for child care and housework (Berkove, 1979; Hooper, 1979; Pleck, 1979).

Just as the balance of power between the genders influences sexual relations in other cultures, North American women's subordinate economic and political status severely limits their sexual freedom. It should come as no surprise that the "battle of the sexes" in the living room spills over into the bedroom.

Although it is less severe in North America than in the Third World, a double standard—unfavorable to women's premarital and extramarital sexual expression, while favorable to such expression by men—has prevailed. Admittedly, this standard is looser than in the past (Hopkins, 1977; Komarovsky, 1976; Peplau, Rubin, & Hill, 1977). Also, it is important to remember that the double standard is stronger among white, lower-middle-class people. It is rare among certain ethnic or racial groups, including working-class U.S. blacks, who do not stigmatize children who are borne out of wedlock (Broderick, 1979; Scanzoni & Scanzoni, 1976). Here, too, women's relative power outside of sexual relationships is important. Although economically oppressed in their own right, lower-class black women are less dependent on men for their livelihood than are white women. Consequently, they may enjoy sex for its own sake rather than expecting it to be an economic bargaining tool (Coleman, 1966).

Unlike their lower-class black counterparts, middle-class white women use sex as a bargaining tool with some hazard to themselves because of the lingering double standard. Specifically, they are tacitly expected to exchange sexual and emotional companionship for economic support from men (Scanzoni, 1970, pp. 4–25). The sexual revolution hasn't changed matters much. Instead of waiting until she marries the "right man" before having sex, today's middle-class woman waits until she *finds* the "right man" to have *premarital* sex (Hunt, 1974).

For some, the goal of courtship continues to be finding the right man to marry. Such arrangements give women veto power over sex and thus a bargaining lever for other things for which sex might be exchanged. The extent to which this veto power operates successfully, or even the desirability of that kind of power in the first place (as compared to true independence and initiative power), can be questioned (Gillespie, 1971, p. 448). Nevertheless, current researchers continue to find that women are less interested in having sex than men (Mancini & Orthner, 1978; Mercer & Kohn, 1979) and have greater power than men when a couple makes the decision to abstain from sexual intercourse (Peplau et al., 1977). If men are really more enthusiastic about sex, it is likely that the traditional pattern of bargaining continues.

## CHANGING BOUNDARIES OF COURTSHIP

Not all North American women view sex as a bargaining tool for finding men who will take care of them. Courtship patterns are changing and these changes could alter the balance of power between the genders. The decrease in the number of people marrying early and staying married weakens the once close connection between successful courtship and marriage. Courtship now occurs for a variety of other purposes, such as for having "a good time," for sexual release only, and for proving one's competence and status. Nevertheless, these changes in themselves may not lead to substantial social change.

The sexual politics of courtship may be especially resistant to change because couples beginning to court often engage in posing—the tendency to fall back on those gender roles that are stereotypically appropriate or safe (Heiss, 1968, p. 82). For example, even if such stereotyped behavior is uncharacteristic, a woman might be careful to appear as sweet and unassertive as possible on the first date so as to make a good impression.

In the next two major sections of this paper, we question the extent to which "posing" continues in sexual encounters (in bars, bedrooms, or the back seats of cars). The following types of questions arise:

1. Do men and women desire (seek) different types of benefits, satisfactions and goals in the courtship process, and if so, what are they, and who actually achieves them?
2. Who may touch whom, and how or where?
3. When sex and sexual signaling occur, to what extent do the values of the society and the gender roles disadvantage one or the other pary in the form, content, timing of the acts or in the benefits to be derived?

## DYNAMICS OF DATING

Despite some speculation that the traditional date is disappearing (Murstein, 1980, p. 780), dating remains a crucial part of courtship for many young people (Bell, 1979, p. 49), although now, with more mixed gender places available and more casualness as the norm; people don't date as much, or they just call it "going out." Dating enables courting partners to get away from their parents and have the opportunity to know each other better. However, there is more to dating than just being alone together. Dating is also a bargaining process in which the man provides certain goods and services in exchange for others provided by the woman. In other words, dating is similar to marriage because it requires negotiations to take place. Perhaps this point would be much clearer if we analyze how the genders use power on the typical date. The best and most enjoyable way to do this is to imagine a traditional date.

When we imagine the classic North American date, the following narration comes to mind. On Tuesday, Herbert Dumple makes the first move. He calls Mildred Smedly, doing his best to sound sophisticated and desirable over the telephone. Herbert asks Mildred out for the following Saturday. Mildred accepts, especially impressed that he phoned a few days in advance. She assesses that this means that Herbert *values* her. She might have refused, even if she had nothing to do but wash her hair, if he phoned only one day before.

On Saturday, Herbert arrives at Mildred's home promptly at 7 P.M. He is neatly attired in a sports jacket and dress slacks. His neat appearance brings home the fact that he values Mildred (jogging shoes and old jeans would be a "putdown") and that he himself is valuable. Herbert's middle-class status or aspirations are clear from his respectable appearance. In other words, he looks like a "good catch."

Mildred isn't ready yet, accidentally on purpose. Consequently, Herbert has about ten minutes to chat with her family. He sits on the loveseat, somewhat anxious about making a good impression, and tries to sound intelligent and responsible. Meanwhile, Mildred's Mom and Dad look him over. The assessment process is so critical that the family has turned off the television set and are even checking out Herbert's manners, asking, "Would you like a snack while you wait?"

Mildred finally comes down to the living room at 7:10 P.M. However, perhaps we are jumping the gun. Before we describe her entrance, it might be useful to speculate about her reasons for being late. Actually, Mildred has two reasons for taking her time, both of which are relevant to our previous discussion of courtship as a bargaining process. First, by being late, she has more time to make herself attractive (put on makeup, fix her hair, make sure she has chosen the right outfit). Second, by being late, she is telling Herbert that she is a valuable person, a woman *worth* waiting for.

At last, Mildred comes down the stairs from her room. She looks "beautiful," at least according to Herbert and her father. Some parent-child negotiations take place concerning where the couple is going and when Mildred can be expected home. "Oh, Mom!" she says, "Can't you trust me?" Finally, the awkward process is over, and Herbert escorts Mildred to his car. He opens the door for her, an excellent example of the posing we described earlier.

Mildred is relieved that Herbert has a car. This increases his marketability. Apparently, he might have some money. She dislikes dating men who expect her to travel on the bus. After all, dates are potential husbands, and it is important to find a good provider.

Mildred and Herbert go to dinner. Again, Herbert provides evidence of his potential as a good provider by taking her somewhere expensive and paying for their meals. Furthermore, he shows that he is appropriately masculine (posing again) by ordering their meals and taking responsibility for assessing the quality of the wine.

During dinner, Mildred tries her best to be a good conversationalist. This means that she asks Herbert about school or his job, focusing on *his* interests and trying her best to sound enthusiastic. Mildred's selfless concern for Herbert's interests is not accidental. After all, she wants to present herself as a valuable person, a potential spouse. She has already established that she is attractive ("beautiful"); her market value could only increase if she also seems empathic and emotionally supportive.

After dinner, the couple goes to Herbert's apartment. He has carefully made sure that his roommates are out so that the two of them can be alone. Mildred and Herbert smoke a couple of joints and share a small bottle of imported wine. Then Herbert begins to make some sexual moves. Now Mildred must make a choice. It is up to Mildred (the woman) to decide "how far to go" (Peplau, Rubin, & Hill, 1977).

Back in the 1950s, Mildred would probably have gone along with Herbert until they engaged in heavy petting. She would have been unlikely to have had sexual intercourse. In those days, many women remained "technical virgins" until marriage because coital experience would have "cheapened them" or decreased their market value for marriage.

The values of the 1950s are over, however. These are the 1980s. More and more women, including young adolescents, are having sex before marriage. Today, a woman's market value might be increased by being a good lover (providing, of course, that she has sex with only one man at a time in a relationship). There are still strong prejudices against women who have many partners.

If Mildred really likes Herbert (she may convince herself she loves him), she will probably have sex. However, she will let Herbert make most of the moves. Although it is acceptable for today's woman to have sex, it is still risqué for her to ask for it.

Mildred and Herbert do have sex. Before they straighten out their hair and clothing, trying to look innocent for the benefit of parents, it is appropriate to analyze the power implications behind Mildred's decision to have sex. Mildred's potential power during her sexual encounter depends heavily on her age. If she is a young adolescent, she is probably trading off sex for Herbert's esteem. Indeed, if this is the case, Mildred may have traditional gender-role attitudes and be looking toward Herbert to fulfill multiple dependency and status needs (Scanzoni & Fox, 1980). Young adolescent women who wait until they are older before having sex often have higher self-esteem and more profeminist attitudes than their more coitally experienced peers (Cvetkovich et al., 1978; Larkin, 1979; Scanzoni & Fox, 1980).

Putting on your Sherlock Holmes hats, you may be confused at this point. How could Mildred be a young teenager? Wasn't she able to order wine at the restaurant? Well, if Mildred wasn't "passing" as an older woman, you have a good point. More importantly, the power implications of having sex are completely different for older, college-age women. If Mildred is a college student, having sex suggests that she feels good about herself. In contrast with younger women, sexually active college women are more independent, autonomous, assertive, and profeminist than their less sexually active peers (Scanzoni and Fox, 1980).

## DATING, POWER, AND EQUITY

Our description of Herbert and Mildred's date provides some insight into how men's and women's different interests are reflected in their experience of power during courtship. Equity theory, which predicts that people prefer relationships in which each party receives equal relative gains (Hatfield & Traupmann, 1980), is useful at this point. Will Mildred and Herbert become a couple? Will they feel secure enough about each other to have sex again? Will Herbert and Mildred eventually have a long-term relationship?

According to equity theory, people in inequitable (or "unfair") relationships (both those receiving too little and those receiving too much) become distressed enough to either balance or end the relationship. According to equity theory, then, Herbert and Mildred will be likely to seek a balanced or fair relationship, especially if they have already made a heavy investment in one another (Walster, Walster, & Berscheid, 1978, p. 6).

As their dating relationship develops, if either Herbert or Mildred feels that he or she is getting a "raw" deal, the injured party will use power ploys to achieve a better position. For example, if Herbert "cheats" on Mildred by sleeping with another woman, she will let him have it during an argument. Mildred will continue to feel distressed until Herbert makes it up to her for cheating, perhaps by being especially considerate or even by purchasing an engagement ring. Such actions would help balance the relationship and would lead to greater happiness for both members of the couple (Hatfield and Traupmann, 1980).

Suppose, however, that Mildred's power ploys have failed. Despite her entreaties, Herbert goes out with even more women. Her friends tell her that he is sleeping around with everyone. Moreover, Herbert is into drugs quite heavily and appears to have become an insensitive lout. Unless she can convince herself that she deserves such treatment (alas, some women do this and stay around), Mildred may end or withdraw from what has become an unsatisfactory relationship. Inequitable relationships are unstable. Both the overbenefited, cheating Herbert and the underbenefited, jealous Mildred are not satisfied with the way things are going (Hatfield & Traupmann, 1980). Motivated by anger and guilt, such people would be more likely than equitable couples to use power ploys or attempt to end their relationships (see Walster, & Traupmann, 1978).

Another important issue for Herbert and Mildred is their evaluation of each other's value or marketability with different dating partners. As described earlier, Herbert and Mildred are constantly assessing each other and themselves. Early on, even Mildred's parents get into the act. This evaluation process continues throughout their relationship. Herbert and Mildred are more likely to stay together if they are well-matched in age, intelligence, educational plans, and good looks (Hill, Rubin, & Peplau, 1976).

Finally, equity theory is relevant to the quality of Herbert and Mildred's sex life together. They are more likely to continue having sex if neither partner feels "ripped off" or overbenefited. Actually, having sex in the first place suggests that this couple feels they are a good match. Couples in inequitable relationships are more likely to stop before "going all the way" (Walster, Walster, & Traupmann, 1978, p. 89). Even more relevant to power during sexual encounters, Mildred and Herbert will have very different feelings about *why* they had sex, depending on whether their relationship is equitable or unfair. If Herbert and Mildred truly make up after their argument about Herbert's affair, they will say that they had sex because *both* wanted to, citing reasons such as "mutual physical desire" and "enjoyment" (Walster, Walster, & Traupmann, 1978, p. 89). On the other hand, if their sexual relationship continues, despite the fact that Mildred still feels she is getting the short end of the stick, sex too would be seen as unfair. Herbert, for example, might feel that Mildred obliged him to make love to her to apologize for his indiscretion. In contrast, if Herbert wanted sex more than Mildred, she might blame him for taking advantage of her here, too.

## STRATEGIES FOR INITIATING NEW RELATIONSHIPS

The discussion of equity theory helps explain the balance of power in long-term relationships. However, it provides very little information about how people actually use power, especially in beginning new relationships. Focusing first on flirtation and then on the process during which one person asks another for a date, we will discuss *how* men and women actually use power with new dating partners.

### Flirtation

A flirtation "is a sequence of behavior, mostly nonverbal, which brings two people into increasing sociosexual intimacy" (Perper & Fox, 1980a, p. 23). To date, the best research on what actually happens during flirtation (as opposed to what people think happens) is by Timothy Perper and Susan Fox.

Clocking over 300 hours of observations of working-class and middle-class single people of varying ages in New Jersey and New York City bars, Perper and Fox have overturned two of our most beloved cultural myths. The first overturned cultural myth is that the man is always the sexual aggressor, eagerly pressing himself on the coy but reluctant woman. At least in the beginning of the flirtation process, men do not "swarm around a woman like bees about a lump of sugar." Instead, the woman often makes the first move. Because her move is subtle—usually nothing more than standing close to her target—it is understandable that the man might erroneously come to believe that *he* started the interaction.

According to the second overturned myth, men know more about flirtations and sex than women. In glaring contrast with this expectation, women are the experts:

> Typically, women are exquisitely familiar with what occurs during flirtations while men are generally quite ignorant. Women can describe in great detail how they and other women flirt and pick up men, and what men do (and just as frequently, what men *do not* do). In contrast, . . . [most] men were unfamiliar with all or most of the events of flirtations. Even quite successful men had no idea how they attracted women and what happened during a flirtation. Often men create vast and complex theories . . . but they seem to possess little or no information. [Perper & Fox, 1980b, p. 4]

Now that we have established that women know more about flirting, at least in bars, it is still appropriate to ask, "Which gender has the most power?" Egalitarians should be delighted to know that flirtations are not under the control of one person. Instead, both genders have equal power.

A successful flirtation is one that will probably result in a new dating or sexual relationship. Such a flirtation depends on the influence or target signaling that the flirt's influence attempts are welcome at *each* stage of the flirtation. To clarify this, we have described the stages of a flirtation in Figure 1.

As you can see, neither gender dominates a successful flirtation. Indeed, it is hard to separate the influencing agent from the influencee. Each person takes a turn at influencing the partner and at signaling that the other's influence attempts are welcome. As the couple's relationship becomes more secure, flirtation strategies become more obvious:

> [A woman] commonly touches the man before he touches her. Her touch is made, typically with the palm of the hand flat, and not with the fingertips, in a light, fleeting and pressing gesture. . . . She might brush against him with her hip or back, she may lean on him briefly, or she might brush against him while she turns to look at something. An alternative is for the woman to remove an otherwise nonexistent piece of lint from the man's jacket (men's jackets in bars collect such lint very readily). [Perper & Fox, 1980a, p. 18]

An important aspect of touching is that it is safe, in that it can be interpreted as accidental. This saves face for the influencing agent should the flirtation prove unsuccessful. Touching during flirtation is similar to body language, a popular strategy for both men and women when they approach a date to have sexual intercourse (McCormick, 1979). This strategy relates to a point made earlier: less obvious kinds of sexual power may be preferred because they are subtle enough to convince a partner that he or she wanted what happened just as much as the influencing agent did.

**Asking for a Date**

As you recall, Herbert Dumple asked Mildred Smedly out. North American gender-role norms are rather strict about who initiates a date. The traditional woman can, at most, make herself attractive. She is not allowed to call the man or start a new relationship. In contrast, the traditional man (shy or not) is responsible for initiating any and all relationships with women. Does the man still have all the power when it comes to initiating a new dating relationship? Perhaps not. Current research sheds light on this issue.

FIGURE 1. *Flirtation in Bars (note that either gender may initiate a flirtation—power is shared; neither partner dominates the outcome)*

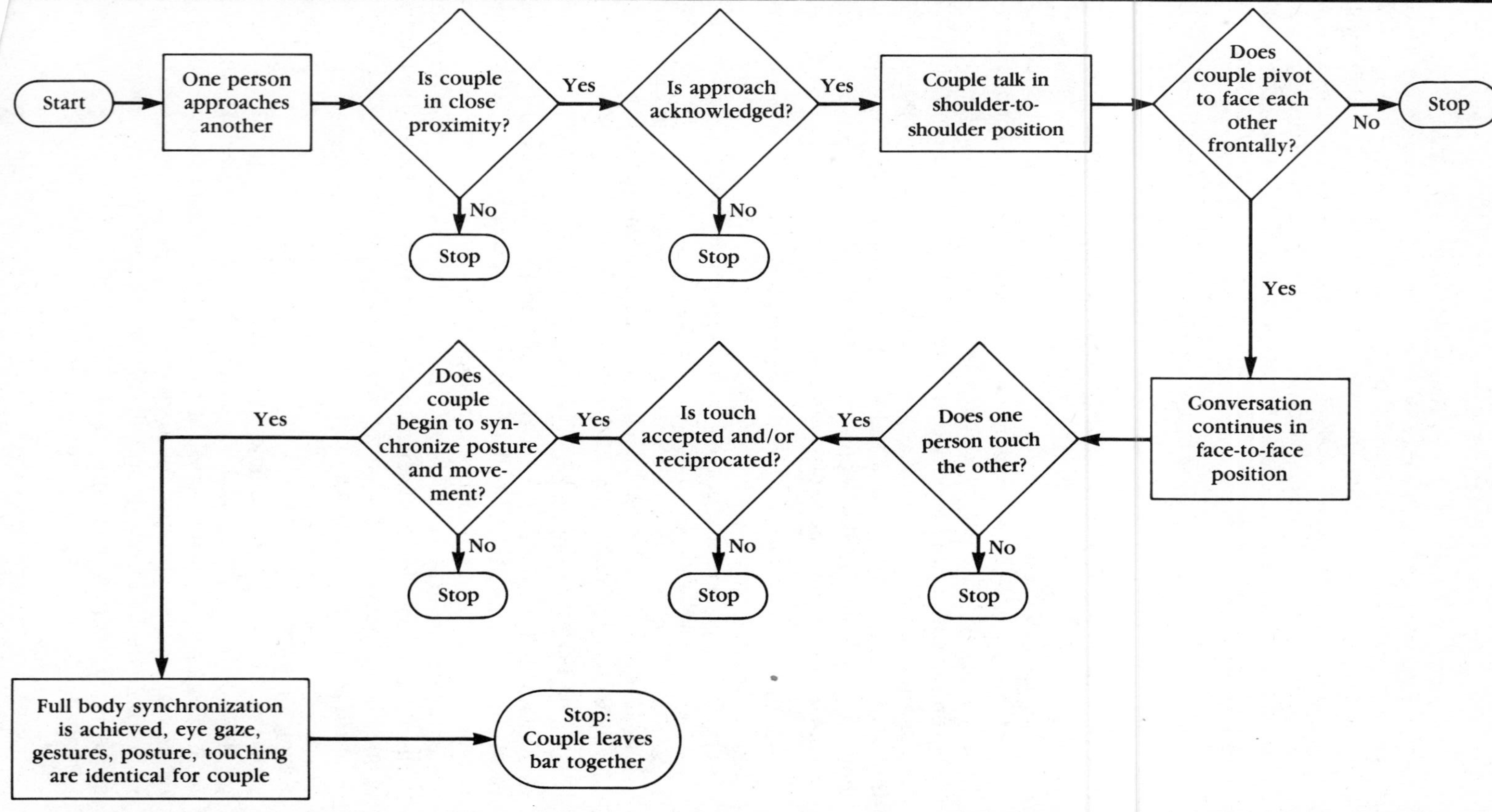


Source: Elizabeth Rice Allgeier and Naomi B. McCormack, *Changing Boundaries: Gender Roles and Sexual Behavior*, figure 3–1, p. 77. © 1983, Palo Alto, Calif., Mayfield Publishing Company. Reprinted by permission.

Research fails to clarify whether or not women take more assertive roles in dating than in the past. Nevertheless, there are strong indications that traditional gender-role norms prevail. Men are more likely to say that they would initiate new heterosexual relationships than women are (Green & Sandos, 1980). Moreover, both gender-typed and androgynous college students report that men typically initiate dates and pay for expenses incurred on dates (Allgeier, 1981).

Men still have most of the power when it comes to initiating new dating relationships. However, not everyone is happy with this situation. Already, some college students are pushing for change (see Allgeier, 1981). Liberals are experimenting with innovative dating patterns. Androgynous people, especially men, tend to have more experiences with female-initiated dates than do gender-typed individuals. Also, some men express dissatisfaction with the traditional date. Men are more positive about women initiating and paying for dates than women are.

In any event, the times may be ripe for change. A recent study at a southern university suggests that college men welcome female sexual initiation. In this study, women students approached strangers with this line: "I have been noticing you around campus. I find you very attractive." After saying this, most of the women are extremely successful in gaining men's verbal compliance with requests to go out on dates, to go to the women's apartments, and especially to go to bed with the women (Clark & Hatfield, 1981). Apparently, more than a few college men enjoy being propositioned. However, as we shall see, wishes aren't always realities.

Women are well advised to be cautious when contemplating whether or not to ask men out. The gender-role norms for male initiative in courtship are far from dead. When college students are asked how they feel about someone who either starts a friendly conversation or invites a co-worker to dinner at a restaurant, responses are stereotyped (Green & Sandos, 1980). Both men and women feel that it is more appropriate for the man than for the woman to take the initiative in either situation. Perhaps this helps explain why women are so conservative. Not surprisingly, women are more positive about men initiating dates than men are (Allgeier, 1981).

There is more to power in courtship than asking someone out. People also have the power to refuse. Women are more pragmatic than men about courtship. They want to size men up before commiting themselves to relationships. Moreover, the double standard may still be operating. Women may be especially reluctant to go along with a man's sexual advances when he comes on "too strong." Clark & Hatfield's (1981) study supports this idea. When men ask strangers on a college campus for dates, they are successful. However, when they ask the new acquaintances to go to their apartments or go to bed with them, they are not greeted with the warm enthusiasm that men give women for these same requests. Instead, most are flatly refused, with such responses as "You've got to be kidding" or "What is wrong with you? Leave me alone" (p.17).

### Changing Boundaries of Dating

We may conclude at this point that North American courtship is not as rigidly bound to the double standard as many of us suspected. Traditional gender-role norms are being challenged in three ways. First, with the exception of young adolescents, sexually active women are not exploited by men. Instead, the coitally experienced woman is likely to be independent and profeminist. Also, she is unlikely to have sex outside of an equitable or balanced relationship. Second, men are not the experts when it comes to picking up dates. If knowledge is power, then women are more powerful than men when it comes to signaling men with whom they would like to become better acquainted. Finally, although it is not known if women are asking men out more than in the past, the times are ripe for change. Some men are highly receptive to women's invitations for dates and sex (Hite, 1981). Probably, the main thing that holds women back is the continued stereotype that such behavior is unfeminine or inappropriate.

Courtship has changed, at least in its preliminary stages. However, what happens once a couple does have sex? In the remainder of this paper, we focus more specifically on the relationship between men and women during sexual intercourse. We also further identify and document the sexual value system—society's evolving rules for playing the courtship game.

## ROLES AND POWER DURING SEXUAL INTIMACY

In general, dominant and extroverted people report engaging in more varied sexual behavior and with more frequency than submissive, introverted people (De Martino, 1963; Eysenck, 1971, 1972; Maslow, 1963). Extroverts of both genders are more likely than passive individuals to be sexual nonconformists, willing to deviate from expected gender roles in their sexual encounters. For example, unlike her passive counterpart, the dominant and extroverted woman may be more likely to take the active sexual role. She is also more willing to experiment with nontraditional coital positions, such as being on top of her partner during sex.

Traditionally, women have been expected to play a relatively passive role in sexual encounters in our own and in some other societies (Ford & Beach, 1951; Rainwater, 1971; Rubin, 1976, pp. 134–154). It is no accident that the stereotype of the sexually passive woman is consistent with both the sexual double standard we have alluded to previously and our culture's idealization of the "passive-receptive" woman (Broverman et al., 1972; McKee & Sherriffs, 1957; Rosenkrantz et al., 1968).

Consistent with the double standard and idealization of the passive-receptive woman, most dating and married couples report that a woman seldom actively initiates a couple's first intercourse (Peplau, Rubin, & Hill, 1977). Generally, the woman is less likely to initiate sex than the man (Bell, 1976; Carlson, 1976; Crain & Roth, 1977). These findings still leave many questions unanswered, however. For example, the need to look feminine might lead a woman to overlook or forget some subtle strategies she uses to give her partner the idea that *he* wants sex. What are the politics of deciding whether and how to have sexual intercourse?

**Seduction and Rejection**

Historically, the whole scenario of the sexual encounter, from initiation and timing to positioning of the bodies, was expected to be initiated by men (Long-Laws, 1979). In contrast, the woman has been expected either to passively go along with men's sexual advances or to refuse to have sex (Ehrman, 1959; Gagnon & Simon, 1973; Komarovsky, 1976; Peplau, Rubin & Hill, 1976, 1977).

Young people's sexual vocabularies characterize men as sexual actors and women as sexual objects. According to Sanders and Robinson (1979, p. 28), women describe the penis with "cute little euphemisms" such as "Oscar," "penie," "ding-a-ling," and "babymaker." In contrast, young men are more likely to use power slang such as "womp," "rod," "pistol," and "stick." Similarly, men use slang for sexual intercourse, such as "poking," "stroking a hole," and "hosing," suggesting that men perceive sex as demonstrations of power. Their language contrasts strongly with women's vague, passive, and romantic images of sex: "doing it," "being inside," "going all the way," and "loving."

Women's typical words for describing sexuality (that is "penis," "vagina," and "make love") reveal attitudinal constraints that contrast strongly with men's verbal flexibility. Unlike women, men are able to communicate about sex with a variety of audiences (Sanders & Robinson, 1979). Less free to talk about sex, women may also feel less free to be sexual actors than are men.

On the other hand, women may feel more comfortable about being sexual actors than they did in the past. A large proportion of both men and women in ongoing relationships report persuading their partners to have sex using such straight-forward approaches as touching, snuggling, kissing, allowing their hands to wander, and asking directly (Jesser, 1978). When asked how men response to their sexual advances, women who ask directly to have sex are *not* more likely to report being rebuffed than those who fail to report asking directly. Predictably, women who are opposed to female sexual modesty and the need for women to pursue their interests inconspicuously are especially likely to consider directly asking their dates to have sex. Equally predictable, men whose partners had directly asked them to have sexual relations are also those who disagreed with the view that women must regard their bodies more modestly than men. These same men are especially likely to disagree with the position that men's dominant interest in women is sexual (Jesser, 1978).

Could sexual role playing be on the wane among today's courting couples? Another study finds strong similarities between men's and women's use of influence in sexual encounters. When asked how they would influence a date to have sex in a hypothetical sexual encounter, both male and female college students prefer indirect strategies. For instance, one student said, "I would test my limits by holding hands, sitting closer to this person, etc." (McCormick, 1979, p. 199). As you recall, using touch as an approach is also popular in flirtations.

Indirect strategies are preferred for good reasons. In their very subtlety, these strategies provide the influencing agent with a haven from possible rejection. For example, imagine that Mildred Smedly uses another indirect approach—environmental manipulation—to influence Herbert Dumple to have sex. After doing her best to set the stage for sex by dimming the lights, providing some liquor, and playing sensual music on the stereo, she is shocked when Herbert makes fun of her. Fortunately, her strategy permits her to avoid the hot seat when Herbert ridicules her.

**Herbert** (in challenging voice): Mildred, are you coming on to me?
**Mildred** (firmly): No, Herbert. I just like that record a lot. Also, candlelight is good for my eyes after a long day of typing my term paper.

Clearly, indirect strategies are useful for having sex. However, seduction, a highly direct and arousal-oriented strategy, is also popular with both men and women for influencing a hypothetical partner to have sex. Here are two quotes from students' essays describing how they would seduce their dates (McCormick, author's file):

> [Female college student:] I would start caressing his body and start kissing his chest, maybe stomach. I would try to be very sexy; doing this especially with lots of eye contact. Probably a few sighs here and there to let him know I feel sexually stimulated. This would probably be all I would do aside from wearing something slinky and bare. I could not get myself to perhaps start unbuckling his pants.
>
> [Male college student:] I would proceed to use my charm and bodily contact to get what I want. (1) If she shys away in a huff, I would stop and try to talk it out. If we got nowhere from there, I would take my ass home. (2) If she gives me the come on, then I would proceed very vigorously. (3) If she pushed away gently, I would tell her what a good time we had, that we are not children, and since we relate so well, we should "Get it on."

Consistent with the stereotype that men are sexual actors and women are sex objects, men say they would use seduction significantly more than women say they would. However, both genders prefer seduction over all other strategies for influencing a potential partner to have sex. Women are clearly capable of experiencing men as sex objects.

Gender differences also disappear when college students are asked how they would avoid sexual intercourse with a turned-on partner. Both men and women prefer direct, obvious strategies. Moralizing—using religious convictions or moral opposition to argue against having sex—is one such strategy. As one volunteer put it, "I would state directly that that type of relationship is reserved for marriage" (McCormick, 1979, p. 199).

Clearly, some of today's young singles are breaking out of sexual role playing. At any rate, the previously discussed findings suggest that male and female college students have the *potential* to enjoy courtship interactions that are free of gender-role stereotypes. Nevertheless, egalitarian readers should be advised to hold their applause. It is important to note that regardless of their gender-role attitudes, the overwhelming majority of college students stereotype men as using all possible strategies to have sex and women as using every strategy in the book to avoid having sex (LaPlante, McCormick, & Brannigan, 1980; McCormick, 1976, 1979). If such stereotyping persists, it is likely that students believe that others want them to engage in sexual role playing and that such behavior will be common with future dating partners.

In contrast with their lack of sexual role playing when asked what they would do within hypothetical sexual encounters with imaginary or future partners, students report strict adherence to gender-role stereotypes during their *actual* courtship experiences. When describing their personal use of power via various strategies, men use strategies significantly more than women do to influence dates to have sex, and women use strategies significantly more than men do when the goal is avoiding sexual intercourse. Complementing this finding, when asked to describe their experiences as influences within sexual encounters, men are more likely than women to report being influenced by all strategies for avoiding sex. Also, women report being more likely than men to be influenced by the majority of strategies for having sex (LaPlante, McCormick, & Brannigan, 1980; McCormick, 1977).

The continued importance of gender roles in sexual encounters is supported by the fact that a higher proportion of women than men say that they use extraordinarily subtle or indirect signals to indicate their sexual interest. For instance, they report using eye contact, changes of appearance or clothing, and changes in tone of voice. Could it be that these women are fearful of "turning off" their partners if they are more sexually assertive? Consistent with such an opinion, many women are hesitant about being assertive with dates with whom they want to have sex, perceiving this as unacceptable to men. Ironically, women may be holding themselves back sexually more than men would desire. Relatively unoffended by sexually assertive women (Jesser, 1978), college men are more positive about women initiating sex than are women (Allgeier, 1981). Just as they would welcome greater female initiative in dating, men also desire more assertive sexual partners. For instance, many older men agree that "it's exciting when a woman takes the sexual initiative" (Tavris, 1978, p. 113).

Overall, the research on strategies for having and avoiding sex has disappointing implications for those who prefer sexual behavior liberated from gender roles. It may be that courtship is a bastion for the strict performance of stereotyped gender-role behavior.

## ARE THE RULES FOR COURTSHIP CHANGING?

The courtship game has changed in three ways. First, thanks to the weakening of the double standard and encouragement from feminists, women are freer to make the first move in a flirtation and to have premarital sex than in the past. Second, men seem to be encouraging women to be more assertive in initiating sexual relationships. Third, given the opportunity, men would reject sex and women would try to have sex with the same strategies that are characteristically used by the other gender.

Despite these changes, the courtship game continues to follow gender-role stereotypes. Men ask women out more than vice versa. Men are more likely to influence a date to have sex; women are morely likely to refuse sex. The persistence of gender-role playing is associated with a number of factors, such as women's more conservative attitudes toward sexuality. Another factor that contributes to the courtship game is that North American society views people who behave "out of role" (that is, passive men and assertive women) as less well adjusted and popular (Costrich et al., 1975).

As the women's liberation movement gains increasing acceptance, the courtship game will probably become less rigid. For instance, although women prefer masculine over feminine men, male college students are *not* more attracted to feminine women than they are to masculine women (Seyfried & Hendrick, 1973). Even more indicative of social change, recent research contradicts earlier reports (Goldberg, Gottesdiener, & Abramson, 1975; Johnson et al., 1978) that men are turned off by profeminist women. Johnson, Holborn, and Turcotte (1979) found that men were more attracted to women who support the feminist movement than they were to those who are described as nonsupporters. As attitudes toward feminist women become more liberal, people may try out more egalitarian ways of dealing with courtship. However, such experimentation is likely to be minimal at first because out-of-role behavior is especially risky within sexual encounters where people already feel emotionally vulnerable.

Some insight into future directions for male-female courtship is provided by a vocal and liberal group of physicians and sex therapists. In the past decade, a number of therapists have contributed their ideas in opinion articles with titles such as "Do men like women to be sexually assertive?," "Who should initiate sexual relations, husband or wife?" and "Who should take the sexual lead—the man or the woman?" In many of these articles, medical personnel and sex therapists indicate that they favor sexual equality in the bedroom for all but those few patients who would experience emotional turmoil as a result of such equality.

If the public continues to be exposed to these liberal ideas, values of future generations will slowly but surely change. It may not be overly optimistic to predict that college students in the year 2000 will be less likely to stereotype strategies for having sex as something only men would do and strategies for avoiding sex as something only women use. Before we get carried away with optimism, however, it is important to note that not all opinion leaders reject the sexist courtship game. Indeed, a powerful backlash by psychiatrists and other sex therapists has indicated that they are highly alarmed by the supposedly explosive impact of the women's liberation movement on power in the sexual encounter. According to this backlash, women who are assertive about sex endanger the security of otherwise solid relationships and make men neurotic, anxious, or insecure. Ruminating about the new impotence allegedly caused by sexually aggressive women, these conservative sex experts advise women to remain sexually passive in the bedroom or, at the very least, to be cautious when taking the sexual initiative with men (Ginsberg, Frosch, & Shapiro, 1972; also see F. Lemere's and G. Ginsberg's commentary in Kroop, 1978). Clearly, if the stereotyped courtship game does die, it will have an agonizing and elongated death rattle.

## REFERENCES


Allgeier, E. R., The influence of adrogynous identification on heterosexual relations. *Sex Roles,* 1981, 7, 321–330.

Bell, R. R. Changing aspects of marital sexuality. In S. Gordon and R. W. Libby (eds.), *Sexuality today and tomorrow.* Belmont, Calif.: Wadsworth, 1976.

Bell, R. R. *Marriage and the family interaction.* Chicago, Ill.: Dorsey Press, 1979

Bem, D. J. Self-perception theory. In L. Berkowitz (ed.), *Advances in experimental social psychology* (Vol. 6). New York: Academic Press, 1972.

Berkove, G. F. Perceptions of husband support by returning women students. *The Family Coordinator,* 1979, *28,* 451–458.

Broderick, C. B. *Marriage and the family.* Englewood Cliffs, N.J.: Prentice-Hall, 1979.

Broverman, I., Vogel, S., Broverman, D., Clarkson, F., & Rosenkrantz, P. Sex role stereotypes: A current appraisal. *Journal of Social Issues,* 1972, *28,* 59–78.

Carlson, J. The sexual role. In F. I. Nye (ed.), *Role structure and analysis of the family.* Beverly Hills, Calif.: Sage, 1976.

Clark, R. D., III, & Hatfield, E. *Gender differences in receptivity to sexual offers.* Unpublished manuscript, 1981. (Available from Dr. Elaine Hatfield, Psychology Department, 2430 Campus Road, Honolulu, HI 96822).

Coleman, J. S., Female status and premarital sexual codes. *American Journal of Sociology,* 1966, *72,* 217.

Collins, B. E., & Raven, B. H. Group structure: Attraction, coalition, communication, and power. In G. Lindzey & E. Aronson (eds.), *The handbook of social psychology* (2d ed., Vol. 4). Reading, Mass.: Addison-Wesley, 1968.

Costrich, N., Feinstein, J., Kidder, L., Maracek, J., & Pascale, L. When stereotypes hurt: Three studies of penalties for sex-role reversals. *Journal of Experimental Social Psychology,* 1975, *11,* 520–530.

Crain, S., & Roth, S. *Interactional and interpretive processes in sexual initiation in married couples.* Paper presented at the meeting of the American Psychological Association, San Francisco, August 1977.

Critchfield, R. Sex in the third world. In C. Gordon & G. Johnson (eds.), *Readings in human sexuality: Contemporary perspectives* (2d ed.). New York: Harper & Row, 1980.

Cvetkovich, G., Grote, B., Lieberman, E. J., & Miller, W. Sex role development and teenage fertility-related behavior. *Adolescence,* 1978, *13,* 231–236.

Davidson, L., & Kramer-Gordon, L. *The sociology of gender.* Chicago: Rand McNally, 1979.

Deckard, B. S. *The women's movement.* New York: Harper & Row, 1975.

Degler, C. *At odds: Women and family in America from the revolution to the present.* New York: Oxford University Press, 1980.

DeMartino, M. F. Dominance-feeling, security-insecurity, and sexuality in women. In M. F. DeMartino (ed.), *Sexual behavior and personality characteristics.* New York: Grove Press, 1963.

Ehrmann, W. *Premarital dating behavior.* New York: Holt, Rinehart, & Winston, 1959.

Eysenck, H. L. Introverts, extroverts, and sex. *Psychology Today,* 1971, *4,* 48–51, 82.

———. Personality and sexual behavior. *Journal of Psychosomatic Research,* 1972, *16,* 141–152.

Ford, C. S., & Beach, F. A. *Patterns of sexual behavior.* New York: Harper & Row, 1951.

French, J. R., Jr., & Raven, B. H. The bases of social power. In D. Cartwright (ed.), *Studies in social power.* Ann Arbor: University of Michigan Press, 1959.

Gagnon, J. H., & Simon, W. *Sexual conduct: The social sources of human sexuality.* Chicago: Aldine, 1973.

Gillespie, D. L. Who has the power? The marital struggle. *Journal of Marriage and the Family,* 1971, *33,* 445–458.

Ginsberg, G. L., Frosch, W. A., & Shapiro, T. The new impotence. *Archives of General Psychiatry,* 1972, *26,* 218–220.

Goldberg, P. A., Gottesdiener, M., & Abramson, P. R. Another put-down of women? Perceived attractiveness as a function of support for the feminist movement. *Journal of Personality and Social Psychology,* 1975, *32,* 113–115.

Gordon, M. The ideal husband as depicted in the nineteenth-century marriage manual. In E. H. Pleck & J. H. Pleck (eds.), *The American Man.* Englewood Cliffs, N.J.: Prentice-Hall, 1980.

Green, S. K., & Sandos, P. *Perceptions of male and female initiators of relationships.* Paper presented at the meeting of the American Psychological Association, Montreal, September 1980.

Hacker, H. M. Gender roles from a cross-cultural perspective. In L. Duberman (ed.), *Gender and sex in society.* New York: Praeger, 1975.

Hatfield, E., & Traupmann, J. Intimate relationships. A perspective from equity theory. In S. Duck & R. Gilmour (eds.), *Personal relationships.* London: Academic Press, 1980.

Heiss, J. (ed.), *Family roles and interaction.* Chicago: Rand McNally, 1968.

Hersch, B. G. A partnership of equals: Feminist marriages in 19th-century America. In E. H. Pleck & J. H. Pleck (eds.), *The American Man.* Englewood Cliffs, N.J.: Prentice-Hall, 1980.

Hill, C. T., Rubin, Z., & Peplau, L. A. Breakups before marriage: The end of 103 affairs. *Journal of Social Issues,* 1976, *32,* 147–168.

Hite, S. *The Hite report on male sexuality.* New York: Knopf, 1981.

Hooper, J. O. My wife, the student. *Family Coordinator,* 1979, *28,* 459–464.

Hopkins, J. R. Sexual behavior in adolescence. *Journal of Social Issues,* 1977, *33,* 67–85.

Hunt, M. *Sexual behavior in the 1970s.* Chicago: Playboy Press, 1974.

Jesser, C. J. Women in society: Some academic perspectives and the issues therein. *International Journal of Sociology of the Family,* 1972, *2,* 246–259.

———. Male responses to direct verbal sexual initiatives of females. *Journal of Sex Research,* 1978, *14,* 118–128.

Johnson, R. W., Doiron, D., Brooks, G. P., & Dickinson, J. Perceived attractiveness as a function of support for the feminist movement: Not necessarily a put-down of women. *Canadian Journal of Behavioral Science,* 1978, *10,* 214–221.

Johnson, R. W., Holborn, S. W., & Turcotte, S. Perceived attractiveness as a function of active vs. passive support for the feminist movement. *Personality and Social Psychology Bulletin,* 1979, *5,* 227–230.

Kinsey, A. C., Pomeroy, W. B., Martin, C. E., & Gebhard, P. H. *Sexual behavior in the human female.* Philadelphia: Saunders, 1953.

Komarovsky, M. *Dilemmas of masculinity: A study of college youth.* New York: Norton, 1976.

Kroop, M. When women initiate sexual relations. *Medical Aspects of a Human Sexuality,* 1978, 12, 16, 23, 28–29.

LaPlante, M., McCormick, N., & Brannigan, G. Living the sexual script: College students' views of influence in sexual encounters. *Journal of Sex Research,* 1980, *16,* 338–355.

Larkin, R. *Suburban youth in cultural conflict.* New York: Oxford University Press, 1979.

Leibowitz, L. *Females, males, families: A biosocial approach.* Belmont, Calif.: Wadsworth, 1978.

Long-Laws, J. *The second X: Sex role and social role.* New York: Elsevier, North Holland, 1979.

Mancini, J. A., and Orthner, D. K. Recreational sexuality preferences among middle-class husbands and wives. *Journal of Sex Research,* 1978, *14,* 96–106.

Maslow, A. H. Self-esteem (dominance feeling) and sexuality in women. In M. F. DeMartino (ed.), *Sexual behavior and personality characteristics.* New York: Grove Press, 1963.

McCormick, N. B. *Impact of sex and sex role on subjects' perceptions of social power in hypothetical sexual interactions.* Paper presented at the meeting of the Western Psychological Association, Los Angeles, April 1976.

———. Gender role and expected social power behavior in sexual decision-making (Doctoral dissertation, University of California at Los Angeles, 1976). *Dissertation Abstracts International,* 1977, *37,* 422-B. (University Microfilms No. 77–1646, 151)

———. Come-ons and put-offs: Unmarried students' strategies for having and avoiding sexual intercourse. *Psychology of Women Quarterly,* 1979, *4,* 194–211.

———. Author's files. Unpublished data, 1976. (Information available from N. McCormick, Ph.D., Department of Psychology, State University of New York College at Plattsburgh, Plattsburgh, NY 12901).

McKee, J., and Sherriffs, A. The differential evaluation of males and females. *Journal of Personality,* 1957, *25,* 356–371.

Mercer, G. W., and Kohn, P. M. Gender difference in the interpretation of conservatism, sex urges, and sexual behavior among college students. *Journal of Sex Research,* 1979, *15,* 129–142.

Murstein, B. I. Mate selection in the 1970s. *Journal of Marriage and the Family,* 1980, *42,* 777–792.

Peplau, L., Rubin, Z., and Hill, C. The sexual balance of power. *Psychology Today,* 1976, *10,* 142–147, 151.

———. Sexual intimacy in dating couples. *Journal of Social Issues,* 1977, *33,* 86–109.

Perper, T., and Fox, V. S. *Special focus: Flirtation behavior in public settings.* Paper presented at the meeting of the Eastern Region of the Society for the Scientific Study of Sex, Philadelphia, April 1980. (a)

———. *Flirtation and pickup patterns in bars.* Paper presented at the meeting of the Eastern Conference on Reproductive Behavior, New York, June 1980. (b)

Pleck, J. H. Men's family work: Three perspectives and some new data. *Family Coordinator,* 1979, *28,* 481–488.

Rainwater, L. Marital sexuality in four cultures of poverty. In D. S. Marshall and R. C. Suggs (eds.), *Human sexual behavior: Variations in the ethnographic spectrum.* New York: Basic Books, 1971.

Raven, B. H. Social influence and power. In I. D. Steiner & M. Fishbein (eds.), *Current studies in social psychology.* New York: Holt, Rinehart & Winston, 1965.

———. *The comparative analysis of power and power preference.* Paper presented at the meeting of the Albany Symposium on Power and Influence, Albany, New York, October 11–13, 1971.

Robinson, W. J. *Woman: Her sex and love life* (17th ed.). New York: Eugenics Publishing, 1929.

Rosenkrantz, P., Vogel, S., Bee, H., Broverman, I., and Broverman, D. Sex role stereotypes and self-concepts in college students. *Journal of Consulting and Clinical Psychology,* 1968, *32,* 287–295.

Rubin, L. B. *Worlds of pain: Life in the working class family.* New York: Basic Books, 1976.

Safilios-Rothschild, C. *Love, sex, and sex roles.* Englewood Cliffs, NJ: Prentice-Hall, Spectrum Books, 1977.

Sanders, J. S., & Robinson, W. L. Talking and not talking about sex: Male and female vocabularies. *Journal of Communication,* 1979, *29,* 22–30.

Scanzoni, J. H. *Opportunity and the family.* New York: Free Press, 1970.

Scanzoni, J. H., and Fox, G. L. Sex roles, family, and society: The 70s and beyond. *Journal of Marriage and the Family,* 1980, *42,* 743–756.

Scanzoni, L., and Scanzoni, J. H. *Men, women, and change.* New York: McGraw-Hill, 1976.

Seyfried, B. A., and Hendrick, C. When do opposites attract? When they are opposite in sex and sex-role attitudes. *Journal of Personality and Social Psychology,* 1973, *25,* 15–20.

Stephens, W. N. *The family in cross-cultural perspective.* New York: Holt, Rinehart & Winston, 1963.

Tavris, C. 40,000 men tell about their sexual behavior, their fantasies, the ideal woman, and their wives. *Redbook Magazine,* February 1978, pp. 111–113.

Walster, E., Walster, G. W., & Berscheid, E. *Equity theory and research.* Boston: Allyn & Bacon, 1978.

Walster, E., Walster, G. W., & Traupmann, J. Equity and premarital sex. *Journal of Personality and Social Psychology,* 1978, *36,* 82–92.

Weber, M. [The theory of social and economic organization] (A. M. Henderson and T. Parsons, eds. and trans.). New York: Free Press, 1964.

Zelnick, M. & Kantner, J. F. Sexual and contraceptive experience of young unmarried women in the United States, 1976 and 1971. *Family Planning Perspectives,* 1977, *9,* 55–71.

———. Reasons for nonuse of contraceptives by sexually active women aged 15–19. *Family Planning Perspectives,* 1979, *11,* 289–296.

———. Sexual activity, contraceptive use and pregnancy among metropolitan-area teenagers: 1971–1979. *Family Planning Perspectives*, 1980, *12,* 230–237.

# 12

WILLIAM J. GOODE

# The Theoretical Importance of Love

*Some sociologists have claimed that romantic love has emerged as an approved basis for marriage only in the United States, and in highly "Americanized" parts of the modern world. According to this view, the common American belief, as stated in a popular song of the 1950s, that "love and marriage go together like a horse and carriage," is historically unique; a far more common belief has held that romantic love and marriage are mutually exclusive. Proponents of this view point out that in the Age of Chivalry in eleventh- and twelfth-century Europe, when romantic love was perhaps first institutionalized and encouraged, the persons who experienced it were married—but not to one another.*

*In the following classic essay, William J. Goode argues that the truth is somewhat more complicated than these sociologists claim, although he agrees that the contemporary United States and a few other societies* are *unusual in the way they view love relationships.*

Source: William J. Goode. "The Theoretical Importance of Love," *American Sociological Review* 34, (1969), pp. 38–47. This paper was completed under a grant (no. M-2526-S) by the National Institute of Mental Health.

Because love often determines the intensity of an attraction[1] toward or away from an intimate relationship with another person, it can become one element in a decision or action.[2] Nevertheless, serious sociological attention has only infrequently been given to love. Moreover, analyses of love generally have been confined to mate choice in the Western World, while the structural importance of love has been for the most part ignored. The present paper views love in a broad perspective, focusing on the structural patterns by which societies keep in check the potentially disruptive effect of love relationships on mate choice and stratification systems.

## TYPES OF LITERATURE ON LOVE

For obvious reasons, the printed material on love is immense. For our present purposes, it may be classified as follows:

1. Poetic, humanistic, literary, erotic, pornographic: By far the largest body of all literature on love views it as a sweeping experience. The poet arouses our sympathy and empathy. The essayist enjoys, and asks the reader to enjoy, the interplay of people in love. The storyteller—Boccaccio, Chaucer, Dante—pulls back the curtain of human souls and lets the reader watch the intimate lives of others caught in an emotion we all know. Others—Vatsyayana, Ovid, William IX Count of Poitiers and Duke of Aquitaine, Marie de France, Andreas Capellanus— have written how-to-do-it books, that is, how to conduct oneself in love relations, to persuade others to succumb to one's love wishes, or to excite and satisfy one's sex partner.[3]

2. Marital counseling: Many modern sociologists have commented on the importance of romantic love in America and its lesser importance in other societies, and have disparaged it as a poor basis for marriage, or as immaturity. Perhaps the best known of these arguments are those of Ernest R. Mowrer, Ernest W. Burgess, Mabel A. Elliott, Andrew G. Truxal, Francis E. Merrill, and Ernest R. Groves.[4] The antithesis of romantic love, in such analyses, is "conjugal" love; the love between a settled, domestic couple.

---

[1]On the psychological level, the motivational power of both love and sex is intensified by this curious fact: (which I have not seen remarked on elsewhere) Love is the most projective of emotions, as sex is the most projective of drives; only with great difficulty can the attracted person believe that the object of his love or passion does not and will not reciprocate the feeling at all. Thus, the person may carry his action quite far, before accepting a rejection as genuine.

[2]I have treated decision analysis extensively in an unpublished paper by that title.

[3]Vatsyayana, *The Kama Sutra*, Delhi: Rajkamal, 1948; Ovid, "The Loves," and "Remedies of Love," in *The Art of Love,* Cambridge, Mass.: Harvard University Press, 1939; Andreas Capellanus, *The Art of Courtly Love*, translated by John J. Parry, New York: Columbia University Press, 1941; Paul Tuffrau, editor, *Marie de France: Les Lais de Marie de France,* Paris L'edition d'art, 1925; see also Julian Harris, *Marie de France*, New York: Institute of French Studies, 1930, esp. Chapter 3. All authors but the first *also* had the goal of writing literature.

[4]Ernest R. Mowrer, *Family Disorganization,* Chicago: The University of Chicago Press, 1927, pp. 158–165; Ernest W. Burgess and Harvey J. Locke, *The Family,* New York: American Book, 1953, pp. 436–437; Mabel A. Elliot and Francis E. Merrill, *Social Disorganization*, New York: Harper, 1950, pp. 366–384; Andrew G. Truxal and Francis E. Merrill, *The Family in American Culture,* New York: Prentice-Hall, 1947, pp. 120–124, 507–509; Ernest R. Groves and Gladys Hoagland Groves, *The Contemporary American Family*, New York: Lippincott, 1947, pp. 321–324.

A few sociologists, remaining within this same evaluative context, have instead claimed that love also has salutary effects in our society. Thus, for example, William L. Kolb[5] has tried to demonstrate that the marital counselors who attack romantic love are really attacking some fundamental values of our larger society, such as individualism, freedom, and personality growth. Beigel[6] has argued that if the female is sexually repressed, only the psychotherapist or love can help her overcome her inhibitions. He claims further that one influence of love in our society is that it extenuates illicit sexual relations; he goes on to assert: "Seen in proper perspective, [love] has not only done no harm as a prerequisite to marriage, but it has mitigated the impact that a too-fast-moving and unorganized conversion to new socio-economic constellations has had upon our whole culture and it has saved monogamous marriage from complete disorganization."

In addition, there is widespread comment among marriage analysts, that in a rootless society, with few common bases for companionship, romantic love holds a couple together long enough to allow them to begin marriage. That is, its functions to attract people powerfully together, and to hold them through the difficult first months of the marriage, when their different backgrounds would otherwise make an adjustment troublesome.

3. Although the writers cited above concede the structural importance of love implicitly, since they are arguing that it is either harmful or helpful to various values and goals of our society, a third group has given explicit if unsystematic attention to its structural importance. Here, most of the available propositions point to the functions of love, but a few deal with the conditions under which love relationships occur. They include:

1. An implicit or assumed descriptive proposition is that love as a common prelude to and basis of marriage is rare, perhaps to be found as a pattern only in the United States.
2. Most explanations of the conditions which create love are psychological, stemming from Freud's notion that love is "aim-inhibited sex."[7] This idea is expressed, for example, by Waller who says that love is an idealized passion which develops from the frustration of sex.[8] This proposition, although rather crudely stated and incorrect as a general explanation, is widely accepted.
3. Of course, a predisposition to love is created by the socialization experience. Thus some textbooks on the family devote extended discussion to the ways in which our society socializes for love. The child, for example, is told that he or she will grow up to fall in love with someone, and early attempts are made to pair the child with children of the

[5]William L. Kolb, "Sociologically Established Norms and Democratic Values," *Social Forces*, 26 (May, 1948), pp. 451–456.

[6]Hugo G. Beigel, "Romantic Love," *American Sociological Review*, 16 (June, 1951), pp. 326–334.

[7]Sigmund Freud, *Group Psychology and the Analysis of the Ego,* London: Hogarth, 1922, p. 72.

[8]Willard Waller, *The Family,* New York: Dryden, 1938, pp. 189–192.

opposite sex. There is much joshing of children about falling in love, myths and stories about love and courtship are heard by children, and so on.

4. A further proposition (the source of which I have not been able to locate) is that, in a society in which a very close attachment between parent and child prevails, a love complex is necessary in order to motivate the child to free him from his attachment to his parents.
5. Love is also described as one final or crystallizing element in the decision to marry, which is otherwise structured by factors such as class, ethnic origin, religion, education, and residence.
6. Parsons has suggested three factors which "underlie the prominence of the romantic context in our culture": (a) the youth culture frees the individual from family attachments, thus permitting him to fall in love; (b) love is a substitute for the interlocking of kinship roles found in other societies, and thus motivates the individual to conform to proper marital role behavior; and (c) the structural isolation of the family so frees the married partners' affective inclinations that they are able to love one another.[9]
7. Robert F. Winch has developed a theory of "complementary needs" which essentially states that the underlying dynamic in the process of falling in love is an interaction between (a) the perceived psychological attributes of one individual and (b) the complementary psychological attributes of the person falling in love, such that the needs of the latter are felt to be met by the perceived attributes of the former and *vice versa*. These needs are derived from Murray's list of personality characteristics. Winch thus does not attempt to solve the problem of why our society has a love complex, but how it is that specific individuals fall in love with each other rather than with someone else.[10]
8. Winch and others have also analyzed the effect of love upon various institutions or social patterns: Love themes are prominently displayed in the media of entertainment and communication, in consumption patterns, and so on.[11]

4. Finally, there is the cross-cultural work of anthropologists, who in the main have ignored love as a factor of importance in kinship patterns. The implicit understanding seems to be that love as a pattern is found only in the United States, although of course individual cases of love are sometimes recorded. The term "love" is practically never found in indexes of anthropological monographs on specific societies or in general anthropology textbooks. It is perhaps not an exaggeration to say that Lowie's comment of a generation ago would still be accepted by a substantial number of anthropologists:

---

[9]Talcott Parsons, *Essays in Sociological Theory,* Glencoe, Ill.: Free Press, 1949, pp. 187–189.

[10]Robert F. Winch, *Mate Selection*, New York: Harper, 1958.

[11]See, e.g., Robert F. Winch, *The Modern Family,* New York: Holt, 1952, Chapter 14.

> But of love among savages? . . . Passion, of course, is taken for granted; affection, which many travelers vouch for, might be conceded; but Love? Well, the romantic sentiment occurs in simpler conditions, as with us—in fiction. . . . So Love exists for the savage as it does for ourselves—in adolescence, in fiction, among the poetically minded.[12]

A still more skeptical opinion is Linton's scathing sneer:

> All societies recognize that there are occasional violent, emotional attachments between persons of opposite sex, but our present American culture is practically the only one which has attempted to capitalize these, and make them the basis for marriage. . . . The hero of the modern American movie is always a romantic lover, just as the hero of the old Arab epic is always an epileptic. A cynic may suspect that in any ordinary population the percentage of individuals with a capacity for romantic love of the Hollywood type was about as large as that of persons able to throw genuine epileptic fits.[13]

In Murdock's book on kinship and marriage, there is almost no mention, if any, of love.[14] Should we therefore conclude that, cross-culturally, love is not important, and thus cannot be of great importance structurally? If there is only one significant case, perhaps it is safe to view love as generally unimportant in social structure and to concentrate rather on the nature and functions of romantic love within the Western societies in which love is obviously prevalent. As brought out below, however, many anthropologists have in fact described love *patterns*. And one of them, Max Gluckman,[15] has recently subsumed a wide range of observations under the broad principle that love relationships between husband and wife estrange the couple from their kin, who therefore try in various ways to undermine that love. This principle is applicable to many more societies (for example, China and India) than Gluckman himself discusses.

## THE PROBLEM AND ITS CONCEPTUAL CLARIFICATION

The preceding propositions (except those denying that love is distributed widely) can be grouped under two main questions: What are the consequences of romantic love in the United States? How is the emotion of love aroused or created in our society? The present paper deals with the first question. For theoretical purposes both questions must be reformulated, however, since they implicitly refer only to our peculiar system of romantic love. Thus: (1) In what ways do various love patterns fit into the social structure, especially into the systems of mate choice and stratification? (2) What are the structural conditions under which a range of love patterns occurs in various societies? These

[12]Robert H. Lowie, "Sex and Marriage," in John F. McDermott, editor, *The Sex Problem in Modern Society,* New York: Modern Library, 1931, p. 146.

[13]Ralph Linton, *The Study of Man,* New York: Appleton-Century, 1936, p. 175.

[14]George Peter Murdock, *Social Structure*, New York: Macmillan, 1949.

[15]Max Gluckman, *Custom and Conflict in Africa*, Oxford: Basil Blackwell, 1955, Chapter 3.

are overlapping questions, but their starting points and assumptions are different. The first assumes that love relationships are a universal psychosocial possibility, and that different social systems make different adjustments to their potential disruptiveness. The second does not take love for granted, and supposes rather that such relationships will be rare unless certain structural factors are present. Since in both cases the analysis need not depend upon the correctness of the assumption, the problem may be chosen arbitrarily. Let us begin with the first.[16]

We face at once the problem of defining "love." Here, love is defined as a strong emotional attachment, a cathexis, between adolescents or adults of opposite sexes, with at least the components of sex desire and tenderness. Verbal definitions of this emotinonal relationship are notoriously open to attack; this one is no more likely to satisfy critics than others. Agreement is made difficult by value judgments: one critic would exclude anything but "true" love, another casts out "infatuation," another objects to "puppy love," while others would separate sex desire from love because sex presumably is degrading. Nevertheless, most of us have had the experience of love, just as we have been greedy, or melancholy, or moved by hate (defining "true" hate seems not to be a problem). The experience can be referred to without great ambiguity, and a refined measure of various degrees of intensity or purity of love is unnecessary for the aims of the present analysis.

Since love may be related in diverse ways to the social structure, it is necessary to forego the dichotomy of "romantic love—no romantic love" in favor of a continuum or range between polar types. At one pole, a strong love attraction is socially viewed as a laughable or tragic aberration; at the other, it is mildly shameful to marry without being in love with one's intended spouse. This is a gradation from negative sanction to positive approval, ranging at the same time from low or almost nonexistent institutionalization of love to high institutionalization.

The urban middle classes of contemporary Western society, especially in the United States, are found toward the latter pole. Japan and China, in spite of the important movement toward European patterns, fall toward the pole of low institutionalization. Village and urban India is farther toward the center, for there the ideal relationship has been one which at least generated love after marriage, and sometimes after betrothal, in contrast with the mere respect owed between Japanese and Chinese spouses.[17] Greece after Alexander, Rome of the Empire, and perhaps the later period of the Roman Republic as well, are near the center, but somewhat toward the pole of institutionalization, for love

---

[16]I hope to deal with the second problem in another paper.

[17]Tribal India, of course, is too heterogeneous to place in any one position on such a continuum. The question would have to be answered for each tribe. Obviously it is of less importance here whether China and Japan, in recent decades, have moved "two points over" toward the opposite pole of high approval of love relationships as a basis for marriage than that both systems as classically described viewed love as generally a tragedy; and love was supposed to be irrelevant to marriage, i.e., noninstitutionalized. The continuum permits us to place a system at some position, once we have the descriptive data.

matches appear to have increased in frequency—a trend denounced by moralists.[18]

This conceptual continuum helps to clarify our problem and to interpret the propositions reviewed above. Thus it may be noted, first, that individual love relationships may occur even in societies in which love is viewed as irrelevant to mate choice and excluded from the decision to marry. As Linton conceded, some violent love attachments may be found in any society. In our own, the Song of Solomon, Jacob's love of Rachel, and Michal's love for David are classic tales. The Mahabharata, the great Indian epic, includes love themes. Romantic love appears early in Japanese literature, and the use of Mt. Fuji as a locale for the suicide of star crossed lovers is not a myth invented by editors of tabloids. There is the familiar tragic Chinese story to be found on the traditional "willowplate," with its lovers transformed into doves. And so it goes—individual love relationships seem to occur everywhere. But this fact does not change the position of a society on the continuum.

Second, reading both Linton's and Lowie's comments in this new conceptual context reduces their theoretical importance, for they are both merely saying that people do not *live by* the romantic complex, here or anywhere else. Some few couples in love will brave social pressures, physical dangers, or the gods themselves, but nowhere is this usual. Violent, self-sufficient love is not common anywhere. In this respect, of course, the U.S. is not set apart from other systems.

Third, we can separate a *love pattern* from the romantic love *complex*. Under the former, love is a permissible, expected prelude to marriage, and a usual element of courtship—thus, at about the center of the continuum, but toward the pole of instutionalization. The romantic love complex (one pole of the continuum) includes, in addition, an ideological prescription that falling in love is a highly desirable basis of courtship and marriage; love is strongly institutionalized.[19] In contemporary United States, many individuals would even claim that entering marriage without being in love requires some such rationalization as asserting that one is too old for such romances or that one must "think of practical matters like money." To be sure, both anthropologists and sociologists often exaggerate the American commitment to romance;[20] nevertheless, a behavioral and value complex of this type is found here.

---

[18]See Ludwig Friedländer, *Roman Life and Manners under the Early Empire* (Seventh Edition), translated by A. Magnus, New York: Dutton, 1908. Vol. 1, Chapter 5, "The Position of Women."

[19]For a discussion of the relation between behavior patterns and the proces of institutionalization, see my *After Divorce,* Glencoe, Ill.: Free Press, 1956, Chapter 15.

[20]See Ernest W. Burgess and Paul W. Wallin, *Engagement and Marriage,* New York: Lippincott, 1953, Chapter 7 for the extent to which even the engaged are not blind to the defects of their beloveds. No one has ascertained the degree to which various age and sex groups in our society actually believe in some form of the ideology.

Similarly, Margaret Mead in *Coming of Age in Samoa,* New York: Modern Library, 1953, rates Manu'an love as shallow, and though these Samoans give much attention to love-making, she asserts that they laughed with incredulous contempt at Romeo and Juliet (pp. 155–156). Though the individual sufferer showed jealousy and anger, the Manu'ans believed that a new love would

But this complex is rare. Perhaps only the following cultures possess the romantic love value complex: modern urban United States, Northwestern Europe, Polynesia, and the European nobility of the eleventh and twelfth centuries.[21] Certainly, it is to be found in no other major civilization. On the other hand, the *love pattern*, which views love as a basis for the final decision to marry, may be relatively common.

## WHY LOVE MUST BE CONTROLLED

Since strong love attachments apparently can occur in any society and since (as we shall show) love is frequently a basis for and prelude to marriage, it must be controlled or channeled in some way. More specifically, the stratification and lineage patterns would be weakened greatly if love's potentially disruptive effects were not kept in check. The importance of this situation may be seen most clearly by considering one of the major functions of the family, status placement, which in every society links the structures of stratification, kinship lines, and mate choice. (To show how the very similar comments which have been made about sex are not quite correct would take us too far afield; in any event, to the extent that they are correct, the succeeding analysis applies equally to the control of sex.)

Both the child's placement in the social structure and choice of mates are socially important because both placement and choice link two kinship lines together. Courtship or mate choice, therefore, cannot be ignored by either family or society. To permit random mating would mean radical change in the existing social structure. If the family as a unit of society is important, then mate choice is too.

Kinfolk or immediate family can disregard the question of who marries whom, only if a marriage is not seen as a link between kin lines, only if no property, power, lineage honor, totemic relationships, and the like are believed to flow from the kin lines through the spouses to their offspring. Universally, however, these are believed to follow kin lines. Mate choice thus has consequences for the social structure. But love may affect mate choice. Both mate choice and love, therefore, are too important to be left to children.

## THE CONTROL OF LOVE

Since considerable energy and resources may be required to push youngsters who are in love into proper role behavior, love must be controlled *before* it appears. Love relationships must either be kept to a small number or they must be so directed that they do not run counter to the approved kinship

---

quickly cure a betrayed lover (pp. 105–108). It is possible that Mead failed to understand the shallowness of love in our own society: Romantic love is, "in our civilization, inextricably bound up with ideas of monogamy, exclusiveness, jealousy, and undeviating fidelity" (p. 105). But these are *ideas* and ideology; *behavior* is rather different.

[21] I am preparing an analysis of this case. The relation of "courtly love" to social structure is complicated.

linkages. There are only a few institutional patterns by which this control is achieved.

1. Certainly the simplest, and perhaps the most widely used, structural pattern for coping with this problem is child marriage. If the child is betrothed, married, or both before he has had any opportunity to interact intimately as an adolescent with other children, then he has no resources with which to oppose the marriage. He cannot earn a living, he is physically weak, and is socially dominated by his elders. Moreover, strong love attachments occur only rarely before puberty. An example of this pattern was to be found in India, where the young bride went to live with her husband in a marriage which was not physically consummated until much later, within his father's household.[22]

2. Often, child marriage is linked with a second structural pattern, in which the kinship rules define rather closely a class of eligible future spouses. The marriage is determined by birth within narrow limits. Here, the major decision, which is made by elders, is *when* the marriage is to occur. Thus, among the Murngin, *galle*, the father's sister's child, is scheduled to marry *due*, the mother's brother's child.[23] In the case of the "four-class" double-descent system, each individual is a member of *both* a matri-moiety and a patri-moiety and must marry someone who belongs to neither; the four-classes are (1) ego's own class, (2) those whose matri-moiety is the same as ego's but whose patri-moiety is different, (3) those who are in ego's patri-moiety but not in his matri-moiety, and (4) those who are in neither of ego's moieties, that is, who are in the cell diagonally from his own.[24] Problems arise at times under these systems if the appropriate kinship cell—for example, parallel cousin or cross-cousin—is empty.[25] But nowhere, apparently, is the definition so rigid as to exclude some choice and, therefore, some dickering, wrangling, and haggling between the elders of the two families.

3. A society can prevent widespread development of adolescent love relationships by socially isolating young people from potential mates, whether eligible or ineligible as spouses. Under such a pattern, elders can arrange the marriages of either children or adolescents with little likelihood that their plans will be disrupted by love attachments. Obviously, this arrangement can-

---

[22]Frieda M. Das, *Purdah*, New York: Vanguard, 1932; Kingsley Davis, *The Population of India and Pakistan*, Princeton: Princeton University Press, 1951, p. 112. There was a widespread custom of taking one's bride from a village other than one's own.

[23]W. Lloyd Warner, *Black Civilization*, New York: Harper, 1937, pp. 82–84. They may also become "sweethearts" at puberty; see pp. 86–89.

[24]See Murdock, *op. cit.*, p. 53 ff. *et passim* for discussions of double-descent.

[25]One adjustment in Australia was for the individuals to leave the tribe for a while, usually eloping, and then to return "reborn" under a different and now appropriate kinship designation. In any event, these marital prescriptions did not prevent love entirely. As Malinowski shows in his early summary of the Australian family systems, although every one of the tribes used the technique of infant betrothal (and close prescription of mate), no tribe was free of elopements, between either the unmarried or the married, and the "motive of sexual love" was always to be found in marriages by elopement. B. Malinowski. *The Family Among the Australian Aborigines*, London: University of London Press, 1913, p. 83.

not operate effectively in most primitive societies, where youngsters see one another rather frequently.[26]

Not only is this pattern more common in civilizations than in primitive societies, but is found more frequently in the upper social strata. *Social* segregation is difficult unless it is supported by physical segregation—the harem of Islam, the zenana of India[27]—or by a large household system with individuals whose duty it is to supervise nubile girls. Social segregation is thus expensive. Perhaps the best known example of simple social segregation was found in China, where youthful marriages took place between young people who had not previously met because they lived in different villages; they could not marry fellow-villagers since ideally almost all inhabitants belonged to the same *tsu*.[28]

It should be emphasized that the primary function of physical or social isolation in these cases is to minimize informal or intimate social interaction. Limited social contacts of a highly ritualized or formal type in the presence of elders, as in Japan, have a similar, if less extreme, result.[29]

4. A fourth type of pattern seems to exist, although it is not clear cut; and specific cases shade off toward types three and five. Here, there is close supervision by duennas or close relatives, but not actual social segregation. A high value is placed on female chastity (which perhaps is the case in every major civilization until its "decadence") viewed either as the product of self-restraint, as among the 17th century Puritans, or as a marketable commodity. Thus love as play is not developed; marriage is supposed to be considered by the young as a duty and a possible family alliance. This pattern falls between types three and five because love is permitted before marriage, but only between eligibles. Ideally, it occurs only between a betrothed couple, and, except as marital love, there is no encouragement for it to appear at all. Family elders largely make the specific choice of mate, whether or not intermediaries carry out the arrangements. In the preliminary stages youngsters engage in courtship under

---

[26]This pattern was apparently achieved in Manus, where on first menstruation the girl was removed from her playmates and kept at "home"—on stilts over a lagoon—under the close supervision of elders. The Manus were prudish, and love occurred rarely or never. Margaret Mead, *Growing Up in New Guinea,* in *From the South Seas.* New York: Morrow, 1939, pp. 163–166, 208.

[27]See Das, *op cit.*

[28]For the activities of the *tsu*, see Hsien Chin Hu, *The Common Descent Group in China and Its Functions,* New York: Viking Fund Studies in Anthropology, 10 (1948). For the marriage process, see Marion J. Levy, *The Family Revolution in Modern China,* Cambridge: Harvard University Press, 1949, pp. 87–107. See also Olga Lang, *Chinese Family and Society*, New Haven: Yale University Press, 1946, for comparisons between the old and new systems. In one-half of 62 villages in Ting Hsien Experimental District in Hopei, the largest clan included 50 percent of the families; in 25 percent of the villages, the two largest clans held over 90 percent of the families; I am indebted to Robert M. Marsh who has been carrying out a study of Ching mobility partly under my direction for this reference: F. C. H. Lee, *Ting Hsien. She-hui K'ai-K'uang t'iao-ch'a,* Peiping: Chung-hua p'ing-min Chiao-yu ts'u-chin hui, 1932, p. 54. See also Sidney Gamble, *Ting Hsien: A North China Rural Community,* New York: International Secretariat of the Institute of Pacific Relations, 1954.

[29]For Japan, see Shidzué Ishimoto, *Facing Two Ways*, New York: Farrar and Rinehart, 1935, Chapters 6, 8; John F. Embree, *Suye Mura,* Chicago: University of Chicago Press, 1950, Chapters 3, 6.

supervision, with the understanding that this will permit the development of affection prior to marriage.

I do not believe that the empirical data show where this pattern is prevalent, outside of Western Civilization. The West is a special case, because of its peculiar relationship to Christianity, in which from its earliest days in Rome there has been a complex tension between asceticism and love. This type of limited love marked French, English, and Italian upper class family life from the 11th to the 14th centuries, as well as 17th century Puritanism in England and New England.[30]

5. The fifth type of pattern permits or actually encourages love relationships, and love is a commonly expected element in mate choice. Choice in this system is *formally* free. In their 'teens youngsters begin their love play, with or without consummating sexual intercourse, within a group of peers. They may at times choose love partners whom they and others do not consider suitable spouses. Gradually, however, their range of choice is narrowed and eventually their affections center on one individual. This person is likely to be more eligible as a mate according to general social norms, and as judged by peers and parents, than the average individual with whom the youngster formerly indulged in love play.

For reasons that are not yet clear, this pattern is nearly always associated with a strong development of an adolescent peer group system, although the latter may occur without the love pattern. One source of social control, then, is the individual's own 'teen age companions, who persistently rate the present and probable future accomplishments of each individual.[31]

Another source of control lies with the parents of both boy and girl. In our society, parents threaten, cajole, wheedle, bribe, and persuade their children to "go with the right people," during both the early love play and later courtship phases.[32] Primarily, they seek to control love relationships by influencing the informal social contacts of their children: moving to appropriate neighbor-

---

[30]I do not mean, of course, to restrict this pattern to these times and places, but I am more certain of these. For the Puritans, see Edmund S. Morgan, *The Puritan Family,* Boston: Public Library, 1944. For the somewhat different practices in New York, see Charles E. Ironside, *The Family in Colonial New York,* New York: Columbia University Press, 1942. See also: A. Abram, *English Life and Manners in the Later Middle Ages,* New York: Dutton, 1913, Chapters 4, 10; Emily J. Putnam, *The Lady,* New York: Sturgis and Walton, 1910, Chapter 4; James Gairdner, editor, *The Paston Letters, 1422–1509,* 4 vols., London: Arber, 1872–1875; Eileen Power, "The Position of Women," in C. G. Crump and E. F. Jacobs, editors, *The Legacy of the Middle Ages,* Oxford: Clarendon, 1926, pp. 414–416.

[31]For those who believe that the young in the United States are totally deluded by love, or believe that love outranks every other consideration, see: Ernest W. Burgess and Paul W. Wallin, *Engagement and Marriage*, New York: Lippincott, 1953, pp. 217–238. Note Karl Robert V. Wikman, *Die Einleitung Der Ehe. Acta Academiae Aboensis (Humaniora),* 11 (1937), pp. 127 ff. Not only are reputations known because of close association among peers, but songs and poetry are sometimes composed about the girl or boy. Cf., for the Tikopia, Raymond Firth, *We, the Tikopia,* New York: American Book, 1936, pp. 468 ff.; for the Siuai, Douglas L. Oliver, *Solomon Island Society,* Cambridge: Harvard University Press, 1955, pp. 146 ff. The Manu'ans made love in groups of three or four couples; cf. Mead, *Coming of Age in Samoa, op cit.,* p. 92.

[32]Marvin B. Sussman, "Parental Participation in Mate Selection and Its Effect upon Family Continuity," *Social Forces,* 32 (October, 1953), pp. 76–81.

hoods and schools, giving parties and helping to make out invitation lists, by making their children aware that certain individuals have ineligibility traits (race, religion, manners, tastes, clothing, and so on). Since youngsters fall in love with those with whom they associate, control over informal relationships also controls substantially the focus of affection. The results of such control are well known and are documented in the more than one hundred studies of homogamy in this country: most marriages take place between couples in the same class, religious, racial, and educational levels.

As Robert Wikman has shown in a generally unfamiliar (in the United States) but superb investigation, this pattern was found among 18th Century Swedish farmer adolescents, was widely distributed in other Germanic areas, and extends in time from the 19th century back to almost certainly the late Middle Ages.[33] In these cases, sexual intercourse was taken for granted, social contact was closely supervised by the peer group, and final consent to marriage was withheld or granted by the parents who owned the land.

Such cases are not confined to Western society. Polynesia exhibits a similar pattern, with some variation from society to society, the best known examples of which are perhaps Mead's Manu'ans and Firth's Tiko-pia.[34] Probably the most familiar Melanesian cases are the Trobriands and Dobu,[35] where the systems resemble those of the Kiwai Papuans of the Trans-Fly and the Siuai Papuans of the Solomon Islands.[36] Linton found this pattern among the Tanala.[37] Although Radcliffe-Brown holds that the pattern is not common in Africa, it is clearly found among the Nuer, the Kgatla (Tswana-speaking), and the Bavenda (here, without sanctioned sexual intercourse).[38]

A more complete classification, making use of the distinctions suggested in this paper, would show, I believe, that a large minority of known societies exhibit this pattern. I would suggest, moreover, that such a study would reveal that the degree to which love is a usual, expected prelude to marriage is corre-

---

[33]Wikman, *op cit.*

[34]Mead, *Coming of Age in Samoa, op cit.* pp. 97–108; and Firth, *op. cit.,* pp. 520 ff.

[35]Thus Malinowski notes in his "Introduction" to Reo F. Fortune's *The Sorcerers of Dobu,* London: Routledge, 1932, p. xxiii, that the Dobu have similar patterns, the same type of courtship by trial and error, with a gradually tightening union.

[36]Gunnar Landtman, *Kiwai Papuans of the Trans-Fly,* London: Macmillan, 1927, pp. 243 ff.; Oliver, *op. cit.,* pp. 153 ff.

[37]The pattern apparently existed among the Marquesans as well, but since Linton never published a complete description of this Polynesian society, I omit it here. His fullest analysis, cluttered with secondary interpretations, is in Abram Kardiner, *Psychological Frontiers of Society,* New York: Columbia University Press, 1945. For the Tanala, see Ralph Linton, *The Tanala,* Chicago: Field Museum, 1933, pp. 300–303.

[38]Thus, Radcliffe-Brown: "The African does not think of marriage as a union based on romantic love, although beauty as well as character and health are sought in the choice of a wife," in his "Introduction" to A. R. Radcliffe-Brown and W. C. Daryll Ford, editors, *African Systems of Kinship and Marriage,* London: Oxford University Press, 1950, p. 46. For the Nuer, see E.E. Evans-Pritchard, *Kinship and Marriage Among the Nuer,* Oxford: Clarendon, 1951, pp. 49–58. For the Kgatla, see I. Schapera, *Married Life in an African Tribe,* New York: Sheridan, 1941, pp. 55 ff. For the Bavenda, although the report seems incomplete, see Hugh A. Stayt, *The Bavenda,* London: Oxford University Press, 1931, pp. 111 ff., 145 ff., 154.

lated with (1) the degree of free choice of mate permitted in the society and (2) the degree to which husband-wife solidarity is the strategic solidarity of the kinship structure.[39]

## LOVE CONTROL AND CLASS

These sociostructural explanations of how love is controlled lead to a subsidiary but important hypothesis: From one society to another, and from one *class* to another within the same society, the sociostructural importance of maintaining kinship lines according to rule will be rated differently by the families within them. Consequently, the degree to which control over mate choice, and therefore over the prevalence of a love pattern among adolescents, will also vary. Since, within any stratified society, this concern with the maintenance of intact and acceptable kin lines will be greater in the upper strata, it follows that noble or upper strata will maintain stricter control over love and courtship behavior than lower strata. The two correlations suggested in the preceding paragraph also apply: husband-wife solidarity is less strategic relative to clan solidarity in the upper than in the lower strata, and there is less free choice of mate.

Thus it is that, although in Polynesia generally most youngsters indulged in considerable love play, princesses were supervised strictly.[40] Similarly, in China lower class youngsters often met their spouses before marriage.[41] In our own society, the "upper upper" class maintains much greater control than the lower strata over the informal social contacts of their nubile young. Even among the Dobu, where there are few controls and little stratification, differences in control exist at the extremes: a child betrothal may be arranged between outstanding gardening families, who try to prevent their youngsters from being entangled with wastrel families.[42] In answer to my query about this pattern among the Nuer, Evans-Pritchard writes:

---

[39]The second correlation is developed from Marion J. Levy, *The Family Revolution in China,* Cambridge, Harvard University Press, 1949, p. 179. Levy's formulation ties "romantic love" to that solidarity, and is of little use because there is only one case, the Western culture complex. As he states it, it is almost so by definition.

[40]E.g., Mead, *Coming of Age in Samoa, op. cit.,* pp. 79, 92, 97–109. Cf. also Firth, *op. cit.,* pp. 520 ff.

[41]Although one must be cautious about China, this inference seems to be allowable from such comments as the following: "But the old men of China did not succeed in eliminating love from the life of the young women.... Poor and middle-class families could not afford to keep men and women in separate quarters, and Chinese also met their cousins.... Girls ... sometimes even served customers in their parents' shops." Olga Lang, *op. cit.,* pp. 33. According to Fried, farm girls would work in the fields, and farm girls of 10 years and older were sent to the market to sell produce. They were also sent to towns and cities as servants. The peasant or pauper woman was not confined to the home and its immediate environs. Morton H. Fried, *Fabric of Chinese Society,* New York: Praeger, 1953, pp. 59–60. Also, Levy (*op cit.,* p. 111): "Among peasant girls and among servant girls in gentry households some premarital experience was not uncommon, though certainly frowned upon. The methods of preventing such contact were isolation and chaperonage, both of which, in the 'traditional' picture, were more likely to break down in the two cases named than elsewhere."

[42]Fortune, *op. cit.,* p. 30.

> You are probably right that a wealthy man has more control over his son's affairs than a poor man. A man with several wives has a more authoritarian position in his home. Also, a man with many cattle is in a position to permit or refuse a son to marry, whereas a lad whose father is poor may have to depend on the support of kinsmen. In general, I would say that a Nuer father is not interested in the personal side of things. His son is free to marry any girl he likes and the father does not consider the selection to be his affair until the point is reached when cattle have to be discussed.[43]

The upper strata have much more at stake in the maintenance of the social structure and thus are more strongly motivated to control the courtship and marriage decisions of their young. Correspondingly, their young have much more to lose than lower strata youth, so that upper strata elders *can* wield more power.

## CONCLUSION

In this analysis I have attempted to show the integration of love with various types of social structures. As against considerable contemporary opinion among both sociologists and anthropologists, I suggest that love is a universal psychological potential, which is controlled by a range of five structural patterns, all of which are attempts to see to it that youngsters do not make entirely free choices of their future spouses. Only if kin lines are unimportant, and this condition is found in no society as a whole, will entirely free choice be permitted. Some structural arrangements seek to prevent entirely the outbreak of love, while others harness it. Since the kin lines of the upper strata are of greater social importance to them than those of lower strata are to the lower strata members, the former exercise a more effective control over this choice. Even where there is almost a formally free choice of mate—and I have suggested that this pattern is widespread, to be found among a substantial segment of the earth's societies—this choice is guided by peer group and parents toward a mate who will be acceptable to the kin and friend groupings. The theoretical importance of love is thus to be seen in the sociostructural patterns which are developed to keep it from disrupting existing social arrangements.

---

[43]Personal letter, dated January 9, 1958. However, the Nuer father can still refuse if he believes the demands of the girl's people are unreasonable. In turn, the girl can cajole her parents to demand less.

# 13

FRANCESCA M. CANCIAN

# The Feminization of Love

*A number of recent studies have shown that both men and women tend to regard women as typically highly skilled at intimate interpersonal relationships and men as typically awkward, unskilled, and unsensitive. In some cases, the female partner in a heterosexual relationship essentially assumes the role of teacher or therapist, relegating the male partner to the subordinate role of student or client. The woman may encourage this definition of her superiority in order to compensate for a perceived overall power disadvantage, or at least the man may attribute such a motive to her, perhaps responding with anger and withdrawal.*

*Most authors who have written on the subject have accepted as correct the popular belief in women's superior skill at intimate relationships. However, Francesca Cancian has pointed out in several publications that women are clearly superior only from the standpoint of a feminine definition of love, in much the same way that men's achievements in the world of work tend to overshadow those of women under a masculine definition of achievement. In the reading that follows, Cancian advocates an "androgynous" view of love, according to which neither men nor women are clearly superior overall, although some individuals are superior to others. The superior individuals, according to this view, are those men and women able to integrate within themselves the instrumental (male) and expressive (female) aspects of love.*

Source: Francesca Cancian, "The Feminization of Love" [*Signs: Journal of Women in Culture and Society* 1986, vol. 11. no. 4] 

A feminized and incomplete perspective on love predominates in the United States. We identify love with emotional expression and talking about feelings, aspects of love that women prefer and in which women tend to be more skilled than men. At the same time we often ignore the instrumental and physical aspects of love that men prefer, such as providing help, sharing activities, and sex. The feminized perspective leads us to believe that women are much more capable of love than men and that the way to make relationships more loving is for men to become more like women.[1] This paper proposes an alternative, androgynous perspective on love, one based on the premise that love is both instrumental and expressive.[2] From this perspective, the way to make relationships more loving is for women and men to reject polarized gender roles and integrate "masculine " and "feminine" styles of love.

## THE TWO PERSPECTIVES

"Love is active, doing something for your good even if it bothers me" says a fundamentalist Christian. "Love is sharing, the real sharing of feelings" says a divorced secretary who is in love again. In ancient Greece, the ideal love was the adoration of a man for a beautiful young boy who was his lover. In the 13th century, the exemplar of love was the chaste devotion of a knight for another man's wife. In Puritan New England, love between husband and wife was the ideal, and in Victorian times, the asexual devotion of a mother for her child seemed the essence of love.[3] My purpose is to focus on one kind of love: long-term heterosexual love in the contemporary Unites States.

What is a useful definition of enduring love between a woman and a man? One guideline for a definition comes from the prototypes of enduring love—the relations between committed lovers, husband and wife, parent and child. These relationships combine care and assistance with physical and emotional closeness. Studies of attachment between infants and their mothers emphasize the importance of being protected and fed as well as touched and held. In marriage, according to most family sociologists, both practical help and affection are part of enduring love, or "the affection we feel for those with whom our lives are deeply intertwined."[4] Our own informal observations often point in the same direction: if we consider the relationships that are the prototypes of enduring love, it seems that what we really mean by love is some combination of instrumental and expressive qualities.

Historical studies provide a second guideline for defining enduring love, specifically between a woman and a man.[5] In precapitalist America, such love was a complex whole that included work and feelings. Then it was split into feminine and masculine fragments by the separation of home and workplace. This historical analysis implies that affection, material help, and routine cooperation all are parts of enduring love.

Consistent with these guidelines, my working definition of enduring love between adults is a relationship wherein a small number of people are affectionate and emotionally committed to each other, define their collective well-being as a major goal, and feel obliged to provide care and practical assistance for each other. People who love each other also usually share physical contact; they communicate with each other frequently and cooperate in some routine tasks of daily life. My discussion is of enduring heterosexual love only; I will for the sake of simplicity refer to it as "love."

In contrast to this broad definition of love, the narrower, feminized definition dominates both contemporary scholarship and public opinion. Most scholars who study love, intimacy, or close friendship focus on qualities that are stereotypically feminine, such as talking about feelings.[6] For example, Abraham Maslow defines love as "a feeling of tenderness and affection with great enjoyment, happiness, satisfaction, elation, and even ecstasy." Among healthy individuals, he says, "there is a growing intimacy and honesty and self-expression."[7] Zick Rubin's "Love Scale," designed to measure the degree of passionate love as opposed to liking, includes questions about confiding in each other, longing to be together, and sexual attraction as well as caring for each other. Studies of friendship usually distinguish close friends from acquaintances on the basis of how much personal information is disclosed, and many recent studies of married couples and lovers emphasize communication and self-disclosure. A recent book on marital love by Lillian Rubin focuses on intimacy, which she defines as "reciprocal expression of feeling and thought, not out of fear or dependent need, but out of a wish to know another's inner life and to be able to share one's own."[8] She argues that intimacy is distinct from nurturance or caretaking and that men are usually unable to be intimate.

Among the general public, love is also defined primarily as expressing feelings and verbal disclosure, not as instrumental help. This is especially true among the more affluent; poorer people are more likely than they to see practical help and financial assistance as a sign of love.[9] In a study conducted in 1980, 130 adults from a wide range of social classes and ethnic backgrounds were interviewed about the qualities that make a good love relationship. The most frequent response referred to honest and open communication. Being caring and supportive and being tolerant and understanding were the other qualities most often mentioned.[10] Similar results were reported from Ann Swidler's study of an affluent suburb; the dominant conception of love stressed communicating feelings, working on the relationship, and self-development.[11] Finally, a contemporary dictionary defines love as "strong affection for another arising out of kinship or personal ties" and as attraction based on sexual desire, affection, and tenderness.[12]

These contemporary definitions of love clearly focus on qualities that are seen as feminine in our culture. A study of gender roles in 1968 found that warmth, expressiveness, and talkativeness were seen as appropriate for women and not for men. In 1978 the core features of gender stereotypes were unchanged although fewer qualities were seen as appropriate for only one sex. Expressing tender feelings, being gentle, and being aware of the feelings of others were still qualities for women and not for men. The desirable qualities for men and not for women included being independent, unemotional, and interested in sex.[13] The only component perceived as masculine in popular definitions of love is interest in sex.

The two approaches to defining love—one broad, encompassing instrumental and affective qualities, one narrow, including only the affective qualities—inform the two different perspectives on love. According to the androgynous perspective, both gender roles contain elements of love. The feminine role does not include all of the major ways of loving; some aspects of love come from the masculine role, such as sex and providing material help, and some, such as cooperating in daily tasks, are associated with neither gender role. In contrast, the feminized perspective on love implies that all of the elements of love are included in the feminine role. The capacity to love is divided by gender. Women can love and men cannot.

## SOME FEMINIST INTERPRETATIONS

Feminist scholars are divided on the question of love and gender. Supporters of the feminized perspective seem most influential at present. Nancy Chodorow's psychoanalytic theory has been especially influential in promoting a feminized perspective on love among social scientists studying close relationships. Chodorow's argument—in greatly simplified form—is that as infants, both boys and girls have strong identification and intimate attachments with their mothers. Since boys grow up to be men, they must repress this early identification, and in the process they repress their capacity for intimacy. Girls retain their early identification since they will grow up to be women, and throughout their lives females see themselves as connected to others. As a result of this process, Chodorow argues, "girls come to define and experience themselves as continuous with others; . . . boys come to define themselves as more separate and distinct."[14] This theory implies that love is feminine—women are more open to love than men—and that this gender difference will remain as long as women are the primary caretakers of infants.

Scholars have used Chodorow's theory to develop the idea that love and attachment are fundamental parts of women's personalities but not men's. Carol Gilligan's influential book on female personality development asserts that women define their identity "by a standard of responsibility and care." The predominant female image is "a network of connection, a web of relationships that is sustained by a process of communication." In contrast, males favor a "hierarchical ordering, with its imagery of winning and losing and the potential for violence which it contains." "Although the world of the self that men describe at times included 'people' and 'deep attachments,' no particular person or relationship is mentioned. . . . Thus the male 'I' is defined in separation."[15]

A feminized conception of love can be supported by other theories as well. In past decades, for example, such a conception developed from Talcott Parsons' theory of the benefits to the nuclear family of women's specializing in expressive action and men's specializing in instrumental action. Among contemporary social scientists, the strongest support for the feminized perspective comes from such psychological theories as Chodorow's.[16]

On the other hand, feminist historians have developed an incisive critique of the feminized perspective on love. Mary Ryan and other social historians have analyzed how the separation of home and workplace in the nineteenth century polarized gender roles and feminized love.[17] Their argument, in simplified form, begins with the observation that in the colonial era the family household was the arena for economic production, affection, and social welfare. The integration of activities in the family produced a certain integration of expressive and instrumental traits in the personalities of men and women. Both women and men were expected to be hard working, modest, and loving toward their spouses, and children, and the concept of love included instrumental cooperation as well as expression of feelings. In Ryan's words, "When early Americans spoke of love they were not withdrawing into a female byway of human experience. Domestic affection, like sex and economics, was not segregated into male and female spheres." "There was a reciprocal idea of conjugal love" that "grew out of the day-to-day cooperation, sharing, and closeness of the diversified home economy."[18]

Economic production gradually moved out of the home and became separated from personal relationships as capitalism expanded. Husbands increasingly worked for wages in factories and shops while wives stayed at home to care for the family. This division of labor gave women more experience with close relationships and intensified women's economic dependence on men. As the daily activities of men and women grew further apart, a new worldview emerged that exaggerated the differences between the personal, loving, feminine sphere of the home and the impersonal, powerful, masculine sphere of the workplace. Work became identified with what men do for money while love became identified with women's activities at home. As a result, the conception of love shifted toward emphasizing tenderness, powerlessness, and the expression of emotion.[19]

This partial and feminized conception of love persisted into the twentieth century as the division of labor remained stable: the workplace remained impersonal and separated from the home, and married women continued to be excluded from paid employment. According to this historical explanation, one might expect a change in the conception of love since the 1940s, as growing numbers of wives took jobs. However, women's persistent responsibility for child care and housework, and their lower wages, might explain a continued feminized conception of love.[20]

Like the historical critiques, some psychological studies of gender also imply that our current conception of love is distorted and needs to be integrated with qualities associated with the masculine role. For example, Jean Baker Miller argues that women's ways of loving—their need to be attached to a man and to serve others—result from women's powerlessness, and that a better way of loving would integrate power with women's style of love.[21] The importance of combining activities and personality traits that have been split apart by gender is also a frequent theme in the human potential movement.[22] These historical and psychological works emphasize the flexibility of gender roles and the inadequacy of a concept of love that includes only the feminine half of human qualities. In contrast, theories like Chodorow's emphasize the rigidity of gender differences after childhood and define love in terms of feminine qualities. The two theoretical approaches are not as inconsistent as my simplified sketches may suggest, and many scholars combine them;[23] however, the two approaches have different implications for empirical research.

## EVIDENCE ON WOMEN'S "SUPERIORITY" IN LOVE

A large number of studies show that women are more interested and more skilled in love than men. However, most of these studies use biased measures based on feminine styles of loving, such as verbal self-disclosure, emotional expression, and willingness to report that one has close relationships. When less biased measures are used, the differences between women and men are often small.

Women have a greater number of close relationships than men. At all stages of the life cycle, women see their relatives more often. Men and women report closer relations with their mothers than with their fathers and are generally closer to female kin. Thus an average Yale man in the 1970s talked about himself more with his mother than with his father and was more satisfied with his relationship with his mother. His most frequent grievance against his father was that his father gave too little of himself and was cold and uninvolved; his grievance against his mother was that she gave too much of herself and was alternately overprotective and punitive.[24]

Throughout their lives, women are more likely to have a confidant—a person to whom one discloses personal experiences and feelings. Girls prefer to be with one friend or a small group, while boys usually play competitive games in large groups. Men usually get together with friends to play sports or do some other activity, while women get together explicitly to talk and to be together.[25]

Men seem isolated given their weak ties with their family and friends. Among blue-collar couples interviewed in 1950, 64 percent of the husbands had no confidants other than their spouses, compared to 24 percent of the wives.[26] The predominantly upper-middle-class men interviewed by Daniel Levinson in the 1970s were no less isolated. Levinson concludes that "close friendship with a man or a woman is rarely experienced by American men."[27] Apparently, most men have no loving relationships besides those with wife or lover; and given the estrangement that often occurs in marriages, many men may have no loving relationship at all.

Several psychologists have suggested that there is a natural reversal of these roles in middle age, as men become more concerned with relationships and women turn toward independence and achievement; but there seems to be no evidence showing that men's relationships become more numerous or more intimate after middle age, and some evidence to the contrary.[28]

Women are also more skilled than men in talking about relationships. Whether working class or middle class, women value talking about feelings and relationships and disclose more than men about personal experiences. Men who deviate and talk a lot about their personal experiences are commonly defined as feminine and maladjusted.[29] Working-class wives prefer to talk about themselves, their close relationships with family and friends, and their homes, while their husbands prefer to talk about cars, sports, work, and politics. The same gender-specific preferences are expressed by college students.[30]

Men do talk more about one area of personal experience: their victories and achievements; but talking about success is associated with power, not intimacy. Women say more about their fears and disappointments, and it is disclosure of such weaknesses that usually is interpreted as a sign of intimacy.[31] Women are also more accepting of the expression of intense feelings, including love, sadness, and fear, and they are more skilled in interpreting other people's emotions.[32]

Finally, in their leisure time women are drawn to topics of love and human entanglements while men are drawn to competition among men. Women's preferences in television viewing run to daytime soap operas, or if they are more educated, the high-brow soap operas on educational channels, while most men like to watch competitive and often aggressive sports. Reading tastes show the same pattern. Women read novels and magazine articles about love, while men's magazines feature stories about men's adventures and encounters with death.[33]

However, this evidence on women's greater involvement and skill in love is not as strong as it appears. Part of the reason that men seem so much less loving than women is that their behavior is measured with a feminine ruler. Much of this research considers only the kinds of loving behavior that are associated with the feminine role and rarely compares women and men in terms of qualities associated with the masculine role. When less biased measures are used, the behavior of men and women is often quite similar. For example, in a careful study of kinship relations among young adults in a southern city, Bert Adams found that women were much more likely than men to say that their parents and relatives were very important to their lives (58 percent of women and 37 percent of men). In measures of actual contact with relatives, though, there were much smaller differences: 88 percent of women and 81 percent of men whose parents lived in the same city saw their parents weekly. Adams concluded that "differences between males and females in relations with parents are discernible primarily in the subjective sphere; contact frequencies are quite similar."[34]

The differences between the sexes can be small even when biased measures are used. For example, Marjorie Lowenthal and Clayton Haven reported the finding, later widely quoted, that elderly women were more likely than elderly men to have a friend with whom they could talk about their personal troubles—clearly a measure of a traditionally feminine behavior. The figures revealed that 81 percent of the married women and 74 percent of the married men had confidants—not a sizable difference.[35] On the other hand, whatever the measure, virtually all such studies find that women are more involved in close relationships than men, even if the difference is small.

In sum, women are only moderately superior to men in love: they have more close relationships and care more about them, and they seem to be more skilled at love, especially those aspects of love that involve expressing feelings and being vulnerable. This does not mean that men are separate and unconcerned with close relationships, however. When national surveys ask people what is most important in their lives, women tend to put family bonds first while men put family bonds first or second, along with work.[36] For both sexes, love is clearly very important.

## EVIDENCE ON THE MASCULINE STYLE OF LOVE

Men tend to have a distinctive style of love that focuses on practical help, shared physical activities, spending time together, and sex.[37] The major elements of the masculine style of love emerge in Margaret Reedy's study of 102 married couples in the late 1970s. She showed individuals statements describing aspects of love and asked them to rate how well the statements described their marriages. On the whole, husband and wife had similar views of their marriage, but several sex differences emerged. Practical help and spending time together were more important to men. The men were more likely to give high ratings to such statements as: "When she needs help I help her," and "She would rather spend her time with me than with anyone else." Men also described themselves more often as sexually attracted and endorsed such statements as: "I get physically excited and aroused just thinking about her." In addition, emotional security was less important to men than to women, and men were less likely to describe the relationship as secure, safe, and comforting.[38] Another study in the late 1970s showed a similar pattern among young, highly educated couples. The husbands gave greater emphasis to feeling responsible for the partner's well-being and putting the spouse's needs first, as well as to spending time together. The wives gave greater importance to emotional involvement and verbal self-disclosure but also were more concerned than the men about maintaining their separate activities and their independence.[39]

The difference between men and women in their views of the significance of practical help was demonstrated in a study in which seven couples recorded their interactions for several days. They noted how pleasant their relations were and counted how often the spouse did a helpful chore, such as cooking a good meal or repairing a faucet, and how often the spouse expressed acceptance or affection. The social scientists doing the study used a feminized definition of love. They labeled practical help as "instrumental behavior" and expressions of acceptance or affection as "affectionate behavior," thereby denying the affectionate aspect of practical help. The wives seemed to be using the same scheme; they thought their marital relations were pleasant that day if their husbands had directed a lot of affectionate behavior to them regardless of their husbands' positive instrumental behavior. The husbands' enjoyment of their marital relations, on the other hand, depended on their wives' instrumental actions, not on their expressions of affection. The men actually saw instrumental actions as affection.[40] One husband who was told by the researchers to increase his affectionate behavior toward his wife decided to wash her car and was surprised when neither his wife nor the researchers accepted that as an "affectionate" act.

The masculine view of instrumental help as loving behavior is clearly expressed by a husband discussing his wife's complaints about his lack of communication: "What does she want? Proof? She's got it, hasn't she? Would I be knocking myself out to get things for her—like to keep up this house—if I didn't love her. Why does a man do things like that if not because he loves his wife and kids? I swear, I can't figure what she wants." His wife, who has a feminine orientation to love, says something very different: "It is not enough that he supports us and takes care of us. I appreciate that, but I want him to share things with me. I need for him to tell me his feelings."[41] Many working-class women agree with men that a man's job is something he does out of love for his family,[42] but middle-class women and social scientists rarely recognize men's practical help as a form of love. (Indeed, among upper-middle-class men whose jobs offer a great deal of intrinsic gratification, their belief that they are "doing it for the family" may seem somewhat self-serving.)

Other differences between men's and women's styles of love involve sex. Men seem to separate sex and love while women connect them,[43] but, paradoxically, sexual intercourse seems to be the most meaningful way of giving and receiving love for many men. A 29-year-old carpenter who had been married for three years said that, after sex, "I feel so close to her and the kids. We feel like a real family then. I don't talk to her very often, I guess, but somehow I feel we have really communicated after we have made love."[44]

Because sexual intimacy is the only recognized "masculine" way of expressing love, the recent trend toward viewing sex as a way for men and women to express mutual intimacy is an important challenge to the feminization of love. However, the connection between sexuality and love is undermined both by the "sexual revolution" definition of sex as a form of casual recreation and by the view of male sexuality as a weapon—as in rape—with which men dominate and punish women.[45]

Another paradoxical feature of men's style of love is that men have a more romantic attitude toward their partners than do women. In Reedy's study, men were more likely to select statements like "we are perfect for each other."[46] In a survey of college students, 65 percent of the men but only 24 percent of the women said that, even if a relationship had all of the other qualities they desired, they would not marry unless they were in love.[47] The common view of this phenomenon focuses on women. The view is that women marry for money and status and so see marriage as instrumentally, rather than emotionally, desirable. This of course is at odds with women's greater concern with self-disclosure and emotional intimacy and lesser concern with instrumental help. A better way to explain men's greater romanticism might be to focus on men. One such possible explanation is that men do not feel responsible for "working on " the emotional aspects of a relationship, and therefore see love as magically and perfectly present or absent. This is consistent with men's relative lack of concern with affective interaction and greater concern with instrumental help.

In sum, there is a masculine style of love. Except for romanticism, men's style fits the popularly conceived masculine role of being the powerful provider.[48] From the androgynous perspective, the practical help and physical activities included in this role are as much a part of love as the expression of feelings. The feminized perspective cannot account for this masculine style of love; nor can it explain why women and men are so close in the degrees to which they are loving.

## NEGATIVE CONSEQUENCES OF THE FEMINIZATION OF LOVE

The division of gender roles in our society that contributes to the two separate styles of love is reinforced by the feminized perspective and leads to political and moral problems that would be mitigated with a more androgynous approach to love. The feminized perspective works against some of the key values and goals of feminists and humanists by contributing to the devaluation and exploitation of women.

It is especially striking how the differences between men's and women's styles of love reinforce men's power over women. Men's style involves giving women important resources, such as money and protection that men control and women believe they need, and ignoring the resources that women control and men need. Thus men's dependency on women remains covert and repressed, while women's dependency on men is overt and exaggerated; and it is overt dependency that creates power, according to social exchange theory.[49] The feminized perspective on love reinforces this power differential by leading to the belief that women need love more than do men, which is implied in the association of love with the feminine role. The effect of this belief is to intensify the asymetrical dependency of women on men.[50] In fact, however, evidence on the high death rates of unmarried men suggests that men need love at least as much as do women.[51]

Sexual relations also can reinforce male dominance insofar as the man takes the initiative and intercourse is defined either as his "taking" pleasure or as his being skilled at "giving" pleasure, either way giving him control. The man's power advantage is further strengthened if the couple assumes that the man's sexual needs can be filled by any attractive woman while the woman's sexual needs can be filled only by the man she loves.[52]

On the other hand, women's preferred ways of loving seem incompatible with control. They involve admitting dependency and sharing or losing control, and being emotionally intense. Further, the intimate talk about personal troubles that appeals to women requires of a couple a mutual vulnerability, a willingness to see oneself as weak and in need of support. It is true that a woman, like a man, can gain some power by providing her partner with services, such as understanding, sex, or cooking; but this power is largely unrecognized because the man's dependency on such services is not overt. The couple may even see these services as her duty or as her response to his requests (or demands).

The identification of love with expressing feelings also contributes to the lack of recognition of women's power by obscuring the instrumental, active component of women's love just as it obscures the loving aspect of men's work. In a culture that glorifies instrumental achievement, this identification devalues both women and love.[53] In reality, a major way in which women are loving is by the clearly instrumental activities associated with caring for others, such as preparing meals, washing clothes, and providing care during illness; but because of our focus on the expressive side of love, this caring work of women is either ignored or redefined as expressing feelings. Thus, from the feminized perspective on love, child care is subtle communication of attitudes, not work. A wife washing her husband's shirt is seen as expressing love, even though a husband washing his wife's car is seen as doing a job.

Gilligan, in her critique of theories of human development, shows the way in which devaluing love is linked to devaluing women. Basic to most psychological theories of development is the idea that a healthy person develops from a dependent child to an autonomous, independent adult. As Gilligan comments, "Development itself comes to be identified with separation, and attachments appear to be developmental impediments.[54] Thus women, who emphasize attachment, are judged to be developmentally retarded or insufficiently individuated.

The pervasiveness of this image was documented in a well-known study of mental health professionals who asked to describe mental health, femininity, and masculinity. They associated both mental health and masculinity with independence, rationality, and dominance. Qualities concerning attachment, such as being tactful, gentle, or aware of the feelings of others, they associated with femininity but not with mental health.[55]

Another negative consequence of a feminized perspective on love is that it legitimates impersonal, exploitive relations in the workplace and the community. The ideology of separate spheres that developed in the nineteenth century contrasted the harsh, immoral marketplace with the warm and loving home and implied that this contrast is acceptable.[56] Defining love as expressive, feminine, and divorced from productive activity maintains this ideology. If personal relationships and love are reserved for women and the home, then it is acceptable for a manager to underpay workers or for a community to ignore a needy family. Such behavior is not unloving; it is businesslike or shows a respect for privacy. The ideology of separate spheres also implies that men are properly judged by their instrumental and economic achievements and that poor or unsuccessful men are failures who may deserve a hard life. Levinson presents a conception of masculine development itself as centering on achieving an occupational dream.[57]

Finally, the feminization of love intensifies the conflicts over intimacy between women and men in close relationships. One of the most common conflicts is that the woman wants more closeness and verbal contact while the man withdraws and wants less pressure.[58] Her need for more closeness is partly the result of the feminization of love, which encourages her to be more emotionally dependent on him. Because love is feminine, he in turn may feel controlled during intimate contact. Intimacy is her "turf," an area where she sets the rules and expectations. Talking about the relationship, as she wants, may well feel to him like taking a test that she made up and that he will fail. He is likely to react by withdrawing, causing her to intensify her efforts to get closer. The feminization of love thus can lead to a vicious cycle of conflict where neither partner feels in control or gets what they want.

## CONCLUSION

The values of improving the status of women and humanizing the public sphere are shared by many of the scholars who support a feminized conception of love; and they, too, explain the conflicts in close relationships in terms of polarized gender roles. Nancy Chodorow, Lillian Rubin, and Carol Gilligan have addressed these issues in detail and with great insight. However, by arguing that women's identity is based on attachment while men's identity is based on separation, they reinforce the distinction between feminine expressiveness and masculine instrumentality, revive the ideology of separate spheres, and legitimate the popular idea that only women know the right way to love. They also suggest that there is no way to overcome the rigidity of gender roles other than by pursuing the goal of men and women becoming equally involved in infant care. In contrast, an androgynous perspective on love challenges the identification of women and love with being expressive, powerless, and nonproductive and the identification of men with being instrumental, powerful, and productive. It rejects the ideology of separate spheres and validates masculine and well as feminine styles of love. This viewpoint suggests that progress could be made by means of a variety of social changes, including men doing child care, relations at work becoming more personal and nurturant, and cultural conceptions of love and gender becoming more androgynous. Changes that equalize power within close relationships by equalizing the economic and emotional dependency between men and women, may be especially important in moving toward androgynous love.

The validity of an androgynous definition of love cannot be "proven"; the view that informs the androgynous perspective is that both the feminine style of love—characterized by emotional closeness and verbal self-disclosure—and the masculine style of love—characterized by instrumental help and sex—represent necessary parts of a good love relationship. Who is more loving: a couple who confide most of their experiences to each other but rarely cooperate or give each other practical help, or a couple who help each other through many crises and cooperate in running a household but rarely discuss their personal experiences? Both relationships are limited. Most people would probably choose a combination: a relationship that integrates feminine and masculine styles of loving, an androgynous love.

## NOTES

I am indebted to Frank Cancian, Steven Gordon, Lillian Rubin, and Scott Swain for helpful comments and discussions.

1. The term "feminization" of love is derived from Ann Douglas, *The Feminization of Culture* (New York: Alfred A. Knopf, 1977).

2. The term "androgyny" is problematic. It assumes rather than questions sex-role stereotypes (agression is masculine, for example); it can lead to a utopian view that underestimates the social causes of sexism; and it suggests the complete absence of differences between men and women, which is biologically impossible. Nonetheless, I use the term because it best conveys my meaning: a combination of masculine and feminine styles of love. The negative and positive aspects of the concept "androgyny" are analyzed in a special issue of *Women's Studies* (vol. 2, no. 2, 1974), edited by Cynthia Secor. Also see Sandra Bem, "Gender Schema Theory and Its Implications for Child Development: Raising Gender-aschematic Children in a Gender-schematic Society," *Signs: Journal of Women in Culture and Society*, 8, no. 4 (1983): 598–616.

3. The quotations are from a study by Ann Swidler, "Ideologies of Love in Middle Class America" (paper presented at the annual meeting of the Pacific Sociological Association, San Diego, 1982). For useful reviews of the history of love, see Morton Hunt, *The Natural History of Love* (New York: Alfred A. Knopf, 1959); and Bernard Murstein, *Love, Sex and Marriage through the Ages* (New York: Springer, 1974).

4. See John Bowlby, *Attachment and Loss* (New York: Basic Books, 1969) on mother-infant attachment. The quotation is from Elaine Walster and G. William Walster, *A New Look at Love* (Reading, Mass.: Addison-Wesley Publishing Co., 1978), 9. Conceptions of love and adjustment used by family sociologists are reviewed in Robert Lewis and Graham Spanier, "Theorizing about the Quality and Stability of Marriage," in *Contemporary Theories about the Family*, ed. W. Burr, R. Hill, F. Nye, and I. Reiss (New York: Free Press, 1979), 268–94.

5. Mary Ryan, *Womanhood in America*, 2d ed. (New York: New Viewpoints, 1979), and *The Cradle of the Middle Class: The Family in Oneida County, N.Y., 1790–1865* (New York: Cambridge University Press, 1981); Barbara Ehrenreich and Deidre English, *For Her Own Good: 150 Years of Experts' Advice to Women* (New York: Anchor Books, 1978); Barbara Welter, "The Cult of True Womanhood: 1820–1860," *American Quarterly* 18, no. 2 (1966), 151–74; Carl N. Degler, *At Odds* (New York: Oxford University Press, 1980).

6. Alternative definitions of love are reviewed in Walster and Walster; Clyde Hendrick and Susan Hendrick, *Liking, Loving and Relating* (Belmont, Calif.: Wadsworth Publishing Co., 1983); Ira Reiss, *Family Systems in America*, 3d ed. (New York: Holt, Rinehart & Winston, 1980), 113–41; Margaret Reedy, "Age and Sex Differences in Personal Needs and the Nature of Love." (Ph.D. diss., University of Southern California, 1977).

7. Abraham Maslow, *Motivation and Personality*, 2d ed. (New York: Harper & Row, 1970), 182–83.

8. Zick Rubin's scale is described in his article "Measurement of Romantic Love," *Journal of Personality and Social Psychology* 16, no. 2 (1970): 265–73; Lillian Rubin's book on marriage is *Intimate Strangers* (New York: Harper & Row, 1983), quote on 90.

9. The emphasis on mutual aid and instrumental love among poor people is described in Lillian Rubin, *Worlds of Pain* (New York: Basic Books, 1976); Rayna Rapp, "Family and Class in Contemporary America," in *Rethinking the Family* ed. Barrie Thorne (New York: Longman, Inc., 1982), 168–87; S.M. Miller and F. Reissman, "The Working-Class Subculture," in *Blue-Collar World*, ed. A. Shostak and W. Greenberg (Englewood Cliffs, N.J.: Prentice-Hall, Inc., 1964), 24–36.

10. Francesca Cancian, Clynta Jackson, and Ann Wysocki, "A Survey of Close Relationships" (University of California, Irvine, School of Social Sciences, 1982, typescript).

11. Swidler.

12. *Webster's New Collegiate Dictionary* (Springfield, Mass.: G. C. Merriam Co., 1977).

13. Paul Rosencrantz, Helen Bee, Susan Vogel, Inge Broverman, and Donald Broverman, "Sex Role Stereotypes and Self-Concepts in College Students," *Journal of Consulting and Clinical Psychology* 32, no. 3 (1968): 287–95; Paul Rosencrantz, "Rosencrantz Discusses Changes in Stereotypes about Men and Women," *Second Century Radcliffe News* (Cambridge, Mass., June 1982), 5–6.

14. Nancy Chodorow, *The Reproduction of Mothering* (Berkeley: University of California Press, 1978), 169. Dorothy Dinnerstein presents a similar theory in *The Mermaid and the Minotaur: Sexual Arrangements and Human Malaise* (New York: Harper & Row, 1976). Freudian and biological dispositional theories about women's nurturance are surveyed in Jean Stockard and Miriam Johnson, *Sex Roles* (Englewood Cliffs, N.J.: Prentice-Hall, Inc. 1980).

15. Carol Gilligan, *In a Different Voice* (Cambridge, Mass.: Harvard University Press, 1982), 32 and 159–61; see also L. Rubin, *Intimate Strangers*.

16. Talcott Parsons and Robert F. Bales, *Family, Socialization and Interaction* (Glencoe, Ill.: Free Press, 1955). For a critical review of family sociology from a feminist perspective, see Arlene Skolnick, *The Intimate Environment* (Boston: Little, Brown & Co., 1978). Radical feminist theories also support the feminized conception of love, but they have been less influential in social science; see, e.g., Mary Daly, *Gyn/Ecology: The Metaethics of Radical Feminism* (Boston: Beacon Press, 1979).

17. I have drawn most heavily on Ryan, *Womanhood* (n. 5 above); Ryan, *Cradle* (n. 5 above); Ehrenreich and English (n. 5 above); Welter (n. 5 above).

18. Ryan, *Womanhood*, 24–25.

19. Similar changes occurred when culture and religion were feminized, according to Douglas (n. 1 above). Conceptions of God's love shifted toward an image of a sweet and tender parent, a "submissive, meek and forgiving" Christ (149).

20. On the persistence of women's wage inequality and responsibility for housework, see Stockard and Johnson (n. 14 above).

21. Jean Baker Miller, *Toward a New Psychology of Women* (Boston: Beacon Press, 1976). There are, of course, many exceptions to Miller's generalization, e.g., women who need to be independent or who need an attachment with a woman.

22. In psychology, the work of Carl Jung, David Bakan, and Bem are especially relevant. See Carl Jung, "Anima and Animus," in *Two Essays on Analytical Psychology: Collected Works of C. G. Jung* (New York: Bollinger Foundation, 1953), 7:186–209; David Bakan, *The Duality of Human Existence* (Chicago: Rand McNally & Co., 1966). They are discussed in Bem's paper, "Beyond Androgyny," in *Family Transition*, 2d ed., ed. A Skolnick and J. Skolnick (Boston: Little, Brown & Co., 1977), 204–21. Carl Rogers exemplifies the human potential theme of self-development through the search for wholeness. See Carl Rogers, *On Becoming a Person* (Boston: Houghton Mifflin Co., 1961).

23. Chodorow (n. 14 above) refers to the effects of the division of labor and to power differences between men and women, and the special effects of women's being the primary parents are widely acknowledged among historians.

24. The data on Yale men is from Mirra Komarovsky, *Dilemma of Masculinity* (New York: W.W. Norton & Co., 1976). Angus Campbell reports that children are closer to their mothers than to their fathers, and daughters feel closer to their parents than do sons, on the basis of large national surveys, in *The Sense of Well-Being in America* (New York: McGraw-Hill Book Co., 1981), 96. However, the tendency of people to criticize their mothers more than their fathers seems to contradict these findings; e.g., see Donald Payne and Paul Mussen, "Parent-Child Relations and Father Identification among Adolescent Boys," *Journal of Abnormal and Social Psychology* 52 (1956): 358–62. Being "closer" to one's mother may refer mostly to spending more time together and knowing more about each other rather than to feeling more comfortable together.

25. Studies of differences in friendship by gender are reviewed in Wenda Dickens and Daniel Perlman, "Friendship over the Life Cycle," in *Personal Relationships*, vol. 2, ed. Steve Duck and

Robin Gilmour, (London: Academic Press, 1981), 91–122, and Beth Hess, "Friendship and Gender Roles over the Life Course," in *Single Life*, ed. Peter Stein (New York: St. Martin's Press, 1981), 104–15. While almost all studies show that women have more close friends, Lionel Tiger argues that there is a unique bond between male friends in *Men in Groups* (London: Thomas Nelson, 1969).

26. Mirra, Komarovsky, *Blue-Collar Marriage* (New York: Random House, 1962) p. 13.

27. Daniel Levinson, *The Seasons of a Man's Life* (New York: Alfred A. Knopf, 1978), 335.

28. The argument about the middle-age switch was presented in the popular book *Passages*, by Gail Sheehy (New York: E. P. Dutton, 1976), and in more scholarly works, such as Levinson's. These studies are reviewed in Alice Rossi, "Life-Span Theories and Women's Lives," *Signs*, 6, no. 1 (1980): 4–32. However, a survey by Claude Fischer and S. Oliker reports an increasing tendency for women to have more close friends than men beginning in middle age, in "Friendship, Gender and the Life Cycle," Working Paper no. 318 (Berkeley: University of California Berkeley, Institute of Urban and Regional Development, 1980).

29. Studies on gender differences in self-disclosure are reviewed in Letitia Peplau and Steven Gordon, "Women and Men in Love: Sex Differences in Close Relationships," in *Women, Gender and Social Psychology*, ed. V. O'Leary, R. Unger, and B. Wallston (Hillsdale, N.J.: Lawrence Erlbaum Associates, 1985), 257–91. Also see Zick Rubin, Charles Hill, Letitia Peplau, and Christine Dunkel-Schetter, "Self-Disclosure in Dating Couples," *Journal of Marriage and the Family* 42, no. 2 (1980): 305–18.

30. Working-class patterns are described in Komarovsky, *Blue-Collar Marriage*. Middle-class patterns are reported by Lynne Davidson and Lucille Duberman, "Friendship: Communication and Interactional Patterns in Same-Sex Dyads," *Sex Roles* 8, no. 8 (1982): 809–22. Similar findings are reported in Robert Lewis, "Emotional Intimacy among Men," *Journal of Social Issues* 34, no. 1 (1978): 108–21.

31. Rubin et al., "Self-Disclosure."

32. These studies, cited below, are based on the self-reports of men and women college students and may reflect norms more than behavior. The findings are that women feel and express affective and bodily emotional reactions more often than do men, except for hostile feelings. See also Jon Allen and Dorothy Haccoun, "Sex Differences in Emotionality," *Human Relations* 29, no. 8 (1976): 711–22; and Jack Balswick and Christine Avertt, "Gender, Interpersonal Orientation and Perceived Parental Expressiveness," *Journal of Marriage and the Family* 39, no. 1 (1977):121–28. Gender differences in interaction styles are analyzed in Nancy Henley, *Body Politics: Power, Sex and Non-verbal Communication* (Englewood Cliffs, N.J.: Prentice-Hall, Inc., 1977). Also see Paula Fishman, "Interaction: The Work Women Do," *Social Problems* 25, no. 4 (1978): 397–406.

33. Gender differences in leisure are described in L. Rubin, *Worlds of Pain* (n. 9 above), 10. Also see Margaret Davis, "Sex Role Ideology as Portrayed in Men's and Women's Magazines" (Stanford University, typescript).

34. Bert Adams, *Kinship in an Urban Setting* (Chicago: Markham Publishing Co., 1968), 169.

35. Marjorie Lowenthal and Clayton Haven, "Interaction and Adaptation: Intimacy as a Critical Variable," *American Sociological Review* 33 (1968): 20–30.

36. Joseph Pleck argues that family ties are the primary concern for many men, in *The Myth of Masculinity* (Cambridge, Mass.: MIT Press, 1981).

37. Gender-specific characteristics also are seen in same-sex relationships. See M. Caldwell and Letitia Peplau, "Sex Differences in Same Sex Friendship" *Sex Roles* 8, no. 7 (1982): 721–32; see also Davidson and Duberman (n. 30 above), 809–22. Part of the reason for the differences in friendship may be men's fear of homosexuality and of losing status with other men. An exploratory study found that men were most likely to express feelings of closeness if they were engaged in some activity such as sports that validated their masculinity (Scott Swain, "Male Intimacy in Same-Sex Friendships: The Impact of Gender-validating Activities" [paper presented at annual meeting of the American Sociological Association, August 1984). For discussions of men's homophobia and

fear of losing power, see Robert Brannon, "The Male Sex Role," in *The Forty-Nine Percent Majority*, ed. Deborah David and Robert Brannon (Reading, Mass.: Addison-Wesley Publishing Co., 1976), 1–48. I am focusing on heterosexual relations, but similar gender-specific differences may characterize homosexual relations. Some studies find that, compared with homosexual men, lesbians place a higher value on tenderness and verbal self-disclosure and engage in sex less frequently. See, e.g., Alan Bell and Martin Weinberg, *Homosexualities* (New York: Simon & Schuster, 1978).

38. Unlike most studies, Reedy (n. 6 above) did not find that women emphasized communication more than men. Her subjects were upper-middle class couples who seemed to be very much in love.

39. Sara Allison Parelman, "Dimensions of Emotional Intimacy in Marriage" (Ph.D. diss., University of California, Los Angeles, 1980).

40. Both spouses thought their interaction was unpleasant if the other engaged in negative or displeasurable instrumental or affectional actions. Thomas Wills, Robert Weiss, and Gerald Patterson, "A Behavioral Analysis of the Determinants of Marital Satisfaction," *Journal of Consulting and Clinical Psychology* 42, no. 6 (1974), 802–11.

41. L. Rubin, *Worlds of Pain* (n. 9 above), 147.

42. See L. Rubin, *Worlds of Pain*; also see Richard Sennett and Jonathan Cobb, *Hidden Injuries of Class* (New York: Vintage, 1973).

43. For evidence on this point, see Morton Hunt, *Sexual Behavior in the 1970s* (Chicago: Playboy Press, 1974), 231; and Alexander Clark and Paul Wallin, "Women's Sexual Responsiveness and the Duration and Quality of Their Marriage," *American Journal of Sociology* 21, no. 2 (1965): 187–96.

44. Interview by Cynthia Garlich, "Interviews of Married Couples" (University of California, Irvine, School of Social Sciences, 1982).

45. For example, see Catharine Mackinnon, "Feminism, Marxism, Method, and the State: An Agenda for Theory," *Signs* 7, no. 3 (1982): 515–44. For a thoughtful discussion of this issue from a historical perspective, see Linda Gordon and Ellen Dubois, "Seeking Ecstacy on the Battlefield: Danger and Pleasure in Nineteenth Century Feminist Thought," *Feminist Review* 13, no. 1 (1983): 42–54.

46. Reedy (n. 6 above).

47. William Kephart, "Some Correlates of Romantic Love," *Journal of Marriage and the Family* 29, no. 3 (1967): 470–74. See Peplau and Gordon (n. 29 above) for an analysis of research on gender and romanticism.

48. Daniel Yankelovich, *The New Morality* (New York: McGraw-Hill Book Co., 1974), 98.

49. The link between love and power is explored in Francesca Cancian, "Gender Politics: Love and Power in the Private and Public Spheres," in *Gender and the Life Course*, ed. Alice S. Rossi (New York: Aldine Publishing Co., 1984), 253–64.

50. See Jane Flax, "The Family in Contemporary Feminist Thought," in *The Family in Political Thought*, ed. Jean B. Elshtain (Princeton, N.J.: Princeton University Press, 1981), 223–53.

51. Walter Gove, "Sex, Marital Status and Mortality," *American Journal of Sociology* 79, no. 1 (1973): 45–67.

52. This follows from the social exchange theory of power, which argues that person A will have a power advantage over B if A has more alternative sources for the gratifications she or he gets from B than B has for those from A. See Peter Blau, *Exchange and Power in Social Life* (New York: John Wiley & Sons, 1964), 117–18.

53. For a discussion of the devaluation of women's activities, see Michelle Rosaldo, "Woman, Culture and Society: A Theoretical Overview," in *Woman, Culture and Society*, ed. Michelle Rosaldo and Louise Lamphere (Stanford, Calif.: Stanford University Press, 1973), 17–42.

54. Gilligan (n. 15 above), 12–13.

55. Inge Broverman, Frank Clarkson, Paul Rosenkrantz, and Susan Vogel, "Sex-Role Stereo-

types and Clinical Judgments of Mental Health," *Journal of Consulting Psychology* 34, no. 1 (1970): 1–7.

56. Welter (n. 5 above).

57. Levinson (n. 27 above).

58. L. Rubin, *Intimate Strangers* (n. 8 above); Harold Rausch, William Barry, Richard Hertel, and Mary Ann Swain, *Communication, Conflict and Marriage* (San Francisco: Jossey Bass, Inc., 1974). This conflict is analyzed in Francesca Cancian, "Marital Conflict over Intimacy," in *The Psychosocial Interior of the Family*, 3d ed. Gerald Handel (New York: Aldine Publishing Co., 1985), 277–92.

# 14

DAVE BARRY

# Designer Genes: An Immodest Proposal for Sexual Realignment

*"Straight from the Heart" is the title of the September 1985 issue of Ms. magazine, a special issue devoted to the subject of men. The editors, Amanda Spake and Ruth Sullivan, explain in their preface, "This special issue on men shows that men and women's views—about each other, about themselves, and about the truly important challenges life offers—are not so different as they may once have seemed."[1] The articles in the issue focus on intimacy, competition and class, friendship, fatherhood, and, of course, that most frustrating and at the same time fulfilling mode of gender interaction, sex.*

*One of the articles in the magazine is a lighthearted look at sexual needs differences between men and women. In "Designer Genes," humorist writer Dave Barry attempts to discuss as diplomatically as possible (though far from delicately!) those seemingly uncontrollable factors that turn the sexual negotiations between males and females into something resembling a cross between a Marx Brothers movie and the SALT II talks.*



[1]Amanda Spake and Ruth Sullivan, "Straight from the Heart," *Ms.* (September 1985), p. 33.

What I think happened is, Mother Nature made some kind of terrible error. I am talking about human sexuality.

When you look at other species, you notice they have everything worked out. Take squid. I haven't bothered to research this, but I'm willing to bet you that when two squids want to have sex, they know *exactly* how to go about it. Probably the male waves his tentacles in a certain way, and the female emits some kind of noxious chemical compound, and the next thing you know they have their suckers all over each other.

Now contrast the effortless suavity of the squid with the sexual behavior of human beings, such as the former hairdresser of my friend Mary Anne. Mary Anne is a television producer who swears that this is an absolutely true anecdote.

This hairdresser, whom I will call Jacques, was leaving the area after having done Mary Anne's hair successfully for several years, and he invited her to his house for one last permanent. It was the old "one last permanent" line, and Mary Anne fell for it.

Things were fine until Jacques put the traditional foul-smelling permanent chemical on her hair. As you probably know, the next step is to wait for about 20 minutes, during which you're supposed to pick up *Glamour* magazine and read an article entitled "12 Common Mistakes Involving Eyeliner." But instead, without warning, Jacques hurled himself into Mary Anne's lap. She perceived this almost immediately as his concept of a sexual advance.

"Jacques," she said. "This is a bad idea."

"Submit to me," Jacques replied, "or there will be *no neutralizer*."

Really, he said that. And it was no idle threat. Jacques claimed that unless he neutralized the permanent chemical, Mary Anne would go bald, which could of course be a real disadvantage to a person working in television, a visual medium. Nevertheless, Mary Anne shoved him off her lap and made it clear by word and gesture that he was being a jerk. Eventually, he apologized and went on with the permanent, and according to Mary Anne it came out very nice.

The point, obviously, is that this would never, ever, have happened elsewhere in the animal kingdom. But this is only one among billions of bizarre activities we human beings engage in because Mother Nature failed to give us a simple, universal, squidlike ritual to perform when we wish to have sex.

What is worse, she made men and women so profoundly different that even if two people do manage somehow to agree that they wish to have sex, they will quickly discover that their purely physical needs differ greatly, in the sense that the amount of time the woman would like to spend in foreplay and lovemaking is roughly equivalent to the amount of time a man would allocate to foreplay, lovemaking, and building a garage. And what is worst of all, even if a man and a woman agree that they want to have sex *and* manage to become comfortable physically, the odds are they will have totally different psychological motivations. Those of you who hate generalizations should leave the room at this time, because I am going to explain briefly how, as I see it, men and women differ in their attitudes toward sex.

- *Women* want sex to be part of a deeper relationship involving commitment, sensitivity to the other's needs, understanding, tenderness, compassion, concern, sharing, and—above all—love.
- *Men* want sex.

"Wait a minute," I hear you women saying. "Not *all* men are like that. What about Paul Newman? What about the Pope? What about *Phil Donahue?*"

Okay. I will give you those three, and a few others, including of course your Significant Other. But this leaves an awful lot of men who basically attach as much emotional significance to the actual sex act as they do to flossing their teeth. Less, in fact, as we are learning more and more every day about the dangers of gum disease.

The vast psychological difference between men and women is the most troublesome of all, because it unfortunately tends to make women think that men have the moral standards of restroom bacteria. Talk to a single woman, and she will tell you about how usually when she dates a male for the first time, he makes a little speech wherein he says that at this point in his life he really does not wish to get involved in a relationship in which he is expected to live with the other person or date the other person exclusively or even necessarily remember the other person's name, but he is nevertheless willing to have sex. Single women call this The Speech, and often when they describe it they stick their fingers partway down their throats to indicate how it makes them feel.

And of course they are right. This truly is repulsive behavior. From their perspective. But that is exactly the problem: their perspective is that of what might as well be a different species altogether. It is as if the blue whale, which mates for life, were criticizing the sexual habits of the dragonfly, which goes through the whole sexual process—meeting, courting, Doing It, and breaking up—without even bothering to land.

Clearly something must be done. The human race has stumbled along for too many thousands of years under the present system, and it has resulted in too many misunderstandings, heartbreaks, divorces, homicides, and totally unnecessary hairdresser attacks.

What can be done, you ask? No doubt you have read articles about how biologists are manipulating genes. The problem is, they're always doing this to life forms that already work just fine, such as cows. As far as I know, there are no major sexual problems with cows. It is *people* who need a major redesign.

So I am proposing that we create a committee of reputable biologists, from both sexes, and ask them to see if they can't whip up a sexually compatible version of the human race. We could have a panel of prominent citizens advising the biologists on moral issues, taking care to avoid citizens who had a particular sexual ax to grind, such as Hugh Hefner or Phyllis Schlafly, because you could end up with a very kinky version of the human race that, for example, wanted to have sex all the time, but only with Republicans.

Assuming we take reasonable precautions, I think genetic manipulation is the way to go. I can think of no greater gift to give to future generations than to put both sexes on exactly the same sexual wavelength, so that everybody could tell instantly who wanted to have sex with whom, and it would always last the perfect length of time and be absolutely terrific for both of them. Or all six of them, depending on what the biologists work out. I think we should keep an open mind about this.

The important thing is that we get rid of the sexual hassles that have obsessed the human race since the dawn of civilization, that have totally dominated our music, our art, our literature, our conversations, our thoughts, our dreams, and our very souls, so we can get on with what we were really put on earth to do. Whatever the hell THAT is.

*Section Four*

# Marriage—Selected Issues

15

KATHLEEN GERSON

# Women's Work and Family Decisions

*In the United States and other Western societies, reaching young adulthood has long required both men and women to make several crucial decisions with lifelong consequences. For men, perhaps the two most crucial decisions have been the choice of a vocation and the choice of a wife. For women, until recently, the choice of a husband overshadowed all other decisions. Few young women considered avoiding marriage or children, and few seriously considered careers that would interfere with their two primary adult roles of wife and mother.*

*In recent years, the number of crucial decisions young women face has increased, and the alternatives open to them have become more varied and complex, especially regarding the choice of work and family roles. This has produced what some observers have called "decision overload" in the young adult years. Perhaps young women now experience more stress and "identity crises" than their mothers and grandmothers did during the same stage of life.*

*The reading that follows reprints the bulk of the first chapter of Kathleen Gerson's book,* Hard Choices. *In it, Gerson summarizes the social and demographic changes that have made young women's choices more difficult, and she describes and illustrates the complexity of the choices.*

Source: Kathleen Gerson, "Women's Work and Family Decisions," pp. 1–21 in *Hard Choices* by Kathleen Gerson, Los Angeles: University of California Press. 

We are in the midst of a "subtle revolution." Even seasoned observers, armed with statistics, are pointing to changes in women's behavior so vast as to warrant this label (Smith, 1979a ). Current concerns about "the new working woman" and "the new choice of motherhood" reflect a growing awareness among experts and lay observers alike of the far-reaching changes taking place in the work and family patterns of American women.

The rising number of female workers is the most obvious indication of the changing position of women.[1] The 1970s witnessed a veritable explosion in the number of women working for pay outside the home. The percentage of women at work rose from 43.3 percent in 1970 to an unprecedented high of 51.2 percent in 1980 (U.S. Department of Labor, 1980:3). For the first time in American history, more women are in the labor force than out of it, and women are likely to continue to stream into the workplace in the coming years. Recent predictions suggest that by 1990 around 70 percent of all women of working age will be employed or looking for a job. For younger groups, this figure is likely to rise even higher (Masnick and Bane, 1980; Smith, 1979b). The scale has thus tipped in favor of the employed woman.

A dramatic drop in women's fertility has accompanied this trend. Despite fears of a population explosion when the children of the baby boom reached childbearing age, the 1970s brought a "baby bust" instead. Although the fertility rate among baby boom mothers rose as high as 3.7 births per woman in the 1955–1959 period, it dropped to about 1.8 births per woman in the 1975–1980 period (Alonso, 1980; Sternlieb et al., 1982).[2] As women's workplace participation reached a historic high, the birthrate also dropped below the replacement rate to a historic low.[3] If current trends continue, the generation now in its prime childbearing years will not bear enough offspring to reproduce itself.

That the rise in the number of women workers occurred alongside a sharp decline in women's fertility is no coincidence. Women's work and family decisions have always been closely connected, and recent changes simply underscore the interactive, indeed inseparable, quality of this relationship.

This study explores the relationship between women's work and family decisions by taking a close look at the women most responsible for recent changes in female work and childbearing patterns. It examines the lives of a strategic group of women now in their prime childbearing years, all members of a generation in which large numbers have departed from the well-worn paths of their forebears. As the generation whose own life choices are most responsible for dramatic demographic shifts, this group is especially well posi-

---

[1]I use the term "work" to refer specifically to work performed outside the home for pay. Whether or not they are paid for what they do, all women (except for a small group of "leisure class" members) work in some way. The significant question is not whether they work, but how they work.

[2]The fertility rate refers to the number of births a woman would have in her lifetime if she kept pace with the age-specific birthrates for the given period (Sternlieb et al., 1982).

[3]The birthrate refers to the number of births per 1,000 population.

tioned to illuminate the causes, consequences, and meaning of the subtle revolution now under way.

Examining the forces that have shaped these women's decisions clarifies the more general process by which women choose between work and family commitments as their work aspirations interact with their desires to bear and rear children. The experiences of these women also show how work and family decisions emerge from the broader social context in which they occur. Proceeding from the lives of this strategically placed group, this study thus presents a model for understanding general processes of human development and a method for analyzing the link between human action and social change.

## CHANGING WORK AND FAMILY PATTERNS

In important respects, American women have often diverged from the model of the homebound, domestic mother. The child-centered housewife is actually a relatively recent historical development and is a social position that has generally been reserved for the more privileged members of the female population.

The rise of the factory system in the nineteenth century promoted the physical, social, and economic separation of the home and the workplace and thus ultimately relegated women to the private sphere. Yet throughout the early stages of industrialization, women contributed directly to the economic support of their families in a variety of ways. In the beginning years of industrial capitalism, many women and children worked alongside men in the factories, withdrawing from the industrial workplace only after male workers fought for and secured a "living" or "family wage" upon which the entire household could depend (Hartmann, 1976; Oakley, 1974b; Smelser, 1959). Many women were never able to withdraw completely from the paid labor force; sizeable segments of working-class and poor women have always worked outside the home for pay (Kessler-Harris, 1981; Tilly and Scott, 1978). Even though most nineteenth-century women did not participate in the paid work force, many took in boarders and lodgers to supplement the family income (Modell and Hareven, 1973).

Early nineteenth-century families were not especially child-centered. Instead, they generally operated as small businesses, looking to all household members, including women and children, to contribute to the "family economy." In order to sustain an acceptable standard of living for the family as a whole, children were often treated in ways that appear decidedly "adult" to modern eyes. Many left home to become apprentices long before the age we now consider appropriate for children to live on their own (Modell et al., 1976). Those who remained at home were expected to fend for themselves without the benefit of doting mothers such as modern children are believed to need.

A lengthy, leisurely childhood and prolonged adolescence are thus modern inventions that came into existence only after the rise of the mass system of education (Demos, 1970; Kett, 1977). If the modern family is expected to gear itself toward the child's needs, then the preindustrial family expected the child to orient himself or herself to its needs (Hareven, 1977). As industrialization proceeded, motherhood only gradually came to assume the idealized, almost mystical, aura that captured the American imagination throughout most of the twentieth century.

The first half of the twentieth century witnessed two paradoxical developments in the position of women. First, after the turn of the century, the size of the female labor force began to grow at a faster pace. In the hundred years between 1800 and 1900, the percentage of women in the paid labor force rose only from about 5 to 20 percent. Yet between 1900 and 1945, the female labor force grew to slightly over 38 percent, gaining 18 percentage points in only fifty years (Blau, 1979:271; Brownlee and Brownlee, 1976:3). During this period, women poured into the workplace both to occupy jobs vacated by men away at war and to fill the expanding job pool in the "pink collar" service sector so central to postindustrial capitalism (Howe, 1977: Oppenheimer, 1970).

Along with the steady rise in the number of working women, this period saw the consolidation of the ideology of female domesticity. This ideology originated in the nineteenth-century notion of "true womanhood," which argued that women are uniquely endowed with the emotional qualities necessary to oversee the private sphere and thus to safeguard society's moral fabric from the corrupting influence of industrialism (Welter, 1966). This ideal of femininity and woman's "proper place" was translated into the belief that mothering is every woman's ultimate fulfillment and should be every woman's highest priority. Ironically, women were encouraged to embrace motherhood just as the birthrate began to plunge and they began to move out of the home in substantial numbers.[4] Thus, Hareven (1977:69) concludes that

> motherhood as a full-time vocation has emerged only since the middle of the 19th century. Ironically, its glorification as a lifelong pursuit for women began to emerge at a time when demographic and social factors were significantly reducing the total proportion of a woman's life actually needed for it.

During the middle decades of the twentieth century, the domestic, nuclear household, whose cornerstone is the housewife-mother, captured the popular imagination as an ideal, if not always the reality. The economic prosperity of the immediate post–World War II era finally enabled large numbers of middle-class and working-class women to attain this domestic ideal. This period spawned the baby boom, promoted the child-centered household, and raised the full-time housewife-mother to a predominant place in American culture. After a long, steady decline dating back well before 1800, the birthrate turned upward in the mid-1930s and then rose even more sharply after World War II. Similarly, after rising sharply during the war, women's labor force par-

[4]For a full consideration of the history of the practice and ideology of "mother love" and its relation to social circumstances, see Badinter (1981). For an analysis of the emergence of the bourgeois, child-centered household in the nineteenth century, see Ryan (1981). Oakley (1974b) presents a historical overview of the rise of the housewife. Ryan (1979) presents a similar overview for American women from colonial times to the present.

**FIGURE 1** *Comparisons between the U.S. Birthrate and the Female Labor Force Participation Rate, 1890–1980*

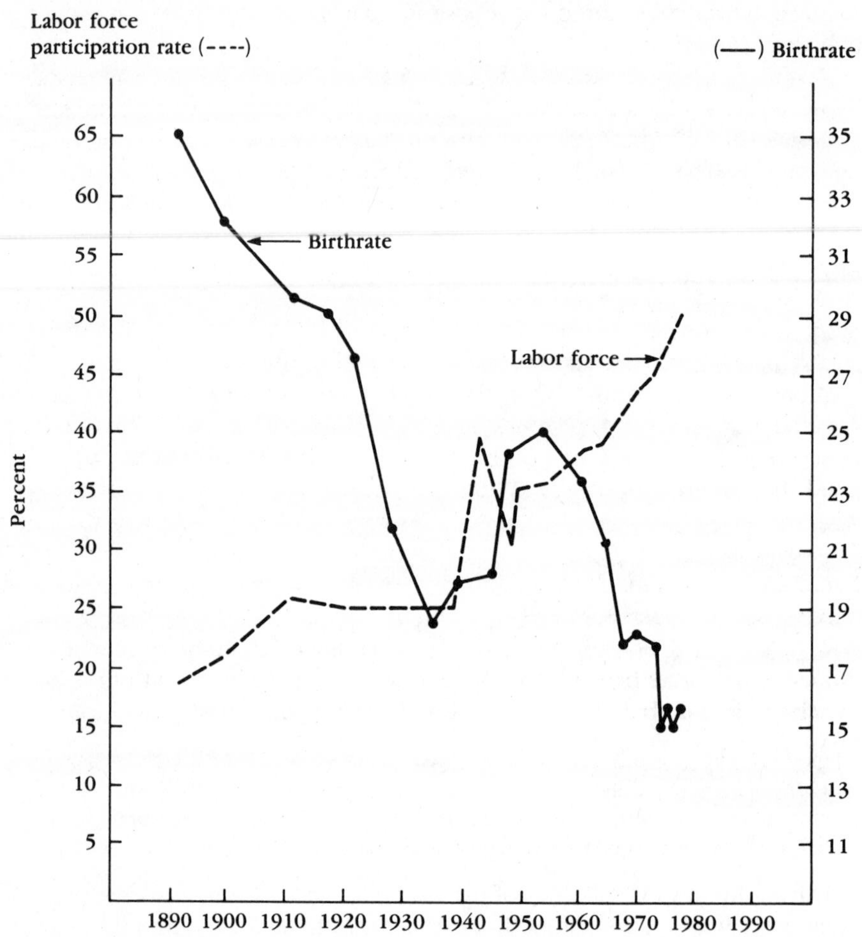


Source: Kathleen Gerson, *Hard Choices: How Women Decide about Work, Career, and Motherhood, Figure 1, p. 6. Berkeley/Los Angeles/London: University of California Press. © 1985 by The Regents of the University of California. Reprinted by permission.*

ticipation dropped precipitously immediately thereafter, reaching wartime levels again only in the mid-1960s.

Figure 1 outlines the major contours of women's fertility and work patterns since the turn of the century. Except during the mid-1930s and mid-1950s, the birthrate has declined steadily since well before the turn of the century. In contrast, except for a brief period immediately following World War II, women's labor force participation has either risen or remained constant over this same time period. The two trends tend to be interactive and inversely related. Since the mid-1950s especially, the birthrate has tended to go down as women's labor force participation has gone up. The figure thus reveals a long-term trend toward women's movement out of the home in the twentieth century. The post–World War II period of resurgent domesticity, and not current patterns, appears to be "a conspicuous and unusual departure" from this overall direction of change (Alonso, 1980:37).

Women's declining fertility and growing ties to the workplace are thus not new developments, but rather extensions of trends that have long been in the making. The roots of recent changes in women's commitments to work and family are deeply embedded in the structure of American society, as well as in virtually all the other advanced industrial nations. Cross-national studies attest to the nearly universal movement of women out of the home under conditions of advanced industrialism. (See, for example, Land, 1979; Lapidus, 1978; Sullerot, 1971; Wilensky, 1968.) Only from the perspective of the immediate post–World War II period do these recent changes appear unexpected. From the perspective of long-term historical change, the 1950s appear more aberrant than typical.

Since the 1950s, the pace of change has quickened dramatically. In slightly more than thirty years, women's labor force participation has risen more than 20 percentage points, from a low of 30.8 percent in 1947 to an all-time high of 51.2 percent in 1980. Similarly, over the last twenty-five years, the birthrate has dropped from an average of 25 children per 1,000 population in 1955 to an average of only 15 in the late 1970s. Notably, this drop has occurred despite the fact that the exceptionally large cohorts of "baby boomers" entered adulthood during the 1970s, placing an especially large number of women in their prime childbearing years. Current patterns in women's work and fertility behavior stand in sharp contrast to the model of female domesticity that attracted so many adherents in the 1950s. Daughters have increasingly departed from their mothers' paths.

The 1950s thus provide the contrast that makes the reemergence of long-gathering trends in the last two decades so striking. Yet recent changes in women's behavior stand out in bold relief not simply because we tend to compare them to the somewhat atypical patterns of the 1950s. Women's current work and family patterns differ qualitatively, and not just quantitatively, from past developments.

First, alterations in the kinds of women who work have accompanied the recent explosion in the proportion of women workers. Historically, the typical woman worker was young, single, and childless. For most, paid employment represented a temporary commitment that ended or was substantially curtailed with marriage and the arrival of children. This is no longer the case. Rather, the biggest increase in women workers since 1950 has occurred among married women, mothers with children (and especially preschool children) in the household, and women aged twenty-five to forty-four. There has also been a notable rise in the percentage of women workers who work full-time, year-round. An increasing proportion of women workers are married, rearing young children, working throughout the middle adult years, and working full-time throughout the year.

Women today have not simply joined the work force in historically high numbers; they have also shown a growing commitment to steady, long-term, full-time workplace attachment. In these important respects, women workers have begun to resemble male workers.[5] Like men, women of all ages and family statuses, and not simply those with few family responsibilities, are building strong work ties. Few, including men and children, have failed to feel the impact of these changes.

Second, the recent sharp drop in the birthrate appears to reflect more fundamental changes in women's orientations toward childbearing and mothering. The decline in the birthrate in the early decades of the twentieth century did not signal a rise in the rate of childlessness of one-child families, as it appears to do today. Historically, the birthrate decline resulted from a drop in average family size, not a rise in childlessness (Bane, 1976; Hofferth and Moore, 1979; Masnick and Bane, 1980). To the contrary, the percentage of ever-married women remaining childless or bearing only one child has also declined until recently—probably because of improved health and increased fecundity among women of childbearing age. Thus, in this earlier period, average family size dropped, but the proportion of women remaining childless or bearing only one child also decreased (Masnick and Bane, 1980).

Recent trends suggest that this historical aversion to childlessness and only children is declining. The cohorts of women now in their prime childbearing years have shown a marked lack of enthusiasm for childbearing, as shown by their increased propensity to remain childless or to have fewer children later in life. Although their ultimate decisions remain an open question, so far these women have exhibited notably higher rates of childlessness than most cohorts of the same age range born earlier in the twentieth century.

Among women born between 1935 and 1939, 80.7 percent had their first child by age twenty-nine and only about 10 percent remained permanently childless. Only 63 percent of those born between 1950 and 1954 had had a child as they neared thirty. This trend appears to be more than just a preference among younger cohorts for postponed childbearing. When asked in 1979 to report their lifetime birth expectations, almost a quarter of the women between ages eighteen and thirty-four said they expected to have either no children or only one child (U.S. Bureau of the Census, 1980a).

Although the link between predictions and actual future behavior is tenuous at best, these forecasts indicate that children are assuming a far less central position in many women's lives than they did thirty years ago. There is considerable controversy among informed analysts concerning the future. Some argue that the voluntary childless rate is declining and that an "echo baby boom" may soon occur as the biological clock runs out of this generation (Housknecht, 1982). Others are convinced that low birthrates are here to stay and

---

[5]The reverse is also true. Men's labor force participation has dropped from 86.4 percent in 1950 to 77.2 percent in 1980 (U.S. Department of Labor, 1980:3). In addition, men tend to work shorter hours and switch careers more often than they did thirty years ago (Hirschhorn, 1977). Men's work patterns thus increasingly resemble the part-time, interrupted model once reserved primarily for women.

that a sizeable proportion (perhaps as large as 20 to 30 percent) of women currently in their prime childbearing years will remain permanently childless (Bloom and Pebley, 1982; Ryder, 1979; Westoff, 1978). Whatever these women finally do, their current behavior signals significant social change. So many women postponing motherhood and acknowledging the possibility of childlessness is in itself consequential. At the very least, as one analyst puts it, we can expect rates of childlessness "considerably higher than the 10 percent rates that prevailed throughout most of the century" (Bloom, 1981:16A).

Since the 1950s, the nondomestic woman has emerged to challenge the predominance of the homemaker-mother. The traditional household composed of a breadwinning husband and homemaking wife dropped from 59.4 percent of all American households in 1950 and 51.2 percent in 1960 to only 30.3 percent in 1980. (When the presence of children in the household is also taken into account, this figure dips even lower.) Increasing numbers of dual-earning couples (with and without children), single-parent households (overwhelmingly headed by women), and single adults living alone or with other unrelated persons (primary individuals) have steadily eroded the dominance of the "traditional" household.[6] The greatest growth has occurred among married couples with a working wife and primary individuals, most of whom live alone (Gerson, 1983: 140).

The domestic woman who builds her life around children and homemaking persists, but she now coexists with a growing number of working mothers and permanently childless women. The nondomestic woman, whether she combines work and motherhood or eschews motherhood altogether, is no longer a statistical, social, or psychological anomaly. Instead, a variety of life patterns more accurately describes the current situation of American women.

## COHORTS AND SOCIAL CHANGE

Recent changes in work and mothering patterns are not distributed equally across the population of women. Rather, these changes have occured primarily through the aging of successive cohorts, whose decisions have differed in important respects from those made by the generations that preceded them.

Younger cohorts of women are much more likely than older cohorts to work. The rise of the woman worker has thus resulted not so much from changes in the behavior of all women, but from the progressive entrance of younger cohorts into the labor force as they reached working age. Women born after 1940, most of whom are now in their twenties and thirties, are most responsible for the steep rise in the percentage of women workers.

---

[6] I use the term "traditional" to refer to women whose primary commitments and orientations are to the home and the domestic sphere. Female domesticity is not a consistently dominant historical pattern. As used here, the term "traditional" thus refers to the type of female homemaker and mother who gained ascendency in the mid-twentieth century, and not to an idealized image that probably never predominated in the more distant past. (See Scott and Tilly, 1975; Tilly and Scott, 1978.)

A similar pattern exists for changes in women's childbearing patterns. Cohorts born after 1944 largely account for the recent sharp decline in the birthrate. Because these women are still moving through their prime childbearing years, their final rates are subject to change. When compared with older cohorts at a comparable age, however, they display notably lower propensities for childbearing.

An additional perspective on the fertility patterns of different generations is gained by comparing the percent remaining childless among different cohorts at different ages. There is an interesting difference between the baby boom mothers born between 1930 and 1940 and the baby boom offspring born between 1945 and 1959. Although only about 20 percent of the women in the older group were childless by the time they reached their late twenties well over 30 percent of the younger group remained childless throughout their twenties. Among those born between 1945 and 1949, almost 20 percent were childless well into their thirties; for those born between 1950 and 1954, over 35 percent were still childless as they approached thirty. Thus, despite improved health standards that helped lower the rate of childlessness throughout the first half of the twentieth century, recent female cohorts have returned to the high childlessness rates that characterized the earlier part of the century.[7]

In sum, younger female cohorts are most responsible for the rise in the percentage of women workers, the decline in the birthrate, and the increasing proportion of childless women in the later stages of their reproductive lives. The personal decisions of young adult women, most of whom came of age in the 1970s, underlie these rapid social changes.

This generation reached adulthood during a period of accelerated social change. Born in the aftermath of World War II, most of its members grew up in so-called traditional households. Ironically, the mothers of this generation are the women who vacated the workplace in large numbers to devote themselves to home and family. Yet the world this generation has inherited, and helped as adults to create, differs greatly from the world it knew as children. As members of a generation on the cutting edge of social change, they have collided with social institutions in flux. They have become both the recipients and the agents of far-reaching changes in work and family life.

Recent demographic changes in women's position can thus be best understood by examining the forces that have shaped the work and family decisions of that generation of women currently in its prime childbearing years. These women's lives offer especially rich clues to understanding the sources, contours, and likely future implications of the subtle revolution in women's behavior.

---

[7]It is difficult to disentangle voluntary and involuntary childlessness. Aside from those with infertility problems, most women who have postponed or rejected motherhood have found the option of childbearing difficult to implement *and* have found other options more attractive. Their choices thus reflect both constraints on their fertility behavior and opportunities to pursue other goals. There is, furthermore, an uneven distribution of fertility as economically disadvantaged women with fewer attractive alternatives to motherhood tend to have more children than educationally advantaged women.

## ALTERNATIVE PATHS IN ADULT DEVELOPMENT

Despite the rising number of women who appear to be breaking from former patterns, those who constitute this strategic generation have not made uniform choices. This group displays a varied range of responses to the structural dilemmas facing all women. Indeed, the experiences encountered by women of all generations may be found to some degree within its ranks.

Many have embraced the patterns of their predecessors; they have married, borne children, and settled down to full-time mothering; they have worked outside the home only intermittently, if at all. Yet a sizeable number of women have departed from this "traditional" path. These women have postponed, and even foresworn, motherhood: they have developed ties to the workplace that resemble the committed, permanent pattern once reserved for men: and they have rejected the domestic path that places children, family, and home above all else. In short, they have moved through their young adult years in markedly different ways from earlier generations. There have always been some women who fit this emerging pattern, but today their numbers are growing on a scale never seen before.

Consider, for example, the diverse paths taken by the following women drawn from the larger group interviewed in this study:

Laura grew up in a "typical" middle-class family. Her father, a middle-level manager for a large utilities company, was happy in his work and able to support his wife and three children with ease. Her mother never worked for pay, devoting herself instead to caring for her family and managing their comfortable suburban home.

Laura never gave much thought to the future when she was young; she always "just assumed" that she would become a wife and mother much like her mother before her. Because there were ample financial resources, she also planned for college. She looked upon this period as a chance to train for a profession, such as teaching or nursing, that would mesh with homemaking. College would also provide the perfect setting, she reasoned, for meeting a man who would support her domestic aspirations.

For Laura, things turned out much as she expected. After two years of post-high school training, she went to work as a nurse. She met her husband, Steve, on the job, and two years later they were married. Because her work did not offer the pay or advancement opportunities that Steve enjoyed as a physician, she began to look forward to trading the long, late hours of nursing for what she imagined would be the more rewarding work of parenting. Because Steve's income rose rapidly, she did not feel financially obligated to remain at a job that had grown tedious. She soon became pregnant and withdrew from the workplace.

Since the birth of her first child, Laura has stayed home with few, if any, regrets. Although she plans to return to work part-time when her two children are older, she states firmly that her family "will always come first." She also resents the undertones of disapproval she senses when she tells inquirers that being a mother is her "career."

Joanne's childhood was not filled with the same advantages as Laura's, but she did grow up with similar expectations. As a repairman, her father struggled to make ends meet. Her mother nevertheless did not work outside the home until Joanne was in the eighth grade. Both parents agreed that the children should have a full-time mother, even if this arrangement entailed forgoing material luxuries. Despite their limited finances, they hoped Joanne would attend college to prepare herself for a "better life" than either of them had achieved.

Joanne, however, did not share her parent's aspirations. She was more interested in dating than in school work and was not inspired by her part-time job as a waitress in a fast-food chain. Thus, when she became pregnant at seventeen, she did not greet this news with disappointment or panic. Instead, much to her parents' chagrin, she married her high school boyfriend and settled down to full-time mothering.

Two children, several sales jobs, and ten years later, Joanne still prefers domesticity to her other options. She occasionally feels social and financial pressure to forsake her domestic commitments for paid work. However, her husband earns enough money as a mechanic to "make ends meet." And every time she searches the want ads, she remembers how much she disliked the few temporary jobs she has held over the years. She then promptly turns her attention back to her children and her home. She is even considering having another child.

These two life histories illustrate the *traditional model* of female development in which an adult woman chooses the domestic life for which she prepared emotionally and practically as a child. Although they have disparate social backrounds, Laura and Joanne share a similar life course trajectory. For each, adult life went according to plan. Neither experienced a substantial change in life goals or emotional priorities as she moved into and through adulthood. Both were also insulated from events that might have caused them to veer off their expected life paths: They were neither pushed out of the home by economic necessity or marital instability nor pulled into the workplace by expanding opportunities. They thus remained committed to the domestic path they assumed was a woman's proper place. In its essentials, these life histories fit well the traditional model of female domesticity that gained momentum during the late nineteenth and twentieth centuries and reached a peak during the post-World War II period.

In contrast, consider the life paths of Elizabeth and Jane:

Elizabeth, like Laura, grew up in a traditional, comfortable, middle-class home. As a lawyer, her father took great pride in supporting his family in style. Indeed, he vetoed the few attempts his wife made to find work outside the home, arguing that children need their mother at home and her working would reflect badly upon both parents. Similarly, he expected his daughter to go to college not to prepare for an occupation, but rather to find a suitable mate. Adopting the messages she received, Elizabeth grew up believing a woman's place is in the home.

Elizabeth, the dutiful daughter, thus married a young engineer soon after college graduation. Within a few years, however, the marriage began to sour. Before she could fully assimilate the implications of her situation, she was divorced and out on her own for the first time in her life. Desperate for a paycheck, she wandered into an employment agency looking for a job, any job. They placed her in a small company, where she started as a receptionist and office manager. She quickly made herself indispensable and over a period of about five years worked her way up the organization to her present position of executive vice-president.

Elizabeth is now in her mid-thirties, and there appear to be few limits on how high she can rise. Rearing a child could, of course, conflict with her career goals. There is little chance that motherhood will interfere with her work, however, for she has foresworn marriage forever and probably childbearing as well. Despite her childhood expectations, home and family just do not fit with the commitments she has developed as an adult. As she looks back over this chain of events, she wonders how she could have come so far from where she began.

Like Laura, Joanne, and Elizabeth, Jane also assumed when she was growing up that she would marry, have many children, and live "happily ever after," just as her parents before her. Her father, a Southern European immigrant, worked day and night to support his large family. Her mother clung tightly to the "old country" ways, which included loyalty to her husband and an almost total devotion to her children. Jane harbored a hidden desire to go to college, but her father opposed such pursuits for women and could not have underwritten the expense in any case.

Jane worked for a short time after high school as a filing clerk. She married two years later and was pregnant within six months of the ceremony.

Shortly after the birth of her daughter, however, she became bored and dissatisfied. Taking care of a baby was not the ultimate fulfillment she had anticipated. Instead, she found motherhood to be a decidedly mixed experience—alternately rewarding and frustrating, joyful and depressing. Although she was reluctant to admit these feelings to herself or others, a growing sense of emptiness plus the need for additional household income spurred her to look for a paid job.

Thus, to keep herself busy and help with the family finances, she took a job as a bank teller. She expected this situation to be temporary, but the appropriate time to leave work never arrived. Her husband, Frank, could not seem to "make it" as a salesman working on commission, and his income consistently fell short of their needs. As time passed, the marriage began to falter. Frank's work difficulties, coupled with his growing desire to have another child, left Jane feeling that she might be happier without Frank than with him.

Just when it seemed that the marriage had become unbearable, Jane's boss offered her a promotion into management, including higher pay, increased responsibility, and more respect from peers and co-workers. The bank was facing affirmative action pressures and had responded by initiating a program designed to advance women who lacked college degrees. Jane was initially worried about the increased pressures the new job would entail, but she was also eager to move ahead. Not coincidentally, she also divorced Frank.

Today, Jane is dedicated to her job, aspires to upper-level management, and has no plans to expand her family beyond her only child. She is convinced, moreover, that her daughter is better off because she left the bulk of child care to someone else who enjoyed the work more than did she.

These lives illustrate an emerging and increasingly common pattern among both middle-class and working-class women that involves *rising work aspirations* and *ambivalence toward motherhood* . Elizabeth and Jane grew up wanting much the same things in life as Laura and Joanne, but adult experiences intervened to push them off their expected life courses. Despite their contrasting class backgrounds, both Elizabeth and Jane experienced similar constraints and opportunities as adults. Not only did their early marriages deteriorate over time, but unanticipated work advancement opportunities also opened to both. Growing work ambitions and a diminishing interest in mothering thus eventually replaced their early domestic aspirations. These examples illustrate the developmental path taken by an increasing proportion of women from both the middle and working classes who grew up believing in the "feminine mystique," only to find that adult life offered a very different set of alternatives.

The next four lives begin from notably different starting points than the first four stories. First, there are the cases of Gail and Mary:

Gail was not attracted to motherhood as a child, but rather hoped to avoid it. Her mother had relinquished a promising career as an artist to raise three children and never seemed to recover from this sacrifice. As her children grew, Gail's mother slipped deeper into depression and frustration.

Gail's father, in contrast, seemed to thrive on both his work and his children. As a successful businessman who had pulled himself out of poverty after the Depression, he encouraged his children, all girls, to aim for whatever they wanted in life. It is not altogether surprising, therefore, that for as long as she could remember Gail wanted to be a lawyer. She knew this was an unusual desire for a girl, but the prohibition against it only fueled her determination.

In major respects, Gail has not waivered from her early plans. She went to college, graduated in the top of third of her class, and entered law school, where she was surprised to find that over 30 percent of her classmates were women. After receiving her law degree, she joined a small law firm and was eventually made a partner. Throughout this period, she never found the time or felt the inclination to marry or have a child.

Now secure in her career, Gail has begun to view children as an option she can afford to consider. Time is running out, however, and no partner is in sight. There have been a few serious relationships with men, but they have all ended badly. She is fast losing confidence that she will find a suitable partner for the joint enterprise of child rearing and has reluctantly concluded that an exclusive commitment to one person for life may not be possible anymore. Because having a child outside of marriage seems unfair to herself and the child, the chances are high that she will never have children. She acknowledges this probability with mild regret.

Mary, like Gail, yearned from an early age for a life beyond the boundaries of home, children, and family. As the oldest of six children in a strict Catholic family, she had few illusions about the constant, often thankless task of rearing children. Her father worked hard as an electrician to keep his children clothed and fed. Her mother also worked hard cooking, washing, cleaning, and generally making sure her numerous children stayed out of trouble. Although Mary remembers her mother as devoted to her duties, she also remembers never wanting to follow her example. Her mother's life seemed stifling, and children seemed more a burden than a fulfillment.

Although she harbored vague ambitions for the independence work could offer, she married within a year of high school graduation. She now admits her primary motivation was to escape her parents' home and the confining atmosphere of her family. Unlike many of her friends, however, she did not rush into motherhood, but instead went to work for a mid-sized corporation.

The work was frustrating at first, but every time she quit, she found staying home was worse. From time to time, she considered starting a family; but both she and her husband had become dependent on her income, and she still viewed children as something she was supposed to but did not want. Rather than getting pregnant, she took a series of clerical jobs. Eventually her persistence paid off, and in her late twenties she was promoted into the lower level of management at a major corporation.

Today Mary is just past thirty. She is more committed to work than ever and still has strong misgivings about becoming a mother, but she also feels the biological clock ticking away. Her husband, who loves young children, is growing impatient to have a child of his own. Mary is beginning to fear that never having a child might condemn her to loneliness later in life. She has recently decided that having one child might be the perfect compromise. With one child, she reasons, she can pursue her growing work ambition without sacrificing completely the pleasures of building a family.

Despite their divergent class and family backgrounds, neither Gail nor Mary found domesticity an appealing option. Even as children, they viewed motherhood apprehensively and hoped for something different out of life. Although Gail formed clear career goals early in childhood and Mary's goals remained vague well into her twenties, both saw children as a potentially dangerous obstacle to achieving other desired life endeavors. For these women, mothering did not represent the ultimate fulfillment to which they could happily devote their lives; rather it threatened to be a trap they wished to avoid.

Like Laura and Joanne, Gail and Mary realized their early life goals and did not substantially change direction over the course of their lives. Because their goals were different from those of traditional women, however, Gail's and Mary's lives developed in a different direction: out of the home, away from motherhood, and toward committed work ties. These women met a set of circumstances in adulthood that enabled them to travel a *nontraditional path*. Their original nondomestic aspirations were supported by the people and institutions they encountered as adults.

In an earlier historical period, these women would have been more likely to have succumbed to the pressures to foreswear career ambitions in favor of childbearing. Today, however, women's social environment is more likely to nuture their work aspirations. Similarly, women today who experience deeply felt ambivalence toward mothering are less likely to repress, deny, or ignore these misgivings than they were in the past, when the sanctions against antimaternal feelings were strong.

The next two women shared Gail's and Mary's high work ambitions and early apprehensions about parenthood. Unlike Gail and Mary, however, they did not meet felicitous circumstances in adulthood that supported these early goals. They thus experienced a marked change of life direction as they turned toward home and children over time:

Susan grew up in a middle-class home, but it was not a happy one. Her parents, who eventually divorced, fought often. Her father worked for an airline and was absent from their home much of the time. Her mother, whom she remembers fondly, worked part-time as a door-to-door saleswoman and occasionally took Susan on these outings. The money her mother received from this intermittent work helped the family over occasional economic rough spots. With her husband generally gone, Susan's mother doted on her two children and wished for them the education and opportunities she never received.

Susan shared her mother's hopes and earned a scholarship to college. She attended college with optimism, but a number of factors ultimately thwarted her career ambitions. First, she met and married John in her senior year. His education required her economic support as well as her attention to the household tasks. Because his career needs collided with hers, she dropped her plans for a business degree and earned a teaching credential instead. She did not particularly like the idea of working with children, but a teaching degree on the primary school level could be earned quickly and promised her job security—or so she thought.

As it turned out, she had a difficult time finding a job and eventually settled for preschool teaching. Despite the low salary, economic constraints have kept her in teaching ever since. She has, not surprisingly, grown steadily weary of the demanding work and lack of chances of advancement.

In contrast, John is beginning to make progress in his architectural career and has begun to complain that he wants more of her attention directed to their life together. Susan can now depend on John for financial support; so she plans to resign and start a family. Ironically, she now looks forward to motherhood as her best chance to escape from the world of children that defines her job.

Vicki's childhood was marked by difficulty. Her father supported his wife and four children on a janitor's salary. Her mother provided little in the way of emotional or economic help, for she was in and out of mental hospitals throughout many of Vicki's early years.

Vicki was never especially oriented toward motherhood. Instead, since she was old enough to know who the police were, she wanted to be a policewoman. She was attracted to the excitement of life on the streets, to the physical and mental challenge. An exciting career also offered the hope of leaving behind her parents' poor existence.

Forced to take the best job she could find after high schook, Vicki became a secretary-clerk. She also took the qualifying exam for police work and passed with high marks. No jobs were available, however, and she returned to her desk job, still hoping for "bigger things."

In the meantime, she met and married Joe. Joe's job as a construction worker required that they move a lot. Vicki found herself changing jobs for the sake of Joe's "career." Once she even turned down the chance to advance because Joe's work came first. She ultimately grew to hate working, for it usually involved taking orders from bosses she did not respect.

Joe also began to pressure her to have children. Children were very important to Joe, for he had been orphaned and wanted to give his children the love he never received. Vicki viewed children as a burden she could do without, but Joe even threatened to leave her if they did not start a family soon. She decided that losing Joe was too heavy a price to pay for her fears and became pregnant in her late twenties.

After the birth of her first child, Vicki discovered that staying home to rear a child was more rewarding than her succession of boring, dead-end jobs. By her mid-thirties, she was a full-time mother of two.

Today she has given up hope of becoming a policewoman, but in return for this sacrifice she feels she has gained the secure home life she never knew as a child. She occasionally considers taking a part-time job, but she hopes she will never have to return to the full-time work she grew to abhor. She worries that, if something ever happened to Joe or the marriage, she would be forced out of the home again.

Susan and Vicki represent a fourth pattern for women that has probably long been in existence but only recently recognized: a woman who harbors deep-seated ambivalance toward mothering and domesticity but over time experiences *falling work aspirations* and begins to see *the home as a haven*. As children, neither Susan nor Vicki identified with the ideal of feminine domesticity, but as adults, they did not meet the supportive environment that greeted Gail and Mary. They ventured into the workplace with high hopes, only to find thwarted opportunities and stifling experiences. In time, work became burdensome, not fulfilling, to these women. They also came to perceive work as a threat to securing the intimacy and support they depended on at home.

Susan and Vicki thus ultimately concluded that mothering was preferable to the frustration of paid work and that it also promised to cement a cherished relationship at home. Despite their early work ambitions and persistent ambivalence toward child rearing, they eventually opted for domesticity over strong work ties.

These two women may seem out of step with their age peers who have found a more supportive environment for rising work aspirations, but they represent a growing group forced into jobs and occupations they find stultifying in order to earn a living. These women also resemble men who find themselves in jobs they would prefer to leave, except for one important difference: Men can weigh the relative costs of remaining in an unsatisfying job versus finding a new one, but few men enjoy the traditional, although shrinking, female option of trading paid work for domestic work. This group of women ultimately reaches occupational roadblocks that lead them to view domestic pastures as greener.

These two examples also demonstrate three important aspects of female development. Many women choose motherhood not to fulfill deep-seated emotional needs, but rather as the best option among a number of unappealing alternatives. Second, an apparent lack of ambition may actually be a well-founded concern for preserving a stable private life. Finally, the erosion of the domestic option, although no loss to women like Gail and Mary who secure work that is rewarding, is perceived as an understandable threat to women like Susan and Vicki who find work a dead-end street. Unlike most men, many women have traditionally had the option *not* to earn a paycheck. As this option erodes, some women's gains are inevitably offset by others' losses.

Each of these eight life histories illustrates the powerful, interactive link between women's work and family decisions. As a group, they also illustrate the varied paths women negotiate through adulthood. Although these are only eight cases amid considerable diversity, they demonstrate four general patterns that a woman's life course can assume, whether she was born into the working or the middle class.

These four patterns are based on two especially important dimensions around which distinct groups of women form. First, women differ in their early expectations about the goals they plan to pursue as adults. Exposed to a diverse, complex set of experiences as children, women, like men, develop a variety of conscious and unconscious aspirations long before they are able to test these wishes as adults. For some, these early images take the shape of well-formed plans in which the future appears as certain as the past. For others, these goals are more amorphous, assuming the form of vague hopes that may or may not be realized.

However misty or clear, these desires form the baseline for adult life. Some plan to build their lives around the traditional feminine commitments to home, husband, and children; these women expect their own lives to resemble the domestic model that has been so prevalent in the recent past. Others view marriage and motherhood with trepidation and aspire to the less traditionally feminine pursuits of work advancement. Because their numbers have been few in the past, members of this latter group may be less convinced that their life choices are guaranteed than are those who start with domestic aspirations. Their lack of certainty, however, in no way diminishes the power of their feelings. The aspirations that women take into adulthood may thus center around domestic or nondomestic goals.

Once established, these early orientations are subjected to the real constraints and opportunities encountered in adulthood, the second dimension that distinguishes groups of women from each other. The social circumstances adults confront can support or undermine their original goals. Initial goals can prove viable, leading one down a life path wholly consistent with early expectations, or these early plans can ultimately turn out to be uninviting or even impossible, encouraging or perhaps requiring individual change. Unexpected events can lead adults to reevaluate their past assumptions and reorient themselves toward the future. Thus, pathways through adulthood may either follow or diverge from one's beginning baseline.

People differ in the extent to which they are exposed to change-inducing experiences. They consequently vary in the degree to which change characterizes their developmental path. When the pace of historical change is slow, most people are insulated from events that might shake up their views of the world or their proper place in it. Under these circumstances, most people tend to assume that their lives are preordained and rooted in the natural order of things. Even during periods of accelerated social change, many are able to move stably through life without veering significantly from an expected path.

Periods of rapid change increase the likelihood of exposure to triggering events that promote and sometimes force individual change. At these times, people who might otherwise assume that the order of their lives is given find that they must undergo personal change in order to adapt to changing social circumstances. These people experience turning points when they abandon old assumptions and confront new possibilities.

## REFERENCES

Alonso, William. 1980. "The Population Factor and Urban Structure." In *The Prospective City*, ed. by Arthur P. Solomon. Cambridge, Mass. MIT Press.

Badinter, Elizabeth. 1981. *Mother Love: Myth and Reality*. New York: Macmillan.

Bane, Mary Jo. 1976. *Here to Stay: American Families in the Twentieth Century*. New York: Basic Books.

Blau, Francine. 1979. "Women in the Labor Force: An Overview." In *Women: A Feminist Perspective*, 2d ed., ed. by Jo Freeman. Palo Alto, Calif.: Mayfield.

Bloom David E. 1981. "Traditional Family Strained by Childlessness, Divorce, Planned Remarriage." *San Francisco Examiner*, May 3: 16A.

Bloom, David, and Anne R. Pebley. 1982. "Voluntary Childnessness: A Review of the Evidence and Implications." *Population Research and Policy Review* 1 (3): 203-224.

Brownlee, W. Elliot and Mary M. Brownlee. 1976. *Women in the American Economy*. New Haven, Conn.: Yale University Press.

Demos, John. *A Little Commonwealth: Family Life in the Plymouth Colony*. New York: Oxford University Press.

Gerson, Kathleen. 1983. "Changing Family Structure and the Position of Women: A Review of the Trends." *Journal of the American Planning Association* 49 (2) (Spring): 138-48.

Hareven, Tamara. 1977. "Family Time and Historical Time." *Daedalus* 106 (Spring): 57–70.

Hartmann, Heidi I. 1976. "Capitalism, Patriarchy, and Job Segregation by Sex." *Signs: Journal of Women in Culture and Society* 1 (Spring): 137–169.

Hirschorn, Larry. 1977. "Social Policy and the Life Cycle: A Developmental Perspective." *Social Service Review* 51 (September): 434–50.

Hofferth, Sandra L. and Kristin A. Moore. 1979. "Women's Employment and Marriage." In *The Subtle Revolution: Women at Work*, ed by Ralph E. Smith. Washington, D. C. : Urban Institute.

Houseknecht, Sharon K. 1982. "Voluntary Childlessness: Toward a Theoretical Integration." Paper presented at the seventy-seventh annual meeting of the American Sociological Association, San Francisco, September.

Howe, Louise Kapp. 1977. *Pink Collar Workers: Inside the World of Women's Work*. New York: Putman.

Kessler-Harris, Alice. 1981. *Women Have Always Worked: A Historical Overview*. Old Westbury, N. Y.: Feminist Press.

Kett, Joseph F. 1977. *Rites of Passage: Adolescence in America, 1790 to the Present*. New York: Basic Books.

Land, Hilary. 1979. "The Changing Place of Women in Europe." *Daedalus* 108 (Spring): 73–94.

Lapidus, Gail. 1978. *Women in Soviet Society*. Berkeley: University of California Press.

Masnick, George, and Mary Jo Bane. 1980. *The Nation's Families: 1960–1990*. Cambridge, Mass.: Joint Center for Urban Studies of MIT and Harvard University.

Modell, John, and Tamara K. Hareven. 1973. "Urbanization and the Malleable Household: An Examination of Boarding and Lodging in American Families." *Journal of Marriage and the Family* 35 (August): 467–79.

Modell, John, Frank F. Furstenberg, Jr., and Theodore Hershberg. 1976. "Social Change and Transitions to Adulthood in Historical Perspective." *Journal of Family History* 1 (Autumn): 7–32.

Oakley, Anne. 1974b. *Woman's Work: The Housewife, Past and Present,* New York: Random House.

Oppenheimer, Valerie K. 1970. *The Female Labor Force in the United States: Demographic and Economic Factors Governing Its Growth and Changing Composition*. Berkeley: University of California, Institute of International Studies.

Ryan, Mary P. 1979 *Womanhood in America: From Colonial Times to the Present*, 2d ed., New York: New Viewpoints.

Ryan, Mary P. 1981. *The Cradle of the Middle Class: The Family in Oneida County, New York, 1790–1865* . New York: Cambridge University Press.

Ryder, Norman B. 1979. "The Future of American Fertility." *Social Problems* 26 (February): 359–370.

Scott, Joan W., and Louise A. Tilly. 1975. "Women's Work and the Family in Nineteenth-Century Europe." *Comparative Studies in Society and History* 17 (January): 36–64.

Smelser, Neil J. 1959. *Social Change in the Industrial Revolution*. Chicago: University of Chicago Press.

Smith, Ralph E. 1979a. "The Movement of Women into the Labor Force." In *The Subtle Revolution: Women at Work*, ed. by Ralph E. Smith. Washington, D.C.: Urban Institute.

———. 1979b. *Women in the Labor Force in 1990*. Washington D.C.: Urban Institute.

Sternlieb, George, James W. Hughes, and Connie O. Hughes. 1982. *Demographic Trends and Economic Reality: Planning and Markets in the '80s.* New Brunswick¿ N.J.: Rutgers Center for Urban Policy Research.

Sullerot, Evelyne. 1971. *Women, Society, and Change.* Trans. by Margaret S. Archer. New York: McGraw-Hill.

Tilly, Louise A., and Joan W. Scott. 1978. *Women, Work, and Family.* New York: Holt, Rinehart and Winston.

U.S. Bureau of the Census. 1980a. "Fertility of American Women: June 1979." *Current Population Reports,* Series p–20, No. 358. Washington, D.C.: U.S. Government Printing Office.

U.S. Department of Labor. 1980. *Perspectives on Working Women: A Databook.* Bulletin 2080. Washington, D.C.: U.S. Government Printing Office.

Welter, Barbara. 1966. "The Cult of True Womanhood: 1820–1860." *American Quarterly* 18 (Summer): 151–74.

Westoff, Charles F. 1978. "Some Speculations on the Future of Marriage and Fertility." *Family Planning Perspectives* 10 (March-April): 79–82.

Wilensky, Harold L. 1968. "Women's Work: Economic Growth, Ideology, and Structure." *Industrial Relations* 7 (May): 235–248.

16

MARION L. KRANICHFELD*

# Rethinking Family Power

*Most sociologists cite the 1960 book* Husbands and Wives *by Robert Blood and Donald Wolfe as the beginning of the research literature on family power. While the question of who dominated within family units might have held some interest for researchers during the 1950s, most people in the United States assumed, rightly or wrongly, that most families were of the Ward and June Cleaver variety with Ward clearly in control.*

*In their classic empirical study, Blood and Wolfe examined family power using what they called a "resource model." In short, they suggested that the power an individual wielded was directly related to the resources he or she controlled—the more resources one had, the more power. The bulk of subsequent research on family theory has evolved directly from that initial study and has further developed resource theory. Most of these family power studies use, as Blood and Wolfe did, a classic sociological definition of power, that is, the ability of a person to carry out his or her will, even if other parties are opposed to it. They then suggest that the ability to use power is based on the resources an individual can call upon to reinforce his or her claim to power.*

*Most family power researchers claim to have found that the most important resource for the establishment of power in the marital dyad is economic power. For instance, working wives have more power in their marriages than nonworking wives, and the more a woman earns, the more power she is likely to exert in the relationship. Throughout this research, relative income has consistently emerged as the most important factor in the balance of power between husbands and wives.*

---

*I would like to thank Gunhild Hagestad for her encouragement and guidance through successive drafts of this article. At certain critical points she has had a major influence on the development of the ideas presented herein.

*This body of literature has received major criticism in the past two decades, but few sociologists concerned with family power have moved outside of the resource model. In the following paper, Kranichfeld does so, viewing family power from a different perspective. The paper is likely to stimulate a new line of research on family power that will broaden the narrow focus on the relative power of spouses in the marriage relationship.*

Source: Marion L. Kranichfeld, "Rethinking Family Power," *Journal of Family Issues* 8, no. 1 (March 1987), pp. 42–56,


---

Although research on power in the family has been ongoing for nearly three decades, the concept of power has proven to be very difficult to work with, particularly at the levels of operationalization and measurement (Olson and Rabunsky, 1972; Turk and Bell, 1972). The last two decade reviews of the subject (Safilios-Rothschild, 1970; McDonald, 1980) present rather disappointing evaluations of the family power literature. In this article, I argue that this research has been fundamentally shaped by an abiding interest in the relative power of men and women, rather than in power in the family per se, and as a consequence we have "missed the boat" on family power. Family power has been masculinized and viewed almost exclusively from a macro-level perspective in which the family has been of interest primarily as a context within which men and women interact and struggle for power, rather than as a realm in and of itself. Researchers have continued to assume that family power is generated by acquiring skills, resources, and status *outside* the family, rather than by acquiring skills for relating to others *within* the family. Much of the family power literature has focused on marriage and marital decision making, but I argue that it is power within the parent-child relationship that is more complex, enduring, and significant. When family power is examined from this micro perspective, women's positions in the family power structure become much clearer.

## BACKGROUND

I begin by defining *family power* as it will be used in this article and by differentiating it from two related concepts, influence and coercion. First, *family power* is the ability of individual members to change the behavior (including thought and affect) of other family members (Cromwell and Olson, 1975). Second, family power involves asymmetry of relations between members with regard to this ability to change the behavior of others, and third, family power reflects family system properties, rather than the attributes of the powerful member (McDonald, 1980). That is, family power exists because of one's relationship within the family system, rather than merely because of one's personal characteristics. *Influence*, which describes a state in which one person has an impact on the behavior of another, is a broader term than power; influence can be intentional or unintentional, whereas power is the capacity to influence another intentionally in the pursuit of specific goals (Huston, 1983). The most important distinction between coercion and power is that coercion is the act of forcing another to do something against their will and requires a conflict of interest, while power does not necessarily involve either action or a conflict of interest. Power is simply a capacity, one that may be used to the detriment of others or that may be used to promote the well-being of others.

Having established this working definition, let us view the past work on power in the family from a broader perspective. From its inception in 1960 with the work of Blood and Wolfe, family power research has been focused primarily on determining the relative power of husbands and wives in marital decision making. Thus the major investigative issue of this field has clearly been power relations *between men and women*. As such, an examination of prevailing thought regarding power and gender informs us about some of the intellectual bedrock on which the family power literature rests. Broad-ranging anthropological studies of power have shown that, while there exists some disagreement in the literature as to whether or not male dominance is universal, there is widespread agreement that sexual asymmetry favoring males exists in many, if not most, societies, that in some cultures the inequality is quite extreme, and that there is no reliable evidence that any society exists or has ever existed in which the opposite pattern holds, that is, where women have general authority over men. Thus in spite of a great deal of variability between cultures regarding the appropriate content of male and female roles, the male role is valued more highly, and men generally have greater economic, political, and religious power than women (Rosaldo, 1974; Mead, 1949).

This near-universal pattern of men's power over women is also reflected in much of what is written about women from other standpoints as well—for example, women's unpaid household labor (Brown, 1982), and men's failure to take on such responsibilities when their wives work (Pleck, 1979); recent feminist writings on women and the family (Thorne, 1982; Cancian, 1985); biologically based theories about power differentials between the genders (Collins, 1975; Tiger, 1970); and Marxist theories about the relationship between sexual asymmetry and economic structure (Leackock, 1972; Zaretsky, 1973). While there have been few direct references made to this larger picture of sexual asymmetry within the family power literature (one notable exception being Gillespie, 1971), this appears to be one of the main assumptions on which family power work rests.

However, there is a discrepancy between the implicit image of women that emerges from much of this literature and the reality in families. That is to say, in spite of all the mental, emotional, and physical hardships that women appear to have experienced simply by virtue of their membership in the female gender, they appear to be remarkably resilient and constructive in their approach to human relations. As a group, women continue to struggle for greater equality and justice, but as individuals *almost never do so by choosing to sever the bonds that connect them to other people,* from which they derive tremendous sustenance and reward. That women are not simply an angry and resentful aggregate informs us that the current literature on women and power tells only part of the story. What, then, are we missing?

## WOMEN'S ROLES

It is evident from a comprehensive reading of any body of literature dealing with power that women are rarely portrayed as having power, *except where and to the extent that they hold the types of power that men generally wield*, in other words, economic, religious, or political power. *Power* appears to be automatically defined as whatever rights men have that women generally do not, and by this definition, women are indeed powerless. When power is viewed from a different perspective, however, it can be seen that women in fact have a great deal of power, of a very fundamental and pervasive nature; so pervasive, in fact that it is easily overlooked. Rapheal (1975, p. 111) notes that

> when power is seen as limited to the political and economic scenes... "male activity is accorded pre-eminence in the public sector" (Freidl, 1967: 97). When power is defined as the ability to bear, educate and determine the personality, the values, beliefs, hates, and loves of each new human member of a society, in fact, to control decisions of who will or will not survive, then females are certainly dominant.... *The power intrinsic in determining the outcome of each new generation is unparalleled* [emphasis added.]

In essence, Raphael is delineating two domains of social power: one internal to the family, and one external to it. The power of this private, internal, micro domain, which has received very little attention, is almost universally the territory of women.

Women's lives are far more involved in the family than are men's. Speaking from a cross-cultural perspective, Rosaldo (1974, pp. 26–28) tells us that while men "have rituals which reinforce the distance between [themselves] and their families ... [that] become a barrier to becoming embedded in an intimate, demanding world ... women's lives are marked by neither privacy nor distance. They are embedded in, and subject to, the demands of immediate interaction." Women invest in and rely more on vertical bonds than do men, and send and receive more intergenerational influence than do men (Hagestad, 1985). Perhaps as a result, women dominate the position of "kinkeeper" in families (Rosenthal, 1985). Kinkeeping is more than a job, it is a career. One-quarter of the kinkeepers in Rosenthal's sample had been taking responsibility for family cohesion for 30 to 75 years. It is not surprising that divorce appears to disrupt men's ties with their families to a greater extent than women's (Hagestad, Smyer, and Stierman, 1984). It should also not be surprising that family transitions are more influential in shaping both the life course and emotional experiences of women than men (Hagestad and Neugarten, 1985). Furthermore, although in many societies institutions outside the home (schools, services for the elderly, and so on) have taken over some of the women's former family functions, none of them provides care or socialization through relationships between individuals, which is the basis of the kind of power discussed here.

Some of the qualities that have been found to differentiate men and women hold implications for differences in family relationships. Analyses of cross-cultural data on sex roles have shown modal patterns that are strikingly widespread, with males being more aggressive, less responsible, less nurturant, and less emotionally expressive than females (D'Andrade, 1966). In a similar vein, Gilligan found that males conceive responsibility as a limit to individual rights, whereas for women, responsibility exists because of one's connection with others, and thus requires response—"an extension rather than a limitation of action" (Gilligan, 1984, p. 38).

The gap between men's and women's family roles appears to be widening at present in our own society. Eggebeen and Uhlenberg (1985, p. 251) found large changes in the organization of men's lives from 1960 to 1980, with "much less time being spent living in families with children present and more time being spent outside marriage." These structural barriers between men and families, which are consequences of recent demographic and social changes, serve to increase men's isolation from family interaction and result in a pattern of increasingly separate spheres of existence of males and females. Rossi (1985) notes that since children are the primary connection between adults and community, there is an increasing gender gap in embeddedness in the caring institutions of society. Hagestad (1986) predicts an increase in matrifocality due to the longer joint survival of mothes and daughters, trends in divorce and remarriage, and nonmarital fertility. She notes that "an increasing proportion of men have only precarious vertical ties, both up and down generational lines, while women's intergenerational ties are more varied, complex, and durable than ever before in human history" (Hagestad, 1986; p. 137).

Women's family roles also have a profound influence on the women's development as individuals and on the kinds of life skills they bring to bear on the problems that confront them and those closest to them. Gutmann (1985) has coined the term ***parental imperative***, which he uses to express the idea that parenthood is a powerful condition, in fact, it is the pivotal stage of the human life cycle and acts as a catalyst in the development of an individual, enlisting normal but powerful narcissistic drives in the service of the new offspring, drawing out latent sex-role polarization in both men and women. Remarkably, Gurmann does not consider gender differences beyond the polarization theme. According to Gutmann's logic, the transformation of narcissism should be far greater in females than in males because of their different biological and social roles in parenthood. For example, any woman who is pregnant, nursing, or caring for a newborn infant is in the process of learning powerful lessons about relinquishing control over her body, her time, and her identity at a fundamental level. She has fewer choices than usual in how she responds to the experience emotionally and intellectually due to hormonal changes, and no choice about whether or not to experience the experience. Most men do not undergo any analogous experience unless and until severe health problems intervene quite late in their lives.

Thus, an extension of Gutmann's logic leads us to the conclusion that women are more likely to change as a response to the demands of parenting than are men, a point that others have made quite explicitly. For example, Ruddick (1982) focuses on the intellectual capacities that she believes white middle-class American women develop as a response to the experience of mothering. Miller (1976) also maintains that change, growth, and intense involvement with others are intimate parts of women's lives in a way that they are not for men, and that, as a result, women develop valuable skills in fostering and guiding the emotional growth of others.

Maternal behavior is certainly influenced by environmental and cultural conditions, and the psychologically intense investment and caring patterns that Ruddick (1982) and Miller (1976) describe likely apply to mothers under relatively "forgiving" conditions, who have access to more or less abundant resources, and who experience relatively little external stress. Under more severe conditions, women may be moved to very different patterns of parental investment: "To give birth to many children, invest selectively based on culturally derived favored characteristics, and hope that a few survive infancy and the early years of life" (Scheper-Hughes, 1985, p. 310). However, these seemingly disparate strategies, one based on intense nurturing and the other on selective neglect, are both directed toward ensuring that, given the particular constraints of their own lives, as many of their children as possible survive and thrive in the environment into which they are born. This is the concern that lies at the core of the "parental imperative," and it is a concern to which women generally devote far more of their time and energy than do men.

Given the mounting evidence that men and women inhabit separate social realities, it makes eminent sense that men and women would hold totally different kinds of social power, and that defining power in normative male terms will tell us little about the kinds of power women wield, and what they use it for. Women are strategists to no less an extent than are men, and they strive to use "all available resources to control the world" around them (Bledsoe, 1976, p. 374). The fact that their world often consists largely of family in no way diminishes women's propensity to seek and use social power. That the incontrovertible source and target of women's power is the family is most evident in cultures in which all other bases of social power are removed beyond the reach of women—patrilineal, patrilocal societies such as China; what power women do have here is based entirely on their success in building "uterine" families—that is, kinship networks based on blood relations (Wolf, 1974).

In sum, if power is defined as the ability to change the behavior of others intentionally, then power is at the core of much of what women do. In fact, women do not just change the behavior of others, they shape whole generations of families. This power to mold the lives of those around her exists over much of a woman's life, from early parenthood, in raising and shaping her children (Ruddick, 1982); to parenthood with adolescents, when she serves as a bridge between the generations above and below her, interpreting each to the other (Hagestad, 1984); to her kinkeeping role throughout adulthood, maintaining family cohesion (Rosenthal, 1985); to later life, when she graduates from primary care in the nuclear family to administration of the extended family, providing support for those who have taken over the demands of active parenting (Gutmann, 1985). Women's power is rooted in their roles as nurturers and kinkeepers, and flows out of their capacity to support and direct the growth of others around them throughout the lifecourse. Women's power may have low visibility from a nonfamily perspective, but women are the lynchpins of family cohesion and socialization, and this is certainly a position of power.

## THE FAMILY POWER LITERATURE

How is it possible to arrive at such a different understanding of family power than the conception that pervades the literature on this topic? What divergent assumptions underlie these two contrasting perspectives that account for the differences between them? The first assumption concerns the relative importance of the two relational axes of the family. As indicated earlier, most of the previous work on family power has been focused on conjugal power. However, when family relationships are analyzed according to two fundamental but often-overlooked criteria—durability of bond and degree of related ness—it becomes abundantly clear that it is the intergenerational tie— that is, the parent-child relationship—rather than the horizontal marital relationship that is of greatest significance in the family. The vertical bond exists over a longer period of time within the individual's life span than does the horizontal tie, and, whereas marriage may be broken by death or divorce, parenthood cannot be. One may have an ex-spouse, but never an ex-child

An examination of families cross-culturally reveals that our focus on the marital bond may be due to an ethnocentric view of the family in which the romantic bond is overemphasized (see, for example Fortes, 1978). In many societies throughout time and across space, the marital relationship has constituted, at best, a union between unrelated lineages, the purpose of which is cooperation in meeting the day-to-day demands of survival, and the opportunity to extend the family lineage through one more generation, rather than the provision of emotional support and romantic gratification. Viewed from this perspective, each marital relationship constitutes one horizontal link connecting two lineages that may never have been and may never again be connected by marriage, while each parent-child bond constitutes one link in a vertical interlocking network of individuals that extends back through time immemorial.

Recently, there has been an increasing emphasis on men's roles as fathers in this society (Lamb et al., in press). However, this too must be understood within a larger context. There is no known society in which men have primary responsibility for child rearing. Research on parenting in our own society has shown that, in general, men spend very little time on a daily basis in contact with their young children. A review of fathering cross-culturally indicates that there is a great deal of variability in the extent to which men invest in their offspring, and this depends on the particular environmental and cultural circumstances (Katz and Konner, 1981; Parke and Suomi, 1981). Thus, it is precisely the fact that we find much variation among men in the extent to which they are involved with children that differentiates them from women.

The problem with the family power research is that marriage has been equated with or substituted for family within it. But marriage is *not* family. In some societies, the husband-wife relationship and, in fact, men themselves are quite peripheral to the family group. But mothers never are. Because it is women who have universally greater access to children, and who are at the intersection of the marital and parent-child relationships, it is women who are in the position of greater power in the family. Further, when we compare power in the two family relational axes from this perspective, it is clear that power in the parent-child relationship is intrinsically more important then power in the conjugal relationship. It is within the parent-child, not the marital relationship, that we find the greatest asymmetry between family members, sweeping changes in the behavior of one individual as a function of the power of another, and the most radical shifts in the balance of power over time.

The second assumption that differentiates these two perspectives on family power concerns the nature of power itself. Because of this emphasis on the marital relationship, the concept of family power has been "masculinized" in several interrelated ways. First, women's power exists at the micro level, and the family power literature has examined the issue from a relatively macro perspective, in which the family is seen mostly in the context of its connections to other societal institutions. For example, in tests of the resource theory of family power, the major model in this field, the resources that women hold universally—that is, skills in relating to and fostering the development of others—have been virtually ignored. Attention has been focused instead on the more typically male resources that are generated outside the family and are the basis for stratification in the larger society: education, income, and so on (Safilios-Rothschild, 1976). Furthermore, some of the concepts that are relied on heavily in the family literature make little or no sense when you look at power from a female perspective. For example, women's power, which derives from the unique position they hold in caring for family members from birth through death, connecting deeply both psychologically and emotionally with others, *requires* tremendous investment in personal relationships. In this context, the principle of least interest, which holds that the person who has *less* invested in a particular relationship will have *greater* power, appears to be a contradiction in terms.

Second, much of the family power research has really investigated the concept of coercion, rather than that of power. Coercion, unlike power, clearly implies forcing the other to do something against his or her will. Much of the family power research has been based on a conflict model of the zero-sum-type game structure, and the most commonly used measures of family power have included self-reports about which member is "the boss" of the family and which member wins when there is disagreement. Sprey (1972, p. 237) suggests that we "start asking family members to tell us what happens in terms of moves and countermoves, threats and promises, aggression and appeasement." This approach to power is based on an understanding of power as the ability to accomplish one's goals despite resistance, a definition that is closer to the spirit of coercion than of power and will not tap much of the power women typically wield. It is ironic that in studies of the family, the one context in which women universally do hold power, power has been defined and measured in such a way that women's power has escaped recognition.

What does this perspective on family power imply for future research directions? First, how should family power be operationalized, if not as marital decision making? We may find that the concept of intergenerational continuity provides some leads in assessing power over the family life cycle. For example, Acock and Bengtson (1978) investigated the similarity between parents and young adults with respect to various behaviors and ideological orientations. Mothers' positions were consistently found to be more predictive of children's positions than were fathers', and Acock and Bengston interpreted their analysis as suggesting that mothers are more influential in most of the areas investigated. This kind of research might prove even more fruitful if we begin thinking in terms of families maintaining continuity, not so much by determining positions that members take on individual issues, as by shaping beliefs about *which* are the important issues on which to take a position (Hagestad and Kranichfeld, 1982).

Second, the approach taken in the family power literature has been almost entirely static, failing to take into account temporal changes with regard to individual, family, or historical time, and I suggest that we need to consider how parent-child power changes over the family development cycle. How do normative changes in family structure affect and differentially affect men's and women's power as parents? Do women "come into power" upon the transition to parenthood? Do women consolidate their power in the internal domain over the course of the family development cycle, as is implied by Gutmann's sex-role polarization hypothesis? How do aging parents and their adult children manage the shifts in balance of power through the later family stages?

In addition, how does parent-child power change with shifts in historical period that affect family functioning? For example, families appear to be increasingly connected to community through children, due to several trends. As an increasing proportion of marriages involve dual-earners, direct adult involvement with communities is attenuated. Similarly, as the process of social change becomes more rapid, families are increasingly dependent on their younger-generation members to serve as bridges that link families to new developments in the larger community. Will children gain greater family power as a consequence? Furthermore, as women gain greater external power through increased participation in the labor force, or through political, economic, and religious recognition, will they relinquish their power in the family to men? I predict that they will not. In fact, it may be that working women do the greater share of child care, not because they are forced to do so by husbands who will not take their share of responsibility, but because it is a means of maintaining control of the internal domain. The biological edge that women have in caring for and connecting with family members makes it unlikely that males will see much point in seriously competing for power in this domain. Women's internal power is the foundation of the rewards that women derive from the family, which simply cannot be replaced by monetary and political returns—the provision of support, and the opportunity for care and connection at deep emotional levels throughout the life span.

## CONCLUSIONS AND IMPLICATIONS

In summary, there is a very real and deeply rooted tension in all societies between those domains of power that are internal and external to the family, a tension based in the biological and social differentiation between male and female that may not be very susceptible to change. There appears to be a good deal of variation between cultures in the exact pattern worked out to accommodate this basic tension, and there is clearly variability in terms of the cost in human life and the amount of misery that is generated as a consequence. But these are all variations *within* the theme. It is clear that women's strong connection to the family is rooted in biology, is part of a human configuration that reaches back to the beginnings of humankind, and is deeply embedded in the social infrastructure of our society.

An understanding of the depth and reach of the kind of power that women hold, taken together with our knowledge of how men's relationships to families are changing in our society, allows us to consider the possibility that women's positions are more secure than they sometimes seem. Many of the painful life situations that women experience because of their powerlessness as a more macro level of society (desertion, physical abuse, teenage pregnancy) occur within the context of the romantic tie, and women's investment and power in vertical bonds are a source of support that reduces women's dependence on and vulnerability to the horizontal tie. Women occupy positions at the very center of the family, affectively and structurally, in contrast to men who seem to be becoming increasingly isolated from the family, and have virtually no substitute for this essential primary group form. From this perspective, the ability to make the decision about what kind of car to buy or where to spend the family vacation (often included in measures of "family power") is nearly reduced to nonsignificance. The message here seems to be that, when it comes to securing the kind of power that exists in the family realm, nothing—not superior physical strength, nor greater economic resources, nor culturally ascribed authority—can substitute for investment, attention, connection, and care.

## REFERENCES

Acock, Alan C. and Vern L. Bengston, 1978. "On the Relative Influence of Mothers and Fathers: A Covariance Analysis of Political and Religious Socialization." *Journal of Marriage and the Family* 40 (August): 519–530.

Bledsoe, Caroline, 1976. "Women's Marital Strategies Among the Kpelle of Liberia." *Journal of Anthropological Research* 32 (Winter): 372–389.

Blood, Robert O. and Donald M. Wolfe. 1960. *Husbands and Wives*. New York: Free Press.

Brown, Clair. 1982. "Home Production for Use in a Market Economy." Pp. 151–167 in *Rethinking the Family: Some Feminist Questions*, edited by Barrie Thorne and Marilyn Yalom. New York: Longman.

Cancian, Francesca M. 1985. "Gender Politics: Love and Power in the Private and Public Spheres." Pp. 253–264 in *Gender and Lifecourse*, edited by Alice S. Rossi, New York: Aldine.

Collins, Randall. 1975. *Conflict and Sociology*. New York: Academic Press.

Cromwell, Ronald E. and David Olson, eds. 1975. *Power in Families*. New York: John Wiley.

D'Andrade, Roy G. 1966. "Sex Differences and Cultural Institutions." Pp. 174–204 in *The Development of Sex Differences*, edited by R. G. Maccoby, Stanford, CA: Stanford University Press.

Eggebeen, David and Peter Uhlenberg. 1985. "Changes in the Organization of Men's Lives: 1960–1980." *Family Relations* 34 (April): 251–257.

Fortes, Meyer. 1978. "Family, Marriage, and Fertility in West Africa." Pp. 17–54 in *Marriage, Fertility and Parenthood in West Africa*, edited by C. Oppong, G. Adaba, M. Bekombo-Prisco, and J. Mogey. Canberra: Australian National University.

Friedl, Ernestine. 1967. "The Position of Women: Appearance and Reality." *Anthropological Quarterly* 40 (July): 97–108.

Gillespie, Dair L. 1971. "Who Has the Power? The Marital Struggle." *Journal of Marriage and the Family* 32 (August): 445–458.

Gilligan, Carol. 1984. *In a Different Voice*. Cambridge, Mass.: Harvard University Press.

Gutmann, David. 1985. "The Parental Imperative Revisited:Towards a Developmental Psychology of Adulthood and Later Life." Pp. 31–60 in *Family and Individual Development*, edited by J. A. Meacham. Basel, Switzerland: Karger.

Hagestad, Gunhild O. 1984. "Women in Intergenerational Patterns of Power and Influence." Pp. 37–55 in *Social Power and Influence of Women*, edited by L. Stamm and C. D. Ryff. Boulder, Colo.: Westview Press.

Hagestad, Gunhild O. 1985. "Older Women in International Relations." Pp. 137–151 in *The Physical and Mental Health of Aged Women*, edited by M. R. Haug, A. B. Ford, and M. Sheafor.

Hagestad, Gunhild O. 1986. "The Aging Society as a Context for Family Life." *Daedalus* (Winter): 119–139.

Hagestad, Gunhild O. and Marion Kranichfeld. 1982. "Issues in the Study of Intergenerational Continuity." Paper presented at the NCFR Theory and Methods Workshop, Washington, D.C.

Hagestad, Gunhild O. and Bernice L. Neugarten. 1985. "Age and Life Course." Pp. 35–61 in *Handbook of Aging and the Social Sciences*, edited by Robert H. Binstock and Ethel Shanas. New York: Van Nostrand Reinhold.

Hagestad, Gunhild O., Michael Smyer, and Karen L. Stierman. 1984. "The Impace of Divorce in Middle Age." In *Parenthood: A Psychodynamic Perspective*, edited by R. Cohen, S. Bernice Cohler, and S. H. Weisman. New York: Guilford Press.

Huston, Ted L. 1983. "Power." Pp. 169–219 in *Close Relationships*, edited by Harold Kelley et al. New York: W. H. Freeman

Katz, Mary M. and Melvin J. Konner. 1981. "The Role of the Father: An Anthropological Perspective." Pp. 155–186 in *The Role of the Father in Child Development*, edited by Michael E. Lamb (second edition). New York: John Wiley and Sons.

Lamb, Michael E., Joseph Pleck, Eric Charnov, and James Levine. In press. "A Biosocial Perspective on Paternal Behavior and Involvement." In *Parenting Across the Lifespan: Biosocial Perspectives*, edited by J. B. Lancaster et al. Chicago: Aldine.

Leacock, Eleanor. 1972. "Introduction." In *Origin of the Family, Private Property and the State*, edited by F. Engels. New York.

McDonald, Gerald W. 1980. "Family Power: The Assessment of a Decade of Theory and Research, 1970–1979." *Journal of Marriage and the Family* 42 (November): 841–854.

Mead, Margaret. 1949. *Male and Female*. New York: William Morrow.

Miller, Jean B. 1976. *Toward a New Psychology of Women*. Boston: Beacon.

Olson, David H. and Carolyn Rabunsky. 1972. "Validity of Four Measures of Family Power." *Journal of Marriage and the Family* 34 (May): 224–233.

Parke, Ross D. and Stephen J. Suomi. 1981. "Adult Male-Infant Relationships: Human and Nonhuman Primate Evidence." Ch. 28 in *Behavioral Development: The Bielefield Interdisciplinary Project*, edited by Klaus Immelman et al. Cambridge, Mass.: Cambridge University Press.

Pleck, Joseph. 1979. "Men's Family Work: Three Perspectives and Some New Data." *Family Coordinator* 28 (October): 481–488.

Raphael, Dana, ed. 1975. *Being Female: Reproduction, Power, and Change*. The Hague, the Netherlands: Mouton.

Rosaldo, Michelle. 1974. *Women, Culture, and Society*. Stanford, CA: Stanford University Press.

Rosenthal, Carolyn. 1985. "Kinkeeping in the Familial Division of Labor." *Journal of Marriage and the Family* 47 (November): 965–974.

Rossi, Alice S. 1985. "Gender and Parenthood." Pp. 161–191 in *Gender and the Life Course*, edited by Alice S. Rossi. New York: Aldine.

Ruddick, Sara. 1982. "Maternal Thinking." Pp. 76–94 in *Rethinking the Family: Some Feminist Questions*, edited by Barrie Thorne and Marilyn Yalom. New York; Longman.

Safilios-Rothschild, Constantina. 1976. "A Macro- and Micro-Examination of Family Power and Love: An Exchange Model." *Journal of Marriage and the Family* 38 (May): 355–362.

Scheper-Hughes, Nancy. 1985. "Culture, Scarcity, and Maternal Thinking: Maternal Detachment and Infant Survival in a Brazilian Shantytown." *Ethos* 31 (Winter): 291–317.

Sprey, Jetse. 1972. "Family Power Structure: A Critical Comment." *Journal of Marriage and the Family* 34 (May): 235–238.

Thorne, Barrie. 1982. "Feminist Rethinking of the Family: An Overview." Pp. 1–24 in *Rethinking the Family: Some Feminist Questions*, edited by Barrie Thorne and Marylon Yalom. New York: Longman.

Tiger, Lionel. 1970. "The Possible Biological Origins of Sexual Discrimination." *Impact of Science on Society* 20 (January-March): 29–44.

Turk, James L. and Norman W. Bell. 1972. "Measuring Power in Families." *Journal of Marriage and the Family* 34 (May): 215–222.

Wolf, Margery. 1974. "Chinese Women: Old Skills in a New Context." Pp. 157–172 in *Woman, Culture, and Society*, edited by Michelle Rosaldo and Louise Lamphere. Stanford, Calif.: Stanford University Press.

Zaretsky, Eli. 1973. *Capitalism, the Family, and Personal Life*. New York: Harper Colophon.

17

LILLIAN B. RUBIN

# The Sexual Dilemma

*If satisfactory marriages are more difficult to achieve today than they were half a century ago, one reason is that spouses expect more from marriage than they used to. For instance, most wives today expect a degree of sexual gratification from their marriages that very few expected just a few decades ago. Also, equally importantly, most husbands now think that they should be able to provide their wives with a high degree of sexual satisfaction. Not long ago, most women seemed content to rely on female relatives and friends for satisfaction of their needs for closeness and intimacy, but now most wives think that a good marriage includes an intimate, emotionally close relationship with the husband.*

*In a provocative and somewhat controversial book published in 1983, sociologist and psychotherapist Lillian Rubin claimed that basic differences between males and females make these new expectations of marriage very hard to attain. In effect, Rubin said that males and females tend to be incompatible because women have a need for emotional closeness and sexual relationships based on intimacy that men in general have limited capacities to meet. Furthermore, Rubin believes that, contrary to the opinions of most sociologists and social psychologists, the male-female differences underlying this incompatibility are not just the result of gender role socialization. Drawing on a reformulation of traditional Freudian theory known as Object Relations Theory, she claims that they result from the male child's having to withdraw identification with his mother to establish his identity as a male. Thus, Rubin believes they will exist as long as the primary parent for most children is a woman. (An explanation rejected by Rubin that is even less palatable to most sociologists and social psychologists, and one with even more pessimistic implications, is that the differences are based in biology.)*

*Whatever their source may be, the male-female differences described by*

*Rubin seem to be real, and they seem not to be diminishing perceptibly. Perhaps the best hope for the immediate future is greater mutual tolerance between men and women based on a better understanding of their differences.*

*In the chapter from* Intimate Strangers *that follows, Rubin draws on her research to illustrate some common sex problems that contemporary couples encounter in their marriages.*



---

*Wife: I say that foreplay begins in the morning.*

*Husband: It seems to me being sexual would make us closer, but she says it works the other way—if she felt closer, there'd be more sex.*

It's a common complaint in marriages—wives and husbands all too often divided as these two are. We wonder about it, ask each other questions, try to persuade the other with reason, and, when that fails, we argue. Sooner or later we make up, telling each other that we'll change. And, in the moment the words are said, we mean them. We try, but somehow the promises aren't fulfilled; somehow, without thought or intention, we slip back into the old ways. The cycle starts again; the struggle is resumed.

We're told by the experts that the problem exists because we don't communicate properly. We must talk to each other, they insist—explain what we need and want, what feels good, what bad. So "communication" has become a household word, the buzzword of the age. We think about it, talk about it, read books, take courses, see therapists to learn how to do it. We come away from these endeavors with resolutions that promise we'll change our ways, that we'll work with our partner on being more open and more expressive about what we're thinking and feeling. But too often our good intentions come to naught, especially when it comes to reconciling our sexual differences.

These are difficult issues, not easily amenable to intervention by talk, no matter how earnest, how compelling our efforts at honesty may be. One couple, aged 33 and married eight years and the parents of two children, told of these differences. Speaking quickly and agitatedly, the wife said:

> Talk, talk, talk! He tries to convince me; I try to convince him. What's the use? It's not the words that are missing. I don't even know if the problem is that we don't understand each other. We understand, all right. But we don't like what we know; that's the problem.

Her husband's words came more slowly, tinged as they were with resignation and frustration.

> I understand what she wants. She wants us to be loving and close, then we can have sex. But it's not always possible that way. We're both busy; there are the kids. It can't be like a love affair all the time, and if we have to wait for that, well [his words trailing off] . . . what the hell, it'll be a long wait.

The wife, speaking more calmly but with her emotional turmoil still evident just below the surface of her words:

> He complains that I want it to be like a love affair, but that's not it. I want to feel some emotion from him; I want an emotional contact, not just a sexual one.

The husband, vexed and bewildered:

> When she starts talking about how I'm sexual but not emotional, that's it; that's where I get lost. Isn't sex emotional, for Christ's sake?

From both busband and wife, an angry yet plaintive cry. It's not words that divide them, however. They tell each other quite openly what they think, how they feel. It just doesn't seem to help in the ways they would wish. But, if it's not a simple matter of communication, then what is it that makes these issues seem so intransigent, so resistant to resolution, even with the best intentions we can muster?

Some analysts of society point to the culture, to the ideologies that have defined the limits of male and female sexuality. Certainly there's truth in that. There's no gainsaying that, through the ages of Western society, women's sexuality has come under attack, that there have been sometimes extreme pressures to control and confine it—even to deny its existence. There's no doubt either that we have dealt with male sexuality with much more ambivalence. On the one hand, it too has been the object of efforts at containment; on the other, we have acknowledged its force and power—indeed, built myth and monument in homage to what we have taken to be its inherently uncontrollable nature.

Such social attitudes about male and female sexuality, and the behavioral ideals that have accompanied them, not only shape our sexual behevior but affect our experience of our own sexuality as well. For culture both clarifies and mystifies. A set of beliefs is at once a way of seeing the world more clearly while, at the same time, foreclosing an alternative vision. When it comes to sex—precisely because it's such a primitive, elemental force—all societies seek some control over it and, therefore, the mystification is greater than the clarification. Thus, for example, Victorian women often convinced themselves that they had no sexual feelings even when the messages their bodies sent would have told them otherwise if they had been able to listen. And, even now, men often engage in complusive sexual behavior that brings them little, if any, pleasure without allowing themselves to notice the joylessness of it. Both behaviors a response to cultural mandates, both creating dissonance, if not outright conflict, when inner experience is at odds with behavioral expectations.

The blueprint to which our sexuality conforms, then, is drawn by the culture. But that's not yet the whole story. The dictates of any society are reinforced by its institutional arrangements and mediated by the personal experience of the people who must live within them. And it's in that confluence of social arrangement and psychological response that we'll come to understand the basis of the sexual differences that so often divide us from each other.

For a woman, there's no satisfactory sex without an emotional connection; for a man, the two are more easily separable. For her, the connection generally must precede the sexual encounter:

> For me to be excited about making love, I have to feel close to him—like we're sharing something, not just living together.

For him, emotional closeness can be born of the sexual contact.

> It's the one subject we never get anywhere on. It's a lot easier for me to tell her what she wants to hear when I feel close, and that's when I get closest—when we're making love. It's kind of hard to explain it, but [trying to find the words] . . . well, it's when the emotions come roaring up.

The issues that divide them around intimacy in the relationship are nowhere to be seen more clearly than here. When she speaks of connection, she usually means intimacy that's born of some verbal expression, some sharing of thought and feeling:

> I want to know what he's thinking—you know, what's going on inside him—before we jump into bed.

For him, it's enough that they're in the same room.

> To me, it feels like there's a nice bond when we're together—just reading the paper or watching the tube or something like that. Then, when we go to bed, that's not enough for her.

The problem, then, is not *how* we talk to each other but *whether* we do so. And it's connected to what words and the verbal expression of emotion mean to us, how sex and emotion come together for each of us, and the fact that we experience the balance between the two so differently—all of which takes us again to the separation and individuation experiences of childhood.

For both boys and girls, the earliest attachment and the identification that grows from it are much larger, deeper, and more all-embracing than anything we, who have successfully buried that primitive past in our unconscious, can easily grasp. Their root is pure eros—that vital, life-giving force with which all attachment begins. The infant bathes in it. But we are a society of people who have learned to look on eros with apprehension, if not outright fear. For us, it is associated with passion, with sex, with forces that threaten to be out of our control. And we teach our young very early, and in ways too numerous to count, about the need to limit the erotic, about our fears that eros imperils civilization.

In the beginning, it's the same for children of either sex. As the child grows past the early symbiotic union with mother, as the boundaries of self begin to develop, the social norms about sexuality begin to make themselves felt. In conformity with those norms, the erotic and emotional are split one from the other, and the erotic takes on a more specifically sexual meaning.

But here the developmental similarities end. For a boy at this stage, it's the emotional component of the attachment to mother that comes under attack as he seeks to repress his identification with her. The erotic—or sexualized—aspect of the attachment is left undisturbed, at least in heterosexual men. To be sure, the incest taboo assures that future sexual *behavior* will take place with a woman other than mother. But the issue here is not behavior but the emotional structure that underlies it.

For a girl, the developmental requirement is exactly the opposite. For her, it's the erotic component of the attachment to a woman that must be denied and shifted later to a man; the larger emotional involvement and the identification remain intact.

This split between the emotional and the erotic components of attachment in childhood has deep and lasting significance for the ways in which we respond to relationships—sexual and otherwise—in adulthood. For it means that, for men, the erotic aspect of any relationship remains forever the most compelling, while, for women, the emotional component will always be the more salient. It's here that we can come to understand the depth of women's emotional connection to each other—the reasons why nonsexual friendships between women remain so central in their lives, so important to their sense of themselves and to their well-being. And it's here also that we can see why nonsexual relationships hold such little emotional charge for men.

It's not, as folklore has held, that a woman's sexual response is more muted than a man's, or that she doesn't need or desire sexual release the way a man does. But, because it's the erotic aspect of her earliest attachment that has to be repressed in childhood if a girl is later to form a sexual bond with a man, the explicitly sexual retains little *independent* status in her inner life. A man may lust after *women*, but a woman lusts after *a man*. For a woman, sex usually has meaning only in a relational context—perhaps a clue to why so many girls never or rarely masturbate in adolescence or early adulthood.

We might argue that the social proscriptions against masturbation alone could account for its insignificance in girls and young women. But boys, too, hear exhortations against masturbation—indeed, even today, many still are told tales of the horrors that will befall them. Yet, except to encourage guilt and secrecy, such injunctions haven't made much difference in its incidence among them.

It would be reasonable to assume that this is a response to the mixed message this society sends to men about their sexuality. On the one hand, they're expected to exercise restraint; on the other, there's an implicit understanding that we can't really count on them to do so—that, at base, male sexuality cannot be controlled, that, after all, boys will be boys.

Surely such differences in the ways in which male and female sexuality are viewed could account for some of the differences between the sexes in their patterns and incidence of masturbation. But I believe there's something else that makes the social prohibitions take so well with women. For with them, an emotional connection in a relationship generally is a stimulus, if not a precondition, for the erotic.

If women depend on the emotional attachment to call up the sexual, men rely on the sexual to spark the emotional, as these words from a forty-one-year-old man, married fourteen years, show:

> Having sex with her makes me feel much closer so it makes it easier to bridge the emotional gap, so to speak. It's like the physical sex opens up another door, and things and feelings can get expressed that I couldn't before.

For women, emotional attachments without sex are maintained with little difficulty or discomfort; for men, they're much more problematic. It's not that they don't exist at all, but that they're less common and fraught with many more difficulties and reservations.

This is the split that may help to explain why men tend to be fearful of homosexuality in a way that women are not. I don't mean by this that women welcome homosexual stirrings any more than men do. But, for women, the emotional and the erotic are separated in such a way that they can be intensely connected emotionally without fear that this will lead to a sexual connection. For men, where the emotional connection so often depends on a sexual one, a close emotional relationship with another man usually is experienced as a threat.

We can see most clearly how deep these differences run when we compare the sexual behaviors of lesbians and homosexual men. Here, the relationships are not muddied by traditional gender differences, suspicions, and antagonisms, and the differences between men and women are stark—there for anyone to see.

In a series of intensive interviews with gay women and men, I was struck repeatedly by the men's ability to take pleasure in a kind of anonymous sex that I rarely, if ever, saw in the lesbian world. For gay women, sex generally is in the context of a relationship—transient perhaps but, for however long it lasts, with genuine elements of relatedness. There are no "fucking buddies" whose names are irrelevant or unknown among lesbians—a common phenomenon with homosexual men. The public bathhouses so popular with many gay men are practically nonexistent for the women because the kind of impersonal, fleeting sexual encounters such places specialize in hold no attraction for most of them.

Among gay men, a friendship that doesn't include sex is rare. With gay women, it's different. Like their straight sisters, lesbians can have intensely intimate and satisfying relationships with each other without any sexual involvement. Certainly a nonsexual friendship will sometimes slide over into a sexual relationship. But, when it does, it's the emotional aspect of the entire relationship, not just the sexual, that's at center stage for the women.

Whether a person is straight or gay, the character of the split between sex and emotion is the same. But the way it's experienced generally is quite different depending upon whether the sexual partner is a woman or a man. Among straight men, because the sexual involvement is with a woman, it calls up the memory of the infantile attachment to mother along with the old ambivalence about separation and unity, about emotional connection and separateness. It's likely, therefore, that it will elicit an intense emotional response—a response that's threatening even while it's gratifying. It's what men look for in their sexual relations with a woman, as these words from a thirty-four-year-old husband tell:

> It's the one time when I can really let go. I guess that's why sex is so important to me. It's the ultimate release; it's the one place where I can get free of the chains inside me.

And it's also what they fear. For it threatens their defenses against the return of those long-repressed feelings for that other woman—that first connection in their lives. So they hold on to the separation between the sexual and emotional, and thereby keep the repression safe. Thus, moments after speaking of sex as the "one place" where he could feel free, the same man spoke of his apprehensions:

> Much as I look for it, sex can also be a problem for me sometimes. I can get awfully anxious and tense about it. If I don't watch it, so much begins to happen that I get scared, like I don't know where I'm at. So that puts a damper on things. I'm a little ashamed to say it, but I can do a whole lot better sexually with someone else—you know, someone I don't care about—than I can with her. With someone like that, it doesn't mess up my insides and get all that stuff boiling around.

"What is this 'stuff' that upsets you so?" I wondered aloud. Discomfited, he lowered his head and muttered, "I don't really know." "Could you try to figure it out for me?" I prodded gently.

> Well, it's really hard to put it into words, but let's see. The closest I can get is to say it feels like something I don't want to know about—maybe something I'm not supposed to know about. [A thoughtful pause] Jesus, I said that, but I'm not even sure what it means. Let's see! It's something like this. If I let it all happen—I mean, let all those feelings just happen—I don't know where it'll end. It's like a person could get caught in them, trapped, so that you could never get out. Hell, I don't know. I've heard people say sex is like going back to the womb. Maybe that's it. Only you came out of the womb, and here it feels like you might never get out again. Does that make any sense to you?

Without doubt the sex act evokes a set of complex and contradictory emotional responses for both women and men—responses that leave them each feeling at once powerful and vunerable, albeit in different ways. For a man, there's power in claiming a woman's body—a connection with his maleness that makes him feel alive, masterful, strong. A thirty-three-year-old man, married eight years, said wistfully:

> When things are quiet between us sexually as they are now, it's not just the sex I miss, it's the contact.

"Do you mean the contact with Marianne?" I asked.

> Yeah, but it's what it stands for; it's not just her. I mean, it's the contact with her, sure, but it's how it makes me feel. I guess the best word for that is "alive"; it makes me feel alive and [searching for the word] I guess you could say, potent.

At the same time, there's anxiety about the intense, out-of-control feelings that are moving inside him—feelings that leave him vulnerable again to the will and whim of a woman.

> I'm not always comfortable with my own sexuality because I can feel very vulnerable when I'm making love. It's a bit crazy, I suppose, because in sex is when I'm experiencing the essence of my manhood and also when I can feel the most frightened about it—like I'm not my own man, or I could lose myself, or something like that.

It deserves a slight detour to comment on the phrase "the essence of my manhood," used by this man to describe his sexual potency and feelings. It makes intuitive sense to us; we know just what he means. Yet it set me to wondering: What is the essence of womanhood?

Some women, I suppose, might say it lies in nurturance, some might speak about mothering, most probably would be puzzled because there would be no single, simple answer that would satisfy. But one thing is sure: For most women, the "essence of womanhood" would not lie in their genitals or in their experience of their sexual powers. That it's such a common experience among men is, perhaps, an effect of their early difficulties in establishing a male identity. Nothing, after all, more clearly separates a boy from his mother than this tangible evidence of his maleness.

This aside now done, let's return to the complex of feelings a man experiences around a sexual connection with a women. There's comfort in being in a woman's arms—the comfort of surrender to the feelings of safety and security that once were felt so deeply, the warming sense of being nurtured and nourished there once again. And there are enchantment and ecstasy to be found there as well—the thrill of experiencing the "essence of manhood," the delight of recapturing the unity with another that had to be forsworn so long ago. But it's also those same feelings that can be felt as a threat. For they constitute an assault on the boundaries between self and other he erected so long ago. And they threaten his manliness, as this culture defines it, when he experiences once again his own dependent needs and wishes.

Thus delight and fear play catch with each other—both evident in the words men use to describe the feelings and fantasies that sex elicits. They speak sometimes of "falling into a dark cavern," and at other times of "being taken into a warm, safe place." They say they're afraid of "being drawn into an abyss," and also that it feels like "wandering in a soft, warm valley." They talk about feeling as if they're drowning, and say also that it's like "swimming in warmth and sunshine." They worry about "being trapped," and exult about feeling "free enough to fly."

Sometimes the same man will describe his feelings with such contradictory words:

> It depends. Sometimes I can get scared. I don't even know exactly why, but I feel very vulnerable, like I'm too wide open. Then it feels dangerous. Other times, no sweat, it's just all pure pleasure.

Sometimes it's different men who speak such widely disparate thoughts. No matter. All together they tell us much about the intensity of the experience, of the pleasure and the pain that are part of the sexual connection.

For a woman, there's a similar mix of feelings of power, vulnerability, and pleasure. There's power in her ability to turn this man who usually is so controlled, so in charge, into what one woman called "a great big explosion" and another characterized as "a soft jellyfish." A thirty-four-year-old woman, married eleven years, put it this way:

> There's that moment in sex when I know I'm in control, that he really couldn't stop anymore because his drive is so great, that I feel wonderful. I feel like the most powerful person in that instant. It's hard to explain in words what that feels like—I mean, the knowledge I have at that second of my own sexual power.

And, alongside this sense of her own power, there's vulnerability also. Thus, sighing in bemusement at the intricacies of her own feelings, she continued.

> But it's funny because there's also that instant when he's about to enter me when I get this tiny flash of fear. It comes and goes in a second, but it's almost always there. It's a kind of inner tensing up. There's a second when instead of opening up my body, I want to close it tight. I guess it's like being invaded, and I want to protect myself against it for that instant. Then he's in and it's gone, and I can get lost in the sexual excitement.

The fear that each of them experiences is an archaic one—the remnants of the separation-unity conflict of childhood that's brought to the surface again at the moment of sexual union. The response is patterned and predictable. He fears engulfment; she fears invasion. Their emotional history combines with cultural mandates about femininity and masculinity to prepare them each for their own side; their physiology does the rest.

For men, the repression of their first identification and the muting of *emotional* attachment that goes with it fit neatly with cultural proscriptions about manliness that require them to abjure the emotional side of life in favor of the rational. Sex, therefore, becomes the one arena where it is legitimate for men to contact their deeper feeling states and to express them. Indeed, all too often, the sex act carries most of the burden of emotional expression for men—a reality of their lives that may explain the urgency with which men so often approach sex. For, if sex is the main conduit through which inhibited emotions are animated, expressed, and experienced, then that imperative and compulsive quality that seems such a puzzle becomes understandable.

But the act of entry itself stirs old conflictual desires that must be contained. This is the moment a man hungers for, while it's also the instant of his greatest vulnerability. As a woman takes him into her body, there are both ecstasy and fear—the ecstasy of union with a woman once again; the fear of being engulfed by her, of somehow losing a part of himself that he's struggled to maintain through the years.

For a woman, the repression of her first *erotic* attachment is also a good fit with the cultural proscriptions against the free expression of her sexuality. But, in childhood, there was no need to make any assault on her first identification with mother and the deep emotional attachment that lay beneath it; no need, either, to differentiate herself as fully and firmly as was necessary for a male child. In adulthood, therefore, she remains concerned with the fluidity of her boundaries, on guard against their permeability—a concern that's activated most fully at the moment of penetration.

This is one of those moments in life when the distinction between fantasy and reality is blurred by the fact that the two actually look so much alike. With entry, her boundaries have been violated, her body invaded. It's just this that may explain why a woman so often avoids the sexual encounter—a common complaint in marriages—even when she will also admit to finding it pleasurable and gratifying once she gets involved. For there are both pleasure and pain—the pleasure of experiencing the union, the pain of the intrusion that violates her sometimes precarious sense of her own separateness. Together, these conflicting feelings often create an inertia about sex—not about an emotional connection but about a sexual one—especially when she doesn't feel as if there's enough emotional pay-off in it to make it worth the effort to overcome her resistance to stirring up the conflict again.

This conflict can be seen in its most unvarnished form in the early stages of relations between lesbians. There's a special kind of ecstasy in their sexual relationship just because it's with a woman—because in a woman's arms the boundaries of separateness fall, the dream of a return to the old symbiosis with mother is fulfilled. But the rapture can be short-lived, for the wish for symbiosis belongs to the infant, not the adult. Once achieved, therefore, ecstasy can give way to fear—fear of the loss of self, which is heightened beyond anything known in the sexual bond with a man.

There's anxiety about boundaries in heterosexual sex, of course. But there's also some measure of safety that exists in this union with one's opposite. For, although sex between a man and a woman can be an intensely intimate experience, there's a limit, a boundary between them that can't be crossed simply by virtue of the fact that they're woman and man. It may, indeed, be one of the aspects of sex with a man that a woman finds so seductive—the ability to satisfy sexual need while still retaining the integrity of a separate sense of self. For, in heterosexual sex, the very physical differences help to reassure us of our separateness while, at the same time, permitting a connection with another that's possible in no other act in human life.

Between two women—just as there was with mother—there's likeness, not difference. Lesbians speak often of the pleasure in this identity, telling of their feeling that loving each other is akin to loving self. But this very identity also raises all the old issues of fusion with a woman and sets the stage for the ambivalent oscillation between desire and fear. This is the central conflict in the early stages of a lesbian relationship—conflict which it must survive if it is to become a lasting one. And it's in their ability to surmount the conflicts these boundary issues produce while, at the same time, maintaining an extraordinary level of intimacy that enduring lesbian relationships may be most instructive for the heterosexual world.

But what about sexual relations between men? Where does male homosexuality fit into this picture? It's different, of course, as these matters of relationship and emotion differ between men and women.

First of all, the boundary problems are not so central for men as for women because, as we have seen, a man develops boundaries that are more rigid and inflexible than a woman's. Therefore, the threat of merger that inheres in the identity between two women will not be a serious issue for men. Rather, the central problem between men is more likely to be related to their difficulty in bridging the distance between them, not in how to maintain it. In fact, to the degree that their boundaries can be penetrated, the threat more likely comes in relations with a woman rather than with a man just because this is the connection that has been the denied one.

Second, because the split between the sexual and the emotional is such a dominant characteristic of male sexuality, relations with men relieve the pressure for an emotional connection that's always present in any interaction with a woman—whether sexual or not. It's this split that permits the kind of impersonal sex so common among homosexual men—sex that's erotically stimulating and exciting yet leaves the emotions relatively untouched; "high sensation, low emotion sex" is the way a male colleague characterized it. And it's this split that, at least until now, has made lasting emotional connections between homosexual men so much less common than among lesbians. When men relate to women, they must confront that split, try to heal it, if their relations are to survive. But, without women in their lives to insist upon the primacy of the emotional connection, it will often get attenuated, if not lost.

As I write these pages, some questions begin to form in my mind. "Is all this," I wonder, "just another way of saying that women are less sexual than men? What about the women we see all around us today who seem to be as easy with their sexuality as men are, and as emotionally detached?"

Without doubt there are today—perhaps always have been—some women for whom sex and emotion are clearly split. But, when we look beneath the behavior of even the most sexually active woman, most of the time we'll see that it's not just sex that engages her. It's true that such a woman no longer needs to convince herself that she's in love in order to have a sexual relationship with a man. But the key word here is *relationship* —limited, yes, perhaps existing only in a transitory fantasy, but there for her as a reality. And, more often than not, such relationships, even when they are little more than fleeting ones, have meanings other than sexual for a woman. For the sexual stimulus usually is connected to some emotional attachment, however limited it may be. And what, at first glance, might seem simply to be a sexual engagement is, in reality, a search for something else.

We need only listen to women to hear them corroborate what I'm saying here. When asked what it is they get in their more casual sexual encounters, even those who consider themselves the most sexually liberated will generally admit that they're often not orgasmic in such transient relationships. "When I was single, I'd sleep with someone who appealed to me right away, no problems," said a recently married twenty-seven-year-old breezily. "Did you usually have orgasms in those relationships?" I asked her. Laughing, she replied, "Nope, that was reserved." "Reserved for what?" I wanted to know. Saucily, "For the guy who deserved it." "And what does that mean?" Finally, she became serious. "I guess it means I have to trust a guy before I can come with him—like I have to know there's some way of touching him emotionally and that I can trust him enough to let him into that part of me."

"What's in it for you?" I asked all the women who spoke this way. "Why get involved at all if it's not sexually gratifying?" Without exception, they said they engaged sexually because it was the only way they could get the other things they need from a man. "What things?" I wanted to know. The answer: Something that told of their need for relationship and attachment rather than sex. They spoke of wanting "hugging more than fucking," of how it "feels good to be connected for a little while." They talk almost urgently of the "need to be held," "to feel needed by someone," of how important it is that "there's someone to give something to and take something from."

It's true, men also will speak of the need to be held and hugged. But orgasm generally is not in question and hugging is seldom an end to be desired in and for itself. In fact, it's one of the most common complaints of women that, even in the context of a stable relationship, such tender physical contact becomes too quickly tranformed into a prelude to sex. "Why can't he just be happy to hold me; why does it always have to lead to fucking?" a woman complains. "I hold her and we hug and cuddle; I like it and I like her to hold me, too. But there's a natural progression, isn't there?" her husband asks, mystified.

Whether in my research or in my clinical work, I hear the same story told—women who are sexually very active yet who only become orgasmic in the context of a relationship with a man they can trust, as these words illustrate. She's a forty-three-year-old woman in a four-year second marriage after having been single for seven years. Talking about some of the experiences of those years as a divorcée, she said:

> There wasn't any dearth of men in my life most of the time, and I learned a lot about myself and how I relate to them during those years. I found out that going to bed with someone was one thing, but getting satisfied sexually was another.
>
> When I got married the first time, I was practically virginal—hardly any experience with anyone but my husband. So I didn't know much about my own sexuality. I mean, I knew I was a very sexual woman, but I thought having orgasms was practically automatic, you know, just a matter of pushing the right buttons, so to speak. What a surprise when I got divorced and started sleeping around with a lot of guys! [With a rueful grin] All of a sudden it seemed like my body had a mind of its own and I just couldn't make it; I couldn't come, I mean. I'd get all hot and

> excited and . . . poof, nothing. I couldn't understand it; I mean, I had no idea what was happening.
>
> Then I got involved with a guy I really liked. It was an honest-to-God relationship with a good man who cared about me as a person, and lo and behold, I was orgasmic again. I didn't get it right away, but after a while, even if you're a dimwit, you get the point.

The flow of words stopped, as if she considered the "point "self-evident. Not certain just what she meant, I asked for an explanation. "What was it you finally 'got'?"

> Well, after a couple of those experiences, I began to realize that something in me would withold having an orgasm when I was with a man I didn't trust. I didn't plan it that way; it just happened. It didn't make any difference how attracted I was to him or how turned on I was, if I didn't trust him in some deep place inside me, then I wouldn't be able to come, and that was that.

Trust is, of course, an issue for men as well. Like the inorgasmic woman, a man too, can become impotent in a sexual encounter with a woman he fears is untrustworthy. In recent years, we have heard more about such men than ever before—perhaps because there are more of them, perhaps only because these issues are more likely to be part of a public discussion these days. But, whatever their number, it's a much less common phenomenon than it is among women. Moreover, when impotence does hit, it's almost as likely to happen in the context of an emotional relationship as it is with a stranger. A thirty-one-year-old cook, married only a short time, spoke of both these moments when experience has taught him that impotency could become an issue for him:

> It's a damned funny business and I can't know exactly when it'll happen. I finally figured out it happens when something scares me—you know, when I figure maybe it's not safe. [Looking perplexed] Sounds a little nuts, doesn't it? What's not safe? I don't know. Sometimes it would be when I was trying to get it on with someone I didn't know—like the first time with a woman. But that's from my past life—[laughing] I mean when I was single. It happens sometimes with LuAnn, too—not a lot, just sometimes. She's great—never makes me feel like I let her down or anything. But it worries me when it happens anyhow. Thing is, I don't really know why, but I think it's the same scared feeling, like something inside me goes,"Uh, oh—better watch out."

"Watch out for what?" I asked. He stood up, paced the room, tried to answer.

> That's the thing; it's hard to put it in words. It's just "better watch out." With some person I don't know, I can figure I don't trust her so much so I get scared. After all, when you're at the peak in sex, you're damned vulnerable—right out there with everything hanging out, so to speak. [With a rush] I mean you're there, man! [Stopping then, as if hearing his own words for the first time, then continuing more calmly] Christ, I guess it's the same with LuAnn, isn't it? It's such an intense experience, sex, that you can't help exposing a lot, so sometimes you can't be sure you can trust *any* woman with it.

Obviously, most men as well as women prefer sex in the context of a relationship with a person to whom they have some emotional attachment. But, in contrast to women, for men, most of the time it's just that—a preference that can be put aside when, for whatever reasons, it cannot be honored. The fullness of the emotional experience may be diminished under conditions that are less than ideal for them, but their sexual pleasure and capacity for orgasm generally are not.

Indeed, for some men, sex is easier, less riddled with conflict, when it comes without emotional attachment. For there are still many men who suffer the madonna-whore split inside themselves—men who love the "good" woman but who lust after the "bad" one, men who can experience their sexuality fully only with a women with whom there is no emotional connection. A 38-year-old accountant, married two years after having been divorced and single for six, said painfully:

> I love Caroline but, damnit, sex just isn't as exciting anymore. I was a regular stud when I was single—always ready, yeah, at your service ma'am, no problems. [Turning to stare out the window which framed a lovely garden] Now it's all changed and I worry like hell about what it's going to do to our marriage. She's patient, but she admits she'd like more sex. But I seem to have lost interest. I go along for a while thinking sex just doesn't matter much to me anymore. Then some woman catches my attention and I feel the flash inside me that says, "Boy would I like to get my hands on *that*." [Bewildered] I don't know! It was the same thing in my first marriage. I'd get it on with women I didn't give a damn about and fly high with it, but with my wife [his words trailing off] . . . I'm scared; I don't want it to happen again. [Retreating suddenly from the obvious emotion in the room, he laughed] What do you think? Do I need a shrink? Am I hiding some deep, dark secret about wanting to fuck my mother? Huh? What about it?

His thirty-one-year-old wife tells her side:

> At the beginning, it was wonderful. I'm sexually pretty free. I mean, I'm not some kind of—what'll I say?—some kind of wild woman, but I'm cool. I like sex and there's not much I wouldn't do sexually. And Randy loved it when we were going together—or at least I thought he did. He acted like it anyway. But not long after we got married, it all changed.

"Then you didn't live together before you got married?" I asked.

> No, we were in two different cities—about five hundred miles apart. So we had weekends together, when we could manage it, and one week's vacation. But we didn't go together very long before we got married. The five hundred miles seemed to get longer and longer, and in a few months we decided to stop fooling around and just do it. [Sighing as she remembered the past] They were wonderful months, though—especially in bed. It was like an explosion when we came together. And now . . . well, most of the time it's just kind of bloop and blah. I finally convinced him that we ought to try some therapy and we've been seeing someone for the last couple of months. But between you and me, I think he needs to do it alone. It's not like I think I'm perfect or anything, but I really think

> this is his problem, not mine. I keep having the feeling that now that we're married, he wishes I were a virgin or something. I know it sounds crazy, but that's what I feel.

"Has the couples therapy helped any? Has anything changed at all?" I wondered aloud.

> Oh yeah, it's better—at least some of the time it is. But I get discouraged sometimes—and scared, too, I guess. It gets better for a while and I get all revved up and hopeful, then he just poops out again. And that's the way it is right now—up and down, up and down, over and over again.

And so it goes: "up and down, over and over again." We make some changes, and the old issues pop up again in new form. We move ahead, and something comes along to push us back. We think about it, wonder about it, fret about it, argue with each other, often forgetting that each step is a gain—a small one, perhaps, but a movement forward which, while it might not take us as far as we would wish, also doesn't permit an easy return to the old ways. Meanwhile, we continue to reach out to each other in yearning—searching for connection, for unity, for emotional release. And again we confront the central dilemma of our relations with each other. For the unity and connection that's at least momentarily possible in this union of two bodies—that makes sex so deeply satisfying—also touches our deepest and earliest fears.

18

NAOMI GERSTEL AND HARRIET GROSS

# The Commuter as Social Isolate: Friends, Kin, and Lovers

*Historically, circumstances have always existed that necessitated husbands and wives to spend some time away from each other. Military service, even in peacetime, routinely requires "separation tours" for its personnel. The families of traveling salesmen develop schedules marked by Dad's departure on Monday morning and his return on Friday evening. Politicians and professional athletes have their seasons of "active duty" that remove them from their homes for varying lengths of time. Across all strata of this and other contemporary societies, the periodic or routine separation of intact families due to the male breadwinner's employment has been accepted, although sometimes grudgingly, by both those left behind and the community at large.*

*Commuter marriage is a relatively new form of the marital relationship, the major characteristic of which is also the separation of husband and wife. It differs, however, from the above arrangements in one important feature—the separation is due to the wife's career. In their book,* Commuter Marriage, *Naomi Gerstel and Harriet Gross examine this unconventional approach to dealing with the pressures that the career goals of both men and women and an ever-tightening job market place on today's marriages. The authors define commuter marriages as "employed spouses who spend at least three nights per week in separate residences and yet are still married and intend to remain so."[1] Their study, based on interviews with a nonrandom sample of fifty commuting couples, gives a detailed portrait of husbands and wives who choose this lifestyle.*

*Gerstel and Gross suggest that the voluntary nature of these arrangements distinguishes them from other separations. On the basis of their findings they also conclude that many of these commuter marriages are motivated not by increased earnings, (as were the former), but by the desire for the personal satisfaction that comes from commitment to a career. The one physical characteristic that differentiates commuter marriages from other forms of marriage is the establishment of a second household.*

*In their book, Gerstel and Gross examine a wide range of topics concerning commuter couples. They look at how the commuting arrangement evolved, how commuting has affected the dyad relationship, and various aspects of nuclear family life, including household maintenance and parenting responsibilities. In the chapter excerpted here, the authors focus on the effects of a commuter marriage on relationships outside the nuclear family.*

Source: Adapted from "The Commuter as Social Isolate: Friends, Kin, and Lovers" by Naomi Gerstel and Harriet Gross, in *Commuter Marriage*: A Study of Work and Family, New York: Guilford Press, 1984, pp. 92–113. 

[1]Gerstel and Gross, *Commuter Marriage*. pp. 1–2.

---

The discussion of commuting has focused on its consequences within the nuclear family. But despite claims to the contrary, the nuclear family is not isolated; it is embedded in a network of other personal relationships. These other relationships—with friends, kin, and even lovers—are significant sources of support, aid, and, occasionally, tension (Bell, 1981; Fischer, 1982; Lee, 1980). Since commuters cannot rely on spouses to the same extent as those who share a home, we might imagine that they would turn frequently to these other relationships.

In this paper, we examine several different types of relationships. First, we ask if commuters turn to friends for both psychological and material support that they would normally get from their husbands or wives. Second, we discuss their ties to kin, in particular to their parents. Third, we look at sexual relationships outside of marriage, whether or not they become more frequent, and what they mean for those who do (and do not) have them.

## THE LOSS OF FRIENDSHIPS WHEN APART

By altering the structure of their marriages, commuter couples also alter their relationships with friends. They discover, often to their own surprise, that one of the great costs of their separation is the restrictions it places on meeting and socializing with others. There is a change, but the change does not involve finding substitutes for the spouse, so much as a general weakening of friendship ties. Why?

### Relationships with Couples

Perhaps the most difficult relationships for commuters to maintain are those with other couples. Many couples assume a commuter marriage is a marriage in trouble or about to dissolve. Others express disapproval, and occasionally such responses result in the disintegration of friendships. However, the breaking-up of friendships does not come simply from skepticism or disapproval. Rather, previous research on individuals living apart from their spouses—military wives away from their husbands (Price-Bonham, 1972), divorced men and women (Hetherington, Cox, & Cox, 1976; Weiss, 1979), widows (Lopata, 1979) and widowers (Gerber, 1977)—suggests that there is a general pattern of exclusion: A spouse living without a mate faces difficulties in maintaining or developing relationships with couples. The commuters' experiences further confirm this pattern.

Most commuters make comments about the "coupledness" of the social world and their resultant exclusion from other couples' leisure activities. Those who remain in the primary home have difficulty maintaining couple friendships that had developed before their spouse began to commute:

> You would be amazed at how little I've been asked out this year. I think people have not asked me because I am single. The same people that asked us together last year won't ask me because Janet [his wife] is away.

For those who moved to new locations, the problem more often involved an inability to develop new friendships with couples:

> Being single makes it more difficult to get to know people. So, I think I do find it more lonely. People tend to think about inviting me only when I'm with my husband.

Note that both of these commuters, like most others, referred to themselves as "singles" when discussing their social worlds. They remain a couple in both a legal sense and an emotional sense. But they are not couples in a social sense. In the absence of a husband or a wife, the marriage—for the purposes of making and keeping friends—does not exist. Other couples will not initiate friendships with them nor will they maintain previously established friendship ties.

In part, this social exclusion may be explained by a perception of the single individual as a sexual menace. Duberman (1974) found that couples, believing that unattached individuals may be sexual threats to their own relationships, do not include them in social gatherings. Some of the commuters' comments suggest that they themselves could see this happening:

> Everybody seems to be just a little bit on guard with me because a single guy around, or a guy without a wife, is always a dangerous quantity in any crowd of people.

However, the perception of sexual threat is only one element contributing to the coupling of the social world. Another element involves the need, or at least desire, to maintain the gender balance that many people seem to see as essential to the smooth flow of leisure activities. As one woman said:

> To be a single woman who has a husband somewhere else makes you an absolute social outcast. You simply don't fit into the very rigid kind of military social system, you know, with wives talking to wives and husbands talking to husbands.

Singles "don't fit in"; they destroy the symmetry of groups composed of pairs. Or as a man put it:

> They don't invite me because I am single. And I can understand it. You try to balance social events. I make it uneven.

He understands the desire for symmetry. But that shared social code precludes his own participation in social gatherings.

"Proper social etiquette" requires equal numbers of each sex. These norms in themselves discourage couples from becoming friends with unattached individuals. For the "single" individual, the consequence is loneliness.

**Relationships with Singles**

As we have suggested, married couples socialize with other married couples. Moreover, Stein (1976), in a study based on intensive interviews, documents that singles socialize primarily with other singles. Because they describe themselves as "singles," we might expect that the commuters could at least form friendships with others who are unattached. But though apart, commuters have an ambiguous status: they are, for social purposes, neither single nor married. The lack of clarity in their position is illustrated in this man's remark:

> They don't know what to do with you. You're an oddball when it comes to social activities. Because they have to pair you off with someone, a woman, and here you are married but not, if you get what I mean. So, how can they pair you?

As "married singles," then, they are usually unable to form independent ties.

Again, sanctions against sexual relationships may explain this isolation. Singles can legitimately ask one another out and even couples can invite the unattached to social gatherings in equal numbers with other singles. But such cross-gender relationships are not available for the "married single" commuters. They cannot legitimately enter into such relationships or at least feel they should not. As one man remarked:

> Um, I am married, so I am not in a position to go out with a woman just for a drink and spend the evening talking. I feel the inhibitions and the community is small enough so any time I go anyplace, I see somebody I know.

But not only small communities prevent such interactions. A woman, living in New York, expected she would become friends with two of her single male colleagues. But she was disappointed:

> Here are these two single divorced men who I would like to say to: "Come over to supper," and they would not have to think about it because I am married. But there is something in the situation that doesn't allow that. They are really confused about how to relate to me. I'm not single, but my husband is not here.

This limitation on cross-gender relationships may be especially problematic for women professionals who are likely to find themselves in a job situation where men outnumber them.

But many commuters not only have trouble developing friendships with those of the opposite sex, they also have difficulty developing friendships with single people of the same sex. As Merton (1957) has argued, participants experience social interaction as rewarding when they share similar statuses and, therefore, similar values or assumptions. Of particular importance here is that marital status seems to contribute to the establishment of a particular set of values and concerns. Often commuters do not share interests with unmarried persons or feel that their personal concerns and needs are different. A woman remarked:

> There's a woman here, a single woman, who I guess I would like to get friendly with. But I get the feeling she cares about different things because she's single. Like she wants to meet men. And she wants to talk about meeting men or not having met them. We just haven't seemed to get that close.

And a man said:

> Well, there's this one single guy in the office whom I like. But when we're outside the office, we just don't see each other. We just don't seem to be able to really get it together. I guess our life situations are just too different. Funny, you wouldn't think marriage would make that kind of difference.

There were, however, a few exceptions to this pattern. Some commuter wives seemed able to form supportive relationships with other women, who tended to be single. When they were able to meet such women, the freedom implied by separation from the spouse promoted the development of the new relationship:

> Relationships when you're apart develop faster. They're easier. Just because of the fact that you spend more time with them. I mean for instance there's this one woman, in particular, we have coffee together in the morning and often dinner. And we sit and talk late. Much more concentrated seeing of each other. If Tony [her husband] had been here, she and I wouldn't spend that much time together.

Such relationships can become more intense in the absence of the spouse:

> When we were together all the time, I didn't have the time or energy and the freedom to just pick myself up and go out with a friend like I do now. Ellen and I get together every Tuesday night and go out to a really nice restaurant. Afterwards, we might go to a movie. Blow a wad of money. Or just sit and have a real good talk. We have a ball. A blast!

But these are exceptions. Such friendships seem to develop only under a number of highly restrictive conditions. First, commuters need the opportunity to meet single individuals, which not all commuters have. Second, they must have a common ground—like the same occupation—that provides similar interests and values sufficient to overcome differences in marital status. Third, they must have a desire to spend a large part of leisure developing such friendships. Not all do. As a result of these restrictive conditions, very few commuters form friendships even with single individuals of the same sex.

### Commuters Perpetuate Their Own Isolation

When couples share a single residence, they typically socialize only with those whom both spouses like (Hess, 1976), even though husbands and wives often disagree about who their friends are or should be (Adams & Butler, 1968; Babchuk, 1965). But, when they are apart, commuters seem to be in a position to develop friendships without considering their spouses' likes or dislikes. However, very few take advantage of this special situation.

Some commuters attribute their willingness to pursue friendships to their lack of material resources. Their second homes are generally small and lack facilities to entertain in. As a result, they suggest that the spouse who travels is not in a position to have people into his or her home. The lack of resources is not, however, limited to the inadequate space and comfort of the second home: Even the commuters who remain behind, or who have a good living arrangement in the second home, do not entertain. Not material resources, but what might be called social resources, prevent them from doing so.

The most important of these social resources is a spouse whose presence permits a division of labor in entertaining. Some described a conventional division of labor that required the presence of both:

> If I am planning to have a dinner party or something like that, it's easier when he's here. It's hard to do alone. When he's here, well, then he can be the host, shake hands, make drinks and so on while I cook.

But for others, while labor was not divided along conventional gender lines, it was nonetheless divided:

> When we have people over, when we're both here, we each do different things. While one is cooking, the other can talk. I think it would be awfully hectic to do it alone.

Though there may or may not be a gender-typed division of labor, there is usually a sharing of tasks to which the commuters have become accustomed and continue to assume is necessary. In the absence of a spouse, socializing becomes burdensome.

Even if they have adequate facilities for entertainment and are not worried about the added labor, they still seem to feel uneasy about asking people over. One man, commenting on his unwillingness to entertain alone, said:

> It just wouldn't feel right without Rebecca [his wife].

Another remarked:

> Because Barbara isn't here, I don't really pursue things. Because I can't, don't want to pursue things alone. I need her for that. It's sort of like waiting. So I've developed acquaintances, not friends. Not people I really see, who I initiate contact with.

These commuter husbands conceive of their marriages as vehicles for socializing. Here, they seem to be speaking not so much of a practical division of labor, but of an emotional division of labor. Perhaps each spouse takes a distinctive role in conversation, in the creation of smooth interactions. When the wife is away, the husband feels unable to replicate the style of interaction he has become accustomed to and now depends on.

Some women, too, said that they do not feel "quite right" inviting people over when their husbands are away. But women add something more:

> I must say I don't entertain at all when Ben is not here. I mean, in terms of social obligations, I don't feel I am obliged to because he is not here.

For her, invitations mean additional work—unnecessary in the absence of her husband. While it is more difficult to socialize, the social obligations of a person living alone are diminished. Part of marriage, at least for a middle-class wife, is the development of a household where entertainment is not only appropriate but expected. These expectations are dropped when the husband is away. One consequence of these decreased expections, however, is fewer friendships.

The problem is the same though heightened for single members of the opposite sex. In those cases where a married person does have a friendship with a single, that relationship is generally fused with the marriage (Hess, 1976). For commuters, this is impossible. Their comments suggest that they do not initiate such friendships because they feel external pressures and internal pressures against doing so:

> Helen and I developed some close friendships with single women when she was here. I just don't see them much anymore. If I invite them, there is a certain artificiality of the relationship that even the greatest honesty in the world can't erase. Sexual faithfulness is not a big thing on my scale of priorities, but that doesn't remove the problem at all with regard to friendships.

A woman expressed the same inhibitions:

> I don't feel like I can go out with a man here, invite him over to dinner or something like that. Well, to be honest, I'm afraid of their intentions and sometimes I'm afraid of my intentions. Sex is always there between a woman and a man. And why place yourself in a situation where it is more likely to be.

For the commuters, too, friendships are arranged to reinforce the solidarity of the couple. Cross-sex friendships in the absence of the spouse reduce that solidarity.

Thus, commuters extend few invitations to both singles and married couples, and as a result, further decrease the likelihood that they will receive invitations. In this sense, then, commuters perpetuate their own isolation.

## THE LOSS OF FRIENDSHIPS WHEN TOGETHER: PRIORITY OF THE MARITAL RELATIONSHIP

Up to this point, we have only discussed the reduced ability to socialize when spouses are apart. But what happens when they are reunited? Apart much of the time, commuters choose to be together as much and as intensely as possible when they are together. When others are included, the intensity of their own interaction diminishes. As Simmel (1950) points out in his analysis of the dyad and triad: "No matter how close a triad may be, there is always the occasion on which two of the three members regard the third as an intruder . . . the sensitive mood of two is always irritated by the spectator" (pp. 135–136). Commuters focus intensely on one another when they reunite, forming just such a "sensitive" union. Third parties are likely to be excluded.

Some commuters' comments illustrate this process of exclusion. One couple, both in their early 30s, spent much time with friends before they began to commute. They enjoy and value such activity but find it appealing only when they also have a great deal of time to share alone with one another. While commuting, they believe that their leisure time should be predominantly for the two of them. Though the wife developed a close friendship with another woman in her husband's absence, she feels that friendship should be curtailed when he returns home:

> We used to be very groupie people and spend a lot of time with our friends. Now we only have weekends together. We get kind of selfish with our time and spend at most one evening with other people. That's kind of hard on us.

Her husband agreed:

> When we're together, there is a desire to spend time by ourselves, take advantage of these marvelous mountains, catch up on all the things that have happened during the week. We really can't be doing these things when other people are around.

Another older couple, both in their 50s, had often entertained before commuting. The wife was a gourmet cook who prepared elaborate meals when entertaining. However, with the onset of commuting, she and her husband became increasingly family-oriented during their short time together. They no longer invite or accept most invitations. As she commented:

> It's fun to have other people in sometimes and to go out or something but now we spend 75 percent, maybe more, of the weekends by ourselves. Because we have to.

And her husband remarked:

> We really don't have time to socialize. There's already so little time together. That bothers me; it bothers me a lot.

When commuters are together, they generally feel that the intensity of their own interactions will be reduced if others are included. They jealously guard the privacy of their already limited reunions. Most of the commuters in this study put a priority on their marital relationship; they reveal their high commitment to their marriages in their willingness to give up other relationships to be together. However, this decision has its costs. Though the choice to eliminate others is made voluntarily, the loss is still felt as very real indeed.

As these findings suggest, either being single or married in a shared residence provide the basis for integration into friendship networks. However, for those who are married but do not share a residence, the situation is very different. For, at the same time that a marriage encourages certain types of relationships, it excludes others. Commuters, who are temporarily single, find themselves excluded from the usual friendships of both the married and the single. For them, marriage plays a role that cannot be played by alternative relationships. Without a shared home, they find it difficult to substitute other people for the spouse and to maintain old friendships. For them marriage is not simply one among many alternative relationships equally available for the distribution of emotions. Rather, there are structural constraints that preclude attachments to others, even when an individual has the desire, available time, and energy to form them. The "coupledness" of the social world, the segregation of singles and marrieds, the requirement of the full marital unit for entertainment, and the priority of the marital relationship are limits that undermine the full use of individual's "affective energy."

Social theorists, analyzing the functions fulfilled by the family in contempoary society, focus on the tasks that involve only the marital dyad and their children. For example, Parsons (1965) argues that: "The home, its furnishings, equipment, and the rest contribute the logistic base for the performance of family functions" (p. 37). However, Parsons (1955) also suggests that the family's functions are limited to the microsociological level, stating:

> The family is not a major agency of integration into the larger society. Its individual members participate . . . but they do so as *individuals not in their roles as family members*. (p. 16, emphasis added)

As the analysis of commuters' friendships suggests, this perspective is limited and omits a major area of family functioning. For married adults, integration into social networks is not "as individuals" but as partners in a marriage. Consequently, the physical separation of spouses has a limiting effect on the breadth and depth of their personal relationships with others.

## RELATIONSHIPS WITH KIN

If friends do not provide company and aid to commuters' spouses, we might expect relatives to. Research on those without a spouse, including both the divorced (McLanahan, Wedemyer, & Adelberg, 1981; Weiss, 1979) and widows and widowers (Arling, 1976) suggests that while they cannot rely on coupled friends, they can and do rely on kin. However, our research suggests that commuters are much less likely to do so. For some, even these relationships become strained. Some of their kin, like some of their friends, take the conventional marriage as a standard and, in doing so, see the commuters as negligent.

But such strained relationships are not typical. Instead, with regard to kin, most commuters resemble the "typical" American middle-class family. Most middle-class couples live at some distance from their relatives. Still, despite their geographic separation, relatives continue to visit with one another and to talk regularly on the phone (Adams, 1966; Lee, 1980; Litwak, 1960). So, too, commuters tend to live at some distance from their relatives, but they continue to visit with kin (an average of about four times a year) and, more often, talk on the phone (an average of about once every two weeks). In short, these relationships were similar to those they had with relatives before they began to commute. As a result, for most commuters, kin certainly could not act as substitutes for the spouse, either in providing daily emotional sustenance or practical help.

A significant minority (about 25 percent) did, however, come to rely on their kin, especially their parents, in extensive ways as a result of commuting. They were able to do so because their relatives lived nearby—either because they lived close before commuting began or because the traveling spouse commuted to a location near kin. In fact, in a few cases, one of the spouses actually moved back in with parents, establishing a home there again. For these commuters, this arrangement includes financial aid and helps alleviate loneliness. As one man, who moved in with his parents while commuting, said:

> I don't have to worry about anything except my work. I let my mother take care of everything else. She feeds me, you know, everything a mother does. Obviously, it could not be permanent. It wouldn't be good for me or for them. But we have a good relationship. I don't have to come home to an empty house. It doesn't cost me anything. It's the optimal arrangement for me right now.

For him, commuting had fewer negative consequences than it did for most: his mother replaced his wife in helping with domestic duties and providing company. However, most others living with their parents do not see this arrangement quite so positively. There were advantages, but also disagreements and conflicts:

> I have a friendly relationship with my parents. But we're very different. They don't understand how I lead my life, like smoking dope or living away from Tina [his wife]. When they're around, I pretty much avoid them. But they're trying to be nice. And it does give me a place to stay. And food in my mouth when I want it.

These relationships had, in the past, been established on the basis of inequality, with the parents having authority over the child. Just as the divorced have difficulty readjusting to sharing a home with parents (Brown, 1979), so, too, do commuters. Because returning to a parental home is sometimes convenient, a few commuters do take advantage of its availability. But when they do, tensions seem inevitable: It is difficult to keep an adequate distance between the two adult generations who now have lives of their own with different values and routines.

Those situations most easy to adjust to involve cases where relatives live nearby and only provide occasional help. Most importantly, they provide emotional support:

> My brother lives nearby and when I am lonesome or want some conversation, I call him or go to see him. It's a pleasure to get reacquainted and to find we really like each other and, I must say, it's nice to know they are here.

> I go see my parents every weekend. It makes the commuting thing easier for me. I know they are here and we are a really close-knit family.

In several cases, when the commuters have young children, their nearby parents provide much needed child care:

> My mother-in-law lives near here and if I need help with the kids, I can just call her up. And Arnold's [her husband] father helps Joey with math. He gives him some kind of constant father figure. It would be much harder to do this whole thing if they weren't available.

The spouse left with the children often experiences burdensome difficulties in trying to provide for them. If relatives live nearby, generally, they are trusted surrogates.

Most of the commuters remain in contact with their families across distances. Unlike friendships, these relationships do not require the presence of both spouses. However, as their relatives are usually living at some distance, the commuters cannot turn to them as substitutes for the daily contact typically provided by a spouse. And, in most cases, when the kin live nearby, commuters tend not to want, or to have, daily contact. Just as Shorter (1975) has remarked: "Kinfolk today extend and complement the conjugal family's egotistical emotional structure. They don't rival it or threaten to break it down" (p. 244). So, too, these kin relationships cannot replace the bonds of spouses.

## EXTRAMARITAL RELATIONSHIPS

Marriage, we have said, provides access to nonsexual relationships. At the same time, it discourages outside sexual relationships.[1] Individuals are restricted by norms prescribing sexual fidelity and, some would suggest, by constant visibility to their spouses (Bell, Turner, & Rosen, 1975; Maykovich, 1976).

But what of those couples who live apart at least some of the time? Commuters say they are constantly confronted by others who expect that they will

[1]Though sexual affairs are more legitimate today than they were in earlier decades, most people still hold the ideal of fidelity. In a recent Roper poll, adults ranked sexual fidelity as a component of a good marriage, below only being in love and being able to talk about one's feelings. And Singh, Walton, and Williams (1976), in a study using a national sample, found that the overwhelming majority of Americans (approximately 75 percent) disapprove of extramarital affairs.

discard monogamy and take advantage of their new found possibilities for sexual freedom. So, too, our popular conceptions would have sailors meeting lovers in every port and traveling businessmen seducing their colleagues. These clichés assume that marriage erects a barrier to extramarital affairs only when the behavior of a husband or wife is under the scrutiny of the other.

For commuters, the spatial and temporal boundaries typically provided by marriage are reduced, resulting in less scrutiny and wider opportunities for extramarital relationships. Furthermore, because the couple is separated, they cannot engage in sex together as often. Do their marriages, with their changed structures, cease to operate as a mechanism of social control over sexual activity? More specifically, do commuters find new sexual partners in the absence of the spouse? And if so, do these relationships replace the marriage as their central emotional relationship?

**Does Freedom Cause Affairs?**

Nearly one third of commuters had affairs while commuting. Those who did but had not before living apart, believe that their increased freedom made these other relationships possible. For example, one man was married 10 years before he and his wife set up two separate residences. During that time, he had had no other sexual relationships. But he felt commuting changed all that:

> I'm having one [an affair] now. I wouldn't be doing it if we weren't commuting. It's simple. My behavior is just less constrained, sexually and otherwise. It's lots of fun. It's like being a kid and going to play baseball when you feel like playing baseball.

A woman, married for six years, clearly saw the separation as an occasion to have sex with another man. Soon after two homes were established:

> I was really feeling my oats. Felt really single for the first time. I probably wouldn't have done it if Thad [her husband] and I had been together. I was sexually turned on to Jack [the "other" man] and I was not about to pass up the opportunity.

Indeed, all but one of the spouses who had affairs while commuting, but not before, believe that commuting made these other relationships possible. They accept the common sense—and sociological—explanation that reduced spatial and temporal boundaries led them to reject sexual boundaries.

However, an analysis of the behavior of the other commuters suggests that interpretation is incorrect, or at least inapplicable, to the majority. The analysis shows that commuters were not more likely to have affairs after they set up two homes than they were while living together. More than half (about 60 percent) of the commuters never, either before or while commuting, engaged in extramarital sex. This figure is very similar to the range found in the general population—50 percent to 70 percent (Athanasious, Shaver, & Tavris, 1976; Hunt, 1974; Ramey, 1977). These figures suggest that commuting does not lead to affairs. But more interestingly, for the purposes of this analysis, we can make a distinction between a "stable" and an "unstable" group of commuters.

The stable group is composed of those individuals who exhibited no change in their extramarital behavior, including those who had no affairs before or while commuting (60 percent) and those who had affairs before commuting and continued to do so (21 percent). The unstable group is composed of those who exhibit change after commuting began. This group includes both cases quoted previously—who did not have affairs before but did while commuting (8 percent) as well as those who had affairs before commuting and did not do so afterwards (11 percent). The combined total of the two stable groups (81 percent) is approximately four times greater than the total of the two unstable groups (19 percent). As the majority exhibit stable behavior, this analysis suggests that physical proximity is not the characteristic of marriage that enables it to serve as a mechanism of social control. In other words, commuting does not cause extramarital affairs.

Finally, there is even more striking evidence that separation does not cause affairs when we see that the majority of those in the unstable group changed in the direction of monogamy. That is, more commuters had affairs while they shared a single residence than did so after they set up separate homes. The rationales they gave for this unexpected behavior change vary greatly. For example, one woman said she had an affair before commuting because she felt hostile toward her husband since she had no job and, simultaneously, he was very involved in his work:

> When we were living together all the time, I got involved with this other guy. Ted [her husband] works very hard and when he works, he doesn't talk. He gets up, leaves the house in the morning, comes home, eats supper and works 'til 3 or 4 in the morning. I was very dissatisfied with that; I was lonesome. I didn't have my own work and so I got involved with this other guy. As soon as I got the job, and knew my life wasn't washed up, it disappeared. It was very dumb. I won't do it again.

Others said that with their present jobs, they are too busy to have affairs. And still others could come up with no explanation for the unexpected change:

> We decided before marriage that marriage wouldn't interfere with that kind of thing. He had some and I had some. And I figure I am getting terribly old because I haven't met anybody in the last few years that I find interesting.

> I've had extramarital affairs. But it hasn't happened since we've been apart. It's crazy, isn't it? I have all the opportunity in the world now and the appetite doesn't seem to be that great.

Many commuters who did not have affairs, however, found that their sexual fantasies increased. Women said:

> I find myself noticing men's bodies a lot more. Thinking about possibilities in bed. But it stops there.

> I daydream more of sexual encounters. Less sex, more fantasy. That makes sense. But no more sex.

Men said:

> Now, while we're apart, my fantasy quotient is probably up. Separation has made me think about it more probably because of my repressed libido. Made me think more in sexual terms about people I'm interested in. But our marriage couldn't take it.

> Sure, when you're apart, you want it more. I notice other women as sexual beings more.

However, for these people—as for most—these fantasies are not translated into activity.

It is clear that other elements—besides time and space apart from their spouse—lead some commuters to extramarital activities. But it is unclear why those who had affairs only after commuting began did so. There are many differences among them. Half are male; half are female. They range in age from 27 to 55. Some see their spouses every weekend; others less frequently. The only thing they clearly have in common is the explanation that increased freedom accounted for their affairs. But because they are such a small minority, the belief that freedom causes affairs remains an inadequate explanation.

These findings suggest that the small minority who believe decreased visibility and increased freedom lead them to affairs are simply using a rationale that helps them understand, and perhaps excuse, their behavior. In most cases, attitudes (that exist prior to separation), rather than the opportunity brought about by separation, seem to be the primary determinant of extramarital liaisons.

**Norms against Sexual Permissiveness**

An examination of the rationales of those who remained monogamous throughout their marital lives will help explain why the increased opportunity for an affair does not, in fact, typically explain its occurrence. Commuters in this stable group use two types of explanations for their abstinence. Some commuters express an overall commitment to an ideology of monogamy. One man said:

> Naturally, I've felt desires. Normal I would say in wanting to, but I haven't primarily because I just don't believe in it.

His wife commented:

> Neither one of us, as far as I know, has ever had a sexual relationship outside of marriage. I guess cause we just don't believe in them. When you're married, you're married.

For the individuals in this group, sexual faithfulness is an essential component of their definitions of marriage.

These commuters are aware of changing sexual mores in contemporary America. Defining themselves in opposition to such changes, they frequently made remarks like: "I'm old fashioned"; "I guess I'm just a traditionalist"; "I'm puritanical." They are not "traditionalist" in that they choose to establish two separate residences. But one type of "deviance" does not mean that they tamper with all traditional marital norms. Restrictions on sexual activities prevail whether their spouses can see them or not.

Not all of the commuters who did not have affairs believe monogamy is the only way to run a marriage. A second group of sexually loyal individuals expressed the fear that they would feel jealous and they would be imposing pain on their spouse if they had affairs. Intellectually, this group thinks sexual liaisons outside of marriage are acceptable. Yet, emotionally they feel that they *themselves*, as individuals, are incapable of such activity and could not deal with it if their mates had affairs. Women were much more likely than men to offer this rationale—to say that they had not engaged in extramarital relationships because of the pain and deception it would involve. As one woman put it:

> On a really intellectual level, I think I can say it is perfectly acceptable for people to be involved with other people. I don't think it would work very well for me. The main problem is deception. And I guess the problem is jealousy of the other person and having to avoid that, having to deceive and to lie about it. It would hurt him very badly.

In contrast, her husband spoke of the more general meaning of marriage and simply said:

> I don't believe in sexual freedom, at least for married people.

Another women expressed the personal orientation, rather than the ideological, in the following way:

> I'm not for it or against it. But we love each other too much to impose that kind of pain. I know being away gives some people a release, makes them turn on.
>
> I have just the opposite reaction. It's like losing your appetite. When you're not hungry, you don't eat. I guess we're just not hungry.

In this case, contrary to what she suggested, her husband was "hungry," but not willing to have an affair:

> I think it has probably crossed my mind more frequently when we are away from each other. There is a need there. But I can't, at least not with another person. It would hurt me if she did it and I think it would hurt her if I did it.

Of course, these are individual attitudes. Spouses differ not only in their rationale for abstention, but, in some cases, their actions: One is opposed to and does not have affairs, while the other does. For example, one woman had an affair when they shared a single home and did not tell her husband. It had been short-lived and she did not feel it "was necessary to dwell on it with him." Her husband, however, did not have affairs because:

> I haven't and I wouldn't because it would hurt Judy [his wife]. I don't like the idea of doing something and not telling her. It's not something I could personally do. I mean I love Judy and that's the reason for not having an affair.

He, like others in this second group, is afraid of the pain an extramarital liaison would cause his wife.

Though this second group may be more likely to change, the end result, for the present, is the same for both groups: none of them engage in extramarital relationships. Marriage is a unique relationship and their commitment to it is unchanged. A changed marital structure—with less proximity and responsibility toward the spouse—does not change the normative attitudes about sexual exclusivity. Rather, these expectations continue to serve as boundaries for sexual activity.

**Who Does Have Affairs?**

Let us turn to the second stable group: those who had affairs before commuting began and continued to do so while living apart. Given their willingness to have affairs, commuting made it somewhat easier:

> If I'm not home by 6:00, she doesn't know and doesn't worry. It obviously makes it easier. I can't tell her. Once, before I started coming up here, I tried and she got incredibly upset. Started screaming at me and crying. And there is no way she is likely to suspect it now.

He was wrong: his wife did suspect it. Her response was to follow suit and have her own flings. But it was her husband's activities, not the residential separation, that led her to do so. Again the increased opportunity brought by separation did not determine such behavior.

Attitudes and rationales for extramarital affairs vary widely. Some commuters suggest they have affairs because of dissatisfaction with their marriages:

> We're very different sexually. She is really not interested in sex. Liz [his wife] is sexually excited about a half-dozen times a year. I'm sexually excited about a half-dozen times a week. I'm not trying to boast. I sometimes seek other people because I miss sex. I would prefer not to. But sometimes I have to.

In this case, dissatisfaction with the marriage provides the legitimate condition to search for alternative sexual relationships. For others, those conditions are provided by the discovery that their spouses are having affairs. They, then, feel they will as well.

> I became aware that Richard [her husband] was considerably more active than I had thought. In order for me to put that in perspective, I have my own relationships. I can understand the significance or lack of significance of them. I don't feel done in or trapped.

Here, a sense of fairness, or even a desire for revenge, overrides the particular attitude toward affairs. Finally, still others simply reject the norms against extramarital sex. They have, instead, a counter ideology:

> I knew from the beginning of our marriage what I wanted for the future. I guess the main reason is I like variation. Why not? You need to develop sexual relationships to have intimate relationships. Now we both agree about this. I don't see why such a big metaphysical fuss is made over this.

His wife did agree:

> Affairs are not correlated with our being apart. We agreed long ago that we were going to have the kind of marriage that included the right for both of us to have sex with other people.

Importantly, these couples who do have affairs, both before and after commuting, maintain a set of normative guidelines for their behavior; they maintain a primary commitment to their marriage. They speak of affairs as "additions" that could not replace their more important marital ties. Therefore, attempts are made to confine such activities to those whom they believe posed no real threat to the more permanent and valued relationship with their spouses:

> It's better to have an affair with a happily married man who is not looking for a life's partner or anything like that. The single man is always falling in love. That's difficult. I choose people who don't threaten my relationship with Jerry [her husband].

> I like having physical relationships with other women. They are nice while they last. But I know there is no future. I wouldn't break up my marriage for them. When they get too serious, that means trouble. I don't allow that to happen. I pull out.

These couples have decided that their relationship with their spouse is special and the distinction made between it and other relationships is not solely sexual. Such other relationships do not affect their desire to maintain a permanent marital commitment. Among this group, marriage still remains subject to a set of normative guidelines, those that Bernard (1973) argues are the only ones viable in contemporary society: "permanence and nonexclusivity." Thus, while those who have affairs speak to the pluralistic character of the normative system, they in no way suggest that norms are unimportant.

Responses of outsiders to commuter marriage involve conceptions of sexual freedom as well as sexual activity. The commuters themselves say people periodically make comments to them about their new found liberties. This popular view, reiterated in the sociological literature on extramarital sex, suggests that marriage acts as a constraint not because of the norms attached to it but because of the daily face-to-face character of its structure. But, as the commuters' experiences suggest, this view is a simplistic one.

Of course, there must be some opportunity. If there were not, there could be no affairs. But, it could be argued that the opportunity for affairs is always available. Few spouses are together 24 hours a day. Most can, and in fact do, interact with members of the opposite sex on a regular basis. Affairs do not have to take place at night in some secret hideaway in order for spouses not "to know." But obviously, even with the relatively high rates of affairs, not all individuals with such opportunities take advantage of their supposed freedom. Instead, they abide by a strongly held set of beliefs. Just because the structure of marriage changes, the rules or guidelines for behavior need not.

Yet we must view these findings with some caution. Perhaps there is the sense among some of these commuters—especially those who had affairs before commuting but not afterwards—that they must compensate for their separation with greater sexual fidelity. Alternative relationships might be more threatening since there is a greater chance for them to become real substitutes. Commuters have already tampered with the marital bond by living in separate residences. To tamper with these bonds even further by starting or even continuing affairs might strain them beyond what the spouses consider acceptable. Yet, the patterns that appear—some continuing to have affairs and others continuing not to do so—are at least suggestive, if not definitive. These patterns suggest that physical proximity is not the determining factor controlling or causing extramarital encounters. Rather, the attitudes of the individual spouses, whether together or apart, are the primary cause. What determines these attitudes cannot be explained by this study. What these data do indicate is that the typical marriage provides access to friendship while it prohibits access to sexual relationships that could replace it.

## CONCLUSION: THE COMMUTER AS SOCIAL ISOLATE

We expected that commuter couples might come to rely on other personal relationships, and even substitute these for their relationships with their spouses. However, in most cases they are unwilling and/or unable to do so. Though the spouses suffer losses in their relationships by being apart, their marriage remains the primary source of aid and support.

Though they may desire to increase the amount of interaction with others, separated spouses typically cannot do so. As far as friends are concerned, social structures and conventions preclude their providing alternative aid and support. Because most live at some distance, kin cannot serve as substitutes for the absent spouse. As for extramarital affairs, normative prohibitions prevent access to sexual partners other than the spouse. As Litwak and Szelenyi (1969) argue:

> Under the impact of modern industrial societies, primary group structures tend to assume a variety of structural forms. Furthermore, these different structures can handle different tasks most effectively. (p. 465)

The "normal" nuclear family, because of its daily face-to-face interaction, is a unique institution that other groups cannot replace. As a result, the physical separation of spouses results in a drastic overall reduction in the amount of interpersonal interaction for each spouse.

The loss of old friends and the inability to make new ones, the failure to substitute kin or lovers may have consequences for the commuters' marriages. In the absence of friends, lovers, and kin, the commuters turn in on one another. These heightened expectations further diminish their ability to get what they want. Ironically, because they are apart, they depend on each other more. The result, perhaps the most difficult part of commuting, is a frequent and pervasive loneliness.

## REFERENCES


Adams, B. N. (1966). *Kinship in an urban setting.* Chicago: Markham.

Adams, B. N., & Butler, J. E. (1968). Occupational status and husband-wife social participation. *Social Forces, 45,* 501–507.

Arling, G. (1976). The elderly widow and her family, neighbors, and friends. *Journal of Marriage and the Family, 38,* 757–768.

Athanasious, R., Shaver, R., & Tavris, C. (1976). Sex (a report to *Psychology Today* readers). *Psychology Today, 4,* 39–53.

Babchuk, N. (1965). Primary friends and kin: A study of of the associations of middle-class couples. *Social Forces, 43,* 483–493.

Bell, R. (1981). *Worlds of friendship.* Beverly Hills, Calif.: Sage.

Bell, R., Turner, S., & Rosen, L. (1975). A multivariate analysis of extramarital coitus. *Journal of Marriage and the Family, 37,* 375–384.

Bernard, J. (1973). *The sex game.* New York: Atheneum.

Brown, P. (1979). Sex differences in divorce. In E. S. Gomberg & V. Franks (eds.), *Gender and disordered behavior* (pp. 101–123). New York: Brunner/Mazel.

Duberman, L. (1974). *Marriage and its alternatives.* New York: Praeger.

Fischer, C. (1982). *To dwell among friends.* Chicago: University of Chicago Press.

Gerber, I. (1977). The widower and the family. In P. Stein, J. Richman, & N. Hannon (Eds.), *The family: Functions, conflicts, and symbols* (pp. 335–337). Reading, Mass.: Addison-Wesley.

Hess, B. (1976). Friendship. In M. Riley, M. Johnson, & A. Foner (eds.), *Aging and society.* (pp. 357–393). New York: Russell Sage.

Hetherington, E. M., Cox, M., & Cox, R. (1976). Divorced fathers. *Family Coordinator, 25,* 417–428.

Hunt, M. (1974). *Sexual behavior in the 1970s.* Chicago: Playboy Press.

Lee, G. R. (1980). Kinship in the seventies: A decade review of research and theory. *Journal of Marriage and the Family, 42,* 923–934.

Litwak, E. (1960). Geographic mobility and extended family cohesion. *American Sociological Review, 25,* 385–394.

Litwak, E. & Szelenyi, I. (1969). Primary group structures and their functions: Kin, neighbors, and friends. *American Sociological Review, 34,* 465–481.

Lopata, H. (1979). *Women as widows.* New York: Elsevier.

Maykovich, M. K. (1976). Attitude vs. behavior in extra-marital sexual relations. *Journal of Marriage and the Family, 38,* 693–699.

McLanahan, S. S., Wedemeyer, N. V., & Adelberg, T. (1981). Network structure, social support and psychological well-being in the single parent family. *Journal of Marriage and the Family, 43,* 601–612.

Merton, R. (1957). *Social theory and social structure.* Glencoe, Ill.: Free Press.

Parsons, T. (1955). *Family, society, and interaction process.* Glencoe, Ill.: Free Press.

Parsons, T. (1965). The normal American family. In S. M. Farber, P. Mustacchi, & R. H. L. Wilson (eds.), *Man and civilization* (pp. 31–50). New York: McGraw-Hill.

Price-Bonham, S. (1972). Missing in action men: A study of their wives. *International Journal of Sociology of the Family, 2,* 202–211.

Ramey, J. W. (1977). Alternative life styles. *Society, 14,* 43–47.

Shorter, E. (1975). *The making of the modern family.* New York: Basic Books.

Simmel, G. (1950). *The sociology of Georg Simmel* (K. H. Wolff, Trans.). New York: Free Press.

Singh, B. K., Walton, B. L., & Williams, J. S. (1976). Extramarital sexual permissiveness: Conditions and contingencies. *Journal of Marriage and the Family, 38,* 701–712.

Stein, P. (1976). *Single.* Englewood Cliffs, N.J.: Prentice-Hall.

Weiss, R. (1979). *Going it alone.* New York: Basic Books.

*Section Five*

# Marriage—The Middle and Later Years

# 19

ELAINE M. BRODY

# Parent Care as a Normative Family Stress

*Traditionally, the human life cycle has been viewed as a process by which individuals acquire certain "adult" roles as they reach maturity and relinquish those roles as they enter old age. In the expected scenario, young men complete their education (a milestone that also marks the end of irresponsible youth), begin employment, marry, and have children. Young women may also work, but their major role is as mother. Couples then spend the next three to four decades fulfilling these roles of worker, spouse, and parent. Eventually, each of these roles may be shed. Parenting usually ends first, followed at some point by work, and for many people, especially women, the marriage ends with the death of a spouse. As life spans lengthen, the period after completion of these roles is increasing.*

*The lengthening life span also means that more people are spending the ends of their lives as frail, extremely elderly persons without the ability to take care of themselves. Gerontologist Elaine Brody suggests that the dependency needs of this growing segment of the population are placing enormous numbers of women "in the middle." These daughters and daughters-in-law are at*

---

Donald P. Kent Memorial Lecture, presented at the 37th Annual Scientific Meeting of The Gerontological Society of America, San Antonio, TX. November 18, 1984. Appreciation is expressed to M. Powell Lawton, Stanley J. Brody, and Peter R. Brody for their helpful comments on an earlier draft of this paper, and to my colleagues at the Philadelphia Geriatric Center--Bernard Liebowitz, M. Powell Lawton, Morton H. Kleban and the late Arthur Waldman--for their support and participation in the research described.

Philadelphia Geriatric Center, 5301 Old York Road, Philadelphia, PA 19191. This lecture is dedicated to my four granddaughters: Hannah and Jodi Karpman and Jocelyn and Rachel Brody.

*the stage in life when, according to the traditional scenario, roles should be decreasing. Children have left home and husbands are beginning to talk of retirement. But the traditional scenario is being acted out less frequently, and many women find their roles in later middle age to be increasing. More women in their forties and fifties are working than ever before, and it is their own retirement they are contemplating. Completion of education or marriage no longer automatically means the children have left home. The empty nest may be refilling, and it may now contain an additional generation.*

*At the same time that these other roles are continuing and expanding, it is likely that at least one elderly parent will need care. In the following selection, Brody overviews what the lengthening life span means in terms of parental care and pressures on families. She suggests that long-term parental care has now become normative—"expectable, though usually unexpected"—and that the stress that caretaking puts on families, especially women, is serious and must be adequately addressed by our institutions and our social policy.*



---

A central theme in Donald Kent's work was the importance of linking research about aging to practice and policy. He wrote:

> Research, policy and practice are . . . not the same, but . . . they are not unrelated . . . policy that is not informed by knowledge may well be worse than worthless; it may be dangerous (1972).

The subject of filial behavior in caring for disabled elderly parents is a case in point. The question "What should adult children do for their dependent elderly parents?" illustrates how values determine whether knowledge is used or ignored in shaping policy decisions. Values also influence the filial behavior of millions of people for whom the question is a salient personal issue. Though the topic of parent care excludes important aspects of family help to the old, it ultimately concerns almost all of us who have had, now have, or may in the future have a parent who is elderly, and all of us who have children and hope to grow old ourselves.

This lecture will argue that parent care has become a normative but stressful experience for individuals and families and that its nature, scope, and consequences are not yet fully understood. Some of the extraordinarily complex factors that interact to determine filial behavior will be explored. A hypothesis will be advanced that may account in part for the myth that adult children nowadays do not take care of their elderly parents as they did in the good old days. I will also comment on some of the ways in which social policy responds to knowledge about filial responsibility.

## HISTORICAL PERSPECTIVES

Answers to the question "What should adult children do . . .?" are profoundly influenced by the pervasive myth that adult children nowadays do not take care of their elderly parents as they did in the good old days.

In 1963, the Gerontological Society of America and Duke University sponsored a symposium to examine the facts in the case. The coveners felt that the three-generation family required consideration. They agreed that many programs for older people were based on social myths that had persisted because the assumptions on which they were founded had not been scrutinized by scholars. In the same year in which the conference papers were published (Shanas & Streib, 1965), Kent characterized a related myth (that of the idyllic three generation household of earlier times) as the "illusion of the Golden Past" (Kent, 1965).

Fifteen years later, the assumptions had been further scrutinized and rejected by much additional research. To the bewilderment of many scholars, the myth had survived nonetheless, prompting Shanas (1979a) to call it a Hydra-headed monster (the monster of Greek mythology that could not be killed).

The 1963 Symposium was a significant watershed in the study of intergenerational relations. There was consensus on facts that are now familiar. Rosow called the conference a "bench mark of the final respects paid to the isolated nuclear family before its interment" (Rosow, 1965, p. 341). Studies had produced compelling evidence to the effect that older people are not alienated from their families. On the contrary, it was clear that strong and viable ties exist among the generations. A consistent theme was the responsible behavior of adult children in helping their parents when need be. Important for our present concern, however, was the conferees' acknowledgement that the effects on those caregivers were hardly touched upon (Streib & Shanas, 1965).

At that time, the number of adults 65 years of age or older had increased by 80 percent in the previous 20 years. But we were not yet fully aware of the second demographic revolution that was occurring—the change in the age structure of the elderly population with increasing proportions of *very* old people.

Less than 400,000 older people were in nursing homes and homes for the aged, a number that would more than double in the next decade. Services and service-supported living arrangements for the noninstitutionalized elderly were virtually non-existent.

Social Security was beginning to take hold in improving the income position of those who were covered, but the income floor was low and incomplete and there was no social insurance against the costs of catastrophic illness in old age. Schorr's classic monograph on the destructive effects of compulsory family economic support of the aged had been published (1960). Yet in most states, the expectation that adult children should provide such support for their parents was still operationalized by harsh LRR (Legally Responsible Relatives) provisions of public assistance programs, imposing severe strains on families (Brody, 1967a).

At the very time that the Symposium was concerned with the *three-*

*generation family,* a cross-national study by Shanas and her colleagues was underway. The data being collected would show that 40 percent of older people with children had great-grandchildren (Shanas et al., 1968, pp. 140–145). The *four generation family* already had become a common phenomenon.

In those early 1960s, most intergenerational research focused on noninstitutionalized older people. Our view at the Philadelphia Geriatric Center (PGC) was looking outward from the doors of a facility whose limited mandate was to provide long-stay residential care for the "well" aged. We were experiencing increasing pressure to admit a special subgroup of the elderly—those who were mentally and/or physically disabled. Older people with dementia were prominent among them. The PGC set a precedent by making a deliberate decision to admit people with that diagnosis, and signaled its determination to provide them with treatment rather than custodial care by convening the first national conference on Alzheimer's disease and related disorders (Lawton & Lawton, 1965).

A series of studies of the changing characteristics of our applicants and of the experiences that brought them to the institution led at once to their families. We found evidence of the impact on all family members of having a dependent elderly relative (Brody, 1966a, 1966b, 1967b, 1969; Brody & Gummer, 1967) and began to explore the social cost of care to families (Lawton & Brody, 1968).

It became clear that institutionalization of the aged did not reflect "dumping" or abandonment, a conclusion reached by others (e.g., Lowenthal, 1964; Townsend, 1965). Rather, it resulted from the chronic disabilities and dependencies of very old people combined with the absence, loss, or incapacities of caregiving families, and a glaring lack of supportive community services. After prolonged and strenuous efforts to care for their parents, adult children reached their limits of endurance.

Our dependent applicants, whom we described as the "older old," had aging children many of whom were grandparents; three fourths of those children were in their 50s and 60s (Brody, 1966b). The crushing reality strains they had experienced often were accompanied by emotional family crisis which peaked during the admission process (Brody & Spark, 1966; Spark & Brody, 1970). The older people felt abandoned, their children were conflicted and suffered intensely from guilt, and multiple relationship problems erupted to create a searing experience for members of all generations in the family.

## PARENT CARE AS A NORMATIVE EXPERIENCE

What had been happening was that *having a dependent elderly parent was becoming a normative experience for individuals and families* and was exceeding the capacities of some of them.

To illustrate—Between 1900 and 1976, the number of people who experienced the death of a parent before the age of 15 dropped from 1 in 4 to 1 in 20, while the number of middle aged couples with two or more living parents increased from 10 perent to 47 percent (Uhlenberg, 1980). At the time of the 1963 Symposium, about 25 percent of people over the age of 45 had a surviving parent, but by the early 1970s, 25 percent of people in their late 50s had a surving parent (Murray, 1973). By 1980, 40 percent of people in their late 50s had a surviving parent as did 20 percent of those in their early 60s, 10 percent of those in their late 60s and 3 percent of those in their 70s (NRTA-AARP, 1981). Ten percent of all people 65 years or older had a child over the age of 65!

Moreover, while the population of older people was increasing, the birthrate was falling, resulting in a marked alteration in the ratio of potential filial caregivers to those in need of care. The odds of being called upon for parent care were increasing radically, and for increasingly older parents and children.

There are no definitive data on the number of people involved in parent care. One of the difficulties in making an estimate is that surveys identify the proportions of older people in need of services but large studies do not gather detailed data from the perspective of all of the various people in the family who are service providers. A problem in collecting data is that more than one child may be helping the same elderly parent, while some may be helping more than one parent or parent-in-law.

Some notion of the dimensions of this situation can be gleaned from various studies, however. For example, estimates of the overall proportion of non-institutionalized elderly in need of help range from 17 percent to 40 percent (see Brody, 1977a for review). For every disabled person who resides in a nursing home, two or more equally impaired elderly live with and are cared for by their families. (Comptroller General of the United States, 1977a). Soldo calculates that two and one quarter million women between the ages of 40 and 59 share their households with elderly kin (1980) and over a million households contain an older person in need of assistance with activities of daily living or mobility—an extreme level of caregiving (Myllyluoma & Soldo, 1980). Soldo's figures, though they are not limited to filial care, reflect only intra-household caregiving. An even larger number of people provide help to old people who do not share their households.

Taken together, these and other findings suggest a very conservative estimate that well over 5 million people are involved in parent-care at any given time. But such cross-sectional data do not speak to the lifetime chances of needing to provide parent care—that is, they do not include people who have provided parent care in the past or who will do so in the future as they and their parents age.

Not only do more people now provide parent care than in the past, but there are differences in the nature and duration of the care provided. Gerontologists need no reminder that chronic illnesses have replaced the acute diseases accounting for most deaths early in this century. As a result, our health systems are struggling to make a major shift in emphasis from acute (i.e., temporary) to chronic (i.e., sustained) care (Brody, S., 1973). People are living longer today after the onset of chronic disease and disability (a phenomenon that has been called "The Failures of Success," Gruenberg, 1977); the number of years of active life expectancy decreases with advancing old age (Katz et al., 1983), and few people reach the end of life without experiencing some period of dependency. More years of dependency mean more years during which there must be someone on whom to depend.

It is *long-term parent care* that has become a normative experience—expectable, though usually unexpected.

The phrase *long-term care* emerged to describe the formal system of government and agencies needed to provide the continuum of sustained helping services dictated by chronicity, though attempts to define it were not made until the late 1970s (Brody, 1977; U.S. National Committee on Vital and Health Statistics, 1978). But the family, virtually unnoticed, had invented long-term care well before that phrase was articulated. The family made the shift from episodic, short-term acute care sooner and more flexibly, willingly, and effectively than professionals and the bureaucracy.

The irony of the myth is that *nowadays adult children provide more care and more difficult care to more parents over much longer periods of time than they did in the good old days.* There is also evidence that adult children now provide more emotional support to the elderly than in the past (Bengtson & Treas, 1980; Hareven, 1982).

At a time when there is a call for new roles for aging adults, a major new role that has emerged for Neugarten's young old (Neugarten, 1974) is that of caregiver for the old old. Can our social values come to regard this role as being as satisfying as second careers of work, volunteer activities, or creative pursuits?

**Research on Filial Behavior**

During the 1960s and 1970s, several major research themes developed, producing a literature too immense to be reviewed here. Particularly relevant are the studies of the role of the family (the informal support system) vis-à-vis government and agencies (the formal support system) in helping the disabled aged. That stream of research found that families, not the formal system, provide 80 to 90 percent of medically related and personal care, household tasks, transportation, and shopping. The family links the old to the formal support system. The family responds in emergencies and provides intermittent acute care. The family shares its home with severely impaired old people who live in the community (Brody, S. et al., 1978), with rates of shared households rising with the advancing age and poor health of the parent(s) (Mindel, 1979; Troll, 1971). It is the dependable family that provides the expressive support—the socialization, concern, affection, and sense of having someone on whom to rely—that is the form of family help most wanted by the old, but that is not usually counted as a service in surveys.

The members of the family who are the principal caregivers were identified as adult daughters (and to some extent daughters-in-law). They are the main helpers to the old who care for their impaired spouses and the main providers of help to the spouseless majority of very old people. They predominate among those who share their homes when the elderly cannot manage on their own. (See Brody, 1978; Horowitz, 1982; Myllyuoma & Soldo, 1980; Shanas, 1979b; Troll, 1971.)

The prominence of women in the parent care role should not obscure the efforts of men, however. Sons also sustain bonds of affection, perform certain gender-defined tasks, and become the "responsible relatives" for the old who have no daughters or none close by. And some sons-in-law are unsung heroes.

**Parent Care as a Stress**

Recently, research on the effects of caregiving has been accelerating. To put the matter in perspective, in the main, having an elderly parent is gratifying and helpful. Older people are a resource to their children, providing many forms of assistance. Most people help their parents willingly when need be and derive satisfaction from doing so. Some adult children negotiate this stage of life without undue strain and experience personal growth during the process. However, when there is an increase in reliance on children to meet a parent's dependency needs, the family homeostasis—whether it is precarious or well-balanced—must shift accordingly. Such shifts have potential for stress, particularly because they augur increasing dependency in the future.

Some people experience financial hardship and some experience declines in their physical health from the arduous tasks of caring for a disabled parent. Certainly, such problems require attention. However, study after study has identified the most pervasive and most severe consequences as being in the realm of emotional strains. A long litany of mental health symptoms such as depression, anxiety, frustration, helplessness, sleeplessness, lowered morale, and emotional exhaustion are related to restrictions on time and freedom, isolation, conflict from the competing demands of various responsibilities, difficulties in setting priorities, and interference with life-style and social and recreational activities (see Archbold, 1978; Cantor, 1983; Danis, 1978; Frankfather et al., 1981; Gurland et al., 1978; Hoenig & Hamilton, 1966; Horowitz, 1982; Robinson & Thurnher, 1979; Sainsbury & Grad de Alercon, 1970).

Though most such research has focused on the "principal caregiver," there are many findings about the effects on the family. The family is affected by interference with its life-style, privacy, socialization, vacations, future plans, and income, and by the diversion of the caregiver's time from other family members and the negative effects on her health.

Emotional support from spouses (Sussman, 1979), siblings (Horowitz, 1982), and other relatives (Zarit et al., 1980), mitigates the caregivers' strains. But when changes in the family homeostasis stimulate interpersonal conflicts, relationships are affected negatively between husbands and wives, among adult siblings, and across the generations.

In short, filial care of the elderly has become normative but stressful, it affects the entire family, and adult children provide more care and affective support than in the good old days. But some aspects of parent care are not well understood as yet: its place in the individual and family life cycle, the inner processes of individuals and families when parent care becomes necessary, and the interaction of values with personal, situational, and environmental factors in determining filial behavior.

**Is Parent Care a "Developmental Stage"?**

Parent care, though normative, does not appear in conceptualizations of what happens during the life course of individual and families.

In a paper given at the 1963 Symposium, Margaret Blenkner made a seminal attempt to conceptualize the inner experience of adult children when parent care becomes necessary. She described the need for the adult child to have the capacity to be depended on by the aging parent and characterized parent care as a developmental stage of life called "filial maturity"—a transitional stage preceding old age. Therapeutic approaches, she urged, should help adult children to meet their parents' dependency needs (rather than to relieve their guilt) and thus to achieve filial maturity (Blenkner, 1965).

Though there are flaws in Blenkner's particular conceptual and therapeutic approach, at the least she issued an implicit challenge to develop appropriate models.

A basic problem with Blenkner's model is that *parent care is not a developmental stage*. Developmental stages are specific to age-linked periods of time while parent care is not.

The "normal" life crises of earlier life usually occur in a somewhat orderly progression as people move serially through more or less well-defined age categories. Those categories are linked to age-specific cognitive, emotional, and physiological developments and capacities. In sharp contrast, the demands of parent care often are incompatible with the adult child's psychological, emotional, and physiological capacities. In fact, the upward trajectory of the increasing demands on aging children often runs counter to the downward trajectory of their declining abilities to meet those demands.

Parent care is not a single "stage" that can be fitted neatly into an orderly sequence of stages in the life course. Among the elderly, age and stage are not the same (Peck, 1968). Young children are "programmed" developmentally for a gradual reduction of dependency, while the dependencies of old age appear with great variability and irregularity, over much wider time spans, and in different sequential patterns. In addition, the timing of the marriages and parenthood of both parent and child influence the ages and stages of adult children when their parents need help. Parent care, therefore, can overlay many different ages and stages in different people and different families, occurring as it does in young adulthood, in middle age, or even in old age. Moreover, since parent care often is a time-extended process (some of the women in our PGC studies had been helping a parent for more than 20 years), it may span several of the caregiver's age periods or stages.

While the largest proportion of parent caring daughters are in their 40s and 50s, as many as one third are either under 40 or over 60. The caregiver may be a grandmother who is experiencing the decrements of aging or she may have young children at home.

Even when they are in the same age group, the situations of parent caring children are extraordinarily variable. One woman in middle age may be engaged in adapting to the onset of chronic ailments and disability; another may be running for Vice President. Health, marital and economic status, living arrangements, geographic distance from the parent, personality, adaptive capacities, and the quality of parent-child relationships vary. The caregiver may or may not be working. Her retirement or that of her spouse may be imminent or already have taken place. Meeting a parent's dependency needs may be concurrent with the "letting go" of one's young adult children. Or, the theoretically empty nest may contain young adult children who have not left it or have returned to it, a phenomenon that has been increasing.

Among the people who called the PGC for help in one typical day were: an exhausted, 70-year-old woman who could no longer go on caring for her disabled 93-year-old mother; a recently widowed 50 year old who had just completed her education in preparation for a return to work, but found that her mother had Alzheimer's disease and could not be left alone; a couple in their late 60s with three frail parents between them; a divorcee of 57 who was caring for two disabled sons, a 6-year-old grandchild, and an 87-year-old wheelchair-bound mother; and a young couple in their early 30s, about to have a first child, who had taken two old people into their home—the wife's terminally ill mother and the confused, incontinent grandmother for whom the mother had been caring.

Such caregivers do not share a single developmental stage of life. A most important consequence of that fact is the absence of behavioral norms for this normative life crisis. Since behavior in different people and families cannot be measured by the same yardstick, there is no simple answer to the question "What should adult children do . . .?"

### The Inner Meaning of Parent Care: A Dialectic of Dependence/Independence

At whatever age or stage the need for parent care arises, the dialectic tension of dependence/independence is a central issue. People vary in the extent to which they have the capacity to meet the dependency needs of others, though growth and change are possible.

As an explanation of the processes that occur, role reversal is a superficial concept at best. (See Goldfarb, 1965 for a discussion of the reasons "role reversal" is inaccurate as a description of dependency on one's child from the perspective of the older person.) Being depended on by one's elderly parent and being depended on by one's young child have different inner meanings. When caring for an infant or child, the future holds promise of a gradual reduction in dependency; caring for an impaired older person presages continuing or increasing dependence. Caregivers have very different reactions to manifestations that are normal and will be dealt with developmentally in the child, but are symptomatic of pathology in the elderly adult—incontinence, for example.

The issue of the older person's dependency on adult children has its origin in the dependency of the helpless infant on the young parent. The inevitable shift in the delicate balance of dependence/independence of the elderly parent and adult child reactivates that child's unresolved conflicts about dependency.

Parent care also stimulates anticipation of the final separation from the parent and of one's potential dependence on one's own children as well. If successful adaptation is to be made, not only must the adult child have the capacity to permit the parent to be dependent, but the parent must have the capacity to be appropriately dependent so as to permit the adult child to be dependable.

There is general acceptance of the proposition that the inevitable vestiges of incompletely resolved crises or earlier stages are reprised and qualify the extent to which later crises are resolved. Since personality continues to develop until the end of life, the way in which the filial crisis is negotiated not only depends on the past, but has implications for the future of the caregiver when she becomes old—and indeed, for that of succeeding generations.

Reactions to the need to provide parent care, of course, range along the theoretical spectrum from health to pathology, as do responses to other life crises. Complex parent care situations occur in the context of the individual's and family's personality and history, qualitative relationships, and coping capacities—all of which qualify the ability to achieve and adapt to the new homeostasis that is required. But the best integrated individual and the best functioning family can be shaken to the core when confronted with reality demands that they cannot meet. It cannot be assumed, as the myth would have it, that the family *is* the problem; more often, the family *has* a problem. Interpretation of "filial maturity" to mean that all of the concrete services needed by the old should be provided by adult children (clearly, a distortion of Blenkner's concept), reinforces the myth by implying that they could do so if only they were "emotionally mature."

When interpersonal problems occur, they are not caused by parent care. Rather, the pressures are such that family relationship problems are reactivated or exacerbated (Brody, 1979). The caregiver's spouse or children may compete with the old person for time and attention. New battles may be fought in the old wars among the siblings. "I do everything for my mother, but my sister/brother is still her favorite." Old loyalties and alliances as well as old rivalries operate.

Given the reality pressures, given the interpersonal and intrapsychic tensions, it is not surprising that the emotional aspects of caregiving have been a consistent theme in research reports. Nor is it surprising that some adult children relinquish tasks of parent care before others think they should. What *is* remarkable is that so many transcend the strains and take so long to reach their limits of endurance.

But to romanticize the family is just as inappropriate as to be judgmental. The romantic view admires those who continue to care for an impaired older person under conditions of such severe strain that there is deprivation and suffering for the entire family. People in such families may be psychologically unable to place the older person in a nursing home, or, as every service worker knows, may be unable to use formal support services that are badly needed. Whatever dynamics are at work—symbiotic ties, the gratification of being the "burden bearer," a fruitless search for parental approval that has never been received, or expiation of guilt for having been the favored child—excessive caregiving may represent not emotional health or heroism or love, but pathology (Brody & Spark, 1966).

Successful resolution of the filial crisis, then, may involve acceptance by adult children of what they can*not* do as well as acceptance of what they can and should do. For their part, successful adaptation to dependency by the elderly involves *their* acceptance of what their adult children cannot do. It is a curious value that encourages others to continue caregiving no matter the personal cost, but ignores the need of some people to be helped to reduce the amount of care they provide.

**Interaction of Inner Processes with Values and Socioeconomic Trends**

Such inner processes interact with values, socioeconomic trends, and other factors in determining behavior.

As the demand for parent care increased dramatically, a broad socioeconomic trend occurred that is associated with changing values. The rapid entry of middle-aged women—the traditional providers of parent care—into the labor force held the potential for affecting their availability for parent care and for increasing the pressures on them and their families.

Betty Friedan's book, which set in motion the women's movement with its changes in values about women's roles, was published in the same year in which the Symposium was held (Friedan, 1963). It was one of a number of factors that were operating to account for women's march to the workplace, not the least of which was that the money was needed. Between 1940 and 1979 the proportion of working married women between the ages of 45 and 54 increased five-fold. At present, 69 percent of all women between the ages of 35 and 44 are in the work force as are 62 percent of those between the ages of 45 and 54, and 42 percent of those in the 55 to 64 age group (U.S. Bureau of Labor Statistics, 1984).

In order to explore the effects of the converging demographic and socioeconomic trends on filial caregiving, our PGC research group surveyed women who were members of families that included three generations of women.[3] We examined possible changes in values about parent care—in attitudes about family care of the aged and filial responsibility, about gender-appropriate roles, and about filial care vis-à-vis help from the formal system. (For methodology and detailed findings see Brody et al., 1982a, 1982b; Brody et al., 1983; Brody et al., 1984a; Lang & Brody, 1983.)

In contradiction to the myth, we found value continuity in that all three generations expressed firm commitment toward filial help for the aged. Value

[3]The Dependent Elderly and Women's Changing Roles (AoA, Grant #90−A−1277). "Women in the Middle" and Care of the Dependent Elderly (AoA, Grant #90−AR−2174).

change was apparent in that large majorities of all generations favored equal roles for men and women—in, for example, the sharing of traditionally female roles such as child care and parent care (though each successively younger generation expressed progressively more egalitarian attitudes).

However, there were many findings indicating tension and conflict between the "new" values about women's roles and the "old" values. For example—Despite the general endorsement of feminist views of the roles of men and women, and though two thirds of the middle generation women were working, they were more likely to expect working daughters than working sons to adjust their work schedules for parent care. But at the same time, a majority of all generations agreed that it is better for a working woman to pay someone to care for her elderly parent than to leave her job to do it herself.

The potentially conflicting values and multiple roles of the middle generation women whom we called the "women in the middle" (Brody, 1981) often led them to have incompatible views. They wanted to be responsible as daughters but not to become dependent on their children in their own old age. Similarly, the granddaughters, at an average age of 23, were the generation most in favor of egalitarian gender roles, but also were the ones most in favor of family care of the aged and the most in favor of grandchildren helping the old—and expression of what we called "grandfilial responsibility." Moreover, those young women expected to work more years than their mothers had expected to work when they were young, but they also expected to marry and have as many children as their mothers had.

Clear statements of these women's values—their "normative expectations [that] serve as guidelines for behavior" (George, 1980)—related to emotional support. Overall, emotional support is what members of all three generations wanted most from their adult children in their own old age. As in other studies, they strongly preferred households separate from their children and did not wish to be financially dependent on them. Family bonds were not equated with economic help, shared households, personal care and instrumental services. But there was variability as well, with preferences differing with the women's lineage position in the family, different situations, social and health status, ethnic backgrounds (Johnsen & Fulcomer, 1984), and according to the specific kind of help needed.

However, the actual behavior of the middle generation women, all of whom had a living elderly mother, demonstrates once again that attitudes and opinions are not always reflected in behavior. Despite their attitudinal acceptance of formal services and their consensus about egalitarian roles, the middle-generation daughters behaved not only in accordance with their unchanged values about family care of the elderly, but in accordance with "traditional" values about women's roles. They were the major source of help to their mothers even though their responsibilities rose steeply as they grew older. In response to the new demography, the older of the daughters (those in their 50s and 60s) provided many more hours of help and did more difficult tasks for their older and more dependent mothers. They also were more likely than the younger daughters to share their households with their mothers—a phenomenon we called the "refilling of the empty nest" (Brody, 1978). In comparison with their elderly mothers when the latter were in their middle years in the good old days, they also provided more emotional support to their elderly parents, provided more emotional and financial support to their own children, and had worked more (Brody et al., 1982b). When faced with competing demands on their time, what these women gave up was their own free time and opportunities for socialization and recreation. Findings such as these led us to be concerned about the mental and physical health of "women in the middle."

## CAREGIVING CAREERS

But being in the middle because of parent care is not a single time-limited episode in the life-course, as data from more recent PGC studies[4] show.

In this research we compared working and nonworking women with respect to their parent care behavior and the effects they experience from caregiving. All of the women in the study were married and were acting as principal caregivers for widowed elderly mothers who required varying amounts of help.

*Care of a particular parent at a particular time proved to be only one phase of these women's careers in caregiving, caregiving careers that extend well into late middle age and early old age.* Almost half of them had helped an elderly father before his death and one third of them had helped other elderly relatives. Twenty-two percent were currently providing help to another elderly relative as well as to their own mothers—to parents-in-law, grandparents, aunts, cousins, and more distant relations. And two thirds of them had children living at home, most under 18 years of age and some (about 10 percent) younger than six. Given the discrepancy in life expectancy for men and women, it is inevitable that many of these women will care for dependent husbands in the future.

To emphasize—*for many women, parent care is not a single time-limited episode in the life course.* Not only can it begin at widely differing ages and be superimposed on more than one of the other individual and family life stages, but dependence/independence issues may be replayed many times. They can be multiple and multi-layered as one's parents and parents-in-law and even grandparents and other elderly relatives require help sequentially or simultaneously. And all of these complex factors operate for the other adult children and their spouses as well, combining to affect parent care in almost infinite variations.

### Do Work and Parent Care Compete?

Another finding from the same study speaks directly to the potential competition between work and parent care. It illustrates the subtle interplay of values, reality pressures, personal characteristics, and other factors in determining filial behavior.

[4]Women, Work, and Care of the Aged: Mental Health Effects (NIMH, Grant #MH35252). Parent Care, Sibling Relationships, and Mental Health (NIMH, Grant #MH35252−04).

The working and nonworking women were providing roughly equal amounts of care to their dependent mothers. Substantial proportions of both groups were experiencing many of the various strains and mental health symptoms referred to above. But simply comparing all of the working women with all of the nonworking women obscured those who were under the most pressure.

We found that *28 percent of our sample of nonworking women had quit their jobs because of their elderly mothers' needs for care. They had been displaced from the work force. A similar proportion of the working women were conflicted: They were considering giving up their jobs for the same reason and some had already reduced the number of hours they worked.*

Women's capacities may indeed be elastic in accommodating many roles, as some researchers have observed. But ultimately, those data indicate, elastic snaps if stretched too thin. To illustrate:

Compared with the other working and nonworking women in the study, the women who had left their jobs were in the most difficult parent care situations and the ones who were considering doing so were very close behind. Both of those groups had more functionally dependent mothers. They experienced more interferences with their life styles and time for their husbands. They had been helping their mothers for longer periods of time and they tended to be the only ones providing that help. And they more often felt that parent care made them feel tied down and as though they had missed out on something in life.

The women who had already quit their jobs were older than any of the other women in the study and they had older mothers. They also had an additional set of problems: they more often shared their households with their mothers (a living arrangement which is a stronger predictor of strain), they reported that parent care had resulted in more deterioration in their health and more of certain mental health symptoms, and they had the lowest family incomes. (See Brody et al., 1984 and Kleban et al., 1984 for detailed reports on these findings.)

Values and socioeconomic considerations also proved to be influential. Compared with the women who had quit their jobs, the women who were thinking of doing so were better educated, held higher level jobs, and to a much greater extent viewed their work as part of a career rather than as "just a job." Within two years after the study, one quarter of all the women in the study had changed their work status; some of the nonworkers entered the labor force (most because the money was needed—to send children to college, for example) and some of the working women had increased or decreased their working hours or were no longer working.

Obviously, patterns of parent care, work, and other role performance must be viewed as long-term processes. As yet, we have no data about this extraordinarily diverse and complex mosaic depicting responses to parent care over the individual and family life-course. Study of women's shifting work and family roles has focused on the earlier stages of their lives; the full story is yet to be written about the shifting of their roles later in life.

Virtually nothing is known about the processes by which different options are selected—processes which have profound implications for clinical approaches and social policy. Caregivers who were not part of our sample may have exercised other options such as nursing home placement of the parent or the redistribution of care in other ways along the informal and formal support systems. Other paths might have been taken by daughters who were not married or by sons.

Given the increasing diversity in women's life courses (cf. Lopata & Norr, 1980), we do not know what choices will be made by future cohorts of women as they move into the parent care years. We do not know how the old behavioral borders that have been measured by research will respond to lifestyle changes, to possible changes in family structure and size, to economic changes, or to changes in mobility patterns, for example.

And what of the myth? How did it fare in the views of the women we studied? To recapitulate the experiences of these "women-in-the middle":

- They were the principal caregivers to their dependent mothers.
- They were in the middle of competing demands on their time and energy.
- They were experiencing many strains as a result of parent care.
- Their "empty nests" had been refilled—for some quite literally, and for all in terms of increased responsibilities.
- Care of their mothers was but one episode in time-extended "caregiving careers" to older relatives.
- Some had quit their jobs to care for their mothers and others were considering doing so or had cut back on the number of hours they worked.

*Yet three fifths of those very same women said that "somehow" they felt guilty about not doing enough for their mothers, and three quarters of them agreed that nowadays children do not take care of their elderly parents as was the case in the good old days.*

## THE MYTH: A HYPOTHESIS

Why is that myth so tenacious in the face of the factual evidence that refutes it? It is important to understand the myth because of its power to inhibit constructive practice and policy approaches.

Many explanations have been advanced for the myth's apparent immortality and it is probable that each of them plays a role. For example—observation of increased mobility and the geographic distance of adult children from their parents; the proliferation of nursing homes and age segregated living arrangements; the visibility of concentrations of old people in places with favorable climates; the taxpayer's fear of the escalating costs of formal system care; the fact, as Shanas (1963) suggested, that those in the helping professions see only the problem situations; and the tendency to romanticize and idealize some vague time in the past.

A hypothesis suggested here is that one possible contributant to the myth's vitality lies at a deeper level and is related to the dependence/independence dialectic:

*The myth does not die because at its heart is a fundamental truth.*

At some level of awareness, members of all generations may harbor the expectation that the devotion and care given by the young parent to the infant and child—that total, primordial commitment which is the original paradigm for caregiving to those who are dependent—should be reciprocated and the indebtedness repaid in kind when the parent, having grown old, becomes dependent.

*The "truth" to which the myth speaks is that adult children cannot and do not provide the same total care to their elderly parents that those parents gave to them in the good old days of their infancy and childhood.* The roles of parent and child cannot be reversed in that sense. The good old days, then, may not be earlier periods in our social history (after all, the myth existed then too), but an earlier period in each individual's and family's history to which there can be no return.

The myth exists because of the disparity between standards and expectations on the one hand and the unavoidable realities on the other hand. The disparity leads to guilt. The myth persists because the guilt persists, reflecting a universal and deeply rooted human theme. That may be why we hear over and over again from adult children "I know I'm doing everything I can for my mother, but somehow I still feel guilty." The fantasy is that "somehow" one should do more. That may be one reason that so many adult children are overwhelmed with guilt when a parent enters a nursing home. It is experienced as the total surrender of the parent to the care of others—the ultimate failure to meet the parent's dependency needs as that parent met the child's needs in the good old days.

Guilt may be a reason that people assert that they and their own families behave responsibly in caring for their old, but that most people do not do so as was the case in the good old days. They need to defend against the guilt and to deny their own negative and unacceptable emotions (emotions such as resentment, anger, and the wish not to be burdened, which add another dimension to the guilt), by feeling that others do not behave as well. "*They* are *really* guilty; I am not."

In completing the feedback loop, by exacerbating the guilt the myth contributes to the strains of parent care. Not only does the myth persist because the guilt persists, but the guilt persists because the myth persists.

To quote Erma Bombeck, "Guilt is the gift that keeps on giving" (1984).

## SOCIAL POLICY

Since the 1963 Symposium, social policy (which expresses the values of the time), has made some progress in applying knowledge about filial behavior. Medicare and Medicaid came into being (1965) and an income floor was established by Supplemental Security Income (SSI, 1974). Medicaid and SSI together eliminated compulsory financial support of the old by their adult children. With Social Security (1935) as a base, the proportion of older people who were wholly dependent on family for economic support dropped from about 50 percent in 1937 to 1.5 percent in 1979 (Upp, 1982). (Note that these figures do not speak to adequacy of income.) Those programs (together with savings, private pensions, etc.) enabled more of the aged to live as they prefer (close to, but not in the same household with, their children) and to realize their wish not to depend on their children for income or the costs of catastrophic illness. There has been considerable development of services and living facilities, though many more are needed.

At present, however, in expressing current values, social policy echoes, uses, and perpetuates the myth, exerting psychological pressure on adult children, increasing their guilt, and adding to their strains by failing to provide services and facilities that are urgently needed to back up their efforts.

The myth is being invoked as a rationale for a philosophy that would shrink the formal support system and encourage its non-use to save public funds. The call to restore the good old days of family values is being operationalized in a variety of ways. For example:

- The states have been encouraged to reinstitute the archaic requirement that people in the grandparent generation be compelled to pay the costs of nursing home care for the great-grandparent generation.
- A variety of cost-containment efforts are limiting nursing home beds, frustrating efforts at quality care, and effectively closing nursing home doors to those who need them most—the "heavy care" Medicaid patients (U.S. GAO, 1983) such as those with Alzheimer's disease (Brody et al., in press). As a result, aging caregivers who have gone beyond the limits of endurance will have no relief. This, though scientists on both sides of the "compression of morbidity" controversy agree that the number of those in need of long-term chronic care will continue to increase, at least for the next few decades (e.g., see Fries, 1984; Schneider & Brody, J., 1983). And this, though it has been shown that community care is not cheaper than nursing home care for severely disabled older people (Comptroller General of the United States, 1977b; Fox & Clauser, 1980).
- Services that would relieve the unrelenting strains on families of non-institutionalized old people should be increasing but are being cut back. Family focused services—notably respite care and day care—are sparse, uneven regionally, and are not funded consistently.

The language used is revealing. The injunction issued is not to "supplant" family services, though research evidence indicates that services strengthen family caregiving (Horowitz, 1982; Zimmer & Sainer, 1978). There are suggestions for "incentives" for families to care, implying that they need to be induced, rather than helped, to do what they want to do and have been doing. Issues are framed artificially as competing propositions such as institutionalization *versus* community care, family (informal) care *versus* formal (government and agencies) care, even respite services to provide temporary relief for caregivers *versus* training programs to build their caregiving skills.

When a "family policy" means cheering the family on to increase its efforts, the effect is to undermine the very family the rhetoric purports to save. The call for filial responsibility masks social irresponsibility, disadvantaging the elderly and the young as well as the middle generation. Binstock (1983) has called attention to the scapegoating of the old. Many policies scapegoat their adult children.

In the future, there could be radical changes in demands for parent care and other long-term support services if bio-medical breakthroughs result in prevention or cure of conditions causing chronic dependency—Alzheimer's disease, for example. But social policy cannot await such major advances. The informal system, which protects the formal system from being overwhelmed, should be supported, not weakened. Overburdening family members can increase the costs to the community of the mental and physical health problems they experience as a result.

Since knowledge has not dispelled the myth, and if the hypothesis advanced here means that one of its aspects is relatively immutable, perhaps the realistic goal is not to slay the Hydra monster but to render it powerless to impede constructive clinical approaches and a sound social policy. As gerontologists, we provide facts which are correctives so that policy based on bias and myth does not go unchallenged.

In a paper presented by co-authors Steve Brody and Don Kent at the 1968 GSA meetings, they said "The union of social research and social action is a long way off, but there are at least signs that such a bridge can be built..." (Brody & Kent, 1968). We have made progress in building that bridge, and our efforts have been increasing. Since the 1963 Symposium, the membership of this organization has risen from 2,000 to 6,000, with an exponential increase in the amount of research.

We cannot do it all, of course. Adult children will continue to care for and about their elderly parents. They will continue to be concerned, to provide affection and emotional support, to do what they are able, and to arrange for the needed services that they cannot supply. (Perhaps those are the only appropriate norms for filial behavior.) The strains families experience are not completely preventable or remediable. But policy should rest on knowledge rather than a myth if it is to create a dependable formal system that forges an effective partnership with the dependable family. Knowledge, properly used, can do much to prevent families from reaching the limits of endurance and can help us as a society to meet our collective filial responsibility.

## REFERENCES

Archbold, P. (1978). Impact of caring for an ill elderly parent of the middle-aged or elderly offspring caregiver. Paper presented at the 31st Annual Meeting of the Gerontological Society, Dallas, Tex., November.

Bengtson, V. L., & Treas, J. (1980). The changing context of mental health and aging. In J. E. Birren & R. B. Sloane (eds.), *Handbook of mental health and aging.* Englewood Cliffs, N. J.: Prentice-Hall.

Binstock, R. H. (1983). The aged as scapegoat. *The Gerontologist, 23,* 136– 143.

Blenkner, M. (1965). Social work and family relationships in later life with some thoughts on filial maturity. In E. Shanas & G. F. Streib (eds.), *Social structure and the family: Generational Relations.* Englewood Cliffs, N. J.: Prentice-Hall.

Bombeck, Erma, quoted by Skow, John (1984). "Erma in Bomburgia," *Time*, July 2, p. 56.

Brody, E. M. (1981). "Women in the middle" and family help to older people. *The Gerontologist, 21,* 471–480.

Brody, E. M. (1979). Aged parents and aging children. In P. K. Ragan (ed.), *Aging Parents.* Los Angeles, CA: University of Southern California Press.

Brody, E. M. (1978). The aging of the family. *The Annals of the American Academy of Political and Social Science, 438,* 13–27.

Brody, E. M. (1977). *Long-term care of older people: A practical guide.* New York: Human Sciences Press.

Brody, E. M. (1977a). Environmental factors in dependency. In Exton-Smith, A. N. & Evans, J. G. (eds.), *Care of the Elderly: Meeting the Challenge of Dependency* (pp. 81–95). London: Academic Press; New York: Grune & Stratton.

Brody, E. M. (1969). Follow-up study of applicants and non-applicants to a voluntary home. *The Gerontologist, 9,* 187–196.

Brody, E. M. (1967a). Aging is a family affair. *Public Welfare,* 129–140.

Brody, E. M. (1967b). The mentally-impaired aged patient: A socio-medical problem. *Geriatrics Digest,* 4, 25–32.

Brody, E. M. (1966a). The impaired aged: A follow-up study of applicants rejected by a voluntary home. *Journal of the American Geriatrics Society, 14,* 414–420.

Brody, E. M. (1966b). The aging family. *The Gerontologist, 6,* 201–206.

Brody, E. M., & Gummer, B. (1967). Aged applicants and non-applicants to a voluntary home: An exploratory comparison. *The Gerontologist, 7,* 234-243.

Brody, E. M., Johnsen, P. T., & Fulcomer, M. C. (1984a). What should adult children do for elderly parents: Opinions and preferences of three generations of women. *Journal of Gerontology, 39,* 736–746.

Brody, E. M., Johnsen, P. T., Fulcomer, M. C., & Lang, A. (1982a). The Dependent Elderly and Women's Changing Roles. Final report on Administration on Aging Grant #90–A–1277.

Brody, E. M., Johnsen, P. T., & Fulcomer, M. C. (1982b). "Women in the middle" and care of the dependent elderly. Final Report on AoA Grant #90–AR–2174.

Brody, E. M., Johnsen, P. T., Fulcomer, M. C., & Lang, A. M. (1983). Women's changing roles and help to the elderly: Attitudes of three generations of women. *Journal of Gerontology, 38,* 597–607.

Brody, E. M., Kleban, M. H., & Johnsen, P. T. (1984). Women who provide parent care: Characteristics of those who work and those who do not. Paper presented at the 37th Annual Meeting of The Gerontological Society of America, San Antonio, Tex., November.

Brody, E. M., Lawton, M. P., & Liebowitz, B. (1984). Senile dementia: Public policy and adequate institutional care. *American Journal of Public Health, 74,* 1381–1383.

Brody, E. M., & Spark, G. (1966). Institutionalization of the aged: A family crisis. *Family Process, 5,* 76–90.

Brody, S. J. (1973). Comprehensive health care of the elderly: An analysis. *The Gerontologist, 13,* 412–418.

Brody, S. J., & Kent, D. P. (1968). Social research and social policy in a public agency. Paper presented at the 21st Annual Meeting of the Gerontological Society, Denver, Col.

Brody, S. J., Poulshock, S. W., & Masciocchi, C. F. (1978). The family care unit: A major consideration in the long-term system. *The Gerontologist, 18,* 556–561.

Cantor, M. H. (1983). Strain among caregivers: A study of experience in the United States. *The Gerontologist, 23,* 597–604.

Cantor, M. H. (1980). Caring for the frail elderly: Impact on family, friends and neighbors. Paper presented at 33d Annual Meeting of The Gerontological Society of America, San Diego, Calif.

Comptroller General of the United States. (1977a). *The well-being of older people in Cleveland, Ohio,* U.S. General Accounting Office, #RD–77–70, Washington, D.C., April 19.

Comptroller General of the United States. (1977b). Report to Congress on *Home Health—The Need for a National Policy to Better Provide for the elderly,* U.S. General Accounting Office, HRD–78–19, Washington, D.C., December 30.

Danis, B. G. (1978). Stress in individuals caring for elderly relatives. Paper presented at 31st Annual Meeting of the Gerontological Society, Dallas, Tex.

Fox, P. D., & Clauser, S. B. (1980). Trends in nursing home expenditures: Implications for aging policy. *Health Care Financing Review,* 65–70.

Frankfather, D., Smith, M. J., & Caro, F. G. (1981). *Family care of the elderly: Publice initiatives and private obligations.* Lexington, Mass.: Lexington Books.

Friedan, B. (1963). *The feminine mystique.* New York: Dell.

Fries, J. F. (1984). The compression of morbidity: Miscellaneous comments about a theme. *The Gerontologist, 24,* 354–359.

George, L. K. (1980). *Role transitions in late life.* Monterey, Calif.: Brooks/Cole.

Goldfarb, A. I. (1965). Psychodynamics and the three-generation family. In E. Shanas & G. F. Streib (eds.), *Social structure and the family: General relations* (pp. 10–45). Englewood Cliffs, N. J.: Prentice-Hall.

Gruenberg, E. M. (1977). The failures of success. *Milbank Memorial Fund Quarterly,* Health and Society, 3–24.

Gurland, B., Dean, L., Gurland, P., & Cook, D. (1978). Personal time dependency in the elderly of New York City: Findings from the U.S.–U.K. cross-national geriatric community study. In *Dependency in the elderly of New York City.* New York: Community Council of Greater New York, 9–45.

Hareven, T. K. (1982). The life course and aging in historical perspective. In T. K. Hareven & K.J. Adams (eds.), *Aging and life course transitions: An interdisciplinary perspective* (pp. 1–26). New York: Guilford Press.

Hoenig, J., & Hamilton, M. (1966). Elderly patients and the burden on the household. *Psychiatra et Neurologia,* Basel, *152,* 281–293.

Horowitz, A. (1982). The role of families in providing long-term care to the frail and chronically ill elderly living in the community. Final report submitted to the Health Care Financing Administration, DHHS, May.

Johnsen, P. T., & Fulcomer, M. C. (1984). "Culture's consequences" in attitudes, opinions, and preferences affecting family care of the elderly. Paper presented at the 37th Annual Meeting of The Gerontological Society of America, San Antonio, Tex., November.

Katz, S., Branch, L. G., Branson, M. H., Papsidero, J. A., Beck, J. C., & Greer, D. S. (1983). Active life expectancy. *The New England Journal of Medicine, 309,* 1218–1224.

Kent, D. P. (1972). Social policy and program considerations in planning for the aging. In D. P. Kent, R. Kastenbaum, & S. Sherwood (eds.), *Research planning and action for the elderly* (pp. 3–19). New York: Behavioral Publications.

Kent, D. P. (1965). Aging—fact or fancy. *The Gerontologist, 5,* 2.

Kleban, M. H., Brody, E. M., & Hoffman, C. (1984). Parent care and depression: Differences between working and nonworking adult daughters. Paper presented at the 37th Annual Meeting of The Gerontological Society of America, San Antonio, Tex., November.

Lang, A., & Brody, E. M. (1983). Characteristics of middle-aged daughters and help to their elderly mothers. *Journal of Marriage and the Family, 45,* 193–202.

Lawton, M. P., & Brody, E. M. (1968). The social cost of care for the elderly. Final report, U.S.P.H.S. Grant #CD00137.

Lawton, M. P., & Lawton, F. (eds.) (1965). *Mental impairment in the aged: Institute on the mentally impaired aged.* Philadelphia, Penn. Philadelphia Geriatric Center.

Lopata, H. Z., & Norr, K. F. (1980). Changing commitments of American women to work and family roles. *Social Security Bulletin,* June, *43,* 3–14.

Lowenthal, M. F. (1964). *Lives in distress.* New York: Basic Books.

Mindel, C. H. (1979). Multigenerational family households: Recent trends and implications for the future. *The Gerontologist, 19,* 456–463.

Murray, J. (1973). Family structure in the preretirement years. *Social Security Bulletin,* October, *36,* 25–45.

Myllyuoma, J., & Soldo, B. J. (1980). Family caregivers to the elderly: Who are they? Paper presented at the 33d Annual Meeting of the Gerontological Society, San Diego, Calif.

Neugarten, B. L. (1974). Age groups in American society and the rise of the young-old. *The Annals of the American Academy of Political and Social Science, 415,* 187–198.

NRTA-AARP (National Retired Teachers Association–American Association of Retired Persons). (1981). National survey of older Americans.

Peck, R.C. (1968). Psychological developments in the second half of life. In B. L. Neugarten (ed.), *Middle age and aging: A reader in social psychology* (pp. 88–92). Chicago: University of Chicago Press.

Roscow, I. (1965). Intergenerational relationships: Problems and proposals. In E. Shanas, & G. F. Streib (eds.), *Social structure and the family: Generational relations* (pp. 341–378). Englewood Cliffs, N.J.: Prentice-Hall.

Sainsbury, P., & Grad de Alercon, J. (1970). The effects of community care in the family of the geriatric patient. *Journal of Geriatric Psychiatry, 4,* 23–41.

Schneider, E. L., & Brody, J. A. (1983). Aging, natural death, and the compression of morbidity: Another view. *The New England Journal of Medicine, 309,* 854–856.

Schorr, A. L. (1960). *Filial responsibility in the modern American family.* Washington, D.C.: U.S. DHEW, Social Security Administration, Government Printing Office, June.

Shanas, E. (1979a). Social myth as hypothesis: The case of the family relations of old people. *The Gerontologist, 19,* 3–9.

Shanas, E. (1979b). The family as a social support system in old age. *The Gerontologist, 19,* 169–174.

Shanas, E. (1963). The unmarried old person in the United States: Living arrangements and care in illness, myth and fact. Paper presented at the International Social Science Research Seminar in Gerontology, Makaryd, Sweden, 1963.

Shanas, E., & Streib, G. F. (eds.). (1965). *Social structure and the family: Generational relations.* Englewood Cliffs, N. J.: Prentice-Hall.

Shanas, E., Townsend, P., Wedderburn, D., Friis, H., Milhøj, P., & Stehouwer, J. (eds.). (1968). *Old people in three industrial societies.* New York: Atherton Press.

Soldo, B. J. (1980). The dependency squeeze on middle-aged women. Presented at Meeting of the Secretary's Advisory Committee on Rights and Responsibilities of Women, Department of Health and Human Services.

Spark, G., & Brody, E. M. (1970). The aged are family members. *Family Process, 9,* 195–210.

Streib, G. F., & Shanas, E. (1965). An introduction. In E. Shanas, & G. F. Streib (eds.), *Social structure and the family: Generational relations.* Englewood Cliffs, N. J.: Prentice-Hall.

Sussman, M. (1979). Social and economic supports and family environment for the elderly. Final report to Administration on Aging, Grant #90–A–316, January.

Townsend, P. (1965). The effects of family structure on the likelihood of admission to an institution in old age: The application of a general theory. In E. Shanas, & G. F. Streib (eds.), *Social structure and the family: Generational relations* (pp. 163–187). Englewood Cliffs, N. J.: Prentice-Hall.

Troll, L. E. (1971). The family of later life: A decade review. *Journal of Marriage and the Family, 33,* 263–290.

Uhlenberg, P. (1980). Death and the family. *Journal of Family History, 5,* 313–320.

U. S. Bureau of Labor Statistics (1984). *Employment and earnings,* Table 3, January.

U. S. General Accounting Office. (1983). *Medicaid and nursing home care: Cost increases and the need for services are creating problems for the States and the elderly.* Washington, D. C.: U. S. General Accounting Office, October 21.

U. S. National Committee on Vital and Health Statistics. (1978). *Long-term health care: Minimum data set,* preliminary report of the Technical Consultant Panel on the Long-Term Health Care Data Set, NCHS, September 8.

Upp, M. (1982). A look at the economic status of the aged then and now. *Social Security Bulletin,* March, *45,* 16–22.

Zarit, S. H., Reever, K. E., & Bach-Peterson, J. (1980). Relatives of the impaired aged: Correlates of feelings of burden. *The Gerontologist, 20,* 649–655.

Zimmer, A. H., & Sainer, J. S. (1978). Strengthening the family as an informal support for their aged: Implications for social policy and planning. Paper presented at the 31st Annual Meeting of the Gerontologial Society, Dallas, Tex.

# 20

ANDREW J. CHERLIN AND FRANK F. FURSTENBERG, JR.

# Styles and Strategies of Grandparenting

*The study of the American family has focused tightly on marriage and, to a lesser extent, on parent-child relations. The conjugal family system in the United States has largely justified this focus since by definition, the central, core relationship in such a family system is marriage. However, even in a conjugal family system, relationships other than those between spouses and between parents and children are important. These other relationships deserve more attention than they have, until recently, received from students of the American family. For instance, children, adolescents, and young adults are all more likely now than previously to have at least one, and up to four, surviving grandparents. The nature of the relationships between grandparents and grandchildren varies widely, but often it is important to both the grandparents and the grandchildren.*

*A recent flurry of publications on grandparents and grandparenting has ended the previous neglect of the topic. Among the most important of these is a book by Andrew J. Cherlin and Frank Furstenberg, Jr., entitled* The New American Grandparent.[1] *The following selection is a summary of the research reported in that book.*

Source: Andrew J. Cherlin and Frank F. Furstenberg, Jr., "Styles and Strategies of Grandparenting," pp. 97–116 in *Grandparenthood,* edited by Vern L. Bengston and Joan F. Robertson. Copyright © 1985 by Sage Publications, Inc. Reprinted by permission of Sage Publications, Inc. This study was supported by grant AG02753 from the National Institute on Aging.

[1]Andrew J. Cherlin and Frank F. Furstenberg, Jr., *The New American Grandparent* (Beverly Hills: Sage, 1985).

There is a great amount of variation in the kinds of relationships that American grandparents have with their grandchildren. Some grandparents are actively involved in their grandchildren's lives, but many others are quite passive and distant. In addition, as we will show in this paper, the relationship can vary from grandchild to grandchild. Some grandchildren may live far from the grandparent, other grandchildren may live with parents who don't get along with the grandparents, and still others may no longer be living with the grandparent's son or daughter as a result of divorce. Under circumstances such as these, grandparents sometimes devote most of their attention to a few grandchildren—or even to just one. This strategy—which we call selective investment—allows them to act like grandparents and feel satisfied with their role, even though they aren't as close to the rest of their grandchildren.

The variation in the styles and strategies of grandparenting is consistent with the general principles that determine the nature of kinship ties in American society. Individuals are allowed to exercise a great deal of discretion in their relations with kin. In his classic account of American kinship, Schneider (1980) characterizes our system as highly voluntaristic. Blood and marriage circumscribe the available pool of kin, but within this pool it is up to individuals to cultivate and maintain ties. Kinship, therefore, has an achieved as well as an ascribed dimension.

This discretionary feature of American kinship is especially salient when divorce and remarriage occur. Our study, which will be described below, was originally designed to investigate what happens to the ties between grandparents and grandchildren when the grandchildren's parents divorce. We found a wide range of responses. Many grandparents became heavily involved in their grandchildren's lives, sometimes to the point of becoming surrogate parents, whereas others drifted apart from their grandchildren. There were no fixed rules about how grandparents should react to a divorce, although a pattern did emerge: With some exceptions, the ties between maternal grandparents and their grandchildren were maintained or strengthened after a divorce; but the ties between paternal grandparents and their grandchildren were often weakened. This difference emerged because mothers usually retain custody of their children after a divorce and many divorced fathers have infrequent contact with their children (Furstenberg, Nord, Peterson, & Zill, 1983). It is therefore more difficult for paternal grandparents to retain close ties to their grandchildren after the disruption of the parents' marriage.

In this paper, however, we will focus on the more general issue of variation in the grandparent-grandchild relationship in intact as well as disrupted families. There have been a number of attempts to classify the styles and meanings of being a grandparent (Neugarten & Weinstein, 1964; Wood & Robertson, 1976; Robertson, 1977; Kivnick, 1982a). All find a diversity of responses that form a continuum from substantial involvement to remoteness. These and other studies (Troll & Bengtson, 1979) also suggest the widespread acceptance in the United States of what we might call the "norm of non-interference": the idea that grandparents should not interfere with the parents in the rearing of the grandchildren.

The previous studies have provided much useful information, but they also have been quite limited. They have tended to be exploratory; geographically, socially, and ethnically limited; and small in size. They cannot tell us whether styles of grandparenting vary systematically by age, ethnicity, or other social and economic characteristics. Moreover, these studies leave us with a rather static view of grandparenting, as if we could pin a label on a grandmother shortly after her first grandchild was born ("fun seeker" or "distant figure") and be sure that the label would remain accurate for all her grandchildren for the rest of her life. As that seems implausible, we need to think more about whether there is a life-course of grandparenting and about the ways in which grandparents may simultaneously maintain different kinds of relationships with different grandchildren. In this paper, we hope to provide some insight into these unresolved issues of styles and strategies of grandparenting.

## THE STUDY

In 1976, data were collected from a nationally representative sample of households containing children between the ages of 7 and 11. The child and his or her primary caretaker—the child's mother in more than 90 percent of the cases—were interviewed. In 1981, all of the children whose parents' marriages had been disrupted by 1976 and a random subsample of children from nondisrupted homes were reinterviewed. The parent of the child also was reinterviewed. During the 1981 interview, the parents were asked to provide the names, addresses, and telephone numbers of the child's grandparents. For currently married grandparents, one spouse was systematically selected to be interviewed. Telephone interviews were conducted by the Institute for Survey Research at Temple University between February and April 1983 with 510 grandparents—82 percent of the names on the final list. In addition, we reinterviewed a small subsample of the grandparents using in-person, semistructured interviews that were taped and subsequently transcribed. We will draw upon these qualitative interviews to interpret and illustrate our quantitative findings.

The 510 grandparent interviews—which form the data for this paper—constitute not a national sample of grandparents but rather the grandparents of a national sample of children. The children in question—whom we refer to as the study children—were almost all between the ages of 13 and 17 by 1983. Our study presents data, then, on grandparents who have teenaged grandchildren and who therefore may be older, on average, than the typical Amercian grandparent. Our focus is on the relationship between the grandparent and a teenaged study child; it is possible that the relationship between these grandparents and their younger grandchildren could be different. We intentionally overrepresented grandmothers in our interviews because most of the parent respondents were female and women are deeply involved in kin networks, according to many studies (Adams, 1968).

## ACTIVITIES

What do grandparents do with teenaged children? We asked the grandparents many questions about their activities with the study children and then, using the statistical technique of factor analysis, examined the responses to see whether there were clusters of activities that some grandparents engaged in but others did not.

One cluster that failed to emerge in our study was the so-called "fun seeker" pattern—consisting of playful, leisure-oriented activities—that was common among the grandparents Neugarten and Weinstein (1964) studied. This pattern was absent not because our grandparents disliked fun but rather because our survey referred to older grandchildren—13 to 18-year-olds, to be specific. The grandparents in the Neugarten and Weinstein sample, it turns out, were much younger than those in our study and were therefore more likely to have had younger grandchildren. In fact, Neugarten and Weinstein found that the fun seeker pattern was less common among grandparents who were over age 65. They ascribed this age difference to trends over time in people's values or to the aging process. We would suggest, in addition, that the difference emerged because grandparents do different things with younger grandchildren than with older grandchildren. Styles of grandparenting, in other words, change as grandchildren and grandparents age. It's easy and natural for grandparents to treat toddlers as sources of leisure-time fun. But no matter how deep and warm the relationship remains over time, a grandmother doesn't bounce a teenager on her knee.

Instead, our factor analyses suggest that what some grandparents do with teenaged children—in addition to the ubiquitous joking, reminiscing, and so forth—is exchange services; and a minority even manage to have a role in how the teenager is being raised. Two groups of activities clustered together. The first was composed of responses to the following four questions: "Over the past 12 months, has (the child) asked for your help with something (s/he) was doing or making? Run errands or chores for you?" and "Over the past 12 months, have you asked (the child) for help with something you were doing or making? Helped (the child) with (his/her) errands or chores?" The first and fourth items refer to flows of assistance from the grandparent to the grandchild; 36 percent and 41 percent, respectively, of the grandparents responded affirmatively to these two items. The second and third refer to assistance from the grandchild to the grandparent; 61 percent and 42 percent, respectively, responded positively to these two items. We formed a scale with a range of zero to four by summing the number of positive responses to these four questions. Most grandparents and grandchildren had a limited exchange of services; but about one third answered positively to at least three of the four questions, and about one sixth answered positively to all four. Grandparents who had very frequent contact with the study child or who were younger were more likely to exchange services. Social class and race, however, appeared to make little difference.

The second cluster of activities that emerged in our analysis measured the extent to which the grandparents were able to exert the type of influence over the grandchild that is typically reserved for parents. The cluster was composed of the responses to the following five questions: "Over the past 12 months, did you discipline (him/her)? Give (the child) advice? Discuss (his/her) problems?" "When you see the child do something you disapprove of, do you correct (him/her) often, sometimes, hardly ever, or never?" and "Do your children consult you before making an important decision about (the child) often, sometimes, hardly ever, or never?" A scale of parentlike behavior with a range of zero to five was formed by summing the number of positive responses to the latter two items. The most common score was zero and the least common was five, reflecting the lack of authority in these matters among most grandparents. Still, nearly half scored three or more and more than one fourth scored four or more.

The grandparents with higher scores on this scale are of particular interest, for they have been able to surmount, at least partially, the powerful norm of noninterference. As with the exchange scale, grandparents who had very frequent contact with the study child or who were younger reported greater amounts of parentlike behavior. In addition, however, race had a strong effect that was not present for the exchange scale: controlling for other effects—including education and income—using the statistical technique of multiple regression, Blacks scored one point higher on this five-point scale than did Whites. It appears that Black grandparents—particularly Black grandmothers—retain more authority over the rearing of their grandchildren. Furthermore, grandparents of study children not living with two biological parents scored 0.4 points higher, other things being equal, as they filled the vacuum left by the absence of a parent. And as with exchange, social class made little difference.

## STYLES OF GRANDPARENTING

These two activity scales demonstrate the kinds of activities that some, but not all, of the grandparents in our sample did with the study children. Our analyses of the correlates of these scales suggested that frequent, or at least regular, contact was a critical determinant of the level of activity. In this section, we combine information from the two scales and from the question about contact ("In the past 12 months, about how often have you seen the child?") to identify the different styles of grandparenting that appear among the grandparents in our sample. Any such classification is somewhat arbitrary; the reader should view the categories given below as illustrative and the percentages as approximations. Moreover, as our discussion of selective investment will show, it is likely that a grandparent can follow different styles with different grandchildren. Still, our telephone survey and follow-up interviews lead us to believe that the styles listed below capture meaningful differences in the ways the grandparents interacted with the study children.

To classify the grandparents according to style, we first divided the scores on each scale into two parts: scores of zero, one, two, or three on the scale of parentlike influence were considered "low"; scores of four or five were considered "high." On the exchange scale, scores of zero, one, or two were considered "low," and scores of three or four were considered "high." Thus, in order to score high on either scale, a grandparent had to respond positively to most of the relevant questions; this rather stringent rule reflected our impression that some grandparents tended to exaggerate the amount of exchange or influence they experienced. We also classified all grandparents according to whether they saw the study child at least once or twice a month versus less often.

On the basis of these distinctions we divided the grandparents into three groups. The "detached" grandparents were those who scored low on both scales and had seen the study child less than once or twice a month over the previous 12 months. The "passive" grandparents were those who scored low on both scales but had seen the child at least once or twice a month. And the "active" grandparents were those who scored high on one or both scales, regardless of how often they had seen the study child.

The percentage of grandparents who were categorized in each of these three groups were as follows: detached, 26 percent; passive, 29 percent; and active, 45 percent. The distinction between detached and passive grandparents seemed critical to us for, as we will illustrate below, some inactive grandparents had only a fleeting, ritual relationship with the study children's daily lives. As we mentioned above, the percentages shouldn't be taken too literally, but they do suggest that roughly one fourth of the grandparents were detached, one fourth were passive, and half were active.

The active category, in turn, can be decomposed into three subgroups. Those who scored high only on the exchange scale we will call "supportive"; those who scored high only on the scale of parentlike influence will be called "authoritative"; and those who scored high on both scales will be called "influential." This further breakdown leads to the following distribution of our sample: detached, 26; passive, 29; supportive, 17; authoritative, 9; and influential, 19.

Thus, we have categorized the grandparents as having one of five styles of grandparenting. As Panel A of Table 1 shows, the detached and passive grandparents were substantially older than other grandparents and the influential grandparents were substantially younger, suggesting that the aging process may have determined, in part, the levels of activity. Panels B and C of Table 1 reveal that the detached grandparents had much lower levels of contact with the study child (a fact that follows from the definition of this category) and lived much farther away—63 percent lived more than 100 miles away. Thus, a clear majority of the detached grandparents faced a strong geographical barrier to a more active role—and yet 15 percent lived within 10 miles of the study child. About half of the passive, supportive, and authoritative grandparents had seen the study child once a week or more during the previous 12 months. It would seem, then, that moderate frequency of visiting is compatible with a passive style or a moderately active one.

The influential grandparents had much higher frequencies of visiting and lived much closer—15 percent, in fact, lived in the same households with study

**TABLE 1** *Percentage of Selected Characteristics of Grandparents by Style of Grandparenting*

| | *Detached* | *Passive* | *Supportive* | *Authoritative* | *Influential* |
|---|---|---|---|---|---|
| A. Age of grandparent: | | | | | |
| Under 65 | 30 | 33 | 44 | 44 | 58 |
| 65 or older | 70 | 67 | 56 | 56 | 42 |
| B. Frequency of visits with study child: | | | | | |
| Once per week or more | 0 | 49 | 54 | 51 | 80 |
| Less than once per week | 100 | 51 | 46 | 49 | 20 |
| C. How far away study child lives: | | | | | |
| Co-reside | 0 | 1* | 5 | 4† | 15* |
| 0–10 miles | 15 | 66 | 56 | 42 | 57 |
| 11–100 miles | 22 | 31 | 21 | 25 | 17 |
| More than 100 miles | 63 | 3 | 18 | 28 | 12 |
| D. Score on family ritual scale: | | | | | |
| 0–1 (low) | 28 | 16 | 19 | 15 | 11 |
| 2–3 (high) | 72 | 84 | 81 | 85 | 89 |
| E. Closeness to study child: | | | | | |
| Is your relationship to the child: | | | | | |
| Extremely close or quite close? | 62 | 74 | 82 | 80 | 90 |
| Fairly close or not very close? | 38 | 26 | 18 | 20 | 10 |
| Weighted n | (160) | (182) | (109) | (57) | (118) |

Note: $p < .05$ for Chi-squared values.
*Total adds up to 101 percent.
†Total adds up to 99 percent.

children. The influential style, as might be expected from the previous analyses of the two scales, is closely tied to very frequent, almost daily contact. As for family-oriented values, the detached grandparents scored sharply lower on a scale that measured family rituals ("In your family, are there special family recipes or dishes? Are there family jokes, common expressions, or songs? Are there ritual or special events that bring the family together?"), although even among this remote group most were able to acknowledge some family rituals.

How these differences affected the relationship with the study child is suggested in Panel E in Table 1, where the answers are displayed to the question, "Is your relationship with the (study child) extremely close, quite close, fairly close, or not very close?" Given the widespread norm in our society that family relationships should be close, it was difficult for a grandparent to admit to an interviewer that her relationship with a grandchild was not close. Thus, even among the detached, a majority responded "extremely close or quite close." But a clear trend still emerged: The detached grandparents were most likely to admit to a "fairly close or not very close" relationship; the passive grandparents were next most likely; the moderately active (supportive and authoritative) less likely; and the influential grandparents least likely of all.

There were no systematic differences in style according to educational attainment, consistent with the low to modest effect of social class we have noted above. But there were sharp racial differences: Of Black grandparents, 63 percent were either authoritative or influential—two styles in which grandparents retained substantial parentlike authority—compared to 26 percent of Whites and 33 percent of other Nonwhites. Only 8 percent of the Black grandparents were classified as passive. Part of this retention of authority, which is extraordinary given the strength of the norm of noninterference elsewhere, can be explained by the higher prevalence of single-parent families among Blacks. In these families grandparents are often called upon to take on a pseudo-parental role. But even among Black grandparents whose grandchildren were living with two biological parents, a majority were classified as authoritative or influential. These differences provide further evidence of the prevalence of strong Black grandparents (especially grandmothers) who play a major role in their children's and grandchildren's lives.

There were more modest sex differences in style. Grandfathers were more likely to be classified as supportive or authoritative and less likely to be detached or passive. This may reflect typically male patterns of relating to family members. But given the small number of grandfathers we were able to interview, we cannot rule out the possibility that the less active grandfathers were less willing to grant an interview, which would bias our sample toward the more active ones.

## SOME EXAMPLES

### The Detached Grandparent

Mrs. Myers, a recently widowed middle-class woman, lives in a northeastern city. While raising her four daughters, she urged them to be self-sufficient and independent in case they were faced with crises such as the death of a husband or a divorce. But partly because of these values, she seems to have created an emotional distance between herself and her children and grandchildren. The last time Mrs. Myers saw any of her nine grandchildren was at Thanksgiving, three and a half months prior to the interview. Three of her daughters (and four of the grandchildren) live out of state. The fourth daughter, the mother of the study child Jessica, 18, and four other children, lives only about 15 miles away; but Mrs. Myers reported that she saw Jessica less than once every two or three months during the previous year. Mrs. Myers feels she has a "nice relationship" with her daughters, but she said "I don't think they tell me everything when there are real problems.... Sometimes I bite the end of my tongue off to keep from asking questions." As for Jessica and her other grandchildren, she said, "I don't feel real, real close with any of them.... Maybe I haven't handled Jessica the way I should have.... I should have made more time for her in my life." When asked what it has meant to her to be a grandmother, Mrs. Myers replied in formal, unemotional terms:

> Well, I'm grateful that I've lived long enough to see the children. And I'm grateful that my children are carrying out the principles, the goals, the ideals that I wanted to put into them. And I hope that my grandchildren put it into their children. You know, to lead the good life, be educated, and to continue your education long after you get out of school.

It seems clear that Mrs. Myers is a remote figure in her grandchildren's lives, much to her current regret. Her parting words to the interviewer were, "If you think of any way to help me deal with my granddaughter, please let me know."

### The Passive Grandparent

Mr. and Mrs. Schmidt live on a farm in a northeastern state; they have three children, nine grandchildren, and three great-grandchildren, most of whom live nearby. Years ago, Mrs. Schmidt's daughter Janice was seriously ill and Mrs. Schmidt kept Janice's daughter Vera, the study child, for months at a time. Now, she sees Vera, 14, once or twice a month. The last time the Schmidts had seen any of their grandchildren was three days prior to the interview. Despite the proximity of their extended family and the regular contact, the Schmidts are careful to keep their distance from their children's and grandchildren's lives. Mr. Schmidt explained:

> Sure, we appreciate our grandchildren, and we do anything we can to help them along, and things like that. But we don't, possibly like some people, some people I think go overboard, maybe they do too much for their grandchildren and things like this. I think they ought to be a little bit left on their own.... I don't think the grandparents should interfere with the parents.

The interviewer read the following story to all the grandparents in our follow-up interviews, and Mrs. Schmidt's response shows how she takes whatever interaction she can get but doesn't press for more:

> ***Interviewer:*** Here's an account of some situations that happen to grandparents, and I'd just like to read them to you and get your reaction. . . . Mrs. Smith lives a half-hour's drive from her son, daughter-in-law, and two grandchildren. Mrs. Smith is unhappy because she doesn't get to see the grandchildren as much as she would like. Sometimes a few weeks go by between visits. She realizes that both her son and her daughter-in-law work full time and that the grandchildren are busy with school activities. But she thinks they could make more of an effort to see her. What, if anything, should she do about it?
>
> ***Mrs. Schmidt:*** [laughter] We run through that right now. All the kids is into everything, you know? Like I was always used to being by myself so much, that if they can come it's all right, and if they can't, they have to live their lives.

There is even some suggestion that the Schmidts might feel a bit burdened by all their grandchildren and the responsibilities they entail.

> ***Interviewer:*** So, are there any other thoughts you have about being a grandmother that I didn't ask you?
>
> ***Mrs. Schmidt:*** I don't know what. I'm just getting too many to keep track of. They're nice to have and so on, but I said when Christmas time come, what in the world are you supposed to do?

Mrs. Schmidt's remark, even though said partly in jest, suggests some ambivalence about her relationships with her grandchildren. But for many grandparents, probably including the Schmidts, the passive style is seen as rewarding and proper. Some passive grandparents even have very high levels of contact with their grandchildren and seem quite pleased with the relationships. Consider Mrs. Waters, who lives in a suburb of a Midwestern city. She lives three houses away from her daughter and four children, one of whom is the 15-year old study child, Linda. Years earlier Linda and her mother had lived with Mrs. Waters for two years after the mother's divorce. Mrs. Waters says she is "extremely close" to Linda, whom she now sees three or four times a week. Yet her visits with Linda are brief, often momentary, as when Mrs. Waters stops by her daughter's house and Linda is going in or out. Linda, who Mrs. Waters says is "very, very busy," never calls her grandmother, nor do they sit down and talk very often. Mrs. Waters explains this as normal behavior for a teenager. She doesn't expect more, and she is satisfied with her relationship with Linda and her older sister Rachel, 18. Although Mrs. Waters speaks wistfully of the time when the grandchildren were younger and would stay overnight at her home or need help with homework, she accepts the fact that those days are over because the grandchildren are older: "Now that's gone because here's Rachel, she's 18 years old; who wants to go and stay with their grandmother at 18 years old [laughter]?" Still, Mrs. Waters derives great satisfaction from her past and present involvement with them. Being a grandmother, she says, has been "a terrific thing. These children have been my life."

### The Influential Grandparent

Mr. Sampson, who has been a widower for 20 years, lives in a middle-class neighborhood of a northeastern city. His grandchild Bob, the study child, has recently gone off to college. Bob and his family live just a half-block away. Before Bob left for college, Mr. Sampson typically saw him two or three times a week.

> ***Interviewer***: How do you (and Bob) usually spend time?
>
> ***Mr. Sampson***: Mostly just talk. Unless there's something we wanted to fix up and all.... And if he has some problem, he'll come over to see me.... And if I need some help, like getting some screens down for putting screens in for the summer, I'll get him to help me bring those down.... You know, we used to take tremendous numbers of trips together and things. I've had him up into Canada, I've had him down in Florida, I've had him out at the lake.

Mr. Sampson pointed out that he had a lot of time to spend with his grandchildren because he was widowed. He gives Bob advice, "like about his relationship in college, that he's going to watch smoking and dope and stuff like that." And if any of his grandchildren do something he disapproves of, "I will very nicely tell them I don't think it's right. And they have never resented that too much on anything." When an interviewer read Mr. Sampson the story about the grandparent who is unhappy because he doesn't get to see enough of the grandchildren, Mr. Sampson, in contrast to most passive grandparents, suggested that the grandparent in the story probably could make more of an effort to go see her grandchildren.

But even influential grandparents must modify their relationships as the grandchildren grow up. Mr. Sampson was well aware that Bob was becoming an adult, and he seemed to have come to terms with the impending change this would bring to their relationship. When asked what it meant to him to be a grandfather, he replied:

> I would hate like thunder not to be one. . . . No, to me it is really part of my life and I would miss a terrible lot of activity, a terrible lot of pleasure and everything else if I did not have grandchildren. . . . All the trips we used to take, it was fun for me, I enjoyed it. . . . I wanted to do it. . . . And I would miss that if it weren't. Of course, I'm missing it now, but I realize that I can't keep up this activity because they have their own lives to lead. And I think that's one thing, grandparents sometimes make a slip on that: they don't realize that the kids are growing up. You've got your own life to live, I don't care what it is. I've lived mine, they've got theirs coming up. Of course I may miss it; I do. I miss the boy because he's away, I don't see him. On the other hand, to help that I get into a tremendous amount of activities of my own.

A minority of the influential grandparents (15percent) were living with the study child, often after their daughters' marriages broke up. These grandparents typically took on the role of a surrogate parent—an intense, rewarding experience, to judge from the interviews, but one that also could be burdensome. When asked what it was like to live with your grandchildren, one grandmother replied, "Well, it's heaven and a hassle, I guess you'd put it." Mrs. Williamson, a 63-year-old Black grandmother from a southern city who lived with her daughter and her granddaughter Susan, 16, described a typical day:

> In the morning, Susan's mom is the first to leave the house.... Sometimes she will wake Susan up before leaving. If not, she will say, "Mom, don't forget to wake Susan up!" So I will make sure that Susan is up. I prepare Susan's breakfast. Mornings that I have to be at work by eight o'clock, I will leave Susan here; she knows what time she is to catch her bus.... When we come in in the evening.... Susan usually gets in about ten minutes 'till four. Her mom and I get in about four thirty.... I prepare all of the meals.... I am the one that will insist that [Susan] eat a good meal, take your vitamin. Susan will do the dishes. Then, after that, there's a period of looking at television, then Susan will get her books. And she is going to finish that homework before going to bed.

Susan, Mrs. Williamson says, "will ask my opinion often quite before asking her mom's." Being a grandparent is "wonderful," Mrs. Williamson told the interviewer, and there were no disadvantages she could think of to having her granddaughter live with her.

## STRATEGIES OF GRANDPARENTING: SELECTIVE INVESTMENT

So far we have examined the relationships between the grandparents and one particular grandchild. Some of the grandparents saw the study children frequently, exchanged services, gave advice, and, in general, seemed to have established intense, warm relationships with the study children. But what about the other grandparents—largely those from the detached or passive groups? Was their greater emotional (and often geographical) distance from the study child typical of their relations with their other grandchildren, or did they have close ties to others? Through design or circumstance, did they evolve strategies to compensate for the weak ties to the study child?

We asked the grandparents, "When was the last time you saw any grandchild?" (Grandparents who lived with the study child were automatically classified as having seen a grandchild "today.") The detached grandparents were much less likely to have seen any grandchild recently than the other grandparents: Half had last seen one a week or more ago; about one-fourth had last seen one a month or more ago. Yet detached grandparents had more grandchildren (12), on average, than did the typical grandparent in the sample (11). Some detached grandparents, then, appeared to be isolated from all of their grandchildren. But others were not: More than a third of the detached grandparents (who, by definition had infrequent contact with the study child) had seen a grandchild that day or the previous day.

Consider Mrs. Grant, a "detached" grandparent who lives in a northeastern city. She doesn't get along well with her daughter-in-law, who is the mother of two of her grandchildren, William, 16, and the study child, Delia, 13. Although she lives only a short drive away, Mrs. Grant rarely sees Delia, who she describes as close to her mother. She told the interviewer that her relationship with Delia was "not very close." Yet Mrs. Grant sees Delia's older brother Wiliam much more often. She feels protective toward him, for he "has always been very, well, he was what you'd call one of those nervous-type babies. I went up and stayed with [the mother] after he was born." Even now, she says, William "gets on his mother's nerves." So Mrs. Grant took a particular interest in him; and now, she says, "he just loves to come here and be with his grandparents." In fact, William wants to attend the local university and live with his grandparents. Mrs. Grant is pleased but torn by this request. She's 72, her health is not great, and she said, "I'm just not up to that responsibility." Thus, although Mrs. Grant may be detached from Delia, she is much more actively involved in William's life. Being a grandmother has its rewards for Mrs. Grant, but the stress of her relationship with her daughter-in-law has taken its toll. "It's just not worth being a grandmother if you have to go through all this hullaballoo, you know, . . . . I get a bit fed up."

Nevertheless, Mrs. Grant's situation shows that grandparents often turn their attention toward particular grandchildren in order to compensate for unsatisfactory relationships with others. We asked the grandparents the following question: "It's not unusual for grandparents to like some grandchildren more than others. Do you have a favorite grandchild?" We felt it would be difficult for grandparents to admit to playing favorites; most prefer to say "I love them all." Yet 30 percent were willing to admit that they had a favorite. (In Mrs. Grant's case, it was William.)

Take, for example, Mrs. Sabatino, who lives in a suburb of a midwestern city. She was classified as a "supportive" grandmother on the basis of her telephone interview, but probing during the follow-up interview suggested that the help was slim—"passive" probably would be the more accurate classification. "I really can't say we do things for him," she said of the study child Christopher, nor could she cite much that Christopher had done for her. She sees him once or twice a month, but when asked whether she felt close to him, she replied, "No, not really, I mean we see him a lot, but not as close as maybe some people would be to their grandson."

However, Mrs. Sabatino does have a favorite: her granddaughter, Nora, 23. Nora, her first grandchild, spent a lot of time at her grandmother's home when she was young. Then Nora's father died. Mrs. Sabatino helped Nora adjust to the loss, and they have remained close ever since. According to Mrs. Sabatino, "We have a very special relationship." This close tie to one grandchild seems sufficient for Mrs. Sabatino; it allows her to think of herself as a person who has good relationships with her grandchildren. When she was read the story about the grandparent who was unhappy because she didn't get to see the grandchildren as much as she would like, Mrs. Sabatino responded:

> I don't think there's really much that she can do. She should just wait and see when they can see her. . . . But I don't think she should feel, if she has a good relationship with the whole family, I don't think she should feel hurt.
>
> ***Interviewer:* So you would advise her to . . .**
>
> Just see them whenever she could and be content.

Mrs. Sabatino, it seems clear, thinks of herself as someone with a good relationship with her whole family. Her strategy of grandparenting seems to be to maintain at least one very close relationship and accept the lack of other close relationships—as with Christopher—as nothing personal. This allows her to express considerable satisfaction about being a grandmother:

> For one thing, I know it's the continuity of the family going on. And it's somebody to love, somebody that comes to see you and that you go to see. And I think it makes you feel that you're not really getting that old.

Thus, it appears to us that many grandparents invest more heavily in their relationships with some grandchildren than with others. There are many reasons why selective investment may be common: Some grandchildren may live closer, some may have parents who get along better with the grandparent, or some may be more in need of help because of a family crisis. Moreover, some may just be more appealing to the grandparent because they are the first born, the last born, or the most outgoing. Consequently, the payoff is likely to be greater for investment in some grandchildren than in others. Often, we suspect, a close tie to one or two grandchildren, coupled with a more distant, ritualistic relationship with the rest, may be sufficient to make grandparents satisfied with their role. They may generalize to all their grandchildren their satisfaction with their relationships with their favorites. Thus, it may not be necessary for grandparents to have equally intense ties to all grandchildren in order to feel good about being a grandparent. Furthermore, equally intense relationships might even be burdensome for an older person with lots of grandchildren. Consciously or not, then, some grandparents have evolved a strategy of selective investment in which a few close ties to grandchildren suffice—in which the part substitutes adequately for the whole.

Given the flexible nature of the American kinship system, grandparents often can choose the grandchildren to whom they pay more attention and can change loyalties as they and their grandchildren age or change places of residence. To be sure, there are constraints on their ability to choose: geographical distance, poor relationships with the middle generation, the limited number of grandchildren they may have, and so forth. Still, this strategy of selective investment fulfills the function of allowing older persons to act as grandparents and to feel as though being a grandparent is an important part of their lives. It may also give grandchildren, who may not have close relations with both sets of grandparents, a better opportunity to experience intense ties to at least one grandparent.

Within families, then, all grandparent-grandchild relations are not equally close, despite the oft-repeated (and usually true) statements of grandparents that they love all their grandchildren. Instead, one often finds wide differences in the strength of the grandparent-grandchild bond, differences that appear to serve the needs of both grandparents and grandchildren to have meaningful, intense relationships with at least some members of the opposite generation.

## CONCLUSION

That there is no single, dominant style of grandparenting is clear from our sample of grandparents. At one extreme are the "detached" grandparents, as we have labeled them. Some of them seem to be remote from all their grandchildren—truly distant figures for whom intergenerational ties, by choice or circumstance, play a small role in life. Older, less imbued with familistic values, perhaps far removed geographically, or emotionally estranged from their children, these people are grandparents only in a symbolic sense. They are recognized by kin and friends as grandparents, but they do little more than fill slots in a geneology. Other grandparents, however, are detached from some but not all of their grandchildren. They may have little to do with the teenager in our study, but they have regular, rewarding contact with other grandchildren. Having adopted a strategy we labeled "selective investment," they focus their efforts and emotions on one or more of the grandchildren who live nearby or are especially personable or in need of help. In this way, they are able to act as grandparents and to compensate for weak ties to other kin.

Thus, a grandparent can be simultaneously detached and involved. Mrs. James, for example, who lives in a northeastern city, has nine children and 40 grandchildren. With such a large family, she can compensate for relationships that are dormant. She sees little of the study child, Henry, who lives with one of her daughters about 20 miles away; but she resides with another daughter and her children, with whom she is deeply involved. Personality differences and geographical mobility constrain the choices of grandparents like Mrs. James concerning involvement with kin. But the flexibility of Amercian kinship patterns allows grandparents like her to selectively take on the grandparent role when and where they can. Grandparents often cannot manage an active, involved role with all of their grandchildren, but in our society they need not do so in order to regard themselves—and to be regarded by others—as "good" or "normal" grandparents. They can achieve the status of grandparenthood by investing in a small proportion of the possible kin ties open to them.

The "passive" grandparents we identified differ from the detached grandparents by their regular contact with the study children. Despite their inactivity, they may serve useful functions merely by being around. They may, for instance, be the "family watchdogs," in Troll's (1983) phrase, who stand ready to offer assistance when needed but otherwise are loath to interfere in the raising of the grandchildren. Most passive grandparents, we believe, derive substantial satisfaction from their relationships with their grandchildren. They consider the regular but often superficial contact with their teenaged grandchildren to be acceptable, proper, and unavoidable given the nature of adolescence. Although they may be nostalgic for the days when the grandchildren were younger, they also can derive satisfaction from watching them mature. Some of the passive grandparents in our study selectively invested in other grandchildren to compensate for the increasing independence of the teenaged study child. The passive grandparents, we submit, best fit the popular image of American grandparents: the loving older person who sees the grandchildren fairly often, is ready to provide help in a crisis, but under normal circumstance leaves parenting strictly to the parent.

We found other grandparents who take on more active roles. They exchange services with the teenaged grandchildren or, in come cases, advise, discipline, and even help rear them. At the extreme are the "influential" grandparents, who see grandchildren quite often and are major figures in the grandchildren's day-to-day lives. The influential grandparents are younger and perhaps therefore more energetic; and they tend to have a familistic value orientation. But the key prerequisite for this style of grandparenting is frequent, almost daily contact with the grandchildren. Indeed, a sizable minority of the influential grandparents resided in the same home with the study children, where they often took on a pseudo-parental role. It is therefore a style that is not open to the large number of grandparents who cannot—because of distance, health, or poor relations with the middle generation—visit so regularly. It is a style that seems to be quite rewarding—90 percent of these grandparents reported that they were "extremely close or quite close" to the study children. But it also can exact costs: It demands a great commitment of time, energy, and sometimes money. It is a style that we often celebrate and mythologize (as if it were the common arrangement in some bygone era—an unproven assertion); but it can be both a joy and a burden for the grandparents involved—"heaven and a hassle," as one grandparent said. On balance, though, we received the impression that the heavenly aspects outweighed the hassle for most of the influential grandparents in our sample.

We found litle evidence that social class made a difference in grandparenting styles. Black grandmothers were much more likely to retain some authority over the rearing of the grandchildren. We say grandmothers rather than grandparents because we were not able to talk to many Black grandfathers. (Of our 51 interviews with Black grandparents, 44 were with grandmothers. Our lack of success in gaining interview access to Black men may be an indicator of their lesser role.) As mentioned above, the authority of Black grandmothers holds up nearly as well when the grandchildren are in two-parent homes as compared to one-parent homes. From our follow-up interviews, as well as from some preliminary interviews at a predominantly Black senior citizen's center in Baltimore, we received the impression that a strong grandmother is an accepted part of Black family patterns. Perhaps this role dates back to family disruptions during slavery or perhaps it is a more recent reaction to high rates of marital disruption or to the difficult economic position of Black men. Regardless, the Black grandmothers with whom we spoke often evinced a degree of authority, intensity, and warmth that made manifest their central roles in their children's and grandchildren's lives.

Although our study focused on grandparents with teenaged grandchildren, we were able to present evidence suggesting that the grandparental role changes as grandparents and grandchildren age. There is, then, a life course of grandparenting, although this life course can follow several diverse patterns. Early on, some grandparents offer substantial assistance in the form of babysitting, gifts, or even co-residence, and they seek leisure-oriented fun from their young grandchildren. The pattern of assistance continues for some, although it is transformed from baby-sitting to direct exchanges of services with the grandchildren. As grandchildren enter adolescence, the "fun seeking" style seems to fade. It can be superseded by mutual assistance, advice-giving, and discussions of problems; or it can be superseded by a passive style in which the grandparent still sees the teenaged grandchildren regularly but is increasingly removed from their world. And as the grandchildren enter adulthood, the grandparents prepare to let go of the relationship, just as parents do. Perhaps the relationship is strengthened again when the grandchildren marry and renew the cycle by producing great-grandchildren.

The styles and strategies we have described in this paper show the kinds of relationships that emerge when the grandchildren are adolescents. There has been speculation that this lifecycle stage is a low-point in grandparent-grandchild relations. Perhaps so. But we found some grandparents who were deeply involved with their adolescent grandchildren and many others who, though passive in style, derived substantial satisfaction from being around to watch their grandchildren grow up.

## REFERENCES

Adams, B. N. (1968). *Kinship in an urban setting.* Chicago: Markham.

Furstenberg, F. F., Jr., Nord, C. W., Peterson, J. L., & Zill, N. (1983). The life course of children of divorce: Marital disruption and parental conflict. *American Sociological Review,* 48, 656–668.

Kivnick, H. Q. (1982a). *The meaning of grandparenthood.* Ann Arbor, Mich.: University of Michigan Research Press.

Kivnick, H. Q. (1982b). Grandparenthood: An overview of meaning and mental health. *Gerontologist, 22,* 59–66.

Neugarten, B. L., & Weinstein, K. K. (1964). The changing American grandparent. *Journal of Marriage and the Family, 26,* 199–204.

Robertson, J. F. (1977). Grandmotherhood: A study of role conceptions. *Journal of Marriage and the Family, 39,* 165–174.

Schneider, D. (1980). *American kinship: A cultural account* (2d ed.). Chicago: University of Chicago Press.

Troll, L. E. (1983). Grandparents: The family watchdogs. In T. Brubaker (ed.), *Family relationships in later life* (pp. 63–74). Beverly Hills, Calif.: Sage.

Troll, L. E., & Bengtson, V. L. (1979). Generations in the family. In W. R. Burr, R. Hill, F. I. Nye, & I. L. Reiss (eds.), *Contemporary theories about the family, Vol. 1* (pp. 127–161). New York: Free Press.

Wood, V. & Robertson, J. F. (1976). The significance of grandparenthood. In J. F. Gubrium (ed.), *Time, roles, and self in old age* (pp. 278–304). New York: Human Sciences Press.

21

MARION TOLBERT COLEMAN

# Surviving and Doing It Well: Options for Older Women

*When we talk about "problems of the elderly," in general, we are talking about problems of elderly women. Many problems of older persons are connected in some manner to the fact that they are alone, and it is usually the women who are alone. Eighty percent of the men but only 40 percent of the women over age sixty-five are married.*

*The statistics on widowhood are depressing. Three-fourths of all wives can expect to be widowed. The median age at widowhood is only fifty-six, and women who are widowed at sixty can expect, on the average, to live another sixteen years. Moreover, a widow has a low probability of finding a new partner. People tend to remarry people with similar backgrounds, for example, divorced people tend to marry divorced people and widows tend to marry widowers. There are not nearly enough widowers for all of the widows. Furthermore, in first marriages men tend to marry women two to three years younger than they are, while in remarriages, the average age gap between spouses increases to about ten years. Thus, widowed women who do remarry are likely to be widowed a second time.*

*Death is not the only reason that older women are single. Divorce now ends almost as many marriages as death of a spouse, and the ex-husband of forty-five who first married twenty years ago is likely to remarry a woman in her thirties. In the following selection, Coleman addresses some of the issues involved in this "feminization of the elderly" and makes some suggestions about how women can best prepare themselves for this period of their lives.*

Source: Adapted for this volume.

Mrs. Rall was my freshman composition professor more years ago than either of us would like to remember. Once the student/teacher relationship ended, I continued to work as her student assistant for three years. Although we spoke little of personal matters during this time, I quickly came to respect her calm assuredness and her ability to fill the roles of wife, mother, and professional.

At the end of my undergraduate schooling, I followed my husband into the military and lost contact with her for several years. In the mid 1970s, in the midst of my own consciousness raising, I dropped in on Mrs. Rall to let her know I was returning to graduate school and to express my thanks for the role model she had provided.

I found on my visit a newly widowed woman who was grateful that her husband's bout with cancer had gone quickly. She was, she informed me, at the age of 50, deciding what she was going to do with herself.

I think the reestablishment of our friendship, this time, for the first time, as women colleagues, has been extremely satisfying to both of us. Although I seldom see her, I always receive her Christmas card that holds a lovely photograph of a flower she has discovered during the year.

Three years ago, another surprise came with her card—the news that she had remet a college classmate who also had been widowed and that they had married. Mrs. Rall was now Mrs. Minch. And because I can't relate to this new identity, I am finally forced to call her Eilene.

Sheryl White's mother was widowed early one morning when her husband had a heart attack in the shower.[1] I think it is significant that I have no recollection of her first name, only as Sheryl's mother. She was a woman who had been completely dependent on her husband—she had never written a check, she had never filled a prescription. And his death completely devastated her.

When I met Mrs. White, her husband had been dead a number of years. She had continued living in the same house, but now kept the shades pulled down tight. She was alone. Sheryl and her brother were adults and on their own. Mrs. White left the house only to drive to the grocery store—the liquor store delivered.

For a number of years, my husband felt it was his duty to stop in and say hello to Sheryl's mother when he went home to Florida for a visit. After three or four trips home, however, he could no longer bear the hour of nonstop weeping that constituted each visit with her.

In 1974, my Uncle Sikes died quite suddenly, leaving behind, as they say, my mother's sister, Aunt Lete. A strikingly beautiful, 52-year-old woman, Aunt Lete was the epitomy of the 1950s wife and mother. She was a flawless hostess for the social events that came along with being wife of the owner of a small corporation. She was a master seamstress, creating $20 copies of the most expensive clothes in the most exclusive stores. And, I'm sure my childhood memo-

[1]This name has been changed.

ries are exaggerated, but I seem to remember that there was always a fresh chocolate cake sitting on the counter of her immaculate kitchen.

Shortly before my uncle's death, he had begun negotiations to sell his steel company. However, at the urging of her children, Aunt Lete brought an end to these plans and, with the children, took over the business herself. In what seemed an incredibly short time, Aunt Lete moved from the dining room to the boardroom.

I offer these three portraits as a means of suggesting that widowhood is a variable, not a constant. And although most of us women keep some awareness, in the back of our minds, that our older years will likely be spent alone, very few of us have probably given much thought to the shape that existence will take. Because the likelihood of spending some time as a single-person household is so great for older women, it is important that we begin to focus more closely on issues pertaining to women in this situation.

The stories of these three women I know seem to capture the extremes of the course a woman's life may take when she is widowed or divorced in later years. Eilene's remarriage is what we have traditionally viewed as the "happy ending." In recent years, however, demographers and other social scientists have repeatedly documented that the chances for finding a second prince with whom to ride off into the sunset are slim and getting slimmer all the time (e.g., Carter and Glick, 1970; McKain, 1969). Furthermore, for those women who do remarry (usually someone older), the chances that they will outlive their new husbands are far too good.

The isolated existence of Mrs. White is a sadly extreme form of the lifestyle into which we stereotypically assume most older women slip when they are faced with confronting the world alone after a lifetime of dependence. And it is true that many women who move through life's roles, from father's child, to husband's wife, to children's mother, have not ever been faced with, as Eilene put it, "deciding what to do with themselves."

I believe that a great number of women, more than one might think, actually do survive the difficult transition to singledom and emerge, as Aunt Lete did, dynamic, independent, and resourceful people. Further, I believe that we should begin to view the scenario typified by my aunt's experience as an optional and perhaps more common happy ending for older widowed or divorced women of the future.

The argument I would like to present is actually a two-fold one. First, just as the problems today's older widowed or divorced women face evolve directly from the life choices made (both personally and societally) in their pasts, the options open to us future older women will be rooted in the decisions that we have made along the way. Second, I would like to argue that the underlying factors, which presently impact the extent to which a widowed or divorced woman's later life will be either a positive or a negative experience, may be different from, and even opposite to, those factors that will have an effect on later years in the future.

For today's older, single women, most problems are related to either their economic situation or their emotional well-being. I would be hard-pressed to say which of the two is the more important in affecting the quality of life. Clearly, poverty is devastating. Yet, as the sketch of Mrs. White's monetarily comfortable, but emotionally desolate, existence conveys, money, by itself, is not sufficient.

Both types of difficulties stem in large part from a lifetime of, first being taught and then putting into practice, dependence on a male. Over the past decade or so, there have been countless reports on the displaced homemaker. Yet even those women who have some work histories are likely to have irregular ones and may now find themselves with inadequate education or skills to successfully compete in today's quickly changing, high-technology oriented, work world.

Emotionally, this dependence takes its toll, as well. Today's older women were not socialized in how to handle independence, much less view that state as a positive or desirable option. They were socialized to appreciate men and to view other women as competition rather than comrades.

In talking with married women in their late 50s and early 60s, I have found a great many who confess that they have few, if any, female friends that they consider intimate. For some, a daughter has become a confidant as she, too, has entered marriage and parenthood. In most cases, however, it is the husband who, over the years, has become the sole emotional support for her. When many of these women find themselves suddenly alone, due to a divorce or the death of their spouse, they discover that they have not only lost the partner, but they have also lost the one person in the world with whom they have shared their grief and pain.

Historically, one of the major sources of support for older women has been the family. Adult children can help fill emotional needs and day-to-day physical needs. Grandchildren can be, not just occasional objects of affection, but persons for whom the older woman can provide nurturance and support. In the event of a child's divorce, the elder woman's role may become an even more active one. Grandmother may find herself once again packing lunches and sorting socks while son or daughter work to support the household.

Of course, not all women find themselves alone or financially strapped when they become widowed or divorced. And for some, the presence of a family may be more of a curse than a blessing. Many women can think of nothing they would less rather do than parent another generation of children. In general, however, economic and emotional well-being and family ties are three of the major variables that impact the present day older woman's quality of life.

For we women who find ourselves facing our last years alone, 20, 30, or 40 years from now, the basic elements of that existence will not be much changed from those that older women encounter today. If anything, the chances for remarriage may be even less likely. And I would not put much hope in the possibility that pairing off with younger men will be anything more than an occasional, quasi-acceptable practice. In short, we will be entering a world populated by other older women. And although the basic problems of this world will be similar to those today's older women face, future older women should, in general, possess a very different set of skills and values with which to confront those problems. Specifically, I believe that older women of the future will be better prepared both economically and emotionally, to deal with the female world they encounter. However, it is at the same time likely that the supportive role the family has played will decrease.

Beginning with the negative side of this futuristic scenario, I believe the increase in both divorce and remarriage rates will affect the structure of the family units one and two generations behind older women and, consequently, the dynamics of the relationships she is able to develop with these family members. It does not take too many changes in partners to create a mass of related, semirelated, pseudo-related individuals. In the process of family disintegration and reformulation, grandparents can oftentimes be left out of the picture. And for an older woman who is alone, the loss of relationships with grandchildren can be devastating.

Older women in the future will be affected, not only by familial choices made by their children and grandchildren, but they will also feel the effects from choices they personally have made. The macro level trends of decreasing family size and increasing rates of childlessness translate, at the micro level, into the fact that more women in the future, as compared to today, will simply not have a biological family base toward which to turn.

At the same time that these demographic changes in family formation result in less support for older women, other demographic changes, primarily in employment patterns, should enhance the quality of their later years. Twenty and thirty years from now, the term "displaced homemaker" may likely apply to a very small minority of women. Whether by choice or out of need, more women will have lengthy work histories. With more emphasis on career types of employment, these women are also more likely to be better prepared financially for their later years.

Employment has more than just financial benefits, however. Over the years, many of these women will come to see themselves as filling multiple roles. In fact, being Joe Brown's secretary or Dave Smith's boss is likely to become as important an identity as being Fred Jones's wife. In the event of the termination of the relationship with Fred, the older woman loses only one of her roles. In contrast to the experiences of Mrs. White and my aunt, whose lives became totally redefined when their husbands died, women in the future should be more likely to have identities, beyond the relationship with spouse, that prevent such a massive upheaval from occurring.

Future older women are also less likely to view living alone as an undesirable or inappropriate female option. The steady rise in age at first marriage means that many women will have spent at least a few of their adult years living alone. The woman who can reflect back nostalgically on early years spent in independence, faces the prospect of future aloneness from a much different perspective than the woman who made sure she found a man before she finished her schooling and thought that something must be wrong with those females who failed to do so.

Another important attitudinal change which women have undergone in recent years is the value they place on their relationship with other women. As stated previously, today's cohort of older women came of age in a 1920s and 1930s culture that taught that a woman's worth was evaluated in terms of the male who selected her, and later by how well she served him. Other women were competition, first in landing a good catch, and later in who did the best job on his ring-around-the-collar. These women are now, in old age, left with only each other, a situation for which they have had no preparation.

Arising out of the effort to change such thinking, the women's movement has had an enormous impact on how women view themselves, and, equally important, on how they view each other. Over the past decade, women have found, among their ranks, major sources of support. They have found, in each other, a closeness and caring which is different than that they experience with men. In small groups, consciousnesses have been raised, not only about political issues, but about personal strengths and abilities, as well. In light of these new relationships women are forming, I would suggest that many older women will view the prospect of later life spent in the company of women as an exciting, eagerly anticipated opportunity.

Of course, not all women have been caught up in the changes of the last few years. Some women will still be at a complete loss and totally unprepared for being alone. Alice Rossi (1985) feels strongly that it will be the duty of those of us women who are strong and successful in our transition from couple to single, to empower those who are weaker. The support networks we have learned to form in recent years will be even more important to maintain in our later years.

Rossi also suggests that women can have extremely rich and rewarding relationships with other women *if* they are careful about whom they choose as friends. For example, a woman who is more comfortable having decisions made for her and has spent her adult life in a marriage relationship in which she has contentedly let her husband take the lead is likely to become frustrated if she finds herself surrounded by women similar to herself. Rossi advises that, as older women form relationships with other women, they should seek out individuals whose personalities compliment or balance their own, a procedure that most have undoubtedly been practicing in choosing men intimates all their lives.

I think the overarching message of Rossi's ideas is that the formation of strong, rewarding relationships with other women is the clearly logical alternative for older women, both now and in the future. What seems a simple solution,however, may not necessarily be so easy to put into practice. In short, women will need to work diligently to ensure that their older years are full and happy.

## REFERENCES

Carter, H. and P. C. Glick. (1970). *Marriage and Divorce: A Social and Economic Study.* Cambridge, Mass.: Harvard University Press.

McKain, W. C. (1969). *Retirement Marriages.* Storrs Agricultural Experiment Station, Monograph 3 (January).

Rossi, A.S. (1985). Personal communication.

*Section Six*

# Divorce and Remarriage

# 22

GRAHAM B. SPANIER AND LINDA THOMPSON

# Moving toward Separation

*It is relatively easy to study trends in divorce rates and to identify categories of people, such as those who marry before age twenty, who are unusually prone to divorce. It is much harder to understand the interaction processes in marriage prior to separation and how and why persons decide to end their marriages. However, considerable progress has been made in recent years toward understanding how persons experience their marriages, and how they experience the movement of their marriages toward dissolution if that occurs.*

*The following selection reports a study of fifty persons (twenty-eight men and twenty-two women) in Pennsylvania who were separated from their spouses (and in some cases divorced) when they were interviewed in the late 1970s. The separations had occurred from a month to twelve years prior to the interviews, and thus the respondents' recollections of events and feelings prior to their separations may not have been entirely accurate. Furthermore, the fifty persons who were interviewed may not be very representative of persons who have separated from their spouses in the United States in recent years. Nevertheless, the study identifies some of the kinds of marital situations that may often precede separation, and it suggests some recent changes in the motivations for ending marriages.*

Source: Graham B. Spanier and Linda Thompson, "Moving toward Separation," pp. 27 and 41–58 in *Parting: The Aftermath of Separation and Divorce,* by Graham B. Spanier and Linda Thompson. 

It is not surprising that most men and women recall the final months of their previous marriages as unhappy. Rating the overall happiness of marriage, a third of the men and almost half of the women recall their marriages as extremely unhappy—the lowest point on our preferred scale. The vast majority of separated and divorced people remember unhappy marriages, with only 8 percent of the men and 4 percent of the women reporting any degree of prevailing happiness. Half of the men and women report that they never or rarely thought that things between them and their spouses were going well. Characterizing the discord, the majority of both men and women did not frequently regret that they married or frequently discuss or consider marital termination. The majority, however, did recall quarreling or getting on each other's nerves at least more often than not. These marriages were apparently endured rather than enjoyed in the final months by most husbands and wives. Not all of the recollections of marriage, however, are so bellicose and grim; a considerable number of men and women recall marriages where calm and detachment reigned.

Calm and detachment may reign because one or both partners refuse to participate in conflicts of interest. We asked participants how they approached disagreement and conflict in the final months of their waning marriages: 22 percent said they tried to avoid it at all costs, 50 percent said conflict was something they disliked but lived with, while 28 percent accepted conflict as normal. In the unstructured interviews, many men and women referred to their own or their partner's conflict tactics to explain the end of their marriage. Rands and her colleagues (1981) suggest three styles of conflicts: avoid, attack, and compromise. The seperated men and women we spoke with did not talk much about compromise; they talked about avoidance and attack.

A middle-aged man described his manner of avoiding conflict in the following way:

> I never was very good at talking about my feelings and often, in order to avoid conflict, I would suppress the way I was feeling and defer to my wife. I think it bothered her when I was too passive, also when I would suppress or not face openly some issues just to avoid conflict. I think if I would have been able to express my feelings earlier while things were good that would have helped us to solve our later problems much easier.

Another man pointed to his wife's avoidance of conflict:

> She just didn't want to talk about any problems. . . . I mean we always talked to each other but not about problems or how we were feeling. She never could really talk about what was bothering her.

It was clear from several reports such as this one that avoidance of conflict had undermined intimacy in marriage. Frustration and anger are common outcomes. A young woman tersely summarized the conflict process in her marriage: "My husband always ran away. Whenever we'd start to argue, he'd leave. He'd never work anything out, and I'd be left fuming."

Attack tactics in conflict can take many forms. A coercive style may include maligning the partner, threats, flagrant self-interest, demands, shouts, and violence. Attack tactics are cruel and uncompromising. They require that the other partner simply give in. One man characterized his wife and marriage in the following way:

> She seemed to be very domineering. I could feel how she needed to be dominant. . . . She would never admit to being wrong about anything. She wanted her way about everything. . . . I just didn't like to get in a hassle, so I would let her have her way a lot of the time.

Another man put it this way:

> Mostly she would start screaming at me, and I would just leave the room. I wasn't used to being screamed at as a kid, so I just didn't like it. . . . I would always give in to her. She always had to have her way.

As another man noted, seething or pouting can be an effective strategy:

> When we would have a disagreement, she would stay angry for quite awhile, kind of pout and not have anything to say to me. I usually would end up apologizing in the end to get things back to normal. Things never got really loud because I just find that sort of thing very unpleasant.

Coercive conflict tactics can escalate into violence (Straus, 1979). A young woman with an explosive husband recalled the conflict in her marriage:

> Usually it was just hysterical screaming and throwing and smashing things. Then he'd start throwing things at me. It was never anything that showed on me; he always seemed to do things that wouldn't leave marks, like hair pulling and arm twisting. It was like he felt, "you're my wife and I'm the boss," and he had to prove it.

Over and over again, the people who had given in to their partner's demands would say, "I should have put my foot down a long time ago." Some were martyrs; some were submissive. Others avoided conflict at all costs. Putting one's foot down means taking an unwavering stand. Coercive tactics by one partner elicit the same from the other (Gottman, 1979; Raush et al., 1974). Particularly in the final months of marriage, many of the participants found mutual compromise or problem-solving impossible.

The content of disagreement provides an overview of the loci of strain in contentious marriages. Affectional and sexual issues seem to be particularly thorny: Over 70 percent of the men and women recall not showing love as a problem in the final months of marriage, while half report that they frequently to always disagreed about demonstrations of affection and sex relations. Disagreements about philosophy of life, things believed important, and the amount of time spent together are also frequent occurrences, while other issues lag somewhat behind in their persistence.

Disagreement about the amount of time spent together suggests the second major theme of disrupted marriages—involvement. The so-called estranged marriage is often just that: Partners keep their distance from each other and lead emotionally and behaviorally separate lives (Goode, 1956; Weiss, 1975). Although having a stimulating exchange of ideas and working on a project together are rare occurrences in these dissolving marriages, half of the husbands and wives continued to confide in their mates more often than not. About half of the men and women also recall laughing or calmly discussing something with their mates at least once or twice a week in these final months of marriage. For many, then, companionship persists until the end of marriage, although not at the level of more stable relationships. Concerning interests outside of the home, a third of the men and almost two thirds of the women report sharing none or very few of these activities with their wives and husbands.

The waning attractiveness of marriage is reflected in the diminution of personal commitment to its continuance. One fourth of the men and women chose the statement representing the lowest level of commitment: "My marriage could have never succeeded, and there was nothing more that I could have done to keep it going." The vast majority recall that by the final months they had already done everything possible to help the marriage succeed with only the desire and hope for success varying among them. Only 12 and 15 percent of the men and women, respectively, desperately wanted their marriages to succeed and would have gone to almost any length to see that it did by the final months. Table 1 shows how the respondents felt about their partner by the time of the final separation. Men were more likely than women to still love their partner or to feel numb, while women were more likely to feel ambivalence, mild affection, or even hate.

Marriage is notoriously different for men and women, and the reconstruction of failed marriages in this study is no exception. In rating dimensions of the dissolved marriage, men recall greater consensus, companionship, compatibility in affectional realms, and harmony than women recall; the first three dimensions noted are significantly different for men and women. Researchers must be cautious about interpreting these differences as indicating actual differences in the emotional and behavioral experience of marriage. Nevertheless, a close examination of the distributions reveals that with very few exceptions, women as a group rate every item evaluating their previous marriage

**TABLE 1** ***Feelings for Partner at the Time of the Final Separation (in percentages)***

| | *Women* | *Men* |
|---|---|---|
| Still loved him/her | 17.7% | 35.2% |
| Still liked, but didn't love him/her | 21.2 | 15.4 |
| Didn't feel much of anything | 17.7 | 27.5 |
| Hated him/her | 18.6 | 4.4 |
| Both loved and hated him/her | 24.8 | 17.6 |
| Total | 100 | 100 |

more negatively than men. Supposing that the items do not have a drastically different meaning for men and women and that there is no gender-linked propensity to blacken the memory of a bygone marriage, it is safe to conclude that the final months of marriage hold fewer positive attractions and are more costly for women than for men.

Previous research with intact and failed marriages supports this conclusion. In global assessments of marital satisfaction and happiness, women typically report their marriages as less satisfying and happy than men (Campbell et al., 1976; Glenn and Weaver, 1978). Such findings are often taken to mean that marriage is less rewarding and more costly for women than for men (Bernard, 1972). In remembrances of failed marriages, women seem to be more sensitive to the problems that existed. In the case of premarital breakups (Hill et al., 1979) and interviews with divorce applicants (Levinger, 1966), women cited more problems and complaints with the relationship than did men. Finally, women reportedly experience more distress in the predivorce period of marital dissolution than do men (Albrecht, 1980; Nager et al., 1977), while men are more apt to evaluate the predivorce time favorably than are women (Albrecht, 1980). It may well be that the terminal stage of marriage is more unpleasant for women than it is for men.

The portrait of the end of marriage just offered is an aggregated one. It represents the typical experience of separated and divorced men and women rather than the actual experience of any individual. Unfortunately, the richness of exceptional cases is lost. The woman who considered herself contentedly married only to come home one day to a note on the kitchen table from her deserting husband is lost in a sample where the overwhelming majority of couples endures a deteriorating marriage and deliberated about its dissolution for months or even years. There are not enough cases where the marriage was truly a happy one for at least one partner to glean an understanding of this exceptional experience. The reports are also reconstructions of marriage—painfully and deliberately constructed accounts of what went wrong (Weiss, 1975). As such, it is unlikely that the descriptions of marriage are objective or would be similar to reports of dissolving marriages gathered concurrently; but recalled experience has an importance of its own (Goode, 1956).

## DELIBERATION AND DECISION

Most separations and divorces are preceded by a period of conflict and deliberation. We asked our respondents about the timing of events in their marital histories that mark phases in the move toward final dissolution. Respondents recalled when they first thought their marriage might end in separation or divorce, first openly discussed divorce with their partner, were first certain that their marriage was going to end, first separated even for a short time, finally separated, and filed for divorce. Similar to Goode (1956), we wanted to look at the timing and sequence of these markers.

Three events of divorce deliberation vary in timing but not in sequence: (1) foreboding of possible breakup; (2) certainty about the end of marriage; and (3) filing for divorce. On the other hand, both discussion about divorce and actual separation can occur anywhere in the sequence. The order of the events and the swiftness of deliberation tell us a lot about the circumstances and anticipation of the end of marriage. Diversity in the spacing of the three deliberation events is presented in Table 2.

As we might expect, the period between thinking separation or divorce might occur and certainty about the event is longer than the period from certainty to filing. In general, the decision period from certainty to filing took about three to four months in our sample, and the timing is similar for men and women. Length of deliberation between foreboding and certainty, however, differs for men and women. The duration for men is about a year (median=12 months), while women were aware of the possibility of separation and divorce for almost two years (median = 22 months) before certainty settled in or struck. Women considered the possibility of breakup earlier in their marriages than men; for example, 16 percent of the women as compared to 8 percent of the men recall experiencing foreboding in the first month of marriage. One woman said, "I knew in the back of my mind from the beginning it would never work." A young woman married three years described her foreboding in this way: "The first year, I kept thinking, 'Oh, it's the first year, it'll get better.' Then it didn't during the second year, and soon I knew that was it." A man married almost 20 years recalled doubts he had had early in the marriage: "I think we both knew as early as the first two years that we had made a mistake. We knew it was not working but we just sort of muddled through." Both foreboding and certainty are subjective markers and may be

**TABLE 2** ***Time between Events of Deliberation and Decision (in percentages)***

| | *Phases* | | | |
|---|---|---|---|---|
| | *Foreboding to certainty* | | *Certainty to filing* | |
| *Time in months* | *Women* | *Men* | *Women* | *Men* |
| Less than 1 | 11.7% | 21.2% | 32.7% | 22.7% |
| 1–6 | 17.1 | 17.6 | 25.7 | 42.6 |
| 7–12 | 9.9 | 10.6 | 20.8 | 12.0 |
| 13–24 | 18.1 | 16.5 | 10.9 | 6.7 |
| More than 24 | 43.2 | 34.1 | 11.9 | 16.0 |
| Total | 100 | 100 | 100 | 100 |
| Median | 22. mo. | 12 mo. | 4 mo. | 3 mo. |

very different for the two partners involved. The timing of events that apply to both partners—discussion of separation and divorce, actual separation, and filing—have very similar distributions for men and women.

Length of marriage is, of course, associated with the duration of deliberation about separation and divorce. The longer the marriage endured, the more time was spent anticipating and moving toward the end of marriage. Time spent in one phase of deliberation is also related to time spent in the other phase. The phase from foreboding to certainty is associated with *less* time given to the phase from certainty to filing ($r = -.25$ for women and $-.45$ for men). Rather than the whole process being slow or swift, then, it seems that haste in one phase is linked with hesitation in another. Duration from foreboding to filing can be considered anticipation time. Women tend to have a longer anticipation period than men (the median is 31 months for women and 18 months for men), although a fifth of both men and women and experience the entire dissolution process in 6 months or less. Having children tended to draw out the deliberation period (gamma =.34).

Open discussion about divorce between marital partners can occur at any time in the dissolution process. For half of the men and women involved, the first open discussion occurred *before* the partner was certain that his or her marriage was going to end. For another 40 percent of the partners, the first discussion coincided with their certainty about the end of marriage. The remaining 10 percent did not discuss divorce with their partners until after they were certain about the end of their marriage. About half of these partners timed the discussion between certainty and filing, while the other half never discussed the divorce or waited until after filing.

For some couples, discussion of divorce recurred throughout the marriage as a serious consideration or as a threat. Many couples vacillated painfully. They talked again and again about whether to separate or to try to mend their marriage. The uncertainty was excruciating. A woman, whose husband had filed for divorce but was still living in the house, portrayed the agony of indecision.

> This sounds weird, but he's trying to stay here, but he wants to go away. He's mixed up. . . . Sometimes I think he still loves me. Just that he's *here*. He's sort of clinging to us. He doesn't want to give us up. Why else would he stay?... He's afraid to have anything to do with me. He says he doesn't love me, but I think he just does things to get back at me. The love is there, but he wants to hurt me. Sometimes he wants to kiss or hold me I can tell, but I won't. He thinks I've hurt him through the years. I don't know. If I did, I didn't know it.

Other couples had batted around breakup as a threat so often that they failed to recognize the importance of the final discussion:

> She started talking a lot about how maybe the marriage was a mistake and maybe we should separate and get a divorce. At first I didn't think she was very serious, I mean she threw the idea of divorce up everytime we had a row right from the first of the marriage, but it was just off the top of her head. She was never serious about it before.

Another man, who admitted that he was not as involved with his wife as she would have wanted, was surprised by their first and only discussion:

> It all happened all of a sudden. Things were just about the same right up till the time she left. We had an argument on a Saturday afternoon. I don't even remember what it was about. Anyway, after the fight, she said that she wanted a divorce and that she wanted half of the money, and that she would leave. I said that that was fine with me, but I really thought she was just bluffing.

It is charitable to call that a discussion; it is more an announcement. For some, there was no discussion and no announcement; the partner just left:

> Nothing made sense to me during those first few months of the separation. I didn't really know what was going on. I kept trying to talk to her and find out what was bothering her, but she wouldn't talk about it. I talked to friends of ours and asked them to find out anything they could. I even asked her mother to find out what was wrong, but nobody would tell me. I found out later that most of them, including her mother, knew about the other man, but nobody would tell me. . . . I was depressed and confused, and I just didn't know what I had done or what to do about it. I figured we could work it out if we tried.

Separation is an event that may occur at any point in the process of marital breakup. The typical pattern is for the man or woman to have thought about the possibility of separation and divorce, discussed the possibility with the partner, reached a level of certainty about the breakup, and finally separated from the partner. Although this is the typical pattern, there is a sizable minority for whom events did not proceed in this way. For example, a quarter of the partners discussed the divorce coincident with the final separation while another 10 percent did not discuss the breakup until after the separation. For 35 percent of the sample, the final separation coincided with their certainty about the end of their marriage. Another 15 percent were not certain until after the final separation. For the most part, these people cited filing as the point of certainty.

More than filing for divorce or the decree, the final separation marks the end of marriage for most people. Those men and women who had a longer deliberation overall (foreboding to filing) were more likely to have a longer period of certainty before the final separation. Those people with the shortest deliberation (0–6 months) were more likely than those with longer anticipation time to be certain that the marriage was ending only when or after someone finally moved out ($X^2 = 41$, df $= 9$, $p < .01$). In our sample, it was rare (7 percent) for both partners to move out of the house at the final separation, and it was more often the wife who moved out (51 percent) than the husband (42 percent).

For about half of our participants, the final separation was the only separation. Among those with a previous separation, the first separation was, of course, much more ambiguous than the final separation, especially in retrospect. One young woman described the period between her first and final separations:

> See, he never could hold a steady job. Beat me and knocked me around. I had him arrested in May, and he spent three days in jail. He cried, said he'd change and begged me to come back. He loved me and couldn't live without me. The same old story. Well, I went back to him in June and things were fine, really good. He treated me wonderful until October or November, then he started mistreating me again. Forced me to do things I didn't want to do. He'd hit me if I gave him coffee that was too hot. He was insane.

For many of those with more than one separation (4 percent of the men and 27 percent of the women), the first separation was the first time the person had any sense that his or her marriage might break up. A third of the men and women separated the first time with *no* prior discussion of ending the marriage and, in retrospect, the first separation occurred before the partner felt certain about the breakup for the majority of partners. A man married 11 years recalled that things started going badly about a year and a half into his marriage when the first child was born. He described the sequel to his first separation:

> She started calling and said she had made a mistake and wanted the family to get together again. She wanted to come back and try again. At first I wasn't sure, but then I got thinking that I would probably always be wondering if we could have made it. I knew I was still in love with her. So, I said okay and I stopped the divorce proceedings, and she moved back in. Well, within two weeks it became obvious that she was just sitting around moping about the other guy and that she was not serious in really trying to make our lives together work. So, I told her to leave.

Although the marriage had been deteriorating for almost a decade, he was not certain that his marriage was over until he discovered that his wife was seeing someone else. In the highly ambiguous situation of bringing a marriage to a close, the presence of "the other man" or "the other woman" may be necessary to clinch certainty.

In comparing the final separation for those who did and those who did not experience a previous separation, men and women with more than one separation were more likely to have openly discussed and be certain about the end of marriage by the time of the last separation than participants who experienced only one, final separation.

The timing and sequence of the above events are important because they tell us something about the anticipation and ambiguity of ending a marriage. Not only are timing and sequence of dissolution events related to the circumstances of marriage and its demise but also to the emotional impact of the breakup. In subsequent discussions, we use duration of the period from foreboding to certainty, the period from foreboding to final separation, the ordering of certainty with final separation, and the occurrence of a previous separation to understand anticipation and ambiguity in movement toward divorce. By the time of the respondents' interviews with us, there was little question that the marriages were over (only 12 percent of the men and women fostered thoughts of reconciliation) although such certainty was imposed on some of the marriage partners.

Recollection of the partner's role performance in marriage was not related to the length of time required to move toward separation. The only exception was among women and men who were parents. Recalled satisfaction with the partner's parenting performance was associated with a slower movement toward separation than among the more dissatisfied partners.

The majority of women and men approached the final months before separation with an inkling, if not a certainty, that the marriage was over. From the husband's vantage point, the longer period from foreboding to final separation was associated with greater consensus (r = .23), but lower companionship (r = −.22) in the final months of marriage. Among wives, however, those who had anticipated the breakup for a longer time recalled less harmony in the final months of marriage (r = .20) than those who had a shorter time from foreboding to final separation.

In general, with our data we did not find that the degree of disappointment with the partner's role performance as parent, provider, housekeeper, sexual partner, companion, or confidant slowed or hastened the movement toward breakup. We also found only slight indications that the time spent anticipating and deliberating the dissolution was associated with the quality of marriage in its terminal stage. We thought, perhaps, that a longer approach to separation might be linked with a calmer, although more distant, marriage near the end. This is somewhat the case among husbands, but among wives there was greater rancor and conflict with a longer approach to separation than with a shorter approach.

Using an index of the extent to which the partner lived up to the respondent's expectations summed across the several domains, the degree of satisfaction with the spouse was connected to the relative timing of separation and certainty about the end of marriage among wives. Wives who were more satisfied with their husband's performance were more likely than disappointed wives to be uncertain that the marriage was over until the final separation—or even after (gamma = .32). The timing of the separation was not related to evaluations of the partner's performance among husbands. Of the four dimensions of marital quality, only affectional expression in the final months of marriage was related to the timing of separation. Among both men and women, the recollection of sexual and affectional imcompatibility in the terminal stage of marriage was related to a longer phase between certainty that the marriage was over and the final separation (gamma = −.34).

Commitment reflects dedication to the continuance of the relationship. It is not surprising that among women the expression of greater commitment in the final months of marriage is connected with disbelief that the marriage was going to end until separation or after; while those women who reported a lag period between certainty about the end of marriage and the final separation were more likely to express less commitment by the final months of marriage (gamma = .34). Among men, commitment in the terminal stage of marriage was unrelated to the timing of certainty and separation.

When does a person finally know that his or her marriage is over? Frederico (1979) says that a person reaches a "point of no return" at which he or she gives up on the idea that the marriage has more emotional gains than costs. At that point, emotional investment in the marriage wanes and can never be recovered. Typically, the marital partner is not aware or is reluctant to accept that the marriage is over. According to Frederico, it is probably only in retrospect that a person can identify the point of no return and recognize his or her strategies for bringing the marriage to a close. The strategies serve to sabotage the marriage and spread out responsibility for its demise, although neither partner may realize what is happening.

The final separation openly declares the end of marriage. Yet a person may reach the point of no return long before the separation. Among both men and women in our sample, sexual and affectional incompatibility in the final months was linked with a longer period between certainty that the marriage is over (the point of no return) and final separation. We cannot say whether certainty led to sexual and affectional upheaval in marriage, or whether such upheaval clinched certainty. Regardless of the causal connection, however, it is clear that sex and affection are at the center of the emotional end of marriage. Women seem to accumulate evidence from realms of marriage other than sex and affection. Their disappointment in their husband's role performance and their own subsiding commitment was linked with their certainty about the end of marriage. Women who were relatively satisfied with their husbands and committed to their marriages more often needed the separation to mark the end of marriage.

## SUGGESTION AND BLAME

Marital dissolution by divorce is typically considered a mutual and voluntary decision (Levinger, 1979), but accounts of failed marriages consistently reveal that one partner wants and pushes for the divorce more than the other partner (Cuber and Harroff, 1965; Goode, 1956; Hunt, 1966; Weiss, 1975). Although an admitted oversimplification, the issue is most often reduced to "the leaver" and "the left" (Weiss, 1975) or the "breaker-upper" and the "broken-up-with" (Hill et al., 1979). Hill and his colleagues regard this differentiation as crucial to understanding everything else about ending relationships.

In our sample, 64 percent of the women claim to have first suggested the divorce, 27 percent pointed to the spouse as having first suggested the divorce, and 9 percent saw the divorce as a mutual conclusion. This distribution is almost identical to that reported by Goode's (1956) divorced women over 20 years ago. Among the men in our sample, 34 percent accept responsibility for the initial suggestion to separate or divorce, 47 percent attribute the suggestion to the spouse, and 19 percent recall a mutual conclusion. Women are clearly more likely than men to suggest the final separation or divorce, although there is also a tendency toward self-bias for women and men in such reports (Hill et al., 1979).

Specifying the leaver and the left does not, however, accurately portray the complexity of control over the process and progress of marital dissolution. Goode (1956) speculates that it is actually more often the husband who first wishes to escape the marriage and, by various strategies of withdrawal and conflict, maneuvers the wife into suggesting a divorce out of sheer exasperation. As evidence, Goode reports that the length of deliberation between serious consideration and filing for divorce is much shorter when the husband suggests the divorce than when the wife suggests the divorce; divorce by mutual conclusion takes the most time.

Our data show that regardless of the phase of deliberation addressed, divorce by mutual conclusion involves a longer deliberation time than it does when one spouse unilaterally suggests the dissolution. We found no evidence that the progress of moving toward final separation or filing for divorce was more swift when the husband suggested the breakup than when the wife suggested the breakup. There were, of course, differences in the duration of phases depending on whether the partner was the leaver or the left. Regardless of gender, the anticipation and deliberation period was longer for those partners who suggested the separation or divorce themselves rather than received the suggestion from the spouse. As markers of duration reflect subjective foreboding and certainty, it is sensible that the partner who finally suggests the end of marriage has had more time to anticipate its demise. Among those on the receiving end of the suggestion, only 28 percent of the women and 30 percent of the men reported that they were very or completely surprised by the idea. The majority of partners suspected that their marriages might end even if they themselves did not suggest the breakup.

It seems plausible that differences in who suggested the separation or divorce was associated with differences in the attractiveness of marriage, but this was not the case among the women in our study. Among men, however, who suggested the divorce was related to marital harmony ($X^2 = 8.8$, $df = 2$, $p < .01$) and commitment to marriage ($X^2 = 9.9$, $df = 2$, $p < .01$) in the final months. Men were more likely to claim that they first suggested the divorce or that it was a mutual decision if they recalled the final months of marriage as lacking harmony and personal commitment. Attributing the initial suggestion to the wife was associated with recollections of greater harmony in and personal commitment to marriage. Although the pattern did not reach statistical significance, it persisted across several other variables among men: Husbands more often attributed the initial suggestion to their partners when the husbands recalled greater companionship in marriage and felt that their wives had lived up to their expectations as parent, provider, sexual partner, and confidant. They were more likely to report a self- or mutually initiated separation or divorce if they recalled less companionship in the final months of marriage and greater disappointment in their wives' role performance.

Among men, then, memories of a good marriage are linked with attributing the first suggestion to end the marriage to the partner. We can infer that men tend to suggest the divorce themselves or cooperate in a mutual decision when they wish to break out of an unattractive marriage. We cannot draw a similar conclusion about women from our data.

Responsibility for the initial suggestion to separate or divorce and blame for the breakup are two different aspects of control over the process of marital dissolution. The respondents were asked, "If you had to assign blame for the breakup of your marriage, whom would you blame?" Table 3 compares the target of blame for the breakup with the source of the initial suggestion to separate or divorce. Very few partners are willing to take the blame for a one-sided breakup (7 percent). Blaming a person outside the relationship is also uncommon (7 percent). Sharing the blame with the spouse is the typical pattern (55 percent), although attributing the blame for the breakup solely to the spouse is quite common (31 percent). As a group, husbands are somewhat more likely to blame their wives for the breakup than the other way around.

The source of the first suggestion to breakup and attribution of blame are related, but a different impression of the dissolution emerges from the two approaches. Separation or divorce by mutual conclusion is associated with sharing of blame for the breakup between partners. Among those who recall that the spouse first suggested the separation or divorce, it is equally likely that these men and women will blame the spouse solely or share the blame with their spouse. In the self-suggested breakup, the tendency is to share the blame. A good proportion of partners, however, attribute blame for the breakup to their spouses even though they themselves initially suggested the separation or divorce. Among the self-suggested cases, women were more likely to share the blame with their husbands while men tended to place the blame squarely on their wives. There is no evidence in these recollections, then, that it is more often the husband that wants to escape the marriage.

Even more than the source of the initial suggestion to end the marriage, we thought the target of blame for the breakup would be linked with recollections of the marital relationship, but our data did not bear this out. For both women and men, the degree to which their marital partners lived up to their expectations in various role domains and the quality of marriage in the final months were not related to how the respondent parceled out blame for the breakup.

## SUMMARY

Many marital partners were disappointed in their mate's role performance. Husbands and wives expressed the greatest disappointment about the mate as companion and confidant. Across domains, women evaluated their husbands

**TABLE 3** ***Source of Suggestion to Separate or Divorce and Target of Blame for Breakup (in percentages)***

| | *Target of blame* | | | | |
|---|---|---|---|---|---|
| *Source of suggestion* | *Myself* | *Spouse* | *Mutual* | *Other person* | *Total* |
| Myself | 9% | 28% | 57% | 6% | 100% |
| Spouse | 7 | 40 | 45 | 8 | 100 |
| Mutual | 0 | 15 | 78 | 7 | 100 |

more severely than men judged their wives. Women were particularly disappointed in their husbands as parents and helpers with household tasks. Although wives had unmet expectations of their husbands regarding those roles traditionally assigned to women, husbands did not display similar disappointment in their wives as providers. Disappointment in one's mate, therefore, revolved around affectional involvement and the husband's failure to share roles traditionally assigned to women. As one woman said,

> After we were married, I realized all he wanted was a housekeeper, bed partner, and maid. . . . [He wanted] someone to do all the housework, and someone who never got tired. I expected more than I got, that's for sure. . . . I wanted someone who was understanding. I thought I should be able to talk to my husband about my feelings and problems, but I couldn't.

For most people, the final months of marriage were characterized by dissension and withdrawal. Companionship, sex, and affection continued to be at the center of disagreement and involvement. Although most husbands and wives had reduced their involvement in the marriage, they were still tied to their partner and still haggled over their independence. One young woman described the haggling in this way:

> He was always checking up on me, calling, "Where was I?" He didn't want me going out by myself, even when he was at work, didn't want me seeing my friends. He couldn't understand why I'd want to go out to dinner with a male friend who was very close, and I hadn't seen in years. Things like that. Married couples were supposed to do everything together. . . . He was so dependent, needed me so much. . . . I wanted us each to have our own separate lives and one together. . . . According to him I was frigid. He was all touchy-feely. He always wanted me next to him, cuddling. I wasn't supposed to sit across the room from him ever, always next to him on the couch. He said if we couldn't be like husbands and wives were supposed to be, then he wanted to be divorced. I agreed.

Women had a bleaker view of marriage in the final months than men. By the time of the final separation, women felt less affection for their mates than men. The terminal stage of marriage may be more unpleasant for women, but they may also be more prepared for the marriage to end.

Disappointment in the partner's role performance did not hasten or delay the pace of moving toward separation. Only children seemed to make a difference: Among both women and men, having children slowed the progress even more. Among husbands, there was some evidence that a longer approach to separation meant less disagreement and less involvement by the final months—a gradual calm and withdrawal. Among wives, however, there was greater dissension and irritation in the final months if the separation was a long time coming.

Typically, partners thought about the possibility of breakup, discussed the possibility with the partner, reached a level of certainty about the end of marriage, and finally separated. For those who did not experience the breakup in this way, it was likely that the open discussion of the divorce, the actual separation, and certainty that the marriage was over all happened at once.

These people tended to have a shorter time between thinking that their marriage might end and believing that it would. For them, there was less anticipation of the end, and the objective events of dissolution—open discussion and actual separation—occurred together and precipitated their certainty about the crumbling of their marriage. For many, an attempted separation preceded the final separation. Particularly among men with more than one seperation, the first separation was likely to be the first time they had any sense that the marriage might be breaking up. Afterward, the final separation usually followed the typical pattern described above.

Among both men and women, sexual and affectional incompatibility in the final months was linked with a longer period between certainty that the marriage was over and the final separation. Sex and affection are the emotional battleground in the dissolving marriage: Partners use sex and affection to sabotage or save the marriage. Shifts in sexual and affectional involvement reflect the partner's ambivalence about the end of marriage. Partners also use sex and affection to gauge the viability of their marriage. A woman married only two years gave the following account of feelings and messages gone amiss:

> We didn't argue. There wasn't anything specific to argue about. . . . He was so unhappy, and I always wondered if it was me. . . . Sometimes he was just depressed and wouldn't do or say anything. I took it as disinterest, especially in me as a woman. I got really jealous of him, of where he spent his time, of when he wasn't with me. He took that as my trying to trap him and just withdrew more.

For those who were reluctant to admit the end of marriage based on its emotional climate, only a physical separation seemed to convince them that the union was over. Moreover, women seemed to be more sensitive than men to the emotional keel of marriage and attended to a wider range of cues when judging the success of and hope for their marriage.

## REFERENCES


Albrecht, S. L. (1980) "Reactions and adjustments to divorce: Differences in the experiences of males and females." *Family Relations, 29,* 59–68.

Bernard, J. (1972) *The Future of Marriage.* New York: World.

Campbell, A., P. E. Converse, and W. L. Rodgers. (1976) *The Quality of American Life.* New York: Russell Sage Foundation.

Cuber, J. F., and P. B. Haroff. (1965) *Sex and Significant Americans.* New York: Pelican Books.

Frederico, J. (1979) "The marital termination period of the divorce adjustment period." *Journal of Divorce, 3,* 93–106.

Glenn, N. D., and C. N. Weaver. (1978) "A multivariate, multisurvey study of marital happiness." *Journal of Marriage and the Family, 40,* 269–282.

Goode, W. J. (1956) *After Divorce (Women in Divorce).* New York: Free Press.

Gottman, J. M. (1979) *Marital Interaction.* New York: Academic Press.

Hill, C. T., Z. Rubin, and L. A. Peplau. (1979) "Breakups before marriage: The end of 103 affairs," in G. Levinger & O. C. Moles (eds.). *Divorce and Separation: Contexts, Causes, and Consequences.* New York: Basic Books.

Hunt, M. (1966) *The World of the Formerly Married.* New York: McGraw-Hill.

Levinger, G. (1979) "A social psychological perspective on marital dissolution," in G. Levinger and O. C. Moles (eds.). *Divorce and Separation: Context, Causes, and Consequences.* New York: Basic Books.

———. (1966) "Sources of marital dissatisfaction among applicants for divorce." *American Journal of Orthopsychiatry, 36*, 803–807.

Nager, L., D. Chiriboga, and L. Cutler. (1977) "Stress and relief during the process of divorce: A psychosocial study." Presented at Western Psychological Association Meetings, Seattle.

Rands, M., G. Levinger, and G. D. Mellinger. (1981) "Patterns of conflict resolution and marital satisfaction." *Journal of Family Issues, 2,* 297–321.

Raush, H. L., W. A. Barry, R. K. Hetel, and M. Swain. (1974) *Communication, Conflict, and Marriage.* San Francisco: Jossey-Bass.

Straus, M. A. (1979) "Measuring intrafamily conflict and violence." *Journal of Marriage and the Family, 41,* 75–88.

Weiss, R. S. (1975) *Marital Separation.* New York: Basic Books.

## 23

GEORGE LEVINGER

# A Social Psychological Perspective on Marital Dissolution

*In the contemporary United States and most of the rest of the Western world, most people think that the success of a marriage should be gauged primarily by how well it serves the needs and desires of the spouses (a condition that, incidentally, has been historically rare). Since few legal barriers discourage divorce, and since how well marriages serve the needs and desires of spouses is hard to measure directly, one might be tempted to try to measure the success of marriages by whether or not they end in separation or divorce, and if they do, by how long they endure.*

*However, the durability of marriages and how successful they are (in hedonistic terms) are only moderately related. For several reasons, unsuccessful marriages can be highly durable, and marriages that are at least moderately successful may end in divorce. In the selection that follows, Levinger sets forth a simple conceptual scheme for dealing with influences on marital durability, including those other than how well marriages serve the needs and desires of the spouses.*

---

Work on this paper was facilitated by Grant GS−33641 from the National Science Foundation. For their valuable comments on an earlier draft, I am indebted to Ann Levinger, Oliver Moles, Phillips Cutright, Marylyn Lacey, and particularly to Zick Rubin. A previous version of this chapter appeared in *Journal of Social Issues*, 1976, 32 (1).

---

The cycle of life is inexorable. What rises eventually descends. What grows eventually perishes. Closely knit interpersonal attachments, too, sooner or later dissolve.

Why do couple relationships dissolve? The grounds are often complex. Determinants of disruption vary on a continuum ranging from entirely voluntary to entirely involuntary. At the involuntary extreme is death. At the voluntary end, either or both partners may clearly choose to break the bond, as occurs in some instances of withdrawal, estrangement, separation, or divorce.

Divorce generally is the end product of a process of estrangement (Goode, 1956; McCall and Simmons, 1966). It is often preceded by numerous little acts that cool the relationship. Before the actual breakup, a sensitive observer can note stepwise detachments or withdrawals:

> The parties to a progressively less rewarding relationship are allowed simply to give it correspondingly less salience in their respective agendas. . . . The two parties thus begin to fade out of each other's lives. [McCall and Simmons, 1966, pp. 198–199]

Intimate relationships are not easily broken. If they do break, however, they seem already to have declined to a point where one or both partners see an alternative state that is more attractive. The more attractive alternative is not necessarily another lover; it may be going it alone or living in groups other than a nuclear family.

There are few actual data on processes of dissolution. Existing data about the afflicted system are generally based on retrospective reports of single spouses or ex-spouses (Goode, 1956; Weiss, 1975) or of exmembers of premarital pairs (Hill, Rubin, and Peplau, 1979). Process data about couple interaction are difficult to obtain, and neither researchers nor couple members themselves are in a position to view such pair processes objectively.

Most instances of pair dissolution, however, contain a mixture of perceived volition and coercion through circumstance. Events inside the relationship, such as poor communication or intermember coordination, are usually only partly accountable for its breakup; external events also exert powerful effects. Discussions of marital disruption must recognize such external factors. For example, one indirect contributor to the increase in voluntary marital separation during the past century has been the decrease of involuntary separation through death (Bane, 1979). Spouses today see only a distant prospect of death parting an unsatisfying union; thus they may have a greater need to consider other forms of separation. External determinants can also be the source of marital conflict or deficiency. One important source is inadequate income; low family income has been a significant correlate of divorce (Cutright, 1971; Norton and Glick, 1979). The private lives of marriage partners are intertwined with events in their surrounding social and economic environment.

## A SOCIAL PSYCHOLOGICAL PERSPECTIVE

This discussion of divorce will view the marriage relationship as a special case of pair relationships in general. In doing so, it builds on two lines of my earlier work—a decade-old integrative review of the literature on marital cohesiveness and dissolution (Levinger, 1965) and a more recent conceptualization of the development of attraction in dyadic relationships (Levinger, 1974; Levinger and Snoek, 1972). Although cognizant that the events affecting marital durability emerge out of the broader sociocultural matrix, I here consider the marital relationship mainly as a dyad. And even though most data about marriage and divorce derive from the work of demographers and family sociologists, my present view will be mainly social psychological.

### Cohesiveness of the Marriage Pair

One approach to the determinants of marital breakup is to conceive the marriage pair as a special case of all other social groups, and to consider its continuation in terms of its cohesiveness:

> The marriage pair is a two-person group. It follows, then, that marital cohesiveness is analogous to group cohesiveness and can be defined accordingly. Group cohesiveness is "the total field of forces which act on members to remain in the group" [Festinger, Schachter, and Back, 1950]. Inducements to remain in any group include the attractiveness of the group itself and the strength of the restraints against leaving it; inducements to leave a group include the attractiveness of alternative relationships and the restraints against breaking up such existing relationships. [Levinger, 1965, p. 19]

A second approach focuses on gradations of interpersonal relationship. Pair relationships are distinguished according to degrees of interpersonal involvement, from the unilateral impression of another to the deeply mutual attachment (Levinger, 1974; Levinger and Snoek, 1972). Consider, in particular, the continuum of interpersonal involvement ranging from superficial contact to profound closeness—as indicated by varying degrees of cognitive, behavioral, and emotional interdependence.

Most pair dissolutions occur long before two acquaintances ever reach any appreciable depth, but data about dissolution pertain almost entirely to the breakup of established pairs. The ending of superficial encounters offers few research problems. In contrast, the phenomena of marital separation and divorce pertain to couples who have had high involvement, sufficient for them to enter into a long-term commitment; yet, at the moment of breakup such involvement may be either low or charged with negativity. My social psychological perspective does not make categorical assumptions about the phenomena of separation or divorce. Without knowing a pair's location on a continuum of relatedness, one can say little about the meaning of its breakup.

**FIGURE 1** *Schema of a Person-Other Relationship*

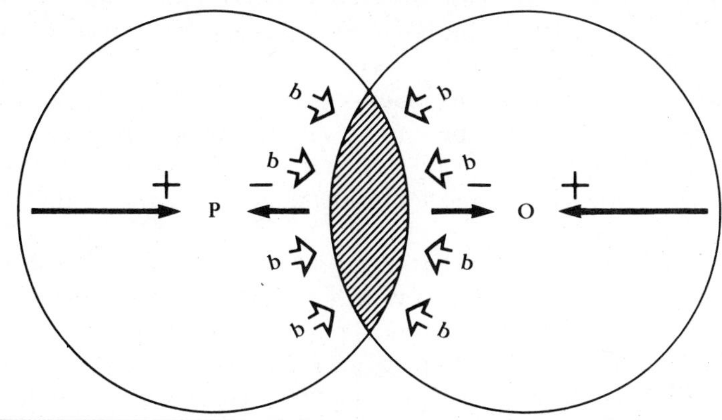


Source: George Levinger and Oliver C. Moles, Eds. *Divorce and Separation: Context, Causes, and Consequences*, figure 3−1, p. 40. New York: Basic Books. Copyright 1979 by The Society for the Psychological Study of Social Issues. Reprinted by permission.

**An image of the pair.** Figure 1 depicts a relationship between Person (P) and Other (O), interpretable according to the above two views. The size of the intersection between P's and O's life circles refers to the degree of their interdependence—substantial in this instance. It refers to a complex of joint property, joint outlook or knowledge, capacities, behaviors, feelings, joint memories and anticipations.

The arrows marked "+," "−," and "b" pertain to different aspects of pair cohesiveness. The positive and negative arrows refer to forces that drive a person either toward or away from a relationship—positive "attractions" such as feelings of comfort or admiration, and negative "attractions" such as discomfort or irritation. It is assumed that one usually has both positive and negative feelings toward an intimate partner. P's net positive attraction tends to be higher, the larger the size of the P−O intersection. Nonetheless, we can imagine persons who feel large interdependence with their partner, but whose feelings are predominantly negative. Resentment or hatred are also forms of bondage or, conversely, being forced to remain together may itself raise negative feelings.

The "b" arrows in Figure 1 refer to barrier forces that act to contain the P−O relationship. Barriers—or psychological "restraining forces" (Lewin, 1951)—affect one's behavior only if one wishes to leave the relationship. In a marriage one's feelings of obligation to the contract or one's fear of community disapproval at its termination are each examples of psychological barriers against breakup.

### Attractions

A person's attraction to membership in a relationship is directly associated with its perceived rewards and inversely with its perceived costs (Thibaut and

Kelley, 1959). At any given moment, each reward or cost is weighted by its respective subjective probability.

Rewards are derived from positive outcomes associated with membership in the relationship. They include the receipt of resources such as love, status, information, goods, services, or money—as conceived in Foa's (1971) scheme of interpersonal resources. The relationship may also bring one support, security, and consensual validation. Costs of membership may include one's time and energy and the various other expenditures demanded from staying in a relationship.

Subjective probability refers to a person's anticipation of how likely it is that a reward will be obtained or a cost incurred. The higher the subjective probability of a reward or cost, the more it is perceived to affect attractiveness. For instance, a man may fancy great pleasure from associating with a wonderful woman he has met but see a low probability of developing the relationship; if he also sees a high probability of receiving a painful rejection, his effective attraction to the woman will be small.

The dissolution of intimate relationships is often marked by a drastic shift in perceived rewards or costs. When relationships are on the upswing, mutual rewards are believed to be highly probable and thoughts of costs are suppressed; later, during disenchantment, one or both partners find the old rewards less probable, and unanticipated costs are now discovered. In some cases, the eventual costs existed from the beginning but neither partner had wanted to see them; in other instances, the components of attraction change markedly over the course of time.

**Barriers**

Discussions of cohesiveness have usually ignored the existence of restraining forces. As originally proposed by Lewin (1951, p. 259), a restraining force affects a person only when he approaches the boundary of a psychological region; he is not restrained unless and until he attempts to cross the boundary. Restraining forces that derive from barriers between people act to keep them apart; barriers around relationships act to keep people together.

Barriers are important for keeping long-term relationships intact. An example is the partnership contract, legitimated by the norms of society. Barriers lessen the effect of temporary fluctuations in interpersonal attraction; even if attraction becomes negative, barriers act to continue the relationship.

If there is little delight in a relationship, however, the existence of strong barriers creates a prison. Such a marital relationship has been called an "empty shell" marriage:

> The atmosphere is without laughter or fun, and a sullen gloom pervades the household. Members do not discuss their problems or experiences with each other, and communication is kept to a minimum. . . . Their rationalization for avoiding a divorce is, on the part of one or both, sacrifice for the children, neighborhood respectability, and a religious conviction that divorce is morally wrong. . . . The hostility in such a home is great, but arguments focus on the small issues, not the large ones. Facing the latter would, of course, lead directly to

separation or divorce, but the couple has decided that staying together overrides other values, including each other's happiness and the psychological health of their children [Goode, 1961, pp. 441–442]

The metaphor of an empty shell marriage evokes contrasting images of "full shell" and "no shell" pairs. A "full shell" marriage would be one in which not only the boundaries but also both partners' attractions are strong.

The left column of Figure 2 shows two distinct instances of "no shell" relationships which differ in their attractiveness. The top left corner refers to premarital or nonmarital relationships between partners who care deeply for one another, but who have not formalized any commitment. The bottom cell refers to partners who are estranged; divorced pairs are significant instances. Figure 2, then, describes a range of instances along two important interpersonal continua; fullness-emptiness of attraction and strength-weakness of boundaries.

**Alternative Attractions**

In almost every marriage, each spouse has numerous relationships with alternative role partners—family, friends, or fellow employees. Each such alternative relationship is the source of its own attractions and constraints; such alternative forces may compete with forces from inside the marriage relationship. Although ties to third parties often enrich the life of the couple, they also demand time and energy and can draw affect away from the pair itself. Images of "open marriage" to the contrary, an extreme commitment to such a relationship can do more to weaken rather than to strengthen marital attractions.

If one partner becomes immersed in relations that consciously exclude the other, the fullness of marital interaction may be threatened—depending, of course, on how the other spouse interprets the action. A jealous partner can perceive even a mild detachment as threatening. Some spouses may not be at all disturbed by their partner's withdrawal or alternate affairs, but such extreme tolerance is rare. A key question is whether the externally involved

**FIGURE 2** *Varying Patterns of Pair Attractions and Barriers*

| ATTRACTIONS | BARRIERS: None (or weak) | BARRIERS: Strong |
|---|---|---|
| Highly Positive | Premarital pairs, uncommitted lovers | Attracted and mutually committed marriages |
| Low or Negative | Strangers, pairs that are now divorced | Empty shell marriages, apathetic and dulled dyads |

Source: George Levinger and Oliver C. Moles, Eds. *Divorce and Separation: Context, Causes, and Consequences*, figure 3–2, p. 42. New York: Basic Books. Copyright 1979 by The Society for the Psychological Study of Social Issues. Reprinted by permission.

spouse will eventually prefer the alternative enough to desire a rupture of the present relationship.

One member's withdrawal, if it proceeds, may indeed lead to the rejection of the entire relationship. Persistent exploration of alternatives is likely to build up a person's "comparison level for alternatives" (Thibaut and Kelley, 1959): The more one samples alternative relations, the more likely one is to find outcomes that appear to exceed those currently obtainable, even if one's present mate is very attractive.

Furthermore, the partner with the wider field of alternatives usually has greater power than the less extended spouse (Waller, 1938). Traditionally, the male partner has had wider latitude than the female, and the female has suffered from a power disadvantage. The woman has stayed home, deepening existing family relationships, while the man is away. Whether as a corporation executive on a trip, a soldier off to the wars, or a cave man searching for better hunting grounds, the husband traditionally has extended his opportunity to compare alternatives without a parallel extension of the wife's opportunities.

## REFERENCES

Bane, M. J. 1979. Marital disruption and the lives of children. In G. Levinger and O. C. Moles (eds.). *Divorce and separation: Context, causes, and consequences*. New York: Basic Books.

Cutright, P. 1971. Income and family events. Marital stability. *Journal of Marriage and the Family, 33*, 291–306.

Festinger, L., Schachter, S., and Back, K. 1950. *Social pressures in informal groups*. New York: Harper.

Foa, U. G. 1971. Interpersonal and economic resources. *Science, 171*, 345–351.

Goode, W. J. 1956. *After divorce*. Chicago: Free Press.

———. 1961. Family disorganization. In R. K. Merton and R. A. Nisbet (Eds.). *Contemporary social problems*. New York: Harcourt, Brace.

Hill, C. T., Rubin, Z., and Peplau, L. A. 1979. Breakups before marriage: The end of 103 affairs. In G. Levinger and O. C. Moles (Eds.). *Divorce and separation: Context, causes, and consequences*. New York: Basic Books.

———. 1965. Marital cohesiveness and disintegration: An integrative review. *Journal of Marriage and the Family, 27*, 19–28.

———. 1974. A three-level approach to attraction: Toward an understanding of pair relatedness. In T. L. Huston (ed.). *Foundations of interpersonal attraction*. New York: Academic Press.

Levinger, G., and Snoek, J. D. 1972. *Attraction in relationship: A new look at interpersonal attraction*. Morristown, N.J.: General Learning Press.

Lewin, K. 1951. *Field theory in social science*. New York: Harper.

McCall, G. J., and Simmons, J. L. 1966. *Identities and interactions*. New York: Free Press.

Norton, A. J., and Glick, P. C. 1979. Marital instability in America: Past, present, and future. In G. Levinger and O. C. Moles (Eds.). *Divorce and separation: Context, causes, and consequences*. New York: Basic Books.

Thibaut, J. W., and Kelley, H. H. 1959. *The social psychology of groups*. New York: Wiley.

Waller, W. 1938. *The family: A dynamic interpretation*. New York: Dryden.

Weiss, R. S. 1975. *Marital separation*. New York: Basic Books.

# 24

LENORE J. WEITZMAN

# Child Support: The National Disgrace

*In 1970, California passed the first no-fault divorce law in the United States, and since then all of the other states have made provisions for some kind of no-fault divorce. Social scientists, members of the legal and judicial systems, and feminists all shared an optimistic view of this sweeping reform. In California, no-fault became the only grounds for divorce. No longer could couples engage in a mudslinging, vindictive process that could turn even mutually agreed-upon uncouplings into vicious battles. Divorce settlements were no longer decided on the basis of who was more at fault. Courts no longer sought to punish offenders and reward victims. Husbands and wives were now to be treated "equally" in settlements, and decisions were made on the basis of fairness.*

*Lenore Weitzman spent ten years researching the consequences of no-fault divorce in California to find out if the new law had indeed fairly treated all parties. Her intensive investigation used a variety of data sources, including a systematic sample of 2,500 court dockets covering a ten year period, some before and some after the enactment of the new divorce law. She also did intensive interviews with California family law judges, attorneys, English legal experts, and divorced men and women. The interviews with judges, lawyers, and divorced persons used a series of hypothetical divorce cases. Some of the most interesting findings in the study are from the predicted outcomes judges and lawyers were asked to make for these cases. One is summarized in the reading that follows.*

*Weitzman's findings clearly show that, while men and women are being treated equally in a formal sense, the consequences for each group are very unequal. For instance, she found that divorced women and their children suffered an average 73 percent drop in their standard of living while the ex-husbands on the average experienced a 42 percent rise in theirs. She found that the only significant asset for most couples is their family home, and thus dividing the property equally means that the home must be sold. In such cases, the children lose not only their intact family, but also their home and their neighborhood. They often change schools, and that too disrupts friendships. Weitzman found young mothers and older housewives to be specially hurt by the new law. In the following selection, she deals with the effects of levels of child support on young divorced mothers.*

Source: Edited with permission of The Free Press, a division of Macmillan, Inc. from *The Divorce Revolution: The Unexpected Social and Economic Consequences for Women and Children in America* by Dr. Lenore J. Weitzman. Copyright © 1985 by Dr. Lenore J. Weitzman.

---

Despite court orders, noncustodial fathers fail to pay $4 billion in child support each year. More than half (53 percent) of the millions of women who are due child support do not receive the court-ordered support.[1] Child support awards that go unpaid and unenforced make a mockery of the judicial system and the value of court orders. They also leave millions of children without the basic necessities of life. If the present system of unenforced child support were to continue unabated, half a generation of American children would suffer years of financial deprivation.

In 1984 Congress unanimously approved legislation to strengthen child support collection through mandatory income withholding and the interception of federal and state tax refund checks to cover past-due support. Margaret Heckler, Secretary of the U.S. Department of Health and Human Services, who lobbied for the congressional action, decried the national disgrace of billions of unpaid dollars owed America's children:

> I . . . feel very strongly the destitution, the desperation, and the simple human suffering of women and children who were not receiving child support payments legally owed them. Frankly it offends my conscience because I believe that a parent's first responsibility is to reasonably provide for the upbringing and welfare of his or her children. To deny that responsibility is a cowardly act.[2]
>
> Fifteen million children live in homes without their fathers. Only 35 percent of these households receive child support and nearly one-third live in poverty. Children deserve to be supported by both their parents. For the sake of America's children, we must put an end to what has become a national disgrace. Our new federal legislation will help states obtain child support orders quickly and pursue them vigorously.[3]

Witnesses at the congressional hearing echoed the Secretary's charges and testified that the "epidemic of nonsupport" had spread to middle- and upper-class fathers.[4] Willful disregard of court orders, a pattern that people assumed was limited to lower-income men, was now common among fathers of all social classes because, it was asserted, judges failed to enforce the law:

> Confronted with overcrowded dockets, judges continue to exhibit a great reluctance to strictly enforce the existing laws. Instead, child support cases are often subjected to broad and inconsistent interpretation, making a mockery of our judicial system. The most pathetic aspect of this entire tragedy is that parents are unnecessarily subjecting their own children to substandard levels of living.
>
> Both the non-paying parents, [and] the legislative and judicial branches [of government] are at fault in this miscarriage of justice.[5]

Key figures in the congressional debates pointed to fathers' flagrant violation of the law: Tennessee Representative Harold Ford bemoaned the ease with which parents were able to escape their legal and moral responsibilities, cheating children out of $4 billion a year.[6] Colorado Representative Patricia Schroeder said it would be a national scandal if you could buy a car, drive it to another state, and not pay for it, but that was what we had allowed nonsupporting fathers to do.[7] She spoke of the tragedy that resulted from the law's tolerance of parents more conscientious about their car payments than their child support.

Noting that single-parent families on public assistance cost the taxpayers $20–$30 billion a year, President Ronald Reagan stressed the need to put the responsibility for support back on the absent fathers:

> The American people willingly extend help to children in need, including those whose parents are failing to meet their responsibilities. However, it is our obligation to make every effort to place the financial responsibility where it rightly belongs—on the parent who has been legally ordered to support his child.[8]

Secretary Heckler stressed the human costs and hardships when child support checks never come:

> Almost eight million single parents share the frustration, and often real hardship, that can result from the failure of absent parents to meet their child support obligation. The disappointment and bitterness which grows out of these situations may add emotional burdens to the financial load these children and their custodial parents frequently face. What may appear to be just a dollars and cents issue has much more far reaching implications for them.
>
> The scope of this problem has grown to the point where it affects not just these children and those who care for them, but society as a whole.[9]

Those who lobbied for the 1984 legislation promised that it would curb the scandalous behavior of wayward parents: Representative Marge Roukema of New Jersey said the landmark bill put the federal government on record that "child support would no longer be treated as a voluntary commitment," and

Margaret Heckler promised "fast track" implementation of the new regulations.[10]

Why do many divorced men feel free to disregard the law and not pay child support? Are they ordered to pay excessive amounts of child support? Or is there something wrong with the system of enforcement? We now turn to these issues.

## THE AMOUNT OF CHILD SUPPORT AWARDED

A useful way of examining child support awards is to think about a hypothetical family and see how the courts would apportion its post-divorce income. One of our hypothetical cases, that of Pat and Ted Byrd, involved the question of child support for their two children, a four-year-old daughter and a six-year-old son. After a seven-year marriage, twenty-seven-year-old Ted Byrd, an accountant, has a net monthly income of $1,000 (after taxes). Pat Byrd has been a housewife and mother throughout the marriage and has no outside income.

In response to the hypothetical Byrd case, the Los Angeles judges proposed a median child support award of $250 for the two children. The attorney's predictions were similar, averaging $271 a month for the two.*

These predictions are somewhat higher than the average child support awards in the sample of court dockets because the hypothetical Ted Byrd's income is above the average income for divorced men. In the 1977 Los Angeles court docket sample, the mean child support order was $126 per month per child. The average child support award in families with two children averaged slightly less per child, presumably due to economies of scale. It was $195 per month per family, or a total of $2,340 a year. (That is about $4,050 a year in 1984 dollars for the support of two children.)

Although these child support awards may seem low, they are comparable with—if not slightly higher than—the national average reported by the U.S. Census Bureau. According to a 1978 census survey, divorced fathers paid an average of $1,951 per year.[11] In 1981 they paid an average of $2,220 per year.[12] These statistics are for the amounts of child support received, because the Census did not report data on the amount of child support awarded to *divorced* women (as distinct from *all* women due child support.)

We do know, however, that the amount of child support actually received by divorced women is invariably less than the amount the court orders. The Census Bureau reports on the difference between the two for all women who were supposed to receive child support in 1981: the mean amount of support ordered was $2,460, but the mean amount paid, including those who received nothing, was $1,510.[13] (These amounts are lower than those for divorced women because they include awards to never-married women for whom compliance is even lower.)

---

*The attorneys' predictions for total support awards were not consistently higher than the judges'. For example, the median alimony award in this case was $200 a month among judges and $150 a month among attorneys.

Among divorced women, black women fared worst in terms of both child support orders and payments. Child support was awarded by the court to 69 percent of the white women, 44 percent of the Hispanic women, and only 34 percent of the black women in 1981. The level of support payments showed the same pattern: the white mother received $2,180; the Hispanic mother, $2,068; and the black mother, $1,640.[14]

When the Census Bureau compared the 1981 child support payments to those in 1978, it found that child support payments actually decreased by about 16 percent in real dollars between 1978 and 1981.*

Another way of looking at the typical child support award is as a percentage of the husband's income. In Ted Byrd's case, $250 out of a new monthly income of $1,000 is 25 percent of his take-home pay for child support. That was about the average percentage in Los Angeles, but was slightly below the average in San Francisco, where child support averaged about one-third of the husband's net income. In national data, child support averaged 13 percent of average male income in both 1978 and 1981.[16]

The percentage of a husband's income awarded in child support varies by the husband's income level, with lower-income men typically being required to pay a greater proportion of their incomes in child support. (However, there is a large amount of variation in data based on different samples.) In the random sample of 1977 court dockets, men who earned less than $10,000 a year were, on average, ordered to pay 20 percent of their gross incomes in child support. The percentage dropped to 10 percent of gross income among men earning $30,000 or more. Along the same lines, Professor Judith Cassetty found regressive child support awards in Michigan data in 1975: men who had gross incomes of over $15,000 contributed, on average, only 11 percent of their incomes to child support.[17]

The same inverse relationship is evident among the divorced husbands in our interview sample. Table 1, which uses net income, shows an even larger disparity between low- and high-income men in the percentages of income ordered for child support. On average, men with net incomes of under $10,000 were ordered to pay 37 percent of their net income in child support, while those with net incomes of $50,000 or more were ordered to pay only 5 percent.

One reason for this difference is that higher-income men are more likely to pay alimony as well as child support, so that the child support figures do not necessarily reflect the full extent of the men's support contributions. Thus if we look at the last column of Table 1, which shows the total amount of support (child support plus alimony—or one or the other), there is less difference between high- and low-income husbands.

One important finding in Table 1 is that no matter what his income level, a divorced man is rarely ordered to part with more than *one-third* of his net income. This one-third limit is surprising because the judges and the attorneys

*However, child support payments as a percentage of average male income remained fairly constant over the years (at 13 percent), since the real income of males declined during this period as well. Average male income was $13,110 in 1978 and $16,520 in 1981.[15]

**TABLE 1** ***Child Support and Alimony Awarded as a Percentage of Husband's Postdivorce Net Income***

| | *Percentage of husband's net income awarded for support* | | |
|---|---|---|---|
| *Husband's net income* | *Child support ordered* | *Alimony ordered* | *Total ordered (either or both)* |
| Under $10,000 | 37% | — | 37% |
| $10–19,999 | 25 | 13% | 25 |
| $20–29,999 | 25 | 30 | 32 |
| $30–49,999 | 10 | 24 | 30 |
| $50,000 or more | 5 | 20 | 19 |

This table is based on weighted sample of interviews with divorced persons, Los Angeles County, 1978.

we interviewed often referred to a *one-half* limit: they said there was an informal rule that judges should never require a man to pay more than one-half of his net income in support. In light of these frequent references to an award limit of 50 percent of the payor's income, we were surprised to find a much lower one-third "ceiling" operating in practice.*

In explaining the awards they set, the California judges stress the need to protect the father's ability to pay by not making the award too burdensome for him. They want to leave him with "enough" money to maintain his motivation to earn, and this means setting aside "enough" income for him. While the judges may not be aware of the extent to which they are allocating income to the father at the expense of his children, they are aware of and clearly express their priority for taking care of his needs first. As one judge said, "you can't touch the goose that lays the golden egg."

This "father first" principle stands out in contrast to the "child first" principle subscribed to by the English judges. The English perspective first considers the children's needs and sets aside enough family income to take care of them. It then allocates the rest of the income to the adults. In California, the procedure is the reverse: the children (and their caretakers) get what is left after money is set aside to meet the father's needs. While the California judges justify their *modus operandi* by saying they need to protect the father's motivation to earn, the bottom line is that he comes first, and his "right" to build a new life comes first, even if his new life is built at the expense of his children and former wife.

The data on the California awards are surprising in another respect: the amounts of support that were awarded were lower than the amounts suggested

*While most of the Los Angeles judges said they were aware of the informal 50-percent rule, only one-third said they themselves follwed it. The other two-thirds said they would award *more* than half of the husband's net income (in combined alimony and child support) where appropriate. This suggests an even larger discrepancy between what judges say they do and what they actually do.

in the judicial guidelines.[18] These guidelines, or schedules as they are typically called, suggest appropriate amounts of support by family income level. While they are intended as a rough norm for temporary orders, close to 60 percent of the judges we interviewed said they consistently relied on them.

Schedules that set uniform award levels have become increasingly popular in recent years, and the 1984 federal child support legislation requires the drafting of optional guidelines throughout the United States. The attorneys we interviewed were generally in favor of such guidelines because they provide predictability and consistency of results, minimize court time necessary to set support awards, facilitate client acceptance of attorney recommendations, and assure that at least minimum standards for support are met.[19] Those who oppose schedules argue that they tend to become rigid rules rather than guidelines, and thereby deprive each case of its uniqueness and opportunity to be heard.

In light of the impetus of the federal law for more widespread use of guidelines in the future, it is disturbing to find that guidelines seem to have the unanticipated effect of depressing award levels because most awards fall into the lower range of the levels set forth in the guidelines. Why is this so? Perhaps the schedules are being read as establishing upper limits, or ceilings, on award levels. Or perhaps attorneys who use the guidelines in negotiations believe that they can never expect to get awards in the upper range of the schedule so they settle for less.

Whatever the reasons, this finding has important policy implications: since the federal legislation of 1984 requires states to draw up child support guidelines, the drafters of these guidelines should be aware that the schedules tend to depress award levels. If a schedule encourages most couples to "settle" for support in the lower and middle ranges specified, drafters might consider setting higher ranges, or using schedules based on a fixed percentage of the payor's gross income, as is done in the schedule used in the state of Wisconsin.[20]

The limited data from other states suggests that the amount of child support and alimony awarded in California is roughly comparable to support awards in other states. For example, a 1983 study of the New Jersey courts concluded that there appears to be an unofficial standard that a total support award will be for "no more than 30 percent of the husband's net pay even when there are small children in the custody of the wife."[21] Researchers in the state of Michigan[22] and in Alberta Province, Canada, have also reported a *de facto* norm whereby no more than one-third of the husband's income is awarded to the wife and children.[23] In Cleveland, Ohio, researchers found that divorced fathers typically retained about 80 percent of their predivorce income.[24]

## THE ADEQUACY OF CHILD SUPPORT AWARDS

Three standards can be used to evaluate the adequacy of child support awards. The first compares awards with the actual costs of raising children and asks if the awards are enough to cover the costs of raising children. The second assesses the reasonableness of the award in terms of the payor's financial resources: Does the father—over 95 percent of those ordered to pay are fathers—have the ability to pay the award? Both of these standards are embodied in the California law, which specifies that support be set in accordance with *needs* and *ability to pay*.[25]

Recent policy discussions of the standards for child support have referred to the first standard as the "cost approach" and the second as the "income sharing approach," terms that were first suggested by University of Maryland economist Barbara Bergmann.[26] The two approaches reflect the fundamental dilemma that all courts (and policy makers) must resolve in establishing standards for child support. The cost approach assumes that there is a basic cost for raising a child that is appropriate for all families. The income sharing approach is more realistic: it assumes that the cost of raising a child depends on the income level of his or her parents.

The two approaches not only produce different numerical results, they also represent different public policy goals. The cost approach, which establishes uniform costs for all families, typically results in lower amounts and assumes a welfare-like basic-needs approach to raising children. As Judith Cassetty, a pioneer in child support research, notes, the income sharing approach, in contrast, results in higher amounts (in middle- and upper-income families) because it is based on "the belief that children should benefit proportionately from the resources of each parent: this means that children would not inevitably suffer a decline in their standard of living in the event of a parental divorce.[27]

A third standard for evaluating child support is to ask if the awards fairly apportion the responsibility between the father and the mother. Here we can compare the financial contributions of the two parents in absolute terms (i.e., the amounts of money they contribute) and relative terms (what percentage of their respective incomes each contributes).

### The Cost of Raising Children[28]

Many different methods have been used to estimate the cost of raising children. Almost all of them involve conservative calculations and produce low estimates. The following analysis relies on one of the most conservative estimates, that of economist Thomas Espenshade. Espenshade estimates that it would cost $85,163 to raise a child to age eighteen in a moderate-income family in 1980. In a low-income family in the United States it would cost $58,238.[29] His calculations include all direct maintenance costs: out-of-pocket expenditures for the child's birth, food, clothing, housing, transportation, medical care, education, and other expenses. A final component included in Espenshade's calculations is the cost of a four-year college education.

*Parents* magazine used a similar procedure, but included an adjustment for yearly inflation and estimated that the cost of raising a child born in 1980, would run to over $175,000.[30]

Before we proceed with this analysis, it is important to note just how conservative Espenshade's estimates are. First, they do not include any costs for child care *services*. Rather, he assumes that someone is "available" to take care of the children—and that someone is there *cost-free*. Obviously, if one has to pay for child care or day care, the cost of children will be much greater.

Second, a brief look at the costs of individual items suggests that Espenshade's estimates are unrealistically low. Consider, for example, his estimates for the cost of a college education. (We have omitted these costs in our calculations below because they may extend beyond age eighteen). Espenshade calculates that *four years* of college will cost a total of $10,000 .[31] This is only $2,500 per year, or $278 per month (for a nine-month academic year). It is difficult to find a public university in the United States today at which the cost of tuition, books, room, board and other living expenses are so low. Private colleges may cost between $10,000 and $15,000 or more each year, with the total cost of four years running more than $40,000. Espenshade's clothing, food, and laundry estimates are likewise unrealistic.

Bearing in mind that these estimates are very low to begin with, let us now look at how they compare with child support awards.

If we use Espenshade's total budget for a moderate-income family ($85,163), and subtract $10,000 cost of college (since college costs may not be included in child support once the child reaches age 18), we find that it averages $4,200 a year to raise one child at a moderate income level. Because of economies of scale, Espenshade calculates that a second child increases the costs by roughly half as much as the cost of the first child, so that the total child-rearing cost for two minor children would be about $6,300 a year. Similarly, for low income standard of living, we find the cost close to $3,000 a year for one child ($2,680 to be precise), and over $4,000 for two children.*

Let us assume that our hypothetical Pat Byrd was raising her children at the "moderate" standard of living. We find that her court-ordered child support award of $250 a month (or $3,000 a year) would give her *$3,300 less* a year than the cost of raising her two children. Even at the lower standard, her court-ordered support is inadequate—$1,020 less than she needs to raise her children at the poverty level.

The inadequacy of court-ordered child support is underscored by another relevant comparison. Pat Byrd's *total* support award—$450 a month for alimony and child support together—is not even as much as she would get from the Aid to Families with Dependent Children (AFDC) program. The California AFDC level of support for a household with two children was $463 per month plus $73 in food stamps, or a total of $536 per month.[32] If this is the amount that the government established as necessary for families at the lowest economic levels, it is evident that Pat Byrd and her children will not be able to live above the poverty level on the child support she was awarded.†

Further, as we have noted, one problem with Espenshade's calculations is that they omit child care expenses, a major cost that Pat Byrd will have to bear.

---

*Since these costs vary between urban and rural areas, and by region, regional consumer price indexes for food, clothing, and housing are available

†New legislation, which was influenced by an earlier report of the findings of this research, established a minimum for child support awards in California as of July 1985.[33]

Since Espenshade's calculations are based on two-parent families, he assumes that one parent, typically the mother, is available full time to care for the child. But if the mother in a single-parent family has to work,[34] she typically must pay someone else to take care of her children. And, as sociologist Karen Seal noted, the cost of child care alone typically exceeds the child support award.[35]

In order to determine adequate child support for such single-parent families, these child care costs should be added to Espenshade's estimates.

A 1980 report of the California Advisory Commission on Child Care compiled the average cost of child care in various California communities at that time.[36] In Los Angeles County, the monthly cost for a preschool child averaged $205 in family day care and $195 in a day-care center for an average of $2,400 a year. If Pat Byrd's daughter was under two years of age, instead of four years old, day care for her would cost another $600 a year. If Pat Byrd works a full day, she will also have to pay for after-school care for her six-year-old son. That will cost her an additional $160 a month in family day care, or $116 a month in an after-school center, for an average of $1,600 a year.

Thus if we assume that Pat Byrd will work full time, her child care costs would be about $200 a month for her daughter ($2,400 ÷ 12) and $133 a month for her son ($1,600 ÷ 12). That adds up to $333 a month—considerably more than her entire child support award of $250 a month. (The child care costs are close to $4,000 a year in contrast to her entire child support award of $3,000 a year.) Of course, if she is lucky enough to get the children into a public day-care center with a sliding fee scale, her costs may be lower, but that typically entails a long waiting list and places her under pressure to go to work immediately.

Quite clearly, child support awards are not adequate to meet the cost of raising children. They fall short of every standard we have used: they are less than the average cost of day care alone, which would leave no child support money for food, or clothing, or housing.

These data suggest the importance of educating those who are setting child support awards about the actual costs of raising children. It is not surprising to find that judges and lawyers underestimate these costs[37] because parents themselves do not realize how much they are spending on their children. In fact, in one study, middle-class parents estimated that they were spending 14 percent of their incomes on their children when they were actually spending 40 percent.[38]

**The Father's Ability to Pay: The Income Sharing Approach**

The second and the preferable approach to establishing a child support award is the income sharing approach. Here the focus is on the family's resources and the father's ability to pay child support.

One frequently hears the complaint that divorced men cannot afford to pay the amount of child support the court has ordered. For example, the president of Fathers' Rights of America portrays the typical divorced man as a conscientious father who is forced to live at the poverty level because he is paying exorbitant child support.[39] Is this claim true? Are most divorced men unable to "afford" the child support award? How do child support awards compare with the fathers' incomes?

There are two standards for evaluating a father's ability to comply with the court order: one examines child support as a percentage of the husband's income; the second evaluates it in relation to standard of living.

Consider first what percentage of the father's income is awarded to child support. If we look back at the far right column of Table 1, we see that it is very rare for any court to order more than 25 percent of a man's income in child support or more than 32 percent of a man's income in combined child support and alimony.* Even though judges *report* that their typical award is closer to one-half of the husband's income, the data from the interviews with divorced persons show that the real proportion is quite different. Instead of a 50/50 division of the husband's income, the typical award is one-third for the wife and two children to two-thirds for the husband. Among upper-income men it is one-fifth to four-fifths: men who earn $50,000 or more a year retain an average of 81 percent of their net incomes for themselves (see Table 1).

The implications of awarding one-third of the family income to the wife and children and leaving two-thirds for the father are immediately apparent when we look at the distribution of family income graphically, as shown in Figure 1.

What happens if men fully comply with the court order: would they have enough left to live on? In a classic study of child support, Michigan law Professor David Chambers found that most fathers would be relatively well off.[40] In fact, 80 percent of the men would live at or above the government's "intermediate" standard budget level if they paid the support the court ordered. Using similar procedures to construct an index of ability to pay, Canadian researchers concluded that 80 percent of the divorced fathers could afford to pay child support and still live comfortably.[41]

**FIGURE 1** *Division of Family Income after Divorce*

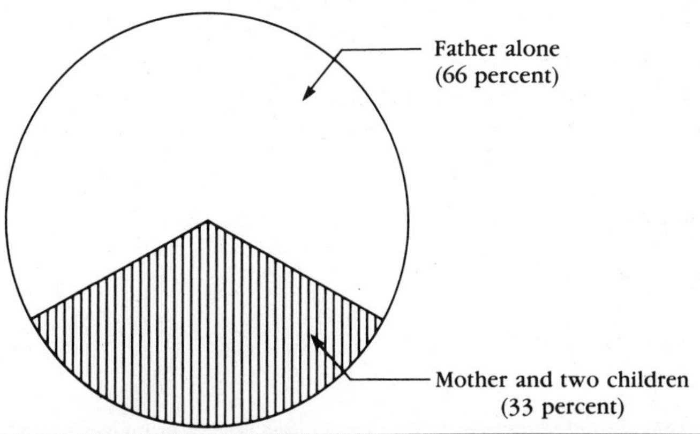


Source: Lenore J. Weitzman, *The Divorce Revolution: The Unexpected Social and Economic Consequences for Women and Children in America*, figure 1, p. 273. New York: Basic Books. © 1985 by the author. Reprinted by permission.

*Men whose net incomes are under $10,000 are the only exceptions—their support awards average 37 percent of their incomes.

Our analysis of the California data also follows Chambers' procedures. The starting point for these computations is the U.S. Department of Labor's standards for a high, intermediate, and lower level budget for an urban family of four for autumn 1977.[42] The basic budgets were devised for a typical family of two adults and two children. (For example, the lower level budget for a family of four was $10,481.) A separate procedure adjusts this budget to other types and sizes of families (depending on family size, age of oldest child, and age of household head).[43] A family of only two persons, for example, with a thirty-five-year old head of the household, would need only 60 percent of the money a family of four would need at a lower level budget. In analyzing the California data,* we found that 73 percent of the divorced men were able to live at or above the lower standard budget. Thus, close to *three-quarters of the California fathers had the "ability to pay" the amount the court ordered without a substantial reduction in their standard of living*. Figure 2 shows that 61 percent of the California fathers would be able to comply fully with the court order and still live above the high standard budget. An additional 12 percent would be living above the lower standard budget. Thus 73 percent of the men could live at a level above the lower standard budget.

Next, Chambers asked what would happen to the men's ex-wives and dependent children if the fathers paid the full amount of child support ordered. Obviously, if the family income stays constant, both the husband and wife cannot maintain the standard of living of the former intact family if they are living in two separate households. In Michigan, Chambers found that 97 percent of the divorced women and children would be living below the poverty line—that is, below the lower standard budget.[44] Similarly, in California, 93 percent of all divorced women would be living below the lower standard budget.

Figure 2 shows the standard of living of California women and children if they had to live on the child support the court ordered. In contrast to the 73 percent of the men who could live comfortably, only 7 percent of the women and children would be living at the same level—even if the support were paid in full. *Almost all of the women and children—fully 93 percent—would be living below the poverty level.*

One of Chambers' conclusions, which is equally applicable to our data, is that "under the levels of child support that are ordered by the court . . . *it is only the women and children whose standards of living decline*, even when the father is making payments."[45] Why does this happen? As Chambers explains:

> . . . a mother with two children needs between 75 and 80 percent of the family's former total income to continue to live at the prior standard. The father will have been ordered by the court to pay around 33 percent of his income. There

---

*Using this procedure, a higher, intermediate, and lower budget was computed for *each* postdivorce family in our interview sample. For each predivorce family, there were two postdivorce families (the husband's and wife's). Postdivorce families were defined as a divorced person, a new spouse or cohabitee (where applicable), and any children whose custody was assigned to that spouse. The actual income of each postdivorce family was then compared with the three standard budgets and ranked according to the level of need.

**FIGURE 2** *Standards of Living if Husband Pays Support**

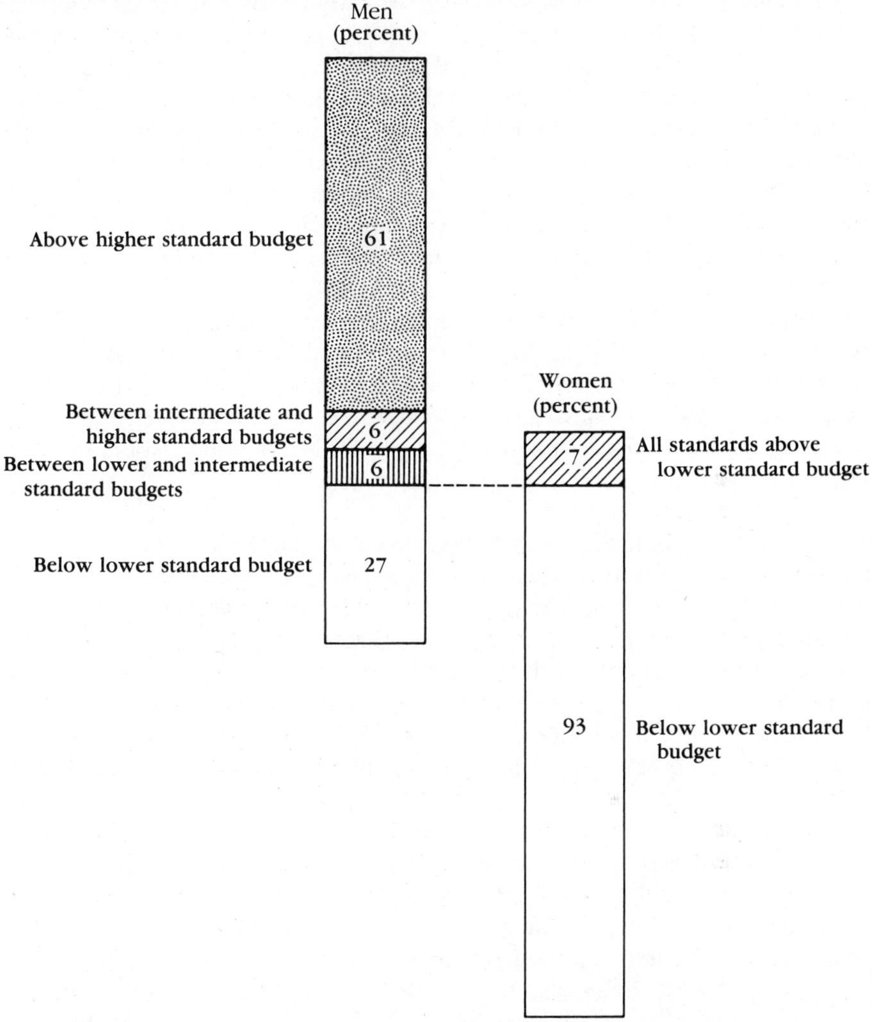

*Income standards of divorced men and women if men pay all support ordered and women live on support.

Based on weighted sample of interviews with divorced persons, Los Angeles County, California. 1978.

Source: Lenore J. Weitzman, *The Divorce Revolution: The Unexpected Social and Economic Consequences for Women and Children in America*, figure 2, p. 275. New York: Basic Books © 1985 by the author. Reprinted by permission.

> remains a painful gap. On the other hand, the father who pays child support and retains two-thirds of his income still remains better off financially than he was before divorce. Four in five fathers can live at or above the Intermediate Standard Budget.[46]

Clearly, women and children cannot live on these awards even if they are paid in full. They must find other financial resources, such as employment or welfare.

The data in this section answer the question of whether men can afford to pay the amounts of child support ordered by the courts with an unequivocal yes. Whether one considers the percentage of the supporter's income or the standard of living he has after paying, the vast majority of divorced fathers can pay child support and still maintain a relatively comfortable standard of living.

Significantly, both divorced men and divorced women agree with this conclusion. When asked, "Can you (or your ex-husband) afford to pay the child support the court ordered?" fully 80 percent of the women and 90 percent of the men say yes. Thus both men and women see the award as reasonable in terms of the husband's ability to pay. Only a small minority feel the awards are excessive.

Along the same lines, when asked about their satisfaction with the amount of child support awarded in their case, the vast majority (91 percent) of *divorced men see the awards as reasonable* in terms of their income. Only 9 percent of the men say they were dissatisfied. (As might be expected, a larger percentage of the *women*, 36 percent, are dissatisfied with the amount of child support awarded and see it as inadequate.)

**The Standard of Equitable Contributions from Husband and Wife**

The final standard for evaluating the adequacy of child support awards is whether they equitably apportion the burden between the two parents. One way of apportioning the financial responsibility for child support would be to ask each parent to contribute half of the child's expenses. Another way would be to ask each parent to contribute according to his or her ability to pay. The latter standard, which is codified in the California law, aims at placing a lesser burden on the spouse with the lower earning capacity, who is typically the wife.

How do the child support awards fare when measured against the first standard, a 50/50 division of expenses? Earlier, in the discussion of the Pat Byrd case, we compared the amount of child support the father would typically be ordered to pay ($3,000 per year) with Espenshade's estimates of the actual cost of raising two children at a moderate income level ($6,300). Setting aside our criticism of Espenshade's cost estimates as too low, we might at first conclude that the child support awards provide close to half of his low estimate. But this is so only if we ignore the wife's contribution of time and child care services which Espenshade conveniently assumes are "free." But there are foregone costs when a mother spends time caring for her children. She is relinquishing wages that she could earn at a paid job and she is avoiding the cost of paying someone else to care for her children.

How much are these forgone costs worth? Even if we use a partial estimate of the cost of child care services, the cost of day care, it would mean that the monetary value of the mother's contribution was *more than twice* as much as the father's (i.e., $4,000 plus $3,300 is $7,300 versus his $3,000 child support award). Once the real cost of the wife's custodial services are recognized, it becomes evident that she is not only bearing more than half of the cost of the children, she is probably contributing the vast majority of it.[47]

Thus, California child support awards typically do not meet the first standard of equity, because the noncustodial father is not required to contribute an equal share of the actual costs of raising his children.

This conclusion is strengthened by an additional fact: the data on noncompliance show that men tend to pay far less than the court has ordered. As a result, the mother is forced to assume an even more disproportionate share of the costs of raising her children after divorce.

The California awards also fall short of the second standard of equity, whereby each parent is expected to contribute according to his or her ability to pay. As we saw earlier, child support is typically set in accordance with the husband's ability to pay while still allowing him to maintain an adequate standard of living. The wife, however, who usually has far less earning capacity, and thus less ability to pay, typically ends up shouldering a disproportionately larger share of the cost of child support. Thus, rather than finding that child support has been apportioned in accord with the second norm of equity—according to the ability of each parent to pay—we find it has been apportioned in *direct contradiction* to that norm, with the heavier burden falling upon the parent who can *least* afford to pay, the custodial mother. This inevitably results in a drastically reduced standard of living for both the mother and the children.

In summary, the data point to three conclusions. First, the amount of child support ordered is typically quite modest in terms of the father's ability to pay. Secondly, the amount of child support ordered is typically not enough to cover even half the cost of actually raising the children. Third, the major burden of child support is typically placed on the mother even though she normally has fewer resources and much less "ability to pay."

## NONCOMPLIANCE: THE PROBLEM OF ENFORCEMENT

The widespread lack of compliance with court-ordered child and spousal support has been well documented by previous research in the United States and Canada. For example, a 1981 survey conducted by the U.S. Census Bureau revealed that less than half of the women who were awarded child support received it as ordered; about 30 percent of the women received partial payments, while another quarter never received a single dollar. Similarly, a 1980 survey of maintenance orders in Alberta, Canada, revealed that only a third of the women received the full amount of the court-ordered support.[49] Another third received less than the full amount, while the final third received nothing.

Our California data *under*estimate the extent of noncompliance because both the docket sample and the interviews were limited to events within the *first year* after the divorce. The 1977 court records that we examined contained complaints from 15 percent of the Los Angeles wives who went back to court to complain of noncompliance within twelve months of following their final decree of divorce.[50] The interview data, however, suggest that this figure greatly underestimates the extent of nonpayment, underpayment, and irregular payment. Many wives reported that they did not file a formal complaint about their husband's noncompliance because they lacked the time, knowledge, or monetary resources to do so. In fact, only about *one-third* of our female interviewees reported that they regularly received the full amount of court-ordered child support in the first year of the court order.* A hefty 43 percent of the women reported receiving little or no child support during that first year. The remaining 22 percent reported having problems either in obtaining the full amount of the order, or in obtaining it on time.

Further, since these interviews were conducted just one year after the divorce became final, it is reasonable to assume that for many of those women noncompliance would become an even greater problem in later years.

There are three consistent findings reported in the research on compliance with child support orders.[51] First, not one study has found a state or county in which even half of the fathers fully comply with court orders.[52] Second, the research suggests that many of the fathers who are ordered to pay support pay it irregularly and are often in arrears. In several studies, the average arrearage is for half or three-quarters of the money owed, and in one study the average reached 89 percent.[53] (While some contribution is certainly preferable to total noncompliance, irregular or infrequent child support payments can create serious hardships for the dependent mother and children.) Third, the research indicates that a very sizable minority of fathers—typically between a quarter and a third—never make a single court-ordered payment.

The problem of noncompliance is particularly serious because child support can make the difference between poverty and nonpoverty for many families. Women who are near the poverty line and receive child support can easily fall below that line if the payments are eliminated. In fact, one U.S. Census Bureau study showed that about a third of the divorced and separated women who did not receive child support fell below the poverty line, compared to only 12 percent of the women who received such support.[54]

Child support payments are also a major determinant of whether or not a woman applies for public assistance. In a 1978 census sample, 38 percent of women who were not receiving child support from the father of their children received public assistance income, compared to only 13 percent of women who had child support income.[55]

The lack of compliance not only causes great economic hardship, it also undermines confidence in the law and in the force of court orders. Our California interviews were replete with complaints about the court's failure to enforce its support orders, the negative or hostile responses of the court officials to requests from nonsupported mothers, and the resulting frustration and disillusionment that women experience when they confront the apparent ease with which a violation of the law is tolerated. As one woman said:

> The whole judicial process is a fraud. You have to hire an expensive lawyer and prepare all these documents for the judge . . . and in the end, all you get is an

---

*Compliance with alimony orders appeared to be somewhat better, probably because alimony tends to be awarded only in higher-income families. Nevertheless, as noted in Chapters 6 and 7, one out of six men was in arrears on spousal support within just six months of the divorce.

order that isn't worth the piece of paper it's written on. It's a sham—a charade! I can't believe our whole system of so-called justice is such a fraud.

Testimony at the 1984 congressional hearings on child support echoed these sentiments. Women throughout the United States testified to their frustration with a legal system that often seems to aid and abet nonsupporting fathers. As one divorced mother said:

> My own children, like thousands of others, have been denied their economic birthright by a father who swore he would never pay a dime in child support, and by courts that have failed to enforce their own orders. The truth is that if a father chooses to be uncooperative, there is little a mother can do.[56]

> I went to court five times between 1972 and 1979, traveling to a distant state and paying attorney fees. The last trip in 1979 cost me $1,300. That court in Media, Pennsylvania, raised the support and required that my former husband pay all medical bills plus almost $2,000 in arrears in a lump sum. When my former husband didn't obey that order, I was told to come back into court—again at my own expense—and sue him for contempt of court. I was told that, even if I did this, I had no guarantee that he would be made to pay. I decided that I couldn't afford to collect my support.[57]

## WHY DON'T FATHERS PAY?

How can we explain the high rate of noncompliance with support orders? One widespread belief is that fathers simply cannot afford to pay child support and alimony ordered by the court. However, Chambers' data from Michigan and our data from California indicate that most divorced fathers could comply with the court orders and still live quite well after doing so. Every study of men's ability to pay arrives at the same conclusion: the money is there. Indeed, there is normally enough to permit payment of significantly *higher* awards than are currently being made.

The suggestion that men cannot afford to pay child support is refuted by a second set of data. If lack of ability to pay were the cause of noncompliance, we would expect the highest rates of noncompliance among men with the lowest incomes. But the California data in Table 2 show little relationship between income and noncompliance (for all men earning less than $50,000 a year). Men with incomes of between $30,000 and $50,000 a year are just as likely to avoid child support payments as are men with incomes of under $10,000 a year.

The Canadian study of support orders found a weak positive relationship between income and compliance, although excellent payers and nonpayers had similar mean incomes.[58] (In that study low income was associated with irregular payment but not with nonpayment.) The Canadian researchers concluded that 80 percent of the fathers could afford to pay.

The one category of men that one might at first assume do not have the ability to pay are those who are unemployed. However, here too compliance is

**TABLE 2** ***Compliance with Child-Support Orders by Father's Postdivorce Gross Income***

| *Father's yearly income* | *Percentage irregular or no payments* |
|---|---|
| Under $10,000 | 27% |
| $10,000–20,000 | 27 |
| $20,000–30,000 | 22 |
| $30,000–50,000 | 29 |
| $50,000 or more | 8 |

This table is based on the combined responses of male and female respondents in the weighted sample of divorced persons. Los Angeles County, 1978.

not related to lowered income. For example, one woman reported that her husband's child support payment record improved when "he went on unemployment because they gave him an allowance for child support so he gave it to me . . . first time he paid steady since the divorce." But another woman with an unemployed husband complained:

> Just because he doesn't have a job doesn't mean his kids can stop eating. When we were married he was out of work sometimes and we managed . . . on the benefits . . . in fact I know he is collecting extra because he has kids, but I never see the money.

Since child support awards are based on the husband's ability to pay, they are adjusted for reduced income and unemployment. Thus even men who are unemployed have the ability to pay what the court orders.

Three other explanations have been offered for why men do not pay: they consider the law unreasonable, they are retaliating for visitation problems, or they are responding to ineffective enforcement. Let us briefly consider the evidence.

The assertion that fathers do not pay child support because they consider the law unreasonable is strongly contradicted by the data. The overwhelming majority of divorced men we interviewed feel that they are responsible for the support of their children. They do not consider the law unfair or unjust. Rather there is a strong moral consensus that "men should support their children." (See also the public opinion data discussed below.) In fact, because the law seems to have widespread moral legitimacy, men who do not pay child support need to rationalize their nonpayment by offering excuses or justification for nonpayment. They think all men, and they themselves, *should* pay child support.

The moral consensus about men's responsibility for their children helps us to evaluate the second reason offered for nonpayment—a response to visitation problems. Here again the empirical data directly contradict the assertion: there is no correlation between compliance and complaints about visitation. That means that men with no visitation problems are just as likely not to pay child support as they are likely to pay. It also means that men who comply with child support awards are just as likely as those who do not comply to say they have some visitation problems. Canadian researchers similarly report the lack of a statistically significant relationship between visitation and compliance.[59]

Clearly some men who do not comply use visitation as an excuse because they need to explain why they are failing to do something which they believe is morally right. As a 1984 editorial in the *Washington Post* put it: "Men claim they have stopped supporting their children because they have been denied visitation rights, but that's an excuse not a justification."[60]

It should be noted that most states explicitly forbid the withholding of child support in retribution for the denial of visitation.[61] Child support belongs to the child. There are separate remedies for the denial of visitation, the most severe being a change in custody.*

There is another datum that suggests that visitation problems are not the cause of noncompliance. A significant portion of women who complained of noncompliance also complained about their ex-husbands *failure* to visit the children. In fact, many of the women we interviewed were as upset about the fathers' lack of parenting (and visitation) as they were about their failure to pay support per se.

The last—and by far the most convincing—explanation for the lack of compliance lies in the absence of—or the failure of judges to use—effective enforcement procedures.

## THE IMPACT OF ECONOMIC CHANGES ON CHILDREN

One of the most persuasive indictments of the system that produces radically different economic circumstances for men and women after divorce lies in the detrimental effects of such economic changes on children in general, and on the mother-child and father-child relationships in particular. While there is a large and growing literature on the effects of divorce on children, it tells us little about how property and support awards directly affect the children of divorce.

The research conducted by Drs. Judith Wallerstein and Joan Kelly provides impressive qualitative evidence on these effects.[63] Wallerstein and Kelly interviewed parents and children in sixty divorcing families in Marin County, California, a relatively affluent community, at three points in time: six months, eighteen months, and five years after separation. While no one would contend that this well-to-do community is typical, the findings of this research are all the more impressive because one might expect the economic impact of divorce to be minimized there.

Wallerstein and Kelly confirm the central role that financial awards play in the lives of men, women, and children after divorce: "virtually every parent in our study was preoccupied with the change in family economics created by the

---

*Joanne Schulman, an attorney at the National Center on Women in Family Law, notes that a common tactic of men who are charged with not paying child support is to counter sue for a change of custody. This puts custodial mothers in the difficult position of having to choose between foregoing child support or fighting a custody challenge.[62]

divorce. . . . [However,] the women in our study were affected by severe economic changes more substantially and more permanently than were the men.[64]

Although a very high percentage of the men in the Wallerstein-Kelly sample paid child support on a more or less regular basis, three-quarters of the women experienced a notable decline in their standard of living. For a third of the women, the economic change was abrupt and severe; few of the women had made any preparation for the drastically diminished economic circumstances they were forced to confront. These changes affect women at every economic level and the stress is no less acute for middle-class women. As Wallerstein and Kelly note:

> While our own sympathies and concern quite naturally tended to be directed more to those whose standard of living moved toward or plummeted below the poverty level, the sudden reduction in available monies was as deeply affecting to women of middle-class means. While such women perhaps worried less about feeding their youngsters adequately or having their car repossessed, the stress of adjusting themselves and their children to living on substantially less money was nonetheless real.[65]

The sharp decline in the mothers' standard of living led to a series of very dramatic changes for their children. It forced the mothers into hectic and exhausting schedules that diminished the time and emotional energy they had available for their children. The extreme pressure to earn money left these mothers with little time for career development, child care, household chores, and a new social life.[66] Children were carried to babysitters early in the morning and picked up on the way home— before or after the rush to do the shopping, prepare dinner, and clean the house. Several mothers, working full time outside the home for the first time in their lives, had to regularly work past midnight to complete their household chores.[67] Thus, the children in these one-parent families not only had less of their fathers; they clearly had less of their mothers as well. As Wallerstein and Kelly describe it:

> Within six months of separation, one-quarter of the mothers interviewed judged themselves to be substantially less available to their children due directly to expanded work schedules and/or new educational demands. One of the ironies of the woman's move toward independence, increased self-esteem, and personal growth was that the children did not always share in the benefits, at least not in the first year. Certainly one of the most pressing dilemmas for the single parent is the difficulty in balancing financial and psychological needs of parent and child in the wake of the separation.[68]

The children of these mothers rarely received compensatory care and attention from other family members: few grandmothers (or other extended-family members) or neighbors were available for assistance. In addition, the fathers typically refused to babysit, even if their schedules would have permitted them to do so. As Wallerstein and Keely note:

> Rather than welcoming the potential time with the child as an opportunity to continue or enrich their relationship, they viewed the mother's request as a

> manipulative exploitation. Some fathers refused, on principle, to be available for the mother's "convenience," even if, for example, she was taking weekly night classes to improve her career or vocational opportunities.[69]

Thus, child-care responsibilities typically fell on the mother alone.

Another major change was that the diminished income available for the wife and children often led to a residential move, and thus to unfamiliar neighborhoods, friends, and schools for the children. Within the first three years, "almost two-thirds of the youngsters had changed their place of residence, and a substantial number of these had moved three or more times."[70] Many of these moves were directly tied to economic factors—the need for cheaper housing, a better job, or more adequate child-care arrangements.

These residential changes represented more than a change in lifestyle and standard of living for the children. They typically caused disruptions in the child's education, close friendships, and neighborhood life. Even when teachers or friends were not particularly helpful, the familiar and relatively stable environment of a school had frequently become an important source of continuity in the child's life.

The effects of these disruptions in the child's home and school environments were heightened because they occurred simultaneously with the child's loss of one parent, and with the onset of greatly reduced care from the other parent. Since many of the mothers had not been employed before the divorce, their children felt altogether abandoned when their mothers had to adopt new work schedules.[71] As a result, the children's basic sense of stability was significantly affected.

The researchers concluded that the quality of care that is given by the custodial parent declines precipitously for a period immediately following divorce.[72] This is a result of the increased stress on both the mother and the children, and the mother's inability to spend as much time with the children after divorce as she did before: the cumulative effect simply makes her physically and psychologically less accessible to her children. Probably most children would be able to adjust satisfactorily to any one of these changes, but their rapid and simultaneous occurence can be overwhelming to almost any child. Thus, the emotional impact of divorce clearly reflects its economic impact.

The economic changes following divorce also have serious detrimental effects on the father-child relationship. Wallerstein and Kelly found that children often compared the economic situation in their mother's and father's household:

> [T]he ambiance of the divorced family is that the economic status of mother and children does not stand alone, but is frequently, and sometimes continually, compared with the standard of living which the family had enjoyed earlier, as well as with the present standard of living of the husband, or the husband's new family.[73]

In cases where the wife and children were experiencing downward mobility and where the father earned very little money, the wife and children were most often compassionate toward the father and protected him. However, when the wife and children experienced downward mobility and the father did not, the discrepancy between the two households was a source of great bitterness. Children in this situation experienced a pervasive sense of deprivation and anger.[74]

Psychologist E. Mavis Hetherington and her colleagues found remarkably similar patterns—downward economic mobility, increased task overload, residential moves, and the disruption of support systems—among white middle class preschool children in Virginia whose parents were divorced.[75]

## CONCLUSION

Children are the tragic victims of the present system of inadequate and unpaid child support. Even though the typical child support award provides less than half the cost of raising a child, chances are that the noncustodial father will not pay it, and the legal system will do nothing about it. Current estimates of noncompliance with child support orders range from 60 to 80 percent.[76] These are appalling statistics for a society that purports to place such a high value on the welfare of its children.[77]

This research reveals that a majority of divorced fathers have the ability to pay court-mandated child support without seriously jeopardizing their own standard of living. A majority also believe they *should* pay. Yet two-thirds of the divorced women we interviewed said that they did not regularly receive the child support that had been ordered by the courts.

In large part, men don't pay because enforcement of child support awards is so lax that noncompliance rarely incurs a penalty. Lawyers, judges, and court personnel are reluctant to use the sanctions the law allows against defaulting fathers. The burden for securing payment therefore falls on the custodial mother, who is already disadvantaged by time and monetary constraints. In addition, the present custody rules may create additional pressures on mothers to accept a lower support award in order to secure and retain custody.

In the end the current legal system places the economic responsibility for children on their mothers and allows fathers the "freedom" to choose not to support their children. The result is that children almost always experience a decline in their standard of living after the divorce. The dislocation from friends, neighborhoods, and family that many of these children endure, and the bitterness and anger they may harbor against one parent or the other, often translate into a pervasively unhappy, distrustful, and pessimistic view of life. This has profound implications for the future of a society which expects more than half of its children to experience the dissolution of their parents' marital relationship before they reach age 18.

Increased public recognition of the national disgrace of unpaid child support has been growing in recent years. As Representative Dan Coats of Indiana said in the 1983 Congressional hearings on child support:

> We see a picture of single mothers struggling to enter and make their way in a marketplace in which many lack the necessary training and experience to successfully compete. The burden for those mothers in providing economic and emotional security for the family is nearly an overwhelming task but even more complicated when they don't receive adequate child support from the fathers.
>
> It is our responsibility to do what we can do to alleviate this shameful child support record. I think ultimately we are faced with a task of reawakening our population to the importance of accepting and fulfilling the responsibility of caring for children that are brought into this world. That responsibility does not end upon separation or divorce but continues to an even greater degree. Fathers have both a legal and a moral obligation to provide child support, and we should do what we can to insure that that is done.[78]

But notwithstanding Representative Coat's proscription, and notwithstanding the 1984 federal legislation that seeks to alter the nonpayment-nonenforcement cycle, the attitudes and practices of judges and lawyers reviewed in this chapter suggest that many courts are moving in the opposite direction; that is, they are asking fathers to contribute minimally, if at all, to child support and making compliance almost discretionary. We have seen that nonsupporting fathers have the economic capacity to pay significantly more than they are currently asked to pay, and substantially more than they are actually paying. In addition, we have seen that noncompliance is just as common among men earning $40,000 a year as among those earning $10,000 or $20,000. The question that therefore lies before us is whether we, as a society, will decide that men should indeed share the financial responsibility for the support of their children (and whether we will revise our divorce laws, court procedures, and enforcement efforts to accomplish this end), or whether we will tolerate the persistence of the present system whereby children and former wives are sentenced to bear the economic brunt of divorce.

## NOTES

1. U.S. Bureau of the Census, "Child Support and Alimony: 1981," *Current Population Reports*, Series P–23, No. 124 (Washington, D.C.: U.S. Government Printing Office, 1983), p. 1 (hereafter cited as "Child Support 1981").

2. Statement in Hearing before the Subcommittee on Public Assistance and Unemployment Compensation of the Committee on Ways and Means, U.S. House of Representatives, Ninety-Eighth Congress, First Session, July 14, 1983, Serial 98–41 (Washington, D.C.: U.S. Government Printing Office, 1984), pp. 34–35 (hereafter cited as "House Hearings 1983").

3. Office of Child Support Enforcement, U.S. Department of Health and Human Services, "Child Support: An Agenda for Action" (Washington, D.C.: U.S. Government Printing Office, 1984) (hereafter cited as "An Agenda").

4. Ruth E. Murphy, statement in "House Hearings 1983," p. 275.

5. Ibid.

6. "Child Support Law Passed," *The Miami Herald*, Aug. 9, 1984, p. 4A (hereafter cited as *Miami Herald*, "Child Support Law").

7. Ibid.

8. Excerpted from Presidential Proclamation, 1983, as cited in "An Agenda," p. 4.

9. Office of Child Support Enforcement, U.S. Dept. of Health and Human Services, "Child Support: New Help Is Available," (August 1984), p. 1.

10. *Miami Herald*, "Child Support Law."

11. U.S. Bureau of the Census, "Child Support and Alimony: 1978," Series P−23, No. 112 (Washington, D.C.: U.S. Government Printing Office, 1981), p. 5, Table B.

12. "Child Support 1981," p. 3, Table B.

13. Ibid., p. 2.

14. Ibid., p. 3, Table B.

15. Ibid., p. 1.

16. Ibid.

17. Judith Cassetty, *Child Support and Public Policy* (Lexington, Mass.: D. C. Heath, 1978), pp. 64−65, Table 4−1.

18. Los Angeles Superior Court, Department 2, Guidelines for Temporary Support Orders, 1978.

19. George Norton, Esq. "A Proposal for Statewide Support Schedules," *Family Law News*, vol. 5, no. 5, September/October 1982, pp. 1−4.

20. Statement of Mary Ann Cook, Wisconsin Department of Health and Social Services, in "House Hearings 1983," pp. 230−240; see also Irwin Garfunkel and Elizabeth Uhr, "A New Approach to Child Support," *The Public Interest* No. 75, Spring 1984, pp. 111−122 (hereafter cited as Garfunkel and Urh, "Approach to Child Support").

21. Summary Report of the New Jersey Supreme Court Task Force on Women in the Courts, New Jersey Judicial College, November 21, 1983, Parsippany, New Jersey, p. 8. The authors of the report state that the New Jersey data are based on testimony from attorneys from all parts of the state and are corroborated by a League of Women Voters' study of all divorces in Bergen County in April, 1978.

22. David Chambers, *Making Fathers Pay* (Chicago:University of Chicago Press, 1979), p. 40 (hereafter cited as Chambers, *Making Fathers Pay*).

23. Canadian Institute of Law Research and Reform, *Matrimonial Support Failures: Reasons, Profiles, and Perceptions of Individuals Involved* (Edmonton, Alberta: Institute of Law Research and Reform, 1981), p. 22 (hereafter cited as Canadian Institute, *Matrimonial Support Failures*).

24. Gloria Sternin and Joseph Davis, "Divorce Awards and Outcomes: A Study of Pattern and Change in Cuyahoga County, Ohio, 1965−1978," *Journal of Family Law*, vol. 20, no. 3, 1981−82, pp. 443−487.

25. *California Civil Code*, Section 4700 (West 1983).

26. Barbara Bergmann, "Setting Appropriate Levels of Child-Support Payments" in *The Parental Child-Support Obligation*, Judith Cassetty, ed. (Lexington, Mass.: D.C. Heath, 1983), pp. 115−118 (hereafter cited as Cassetty, *Parental Child-Support*).

27. Judith Cassetty, "Emerging Issues in Child-Support Policy and Practice," in *Parental Child-Suppport*, pp. 5−6.

28. Portions of this discussion were first presented in Lenore J. Weitzman and Ruth B. Dixon, "Child Custody Awards," *University of California at Davis Law Review*, vol. 12, no. 2, Summer 1978, pp. 473−521; and Lenore J. Weitzman, "The Economics of Divorce," *University of California at Los Angeles Law Review*, vol. 28, no. 6, August 1981, pp. 1181−1268 (hereafter cited as Weitzman, "The Economics of Divorce").

29. Thomas Espenshade, "Raising a Child Can Now Cost $85,000," *Intercom*, September 1980, pp. 10, 11 (hereafter cited as Espenshade, "Raising a Child").

30. Thomas Tilling, "Your $250,000 Baby," *Parents*, November 1980, p. 83.

31. Espenshade, "Raising a Child," pp. 9−11.

32. See *California Welfare and Institutions Code*, Sections 11450, 11453.1 (West 1980 & Supp. 1981).

33. April 1985 interview with Sue North, legislative aide to California Assemblyman Art Agnos, sponsor of A.B. 1527 citing Weitzman, "The Economics of Divorce," and *California Civil Code* § 4720 (West Supp. 1985).

34. While 42 percent of all *married* women with children under six years of age were in the labor force in 1978, 60 percent of the *divorced* women with preschool children were working. Ralph E. Smith, "The Movement of Women into the Labor Force" in *The Subtle Revolution*, Ralph E. Smith, ed. (Washington, D.C.: The Urban Institute, 1979).

35. Karen Seal, "A Decade of No-Fault Divorce," *Family Advocate*, vol. 1, no. 4, Spring 1979, pp. 10, 14.

36. The figures were compiled by Joan P. Emerson of the Bay Area Child Care Project and reported by the Children's Council of San Francisco. The figures for full-time care are generally based on a ten-hour day, but the hours of care range from eight to twelve hours per day for a five-day week.

37. When I ask judges to estimate the cost of food and the cost of clothing for children of various ages in judicial training seminars, their estimates are typically less than the poverty standards established by the U.S. government.

38. Thomas Espenshade, "The Value and Cost of Children," *Population Bulletin*, vol. 32, 1977, p. 43.

39. Gerald and Myrna Silver, *Weekend Fathers* (Los Angeles: Stratford Press, 1981).

40. Chambers, *Making Fathers Pay*, p. 47, Figure 4.2.

41. Canadian Institute, *Matrimonial Support Failures*, p. 22.

42. Bureau of Labor Statistics, U.S. Department of Labor, *Three Standards of Living for an Urban Family of Four Persons*, 1967. This budget is computed for a four-person urban family (husband and wife and two children) and kept current by frequent adjustments. See, for example, McCraw, "Medical Care Costs Lead Rise in 1976–1977 Family Budgets," *Monthly Labor Review*, November 1978, p. 33.

43. Bureau of Labor Statistics, U.S. Department of Labor, *Revised Equivalence Scale for Estimating Equivalent Incomes or Budget Costs by Family Type*, Bulletin No. 1570–2 (1968).

44. Chambers, *Making Fathers Pay*, p. 48.

45. Ibid.

46. Ibid.

47. In fact, a Louisiana court held that because the custodial parent contributes day-to-day care, it is not appropriate to divide support evenly between the two parents. *Arceneaux v. Arceneaux* 426 So.2d 745 (La. App. 1983).

48. "Child Support 1981." Along the same lines, a 1975 nationwide poll showed that only 44 percent of divorced mothers were awarded child support and that of those mothers, only 47 percent were able to collect the support regularly, 29 percent collected it "sometimes" or "rarely," and the remaining 21 percent had never collected even a single dollar of child support the court had ordered. Barbara Bryant, *American Women Today and Tomorrow* (Washington, D.C.: National Commission on the Observance of International Women's Year, U.S. Government Printing Office, 1977), p. 24.

49. Canadian Institute, *Matrimonial Support Failures*, p. 3.

50. That is, they filed an order to show cause why their ex-spouse should not be found in contempt of court for failing to pay alimony or child support.

51. This is summarized from a more extensive review of the literature in Lenore J. Weitzman, *The Marriage Contract: Spouses, Lovers, and the Law* (New York: The Free Press, 1981).

52. The reported percentages for full compliance vary from a low of 22 percent of all fathers (in a 1973 study of AFDC fathers cited in Carol Adaire Jones, Nancy M. Gordon, and Isabel V. Sawhill, "Child Support Payments in the U.S.," *Urban Institute Working Paper* No. 992–03, 1976, p.

78), to a high of 38 percent (in a study covering the first year after the court order discussed in Kenneth Eckhardt, "Deviance, Visibility, and Legal Action: The Duty to Support," *Social Problems*, vol. 15, 1968, pp. 470–77).

53. Fred H. Steininger, "Study of Divorce and Support Orders in Lake County, Indiana, 1956–1957," cited in Henry Foster and Doris Jonas Freed, *Law and the Family—New York* (Rochester, N.Y.: Lawyers Cooperative Publishing Co., 1966). p. xv.

54. U.S. Bureau of the Census, "Divorce, Child Custody, and Child Support," *Current Population Reports*, Series P–23, No. 84, June 1979, pp. 3–4.

55. Ibid.

56. Statement of Gail Forsythe, "House Hearings 1983," p. 105.

57. Ibid.

58. Canadian Institute, *Matrimonial Support Failures*, p. 20.

59. Ibid.

60. *Washington Post*, Jan. 16, 1984, editorial page.

61. The *California Civil Code* states that a noncustodial parent's duty to make child support payments is not affected by the custodial parent's frustration of visitation rights by refusing access to the hild or by moving out of state. *California Civil Code*, Section 4382 (West 1983) Added by Stats. 1980, c. 237, p. 480, Section 1. The rationale for this rule is that the child should not be deprived of food and clothing because of the custodial parent's actions.

62. Interview with Joanne Schulman, staff attorney, National Center on Women and Family Law, New York City, New York, January 8, 1985.

63. Judith S. Wallerstein and Joan Kelly, *Surviving the Breakup: How Children and Parents Cope with Divorce* (New York: Basic Books, 1980).

64. Ibid., p. 22.

65. Ibid.

66. Ibid., p. 231.

67. Ibid., p. 25.

68. Ibid.

69. Ibid.

70. Ibid., p. 183.

71. Ibid., p. 42.

72. Ibid.

73. Ibid., p. 231.

74. Ibid.

75. E. Mavis Hetherington, "Children and Divorce" in *Parent-Child Interaction: Theory, Research and Prospects*, R. W. Henderson (ed.) (New York: Academic Press, 1981).

76. Cassetty, *Parental Child-Support*, p. 3.

77. Ibid.

78. Testimony of Dan Coats, "House Hearings 1983," p. 84.

# 25

MARION GRAHAM

# Working Your Fingers to the Bone

*In* The Divorce Revolution, *Lenore Weitzman notes that two specific groups of women have been most seriously affected by the changes brought about by no-fault divorce: young women with small children and older housewives—the two groups of women who have always been particularly vulnerable in the event of divorce. Heather Ross and Isabel Sawhill were among the first researchers to study female-headed households and alert policy makers that these families were becoming the largest segment of the poverty population.*[1] *In 1976, one year after their study was published, Diana Pearce coined the phrase "the feminization of poverty" to sensitize people to this phenomenon.*[2]

*By the mid 1980s two-thirds of all poor adults were women. The previous reading from Weitzman's book focuses on mothers and specifically on her study's findings on court orders for child support payments and compliance with those orders. The following selection is written by a divorced mother about her inability to maintain an adequate standard of living. It is a personal essay rather than a research piece. We believe, however, that the words with which one woman relates her struggle provide a kind of understanding that numerical data cannot provide.*

---

[1]Heather L. Ross and Isabel V. Sawhill, *Time of Transition: The Growth of Families Headed by Women* (Washington, D.C.: Urban Institute, 1975).

[2]Diana Pearce, "The Feminization of Poverty: Women, Work, and Welfare," *Urban and Social Change Review*, February 1978, p. 28.

Source: Marion Graham, "Working Your Fingers to the Bone," pp. 165–168 in *For Crying Out Loud: Women in Poverty in the United States*, edited by Rochelle Lefkowitz and Ann Withorn, New York: Pilgrim Press. 

---

I was born in Boston, the youngest of a four-girl family. When I was thirteen my father's firm went bankrupt and he found himself out of a job. My family were so ashamed they wouldn't tell their friends that they had to move from the suburbs to a three decker in Boston, even though they weren't really poor. Now I know a lot of people who would love to move out of the projects into a three decker.

In 1960 I got married. I left my good job with the telephone company when I was pregnant with my first child, in 1961. I really looked forward to being home with my children. Nobody worked that I knew. During the Sixties I was always pregnant when everybody was out rebelling against everything. I was too pregnant to rebel, so I have to rebel now! I have five kids. They are now twenty-four, twenty-two, twenty, nineteen, and sixteen.

When I saw how my marriage was disintegrating, I did work at home for marketing research companies, and I did typing for college students, just to try to make money. I had planned for two or three years to get a divorce before I did. But I never had the money to do it. I knew I had to have a job in order to save the money to go to a lawyer. I couldn't leave the kids; there was no day care. Finally, I had to go on welfare because my husband did not pay enough support, and sometimes he did not pay at all.

When I started working full-time again, I thought it was going to be wonderful, that I wasn't going to be poor anymore. I was going to be away from the bureaucracy; they couldn't call me in anytime they wanted to. Even then, though, I still earned so little that I was eligible for a housing subsidy, Medicaid, and food stamps. I remember at the time being ashamed to let people where I worked know that I was poor enough for food stamps. And I hated that.

About three years ago they came out with some new "poverty line," that's what they called it, and they decided I earned too much for most of those other benefits. I only grossed something like $8,600 at the time, but it was still too much for them, so they cut me off. I still had the same needs I had before, but suddenly I was no longer poor. I guess I was supposed to be proud.

Since then I got a raise, so I thought things would be OK, but then I lost my housing subsidy because I earned too much. I ended up having to take an apartment that cost exactly seven times what I had paid with a subsidy. My rent

---

Marion Graham was originally interviewed for *We Need a Change,* a collection of interviews produced for the University of Massachussetts/Boston Conference on Women and Poverty, held in April 1984. Jean Humez and Melissa Shook conducted the original interview. In July 1985, Ann Withorn updated, edited, and expended the interview.

came to half of my net pay. Just the rent. After that sometimes I would get to work but not be able to pay for lunch. I had my subway tokens, but no money to eat. Every week they take something different out of my salary. Life insurance, disability insurance, union dues, retirement benefits are all good, but you don't get much to live on. Now, finally, I can buy *Woman's Day* and *Family Circle* magazines—that used to be my dream.

How you dress for work, the hours and flexibility, transportation, whether you can bring a lunch—all these nitty gritty things make a big difference in how you can live on a low salary. You just cannot afford to take some jobs even if they sound interesting because you have to spend too much money on clothes or transportation. It's sad. I couldn't afford to work at a place where I had to dress up, for instance. You can't "dress for success" on a secretarial salary. It's an invisible poverty.

You think you're not poor because you are working, so you don't even ask for the information about benefits you need. And nobody tells you that you might be eligible, because they think you are working and all set. Also, it is even harder to ask for things from your family, because if you are working you should have the money. I feel bad, though, that I don't have more chance to help my family. I can't afford it, even though I'm working.

The average pay in my union of clerical and hospital workers is $11,000. That's not much—it is poverty for a woman who is trying to raise a family. When people need child care they have to pay for it, and they can't afford it. I don't need child care, but the health insurance, which I had to wait two years for, costs a lot. And I couldn't get it for my son, who is twenty and has juvenile diabetes.

Not having money affects everything about how you feel. I used to feel lousy about myself. I thought I was supposed to be set, to have slice of the American pie. Now I was a big person and I worked and everything and I was supposed to get there. But instead I found myself just with a job and no money. When I reached forty I was so depressed.

Now I have learned that I am not alone, that it is not my fault. The average secretary around here makes $14,000. So we are just over the line for many benefits, but we still have expenses we can't meet. That makes some women, who don't understand how it works, take it out on women on welfare. They blame them for getting something they can't have, instead of blaming the rules, which keep them from getting anything. Some secretaries may think, "I am better off than they are," instead of seeing how we have similar problems. But they are afraid of the label that would be put on them if they identify with welfare. I don't do that because I have been there and I know both, and I know that none of it is good. It's bad to be on welfare, and it is bad to be working and have no money.

As secretaries here we have worked hard to do things together so that we can know each other as people, because at work we are all separated in our individual little offices. We go on picnics together, or to dinner, just to get to know each other. Although they don't pay us much, they act like we can never be absent or the world will fall apart, so we have to cover for each other, and we can't do that if we don't know each other. I keep saying, if we are so important why don't they pay us more? But they don't, so we have to help each other.

The hardest thing about being a secretary is that people think there is something wrong with being a secretary. You are an extension of your typewriter, you are a piece of furniture, you aren't really important. They always say, "You are overqualified," but many people with degrees still can't do the job; it's hard and important. We don't have money or status. For instance, my job now is strictly administrative work, detail and organizing. I don't even have a typewriter any more, but I am still listed on a secretarial line because it's cheaper to keep me that way. I hope the comparable-worth stuff will help us some, even though they will fiddle around with it forever.

They act like all secretaries are young girls waiting to get married who don't need much money. But that is not how it is. Besides that, young girls, like my daughter, want money too, to save, to do what they want. So nobody deserves bad wages.

It's also frustrating that so many people, like my family, think unions are "low class" and are afraid of them, even when they need them. My mother told me not to "upset management" when I became a steward. I told her that was the whole point.

I think our union should invite women on welfare to come talk about what they get and don't get. And to let people know about benefits. That would be a help and could bridge the gap and keep working women from looking down on welfare mothers, or say they aren't working. We need to make alliances; it is sad that we haven't done it.

I have to admit that I am thrilled that my income has doubled in the past six years. It took a lot of hard work and I am proud. But I still don't have enough money, and that's the bottom line.

*Section Seven*

# Family Influences on Human Development

# 26

ADRIENNE RICH

# Anger and Tenderness

*Our culture tells us that one of our most important adult roles, if we choose to take it on, is parenthood. When we bear and rear a child we assume responsibility for another human life. For a woman who is suddenly redefined as mother, the responses can span the spectrum from ecstasy to terror, from frustration to unparalleled satisfaction.*

*Germaine Greer (Reading 31) suggests that modern Western society acknowledges that mothering is a learned behavior, but fails to provide a culture in which that learning is offered. Each mother must "reinvent childbirth," and this isolation is largely responsible for many mothers' negative feelings.*

*Poet Adrienne Rich focuses on her own experience with these feelings in* Of Woman Born. *She writes in the forward to her book, "I did not choose this subject; it had long ago chosen me."*[1] *She goes on to say that her purpose in researching and writing the book was to extend feminist theory into an examination of the institution of motherhood as it has developed in patriarchal societies. However, her own experiences in pregnancy, childbearing, and child rearing made her realize that she could not complete the task without drawing upon her personal feelings. Thus, her study has the subtitle,* Motherhood as Experience and Institution. *From the standpoint of institution, Rich provides a carefully researched, feminist, historical overview of motherhood. Among other subjects, she examines the relatively new concept of full-time mother, traces the fascinating but grizzly history of childbirth and obstetrics, and examines the relationship between mothers and sons and mothers and daughters. The*

[1]Rich, *Of Woman Born,* p. xiv.

*following selection is from the first chapter of her book, in which she reflects on her own experience as a mother.*



---

Entry from my journal, November 1960

My children cause me the most exquisite suffering of which I have any experience. It is the suffering of ambivalence: the murderous alternation between bitter resentment and raw-edged nerves, and blissful gratifaction and tenderness. Sometimes I seem to myself, in my feelings toward these tiny guiltless beings, a monster of selfishness and intolerance. Their voices wear away at my nerves, their constant needs, above all their need for simplicity and patience, fill me with despair at my own failures, despair too at my fate, which is to serve a function for which I was not fitted. And I am weak sometimes from held-in rage. There are times when I feel only death will free us from one another, when I envy the barren woman who has the luxury of her regrets but lives a life of privacy and freedom.*

And yet at other times I am melted with the sense of their helpless, charming and quite irresistible beauty—their ability to go on loving and trusting—their staunchness and decency and unselfconsciousness. *I love them.* But it's in the enormity and inevitablity of this love that the sufferings lie.

*April 1961:*

A blissful love for my children engulfs me from time to time and seems almost to suffice—the aesthetic pleasure I have in these little, changing creatures, the sense of being loved, however dependently, the sense too that I'm not an utterly unnatural and shrewish mother—much though I am!

*May 1965:*

To suffer with and for and against a child—maternally, egotistically, neurotically, sometimes with a sense of helplessness, sometimes with the illusion of learning wisdom—but always, everywhere, in body and soul, *with* that child—because that child is a piece of oneself.

To be caught up in waves of love and hate, jealousy even of the child's childhood; hope and fear for its maturity; longing to be free of responsibility, tied by every fibre of one's being.

That curious primitive reaction of protectiveness, the beast defending her cub, when anyone attacks or criticizes him—And yet no one more hard on him that I!

---

*The term "barren woman" was easy for me to use, unexamined, fifteen years ago. As should be clear throughout this book, it seems to me now a term both tendentious and meaningless, based on a view of women which sees motherhood as our only positive definition.

*September 1965:*

> Degradation of anger. Anger at a child. How shall I learn to absorb the violence and make explicit only the caring? Exhaustion of anger. Victory of will, too dearly bought—far too dearly!

*March 1966:*

> Perhaps one is a monster—an anti-woman—something driven and without recourse to the normal and appealing consolations of love, motherhood, joy in others . . .

Unexamined assumptions: First, that a "natural" mother is a person without further identity, one who can find her chief gratification in being all day with small children, living at a pace tuned to theirs; that the isolation of mothers and children together in the home must be taken for granted; that maternal love is, and should be, quite literally selfless; that children and mothers are the "causes" of each others' suffering. I was haunted by the stereotype of the mother whose love is "unconditional"; and by the visual and literary images of motherhood as a single-minded identity. If I knew parts of myself existed that would never cohere to those images, weren't those parts then abnormal, monstrous? And—as my eldest son, now aged twenty-one, remarked on reading the above passages: "You seemed to feel you ought to love us all the time. But there *is* no human relationship where you love the other person at every moment." Yes, I tried to explain to him, but women—above all, mothers—have been supposed to love that way.

From the fifties and early sixties, I remember a cycle. It began when I had picked up a book or began trying to write a letter, or even found myself on the telephone with someone toward whom my voice betrayed eargerness, a rush of sympathetic energy. The child (or children) might be absorbed in busyness, in his own dreamworld; but as soon as he felt me gliding into a world which did not include him, he would come to pull at my hand, ask for help, punch at the typewriter keys. And I would feel his wants at such a moment as fraudulent, as an attempt moreover to defraud me of living even for fifteen minutes as myself. My anger would rise; I would feel the futility of any attempt to salvage myself, and also the inequality between us: my needs always balanced against those of a child, and always losing. I could love so much better, I told myself, after even a quarter-hour of selfishness, of peace, of detachment from my children. A few minutes! But it was as if an invisible thread would pull taut between us and break, to the child's sense of inconsolable abandonment, if I moved—not even physically, but in spirit—into a realm beyond our tightly circumscribed life together. It was as if my placenta had begun to refuse him oxygen. Like so may women, I waited with impatience for the moment when their father would return from work, when for an hour or two at least the circle drawn around mother and children would grow looser, the intensity between us slacken, because there was another adult in the house.

I did not understand that this circle, this magnetic field in which we lived, was not a natural phenomenon.

Intellectually, I must have known it. But the emotion-charged, tradition-heavy forum in which I found myself cast as the Mother seemed, then, as ineluctable as the tides. And, because of this form—this microcosm in which my children and I formed a tiny, private emotional cluster, and in which (in bad weather or when someone was ill) we sometimes passed days at a time without seeing another adult except for their father—there *was* authentic need underlying my child's invented claims upon me when I seemed to be wandering away from him. He was reassuring himself that warmth, tenderness, continuity, solidity were still there for him, in my person. My singularity, my uniqueness in the world as *his mother*—perhaps more dimly also as Woman—evoked a need vaster than any single human being could satisfy, except by loving continuously, unconditionally, from dawn to dark, and often in the middle of the night.

In a living room in 1975, I spent an evening with a group of women poets, some of whom had children. One had brought hers along, and they slept or played in adjoining rooms. We talked of poetry, and also of infanticide, of the case of a local woman, the mother of eight, who had been in severe depression since the birth of her third child, and who had recently murdered and decapitated her two youngest, on her suburban front lawn. Several women in the group, feeling a direct connection with her desperation, had signed a letter to the local newspaper protesting the way her act was perceived by the press and handled by the community mental health system. Every woman in that room who had children, every poet, could identify with her. We spoke of the wells of anger that her story cleft open in us. We spoke of our own moments of murderous anger at our children, because there was no one and nothing else on which to discharge anger. We spoke in the sometimes tentative, sometimes rising, sometimes bitterly witty, unrhetorical tones and language of women who had met together over our common work, poetry, and who had found another common ground in an unacceptable, but undeniable anger. The words are being spoken now, are being written down; the taboos are being broken, the masks of motherhood are cracking through.

For centuries no one talked of these feelings. I became a mother in the family-centered, consumer-oriented, Freudian-American world of the 1950s. My husband spoke eagerly of the children we would have; my parents-in-law awaited the birth of their grandchild. I had no idea of what *I* wanted, what *I* could or could not choose. I only knew that to have a child was to assume adult womanhood to the full, to prove myself, to be "like other women."

To be "like other women" had been a problem for me. From the age of thirteen or fourteen, I had felt I was only acting the part of a feminine creature. At the age of sixteen my fingers were almost constantly ink-stained. The lipstick and high heels of the era were difficult-to-manage disguises. In 1945 I was writing poetry seriously, and had a fantasy of going to postwar Europe as a journalist, sleeping among the ruins in bombed cities, recording the rebirth of civilization after the fall of the Nazis. But also, like every other girl I knew, I spent hours trying to apply lipstick more adroitly, straightening the wandering seams of stockings, talking about "boys." There are two different compartments, already, to my life. But writing poetry, and my fantasies of travel and self-sufficiency, seemed more real to me; I felt that as an incipient "real woman" I was a fake. Particularly was I paralyzed when I encountered young children. I think I felt men could be—wished to be—conned into thinking I was truly "feminine"; a child, I suspected, could see through me like a shot. This sense of acting a part created a curious sense of guilt, even though it was a part demanded for survival.

I have a very clear, keen memory of myself the day after I was married: I was sweeping a floor. Probably the floor did not really need to be swept; probably I simply did not know what else to do with myself. But as I swept that floor I thought: "Now I am a woman. This an age-old action, this is what women have always done." I felt I was bending to some ancient form, too ancient to question. *This is what women have always done.*

As soon as I was visibly and clearly pregnant, I felt, for the first time in my adolescent and adult life, not-guilty. The atmosphere of approval in which I was bathed—even by strangers on the street, it seemed—was like an aura I carried with me, in which doubts, fears, misgivings, met with absolute denial. *This is what women have always done.*

Two days before my first son was born, I broke out in a rash which was tentatively diagnosed as measles, and was admitted to a hospital for contagious diseases to await the onset of labor. I felt for the first time a great deal of conscious fear, and guilt toward my unborn child, for having "failed" him with my body in this way. In rooms near mine were patients with polio; no one was allowed to enter my room except in a hospital gown and mask. If during pregnancy I had felt in any vague command of my situation, I felt now totally dependent on my obstetrician, a huge, vigorous, paternal man, abounding with optimism and assurance, and given to pinching my cheek. I had gone through a healthy pregnancy, but as if tranquilized or sleep-walking. I had taken a sewing class in which I produced an unsightly and ill-cut maternity jacket which I never wore; I had made curtains for the baby's room, collected baby clothes, blotted out as much as possible the woman I had been a few months earlier. My second book of poems was in press, but I had stopped writing poetry, and read little except household magazines and books on child-care. I felt myself perceived by the world simply as a pregnant woman, and it seemed easier, less disturbing, to perceive myself so. After my child was born the "measles" were diagnosed as an allergic reaction to pregnancy.

Within two years, I was pregnant again, and writing in a notebook:

*November 1956:*

> Whether it's the extreme lassitude of early pregnancy or something more fundamental, I don't know; but of late I've felt, toward poetry,—both reading and writing it—nothing but boredom and indifference. Especially toward my own and that of my immediate contemporaries. When I receive a letter soliciting mss., or someone alludes to my "career," I have a strong sense of wanting to deny all responsibility for and interest in that person who writes—or who wrote.

> If there is going to be a real break in my writing life, this is as good a time for it as any. I have been dissatisfied with myself, my work, for a long time.

My husband was a sensitive, affectionate man who wanted children and who—unusual in the professional, academic world of the fifties—was willing to "help." But it was clearly understood that this "help" was an act of generosity; that *his* work, *his* professional life, was the real work in the family; in fact, this was for years not even an issue between us. I understood that my struggles as a writer were a kind of luxury, a peculiarity of mine; my work brought in almost no money: it even cost money, when I hired a household helper to allow me a few hours a week to write. "Whatever I ask he tries to give me," I wrote in March 1958, "but always the initiative has to be mine." I experienced my depressions, bursts of anger, sense of entrapment, as burdens my husband was forced to bear because he loved me; I felt grateful to be loved in spite of bringing him those burdens.

But I was struggling to bring my life into focus. I had never really given up on poetry, nor on gaining some control over my existence. The life of a Cambridge tenement backyard swarming with children, the repetitious cycles of laundry, the night-wakings, the interrupted moments of peace or of engagement with ideas, the ludicrous dinner parties at which young wives, some with advanced degrees, all seriously and intelligently dedicated to their children's welfare and their husbands' careers, attempted to reproduce the amenities of Brahmin Boston, amid French recipes and the pretense of effortlessness—above all, the ultimate lack of seriousness with which women were regarded in that world—all of this defied analysis at that time, but I knew I had to remake my own life. I did not then understand that we—the women of that academic community—as in so many middle-class communities of the period—were expected to fill both the part of the Victorian Lady of Leisure, the Angel in the House, and also the Victorian cook, scullery maid, laundress, governess, and nurse. I only sensed that there were false distractions sucking at me, and I wanted desperately to strip my life down to what was essential.

*June 1958:*

> These months I've been all a tangle of irritations deepening to anger: bitterness, disillusion with society and with myself; beating out at the world rejecting out of hand. What, if anything, has been positive? Perhaps the attempt to remake my life, to save it from mere drift and the passage of time . . .
>
> The work that is before me is serious and difficult and not at all clear even as to plan. Discipline of mind and spirit, uniqueness of expression, ordering of daily existence, the most effective functioning of the human self—these are the chief things I wish to achieve. So far the only beginning I've been able to make is to waste less time. That is what some of the rejection has been all about.

By July of 1958 I was pregnant again. The new life of my third—and, as I determined, my last—child, was a kind of turning for me. I had learned that my body was not under my control; I had not intended to bear a third child. I knew now better than I had ever known what another pregnancy, another new infant, meant for my body and spirit. Yet, I did not think of having an abortion. In a sense, my third son was more actively chosen than either of his brothers; by the time I knew I was pregnant with him, I was not sleepwalking any more.

*August 1958 (Vermont):*

> I write this as the early rays of the sun light up our hillside and eastern windows. Rose with [the baby] at 5:30 A.M. and have fed him and breakfasted. This is one of the few mornings on which I haven't felt terrible mental depression and physical exhaustion.
>
> . . . I have to acknowledge to myself that I would not have chosen to have more children, that I was beginning to look to a time, not too far off, when I should again be free, no longer so physically tired, pursuing a more or less intellectual and creative life. . . . The *only* way I can develop now is through much harder, more continuous, connected work that my present life makes possible. Another child means postponing this for some years longer—and years at my age are significant, not to be tossed lightly away.
>
> And yet, somehow, something, call it Nature or that affirming fatalism of the human creature, makes me aware of the inevitable as already part of me, not to be contended against so much as brought to bear as an additional weapon against drift, stagnation and spiritual death. (For it is really death that I have been fearing—the crumbling to death of that scarcely-born physiognomy which my whole life has been a battle to give birth to—a recognizable, autonomous self, a creation in poetry and in life.)
>
> If more effort has to be made then I will make it. If more despair has to be lived through, I think I can anticipate it correctly and live through it.
>
> Meanwhile, in a curious and unanticipated way, we really do welcome the birth of our child.

There was, or course, an economic as well as a spiritual margin which allowed me to think of a third child's birth not as my own death-warrant but as an "additional weapon against death." My body, despite recurrent flares of arthritis, was a healthy one; I had good prenatal care; we were not living on the edge of malnutrition; I knew that all my children would be fed, clothed, breathe fresh air; in fact it did not occur to me that it could be otherwise. But, in another sense, beyond that physical margin, I knew I was fighting for my life through, against, and with the lives of my children, though very little else was clear to me. I had been trying to give birth to myself; and in some grim, dim way I was determined to use even pregnancy and parturition in that process.

Before my third child was born I decided to have no more children, to be sterilized. (Nothing is removed from a woman's body during this operation; ovulation and menstruation continue. Yet the language suggests a cutting- or burning-away of her essential womanhood, just as the old word "barren" suggests a woman eternally empty and lacking.) My husband, although he supported my decision, asked whether I was sure it would not leave me feeling "less feminine." In order to have the operation at all, I had to present a letter, counter-signed by my husband, assuring the committee of physicians who approved such operations that I had already produced three children, and stating my reasons for having no more. Since I had had rheumatoid arthritis for some years, I could give a reason acceptable to the male panel who sat on my case; my own judgement would not have been acceptable. When I awoke from the operation, 24 hours after my child's birth, a young nurse looked at my chart and remarked coldly: "Had yourself spayed, did you?"

The first great birth-control crusader, Margaret Sanger, remarks that of the hundreds of women who wrote to her pleading for contraceptive information in the early part of the 20th century, all spoke of wanting the health and strength to be better mothers to the children they already had; or of wanting to be physically affectionate to their husbands without dread of conceiving. None was refusing motherhood altogether, or asking for an easy life. These women—mostly poor, many still in their teens, all with several children—simply felt they could no longer do "right" by their families, whom they expected to go on serving and rearing. Yet there always has been, and there remains, intense fear of the suggestion that women shall have the final say as to how our bodies are to be used. It is as if the suffering of the mother, the primary identification of woman *as* the mother—were so necessary to the emotional grounding of human society that the mitigation, or removal, of that suffering, that identification, must be fought at every level, including the level of refusing to question it at all.

"Vous travaillez pour l'armée, madame?" (You are working for the army?), a Frenchwoman said to me early in the Vietnam war, on hearing I had three sons.

*April 1965:*

> Anger, weariness, demoralization. Sudden bouts of weeping. A sense of insufficiency to the moment and to eternity . . .
>
> Paralyzed by the sense that there exists a mesh of relations, between e.g. my rejection and anger at [my eldest child], my sensual life, pacifism, sex (I mean in its broadest significance, not merely physical)—an interconnectedness which, if I could see it, make it valid, would give me back myself, make it possible to function lucidly and passionately—Yet I grope in and out among these dark webs—
>
> I weep, and weep, and the sense of powerlessness spreads like a cancer through my being.

*August 1965, 3:30 A.M.:*

> Necessity for a more unyielding discipline of my life.
> Recognize the uselessness of blind anger.
> Limit society.
> Use children's school hours better, for work & solitude.
> Refuse to be distracted from style of life.
> Less waste.
> Be harder & harder on poems.

Once in a while someone used to ask me, "Don't you ever write poems about your children?" The male poets of my generation did write poems about their children—especially their daughters. For me, poetry was where I lived as no-one's mother, where I existed as myself.

The bad and the good moments are inseparable for me. I recall the times when, suckling each of my children, I saw his eyes open full to mine, and realized each of us was fastened to the other, not only by mouth and breast, but through our mutual gaze: the depth, calm, passion, of that dark blue, maturely focused look. I recall the physical pleasure of having my full breast suckled at a time when I had no other physical pleasure in the world except the guilt-ridden pleasure of addictive eating. I remember early the sense of conflict, of a battleground none of us had chosen, of being an observer who, like it or not, was also an actor in an endless contest of wills. This was what it meant to me to have three children under the age of seven. But I recall too each child's individual body, his slenderness, wiriness, softness, grace, the beauty of little boys who have not been taught that the male body must be rigid. I remember moments of peace when for some reason it was possible to go to the bathroom alone. I remember being uprooted from already meager sleep to answer a childish nightmare, pull up a blanket, warm a consoling bottle, lead a half-asleep child to the toilet. I remember going back to bed starkly awake, brittle with anger, knowing that my broken sleep would make next day a hell, that there would be more nightmares, more need for consolation, because out of my weariness I would rage at those children for no reason they could understand. I remember thinking I would never dream again (the unconscious of the young mother—where does it entrust its messages, when dream-sleep is denied her for years?)

For many years I shrank from looking back on the first decade of my children's lives. In snapshots of the period I see a smiling young woman, in maternity clothes or bent over a half-naked baby; gradually she stops smiling, wears a distant, half-melancholy look, as if she were listening for something. In time my sons grew older, I began changing my own life, we began to talk to each other as equals. Together we lived through my leaving the marriage, and through their father's suicide. We became survivors, four distinct people with strong bonds connecting us. Because I always tried to tell them the truth, because their every new independence meant new freedom for me, because we trusted each other even when we wanted different things, they became, at a fairly young age, self-reliant and open to the unfamiliar. Something told me that if they had survived my angers, my self-reproaches, and still trusted my love and each others', they were strong. Their lives have not been, will not be, easy; but their very existences seem a gift to me, their vitality, humor, intelligence, gentleness, love of life, their separate life-currents which here and there stream into my own. I don't know how we made it from their embattled childhood and my embattled motherhood into a mutual recognition of ourselves and each other. Probaby that mutual recognition, overlaid by social and traditional circumstance, was always there, from the first gaze between the mother and the infant at the breast. But I do know that for years I believed I should never have been anyone's mother, that because I felt my own needs acutely and often expressed them violently, I was Kali, Medea, the sow that devours her farrow, the unwomanly woman in flight from womanhood, a Nietzschean monster. Even today, rereading old journals, remembering, I feel grief and anger; but their objects are no longer myself and my children. I feel grief at the waste of myself in those years, anger at the mutilation and manipulation of the relationship between mother and child, which is the great original source and experience of love.

On an early spring day in the 1970s, I meet a young woman friend on the street. She has a tiny infant against her breast, in a bright cotton sling; its face is pressed against her blouse, its tiny hand clutches a piece of the cloth. "How old is she?" I ask. "Just two weeks old," the mother tells me. I am amazed to feel in myself a passionate longing to have, once again, such a small, new being clasped against my body. The baby belongs there, curled, suspended asleep between her mother's breasts, as she belonged curled in the womb. The young mother—who already has a three-year-old—speaks of how quickly one forgets the pure pleasure of having this new creature, immaculate, perfect. And I walk away from her drenched with memory, with envy. Yet I know other things: that her life is far from simple; she is a mathematician who now has two children under the age of four; she is living now in the rhythms of other lives—not only the regular cry of the infant but her three-year-old's needs, her husband's problems. In the building where I live, women are still raising children alone, living day in and day out within their individual family units, doing the laundry, herding the tricycles to the park, waiting for the husbands to come home. There is a baby-sitting pool and a children's playroom, young fathers push prams on weekends, but child-care is still the individual responsibility of the individual woman. I envy the sensuality of having an infant of two weeks curled against one's breast; I do not envy the turmoil of the elevator full of small children, babies howling in the laundromat, the apartment in winter where pent-up seven- and eight-year-olds have one adult to look to for their frustrations, reassurances, the grounding of their lives.

Most of the literature of infant care and psychology has assumed that the process toward individuation is essentially the *child's* drama, played out against and with a parent or parents who are, for better or worse, givens. Nothing could have prepared me for the realization that I *was* a mother, one of those givens, when I knew I was still in a state of uncreation myself. That calm, sure, unambivalent woman who moved through the pages of the manuals I read seemed as unlike me as an astronaut. Nothing, to be sure, had prepared me for the intensity of relationship already existing between me and a creature I had carried in my body and now held in my arms and fed from my breasts. Throughout pregnancy and nursing, women are urged to relax, to mime the serenity of madonnas. No one mentions the psychic crisis of bearing a first child, the excitation of long-buried feelings about one's own mother, the sense of confused power and powerlessness, of being taken over on the one hand and of touching new physical and psychic potentialities on the other, a heightened sensibility which can be exhilarating, bewildering, and exhausting. No one mentions the strangeness of attraction—which can be as single-minded and overwhelming as the early days of a love affair—to a being so tiny, so dependent, so folded-in to itself—who is, and yet is not, part of oneself.

From the beginning the mother caring for her child is involved in a continually changing dialogue, crystallized in such moments as when, hearing her child's cry, she feels milk rush into her breasts; when, as the child first suckles, the uterus begins contracting and returning to its normal size, and when later, the child's mouth, caressing the nipple, creates waves of sensuality in the womb where it once lay; or when, smelling the breast even in sleep, the child starts to root and grope for the nipple.

The child gains her first sense of her own existence from the mother's responsive gestures and expressions. It's as if, in the mother's eyes, her smile, her stroking touch, the child first reads the message: *You are there!* And the mother, too, is discovering her own existence newly. She is connected with this other being, by the most mundane and the most invisible strands, in a way she can be connected with no one else except in the deep past of her infant connection with her own mother. And she, too, needs to struggle from that one-to-one intensity into new realization, or reaffirmation, of her being-unto-herself.

The act of suckling a child, like a sexual act, may be tense, physically painful, charged with cultural feelings of inadequacy and guilt; or, like a sexual act, it can be a physically delicious, elementally soothing experience, filled with a tender sensuality. But just as lovers have to break apart after sex and become separate individuals again, so the mother has to wean herself from the infant from herself. In psychologies of child-rearing the emphasis is placed on "letting the child go" for the child's sake. But the mother needs to let it go as much or more for her own.

Motherhood, in the sense of an intense, reciprocal relationship with a particular child, or children, is *one part* of female process; it is not an identity for all time. The housewife in her mid-forties may jokingly say, "I feel like someone out of a job." But in the eyes of society, once having been mothers, what are we, if not always mothers? The process of "letting-go"—though we are charged with blame if we do not—is an act of revolt against the grain of patriarchal culture. But it is not enough to let our children go; we need selves of our own to return to.

To have borne and reared a child is to have done that thing which patriarchy joins with physiology to render into the defintion of femaleness. But also, it can mean the experiencing of one's own body and emotions in a powerful way. We experience not only physical, fleshly changes but the feeling of a change in character. We learn, often through painful self-discipline and self-cauterization, those qualities which are supposed to be "innate" in us: patience, self-sacrifice, the willingness to repeat endlessly in the small, routine chores of socializing a human being. We are also, often to our amazement, flooded with feelings both of love and violence more intense and fiercer than any we had ever known. (A well-known pacifist, also a mother, said recently on a platform: "If anyone laid a hand on *my* child, I'd murder him.")

These and similar experiences are not easily put aside. Small wonder that women gritting their teeth at the incessant demands of child-care still find it hard to acknowledge their children's growing independence of them; still feel they must be at home, on the *qui vive,* be that ear always tuned for the sound of emergency, of being needed. Children grow up, not in a smooth ascending curve, but jaggedly, their needs inconstant as weather. Cultural "norms" are marvelously powerless to decide, in a child of eight or ten, what gender s/he will assume on a given day, or how s/he will meet emergency, loneliness, pain, hunger. One is constantly made aware that a human existence is anything but linear, long before the labyrinth of puberty; because a human being of six is still a human being.

In a tribal or even a feudal culture a child of six would have serious obligations; ours have none. But also, the woman at home with children is not believed to be doing serious work; she is just supposed to be acting out of maternal instinct, doing chores a man would never take on, largely uncritical of the meaning of what she does. So child and mother alike are depreciated, because only grown men and women in the paid labor force are supposed to be "productive."

The power-relations between mother and child are often simply a reflection of power-relations in patriarchal society: "You will do this because I know what is good for you" is difficult to distinguish from "You will do this because I can *make* you." Powerless women have always used mothering as a channel—narrow but deep—for their own human will to power, their need to return upon the world what it has visited on them. The child dragged by the arm across the room to be washed, the child cajoled, bullied, and bribed into taking "one more bite" of a detested food, is more than just a child which must be reared according to cultural traditions of "good mothering." S/he is a piece of reality, of the world, which can be acted on, even modified, by a woman restricted from acting on anything else except inert materials like dust and food.

When I try to return to the body of the young woman of twenty-six, pregnant for the first time, who fled from the physical knowledge of her pregnancy and at the same time from her intellect and vocation, I realize that I was effectively alienated from my real body and my real spirit by the institution—not the fact—of motherhood. This institution—the foundation of human society as we know it—allowed me only certain views, certain expectations, whether embodied in the booklet in my obstetrician's waiting room, the novels I had read, my mother-in-law's approval, my memories of my own mother, the Sistine Madonna or she of the Michelangelo *Pietà,* the floating notion that a woman pregnant is a woman calm in her fulfillment or, simply, a woman waiting. Women have always been seen as waiting: waiting to be asked, waiting for our menses, in fear lest they do or do not come, waiting for men to come home from wars, or from work, waiting for children to grow up, or for the birth of a new child, or for menopause.

In my own pregnancy I dealt with this waiting, this female fate, by denying every active, powerful aspect of myself. I became dissociated both from my immediate, present, bodily experience and from my reading, thinking, writing life. Like a traveler in an airport where her plane is several hours delayed, who leafs through magazines she would never ordinarily read, surveys shops whose contents do not interest her, I committed myself to an outward serenity and a profound inner boredom. If boredom is simply a mask for anxiety, then I had learned, as a woman, to be supremely bored rather than to examine the anxiety underlying my Sistine tranquility. My body, finally truthful, paid me back in the end: I was allergic to pregnancy.

But this reaction against the body is now coming into synthesis with new inquires into the actual—as opposed to the culturally warped—power inherent in female biology, however we choose to use it, and by no means limited to the maternal function.

My own story is only one story. What I carried away in the end was a determination to heal—insofar as an individual woman can, and as much as possible with other women—the separation between mind and body; never again to lose myself both psychically and physically in that way. Slowly I came to understand the paradox contained in "my" experience of motherhood; that, although different from many other women's experiences it was not unique; and that only in shedding the illusion of my uniqueness could I hope, as a woman, to have any authenic life at all.

# 27

JEROME KAGAN

# The Powers and Limitations of Parents

*Since the appearance of Dr. Spock's* Baby and Child Care *in the 1950s, parents have come to rely more and more on the advice of experts as they rear their children. Bookstores now offer scores of volumes on birthing, nursing, punishing, and potty training. Developmental stages about which our grandmothers did not even care are now viewed as major events that we must handle properly if our children are to become healthy, stable individuals.*

*Although much of this literature has benefited parents, it conveys two subtle underlying messages. First, it says that parents cannot adequately rear children on their own, that their own nurturing feelings are not adequate to ensure the healthy development of their offspring. Luckily, the experts remind us, their advice is there for the taking. The second and more serious message of this literature teaches that parents are responsible for the way their children turn out. If one does not reward consistently, punish properly, or stimulate adequately, the result is likely to be an inferior adult.*

*Harvard Professor Jerome Kagan is a world-reknowned expert on child development, whose ideas about the development of children and the part parents play in that development differ from those of the popular experts. In the preface to his recent book,* The Nature of the Child, *he writes:*

> Most modern American parents hold two strong beliefs. The first is that they have only a few years to set the course of their child's life. If they fail to implement the proper actions, the child is doomed. The second, potentially faulty, premise is that physical affection and firmness are the two vital ingredients. The first promotes self-confidence; the second prevents self-indulgence. Although there is insufficient scientific support for either of these views, they are so

strongly held by most parents that it is hard to persuade them that they are folk beliefs.[1]

*In the following selection, Kagan continues this line of thought and offers some provocative ideas on parental influence or the lack thereof.*

Source: Jerome Kagan, *The Power and Limitations of Parents.* Austin, Tex.: Hogg Foundation for Mental Health (1986). © Hogg Foundation for Mental Health, 1986. Reprinted with permission of the publisher and the author.

[1]From Jerome Kagan, *The Nature of the Child* (New York: Basic Books, 1984), p. xv.

---

This paper is about the mystery of human development. Because human development is of such concern to all of us, whether citizens or parents, we care about the facts that are true. We want certain beliefs to be valid, and we resist giving credence to facts we do not like.

Major changes have occurred in our views of family and child since the early 18th century. In the first place, historical changes made possible a large middle class that could afford to relieve women of the task of gathering food and so give them more time for leisure. As European cities grew and a larger middle class emerged, three beliefs—which are still with us—became established. In my view these beliefs are stronger now than they were two-and-a-half centuries ago.

The first belief is that the experiences of the infant in the family set the course of the child's development, and once these original qualities are established they are difficult to change. The second belief is that the most critical ingredient for the child's psychological growth is the mother's love. And beginning in the late 19th century this love had to be physical—embraces and kisses—rather than only verbal affirmations. The third belief is that the mother is the central figure in the child's development.

Although each of these beliefs might be true, the scientific basis for their truth remains meager. If a petit jury were to decide on the truth of these statements, I suspect they would determine that they should be tried in the court of science to see how innocent or guilty they are.

We now ask why these three beliefs grew so strong. Of the many revelant factors, I suggest that three were most central. I've already mentioned one—namely, the rise of a powerful middle class that did not need female labor. However, women needed an assignment, and all citizens agreed on one that was important. Total devotion to raising the infant and child became the central mission for the married woman. As a result, the dignity of women in the West rose considerably. European and American women have more dignity in this century, and especially during the last two decades, than they ever had in any society in the past.

An important corollary of the rise in dignity was the awarding of an enhanced importance to love and affection. As I read history, it appears that whenever a society celebrates women it also celebrates the moods and acts of love and affection.

The third factor involves the set of philosophical premises we call the Protestant tradition. The assumption that the mother was a central figure and that love should be in the family, not outside the family, was an important credo in the Protestant Reformation. Luther was troubled by the high rate of adultery in his society and urged men to select wives who would be not only good mothers but also attractive and gratifying love objects, as well. A final component of the Protestant credo is the imperative to train character. The task of training character belongs to the mother.

I trust you appreciate that the belief in the power of early experience, the significance of love, and the centrality of the mother cannot be as true as contemporary magazines and books imply. With so many other factors influencing the growing child, the assumptions that stem from these beliefs must be less valid than current ideology pretends.

## TWO DEVELOPMENTAL STORIES

Human development has two different stories to tell. One describes the growth of the universal characteristics that are present in all human beings because humans possess a particular set of genes. Humans have a generative language , apes do not; humans experience guilt, shame, and pride; apes do not; humans create laws and mathematics, and apes do not. As long as a child is not locked in a closet or confined to a basement, he or she will resemble other children around the world. The reasons for this universality comprise an interesting story, especially to psychologists, psychiatrists, and pediatricians. The moral of the story is that regardless of the family in which a child grows, he or she will demonstrate some of these universal qualities.

The second plot, which is of greater interest to citizens, seeks to explain the psychological differences among us. One hundred people, of any age, are different. In textbooks this idea is called personality. And therefore it is interesting to ask what factors create different personalities.

I shall deal first with the universals and then turn to what we know about the causes of personality.

## BIOLOGICAL PREPAREDNESS

As the brain grows in accord with its genetic script, the infant becomes able to behave and think in new ways. A six-month-old can neither understand nor speak language no matter what parents do because the brain is not sufficiently mature. However, when the child is twelve to fifteen months old it has reached a level of maturity that enables it to use the experiences of hearing speech to begin to utter words. We say that children are biologically prepared to learn, as long as they hear some language. The key phrase is "biologically prepared."

Zoologists say that birds are biologically prepared to sing the song of their species if they hear that song. So if a canary, hatched and raised in a laboratory and isolated from all birds, hears on tape the song of a canary at the right time in its development, it will later sing its proper song. All the bird needs is a brief exposure. Let us now examine four examples of biological preparedness in the psychological growth of children.

**The Growth of Memory**

At around eight to ten months of age the human brain reaches an important milestone when the number of synapses in most parts of the brain has reached a peak. As a result the infant can now retrieve memories of the past, as you can remember what you ate for breakfast or what you did last evening. Before infants are eight months old they cannot retrieve the past because their brains are not sufficiently mature to permit them to reach back and recall what happened a minute earlier. After eight months they can. As a result, infants become vulnerable to a special form of anxiety.

One basic occasion for anxiety is remembering the past and comparing it with the present and noting that the two memories do not correspond. Now the person has a problem and if he or she cannot solve that cognitive problem, anxiety results. If the engine on a jet sounds odd, you only become anxious if you can remember what the engine ordinarily sounds like. If you could not retrieve that sound you would not become anxious. You may have noticed that older people who begin to lose their recall memory become less anxious.

At about eight months babies begin to show fear of strangers and fear of separation from their caretakers. You may remember that at about eight to nine months your own child cried when you left the house. A four-month-old rarely cries to that event. The eight-month-old cries because, as the mother leaves, he or she is able to compare the memory of her presence moments ago with the current perception that she is absent. The infant cannot understand that inconsistency and so has a problem. The mother was present moments ago but is not present now. As a result the infant becomes anxious.

The anxieties of infancy are a nice illustration of the principle of preparedness. All infants are prepared to become anxious about unfamiliar people and separation from their mothers at a certain age because of the maturation of the brain.

**Moral Sense and Empathy**

A second example of preparedness that is equally important to our species concerns our moral sense. The tree of knowledge allegory in the Bible may be the wisest statement ever written about humans. You will remember that when Adam and Eve ate from the tree of knowledge God warned them that from then on humans would be different from animals because they would know the difference between right and wrong. Every moral philosopher has acknowledged, in one way or another, that deep truth about our species.

But, after the First World War, American psychology was caught up in a rampant and dogmatic environmentalism that implied that if you didn't teach a child right from wrong he might never know the difference. Psychologists taught their students in the thirties and forties that if a parent did not punish a child and inform him what was right and what was wrong, that child might grow up to be a criminal. But Genesis and Kant were closer to the truth. All children with an intact brain will, between seventeen and twenty-four months, become concerned with broken and flawed objects. This is a time when a child may point to a frayed thread on its shirt and say to the mother, "Mommy, look." The child understands there is something wrong with the shirt. This concern with right and wrong is a prepared characteristic, no different from speech or the improvement in memory at one year.

Another quality that appears at this time is empathy for the emotional state of another. Two-year-olds who live with human beings are able to infer that a person or an animal might be suffering or feeling distress. Hume, the Scottish philosopher, called that feeling sympathy and regarded it as the most fundamental human emotion. Psychologists call it empathy. Empathy for the state of another is a fundamental human emotion that does not have to be taught. It will emerge in all children in the second year. The two-year-old who is capable of empathy has also matured enough to know that if he or she caused the distress of another guilt will also appear. Like empathy, guilt does not have to be taught. Thus humans are biologically prepared to possess a minimal conscience.

Modern psychiatry made a mistake when it invented the word psychopath to apply to criminals. Applying that word to someone who murders with no emotion implies that the killer never had a conscience at any point in his development. I doubt that. As long as the killer was not brain damaged, he once knew right from wrong, and at age two had empathy. What may have happened was that life experiences during childhood and adolescence impaired his adult capacity for empathy. One may lose temporarily a basic human emotion—love is a good example. If a woman is rejected in love twelve times it will become harder for her to fall in love the next time the occasion arises. The experiences of life can reduce the adult capacity for empathy, but every child has that capacity.

**Preparedness for Responsibility**

Jean Piaget, one of the great psychologists of the twentieth century, said that children passed through stages of intellectual development and that one important stage occurred at about six or seven years of age, although children living in isolated, illiterate villages without schools pass through this stage two or three years later. I believe that at this time the brain has matured in new ways permitting a new set of mental abilities to be actualized.

You will remember that the Catholic church does not require confession of a child before age seven; English Common Law did not view a child as responsible for a crime prior to seven years of age. These facts mean that our ancestors, long before there was child psychology, understood that something profound happens to a child at about seven years of age. In my work in rural Guatemala I found that parents with eight or nine children who did not know their ages would assign a boy the cutting of a new field for corn or assign to a daughter the responsiblity of caring for an infant at about seven or eight years of age. Thus it must be that children are giving off some sign informing their parents they are ready for responsibility.

A second characteristic that occurs at this age is the talent to compare oneself to others. Now the child understands that he or she is prettier, less brave, or a better reader than a friend. A four-year-old cannot compare him or herself with another. This competence or ability to understand how one's qualities compare with those of a larger group has a major effect on the sense of self or self-concept. One of the components of the self-concept is the result of a psychological comparison of self with others. A child cannot know how intelligent he or she is unless he evaluates the other children in his classroom or neighborhood. Without comparative information there is no way to know how attractive, strong, brave, or intelligent one is.

### Recognition of Inconsistency

The last preparedness I shall discuss is more abstract but is critical for human functioning. As puberty begins another important maturational change occurs. By twelve or thirteen years of age adolescents begin to examine their beliefs on a particular theme, and if they detect inconsistency among these beliefs they become troubled. Consider the following illustration. An eight-year-old boy can hold these two beliefs and yet not feel uneasy—"My father is a wonderful man;" "My father yells at my mother." Although these ideas are inconsistent, an eight-year-old does not sense their lack of concordance. By contrast, a thirteen-year-old cannot help but sense the inconsistency and is driven to resolve it.

Adolescents experience the dissonance that is inherent in their sets of beliefs about God, sex, family, and their future. The tension and stress we attribute to adolescence has less to do with an increase in sex hormones than with a new ability to recognize that one's beliefs are discordant.

This special psychological tension is stronger in the West than in isolated village communities around the world where almost everybody in the community holds the same set of beliefs. As a result, there is little inconsistency and adolescence is a less troubling period than in Western communities where there is so much pluralism in ideology.

Each of these phenomena, the anxiety of infancy as well as the cognitive dissonance of adolescence, will appear whether ones's parents are kind or cruel, permissive or restrictive.

## PERSONALITY

I now turn to the second developmental story which asks how one can account for the differences among children and adults. In order to begin this discussion we have to decide what specific differences we will consider as important. Should we concentrate on swimming ability, how long a person sleeps, or whether a person laughs with gusto at jokes? Each culture values a small number of human qualities, awarding them more seriousness than others.

I believe that four such qualities valued in contemporary American society are: the acquistion of technical abilities, especially academic ones; differences in wealth and status; differences in the ability to enter into close and satisfying social relationships with others; and, finally, differences in happiness. Americans want to know why people differ on these four psychological qualities. Depending upon which of the four you pick, the profile causative forces will be different.

**Influencing Factors**

I now want to suggest six conditions which I believe contribute to the differences in technical ability, status, social relationships, and happiness that we see among adults. Depending upon which criterion you pick the balance of the six conditions will vary. Although the six conditions do not exhaust the domain of causative factors, they are important. You will also note at the end of the discussion that only one of the six is completely within the power of the parent. The remaining five are harder for parents to influence, although they are not beyond their will.

**1. Biological temperament.** The biological temperament of the infant is one of the most basic factors. The biological and psychological differences among infants that we call temperamental can be genetic or prenatal. Babies differ in activity level, irritability, and in how easily they establish a schedule when they return home from the hospital. The tempermental quality I wish to dwell on is one that our research group has been studying for almost eight years.

During the second year of life one sees infants who are extremely timid, fearful, cautious, and shy. They rush to their mother if a stranger comes into the house, and they cry when taken to the doctor. They don't let their mother leave them the first month or two of nursery school and cling whenever they're in an unfamiliar situation, at least until they have become more relaxed. We believe about 10 to 15 percent of children who behave this way were born with a biological predispositon to develop this style. Obviously, it is possible to make a child shy and timid through family experiences.

Another 15 percent of children are born with a predisposition to develop a more sociable, outgoing, and fearless behavioral style. It is hard to frighten such children. We have been following two groups of children who were noted in the second or third year of life to be either timid and shy or sociable and outgoing. We had to observe over 400 volunteer children in our laboratory in order to find these 100 children—50 who are consistently shy and timid and 50 who are sociable, fearless and outgoing. The children in the middle are less consistent. We have followed these children for six years and find remarkable consistency in their styles of behavior. We believe this consistency is due, in part, to differences in the biochemistry of their brains.

Deep in our brains there is an area called the limbic lobe which is the origin of the stress circuits that discharge when we are frightened. The activity of these stress circuits leads us to secrete cortisol, a hormone of the adrenal gland, increases the tension in our muscles, and makes our hearts beat faster.

The timid, shy children are reactive in all three of the stress circuits—namely, the pituitary-adrenal axis, the motor system, and the sympathetic chain. The fact suggests that the limbic lobe in the shy, timid children is at a lower threshhold of excitability to events that are unfamiliar or challenging.

However, some of these children have changed. We have seen parents of timid two-year-olds gently urge their children to be less shy, and over the years these children have changed. Specifically, about half of our timid, shy children at seven-and-a-half years of age are not extremely shy or timid. However, many families are fatalistic about their children and do not make gentle efforts to alter the child's temperamental qualities. When timid children enter school, many become isolated and loners. If such children come from middle-class families who promote high academic standards they are likely to choose an academic vocation such as history, poetry, or science. I believe that T. S. Eliot was one of these children.

If, on the other hand, the parents put excessive pressure on the child to succeed in some domain and the child does not have successes, that child may become extremely anxious and may show pathology later in life.

**2. Birth order.** A second condition contributing to personality differences is the child's birth order; that is, whether the child is first, second, or third born. If we compared a thousand first borns with a thousand later borns we would find that, among middle-class Americans, first borns are generally more responsible and seek to control their environment. First borns get better grades, end up going to better colleges, and, as adults, commit fewer crimes. When a stress or challenge occurs first borns are less likely to develop symptoms.

By contrast, when later borns are faced with stress they are more likely to develop problems. Later borns are more pragmatic, less idealistic, and a little more likely to be rebellious. Historical studies show that more of the rebels and terrorists of the world are later borns, and more of the idealists and abstract thinkers are first borns. For example, Trotsky the activist was a later born, Marx the scholar a first born.

Let me try to explain these differences. To a first born growing up in a traditional middle-class home, the world looks orderly. Parents are nurturant, predictable, kind people who set high standards. The child is closely attached to and identified with them and the child looks at the world as a just place where, if you do what you are told, all will be well. As first borns enter the period of childhood they ask their parents, "What is it that you want me to do? I will do it."

But the world looks different to a later born. Imagine a later born lying in his crib when suddenly a first born unpredictably shows up and intrudes into the sphere of the younger child. When a later born talks to his older sibling the latter doesn't necessarily reply, but he may seize a toy or pinch the child. Additionally, the first born can stay up until 10 o'clock, while the later born has to go to bed at sunset. Imagine these experiences happening week after week, year after year.

What might you predict to be the consequences of this regimen? One reasonable prediction is that later borns should see the world as a little less fair and just, while first borns should be more concerned with the approval of authority and less prone to disagree with or rebel against authority. First borns should want to keep harmonious relationships with authority and have less hostile feelings toward authority. If, as an adult, the person picks science as a vocation, one might predict that if a new scientific theory opposed what authority believed to be correct, and, therefore, threatened the society, the first born would be more likely to question the new idea. The more defiant later born would be more likely to favor it.

We are talking here about theories for which citizens have strong opinions. Educated citizens cared when Copernicus and Darwin said that the Bible's interpretation of the heavens or of man's place in nature was wrong. By contrast, the laser, although a brilliant discovery, did not threaten the average person's beliefs about man and nature. We are concerned here not with brilliant discoveries but with brilliant, new ideas about which most people have fixed beliefs.

Frank Sulloway, a young historian, has done research on this issue. He studied a large number of revolutions in science where the themes were of concern to the society. Some of these revolutions included the ideas of Copernicus, Francis Bacon, Freud, and, of course, Darwin. He then sought to determine what the eminent scientists of the time said about each revolutionary idea in a ten-year period after its original discovery. Was the scientist for or against the new idea and was he a first or later born? In studies of a dozen different scientific revolutions and many hundreds of scientists, he found that those who agreed with a new idea were likely to be later borns, while those who opposed it were likely to be first borns.[1] Thus one's attitude about a new scientific idea is influenced by one's ordinal position and seems to have little to do with that child's specific relationship to its parents.

3. **Parental influence.** Parents assume importance in our third condition, which deals with parental behavior toward the child. Parental behavior tends to assume its greatest importance during the first six or seven years of life.

There are three experiences that parents can provide that have a profound influence on their children. One of the least impeachable facts in child development is that the child's mental development will be stimulated if a parent provides a great deal of variety for the infant. Hence, parents who play with and talk to their children and present them with tameable variety will promote their children's mental development. Obviously, this variety can be supplied by a babysitter or a daycare center.

Some of the intellectual differences between a working- and a middle-class child are apparent by two to three years of age. Although working-class moth-

---

[1]Sulloway, F. Family constellations, sibling rivalry and scientfic revolutions. Unpublished manuscript, 1972.

ers love their children, they generally provide less variety during the period of infancy. It is not clear why they behave this way. Perhaps they don't believe in the effectiveness of presenting variety to the child.

A second way parents influence their children is through praise and punishment. The child does learn values in accord with what is rewarded and punished. Thus if parents discipline a child for dirtying his shirt or not cleaning his hands and do so consistently, they will get a five-year-old who is a little worried about keeping his shirt and hands clean. If a parent praises schoolwork, the child will become more concerned with doing well in school, at least during the early years of school.

A final source of parental influence involves communicating to the child that the parents value him or her. This experience is more important in our society in this century than it was in the past. You will recall that human beings have a natural tendence to evaluate themselves as good or bad. We all want our consciences to be gentle with us. When the day is done and we ask ourselves in the quiet of the evening, "How are you doing?" we want to be able to answer, "I am a good person." We are essentially moral creatures; in our daily lives we are engaged in a moral mission. A child growing up in a Third World village has to gather wood for the family, prepare supper, or wash clothes in the river. As a result it is obvious to such children that they are good. These seven-year-olds know that they are making a contribution to the family's vitality. Hence no adult has to say to them—and they usually don't—"I love you very much, Maria." Maria has less of a need for this communication because she knows she is of value.

In a society like ours, however, where children make no economic contribution to the family they have to be reassured about their goodness. That is one reason why love, the communication of value, has become so important. Historical changes made loving children, and the communication of love to children, important.

Loving a child does not necessarily mean giving that child a great deal of physical affection. John Stuart Mill recalled that his father was a wonderful person but not an emotionally close one. I have been reading an autobiography by a colleague, George Homans, who is now an emeritus professor. He writes of his father, "I could not have been blessed with a better father. I always enjoyed being with him, I respected him. Yet, I must say, I never felt emotionally close to him." A child can feel loved and can love a parent, even though there is not a great deal of physical affection between them. Some young Americans have a hard time understanding that idea because our culture has come to equate parental love with kissing and embracing.

4. **Identification with role models.** The fourth set of conditions is, in my opinion, the most important, and almost every philospher has made this point, but we continue to forget it. In modern dynamic pyschology the phenomenon I am referring to is called identification. Let me explain this idea. The child believes that some of the qualities of his or her parents also belong to the child. The child, as well as the adult, go beyond the objective facts and con-

clude, "I have the same last name as my family, I have the same color hair as my father, and my aunt noticed that my father and I both have dimples in our chins." The child goes beyond those facts and concludes that "because my father is popular I must be popular too; because my father is talented, I must be talented." Or the child can conclude, "No one respects my father, therefore no one will respect me." An identification with the parent can be positive or negative.

I believe that a parent's most important influence on a child originates in his or her status as a role model with whom that child can identify. One problem is that most parents find it difficult to hide their deep qualities, especially if these are undesirable. If a child perceives that the mother is competent, kind, nuturing, and attractive, then, fair or unfair, that seven-year-old girl will feel better about herself than she would otherwise. But if the mother is incompetent, not liked, and perceived to be unjust, then the child, even though she possesses none of those qualities, will feel bad, perhaps guilty. Many schizophrenics have identified with a rejecting mother they labeled as bad. As a result, they have these anxious feelings about themselves. A typical statement from a young schizophrenic woman to her psychiatrist is, "I'll tell you my problem, deep inside of me there is a great deal of evil." That feeling is a result of identification with a parent whom one perceives as bad.

Even though parents have limited control over how they present themselves to their children, it is their strongest power for it will influence the child's conception of self for many years. The child can also identify with his or her class or ethnic group. A child who is a member of a disadvantaged minority group is likely to perceive his or her group to be rejected by the larger society. As a result, the child will feel anxiety. In contemporary American society, disadvantaged Hispanic and Black children live with this burden if they identified with their ethnic group when they were young. Even though some grow up to be sucessful, they can carry the vulnerability for many years. A book that will bring a tear to your cheek, written by John Henry Wideman, is about a pair of Black brothers growing up in a ghetto in Pittsburgh. The older brother, a professor of English at the University of Wyoming, has written three novels and is respected in his community. His younger brother is serving a life sentence in a Pennsylvania prison for murder. The older brother, in an attempt to understand his younger brother, wrote a book called *Brothers and Keepers.*[2] In this book he confesses that although he is a professor of English who has written many books, every morning when he wakes up he is afraid he will be discovered. That feeling of vulnerability is a product of an earlier identification. Mr. Wideman may go to his grave anxious and suspecting that one day the larger society will discover this mysterious lack of goodness.

**5. Success and failure.** A fifth condition that influences the child resides in actual environmental successes and failures. Success in school depends in part on the size of the school. Many studies show that if the talent of a child is held

---

[2]Wideman, John Edgar. *Brothers and Keepers*. New York: Holt, Reinhart, and Winston, 1984.

constant, the probability of that child being successful is higher if he or she goes to a small school than to a very large one. Similarly, whether the peer group accepts or rejects the child is important. My colleague George Homans was not very popular with his peers and he writes that his classmates bullied and teased him. As a result he decided that he would become talented in schoolwork. The rejection by his peers and the subsequent decision set his life career.[3] It had less to do with his parents that with his experiences in school.

**6. Chance and history.** Finally we consider chance as a factor. Unlike the Chinese and the Malaysians, we in the West are less willing to acknowledge the role of chance in our lives. The Greeks acknowledged the power of the god's moods. You will remember that in *The Odyssey,* Athena decides what will happen to Odysseus; maybe she will cause a storm or arrange conditions to beach his boat on the rocks. But Americans want to believe that each is a master of his or her fate. If an adult is successful, he wants to believe that he did it through talent and motivation. If one fails, he or she did something wrong. And in our theories of human development we give chance events very little power.

Let me cite a few factors that are outside the control of children or families and, therefore, from that perspective are chance events. What was the size of the town in which the child grew up? If one leafs through *Who's Who in America* and notes the places where each person grew up, you will find that over 60 percent came from towns under 50,000 although the vast majority of Americans grow up in urban areas. How can we explain that anomaly?

Consider a nine-year-old girl with an I. Q. of 120 who is skilled and has kind parents. On the one hand, let us have her grow up in Salado, Texas; on the other in Chicago. In Salado there will be very few girls as talented as she, and if she stays there through high school she will graduate as a seventeen-year-old who feels very good about herself because she has compared herself with the other girls in the town and realized that she was in the top 5 percent. In Chicago she will know over two-hundred girls who are more talented and pretty than she and, as a result, she will learn humility.

That's why those listed in *Who's Who* spent their childhoods in small towns. Among the first group of astronaut candidates, three-quarters grew up in small towns—towns without great museums, large aquariums, or six-story libraries.

If one is going to succeed in an extraordinary way it is necessary to have an illusion about the self. The adolescent must believe that he or she is much better than others are. Illusion is harder to establish if there are several hundred children one's own age who are more talented, attractive, or courageous.

Historical events that influence the entire society comprise another chance factor. The Depression of the 1930s is one example. Sociologists have found that if a child was between seven and fifteen years of age during the Depression, his adult behavior was influenced profoundly. Many who were adoles-

---

[3]Homans, G. C. *Coming to My Senses.* New Brunswick, N.J.: Transaction Books, 1984.

cents in Europe after World War I, the spiritual war that was to solve all of the world's probems, became skeptics for the rest of their lives.

An American youth in high school or college during the Vietnam War was also influenced in a serious way. I would like to find two hundred 35-year-olds who were ages fifteen to eighteen during the Vietnam protests in cities like San Francisco, Chicago, New York, and Boston and compare them with similar groups who are five years younger or five years older. I believe that I would find profound differences among these groups because of the experiences that occurred to them during the Vietnam era. These experiences had little to do with the kindness or meanness of their parents but were the result of events that were totally outside familial control.

With computers gaining ascendance, a child between seven and fifteen years old today will be influenced by the introduction of computers into the schools and society.

## CONCLUSION

I have listed six factors that can have important effects on the growth of children. Two involve parents. They pertain to what parents do and what they are—their actual practices with their children and how they are viewed as role models for identification. But parents have far less control over the other four factors. That is why I said earlier that parents have power but that power is constrained. The limitation does not mean that parents should not invest effort and care in rearing children. They should be loving and conscientious as parents and should reflect on their actions. Indeed, they cannot do otherwise, for humans are prepared to believe that they can have an effect on the world. But they also must realize that the growing child is a product of the coming together of many, many coherent events, including the child's temperament, historical era, and birth order. An individual life is a complex story with many collaborators.

# 28

Judith Blake

# The Only Child in America: Prejudice versus Performance

*Many of the characteristics of the family in which a person grows up may affect the kind of adult that person becomes. Among the more tangible of these characteristics is whether or not one has siblings (brothers and/or sisters), and if so, how many.*

*In the reading that follows, Judith Blake summarizes much of what has been learned in recent years about the effects of being an only child, and incidentally, she also presents considerable evidence on the effects of number of siblings on those who have them. She emphasizes evidence that indicates the advantages of being an only child, and indeed makes it clear that being an only child does not bring as much disadvantage as popular belief holds.*

*On the other hand, evidence on the effects of sibship size (number of children in the family) is still rather limited, and it is possible that typical disadvantages of being an only child await discovery by social and behavioral scientists. One largely unexplored issue is how well only children fare in their marriages and other intimate relationships, although Blake points out that they are not much more likely to divorce than are other persons.*

Source: Reprinted with the permission of the Population Council, from Judith Blake, "The only child in America: Prejudice versus performance," *Population and Development Review* 7, no. 1 (March 81): 43–54.

Being an only child is widely regarded as a significant handicap. Indeed, this belief appears to be so generally accepted that research psychologists Thompson and Maltes suggest that it is a "cultural truism"—an unchallengeable given.[1]Going beyond her own research, Thompson has noted, in a 1974 review of the popular and scientific literature on the effects of birth order and family size, that only children are usually viewed as being selfish, lonely, and maladjusted.[2] A 1977 survey of the literature on the only child by another psychologist, Toni Falbo, stated that the presence of siblings is popularly assumed to have both positive and negative effects, but the lack of siblings is believed to have only negative consequences.[3]

In my own work, I have used the mechanism of nationwide surveys to test public views about the only child in the United States. In 1950, a question was asked whether being an only child is an advantage or a disadvantage. Seventy-six percent of respondents said that being an only child is a disadvantage. The same question, asked again on three occasions during the 1970s, produced similar results, although there was a small decline, in the 1977 survey, to 67 percent saying "disadvantaged." In this most recent study, respondents who believed the only child to be at a disadvantage were asked to specify the single most important handicap they had in mind. Sixty percent cited a personality or character defect—self-centered, domineering, anxious, quarrelsome, "spoiled," or "overprotected." An additional 22 percent claimed tht the only child has a lonely childhood. Yet, only 2 percent of respondents believed, or even when asked directly, that the major disadvantage suffered by only children is prejudice from teachers, neighbors, relatives, or other children.

It is not remarkable, therefore, that my analysis of over 40 years of nationwide American surveys on reproductive preferences finds the one-child response to be almost an empty cell. Similar results have come out of major fertility surveys of American women in the reproductive ages that have been taken from time to time since 1955.[1] Additionally, the Bureau of the Census Current Population Survey asks questions on the number of children wives expect to have and the number they have had, by various ages. Although Census Bureau experts Maurice Moore and Martin O'Connell document a rise between 1960 and 1976 in the proportion of wives expecting to have one child—from 7 percent to 11 percent—not all of this increase necessarily reflects perferences.[5] As couples marry later, delay childbearing, and divorce more freqently, the expectation of one child is, in many cases, probably only realistic. Indeed, the proportions expecting to have one child are considerably more modest than the proportions having one child. According to the Census Bureau, among married women aged 30–31, the percentage who had only one birth increased from 11.9 in 1970 to 17.9 in 1978.[6] In effect, few people actually prefer to have a single child, more people realistically asses that this is how they will end up (given their marital patterns and childbearing delays), and an even higher percentage actually have only one birth (although this result may not have been "expected"). Even in this era of low birth rates, at least two children are preferred by all but a small percentage of Americans.

Do the actual attributes and behaviors of only children warrant the unflattering evaluations that seem to prevail? Aside from its intrinsic scientific interest, this question has increasingly practical implications. Like the United States, many countries in the developed world will be experiencing rising proportions of single-child families if, for no other reason, because of skyrocketing divorce rates and, in some cases, delayed first births. The leaders of one quarter of the world's population, China, are now setting the single-child family as a national goal, in an effort to hasten not only zero population growth, but population decline. Are couples in these countries faced with a trade-off between nurturing excess seeds and producing a single bad one?

Until recently, social science has had little to say on this topic. Interest in the only child has been marginal, and such work as has appeared typically has addressed the subject solely in the context of other more pressing matters. Consequently, research on singletons often is fraught with methodological incomparabilities. For example, many studies have grouped only children and first-borns from families of all sizes. Most research, even when distinguishing only children from first-borns, has been based on small samples (sometimes fewer than 100 cases) and has been composed of subjects selected for particular attributes—eminent persons, geniuses, college students, inhabitants of mental institutions, alcoholics, and so on. Conclusions about the characteristics of only children based on such "retrospective" samples are, of course, highly suspect. Needed are large, heterogeneous samples, chosen according to some statistically rational sampling scheme, rather than samples self-selected for either superior performance or debilitating malfunction. It is obviously crucial, as well, to control for different characteristics of parents—for example, education, income, occupation—and for whether the home was broken during the subject's childhood.

Beginning with the mid-1970s, studies of this sort have started to appear. In general, they have concentrated on a single dependent variable, such as a measure of intelligence, and they have involved very young samples. Moreover, the only child rarely has been the focus of attention. Reports about only children have emerged as a consequence of a general concern with birth order and family size. Nonetheless, the results are of major importance in establishing a scientific base for inquiry into the consequences of being an only child.

For example, in a now-classic article published in 1973,[7] Belmont and Marolla presented results of their work on birth order, family size, and intelligence among the total population of men (400,000) born in the Netherlands from 1944 through 1947 who still resided in Holland at the time they reached age 19. At that age, they had to appear for an examination to determine their fitness for military service. Part of that examination included a psychometric test of intellectual performance, the Raven Progressive Matrices. This instrument tests nonverbal intelligence and, hence, is relatively free of a bias favoring upper social and economic groups who are more verbally facile and the less-advantaged. Information was also available on the subject's sibsize and birth order, as well as on the father's occupation, the latter serving as a control for social class. Belmont and Marolla's principle findings related to the separate effects of family size and birth order on intellectual performance, controlling for social class. Of interest here is that, although first-born children and children from small families (one to three children) achieved the highest scores, only children did not do as well as expected given the fact that they were the first-borns from the smallest possible family. Only children did slightly less well than first-borns in four-child families and then the youngest children in two-child families. The differences are not great (although statistically significant), but they are unexpected.

Following up on Belmont and Marolla, Zajonc used the same data to attempt to interpret the family size and birth-order difference.[8] His thesis, the confluence model, was that as family size goes up, the intellectual environment of the nuclear family goes down because it becomes heavily weighted with infantile minds. Hence, progressively younger children not only receive less parental attention than did the oldest child, but the overall family configuration has become more and more intellectually "babyish." As family size becomes very large, a parabolic effect occurs—older children become pseudo-parents—so that the negative effect of the large family is mitigated for younger children. But, why is the only child at a disadvantage compared with children in small families? Because, Zajonc postulates, it has no one to teach, as do older children in families of one or more siblings. The only child shares this disability with the last-born child in all families.

In pointing out this anomaly, we should stress that only children do better than most subjects in the birth order/family size matrix. Out of 45 categories of birth order/family size in the Belmont-Marolla data, the score for the only child is exceeded by only five categories—both children in the two-child family, the first two in the three-child family, and the oldest in the four-child family. Moreover, the differences are small. Given the marginal differences, Falbo has suggested that the effects may be due to factors other than the teaching influence cited by Zajonc.[9] For example, only children are more likely to come from homes broken by death or divorce. Controls are needed for this problem.

This point is highlighted by further findings of Zajonc's concerning the only child and children from small families: the relative intelligence test scores among these birth orders tend to shift somewhat, depending on ages at which the children are tested. Among subjects in late adolescence, such as American National Merit Scholarship test-takers studied by Breland, the pattern found among Dutch males is replicated. But among younger subjects, such as a sample of 11-year-old Scottish children, only children score the highest of all birth order/family size combinations; and in France only children aged 6–14 had the highest intelligence scores except for the second of two-child families.[10] Such minor anomalies among children in small families remain to be explained, but of interest here is the clear intellectual advantage of only children relative to those from most family size/birth order statuses.

The fact that only children have been found, in study after study, to be intellectually advantaged, does not bear on the persistent popular belief that singletons are "spoiled," maladjusted, asocial, lonely, and self-centered. In a recent review of the literature on the only child, Falbo concludes that no evidence supports such popular stereotypes, but, at that time of her review in 1977, no compelling evidence was available to cast doubt on them either.[11]

Now, as a consequence of independent work by Claudy, Farrell, and Dayton, on the one hand, and the author, on the other, it is possible to offer some systematic assessment of the social and personal attributes of only children, as well as of their educational and occupational achievements. The findings suggest that only children either do not differ from children in small families or are superior to children with siblings. They are most certainly ahead, on the average, of children from large families (six or more children). These findings hold whether we consider children from unbroken parental marriages or from broken and unbroken ones combined. They hold even controlling for the fact that only children tend to come from more educated and advantaged families. Although numerous personal attributes have gone unmeasured, these results argue that the disadvantages of being an only child may lie primarily in the eye of the socioculturally biased beholder.

The research by Claudy, Farrell, and Dayton[12] used data from Project Talent, a large-scale, longitudinal study concerned with the nature and development of younger people's talents in the United States. Talent involved a 4.5 percent sample of 400,000 students in 1,255 American high schools (grades 9–12). Beginning in 1960, and, for follow-up subsamples, one, five, and eleven years later, these students were given a battery of cognitive, personality, achievement, attitudinal, and health-related tests. Claudy and his colleagues focused their analysis on a subsample of 3,331 only children and children from two-child families. No birth-order distinction was made from unbroken, two-parent homes. The results of this study partialled out the effects of socioeconomic differences between only and two-child families.

To summarize the results briefly, only children performed significantly better cognitively than did children from two-child families. Of the 32 possible differences between the two groups, only children scored higher in 25 instances, were equal in four, and lower in only three. As the authors say, "a sign test applied to these directionality differences shows that onlies were significantly higher in cognitive abilities overall."[13] These results suggest that the marginal underperformance of only children in the Belmont and Marolla findings and in Breland's analysis of the National Merit Scholarship Qualification Tests may be due to a lack of controls in these analyses, for the fact is that only children are more likely to come from broken homes.

Claudy and his colleagues found that only children were more mature, socially sensitive, tidy, and "cultered," but somewhat less sociable. They did not differ from children in two-child families in calmness, impulsiveness, self-confidence, drive, vigor, or leadership. Only children appear to be more like adults than other children. They imitate not only adult linguistic behavior, but other adult behavior as well. Their "reference group" is more likely to be composed of adults than is the case for children having a sibling. With the effect of parents' occupations partialled out, the occupational interests of only children favored science, mathematics, music, and literary fields, whereas children from two-child families veered more toward sports, hunting and fishing, and mechinical pursuits. Only children preferred more solitary activities (like reading), over group-oriented and practical ones. As to health, only children did not differ from non-onlies. Only children had higher academic skills and higher need to achieve; however the differences in this area were small. The follow-up, when the oldest subjects were age 29, showed only children to have greater academic achievement, to have married better educated spouses, to have had fewer children, to be less likely to divorce (at least by a young age), and to differ in subjective "life satisfaction," from those subjects who had a sibling.

The author's analysis is based on a widely used data bank, the General Social Science Surveys, conducted annually between 1972 and 1978 by the National Opinion Research Center (NORC) of the University of Chicago.[14] These surveys took place during the early spring in each year and covered 10,652 respondents for all years combined. Approximately 1,500 respondents were interviewed each year for approximately one hour. Each survey was an independently drawn sample of English-speaking men and women living in noninstitutional arrangements within the continental United States. The early surveys used a modified probability sample design; from the mid 1970s onward a full probability sample was employed.

This analysis treats the entire set of surveys for the 1970s as one body of data. In each year, a question was asked concerning how many siblings respondents had. It is thus possible to disaggregate the data set according to the sibsize of the respondents. There are a total of 627 only children in the entire data set. To our knowledge, this is the largest heterogeneous sample of adult singletons that has been studied to date and that can be compared with respondents from families of other sizes, although this is an interesting by-product of our research that receives attention elsewhere.

The National Opinion Research Center data have other desirable properties. There is extensive information concerning the educational, occupational, financial, and religious background of respondents' parents, the educational, occupational, and religious attributes of spouses, and numerous demographic, socioeconomic, and cultural data on the respondents themselves. There are, as well, for almost every year, data on a variety of indexes of personal-social adjustment and satisfaction in life; sociability and group membership; attitudes toward social and political institutions and social issues; and family behavior. Finally, it is possible to control for whether respondents were from broken or unbroken homes by the age of 16. It is not possible to distinguish among various birth orders. However, the only child can be compared with respondents from two-child families, both of which birth orders exceeded the only child on the Dutch intelligence tests and in the American National Merit Scholarship analysis. It is thus possible to view the only child against its two most powerful competitors—children in two-child families.

Before describing our findings on only children themselves, we may glance briefly at their family backgrounds. According to almost every measure, only children chose their parents well. The parents of only children far exceed the mothers and fathers of respondents from large families on every measure of achievement and are highly competitive with the parents of small families. The educational level of both parents of only children is almost identical to that of respondents from two- and three-child families (see Table 1). Among the fathers of all birth orders, those who sired singletons are least represented in the grade-school category and have the highest proportions completing high school. Singletons' fathers are almost equal in college preparation to fathers who produced two offspring. The mothers of only children also make an educational showing that vies with that of mothers of two.

With regard to occupational prestige, as shown in Table 2, fathers of only children are equal to fathers of two. Additionally, insofar as city life has cultural advantages for a growing youngster, singletons were the most advantaged in adolescence. Compared with every other family size, fewer only children lived in a rural setting at age 16, and more lived in a large city (see Table 3). Evaluations by respondents of their family's income when they were teenagers (Table 4) puts only children in as advantaged a situation as children from two-child families.

In only one major respect were only children handicapped—fewer grew up through mid-adolescence with both parents. Only 66 percent of only children still lived with both parents by age 16, whereas among respondents from two-child families 79 percent came from unbroken households. The parents of only children were disproportionately separated by both death and divorce, leaving a higher percentage of only children with their mothers than was the case for respondents of any other birth order. Only children also resided disproportionately with relatives other than a parent. It is hardly surprising, therefore, that more of the singletons' mothers worked after marrying and

**TABLE 1** ***Educational attainment of respondent's parents by sibsize (percent distribution)***

| *Respondent's sibsize* | *Some high school or less* | *Completed high school* | *Some college* | *Completed college* | *Total* |
|---|---|---|---|---|---|
| Father | | | | | |
| 1 | 48 | 29 | 11 | 12 | 100 |
| 2 | 49 | 27 | 9 | 15 | 100 |
| 3 | 52 | 27 | 10 | 11 | 100 |
| 4 | 58 | 24 | 9 | 9 | 100 |
| 5 | 67 | 20 | 7 | 6 | 100 |
| 6 | 73 | 17 | 4 | 6 | 100 |
| 7 + | 84 | 11 | 3 | 2 | 100 |
| Mother | | | | | |
| 1 | 45 | 37 | 9 | 9 | 100 |
| 2 | 42 | 40 | 11 | 7 | 100 |
| 3 | 45 | 38 | 10 | 7 | 100 |
| 4 | 56 | 29 | 9 | 6 | 100 |
| 5 | 58 | 32 | 6 | 4 | 100 |
| 6 | 69 | 23 | 5 | 3 | 100 |
| 7 + | 81 | 15 | 3 | 1 | 100 |

**TABLE 2** ***Prestige of respondent's father's occupation by sibsize (percent distribution)***

| *Respondent's sibsize* | *1* | *2* | *3* | *4* | *Total* |
|---|---|---|---|---|---|
| 1 | 16 | 22 | 31 | 31 | 100 |
| 2 | 15 | 26 | 31 | 30 | 100 |
| 3 | 17 | 24 | 35 | 24 | 100 |
| 4 | 19 | 25 | 35 | 21 | 100 |
| 5 | 23 | 25 | 38 | 14 | 100 |
| 6 | 24 | 21 | 41 | 14 | 100 |
| 7+ | 27 | 17 | 47 | 9 | 100 |

Note: The four categories of occupational prestige used in this table have been derived from a continuous variable ranging from 1 to 89. In this table, the categories range from "low" (1) to "high" (4).

worked while the child was a preschooler. It would appear that being an only child is frequently a result of marital disruption, rather than choice, on the part of the youngster's parents.

Turning to the characteristics of the respondents themselves, we find (after controlling for the educational attainment of both parents, the respondent's own race, age, sex, religion, and community size and economic status during adolescence) that singletons have marginally higher educational achievement than respondents who had one sibling. As shown in Table 5, starting with respondents from three-child families, educational achievement declines sharply with increasing family size.

The slight advantage in educational achievement enjoyed by only children is somewhat more marked when the regression is run for respondents from unbroken homes. Again, in this case as well, educational attainment declines regularly with increases in family size. Quite clearly, as with the findings by Claudy and his colleagues, only children measure up well in educational achievement.

**TABLE 3** ***Size of community in which respondent resided during adolescence (percent distribution)***

| *Respondent's sibsize* | *Rural* | *Fewer than 50,000* | *50,000–250,000* | *Suburb of large city* | *250,000+* | *Total* |
|---|---|---|---|---|---|---|
| 1 | 16 | 34 | 17 | 8 | 25 | 100 |
| 2 | 21 | 32 | 15 | 12 | 20 | 100 |
| 3 | 26 | 33 | 15 | 9 | 17 | 100 |
| 4 | 27 | 33 | 14 | 9 | 17 | 100 |
| 5 | 32 | 33 | 12 | 7 | 16 | 100 |
| 6 | 38 | 31 | 11 | 5 | 15 | 100 |
| 7+ | 51 | 26 | 9 | 3 | 11 | 100 |

**TABLE 4** ***Respondent's estimate of family income during adolescence (percent distribution)***

| *Respondent's sibsize* | *Below average* | *Average* | *Above average* | *Don't know* | *Total* |
|---|---|---|---|---|---|
| 1 | 22 | 57 | 20 | 1 | 100 |
| 2 | 21 | 57 | 21 | 1 | 100 |
| 3 | 26 | 55 | 18 | 1 | 100 |
| 4 | 26 | 57 | 16 | 1 | 100 |
| 5 | 32 | 56 | 11 | 1 | 100 |
| 6 | 36 | 53 | 11 | — | 100 |
| 7+ | 44 | 48 | 7 | 1 | 100 |

Of interest also is the fact that, taking account of respondent's own education and occupational prestige, only children marry spouses whose education is roughly equal to that of respondents coming from two-child families.

Turning to occupational achievement, after controls for educational attainment, age, race, religion, and community size at age 16, Table 6 shows that male singletons exceed those from all other birth orders, including those from two-child families. Moreover, male singletons marry women from higher prestige occupations, even controlling for the spouse's education, the man's education, and his own occupational achievement.

Interestingly, the occupational advantage enjoyed by male singletons, relative to those from other sibsizes, is not so clearly reflected in the behavior of women—either with regard to their own occupational achievement, or to that of their spouses. Female only children, although above the mean in occupational attainment, did not do as well as did those from two-child and three-

**TABLE 5** ***Educational attainment of respondents (years of schooling) (adjusted deviation from grand mean)***

| *Respondent's sibsize* | *Unbroken parental homes* | *All types of parental homes* |
|---|---|---|
| 1 | .78 | .74 |
| 2 | .68 | .69 |
| 3 | .32 | .35 |
| 4 | .22 | .18 |
| 5 | −.12 | −.10 |
| 6 | −.25 | −.24 |
| 7+ | −.76 | −.73 |
| Grand Mean | 11.91 | 11.67 |

Note: These deviations have been adjusted through multiple regression analysis for the respondent's parents' educational levels and religion and the respondent's age, sex, race, urban/rural background, and economic level when an adolescent.

**TABLE 6** ***Prestige of respondent's occupation (adjusted deviation from the grand mean)***

| | *Men* | | *Women* | |
|---|---|---|---|---|
| *Respondent's sibsize* | *Unbroken parental homes* | *All types parental homes* | *Unbroken parental homes* | *All types parental homes* |
| 1 | 2.03 | 1.50 | .45 | .20 |
| 2 | .12 | .20 | .97 | 1.03 |
| 3 | −.30 | −.14 | .92 | .86 |
| 4 | .41 | .18 | .60 | .20 |
| 5 | .94 | .84 | .63 | .90 |
| 6 | −.15 | −.24 | −1.06 | −.75 |
| 7+ | −.93 | −.74 | −1.43 | −1.39 |
| Grand Mean | 40.40 | 39.60 | 38.77 | 37.88 |

Note: These deviations have been adjusted, through multiple regression analysis, for the respondent's age, race, religion, educational attainment, urban/rural background, and income. See also note to Table 2.

child families. Moreover, those who came from unbroken homes did not perform any better. Additionally, female singletons did not marry men of as high occupational status as did female respondents from two- or three-child families. We should caution that none of the differences is large, however.

Singletons and those from two-child families are also less likely ever to have received public assistance as adults than respondents coming from larger families. This result partials out the confounding effects of educational and occupational achievement and such other attributes as race, age, and religion.

Are only children dissatisfied, malajusted, and asocial? Four indicators of happiness and life satisfaction are available from the NORC survey— respondents' self-evaluations of their own general happiness and their satisfaction with their health, with a hobby or hobbies, and with their jobs. When compared to those from families of two or three children, singletons either are no different with regard to happiness and satisfaction or are happier and more satisfied. The possible exception to this generalization relates to hobbies, but the differences are small. Only children see themselves as happier and more satisfied than do persons from really large families (six or more children). This result holds true even when confounding differences in social and economic status are controlled.

What of expectations about the motives and goodwill of other people? Are singletons optimistic about the generally benign nature of human interaction, or are they suspicious, guarded, and mistrustful? In general, as with other measures, differences by sibsize are small when background characteristics have been controlled. Nonetheless, those differences that do exist suggest that only children are optimistic that other people will be helpful and fair. Children from large families, by contrast, are less sanquine about other people's motives. Singletons are marginally less likely to believe that others can be trusted than are those from other small families, but they are more trusting than those from large families.

Are NORC respondents who are only children as sociable and affiliative as those who have had siblings? One indicator of such behavior is membership in voluntary organizations (over and above church membership). Table 7 suggests little difference by sibsize when background variables are controlled but indicates a slightly lower average number of memberships for singletons than for those having siblings. Additional questions concerning the number of times a year the respondent spent an evening with relatives or friends show singletons are least likely, of all respondents, to spend an evening with relatives, and they are less likely than are respondents from two-child families to spend an evening with friends, although differences are not great.[15] The evidence does point, therefore, to somewhat less sociability on the part of singletons—a result consistent with previous work.

As a final measure of social adjustment, we may take marital stability. Are singletons more likely to have unstable marriages? Again, compared to those from two- and three-child families, there are no differences in proportions ever-divorced. The proportions ever-divorced for those respondents from all small families are slightly higher than those from larger families, but the differences are in no case noteworthy.

Aside from personal and social adjustment, a major problem in modern societies is that of alienation from social and political institutions. The NORC surveys have devoted many questions to this topic. Analysis of the results of these questions demonstrates that singletons are as supportive of science, medicine, business, educational institutions, the press, and the clergy as are those

**TABLE 7** ***Sociability and affiliation of respondent's (adjusted deviations from the grand mean)***

| *Respondent's sibsize* | *Number of nonchurch organizational memberships* | *Frequency of evening with relatives* | *Frequency of evening with friends* |
|---|---|---|---|
| 1 | −.15 | −.17 | −.08 |
| 2 | .06 | −.06 | .10 |
| 3 | −.05 | −.11 | .02 |
| 4 | .06 | −.01 | .02 |
| 5 | .02 | .09 | .02 |
| 6 | .06 | .06 | .01 |
| 7+ | −.05 | .08 | −.09 |
| Grand Mean | 1.90 | 4.57 | 3.96 |

Note: "Membership" is adjusted for age, race, sex, religion, educational attainment, rural urban background, and income. "Relatives" and "Friends" are, in addition, adjusted for the number of children the respondent has. In the case of both "Relatives" and "Friends" the frequency ranges from "Never" (1) to "More than once a week" (7).

from two- and three-child families. The same is true of only children's confidence in the Congress, the Supreme Court, and the Presidency.

In one final respect, only children are uniquely adusted. In a world that seems increasingly to require fertility control, singletons prefer smaller families, on the average, than do respondents from any other family size of orientation (Table 8). The total number of children they actually have, and expect to have, is commensurably modest. Only children do not, however, disproportionately desire to have a one-child family themselves.

To conclude, research findings on the only child do not support the negative stereotypes that still persist about singletons. On average, only children are intellectually superior and achieve higher educational and occupational status. They have no obvious character or personality defects; they have attitudes appropriate to good citizens of the body politic, their family behavior is not disruptive, and they are unlikely to be public charges. Even partialling out the positive effects of their relatively advantaged social and economic status, they tend to count themselves happy, and to be satisfied with important aspects of life—notably jobs and health.

Hence, rather than emphasizing marginal differences between only children and those who have one or two siblings, it seems more important to note that on every measure children from small families, including only children, fare better than do those from large families.

Why do unflattering stereotypes about the only child persist? One possible explanation, or course, is that the research reported here has failed to capture aspects of the personalities of only children that other people find abrasive or otherwise unattractive. In unmeasured, but important ways, only children may be less cooperative, less extending to others, less socially engaging, more individualistic and autonomous. Even the positive findings reported here do not

**TABLE 8** ***Respondent's family size preferences and actual-plus-expected family size (adjusted deviations from the grand mean)***

| *Respondent's sibsize* | *Ideal number of children* | *Actual-plus-expected number of children* |
|---|---|---|
| 1 | −.19 | −.19 |
| 2 | −.15 | −.21 |
| 3 | −.10 | −.06 |
| 4 | −.03 | −.06 |
| 5 | .03 | .09 |
| 6 | .07 | .01 |
| 7+ | .17 | .20 |
| Grand Mean | 2.68 | 2.58 |

Note: These deviations have been adjusted, through multiple regression analysis, for the respondent's age, sex, race, religion, education, rural/urban background, and income.

show sociability to be the only child's strong suit. The possibility that significant variables have been ignored cannot be dismissed out of hand.

Two other explanations are also plausible. One is that, in human history, only children and those with few siblings have always been at an advantage in at least some respects. Impartible inheritance of land and wealth certainly argues for this point. Yet, what was an advantage for the individual was not necessarily in the interest of societal survival, under conditions of high infant and child mortality. Hence, those societies that survived were ones that built strong pronatalist sentiments into their belief structures—including prejudice against singletons. This prejudice set the minimal acceptable number of surviving births at two and, presumably, was a factor motivating parents to have more births than would have been the case had the singleton not been disvalued.[16]

Second, it is also more likely that only children are becoming progressively more advantaged over time, because the modern world is geared to rewarding individual talent over group effort or family backing. In effect, not only have the rewards to parents for having many children largely disappeared in urban, mobile, technological societies, but the rewards to siblings from having strong brothers and well-married sisters have also faded. Remaining are the disadvantages of large families—particularly competition for parental resources during the growing-up period.

The results presented here encourage social scientists to continue to examine the effects of differential family size. But, these findings also suggest that the burden of demonstrating deleterious consequences for singletons has been shifted to the critics of the only child.

## NOTES

1. The unpublished research by Thompson and Maltes is discussed in V.D. Thompson, "Family size: Implicit policies and assumed psychological outcomings," *Journal of Social Issues* 30, no. 4(1974): 93–124.

2. Thompson, cited in note 1, p. 96.

3. T. Falbo, "The only child: A review," *Journal of Individual Psychology* 33, no. 1(May 1977): 47–61.

4. I have analyzed the 1955 and 1960 Growth of American Families Studies and the 1965, 1970, and 1975 National Fertility Studies, as well as the 1973 and 1976 National Surveys of Family Growth. All shows fractional proportions of respondents intending or expecting or desiring to have one child.

5. M. J. and M. O'Connell, *Perspectives on American Fertility.* U.S. Bureau of the Census. Current Population Reports: Special Studies, Series P–23, no. 70 (July 1978): Table 3–3, p. 25.

6. U.S. Bureau of the Census, Current Population Reports, Series P–20, no. 341 (October 1979): Table 7, p. 34.

7. L. Belmont and F. A. Marolla, "Birth order, family size, and intelligence", *Science* 182 (14 December 1973): 1096–1101.

8. R. B. Zajonc and G. B. Markus, "Birth order and intellectual development," *Psychological Review* 82, no. 1 (1975): 74–88; and R. B. Zajonc, "Family configuration and intelligence," *Science* 192(16 April 1976): 227–236.

9. T. Falbo, "Sibling tutoring and other explanations for intelligence discontinuties of only and last borns." *Journal of Population* 1, no. 4(Winter 1978): 349–363.

10. Zajonc, cited in note 8.

11. Falbo, cited in note 3.

12. J. G. Claudy, W. S. Farrell, Jr., and C. W. Dayton, *The Consequences of Being an Only Child: An Analysis of Project Talent Data* (Palo Alto, California: American Institutes for Research. 1979).

13. Claudy, Farrell, and Dayton, cited in note 12, p. 33.

14. For a complete listing of the questions used in every year of the NORC surveys, together with the marginals for each question, see J. A. Davis, *General Social Surveys, 1972–1978: Cumulative Data* (Chicago: National Opinion Research Center. 1978). In performing the present analysis, I have used the cumulative tapes that were made available by the Social Data Archive, Institute for Social Science Research, University of California, Los Angeles. I am indebted to Sandra Rosenhouse for assistance with data processing and analysis.

15. Since only children do not have siblings and are more likely to have come from broken homes, they have fewer relatives, on average, with whom to spend an evening. It was not possible to control for the number of available relatives among respondents from various sibsizes.

16. The desire to avoid having an only child was one of the most frequent reasons offered by respondents in the Indianapolis Study when they were asked why they wanted a second child. See E. S. Solomon, J. E. Clare, and C. F. Westoff, "Fear of childness, desire to avoid having an only child, and children's desires for siblings," *Milbank Memorial Fund Quarterly* 34, no. 2 (April 1956): 160–177.

29

E. MAVIS HETHERINGTON AND KATHLEEN A. CAMARA

# The Effects of Family Dissolution and Reconstitution on Children

*The breakup of a marriage usually brings pain and discomfort to everyone involved, but for at least a substantial minority of divorcing spouses, the final separation and the divorce bring a sense of relief. For the "children of divorce," on the other hand, the parental separation and its aftermath are rather consistently associated with strong negative feelings (some of which may be lingering effects of influences prior to the parental separation). There almost always seem to be some negative effects, but precisely how children are affected by a parental separation, by living in a one-parent home, and by remarriage of the custodial parent seems to depend on a number of variables, many of which are discussed in the reading that follows. The selection excerpts, from a paper on the effects of family dissolution and reconstitution on both adults and children, the portions that deal primarily with children.*

*Although the literature on the effects on children of parental separation and divorce is extensive, many questions remain unanswered. For instance, have the negative effects become less severe as divorce has become more common and as the children of divorce have less reason to feel different from most of their peers? Do some negative effects often persist into adulthood, leaving persons whose parents divorced less well adjusted, on the average, than other adults?*

Source: Adapted from "Families in Transition: The Process of Dissolution" by E. Mavis Hetherington and Kathleen A. Camara in *Review of Child Development Research: Volume 7, The Family*, pp. 398–431 by permission of The University of Chicago Press.  Published 1984.

---

Divorce, life in a one-parent family, and remarriage are becoming increasingly common experiences in the lives of parents and children. Past psychological and sociological research on divorce has focused on the effects of changes within family structure on the intellectual, social, and psychological functioning of children and adults. A sizable body of literature now exists on the outcomes of divorce for family members. However, until recent years, little attention has been paid to the process of transition represented by separation, divorce, life in a one-parent family, and remarriage or to the factors that may lead to reduced or increased risk of disturbance for children and adults. Families experiencing divorce are faced with a number of changes including the diminution of financial resources, changes in residence, assumption of new roles and responsibilities, establishment of new patterns of intrafamilial interaction, reorganization of routines and schedules, and eventually the introduction of new relationships into the existing family. The nature of these changes demands resources that generally extend beyond those possessed by individual family members. It is our intent there to examine the nature of divorce and subsequent transitions in family life that accompany the structural changes in the family.

## FACTORS MEDIATING THE EFFECTS OF DIVORCE

Although we are still at a preliminary stage in our understanding of the nature of divorce and separation, recent studies have provided empirical evidence for the identification of several elements of family interaction accompanying the divorce and postdivorce process which are related to family functioning. The amount of conflict that persists among family members, the loss or unavailability of one parent, changes in the relationship between parents and children, and changing responsibilities and roles of family members are some of the most salient changes in family relationships that influence the outcome of divorce.

### Conflict

There are few divorces that are not preceded and accompanied by conflict and acrimony, and in many cases conflict is continued or escalated following separation and divorce (Hess & Camara, 1979; Hetherington et al., 1982; Wallerstein & Kelly, 1980). Many parents report that contacts with the legal system tend to intensify family problems as the divorcing couple attempts to settle issues of custody, visitation, and divorce. Both conflict between spouses or ex-spouses and between parents and children can lead to the development of behavior disorders in children (Emery & O'Leary, 1982; Hess & Camara, 1979; Hetherington et al., 1982; McDermott, 1968, 1970; Rutter, 1979a, 1979b; Wallerstein & Kelly, 1980; Westman, Cline, Swift, & Kramer, 1970). Interparental conflict to which the child has not been directly exposed does not appear to be associated with psychopathology in children (Hetherington et al., 1982; Porter & O'Leary, 1980; Rutter, Yule, Quinton, Rowland, Yule, & Berger, 1974).

The relationship between family conflict and behavior disorders is closer and more consistently found for boys than for girls (Block, Block, & Morrison, 1981; Cadoret & Cain, 1980; Emery & O'Leary, 1982; Hess & Camara, 1979; Hetherington et al., 1979; Porter & O'Leary, 1980; Rutter, 1971; Wolkind & Rutter, 1973). When family conflict occurs, boys are more often exposed to parental battles and disagreements and get less support than girls (Hetherington et al., 1982). Boys are more likely to respond to stressful situations with undercontrol and girls with overcontrol (Emery, 1982). There also is a suggestion that males interpret family disagreements less favorably than do females (Epstein, Finnegan, & Gythell, 1979).

Although conflict has harmful effects in both one- and two-parent households, the effects of conflict are more deleterious in divorced families than in nondivorced families. This seems to be attributable to the protective buffering effect that a very good relationship with either parent can play in attenuating the effects of disharmony in a two-parent household, whereas only an exceptionally good relationship with the custodial parent can serve this function in a divorced family. The noncustodial parent who is not available to mediate in day-to-day altercations is not an effective buffer, although highly available noncustodial parents have more impact than those who are less available (Hess & Camara, 1979; Hetherington, Cox, & Cox, 1979). It should be noted that the cluster of stressful events associated with divorce may initially result in more disrupted functioning in divorced families than in conflict-ridden nondivorced families, however, in the long run if children go into a stable one-parent household the escape from conflict is likely to enhance their adjustment (Hess & Camara, 1979; Hetherington et al., 1982; Wallerstein & Kelly, 1980).

There is support for the position that it is in part the conflict associated with divorce rather than the loss and separation that leads to conduct disorders, since death of a parent is less likely to lead to such behavior problems (Douglas, Ross, Hammond, & Mulligan, 1966; Gibson, 1969; Gregory, 1965).

### Attachment, Separation, and Loss

Many theorists view issues of attachment and loss as being central in the divorce process (Bowlby, 1973; Goldstein, Freud, & Solnit, 1973; Weiss, 1975). These factors play an important role for both the divorcing adults and their children.

**Parent-child attachment and loss.** One of the most important things to keep in mind about the decision to divorce is that it is a decision made by parents and not by children, and it is usually viewed as a solution to the problems of parents and not those of children. Children more often perceive divorce as a cause than as a resolution of their difficulties (Hetherington et al., 1982; Wallerstein & Kelly, 1980), and most children respond negatively to the separation and loss of a parent involved in divorce. Although the specific response to divorce varies with the developmental status of the child, common immediate responses at all ages are anger, anxiety, depression, dependency, yearning for the lost parent, and fantasies of reconciliation.

Laws regarding custody have changed recently, and few states have laws that advocate the preferential status of mothers as custodial parents. However, judges still are more likely to award custody to mothers than to fathers (Lindeman, 1977; Minuchin, 1974; Pearson, Munson, & Thoennes, 1982; Weitzman & Dixon, 1979). The new sex-neutral custody laws have tended to increase custody disputes and the number of fathers requesting custody with little increase in the number of fathers gaining sole custody and very modest increases in the number of fathers gaining joint, shared, or split custody (Emery, Hetherington, & Fisher, 1984; Lindeman, 1977; Pearson, Munson, & Thoennes, 1982; Weitzman & Dixon, 1979). It has been reported that fathers with joint custody are more likely than those only with visitation rights to remain involved with their children (Greif, 1979). However, since fathers who desire or fight for joint custody may be more involved with their children before the divorce, it is difficult to interpret this finding.

The absence of a father in the household usually means less social, emotional, and financial support, and less help for the mothers in decision making, child rearing, and household tasks. However, in marriages where the father has been distant, uninvolved, and nonsupportive, there may be little to lose and much to gain from opportunities for new relationships, self-sufficiency, and relief from conflict. For children, the absence of a father may mean the loss of emotional support, an effective role model, agent of socialization, trainer of skills, disciplinarian, and buffering agent. Considerable research evidence has accumulated that fathers respond differently to their children than do mothers and that fathers may play a unique role in the socialization of children. In addition, children respond in a different way to fathers than to mothers. This is particularly apparent in the area of discipline and compliance where children tend to be less disruptive and more obedient with fathers than with mothers (Hetherington et al., 1982).

Furstenberg recently has reported that by two years after divorce many children see their noncustodial fathers rarely or not at all (Furstenberg, 1982). Thus for many children divorce means true loss of the noncustodial parent accompanied by increased salience of the custodial parent. Conflicts about visitation, remarriage, the birth of new children in a remarriage, and geographical distance all contribute to diminished contact between noncustodial parents and their children. An important finding is that fathers' postdivorce relationships cannot be predicted from their predivorce relationships with their children. Many previously intensely attached fathers cannot tolerate part-time parenting and become disengaged, other fathers who had little predivorce contact with their children become active, competent parents.

The experience of visitation is often stressful for both parents and children. The intense scheduled contact and the desire to entertain the child, to be what Weiss has called a "tour guide father," is an abnormal way for parents and children to interact. In addition, Wallerstein has reported that the "datelike" quality of visitation may make fathers and daughters apprehensive about their encounters. As children become older and would normally become increasingly involved with peers, they may begin to view enforced visits with their fathers as a burden and an interference with their social lives.

Fathers are more likely to maintain contact with sons than with daughters (Hess & Camara, 1979) and the visits are longer between fathers and sons than between fathers and daughters (Hess & Camara, 1979; Hetherington et al., 1982). In addition, as sons grow older, mothers are more likely to yield them to their fathers, especially if the father has remarried and the mother has not, or if the son is difficult to handle (Furstenberg, Spanier, & Rothschild, 1982; Hetherington et al., 1982). There is some indication that continued contact with fathers may be more important in the adjustment of sons than daughters (Hetherington et al., 1982; Santrock & Warshak, 1979). Santrock and Warshak (1979) report that elementary school-aged children adjust better in the custody of the same-sexed parent. The samples in this study are small, and the study must be replicated before great weight is put on the findings. Camara (1982), in a preliminary report of findings of a study of early elementary school-aged children, found that a positive relationship with the same-sexed parent was associated with children's social competence with same-sexed peers. Although sustained contact with the father may not be as important in the development of self-control, sex typing, and cognition in girls as in boys, there is evidence that there may be a delayed effect on girls of lack of availability of a father that may emerge in the form of precocious sexual preoccupation and disruption in heterosexual relations in adolescence (Hetherington, 1972; Wallerstein & Kelly, 1980).

### Changes in Parent-child Relations Following Divorce

Changes in parent-child relations are associated with the emotional responses and adjustment of individual family members and with the redefinition of roles and responsibilities in the restructured family.

**The altered parent.** In the period immediately following separation and divorce, the emotional disturbance experienced by family members often exacerbates children's and parents' distress. Children often encounter greatly altered parents; although the parents are physically the same, their behavior seems unfamiliar and unpredictable. In this period parents show wide mood swings from soaring euphoria as they contemplate the opportunities for a more gratifying, less conflictual life-style and crashing depressions as they confront the difficulties in attaining this goal. Robert Weiss has likened this emotional lability to riding on an elevator with only two buttons—penthouse and basement.

Other symptoms in adults that often accompany divorce include the inability to work effectively, poor health, weight changes, insomnia and sleep disturbances, sexual dysfunction, lethargy, and increased drinking, smoking, and drug use (Bloom et al., 1978; Goode, 1956; Hetherington et al., 1982). Although continued contact with the noncustodial parent can have important positive effects on children and custodial mothers, the adjustment and emotional problems of the custodial parents are particularly important in determining the coping and adaptation of children in one-parent households, following divorce. The important point is that children with a custodial parent who is ill, withdrawn, depressed, anxious, or dissatisfied are at increased risk of encountering parent-child relationships associated with adverse emotional outcomes. It should be kept in mind that both the parents and the children are undergoing a stressful experience. The angry, preoccupied, and depressed parent may be unable to respond to the needs of the distressed child and the demands, anxiety, and rage of the child may exacerbate the tensions of the parent.

**Parenting.** In the period surrounding separation and divorce, both parents express concern about their relations with their children and their competence as parents. This is marked in divorced mothers of sons, who report themselves to have more problems in child rearing and to be more helpless, stressed, incompetent, and depressed than do divorced mothers of daughters (Colletta, 1979; Hetherington et al., 1982). However, in general, noncustodial parents, whether they are mothers or fathers, experience fewer stresses in day-to-day child rearing but feel more dissatisfied, deficient, powerless, and shut out in their relations with their children (Furstenberg et al., 1982; Hetherington et al., 1982).

In the period accompanying divorce there is often what has been called a diminished capacity to parent (Wallerstein & Kelly, 1980), a breakdown in parent behaviors, followed by improvement in child-rearing practices in the second year after the divorce. During the first year following divorce both parents communicate less with their children, are more erratic in enforcing discipline, are less affectionate, and make fewer maturity demands (Hetherington et al., 1982).

Immediately following the divorce, noncustodial fathers may actually spend more time with their children than they did before the divorce, but this contact rapidly diminishes (Furstenberg et al., 1982; Hetherington et al., 1982). Fathers become more indulgent and permissive and less available following divorce (Hetherington et al., 1982), however, divorced fathers have less difficulty controlling their children and gaining compliance than do divorced mothers.

Both divorced and remarried mothers experience more difficult in their role as parents than do nondivorced mothers (Furstenberg et al., 1982; Hetherington et al., 1982; Zill, 1983). Custodial mothers of young children usually tend to increase their use of power assertive, restrictive, and negative sanctions

(Burgess, 1978; Colletta, 1979; Hetherington et al., 1982; Kriesberg, 1970; Phelps, 1969). They are inconsistently and ineffectually authoritarian, particularly in their relations with sons. Custodial mothers and sons often get involved in escalating reciprocal cycles of coercive behavior. Divorced mothers in comparison to nondivorced mothers seem more often to instigate aggression and noncompliance in sons and to have more difficulty terminating their sons' coercive behavior once it has begun (Hetherington et al., 1982; Patterson, 1982).

In both one- and two-parent families high stress accompanied by dissatisfaction with support systems is associated with more restrictive and harsher parent-child relationships (Collette, 1979). The combination of poor control and infantilization of young children by divorced mothers may be more common for mothers of younger than older children (Wallerstein & Kelly, 1979; Weiss, 1975) and in middle than lower socioeconomic status one-parent families (Colletta, 1979).

In one-parent families older children may assume more power and responsibility in the family and participate more actively in decision-making processes (Fulton, 1979; Kurdek & Siesky, 1979; Weiss, 1979a, 1979b). Eldest children in particular are likely to find themselves assuming increased responsibility for child care (Zill, 1983). Although the household tasks and chores assigned may not differ in one- and two-parent homes, children in one-parent households tend to perceive themselves as having greater responsibilities than do their peers from two-parent households. The presence of a second adult in the home may alter the context of children's participation so that children in two-parent households perceive their chores as "helpful," while children in one-parent households perceive their assistance as "necessary" for family functioning (Camara, 1980).

Weiss (1979b) has argued that this increased power and responsibility may be associated with self-sufficiency in children and egalitarian, friendly, companionate relationships between divorced parents and their adolescent children. Children become juniors partners in the family. However, the push toward the assumption of adult roles and responsibilities, toward what Weiss (1979b) has called "growing up faster," in some school-aged and adolescent children is also associated with resentment, feelings of helplessness, precocious sexuality, and withdrawal from the family (Kelly, 1978; Wallerstein, 1978; Wallerstein & Kelly, 1980).

Custodial parents, in attempting to deal with task overload, may assign too many, or too difficult, or age-inappropriate tasks to their children. In addition, parents in their distress may expect children to act as an emotional support or fill some of the roles of the divorced spouse. This may involve inappropriate self-disclosure by the parents which escalates the anxiety of the child. Role reversals where children are offering support to parents are common. Thus, relief for a disturbed or overburdened parent may result in an overburdened or emotionally enmeshed child. If the child is unwilling or unable to respond to the needs of the parent, the child may feel overwhelmed, incompetent, guilty, and resentful.

## Parent-Child Relations and the Adjustment of Children

In the period immediately following divorce children may be more aggressive, noncompliant, whining, nagging, dependent, and unaffectionate with their parents, teachers, and peers. This response is more intense and enduring in boys than in girls. If they are not exposed to additional stresses both boys and girls show markedly improved adjustment in the two years following divorce, although at this time boys from divorced families are still manifesting more problems than those from nondivorced families. Two recent nationwide surveys show that boys from divorced families show more problems in school and difficulties in self-control and aggression than do girls or children from nondivorced families (Guidubaldi, Perry, & Cleminshaw, 1983; Zill, 1983). However, it should be noted that the vast majority of children in divorced families function as well as those in nondivorced families.

The deleterious outcomes for children have been found to be related to changes in family functioning following divorce rather than attributable to family structure. During periods of high stress, children require more structure and stability as well as more nurturance and support in their environments (Hetherington et al., 1982). Problems in adjustment are least likely to occur if children find themselves in a warm, predictable, secure, conflict-free environment. Emotional disturbance in children is minimized if household routines are well organized, if discipline is authoritative and consistent (Hetherington et al., 1982), if there is warmth, support, and good communication between parents and child (Hess & Camara, 1979; Hetherington et al., 1982; Jacobson, 1978; Wallerstein & Kelly, 1980), and if the custodial parent is happy and well adjusted (Hetherington, Cox, & Cox, 1981; Wallerstein & Kelly, 1980). In addition, the continued relation between the divorced parents plays a significant role in successful coping in children. Low conflict and absence of mutual denigration, high support and agreement on child rearing and discipline, and frequent contact with the noncustodial parent, if that parent is not extremely deviant or destructive, are associated with positive adjustment in children (Hess & Camara, 1979; Hetherington et al., 1982; Nelson, 1981; Wallerstein & Kelly, 1980). Many effective divorced families continue to function as an integrated parenting system after divorce, although the divorced spouses are living in different households.

## Effects of Remarriage on Children

The remarriage of parents has particular significance for the children involved. It is reasonable to assume that remarriage may present a child with additional adjustments which may be stressful and difficult (Duberman, 1975; Langer & Michael, 1963; Messinger, 1976; Visher & Visher, 1979; Wilson, Zurcher, McAdams, & Curtis, 1975). The remarriage may signify the finality of the parents' divorce and may end children's fantasies of reconciliation. In addition, alterations in relationships with the biological parents may occur as well as the need to adapt to the stepparent and his or her kin. There is some evidence to

suggest that involvement and visitation by noncustodial fathers diminish markedly after remarriage (Furstenberg, Spanier, & Rothschild, 1980; Hetherington et al., 1981). Frequently, fathers reduce their participation in their first family as they become involved in a new relationship, particularly when the former spouse remains single. When divorced men or women defer marriage, they are more likely to share parental responsibilities more equally than when one or both remarry (Camara et al., 1981; Furstenberg et al., 1980). It should be noted that continued involvement with the child by a divorced father even after remarriage leads to positive outcomes for children, especially for boys (Camara et al., 1981; Hess & Camara, 1979; Hetherington et al., 1981).

Bernard (1972) acknowledges that many variables may influence the successful integration of family members into the stepfamily unit, in particular, the timing and method of introduction of a new spouse into the family and the age, sex, and attitude of children. Adolescents, particularly those in the custody of the remarried parent, appear to have the most complex reactions (Bernard, 1972; Hetherington et al., 1981). Children in the preadolescent and adolescent period (ages 9–15) are less likely to accept even a good stepparent than are younger or older children (Hetherington et al., 1981). In addition, in blended families in which both sets of children reside in the same household, both parents are more likely to report high rates of marital conflict, disagreement about child rearing, dissatisfaction with the spouse's parental role, and differential treatment of natural children and stepchildren (Hetherington et al., 1981).

Most researchers note the great variability in responses of stepparents to stepchildren (Bossard, 1956; Camara et al., 1981; Fast & Cain, 1966; Hetherington et al., 1981). Fast and Cain (1966) conclude that no matter how much skill a stepparent possesses in adopting a parent role, he cannot succeed because social norms make it inappropriate for him to do so. Attempts to reproduce the nuclear family in the "step" situation cannot succeed since the stepfamily must be considered a structurally different type of child-rearing unit.

Stern (1978) has suggested that it may take up to two years for stepfathers to form a friendly relationship with their stepchildren and to achieve a partnership in a disciplinary role with their wives. Hetherington et al. (1981) reported that many stepfathers tended either to be disengaged and inattentive and to give the mother little support in child rearing, or to be extremely actively involved in child rearing and often restrictive in dealing with their stepchildren, especially stepsons. However, the most effective role for the stepfather seemed to be one where he supported the mother's discipline rather than trying either to take over or to totally relinquish responsibility. If the natural parent welcomed the involvement of the stepparent, and if the stepparent was an authoritative parent, warm, willing to set consistent limits and to communicate well with the stepchild, children in stepparent families, particularly boys, functioned better than those in unremarried families or conflict-ridden, nondivorced families (Hetherington et al., 1981). However, a recent national survey of American children suggests that these conditions may be difficult to attain. Zill (1983) found that mothers and teachers report that children in step-

father families show more problems in the home and in the school than do children from nondivorced families. Less is known about the influence of stepmothers on the behavior of children since most children reside with their biological mothers.

It seems likely that in future years more children and adults are going to experience living in a diverse array of family forms. The research to date suggests that divorce and remarriage involve a reorganization and modification of family relationships rather than the termination of family relationships. The relationships become increasingly complex with the introduction of a broader network of kin in reconstituted families. The long-term impact of these transitions in family relations on parents and children remains unknown.

## REFERENCES


Bernard, J. *The future of marriage.* New York: Bantam, 1972.

Block, J. H., Block, J., & Morrison, A. Parental agreement-disagreement on childrearing orientations and gender-related personality correlates in children. *Child Development*, 1981, *52*, 965–985.

Bloom, B. L., Asher, S. J., & White, S. W. Marital disruption as a stressor: A review and analysis. *Psychological Bulletin*, 1978, *85*, 867–894.

Bossard, J. H. S. *The large family system.* Philadelphia: University of Pennsylvania Press, 1956.

Bowlby, J. *Attachment and loss, vol. 2. Separation, anxiety, and anger.* New York: Basic Books, 1973.

Burgess, R. L. *Project interact: A study of patterns of interaction in abusive, neglectful, and control families.* Final Report. National Center on Child Abuse and Neglect, 1978.

Cadoret, R. J. & Cain, C. Sex differences in predictors of antisocial behavior in adoptees. *Archives of General Psychiatry*, 1980 *37*, 1171–1175.

Camara, K. A. Children's construction of social knowledge: Concepts of family and the experience of parental divorce. (Doctoral dissertation, Stanford University, 1979). *Dissertation Abstracts International*, 1980, *40*, 3433B.

Camara, K. A. *Social interaction of children in divorced and intact households.* Paper presented at the Tenth International Congress of Psychiatry and Allied Professions, Dublin, July 1982.

Camara, K. A., Weiss, C. P., & Hess, R. D. *Remarried fathers and their children.* Paper presented at the biennial meeting of the Society for Research in Child Development, Boston, April 1981.

Colletta, M. D. Support systems after divorce: Incidence and impact. *Journal of Marriage and the Family*, 1979, *41*, 837–846.

Douglas, J. W. B., Ross, T. M., Hammond, W. A., & Mulligan, D. G. Delinquency and social class. *British Journal of Criminology*, 1966, *6*, 294–302.

Duberman, L. *The reconstituted family: A study of remarried couples and their children.* Chicago: Nelson-Hall, 1975.

Emery, R. E. Marital turmoil: Interpersonal conflict and the children of discord and divorce. *Psychological Bulletin*, 1982, *92*, 310–330.

Emery, R. E., Hetherington, E. M., & Fisher, L. Divorce, children and social policy. In H. Stevenson & A. Siegel (Eds.). *Children and social policy.* Chicago: University of Chicago Press, 1984.

Emery, R. E., & O'Leary, K. D. Children's perceptions of marital discord and behavior problems of boys and girls. *Journal of Abnormal Child Psychology*, 1982, *10*, 11–24.

Epstein, N., Finnegan, D., & Gythell, D. Irrational beliefs and perceptions of marital conflict. *Journal of Consulting and Clinical Psychology*, 1979, *67*, 608–609.

Fast, I., & Cain, A. C. The stepparent role: Potential for disturbances in family functioning. *American Journal of Orthopsychiatry*, 1966, *36*, 485–491.

Fulton, J. A. Parental reports of children's post-divorce adjustment. *Journal of Social Issues*, 1979, *35*, 126–139.

Furstenberg, F. F. *Remarriage.* 1982 Report to Planning Committee on Divorce, National Academy of Science Meeting, Stanford, Calif.

Furstenberg, F. F., Spanier, G. B., & Rothschild, N. *Patterns of parenting in the transition from divorce to remarriage.* Paper presented at the NICHD, NIMH, and NIA Conference on Women: A Developmental Perspective, Washington, D.C., 1980.

Furstenberg, F. F., Spanier, G. B., & Rothschild, N. Patterns of parenting in the transition from divorce to remarriage. In P. W. Berman & E. R. Ramey (eds.), *Women: a developmental perspective.* NIH Publication No. 82–2298, 1982.

Gibson, H. B. Early delinquency in relation to broken homes. *Journal of Child Psychology and Psychiatry and Allied Disciplines*, 1969, *10*, 195–204.

Goldstein, J., Freud, A., & Solnit, A. *Beyond the best interests of the child.* New York: Free Press, 1973.

Goode, W. J. *After divorce.* New York: Free Press, 1956.

Gregory, I. Anterospective data following childhood loss of a parent. *Archives of General Psychiatry*, 1965, *13*, 110–120.

Greif, J. B. Fathers, children, and joint custody. *American Journal of Orthopsychiatry*, 1979. *49*, 311–319.

Guidubaldi, J., Perry, J. D., & Cleminshaw, H. K. The legacy of parental divorce: A nationwide study of family status and selected mediating variables in children's academic and social competencies. *School Psychology Review*, 1983, *2*, 148.

Hess, R. D., & Camara, K. A. Post-divorce family relations as mediating factors in the consequences of divorce for children. *Journal of Social Issues*, 1979, *35*, 79–96.

Hetherington, E. M. Effects of father absence on personality development in adolescent daughters. *Developmental Psychology*, 1972, *7*, 313–326.

Hetherington, E. M., Cox, M., & Cox, R. Family interaction and the social emotional and cognitive development of children following divorce. In V. Vaughan & T. B. Brazelton (eds.). *The family: Setting priorities.* New York: Science & Medicine Publishing Co., 1979.

Hetherington, E. M., Cox, M., & Cox, R. Divorce and remarriage. Paper presented at the meeting of the Society for Research in Child Development, Boston, April 1981.

Hetherington, E. M., Cox, M., & Cox, R. Effects of divorce on parents and children. In M. Lamb (ed.), *Nontraditional families.* Hillsdale, N.J.: Erlbaum, 1982.

Jacobson, D. S. The impact of divorce/separation on children. III. Parent-child communication and child adjustment, and regression analysis of findings from overall study. *Journal of Divorce*, 1978, *2*, 175–194.

Kelly, J. B. *Children and parents in the midst of divorce: Major factors contributing to differential response.* Paper presented at the National Institute of Mental Health Conference on Divorce, Washington, D.C., 1978.

Kriesberg, L. *Mothers in poverty: A study of fatherless families.* Chicago: Aldine, 1970.

Kurdek, L. A., & Siesky, A. E. An interview study of parents' perceptions of their children's reactions and adjustment to divorce. *Journal of Divorce*, 1979, *3*, 5–18.

Langer, T. S., & Michael, S. T. *Life stress and mental health.* New York: Free Press, 1963.

Lindeman, J. *Contested custody and the judicial decision-making process.* Ph.D. dissertation, Florida State University, College of Social Sciences, 1977.

McDermott, J. F. Parental divorce in early childhood. *American Journal of Psychiatry*, 1970, *124*, 1424–1432.

McDermott, J. F. Divorce and its psychiatric sequelae in children. *Archives of General Psychiatry*, 1970, *23*, 421–427.

Messinger, L. Remarriage between divorced people with children from a previous marriage: A proposal for preparation for remarriage. *Journal of Marriage and Family Counseling*, 1976, *2*, 193–200.

Minuchin, S. *Families and family therapy.* Cambridge, Mass.: Harvard University Press, 1974.

Nelson, G. Moderators of women's and children's adjustment following parental divorce. *Journal of Divorce*, 1981, *4*, 71–83.

Patterson, G. R. *Coercive family process.* Eugene, Ore.: Castalia, 1982.

Pearson, J., Munson, P., & Thoennes, N. Legal change and child custody awards. *Journal of Family Issues*, 1982, *3*, 5–24.

Phelps, D. W. Parental attitudes toward family life and child behavior of mothers in two-parent and one-parent families. *Journal of School Health*, 1969, *89*, 413–416.

Porter, B., & O'Leary, K. D. Marital discord and childhood behavior problems. *Journal of Abnormal Child Psychology*, 1980, *8*, 287–295.

Rutter, M. Parent-child separation: Psychological effects on the children. *Journal of Child Psychology and Psychiatry and Allied Disciplines*, 1971, *12*, 233–260.

Rutter, M. Protective factors in children's responses to stress and disadvantage. In M. W. Kent & J. E. Rolf (eds.), *Primary prevention of psychopathology. Vol. 3.* Hanover, N.H.: University Press of New England, 1979. (a)

Rutter, M. Maternal deprivation, 1972–1978: New findings, new concepts, and approaches. *Child Development*, 1979, *50*, 283–305. (b)

Rutter, M., Yule, B., Quinton, D., Rowland, O., Yule, W., & Berger, M. Attainment and adjustment in two geographical areas. III. Some factors accounting for area differences. *British Journal of Psychiatry*, 1974, *125*, 520–533.

Santrock, J. W., & Warshak, R. A. Father custody and social development in boys and girls. *Journal of Social Issues*, 1979, *35*, 112–125.

Stern, P. N. Stepfather families: Integration around child discipline. *Issues in Mental Health Nursing*, 1978, *1*, 50–56.

Visher, E. B., & Visher, J. S. *Stepfamilies: A guide to working with stepparents and stepchildren.* New York: Brunner/Mazel, 1979.

Wallerstein, J. S. *Children and parents 18 months after parental separation: Factors related to differential outcome.* Paper presented at the National Institute of Mental Health Conference on Divorce. Washington, D.C., February 1978.

Wallerstein, J. S., & Kelly, J. B., Children and divorce: A review. *Social Work*, 1979, 468–475.

Wallerstein, J. S., & Kelly, J. B. *Surviving the breakup: How children and parents cope with divorce.* New York: Basic Books, 1980.

Weiss, R. *Marital separation.* New York: Basic Books, 1975.

Weiss, R. S. *Going it alone.* New York: Basic Books, 1979 (a)

Weiss, R. S. Growing up a little faster: The experience of growing up in a single-parent household. *Journal of Social Issues*, 1979, *35*, 97–111. (b)

Weitzman, L. J., & Dixon, R. B. Child custody awards: Legal standards and empirical patterns for child custody, support, and visitation after divorce. *University of California at Davis Law Review*, 1979, *12*, 473–521.

Westman, J. D., Cline, D. W., Swift, W. J., & Kramer, D. A. The role of child psychiatry in divorce. *Archives of General Psychiatry*, 1970, *23*, 416–420.

Wilson, K. L, Zurcher, L., McAdams, D. C., & Curtis, R. L. Stepfathers and stepchildren: An exploratory analysis from two national surveys. *Journal of Marriage and the Family*, 1975, *37*, 526–536.

Wolkind, W., & Rutter, M. Children who have been "in care"—an epidemiological study. *Journal of Child Psychology and Psychiatry and Allied Disciplines*, 1973, *14*, 97–105.

Zill, N. *Happy, healthy, and insecure.* New York: Doubleday, 1983

*Section Eight*

# Controversial Perspectives on the Contemporary Family and the Future

30

CHRISTOPHER LASCH

# The Flight from Feeling: Sociopsychology of the Sex War

*Some of the most controversial commentary on the American family in recent years has come from Christopher Lasch, history professor, social critic, and member of the so-called* New York Review of Books *intellectual group. Although he is an intellectual, his commentary on the American family in some ways resembles that of anti-intellectual conservatives, such as the religious fundamentalists in the Moral Majority. For instance, both Lasch and members of the Moral Majority negatively evaluate most of the recent changes in the American family.*

*Most social and behavioral scientists who study the family take a much more positive view of recent changes, most of which they claim are adaptations to changes in other parts of society. Thus, recent changes are claimed to tend to make the family stronger and more viable. However, a few family social scientists find what they consider to be a basic truth in Lasch's commentary. They point out, for instance, that when marriage becomes hedonistic, some of the consequences can be very antihedonistic. That is, when the primary purpose of marriage becomes the pleasure and satisfaction of the married person, the resulting instability and insecurity in marriage may make marital satisfaction more difficult to attain.*

Source: Reprinted from *The Culture of Narcissism* by Christopher Lasch. By permission of W. W. Norton & Company, Inc.

*Suddenly she wished she was with some other man and not with Edward. . . . Pia looked at Edward. She looked at his red beard, his immense spectacles. I don't like him, she thought. That red beard, those immense spectacles. . . .*

*Pia said to Edward that he was the only person she had ever loved for this long. "How long is it?" Edward asked. It was seven months.*

*Donald Barthelme*

*I think more and more. . . . that there is no such thing as rationality in relationships. I think you just have to say okay that's what you feel right now and what are we going to do about it. . . . I believe everybody should really be able to basically do what they want to do as long as it's not hurting anybody else.*

*Liberated Bridegroom*

Bertrand Russell once predicted that the socialization of reproduction—the supersession of the family by the state—would "make sex love itself more trivial," encourage "a certain triviality in all personal relations," and "make it far more difficult to take an interest in anything after one's own death." At first glance, recent developments appear to have refuted the first part of this prediction. Americans today invest personal relations, particularly the relations between men and women, with undiminished emotional importance. The decline of childrearing as a major preoccupation has freed sex from its bondage to procreation and made it possible for people to value erotic life for its own sake. As the family shrinks to the marital unit, it can be argued that men and women respond more readily to each other's emotional needs, instead of living vicariously through their offspring. The marriage contract having lost its binding character, couples now find it possible, according to many observers, to ground sexual relations in something more solid than legal compulsion. In short, the growing determination to live the moment, whatever it may have done to the relations between parents and children, appears to have established the preconditions of a new intimacy between men and women.

This appearance is an illusion. The cult of intimacy conceals a growing despair of finding it. Personal relations crumble under the emotional weight with which they are burdened. The inability "to take an interest in anything after one's death," which gives such urgency to the pursuit of close personal encounters in the present, makes intimacy more elusive than ever. The same developments that have weakened the tie between parents and children have also undermined relations between men and women. Indeed the deterioration of marriage contributes in its own right to the deterioration of care for the young.

This last point is so obvious that only a strenuous propaganda on behalf of "open marriage" and "creative divorce" prevents us from grasping it. It is clear, for example, that the growing incidence of divorce, together with the ever-present possibility that any given marriage will end in collapse, adds to the instability of family life and deprives the child of a measure of emotional security. Enlightened opinion diverts attention from this general fact by insisting that in specific cases, parents may do more harm to their children by holding a marriage together than by dissolving it. It is true that many couples preserve their marriage, in one form or another, at the expense of the child. Sometimes they embark on a life full of distractions, that shield them against daily emotional involvements with their offspring. Sometimes one parent acquiesces in the neurosis of the other (as in the family configuration that produces so many schizophrenic patients) for fear of disturbing the precarious peace of the household. More often the husband abandons his children to the wife whose company he find unbearable, and the wife smothers the children with incessant yet perfunctory attentions. This particular solution to the problem of marital strain has become so common that the absence of the father impresses many observers as the most striking fact about the contemporary family. Under these conditions, a divorce in which the mother retains custody of her children merely ratifies the existing state of affairs—the effective emotional desertion of his family by the father. But the reflection that divorce often does no more damage to children than marriage itself hardly inspires rejoicing.

## THE BATTLE OF THE SEXES: ITS SOCIAL HISTORY

While the escalating war between men and women has psychological roots in the disintegration of the marital relation, and more broadly in the changing patterns of socialization, much of this tension can be explained without reference to psychology. The battle of the sexes also constitutes a social phenomenon with a history of its own. The reasons for the recent intensification of sexual combat lie in the transformation of capitalism from its paternalistic and familial form to a managerial, corporate, bureaucratic system of almost total control: more specifically, in the collapse of "chivalry"; the liberation of sex from many of its former constraints; the pursuit of sexual pleasure as an end in itself; the emotional overloading of personal relations; and most important of all, the irrational male response to the emergence of the liberated woman.

It has been clear for some time that "chivalry is dead." The tradition of gallantry formerly masked and to some degree mitigated the organized oppression of women. While males monopolized political and economic power, they made their domination of women more palatable by surrounding it with an elaborate ritual of deference and *politesse*. They set themselves up as protectors of the weaker sex, and this cloying but useful fiction set limits to their capacity to exploit women through sheer physical force. The counterconvention of *droit de seigneur*, which justified the predatory exploits of the privileged classes against women socially inferior to themselves, nevertheless showed that the male sex at no time ceased to regard most women as fair game. The long history of rape and seduction, moreover, served as a reminder that animal strength remained the basis of masculine ascendancy, manifested here in its most direct and brutal form. Yet polite conventions, even when they were no more than a façade, provided women with ideological leverage in their struggle to domesticate the wildness and savagery of men. They surrounded essentially exploitive relationships with a network of reciprocal obligations, which if nothing else made exploitation easier to bear.

The symbiotic interdependence of exploiters and exploited, so characteristic of paternalism in all ages, survived in male-female relations long after the collapse of patriarchal authority in other areas. Because the convention of deference to the fair sex was so closely bound up with paternalism, however, it lived on borrowed time once the democratic revolutions of the eighteenth and nineteenth centuries had destroyed the last foundations of feudalism. The decline of paternalism, and of the rich public ceremonial formerly associated with it, spelled the end of gallantry. Women themselves began to perceive the connection between their debasement and their sentimental exaltation, rejected their confining position on the pedestal of masculine adoration, and demanded the demystification of female sexuality.

Democracy and feminism have now stripped the veil of courtly convention from the subordination of women, revealing the sexual antagonisms formerly concealed by the "feminine mystique." Denied illusions of comity, men and women find it more difficult than before to confront each other as friends and lovers, let alone as equals. As male supremacy becomes ideologically untenable, incapable of justifying itself as protection, men assert their domination more directly, in fantasies and occasionally in acts of raw violence. Thus the treatment of women in movies, according to one study, has shifted "from reverence to rape."

Women who abandon the security of well-defined though restrictive social roles have always exposed themselves to sexual exploitation, having surrendered the usual claims of respectability. Mary Wollstonecraft, attempting to live as a free woman, found herself brutally deserted by Gilbert Imlay. Later feminists forfeited the privileges of sex and middle-class origin when they campaigned for women's rights. Men reviled them publicly as sexless "she-men" and approached them privately as loose women. A Cincinnati brewer, expecting to be admitted to Emma Goldman's hotel room when he found her alone, became alarmed when she threatened to wake the whole establishment. He protested, "I thought you believed in free love." Ingrid Bengis reports that when she hitchhiked across the country, men expected her to pay for rides with sexual favors. Her refusal elicited the predictable reply: "Well, girls shouldn't hitchhike in the first place."

What distinguishes the present time from the past is that defiance of sexual conventions less and less presents itself as a matter of individual choice, as it was for the pioneers of feminism. Since most of those conventions have already collapsed, even a woman who lays no claim to her rights nevertheless finds it difficult to claim the traditional privileges of her sex. All women find themselves identified with "women's lib" merely by virtue of their sex, unless by strenuous disavowals they identify themselves with its enemies. All women share in the burdens as well as the benefits of "liberation," both of which can be summarized by saying that men no longer treat women as ladies.

## THE SEXUAL "REVOLUTION"

The demystification of womanhood goes hand in hand with the desublimation of sexuality. The "repeal of reticence" has dispelled the aura of mystery surrounding sex and removed most of the obstacles to its public display. Institutionalized sexual segregation has given way to arrangements that promote the intermingling of the sexes at every stage of life. Efficient contraceptives, legalized abortion, and a "realistic" and "healthy" acceptance of the body have weakened the links that once tied sex to love, marriage, and procreation. Men and women now pursue sexual pleasure as an end in itself, unmediated even by the conventional trappings of romance.

Sex valued purely for its own sake loses all reference to the future and brings no hope of permanent relationships. Sexual liaisons, including marriage, can be terminated at pleasure. This means, as Willard Waller demonstrated a long time ago, that lovers forfeit the right to be jealous or to insist on fidelity as a condition of erotic union. In his sociological satire of the recently divorced, Waller pointed out that the bohemians of the 1920s attempted to avoid emotional commitments while eliciting them from others. Since the bohemian was "not ready to answer with his whole personality for the consequences of the affair, nor to give any assurance of its continuance," he lost the right to demand such an assurance from others. "To show jealousy," under these conditions, became "nothing short of a crime. . . . So if one falls in love in Bohemia, he conceals it from his friends as best he can." In similar studies of the "rating and dating complex" on college campuses, Waller found that students who fell in love invited the ridicule of their peers. Exclusive attachments gave way to an easygoing promiscuity as the normal pattern of sexual relations. Popularity replaced purity as the measure of a woman's social value; the sentimental cult of virginity gave way to "playful woman-sharing," which had "no negative effect," as Wolfenstein and Leites pointed out in their study of movies, "on the friendly relations between men."[1] In the thirties and forties, the cinematic fantasy in which a beautiful girl dances with a chorus of men,

---

[1]The transition in American movies from vamp to the "good-bad girl," according to Wolfenstein and Leites, illustrates the decline of jealousy and the displacement of sexual passion by sexiness. "The dangerousness of the vamp was associated with the man's intolerance for sharing her with other men. Her seductive appearance and readiness for love carried a strong suggestion that there had been and might be other men in her life.... The good-bad girl is associated with a greater

favoring one no more than the others, expressed an ideal to which reality more and more closely conformed. In *Elmtown's Youth*, August Hollingshead described a freshman girl who violated conventional taboos against drinking, smoking, and "fast" behavior and still retained her standing in the school's most prominent clique, partly because of her family's wealth but largely by means of her carefully calibrated promiscuity. "To be seen with her adds to a boy's prestige in the elite peer group. . . . She pets with her dates discreetly—never goes too far, just far enough to make them come back again." In high school as in college, the peer group attempts through conventional ridicule and vituperation to prevent its members from falling in love with the wrong people, indeed from falling in love at all; for as Hollingshead noted, lovers "are lost to the adolescent world with its quixotic enthusiasms and varied group activities."

These studies show that the main features of the contemporary sexual scene had already established themselves well before the celebrated "sexual revolution" of the sixties and seventies: casual promiscuity, a wary avoidance of emotional commitments, an attack on jealousy and possessiveness. Recent developments, however, have introduced a new source of tension: the modern woman's increasingly insistent demand for sexual fulfillment. In the 1920s and 1930s, many women still approached sexual encounters with a hesitance that combined prudery and a realistic fear of consequences. Superficially seductive, they took little pleasure in sex even when they spoke the jargon of sexual liberation and professed to live for pleasure and thrills. Doctors worried about female frigidity, and psychiatrists had no trouble in recognizing among their female patients the classic patterns of hysteria described by Freud, in which a coquettish display of sexuality often coexists with powerful repression and a rigid, puritanical morality.

Today women have dropped much of their sexual reserve. In the eyes of men, this makes them more accessible as sexual partners but also more threatening. Formerly men complained about women's lack of sexual response; now then find this response intimidating and agonize about their capacity to satisfy it. "I'm sorry they ever found out they could have orgasms too," Heller's Bob Slocum says. The famous Masters-Johnson report on female sexuality added to these anxieties by depicting women as sexually insatiable, inexhaustible in their capacity to experience orgasm after orgasm. Some feminists have used the Masters report to attack the "myth of the vaginal orgasm," to assert women's independence of men, or to taunt men with their sexual inferiority. "Theoretically, a woman could go on having orgasms indefinitely if physical exhaustion did not intervene," writes Mary Jane Sherfey. According to Kate Millett, "While the male's sexual potential is limited, the female's appears to be biologically nearly inexhaustible." Sexual "performance" thus becomes another weapon in the war between men and women; social inhibitions no longer

---

tolerance for sharing the woman. . . . In effect, the woman's attraction is enhanced by her association with other men. All that is needed to eliminate unpleasantness is the assurance that those these relations were not serious."

prevent women from exploiting the tactical advantage which the current obsession with sexual measurement has given them. Whereas the hysterical woman, even when she fell in love and longed to let herself go, seldom conquered her underlying aversion to sex, the pseudoliberated woman of *Cosmopolitan* exploits her sexuality in a more deliberate and calculating way, not only because she has fewer reservations about sex but because she manages more successfully to avoid emotional entanglements. "Women with narcissistic personalities," writes Otto Kernberg, "may appear quite 'hysterical' on the surface, with their extreme coquettishness and exhibitionism, but the cold, shrewdly calculating quality of their seductivenesss is in marked contrast to the much warmer, emotionally involved quality of hysterical pseudo-hypersexuality."

## TOGETHERNESS

Both men and women have come to approach personal relations with a heightened appreciation of their emotional risks. Determined to manipulate the emotions of others while protecting themselves against emotional injury, both sexes cultivate a protective shallowness, a cynical detachment they do not altogether feel but which soon becomes habitual and in any case embitters personal relations merely through its repeated profession. At the same time, people demand from personal relations the richness and intensity of a religious experience. Although in some ways men and women have had to modify their demands on each other, especially in their inability to exact commitments of lifelong sexual fidelity, in other ways they demand more than ever. In the American middle class, moreover, men and women see too much of each other and find it hard to put their relations in proper perspective. The degradation of work and the impoverisment of communal life force people to turn to sexual excitement to satisfy all their emotional needs. Formerly sexual antagonism was tempered not only by chivalric, paternalistic conventions but by a more relaxed acceptance of the limitations of the other sex. Men and women acknowledged each other's shortcomings without making them the basis of a comprehensive indictment. Partly because they found more satisfaction than is currently available in casual relations with their own sex, they did not have to raise friendship itself into a political program, an ideological alternative to love. An easygoing, everyday contempt for the weaknesses of the other sex, institutionalized as folk wisdom concerning the emotional incompetence of men or the brainlessness of women, kept sexual enmity within bounds and prevented it from becoming an obsession.

Feminism and the ideology of intimacy have discredited the sexual stereotypes which kept women in their place but which also made it possible to acknowledge sexual antagonism without raising it to the level of all-out warfare. Today the folklore of sexual differences and the acceptance of sexual friction survive only in the working class. Middle-class feminists envy the ability of working-class women to acknowledge that men get in their way without becoming manhaters. "These women are less angry at their men because they don't spend that much time with them," according to one observer. "Middle-class women are the ones who were told men had to be their companions."[2]

**FEMINISM AND THE INTENSIFICATION OF SEXUAL WARFARE**

Not merely the cult of sexual companionship and "togetherness" but feminism itself has caused women to make new demands on men and to hate men when they fail to meet those demands. Feminist consciousness-raising, moreover, has had irreversible effects. Once women begin to question the inevitability of their subordination and to reject the conventions formerly associated with it, they can no longer retreat to the safety of those conventions. The woman who rejects the stereotype of feminine weakness and dependence can no longer find much comfort in the cliché that all men are beasts. She has no choice except to believe, on the contrary, that men are human beings, and she finds it hard to forgive them when they act like animals. Although her own actions, which violate the conventions of female passivity and thus appear to men as a form of aggression, help to call up animal-like actions in males, even her understanding of this dynamic does not make it any easier to make allowances for her adversary. "You aren't willing to compromise. Men will never be as sensitive or aware as women are. It's just not in their nature. So you have to get used to that, and be satisfied with . . . either sexual satisfaction or theoretical intelligence or being loved and *not* understood or else being left alone to do the things you want to do."

A woman who takes feminism seriously, as a program that aims to put the relations between men and women on a new footing, can no longer accept such a definition of available alternatives without recognizing it as a form of surrender. The younger woman rightly replies that no one should settle for less than a combination of sex, compassion, and intelligent understanding. The attempt to implement these demands, however, exposes her to repeated disappointments, especially since men appear to find the demand for tenderness as

---

[2]Psychiatric and sociological studies of working-class life confirm these observations. "An American middle-class wife tends to expect her husband to treat her as an equal," wrote a psychiartrist in 1957. ". . . She expects cooperation, sharing of responsibility, and individual consideration . . . In the lower-class family of Italians, . . . the wife . . . does not expect to be treated as an equal. Rather she expects him to make the chief decisions, relieving her of the responsibility so that she can tend to the needs of the large brood of children." Rainwater, Coleman, and Handel reported in their study of working-class wives: "Middle class wives tend to see a greater interchangeability between the marriage partners in handling the work that must be done. There is much more interest in doing things together, whether it be the dishes or painting the walls; 'togetherness' is largely a middle class value."

In the twenty years since these descriptions were written, the ideology of marital companionship has made headway in working-class, as well as middle-class families, while feminism, penetrating finally into the consciousness of working-class women, has made conventional sexual stereotyping suspect and has thus made it hard for people to indulge in routine depreciation of the opposite sex without self-consciousness. As working-class women begin to assert their rights or at least to listen to feminist ideas, their husbands see in this turn of events another blow to their own self-respect, the crowning indignity heaped on the workingman by a middle-class liberalism that has already destroyed his savings, bused his children to distant schools, undermined his authority over them, and now threatens to turn his wife against him.

threatening to their emotional security as the demand for sexual satisfaction. Thwarted passion in turn gives rise in women to the powerful rage against men so unforgettably expressed, for example, in the poems of Sylvia Plath.

> No day is safe from news of you,
> Walking about in Africa maybe, but thinking of me.

Women's rage against men originates not only in erotic disappointments or the consciousness of oppression but in a perception of marriage as the ultimate trap, the ultimate routine in a routinized society, the ultimate expression of the banality that pervades and suffocates modern life. For the heroine of *The Bell Jar*, marriage represents the apotheosis of the everyday: "It would mean getting up at seven and cooking him eggs and bacon and toast and coffee and dawdling about in my nightgown and curlers after he'd left work to wash up the dirty plates and make the bed, and then when he came home after a lively, fascinating day he'd expect a big dinner, and I'd spend the evening washing up, even more dirty plates till I fell into bed, utterly exhausted." If the man protests that he is exhausted too, and that his "fascinating day" consists of drudgery and humiliation, his wife suspects that he wishes merely to give her domestic prison the appearance of a rose-covered cottage.

In theory, it should be possible for feminists to advance beyond the present stage of sexual recrimination by regarding men simply as a class enemy, involuntarily caught up in the defense of masculine privilege and therefore exempt from personal blame. The symbiotic interdependence of men and women, however, makes it hard to attain such intellectual detachment in everyday life. The "class enemy" presents himself in ordinary existence as a lover, husband, or father, on whom women proceed to make demands that men usually fail to meet. According to the feminists' own analysis of the way in which the subjection of women damages women and impoverishes the emotional life of men, men cannot possibly meet the full erotic demands of women under the existing sexual arrangements; yet feminism itself gives those demands the strongest ideological support. It therefore intensifies the problem to which it simultaneously offers the solution. On the one hand, feminism aspires to change the relations between men and women so that women will no longer be forced into the role of "victim and shrew," in the words of Simone de Beauvoir. On the other hand, it often makes women more shrewish than ever in their daily encounters with men. This contradiction remains unavoidable so long as feminism insists that men oppress women and that this oppression is intolerable, at the same time urging women to approach men not simply as oppressors but as friends and lovers.

## STRATEGIES OF ACCOMMODATION

Because the contradictions exposed (and exacerbated) by feminism are so painful, the feminist movement has always found it tempting to renounce its own insights and program and to retreat into some kind of accommodation with the existing order, often disguised as embattled militancy. In the nineteenth century, American feminists edged away from their original programs, which envisioned not only economic equality but a sweeping reform of marriage and sexual relations, into a protracted campaign for women suffrage. Today many feminists argue, once again in the name of political realism, that women need to establish their influence within the two-party system, as a kind of loyal opposition, before they can raise broader issues. Such tactics merely serve to postpone the discussion of broader issues indefinitely. Just as the women's rights movement of the nineteenth century drew back from discussions of love and marriage when they met with public hostility, so strong forces in the National Organization for Women today propose to improve woman's image, to show that feminism in no way threatens men, and to blame "social conditions" or bad attitudes, not male supremacy, for the subordination of the female sex.

More subtle forms of accommodation pose as radical challenges to mainstream feminism and the status quo. Some militants have revived discredited theories of matriarchal origins or myths of the moral superiority of women, thereby consoling themselves for the lack of power. They appeal to the illusory solidarity of sisterhood in order to avoid arguments about the proper goals of the feminist movement. By institutionalizing women's activities as "alternatives to the male death-culture," they avoid challenging that culture and protect women from the need to compete with men for jobs, political power, and public attention. What began as a tactical realization that women have to win their rights without waiting for men to grant them has degenerated into the fantasy of a world without men. As one critic has noted, the movement's "apparent vigor turns out to be mere busyness with self-perpetuating make-work: much of it serving in the short run to provide its more worldly experts with prestige, book contracts, and grants, its dreamers with an illusory matriarchal utopia."

"Radical lesbians" carry the logic of separation to its ultimate futility, withdrawing at every level from the struggle against male domination while directing a steady stream of abuse against men and against women who refuse to acknowledge their homosexual proclivities. Proclaiming their independence from men, militant lesbians in fact envision a protected enclave for themselves within a male-dominated society. Yet the form of surrender—the dream of an island secure against male intrusion—remains attractive to women who repeatedly fail to find a union of sexuality and tenderness in their relations with men. As such disappointments become more and more common, sexual separatism commends itself as the most plausible substitute for liberation.

All these strategies of accommodation derive their emotional energy from an impulse much more prevalent than feminism: the flight from feeling. For many reasons, personal relations have become increasingly risky—most obviously, because they no longer carry any assurance of permanence. Men and women make extravagant demands on each other and experience irrational rage and hatred when their demands are not met. Under these conditions, it is not surprising that more and more people long for emotional detachment or "enjoy sex," as Hendin writes, "only in situations where they can define and limit the intensity of the relationship." A lesbian confesses: "The only men I've ever been able to enjoy sex with were men I didn't give a shit about. Then I could let go, because I didn't feel vulnerable."

Sexual separatism is only one of many strategies for controling or escaping from strong feeling. Many prefer the escape of drugs, which dissolve anger and desire in a glow of good feeling and create the illusion of intense experience without emotion. Others simply undertake to live alone, repudiating connections with either sex. The reported increase in single-member households undoubtedly reflects a new taste for personal independence, but it also expresses a revulsion against close emotional attachments of any kind. The rising rate of suicide among young people can be attributed, in part, to the same flight from emotional entanglement. Suicide, in Hendin's words, represent the "ultimate numbness."

The most prevalent form of escape from emotional complexity is promiscuity: the attempt to achieve a strict separation between sex and feeling. Here again, escape masquerades as liberation, regression as progress. The progressive ideology of "nonbinding commitments" and "cool sex" makes a virtue of emotional disengagement, while purporting to criticize the depersonalization of sex. Enlightened authorities like Alex Comfort, Nena and George O'Neill, Robert and Anna Francoeur insist on the need to humanize sex by making it into a "total experience" instead of a mechanical performance; yet in the same breath they condemn the human emotions of jealousy and possessiveness and decry "romantic illusions." "Radical" therapeutic wisdom urges men and women to express their needs and wishes without reserve—since all needs and wishes have equal legitimacy—but warns them not to expect a single mate to satisfy them. This program seeks to allay emotional tensions, in effect, by reducing the demands men and women make on each other, instead of making men and women better able to meet them. The promotion of sex as a "healthy," "normal" part of life masks a desire to divest it of the emotional intensity that unavoidably clings to it: the reminders of earlier entanglements with parents, the "unhealthy" inclination to re-create those relations in relation with lovers. The enlightened insistence that sex is not "dirty" expresses a wish to sanitize it by washing away its unconscious associations.

The humanistic critique of sexual "depersonalization" thus sticks to the surface of the problem. Even while preaching the need to combine sex with feeling, it gives ideological legitimacy to the protective withdrawal from strong emotions. It condemns the overemphasis on technique while extolling sexual relations that are hermetically free of affect. It exhorts men and women to "get in touch with their feelings" but encourages them to make "resolutions about freedom and 'non-possessiveness,'" as Ingrid Bengis writes, which "tear the very heart of intimacy." It satirizes the crude pornographic fantasies sold by the mass media, which idealize hairless women with inflated mammaries, but it does so out of an aversion to fantasy itself, which so rarely conforms to social definitions of what is healthy minded. The critics of dehumanized sex, like the critics of sport, hope to abolish spectatorship and to turn everyone into a participant, hoping that vigorous exercise will drive away unwholesome thoughts. They attack pornography, not because they wish to promote more complicated and satisfying fantasies about sex, but because, on the contrary, they wish to win acceptance for a realistic view of womanhood and of the reduced demands that men and women have a right to make of each other.

31

GERMAINE GREER

# A Child Is Born

*Few books of this decade are likely to generate as much controversy, arouse as much anger, and stimulate as many minds as Germaine Greer's massive work on the human politics of reproduction,* Sex and Destiny. *Greer is aware of the wrath she may invoke by suggesting that the Western concern with world overpopulation may represent our effort to force our cultural values on the rest of the world more than an effort to protect the health of those populations in what we term developing or underdeveloped countries. We see the sensitivity of this argument reflected in the fact that many, if not most, of the persons from whom she gathered data are thanked anonymously in her acknowledgments in order to protect their own careers. An even stronger indication of the volatile nature of her subject is the fact that the volume begins with a warning to the reader.*

*Because the chapter from* Sex and Destiny *entitled "A Child Is Born" is too long to reprint in its entirety, we must edit out a substantial portion. The chapter presents two arguments; the first is Greer's viewpoint on how Westerners view child rearing and childbearing, and the second is her description of how the rest of the world views those two activities. Both aspects of Greer's argument are vital, but we can present only the Western portion of the analysis. Thus, as you read the following paper, bear in mind that Greer simultaneously offers a picture of childbearing and child rearing in nonwesternized parts of the world as extremely humane, mindful of the welfare of mothers during the birth process, and child-centered once the infant enters the family group.*

In World Population Year (1974), the location chosen for the international conference was Bucharest. The choice was perhaps unfortunate, for the raison d'e^tre behind the whole jamboree was fear of the population explosion and the promotion of birth control programs. Just the year before, the Rumanian government had outlawed abortion and banned the sale of contraceptives, because the decline in population growth and the increasing senility of the population had been construed as a threat to the country's economic future. When the foreigh minister met with the press, among the questions he was asked was whether such Draconian measures were not tantamount to forced childbirth. The minister had trouble understanding the question, which was rephrased for him. "Does that mean that unwanted children are being born in Rumania?" "Of course not!" snapped the minister. The question was based upon the common Western assumption that the only people who want children are those who conceive them. The minister's answer might have been based upon a different premise, that a child wanted by someone, in this case the Rumanian government, could not have been called unwanted. On the other hand, he might have been referring to the fact that after an initial baby boom, during which the country literally ran out of diapers and baby foods, the birthrate had settled back at its earlier, unsatisfactory level.[1]

The Rumanian example is just one of many which could be cited to show that even the governments of totalitarian countries cannot counteract the profound lack of desire for children which prevails in Western society, especially among upwardly mobile social groups. Governments may present themselves as pro-children, but governments are interested not in children themselves but in recruiting the work force of the future. The methods they may adopt are extremely limited, for no suggestion of forced childbirth will be tolerated, even in conspicuously unfree societies like Rumania. "Every child a wanted child" is the slogan, but the modern Western infant is wanted by fewer people than any infants in our long history, not only by fewer parents but by smaller groups of people. Historically, babies have been welcome additions to society; their parents derived prestige and pleasure and pride from their proximity and suffered little or no deterioration in the quality of their lives, which could even have been positively enhanced by their arrival. Parents, themselves still relatively junior in the social hierarchy, had not to cudgel their brains to decide if they were ready for the experience, for they were surrounded by people who watched their reproductive career with passionate interest, who would guide them through the fears and anguish of childbirth and take on a measure of responsibility for child rearing. Historically, human societies have been pro-child; modern society is unique in that it is profoundly hostile to children. We in the West do not refrain from childbirth because we are concerned about the population explosion or because we feel we cannot afford children, but because we do not like children.

Conventional piety is still such that to say such a thing is shocking. Parents will point angrily to the fact that they do not beat or starve or terrorize their children, but struggle to feed, house, clothe, and educate them to the best of their ability. Our wish that people who cannot feed, house, clothe, and educate their children adequately not have them is born of our concern for the children themselves, or so most of us would claim. At the heart of our insistence upon the child's parasitic role in the family lurks the conviction that children must be banished from adult society. Babies ought not to be born before they have rooms of their own: when they are born they must adhere to an antisocial timetable. Access to the adult world is severely rationed in terms of time, and in any case, what the child enters is not the adult's reality but a sort of no-man's-land of phatic communication. Mothers who are deeply involved in exploring and developing infant intelligence and personality are entitled to feel that such a generalization is unjust, but even they must reflect that they share the infant's ostracized status. No one wants to hear the fascinating thing that baby said or did today, especially at a party. Mother realizes she is becoming as big a bore as her child and can be shaken by the realization. The heinousness of taking an infant or a toddler to an adult social gathering is practically unimaginable; as usual, the discomfort and uneasiness are manifested as concern. A baby may be produced and brandished momentarily, but then it must disappear. Otherwise well-meaners begin cooing about its being time for bed; the more baby chirps and chatters and reaches for necklaces and earrings, the more likely it is to be told that it is a poor little thing. Restaurants, cinemas, offices, supermarkets, even Harrods auction rooms, are all no places for children. In England, restaurants mentioned in *The Good Food Guide* boldly advise parents to "leave under-fourteens and dogs at home": their object in doing so is to increase their patronage by vaunting their child-free condition.[2]

Adults cannot have fun while kids are around; kids must be "put down" first. Drinking and flirting, the principal expressions of adult festivity, are both inhibited by the presence of children. Eventually our raucousness wakes them and they watch our activities through the stair rails and learn to despise us. In lieu of our real world we offer them a fake one, the toy world. Parents shocked by some family crisis try to mend the cracks in the nuclear family by dating their children, abjectly courting them. The scale and speed of our world is all anti-child; children cannot be allowed to roam the streets, but must run a terrifying gauntlet to get to the prime locus of their segregation, school. They cannot open doors or windows, cannot see on top of counters, are stifled and trampled in crowds, hushed when they speak or cry before strangers, apologized for by harassed mothers condemned to share their ostracized condition.

As we shall see, the state's desire for children is powerless against the anti-child thrust of the Western lifestyle. Western industrialized society is gerontomorphic. Life has become so complex that induction into adult society takes many years and effectively isolates the socialized adult from the unsocialized child. There is so little interpenetration between the worlds of the child and the adult that we can easily call to mind whole districts of our inner cities where no child is ever seen. The adult who elects to spend time with a child must take time off from his immediate interests and make a special effort. Communication is strained, artificial, and often illusory, and the children less often fooled about the real nature of the case than their egregious parents. The general tendency to separate children from parents, which has always characterized Northwestern Europe, has intensified with the development of consumer society. The most privileged people in protestant Europe have traditionally seen least of their children, and upwardly mobile groups have assumed the upper-class pattern. The new baby has its own room, is put to bed awake and not picked up until the time is right and routine says it will not thereby be "spoiled." The child goes away to school and learns "self-reliance." Children learn to treat adults, all of whom stand in paternal authoritarian relationship to them, with a sort of hypocritical deference. All their spontaneous contacts are with their peer group, with whom they are likely to share antisocial ritual behavior. The child world was further alienated from the adult world by the creation of the buffer state, "teenager." Old age is absurd, isolated, disgusting, so alien that it serves as a bait for juvenile thugs to bash, rape, and rob.

If the truth is that we of the industrialized West do not like children, the corollary is equally true: our children do not like us. It is blasphemy to deny that parents love their children (whatever that may mean), but it is nevertheless true that adults do not like children. People of different generations do not consort together as a matter of preference: where a child and an old person develop any closeness, we are apt to suspect the motives of the old person. Most social groupings tend to be formed of individuals in the same age set and social circumstances, and even within the family, parents and children spend very little time in each other's company. The family which sits down at the table together most nights in the week is now an exception in many of the well-to-do suburbs in the United States. Food advertising often shows mothers preparing single-portion frozen dinners for individual family members. Families used to meet only to eat; nowadays a commoner pattern has the kids being fed earlier and of different foods from those which will be eaten later by the adults.

We generally try to explain our separation from our children as a system adopted for their own good; they must not work but learn, and so they are passive subordinates in the family structure. Serious matters are not discussed with them because it might confuse and worry them; they are offered a kind of conversational pablum out of consideration. So much adult amusement stems from matters ribald or malicious that even lighthearted conversation is censored for the younger generation. The children capitulate by concealing their own diversions; where once parents sent them to bed before a party, they wait until their parents are in the Bahamas before planning their jubilee.

The inability to enjoy the company of children is for many adults a source of guilt. Because children spend most of their time with their peers, they are unable to participate intelligently in an adult conversation. They have not learned to listen and learn from unselfconscious discussions which are not primarily directed at them. Children paraded in front of adults are too often silent and coy or else dominate the conversation with tedious twaddle, unenlivened by complexity or spontaneity. It is anathema to admit being bored by one's own children, but it is understood that one's children will bore anyone else who has to spend time with them and that the company of the children of others is all the things one would never admit about the company of one's own.

The gulf that yawns between adult society and the world of children in the "Anglo-Saxon" West is by no means universal. There are societies where adults and children laught at the same jokes, where adults would not dream of eating their evening meal without their children about them and would not inhibit discussion of serious matters because children were present. In fact, such societies are still more populous than our own. There are huge cities which are practically run by children, children who support their parents and their sibs by their skills and initiative, where children and adults inhabit the same cruel world and survive by clinging to each other. But these are the societies whose children, we think, should not be born.

The state's institutionalized desire for children is, obviously, a desire for productive adults, rather than for children themselves. This pressure is expressed through other institutions, those dealing directly with the production of these grade-A humans, and which are constantly struggling to improve the product by further sophistication of the technology. The most fantastic elaboration of this process would bypass the role of mother altogether. When asked on an ABC television program whether he thought that artificial wombs were a possibility, Professor Joseph Fletcher replied:

> Yes, yes. I—I foresee it with urgent approval.... If I were an embryologist I should be eager for the day when I could actually see, let's say through a glass container, a conceptus develop from fertilization through to term.... It seems to me that what is known as artificial gestation.... in such a non-uterine container is the most desirable thing in the world for me to imagine.... Great thing.... I hope it comes soon. I think it will.

His co-guest on the program, Dr. André Hellegers, ventured to suggest a different point of view:

> I have a misgiving about what I would call the increasing objectivization of children.... children as a product of artifice. I think it's already terribly difficult for an American child today to come home with a C minus instead of an A and I think this intolerance towards imperfection, I have some considerable misgivings about.[3]

The "objectivization," or reification, of which Dr. Hellegers was speaking is already far advanced. Dr. Hellegers would draw the line at trying to screen out children of C minus academic ability in utero, but he would be out of line with the consensus if he did not accept "therapeutic" abortion in some cases, perhaps even including the relatively mild cases of Down's syndrome, and he would almost certainly endorse the drive towards perfectibility in correcting minor disfigurements and straightening teeth. People who cannot afford to pay orthodontists' huge bills had better not have children. Reproduction in the highly developed world has a become kind of manufacture: doctors do not want children for themselves; they want better children, just as industry demands a better mousetrap, or a bigger, brighter, more regularly formed, utterly flawless (and tasteless) tomato. Such a desire is not tantamount to an encouragement to any woman to bear a child; it functions instead as a challenge and a multifarious source of anxiety.

If we continue along the path of trying to see who, if anyone, wants children around, we come next to the child's kin group. It used to be a truism of feminist theory that women were railroaded into motherhood by the expectations of their parents and their in-laws. In the view of this writer, such forms of persuasion and pressure as the kin group can bring to bear pale into utter insignificance next to the powerful disincentives which are offered by the actual social context in which the would-be childbearer lives. A distant mother or a mother-in-law who is plainly waiting around for the good news can be disregarded. Only in the rarest instance does she have any economic power to coerce the birth of a grandchild, and she is hardly any more likely to be actively involved in the rearing of a grandchild, especially in the socially mobile groups which characterize the American (and the EEC) dream. None of us thinks that one generation has a right to the children of the next generation, not only because it gives no help in raising children but because in our view the exercise of such a right would represent an intolerable intrusion into the rights of the individual. Only two people have the right to want a child, its parents, and even then the father has no a priori right to want a child from an unwilling woman.

One of the reasons we so firmly believe that the only people with the right to want a child are its parents is that we see quite clearly that bearing and raising a child is an ordeal. The individuals whom we have painstakingly inducted into child-free society and established there, with a lifestyle centered entirely upon achievement and self-gratification, have now to disrupt that pattern. The sacrifice is enormous, and they are to expect no reward or recompense. If the management of childbearing in our society had actually been intended to maximize stress, it could hardly have succeeded better. The childbearers embark on their struggle alone; the rest of us wash our hands of them.

From conception, pregnancy is regarded as an abnormal state, which women are entitled to find extremely distressing. Such an attitude is itself the product of the fact that western women are pregnant so seldom, but even so, pregnancy is not simply viewed as a natural, if rather peculiar, condition but as an illness, requiring submission to the wisdom of health professionals and constant monitoring, as if the fetus were a saboteur hidden in its mother's soma. Though some women will freely admit that they feel more comfortable pregnant than they ever felt when enduring the monthly cycle of depression, tension, *Mittelschmerz,* and menstruation, their number is not likely to be increased by the fact that most women expect to feel rotten and look worse. The well-documented disabilities—morning sickness, caries, cravings, incontinence, toxemia, thrombosis, fluid retention, skin eruptions, piles, sleeplessness, varicose veins—range from the undignified to the unbearable. Bitterest irony of all, of the palliatives offered by the medical profession for the disorders of pregnancy, so many of them the result of cultural practices and not of the condition itself, there is hardly one effective drug which is not also damaging to the development of the fetus.[4] The pregnant woman also finds that she is to forgo the drugs upon which our society depends, alcohol, caffeine, and nicotine.

Perhaps more difficult to bear than the physical discomforts of pregnancy is the psychic discomfort of feeling unattractive. The feeling has less to do with the behavior of the woman's mate than it has to do with the accepted aesthetic of female appearance. Societies which place a high premium on childbearing feature styles of female dress which accept breasts and bellies, whether softly accentuated by the sari, rounding out the salwar or pushing out the high-wasted front-opening full-skirted frocks of the vanishing European peasantry. The preferred shape of Western women, narrow-hipped and small-breasted, is desirable partly because of its denial of fecundity. Even those few women who feel at ease with their own soft and ample bodies are sorely tried whenever they are obliged to choose clothes. Women who want to breast feed will find that very few clothes which will open to free the breast can be found, so we have the multiple irony that they are forced to make a display of what most people would rather not see. Because the pregnant woman is unlikely to have seen pregnancy in her immediate family, she is ill prepared for the changes her body goes through, from the swelling, darkened nipples and engorged veins of early pregnancy to the wallowing bulk of the last weeks, she may well find them alarming and disgusting.

It is to be hoped that there are very few men who react as violently as Maurice Utrillo to the physical signs of pregnancy; when he saw pregnant women in the street, "he would chase them and pull their hair and try to kick them in the stomach."[5] Unfortunately, this extreme behavior may not be altogether rare. Dr. Anson Shupe of the Center for Social Research and Dr. William Stacey of the Center on Domestic Violence at the University of Texas at Arlington found that of 2,638 women who entered shelters for battered wives in Dallas and Denton or used the shelter hot lines, fully 42 percent had been attacked when they were pregnant.[6] The roles of sex object, as stereotyped in our culture, and mother, as it is biologically determined, are antagonistic. Men may be baffled and enraged when their playmate becomes a parturient monster, but women are even more bamboozled by the demands of the dual role. Should they or should they not engage in sexual intercourse during pregnancy? Not to is to "let the child come between them"; there is no helpful rule which says that a father must nourish the fetus with his seed, or that he must protect it by practicing self-control. If husbands grow fractious, pregnant wives are to try to placate them; if wives are desirous, they may court rejection.

While the pregnant woman does not have to be protected from exertion, for like most people in our society she is more likely to take too little exercise than too much, she ought to be protected from anxiety. There are too many genuinely unknowable aspects of childbirth for a mother to be unaware of risk, yet genuine psychoprophylaxis is the last thing that modern obstetrics can offer. Most Western women face a pregnancy fundamentally alone. They sally forth alone on their endless round of visits to the obstetrician, the clinic, the hospital, abondoning their own enviornment and entering a series of unfamiliar settings in a submissive posture. The women who have given up paid employment to have a baby move from gossipy collectivity to isolation and introspection in an empty house, at a time when neither isolation nor introspection is good for them. Women who fear the consequences of loneliness and brooding fight to remain at jobs they are perfectly capable of doing, even to the extent of concealing their pregnancies almost to the end. As soon as a pregnancy is admitted, the mother-to-be is bombarded with contradictory advice, and not only from well-meaning amateurs but from the health professionals themselves. Some doctors routinely prescribe diuretics, others detest the idea. Some are so keen on small babies that they keep the mothers half starved and increase the risk of toxemia. Some urge women to undergo amniocentesis when others would oppose it.

Childbirth in our society is not conducted in an orderly, predictable way but half experimentally. It is a hand-to-mouth business, changing weekly according to the fads and fashions which sweep the medical world, bringing riches and fame to their proponents. Every fad is presented as the newest medical breakthrough, the meticulously researched result of increased technological know-how, and each gains a measure of acceptance because of women's anxiety. Within the span of one woman's childbearing years we have seen diethylstilbestrol administered for bigger and better babies; decompression chambers for easier labor and smarter children; thalidomide and its sister catastrophes; the Lamaze or gymnastic approach; every kind of anesthesia and induction, and the seesawing battle between high forceps and caesarians, to name but a few. Women who have "been through it" naturally seek to find converts to the methods used on them, in order to allay their own anxiety. Women whose experiences caused rage and bitterness are expected to hold their tongues. Fortunately, perhaps, once the immediate interest in the management of childbirth has waned, very few women trouble to read the rueful follow-up information about the methods they chose. There is after all nothing they can do to right the consequences of an induction, or to restore to their children those first days passed in a drugged daze or the brain cells that died while technicians disagreed.[7] The women who have still to become pregnant will not have the benefit of their collective experience; they must pick a haphazard course across terrain which has been charted in various and contradictory ways, and which guide they choose is simply, shockingly, a matter left to blind chance.

The fortuitousness of the method of management of childbirth stands in sharp constrast to the deliberateness with which the prospective parents must approach the childbearing project, timing it carefully, making sure that they can afford it. From the beginning, childbearing involves investment, as the mother-to-be acquires her special wardrobe and the infant's layette is assembled and the doctor is paid and the hospital is booked and so forth and so on endlessly. In the case of a student of mine in the United States, the doctor demanded to be paid in advance before he would agree to preside at the delivery. Everything about the wanted child's arrival is calculated, everything, that is, except how he and his mother shall be treated. If ours was a society which welcomed and enjoyed children, and if each parturient woman was surrounded by people who wanted her child even more than she did, she could ease her feelings of responsibility and inadequacy. If ours was a society with collective notions of normative behavior for parents, parents could escape the crushing responsibility for the ills that befall the children, provided they were aware that they had fulfilled all expectations. Where there are no shared expectations there can be no feeling of having done the right thing. Western mothers enter on childbirth punctiliously—the ones who are not "feckless," that is—and consciously, self-consciously, strive to go about it intelligently and carefully, but even that is not forgiven them. The very people who exploit their conscientiousness to increase their own influence—and income—will be the first to tell them that their lack of spontaneity is in itself a cause of uncomfortable pregnancy or tension during the birth or difficulties with feeding or failure to caress the baby adequately.

The gestation period of humans is only nine months, too short a time for any individual to get a grasp of the whole spectrum of ideas about pregnancy mangement and her own place in it. The decisions which any mother makes are partly rational and informed and partly irrational and emotional. Eventually the mother may wish to say that she behaved in certain ways instinctively, but in fact intelligence and emotion play a more significant part in mothering than does instinct. Mothering behavior is learned, but not in our society by custom and example. Each mother has, as it were, to reinvent childbirth: she has joined the competition for the bigger, better, brighter baby. On the widely accepted priciple that parenthood is too important a function to be left to amateurs, the Swedish government has instituted a nationwide scheme to teach Swedes how to do it, although there is no more agreement about the right way to do it in Sweden than there is anywhere else in the protestant world.

It follows from the middle of conflicting demands made upon her that the mental strain of pregnancy for an intelligent, self-regulating female must be much more upsetting than the physical concomitants of her condition. The stress can only be increased by the fact that although everyone agrees that the woman who has wished this extraordinary dilemma upon herself must bear the total responsibility for the outcome, she will not be allowed complete freedom of choice in the matter. Her family doctor will have ideas of his own about the best management of her pregnancy; after all, he is much more used to pregnancies than she is. Her first problem is to find out what her doctor's fixed ideas are and whether they are acceptable to her or not. Her doctor may agree to discuss them frankly with her, but he is much more likely to try to extort confidence in himself at the expense of minimizing the disagreements among the members of his profession. The more experience he has the more likely he is to want a biddable patient, especially if she is too intelligent to be fobbed off with oversimplified accounts of why he is choosing a certain course of action. He also comes in with the considerable advantage of knowing what he wants, while his "patient" is still trying to find out what she wants. As an expert and a detached professional, he will make decisions which she, not he, has to live with. The doctor who counsels a woman to accept a method of birth which has adverse consequences for her or her child may do so with impunity. The woman who trusts him has only herself to blame, for no one can be found who will share the blame with her. The more malpractice suits proliferate, the more conservative the procedures doctors will choose; the high proportion of caesarians carried out in the U. S. can probably be explained by some such irrelevant factor. Babies plucked out of opened abdomens escape many of the perils of the struggle down the birth canal, but they are born anesthetized, and their mothers have missed out on the experience too. The first days of life are poisoned.

The woman who demands the right to make her own decisions will find herself conducting a running battle with health professionals. There are good grounds, for example, for giving birth at home, but a woman who chooses to do so may find herself abandoned by the people who should help her. In some parts of North America she may be breaking the law; if she can find a midwife to attend her, the midwife may go to jail.[8] On the other hand, she may find herself in worse danger because the only help she can find is inexpert. Obstetricians may refuse to attend her at home for fear of eventual malpractice suits. Home is less bacterially pathogenic than the hospital, is a less stressed and stressing environment, yet for more and more women birth at home is not a realistic possibility.[9] A primipara might be told that if she gives birth at home she is solely responsible for the consequences, so that the advantages of home confinement are effectively negated by the imposition of anxiety. The British home confinement system is being wound down; the flying squads which would attend home births if any difficulty arose no longer exist. The official policy is to have all births carried out in hospitals, as they are in Sweden, which has an extremely low rate of perinatal complication and death, and in the United States, where the consequences are much less impressive.[10]

Much has been written on the inappropriateness of the hospital as the setting for the birth of children, but the logistics of delivery of health services force the continuation and intensification of the trend to manage births in the atmosphere of crisis and disease. Even when induction and caesarian sections are not performed on slight justification, with appalling results for mother and child, hospital birth takes place among strangers and is subordinated to their routine. There is no room for the family to celebrate one of the climatic points in its life cycle. The only other family member allowed to be present is the mother's lover or husband, or someone purporting to be one or the other; the presence of a sex partner as the only lay helper in the birthplace is an unusual circumstance, in historical terms, and it dramatizes the fact that the basic unit of consumer society is not the family but the couple.

Ironically, because hospitals are geared to deal with crises, a birth which presents no complications may be worse attended in hospital than it would have been at home. The commonest complaint of women undergoing hospital chidldbirth in Britain as long ago as 1947, and ever since, was that they had been left alone during labor.[11] Labor, as its name implies, is very hard work; a laboring woman needs support and sustenance and reassurance. Writhing like a beached whale on a trolley in a corridor is no way to get any of these. Even when hospitals have taught women what to expect in prenatal classes, the staff is still capable of telling a woman who knows that she is in second stage labor and dilation is well advanced that she has hours to go and mustn't be naughty and clamor for assistance when the need of others is so much greater. Nevertheless the woman who can get on with the business without interference is in better shape than the one who has been taken over by the doctors, fighting to stay aware in delivery rooms which exist to deliver drugs and surgical procedures, helpless in the stupid lithotomy position, befuddled, bamboozled, and humiliated.

Yet women continue to want to bear children. They may say that they want to experience childbirth. What they can mean by that when there is no telling whether they will be allowed to experience it, given the agressiveness of childbirth managment, or whether it will not simply consist of torture and terror, is not at all clear. Far too many women have no experience of birth at all, but simply of anesthesia. Others have a confused, hallucinatory recollection which has more to do with narcotics than any natural event; others felt fear and loneliness and resentment, humilation and defeat, and pain natural and induced. Some speak of an experience dramatic, rewarding, deeply pleasurable, a vast whole-body orgasm. Having had one child does not mean that one will know about the next time; it is probably true to say that no two births are the same, yet the degree of contrast between one birth and the next in the childbearing career of a single Western woman can be utterly disorienting and unpredictable. Women who want the experience of childbirth are in the curious position of desiring the unknown.

If the only persons to suffer in the chaos of childbirth management were the mothers, female stoicism might override self-preservation, as always, in the interest of better babies. Instead, an increasing number of voices can be heard sternly insisting on the importance of the birth experience for the future development of the child, its capacity for bonding, affection, orgasm, sociability, and so forth. Again we have the typical mix of impotence and responsibility which characterizes the twentieth-century western parent. The threat of damage to the child's future is much more disturbing to women than the prospect of pain or torment or disfigurement to themselves. The very women who would take their responsibility most seriously in this regard are the ones who would experience the most stress in fulfilling it. Proponents of birth control often point to the phenomenon that the birthrate falls as the educational level rises, and see in that a sign that literacy and investigative intelligence lead to informed choices and a greater measure of control. They could interpret the phenomenon in a less positive way: the more women know about childbirth, the more likely they are to refuse to undergo it. Further, educated women are more likely to encounter institutionalized, sophisticated health care, so the reality of the experience is actually different for them and has very little to recommend it. When we encounter eugenists lamenting the unwillingness of the brightest women to reproduce, we might suggest to them that they give some thought to making childbirth less of an ordeal.

The closer women draw in social and economic status to the male level, the more disruptive childbirth becomes. In order to compete with men, western woman has joined the masculine hierarchy, and cultivated a masculine sense of self. The acknowledgement of her pregnancy means that she must step down from all that and enter the psychological equivalent of the birth hut; what happens to her there can have convulsive effects upon what she has come to think of as unalterable, her personality. In exchange for her settled self-image she has a body which inexorably goes about its own business, including biochemical changes in the brain. From this time forward her attention will be divided. The period following the birth of a child has been called a fourth trimester; mother and child remain attached as it were by an invisible umbilical cord.[12] A mother is no longer self-sufficient but at the mercy of the child's indomitable love and egotism. The drastic nature of the psychological process has never been explained, but there is a growing body of evidence that carrying a child to term results in a bond which cannot be broken without causing enduring anguish to the mother. Adoption at birth is much less manageable in terms of emotional sequelea than abortion.[13] Miscarriage and stillbirth are also experienced as disasters, although society callously ignores them.[14] The woman who becomes a mother vastly increases her capacity for pain and her vulnerability. If she returns to work and brings baby to the office, the divided nature of her attention is obvious. She may encounter support as she breast feeds in the board room, but she will also encounter ridicule. If she stays at home for her two years paid leave, supposing she has such an unusual privilege, and returns to work without loss of seniorty, she is not the same worker who left to bear a child. Asking her to continue as if nothing had happened is absurd. Contemplated throught the eyes of the ostracized dyad mother-and-child, the world of business may well seem cruel and silly, and a key to the executive washroom a poor reward. Meanwhile the child's development is taken over by professionals: the mother begins her long struggle with guilt.

The woman who becomes a mother suffers a crushing loss of status; as a "patient" she was at the bottom end of the health professionals' social hierarchy. At home she is a solitary menial. Fewer and fewer women can expect the support of another family member during their maternal isolation, and fewer still could expect or would welcome the help and support of neighbors. Modern dwellings are arranged in such a way that housewives carry out identical tasks in isolation from one another, in suburbs which are deserted by day except for their lonely selves and their babies. The mother who has a car may break out of her isolation without too much difficulty; she will also have a place to feed baby which is not a public lavatory. If she has to rely on public transport, the ordeal of escaping from her suburb may well prove too intimidating. Watching mothers trying to juggle their parcels and the baby while stowing their strollers on London buses is an unedifying pastime. Watching airline stewardesses ignoring women with children and fawning on businessmen is equally unedifying, especially as time was when mothers with infants were given special attention. Outside English supermarkets rows of parked baby carriages can be seen, because the merchants who take billions of pounds from mothers' purses cannot be bothered to design a facility to accommodate them. Instead they have the gall to announce that perambulators and strollers are not permitted inside the store. Feminists are often accused of downgrading motherhood. The accusation is ridiculous: motherhood hit rock bottom long before the new feminist wave broke. The wave itself was caused by the groundswell.

As a mother, the young woman who once moved freely through her varied and stimulating environment as a working girl now finds herself segregated and immobilized. The collapse in the quality of her life will have to be expiated by her infant, who has to deal with the barrage of her full attention. The best mother in the world cannot continue for long on a diet of dreary routine chores and insatiable infant demand; if she is not to suffer from serious psychic deprivation she must have stimulation and communication from supportive peers, as well as rest. The unfamiliarity of the mothering situation itself makes for anxiety; isolation and exhaustion complicate the picture. Women who planned their babies, and therefore believe sincerely that they wanted them, find themselves driven to desperation. They did not know that motherhood was like this: how could they have known? They write angry books about the lie of mother love. Human societies before our own have known that mother love does not well up unbidden to lull women into bearing the unbearable. The mother who will love her child must be allowed to take pleasure in it. Caressing and cuddling are behaviours which must be reinforced, not forced. The baby who brings its mother new prestige, new leisure, prettier clothes, and better food is vastly more lovable than the baby attended by loneliness, drudgery, and anxiety. If mothering is not positively reinforced, women will cease to do it, whether contraception and abortion are legal or illegal, easy or dangerous. In our immediate past, mothering was negatively reinforced by the severe limitations on women's options; in our arrogant ethnocentricity we have interpreted the popularity of motherhood in other cultures as reflecting nothing but the paucity of options. It is logical and sensible for a Western woman to wish to avoid childbirth, but it is wrongheaded of her to judge women in contrasting circumstances and assume that childbearing is as profitless and unreasonable for them as it would be for her.

If we turn birth from a climactic personal experience into a personal disaster, it matters little that the result is more likely to be a live child. Women will not long continue to offer up their bodies and minds to such brutality, especially if there is no one at home to welcome the child, to praise the mother for her courage and to help her raise it. In fact, peasant communities are more levelheaded and skeptical of us and our methods than we realize and they have resisted the intrusion of our chromium-plated technology more successfully than we like to think. They know that death attends too frequently in the tradional birthplace, but they also know that there are worse fates than death. Nevertheless, all that stops our technology from reaching into every hut and hovel is poverty: the cultural hegemony of Western technology is total. The voices of a few women raised in warning cannot be heard over the humming and throbbing of our machines; which is probably just as well, for if we succeed in crushing all pride and dignity out of childbearing, the population explosion will take care of itself.

## NOTES

1. John F. Besemeres, *Socialist Population Politics* (New York, 1980), pp. 271, 272.

2. Christopher Driver, ed., *The Good Food Guide* (London, 1979), p. 83.

3. ABC transcript of interview conducted by Bob Clark, August 13, 1978.

4. For a summary of the evidence about the use of drugs during pregnancy, see L. D. Sabath, Agneta Philipson, and David Charles, "Ethics and the Use of Drugs During Pregnancy," *Science,* vol. 202 (November 3, 1978), pp. 540–41; also Marcus A. Klingberg and Cheri M. Papier, "Teratoepidemology," *Journal of Biosocial Science,* vol. 11 (1979), pp. 234–51.

5. Robert Coughlan, *The Wine of Genius* (London, 1952), p. 58.

6. "Battered Women: Study Shows Their Plight a 'Family Problem,' " *UTA Magazine,* vol 5, no. 1 (September 1982), p. 15.

7. Some idea of the complexity of the problem may be gained from Watson A. Bowes, "Obstetrical Medication and Infant Outcome: A Review of the Literature," in *The Effects of Obstetrical Medication on Fetus and Infant* (Monographs of the Society for Research in Child Development, no. 35, pt. 4), pp. 3–23.

8. Sheryl Burt Ruzek, *The Women's Health Movement: Feminist Alternives to Medical Control* (New York, 1978), pp. 59–60.

9. Juith Randall, "Too Many Caesarians?" *Parents' Magazine,* November 1978, quoting Dr. Albert Havercamp of Denver General Hospital; Frederick M. Ettner, "Hospital Technology Breeds Pathology," *Women and Health,* vol. 2, no. 2.

10. R. Beard et al., eds., *The Management of Labour: Proceedings of the Royal College of Obstetricians and Gynaecologists, 1975,* mimeographed, pp. 218–34. Brigitte Jordan, *Birth in Four Cultures: A Cross-Cultural Investigation of Childbirth in Yucatán, Holland, Sweden, and the United States* (Montreal, 1980), pp. 94–5.

11. *Maternity in Britain: A Survey of Social and Economic Aspects of Pregnancy and Childbirth Undertaken by a Joint Committee of the Royal College of Obstetricians and Gynaecologists and the Population Investigation Committee* (Oxford, 1948), p. 72.

12. Sheila Kitzinger, *Women as Mothers* (Glasgow, 1978), p. 195. This chapter should be read in conjunction with this excellent book, which while taking a less saturnine view than my own, makes many of the same points in a fuller, more convincing way.

13. Joss Shawyer, "Death by Adoption," seen in typescript, 1977.

14. Susan Borg and Judith Lasker, *When Pregnancy Fails* (Boston, 1981), passim.

# 32

BARBARA EHRENREICH

# *Playboy* Joins the Battle of the Sexes

*Feminist writer Barbara Ehrenreich says she found herself approaching the study of the male in contemporary United States with antagonism. However, as she became more deeply involved in her research and writing, she began moving slowly from that initial stance through one of understanding to, ultimately, a sense of impatience. The product of her journey,* The Hearts of Men, *is a book that, in a sense, views the battle of the sexes from the male side of the bleachers. Ehrenreich concludes the preface to her work with the hope that it may bring the sexes a little closer together in their struggle "toward a more generous, dignified, and caring society."*[1]

*Historically, we know that the Industrial Revolution had a profound impact on the family by removing the workplace from the home. With this move, the once vital roles of wife and children as contributors to the family's livelihood were eliminated. Simultaneously, husbands received the new label of breadwinner (or were deemed failures if they refused it). One result of this series of changes was that the balance of independence/dependence between husbands and wives tipped precariously. The marital partnership was now based on the exchange or sharing of* his *wages for housekeeping and childcare services. The equity of such a trade may seem questionable. A working man could live easily, if not quite as comfortably, without all these other folks along for the ride, whereas a woman whose strong points might include the ability to bake a pie crust that does not get soggy and to keep a five-year-old clean may not have much market value.*

---

[1]Ehrenreich, *Hearts of Men*, p. 13.

*We might ask, "Why would men agree to such an unequal arrangement?" Would not men, if they were given a choice, prefer to keep their money for themselves and use it for such food, household maintenance, and such female companionship as they need or desire? Ehrenreich suggests that it is the "breadwinner ethic," the ideology that men should grow up and become responsible adults (the reader may translate this as "get married and support their families") that has kept men in their grey flannel suits catching the 6:45 into the city.*

*Thus, Ehrenreich explains, by the 1950s a pattern was set, and women who moved beyond the marriageable age still unclaimed were considered rejects while men who failed to grab a bride were deemed irresponsible. However, it was also during this time that the first major rumblings of male discontent quietly and subtly surfaced.* The Hearts of Men *traces the journey of men in their efforts to "break with the responsibilities of breadwinning, without, somehow, losing their manhood."*[2]

*Ehrenreich's volume in many ways parallels Betty Friedan's* The Feminine Mystique. *Just as Friedan uncovers the roots of "the disease with no name" that plagued the women of the 1950s, Ehrenreich traces the emergence of the new male by focusing on the impacts of such social phenomena as the beatniks, the discovery of the Type A personality, the hippies, and the human potential movement on the man in the grey flannel suit. She ends her analysis of the events of the last three decades with a provocative hypothesis about the recent antifeminist backlash begun by women in the 1970s, namely, that these women are not resisting the entrance of women into the marketplace so much as they are fighting the attempts of men to discard their responsibilities as heads of households. The chapter excerpted here is an early one in which she describes how she believes Hugh Hefner and his creation of the* Playboy *lifestyle was a step toward the shedding of the breadwinner ethic.*

Source: "*Playboy* Joins the Battle of the Sexes" by Barbara Ehrenreich in *The Hearts of Men*. Copyright 1983 by Barbara Ehrenreich. Reprinted with permission of Doubleday and Company, Inc.

---

*I don't want my editors marrying anyone and getting a lot of foolish notions in their heads about "togetherness," home, family, and all that jazz.*

*Hugh Hefner*

The first issue of *Playboy* hit the stands in December 1953. The first centerfold—the famous nude calendar shot of Marilyn Monroe—is already legendary. Less memorable, but no less prophetic of things to come, was the first feature article in the issue. It was a no-holds-barred attack on "the whole

---

[2]Ibid., p. 28.

concept of alimony," and secondarily, on money-hungry women in general, entitled "Miss Gold-Digger of 1953." From the beginning, *Playboy* loved women—large breasted, long-legged young women, anyway—and hated wives.

The "Miss Gold-Digger" article made its author a millionaire—not because Hugh Hefner paid him so much but because Hefner could not, at first, afford to pay him at all, at least not in cash. The writer, Burt Zollo (he signed the article "Bob Norman"; even Hefner didn't risk putting his own name in the first issue), had to accept stock in the new magazine in lieu of a fee. The first print run of 70,000 nearly sold out and the magazine passed the one million mark in 1956, making Hefner and his initial associates millionaires before the end of the decade.

But *Playboy* was more than a publishing phenomenon, it was like the party organ of a diffuse and swelling movement. Writer Myron Brenton called it the "Bible of the beleaguered male."[1] *Playboy* readers taped the centerfolds up in their basements, affixed the rabbit-head insignia to the rear windows of their cars, joined Playboy clubs if they could afford to and, even if they lived more like Babbits than Bunnies, imagined they were "playboys" at heart. The magazine encouraged the sense of membership in a fraternity of male rebels. After its first reader survey, *Playboy* reported on the marital status of its constituency in the following words: "Approximately half of PLAYBOY'S readers (46.8%) are free men and the other half are free in spirit only."[2]

In the ongoing battle of the sexes, the *Playboy* office in Chicago quickly became the male side's headquarters for wartime propaganda. Unlike the general-audience magazines that dominated fifties newsstands—*Life, Time,* the *Saturday Evening Post, Look,* etc.—*Playboy* didn't worry about pleasing women readers. The first editorial, penned by Hefner himself, warned:

> We want to make clear from the very start, we aren't a "family magazine." If you're somebody's sister, wife, or mother-in-law and picked us up by mistake, please pass us along to the man in your life and get back to your *Ladies' Home Companion*.

When a Memphis woman wrote in to the second issue protesting the "Miss Gold-Digger" article, she was quickly put in her place. The article, she wrote, was "the most biased piece of tripe I've ever read," and she went on to deliver the classic anti-male rejoinder:

> Most men are out for just one thing. If they can't get it any other way, sometimes they consent to marry the girl. Then they think they can brush her off in a few months and move on to new pickings. They *ought* to pay, and pay, and pay.

The editors' printed response was, "Ah, shaddup!"

Hefner laid out the new male strategic initiative in the first issue. Recall that in their losing battle against "female domination," men had been driven from their living rooms, dens, and even their basement tool shops. Escape seemed to lie only in the great outdoors—the golf course, the fishing hole, or the fantasy world of Westerns. Now Hefner announced his intention to reclaim *the indoors for men.* "Most of today's 'magazines for men' spend all their time out-of-doors—thrashing through thorny thickets or splashing about in fast flowing streams," he observed in the magazine's first editorial. "But we don't mind telling you in advance—we plan spending most of our time inside. We like our apartment." For therein awaited a new kind of good life for men:

> We enjoy mixing up cocktails and an *hors d'oeuvre* or two, putting a little mood music on the phonograph and inviting in a female acquaintance for a quiet discussion on Picasso, Nietzsche, jazz, sex.

Women would be welcome after men had reconquered the indoors, but only as guests—maybe overnight guests—but not as wives.

In 1953, the notion that the good life consisted of an apartment with mood music rather than a ranch house with barbecue pit was almost subversive. Looking back, Hefner later characterized himself as a pioneer rebel against the gray miasma of conformity that gripped other men. At the time the magazine began, he wrote in 1963, Americans had become "increasingly concerned with security, the safe and the sure, the certain and the known . . . it was unwise to voice an unpopular opinion . . . for it could cost a man his job and his good name."[3] Hefner himself was not a political dissident in any conventional sense; the major intellectual influence in his early life was the Kinsey Report, and he risked his own good name only for the right to publish bare white bosoms. What upset him was the "conformity, togetherness, anonymity and slow death" men were supposed to endure when the good life, the life which he himself came to represent, was so close at hand.[4]

In fact, it was close at hand, and, at the macroeconomic level, nothing could have been more in conformity with the drift of American culture than to advocate a life of pleasurable consumption. The economy, as Riesman, Galbraith, and their colleagues noted, had gotten over the hump of heavy capital accumulation to the happy plateau of the "consumer society." After the privations of the Depression and the war, Americans were supposed to enjoy themselvs—held back from total abandon only by the need for Cold War vigilance. Motivational researcher Dr. Ernest Dichter told businessmen:

> We are now confronted with the problem of permitting the average American to feel moral . . . even when he is spending, even when he is not saving, even when he is taking two vacations a year and buying a second or third car. One of the basic problems of prosperity, then, is to demonstrate that the hedonistic approach to his life is a moral, not an immoral one.[5]

This was the new consumer ethic, the "fun morality" described by sociologist Martha Wolfenstein, and *Playboy* could not have been better designed to bring the good news to men.

If Hefner was a rebel, it was only because he took the new fun morality seriously. As a guide to life, the new imperative to enjoy was in contradiction with the prescribed discipline of "conformity" and *Playboy*'s daring lay in facing the contradiction head-on. Conformity, or "maturity," as it was more affirmatively labeled by the psychologists, required unstinting effort: developmental "tasks" had to be performed, marriages had to be "worked on," individual whims had to be subordinated to the emotional and financial needs of the family. This was true for both sexes, of course. No one pretended that the adult sex roles—wife/mother and male breadwinner—were "fun." They were presented in popular culture as achievements, proofs of the informed acquiescence praised as "maturity" or, more rarely, lamented as "slow death." Women would not get public license to have fun on a mass scale for more than a decade, when Helen Gurley Brown took over *Cosmopolitan* and began promoting a tamer, feminine version of sexual and material consumerism. But *Playboy* shed the burdensome aspects of the adult male role at a time when businessmen were still refining the "fun morality" for mass consumption, and the gray flannel rebels were still fumbling for responsible alternatives like Riesman's "autonomy." Even the magazine's name defied the convention of hard-won maturity—*Playboy*.

*Playboy*'s attack on the conventional male role did not, however, extend to the requirement of earning a living. There were two parts to adult masculinity: One was maintaining a monogamous marriage. The other was working at a socially acceptable job; and *Playboy* had nothing against work. The early issues barely recognized the white-collar blues so fashionable in popular sociology. Instead, there were articles on accoutrements for the rising executive, suggesting that work, too, could be a site of pleasurable consumption. Writing in his "*Playboy* Philosophy" series in 1963, Hefner even credited the magazine with inspiring men to work harder than they might: ". . . *Playboy* exists, in part, as a motivation for men to expend greater effort in their work, develop their capabilities further and climb higher on the ladder of success." This kind of motivation, he went on, "is obviously desirable in our competitive, free enterprise system," apparently unaware that the average reader was more likely to be a white-collar "organization man" or blue-collar employee rather than a free entrepreneur like himself. Men should throw themselves into their work with "questing impatience and rebel derring-do." They should overcome their vague, ingrained populism and recognize wealth as an achievement and a means to personal pleasure. Only in one respect did Hefner's philosophy depart from the conventional, Dale Carnegie-style credos of male success: *Playboy* belived that men should make money; it did not suggest that they share it.

*Playboy* charged into the battle of the sexes with a dollar sign on its banner. The issue was money: Men made it; women wanted it. In *Playboy*'s favorite cartoon situation an elderly roué was being taken for a ride by a buxom bubblebrain, and the joke was on him. The message, squeezed between luscious full-color photos and punctuated with female nipples, was simple: You can buy sex on a fee-for-service basis, so don't get caught up in a long-term contract. Phil Silvers quipped in the January 1957 issue:

> A tip to my fellow men who might be on the brink of disaster: when the little doll says she'll live on your income, she means it all right. But just be sure to get another one for yourself.[6]

Burt Zollo warned in the June 1953 issue:

> It is often suggested that woman is more romantic than man. If you'll excuse the ecclesiastical expression—*phooey!*... All woman wants is security. And she's perfectly willing to crush man's adventurous, freedom-loving spirit to get it.[7]

To stay free, a man had to stay single.

The competition, meanwhile, was still fighting a rearguard battle for patriarchal authority within marriage. In 1956, the editorial director of *True* attributed his magazine's success to the fact that it "stimulates the masculine ego at a time when man wants to fight back against women's efforts to usurp his traditional role as head of the family."[8] The playboy did not want his "traditional role" back; he just wanted out. Hefner's friend Burt Zollo wrote in one of the early issues:

> Take a good look at the sorry, regimented husbands trudging down every woman-dominated street in this woman-dominated land. Check what they're doing when you're out on the town with a different dish every night... Don't bother asking their advice. Almost to a man, they'll tell you marriage is the greatest. *Naturally.* Do you expect them to admit they made the biggest mistake of their lives?[9]

This was strong stuff for the mid-fifties. The suburban migration was in full swing and *Look* had just coined the new noun "togetherness" to bless the isolated, exurban family. Yet here was *Playboy* exhorting its readers to resist marriage and "enjoy the pleasures the female has to offer without becoming emotionally involved"—or, of course, financially involved. Women wrote in with the predictable attacks on immaturity: "It is... the weak-minded little idiot boys, not yet grown up, who are afraid of getting 'hooked.' " But the men loved it. One alliterative genius wrote in to thank *Playboy* for exposing those "cunning cuties" with their "suave schemes" for landing a man. And, of course, it was *Playboy*, with its images of cozy concupiscence and extra-marital consumerism, that triumphed while *True* was still "thrashing through the thorny thickets" in the great, womenless outdoors.

One of the most eloquent manifestos of the early male rebellion was a *Playboy* article entitled, "Love, Death and the Hubby Image," published in 1963. It led off with a mock want ad:

> TIRED OF THE RAT RACE?
> FED UP WITH JOB ROUTINE?
>
> Well, then... how would you like to make $8,000, $20,000—*as much as $50,000 and More*—working at Home in Your Spare Time? No selling! No commuting! No time clocks to punch!
>
> BE YOUR OWN BOSS
>
> Yes, an Assured Lifetime Income can be yours *now*, in an easy, low-pressure, part-time job that will permit you to spend most of each and every day as *you please!*—relaxing, watching TV, playing cards, socializing with friends!...

"Incredible though it may seem," the article began, "the above offer is completely legitimate. More than 40,000,000 Americans are already so employed..." They were, of course, wives.

According to the writer, William Iversen, husbands were self-sacrificing romantics, toiling ceaselessly to provide their families with "bread, bacon, clothes, furniture, cars, appliances, entertainment, vacations, and country-club memberships." Nor was it enough to meet their daily needs; the heroic male must provide for them even after his own death by building up his savings and life insurance. "Day after day, and week after week the American hubby is thus invited to attend his own funeral." Iversen acknowledged that there were some mutterings of discontent from the distaff side, but he saw no chance of a feminist revival: The role of the housewife "has become much too cushy to be a abandoned, even in the teeth of the most crushing boredom." Men, however, had had it with the breadwinner role, and the final paragraph was a stirring incitement to revolt:

> The last straw has already been served, and a mere tendency to hemophilia cannot be counted upon to ensure that men will continue to bleed for the plight of the American woman. Neither double eyelashes nor the blindness of night or day can obscure the glaring fact that American marriage can no longer be accepted as an estate in which the sexes shall live half-slave and half-free.[10]

*Playboy* had much more to offer the "enslaved" sex than rhetoric: It also proposed an alternative way of life that became ever more concrete and vivid as the years went on. At first there were only the Playmates in the centerfold to suggest what awaited the liberated male, but a wealth of other consumer items soon followed. Throughout the late fifties, the magazine fattened on advertisements for imported liquor, stereo sets, men's colognes, luxury cars and fine clothes. Manufacturers were beginning to address themselves to the adult male as a consumer in his own right, and they were able to do so, in part, because magazines like *Playboy* (a category which came to include imitators like *Penthouse, Gent,* and *Chic*) allowed them to effectively "target" the potential sybarites among the great mass of men. New products for men, like toiletries and sports clothes, appeared in the fifties, and familiar products, like liquor, were presented in *Playboy* as accessories to private male pleasures. The new male-centered ensemble of commodities presented in *Playboy* meant that a man could display his status or simply flaunt his earnings without possessing either a house or a wife—and this was, in its own small way, a revolutionary possibility.

Domesticated men had their own commodity ensemble, centered on home appliances and hobby hardware, and for a long time there had seemed to be no alternative. A man expressed his status through the size of his car, the location of his house, and the social and sartorial graces of his wife. The wife and home might be a financial drag on a man, but it was the paraphernalia of family life that established his position in the occupational hierarchy. *Playboy*'s visionary contribution—visionary because it would still be years before a significant mass of men availed themselves of it—was to give the means of status to the single man: not the power lawn mower, but the hi-fi set in mahogany console; not the sedate, four-door Buick, but the racy little Triumph; not the well-groomed wife, but the classy companion who could be rented (for the price of drinks and dinner) one night at a time.

So through its articles, its graphics and its advertisements *Playboy* presented, by the beginning of the sixties, something approaching a coherent program for the male rebellion: a critique of marriage, a strategy for liberation (reclaiming the indoors as a realm for masculine pleasure) and a utopian vision (defined by its unique commodity ensemble). It may not have been a revolutionary program, but it was most certainly a disruptive one. If even a fraction of *Playboy* readers had acted on it in the late fifties, the "breakdown of the family" would have occurred a full 15 years before it was eventually announced. Hundreds of thousands of women would have been left without breadwinners or stranded in court fighting for alimony settlements. Yet, for all its potential disruptiveness, *Playboy* was immune to the standard charges leveled against male deviants. You couldn't call it anti-capitalist or un-American, because it was all about making money and spending it. Hefner even told his readers in 1963 that the *Playboy* spirit of acquisitiveness could help "put the United States back in the position of unquestioned world leadership." You *could* call it "immature," but it already called itself that, because maturity was about mortgages and life insurance and *Playboy* was about fun. Finally, it was impervious to the ultimate sanction against male rebellion—the charge of homosexuality. The playboy didn't avoid marriage because he was a little bit "queer," but, on the contrary, because he was so ebulliently, even compulsively, heterosexual.

Later in the sixties critics would come up with what seemed to be the ultimately sophisticated charge against *Playboy*: It wasn't really "sexy." There was nothing erotic, *Time* wrote, about the pink-cheeked young Playmates whose every pore and perspiration drop had been air-brushed out of existence. Hefner was "puritanical" after all, and the whole thing was no more mischievous than "a Midwestern Methodist's vision of sin."[11] But the critics misunderstood *Playboy*'s historical role. *Playboy* was not the voice of the sexual revolution, which began, at least overtly, in the sixties, but of the male rebellion, which had begun in the fifties. The real message was not eroticism, but escape—literal escape, from the bondage of breadwinning. For that, the breasts and bottoms were necessary not just to sell the magazine, but to protect it. When, in the first issue, Hefner talked about staying in his apartment, listening to music and discussing Picasso, there was the Marilyn Monroe centerfold to let you know there was nothing queer about these urbane and indoor pleasures. And when the articles railed against the responsibilities of marriage, there were the nude torsos to reassure you that the alternative was still within the bounds of heterosexuality. Sex—or Hefner's Pepsi-clean version of it—was there to legitimize what was truly subversive about *Playboy*. In every issue, every month, there was a Playmate to prove that a playboy didn't have to be a husband to be a man.

## NOTES

1. Quoted in Joe L. Dubbert, *A Man's Place: Masculinity in Transition* (Englewood Cliffs, N.J.: Prentice-Hall, Inc., 1979), p. 269.

2. "Meet the *Playboy* Reader," *Playboy*, April 1958, p. 63.
3. Hugh Hefner, "The Playboy Philosophy," *Playboy*, January 1963, p. 41.
4. Frank Brady, *Hefner* (New York: Macmillan Pub. Co., Inc., 1974), p. 98.
5. Quoted in Douglas T. Miller and Marion Nowak, *The Fifties* (Garden City, N.Y.: Doubleday & Company, Inc., 1977), p. 119.
6. Phil Silvers, "Resolution: Never Get Married," *Playboy*, January 1957, p. 77.
7. Burt Zollo, "Open Season on Bachelors," *Playboy*, June 1953, p. 37.
8. Quoted in Myron Brenton, *The American Male* (New York: Coward, McCann, 1966), p. 30.
9. Zollo, "Open Season."
10. William Iverson, "Love, Death and the Hubby Image," *Playboy*, September 1963, p. 92.
11. "Think Clean," *Time*, March 3, 1967, p. 76.

# 33

WILLIAM MARTIN

# Two Cheers for the Moral Majority

*Few social/political/philosophical movements in recent years have grown as quickly and enraged as many as the "pro-family, Moral Majority, New Right." Its highly vocal constituency has drawn very clear lines between good and bad and between acceptable and nonacceptable solutions to the serious problems facing our society. Because of the intimate substance of its arguments, the unsubtle tactics of its leaders, and the sometimes damning nature of its solutions, few persons have a neutral opinion of the movement.*

*Thus, it may seem ironic that a sociologist, a member of a profession often stereotyped as liberal in its political views, would write an essay that asks readers to reexamine their feelings about this group. And it seems even more ironic in light of the fact that Martin has devoted a number of years to the critical study of television evangelists and the Christian New Right. Martin says, however, that he feels we have been so steeped for so long in the criticisms of this group that we really do not bother to listen. If we were to listen, as he did in his research, he thinks we might agree with many of their arguments. At the same time, in his view, when we begin to recognize that the liberal rhetoric has not worked very well in holding families together or producing a healthy new generation of young people, it is obvious that we need to look at some alternatives. When asked what kind of response he received to the article, Martin answered, "A lot of people said that they really didn't disagree with me—they just wouldn't say it in public!"*

Source: William Martin, "Two Cheers for the Moral Majority." Originally published in *The Texas Humanist* 7, no. 4 (March–April 1985).

Who are these people anyway, and how dare they call themselves "pro-family," as if to suggest that those who disagree with them are somehow "anti-family"? Well, some probably use pious rhetoric about the family to mask a primary interest in rapacious profit-seeking. Some are driven by intolerance for ambiguity to accept absolute answers from egomaniacal God-hucksters. Some feel desperately threatened by the spector of a society in which women and homosexuals enjoy equal rights and in which stimulating media depictions of sexual or violent activity are not repressed by the state. A great many, however, are people who work hard, love their families, pay their bills and taxes, and are troubled, frightened, and mad as hell over what they have seen happening to their country in recent decades. There was a time, not so long ago, when it was fashionable to observe, over Brie and Chablis, that they were neither moral nor a majority. In fact, though we may honestly disagree with them at several crucial points, they may be both, and we may have something to learn from them.

Whether one is watching Jerry Falwell or Pat Robertson, reading books by Tim and Beverly LaHaye, looking at James Dobson films, sitting through a Bill Gothard conference, or hearing Phyllis Schlafly address an Eagle Forum, one finds a great deal of agreement in "pro-family" circles about the threat to the American family. The litany is familiar. Nearly half of all marriages end in divorce, 12 million children under 18 live with one divorced parent, a million children a year experience dissolution of their family, and 45 percent of American children will spend at least part of their lives before age 18 with a divorced parent. Nearly one in five births is illegitimate; in New York City and Washington, D.C., illegitimate babies outnumber legitimate ones. Eleven million unborn children—a million a year—have been aborted since the *Roe v. Wade* decision in 1973. Twenty million Americans have herpes, 3 million have gonorrhea, new strains of syphillis and other venereal diseases have appeared, and the AIDS epidemic is causing a panic among homosexuals and heterosexuals alike. Hundreds of thousands of children are sexually abused and in Los Angeles alone, an estimated 30,000 are exploited for pornography and prostitution.

Sixty percent of women with school-age children work, leaving millions of pre-school children in day-care centers and more than 2 million latch-key children without adult supervision for long periods each day, yet marriage and motherhood are often portrayed in the media and by feminists as unrewarding, unfulfilling, boring, and even enslaving. Alcohol problems trouble 22 percent of American homes, nearly double the 12 percent recorded in 1974. More than half the population has used marijuana and 20 percent has used harder drugs. Crime and violence—in the streets, in the schools, in the homes, in the media—have stripped us of the freedom and peace of mind that characterized the lives of our childhood and that ought to be characteristic of the lives of our children. So it goes.

The pro-family movement not only agrees about the nature of the problem, but it is impressively united in assessing the blame for this catalogue of social and personal ills. Among its key culprits are feminists, political collectivists, social scientists, evolutionists, and, of course, the all-purpose evil-seekers and

-doers, Secular Humanists. I have, in other contexts, offered criticism of various positions espoused by the movement known as the Christian New Right (for example, "God's Angry Man," *Texas Monthly*, April 1981, and "The Guardians Who Slumbereth Not," *Texas Monthly*, Nov. 1982). I do not recant what I have written on these subjects. I still believe the hysterical attack on secular humanism is dangerously misleading, the refusal to wrestle with the profound implications of cultural relativism intellectually myopic, the parody known as "scientific creationism" an obscurantist threat to American leadership in science, the belief that restoration of school prayer will have much effect on crime of drug abuse or sexual promiscuity touchingly naive, the radical individualism destructive of community, and the emphasis on a father-dominated home not only demeaning to women and embarrassing to men but a hindrance to the kind of healthy family the movement seeks. Having said that, however, I admit to occasional surprise at the degree to which I find myself vaguely comfortable with some of the concerns of the Moral Majority and their colleagues in the Christian New Right.

Analysts of the pro-family movement often describe its advocates and adherents as people outside the mainstream, people troubled by rapid change and suffering from various sorts of economic, social, physical, or psychic deprivations. There is some truth to that analysis, but the point I want to consider is the more straight-forward possibility that a sizable chunk of the people who comprise and support the pro-family movement are drawn to it because they genuinely believe the family is in serious trouble, that this trouble has serious implications for both individuals and society as a whole, and that they want to do what they can to help.

The fact that America has survived widespread social change in the past has often been taken as a sign that what we face at present is not so much a crisis as a predictably recurring bit of rough water that we will navigate successfully in our passage to new, exciting, and satisfying forms of family life. I am more pessimistic. I think the family as an institution is in a lot of trouble, and I am not sure things are going to get better. I hope they do. I will not likely join the Moral Majority or any other indentifiable component of the pro-family movement in their efforts to improve the situation, but if they bring about improvements, I might occasionally offer, say, two cheers. Let me elaborate on that a bit.

To begin, we should admit that the problems delineated by the pro-family movement are real, deep, and serious. Consider, for example, divorce. It was common in the 1970s to find popular books and sociological studies that indicated divorce might not only be creative and painless, but of considerable positive benefit to everybody concerned, including the children. A lot of people wanted to hear that, some people wanted to say it, and, for a time, the evidence appeared to support it. Increasingly, however, the evidence seems to be leading us in a different direction. It now appears that painless divorce is a myth. Divorce is a traumatic occurrence for everyone involved—husbands, wives, and children—and a substantial percentage of those involved, particularly the children, experience longstanding negative effects. Albert Solnit, director of the Yale Child Study Center, has called divorce "one of the most serious and complex mental-health crises facing children of the '80s."

Please do not misread my attitude as one of smugness or judgment. Certainly, there are situations in which it is better to get a divorce than to stay married. Certainly, there are situations in which one partner may wish to stay married and the other does not permit an effective choice. And certainly, most people who have been married for any substantial length of time can understand how divorces can happen to good and honorable people who love their children and are deeply concerned to protect them from harm.

And yet, all that notwithstanding, divorce is still an occurrence quite likely to have serious negative effects on those it touches. In their important study of divorce, *Surviving the Breakup: How Children Actually Cope* (1980), Judith Wallerstein and Joan Kelly found that virtually all children respond to news of their parents' divorce in uniform fashion, characterized by shock, surprise, depression, denial, anger, low self-esteem, guilt, and feelings that their world has been shattered and that the rules no longer make sense. Further, hardly a child they studied did not cling to a fantasy of magical reconciliation. Even more striking was their finding far more turmoil than expected, even long after the divorce. Ten years later, for example, only one quarter of the children were described as doing well. Half were "muddling through" but still experiencing significant periods of unhappiness and diminished self-esteem. A final one quarter were still bruised; some had been that way before the divorce, but most of their difficulties appeared connected to the divorce. About one third experienced far-reaching change once again when their parents remarried.

In other research, Richard Kulka and Helen Weingarten, of the Social Research Center at the University of Michigan, have concluded from two national surveys of adult Americans that young adults (ages 21–34) from divorced families are less likely to describe themselves as "very happy" and more likely to report symptoms of poor physical health than are those from intact families.

These matters require and are receiving more study. We cannot say with certainty that instability in the family will make other key social institutions unstable. But if a million children a year experience divorce, and one-quarter of those—approximately 250,000 people—are still suffering rather seriously after 10 years, it would be naive to believe we are not going to feel some bad effects.

As to the question of optimal arrangements for intact families, the pro-family movement's frequent criticism of day-care centers and its related efforts to keep women at home often overlook the fact that many women have little choice in the matter and that, when there is a choice, it is no more fair for women to be assigned the home duty than for men—or, to put it another way, that it is no more fair for the man to have to go out everyday and for the woman to be able to stay home. In fairness, however, it should be noted that members of the pro-family movement generally favor "flex-time" arrangements that allow parents to be at home when their children need them, and also advocate having people perform work at home when the nature of their jobs permits. Further, many evangelical churches provide good quality day care for parents who work, whether or not they have another option.

It is worth noting that it is not aberrant to believe that children may flourish better in the company of a parent who loves them, enjoys being with them, and has a responsive attitude toward them, than at a day-care center. The evidence indicates that children do best in a situation in which at least one and preferably more than one person is irrationally attached to them. The popular assertion that what children need is "quality time" is, in large measure, an illusion, a rationalization offered by people who do not wish or who feel guilty about not being able to spend "quantity time" with their offspring. Children need quality time, to be sure, but they need it in substantial quantities. For years, the system has worked unfairly in pressuring women to bear the burden of child care. The system has changed. Now it is unfair to children.

The family, with both male and female roles represented, is an admirably efficient institution for rearing children. I do not believe women should bear a disproportionate share of the responsibility for child-rearing. If there are things they do best, whether by gender, individual temperament, or socialization, they might do well to concentrate in those areas, but there is plenty for two people to do. I do believe that people who do not want to devote sufficient time to rear sound and emotional healthy children should not give birth to them.

On the other hand, I am uncomfortable with abortion as a popular means of avoiding responsibility for children. I believe there are cases in which abortion may be the least undersirable of two truly difficult alternatives. I find it difficult to justify a million abortions a year. I am uncomfortable with much of the pro-family rhetoric about "killing babies" and "medical holocaust," and yet, a fetus, if allowed to live—that is to say, if not killed—has from the moment of conception all the genes and chromosomes it will ever have and, as it grows, comes to look a lot like a baby. I am generally in favor of keeping babies alive. And I suspect that talk of moving to other steps—of deciding, for example, to get rid of other inconvenient populations—is not entirely outrageous.

I also suspect that the sexual freedom encouraged by mass media is overrated, that it does not lead to emotional health, psychologically satisfying intimate relationships, or even to deep sexual fulfillment. Usually, people who take a full run at the liberated single life tire of it and seek something more lasting. Similarly, only a decade ago, hundreds of thousands of people talked optimistically of "open marriage."Almost nobody who tried to put it into practice is still married to the same partner. It is probably the case that, for good or ill, most of us hold somewhat more relaxed views of sexuality than those with which we were reared. It is probably also the case that most of us who have children feel some dis-ease when we walk through our living rooms and find our children watching television programs that portray or discuss sexual behavior in astonishingly explicit terms, with seldom a hint that such behavior may have unanticipated problematic consequences—perhaps because it is exploitative, perhaps because it may result in devastating and incurable venereal disease, perhaps because it is potentially injurious to third parties, perhaps because, though tender and appropriate for adults, it may be too advanced for the minds and emotions of children.

The sexual world depicted in pornography is even more disquieting. I am uneasy with any form of censorship, but I am also uneasy with a society in which children can buy *Hustler* magazine at the Stop 'n' Go and in which "adult" newsstands and "art" cinemas offer customers the vicarious experience of pedophilia, bestiality, and sado-masochism to the point of physical injury and extreme degradion. It is sometimes said that pornography can serve as an aid to more satisfying sexual relationships. That may be so, I am reasonably certain that is not its only possible result.

In short, I find myself in moderate sympathy with a good many of the fears and apprehensions of the pro-family movement. By virtue of having sent them a donation to insure receipt of their literature, I have a card proclaiming that I am a member of the Moral Majority, but I neither attend their meetings nor wear a little baby-feet pin in my lapel. On the other hand, I have declined to assist the American Civil Liberties Union in the defense of a pornographer and, until they went to college, I usually had a fairly good idea where my children were and who was with them. I don't drink Coors beer when there is something else available, because Joseph Coors is one of the key Sugardaddy Warbucks of the New Right. But if the Reverend Donald Wildmon could convince me that it would help reduce the explicit sex and violence on my TV screen, I might switch brands of razor blades or toothpaste. Significantly, surveys indicate that 33 million Americans say they feel much the same way.

What all this amounts to, obviously, is a somewhat inconsistent and wishy-washy moral testimony. But I suspect many readers may feel a similar anxiety and ambivalence, and we are not alone. Large-scale social surveys reveal that millions of people who would not regard themselves as members of the pro-family movement—indeed, who differ with it strenuously on various issues—nevertheless concede that it may have its good points. We are not likely to launch any crusades ourselves, but we might not be seriously disturbed if they got porn shops closed down, arrested all the drug dealers, put the prostitutes out of business, and sanitized the media. We won't get too excited about the crusade to get prayer and Bible reading back into the schools, but we are likely to feel that it might do our children good if somebody took the time to talk to them seriously and convincingly about such matters as cheating and lying and stealing. We may defend a liberal morality at parties and among our friends, but we are likely to hope that our children will adopt a reasonably conservative version.

At least part of what is happening here, insofar as this describes us, is that we do not have our own lives put together in a way that completely satisfies us. We may feel, perhaps correctly, that we can keep our moral center intact, because our upbringing instilled in us a clear sense of right and wrong. But we may be less confident that we have provided our children with comparable moral conviction. And if we have not done that, the results, or what we fear the results might be, may be making us uneasy. That anxiety, and our success or failure in dealing with, probably have important implications for the eventual success or failure of the pro-family movement.

As pollster and social analyst Daniel Yankelovich has pointed out, we can find instruction in recalling how the nation responded to two recent social movements: the New Left and the feminist movement. I both cases, many people who expressed sympathy for the movements disagreed with many of their more extreme positions. In the case of the New Left, the issue that drew people together was Vietnam. When the war was over, talk of "power to the people" and the evils of private property faded away and the New Left became a memory. In the case of the feminist movement, there were sufficient issues of substance to attract and hold millions of women and a sizable contingent of men long past the days of bra burning and calls for dissolution of the family. It has become one of the most significant and influential social movements of our lifetime.

If only our choices are between the restrictiveness urged by the pro-family movement and a continuing permissiveness and unwillingness to formulate and articulate substantial moral and ethical positions, I suspect the pro-family movement will enjoy continued and increased success. When societies threaten to go out of control, it is not uncommon for them to choose restrictiveness over the threat of chaos. If, on the other hand, more moderate and liberal elements of the society are willing to take the time to examine and work out defensible positions and policies—in churches, schools, and other groups, or in social scientific research such as that reported by Robert N. Bellah's research team in the new book, *Habits of the Heart*—on such matters as divorce, child-rearing arrangements, abortion, promiscuity, pornography, alcohol and other drugs, work and economic policies that directly affect the family, and a pluralism that does not deny or preclude some common core of values, it is plausible, even probable, that the more extreme positions represented in the pro-family movement will fade away as have such minority ideological movements as the New Left and the John Birch Society.

I know which of these options I prefer. I am not sure that is the way it will turn out. Things do not always work out for the best. Societies do go into decline. Often, it is when they surrender a core of values on which most of their members can agree, and the center no longer holds. I do not regard the future of the American family as particularly rosy. At the same time, there are indications that we are not so far gone as to justify despair. The increased concern for the family manifested by a wide spectrum of the population is one of these hopeful signs.

## About the Editors

**Norval D. Glenn** is Ashbel Smith Professor of Sociology at The University of Texas at Austin. He is the editor of the *Journal of Family Issues,* is a former editor of *Contemporary Sociology,* and is on the editorial boards of the *Journal of Marriage and the Family,* the *Public Opinion Quarterly,* and *Social Indicators Research.* For the past fifteen years his research has centered primarily on aspects of marriage and family in the United States.

**Marion Tolbert Coleman** is a program officer at the Hogg Foundation for Mental Health and Adjunct Assistant Professor of Sociology at The University of Texas at Austin. She is deputy editor of the *Journal of Family Issues.* Her current research focuses on families of the mentally ill and the gender balance of power in married couples.

## A Note on the Type

The text of this book was set in 10/12 Garamond Light via computer-driven cathode ray tube. Claude Garamond (1480–1561), the respected French type designer and letter cutter, produced this beautiful typeface for François I at the king's urging. Garamond is a fine example of the Old Style typeface, characterized by oblique stress and relatively little contrast between thicks and thins. Full of movement and charm, this elegant face influenced type design down to the end of the eighteenth century.

Composed by The Saybrook Press, Old Saybrook, Connecticut.

Printed and bound by Malloy Lithographing, Inc., Ann Arbor, Michigan.